To: four parents
   two spouses
   five children

Preface

Aims of the book

This book is a general account of the contemporary population of Britain. It describes the demographic characteristics of the British people; their fertility, marriages, and households, their death rates, their distribution, migration, and ethnic composition. It offers explanations for some of the patterns and trends. It suggests where the trends may be going and why they may be important. The authors hope that their book will be a useful introduction to the demographic background of contemporary issues.

It is important to keep in mind what demography can and cannot tell us. Population statistics and processes are not things in themselves. They are 'visible signs of what has been happening below the surface and reveal collective attitudes towards life and death, at times almost sub-conscious and usually kept hidden' (Aries 1983). A society's demography can be regarded as a formalization and generalization of the risks of the membership of that society (Schofield and Coleman 1986). These risks—of favourable as well as unpleasant events—are one way of measuring the consequences of the way people live and behave, and the effects of the social and material environment in which they live. Part of that environment is itself demographic. Demographic analysis can show how the mass consequences of millions of individual decisions will in turn generate population growth or decline, or changes in the age structure, which may have an effect on the life chances of individuals, though these may not necessarily be the same individuals as those whose behaviour caused the changes.

The vital events with which demography is concerned are usually unambiguous and easily measurable. Statistics based on them can act as an interchangeable hard currency with which societies and their trends can be compared. Students of many disciplines employ demographic measures and ideas, and contribute to each other's understanding. The analyst of these trends must draw upon a wide variety of knowledge from biology, economics, geography, history, sociology, and other subjects in his search for causes and consequences.

This book was begun more years ago than either of the authors care to admit. Since then, demographic trends and, even more, demo-

The British Population

Patterns, Trends, and Processes

David Coleman
and
John Salt

OXFORD UNIVERSITY PRESS
1992

Oxford University Press, Walton Street, Oxford OX2 6DP

Oxford New York Toronto
Delhi Bombay Calcutta Madras Karachi
Petaling Jaya Singapore Hong Kong Tokyo
Nairobi Dar es Salaam Cape Town
Melbourne Auckland

and associated companies in
Berlin Ibadan

Oxford is a trade mark of Oxford University Press

Published in the United States
by Oxford University Press, New York

British Library Cataloguing in Publication Data
Coleman, D. A. (David A.)
The British population: patterns, trends and processes,
1. Great Britain, Population, Demographic aspects
1. Title   II. Salt, John 1942–
304.60941
ISBN 0-19-874097-2
ISBN 0-19-874098-0 pbk

Library of Congress Cataloging-in-Publication Data
Coleman, David.
    The British population: patterns, trends, and processes/David
  Coleman and John Salt.
    Includes bibliographical references and index.
    1. Great Britain—Population.   I. Salt, John.   II. Title.
  H88583.C81   1991 804.8'0911—dc20   90-46808
ISBN 0-19-874097-2
ISBN 0-19-874098-0 pbk

Set by Best-set Ltd, Hong Kong

Printed in Great Britain by
Biddles Ltd Guildford & Kings Lynn

graphic thinking have developed so much that the book has gone through a number of editions before even being published. When we started it seemed surprising that there had been so few attempts (e.g. Kelsall 1970, 1989, OPCS 1978*c*) to produce a description of the British population and an analysis of its trends. We are now less surprised. The capacity of the British population to change its demographic behaviour, and the ability of its academic observers to develop new explanations for it, set a daunting pace.

Most books on British demography are either about populations of the past (the majority) or about contemporary issues (e.g. Ermisch 1983, 1990, Joshi 1989). Few (e.g. Tranter 1979) combine the two. We felt it was essential to do so, even though neither of us pretends to be a historian. Many characteristics of Western demography and of Western societies, not the least their pre-eminent economic position, cannot be understood without reference to their unique historical demographic development. And within that special Western system, British patterns of mortality and household seem exceptionally moderate; signs perhaps, among other things, of a more tranquil political evolution than that enjoyed by most of our Continental neighbours.

Despite its long gestation, this book is still incomplete. For example, far too little is said about Scotland and Northern Ireland, and almost nothing on their population history (see Flinn *et al.* 1977, Connell 1950*a*, Goldstrom and Clarkson 1981, Coleman 1990*b*). Their special features warrant sections of their own, for which there was simply no space. However, much of what is said about the whole country applies equally to England, Wales, and Scotland. Regional differences in Britain are, and have generally been in the past, much more subdued than on the Continent. The special regime of fertility, marriage, and migration in Ireland, including Northern Ireland, has stood alone in Western Europe since the nineteenth century (Compton 1978, 1981). Some special aspects of Northern Irish fertility are considered in Chapter 12, but much of interest has had to be omitted. Special reference is made to Scotland where patterns differ, especially in Chapters 3 and 8–11.

One of the most striking differences between the nations of the United Kingdom is the relative stagnation or even decline of the populations of Scotland and Northern Ireland in the twentieth century, not least by migration to England, compared with England's growth. The migrants do, however, make a further contribution to English, as well as to British demography: 21 per cent of the population of the British Isles who were born in Wales were living in England in 1981, as were 14 per cent of the Scots, 12 per cent of people born in Northern

Ireland, and 14 per cent of people born in the Irish Republic. Altogether these made up 2.1 million, or 5 per cent of the English population, in 1981.

Other topics in this book enjoy more attention than their demographic importance merits. They include certain risks to health such as nuclear radiation, considered in Chapter 7, which have dominated public concern to the detriment of the consideration of other, more substantial hazards. Others, such as the comments on marital choice in Chapter 5, happen to have been favourite topics of one of the authors. No doubt there are many other examples of imbalance.

Sources of data and their analysis

The book does not attempt to describe sources of data in detail, or the methods used to analyse demographic material, beyond the minimum required to make sense of the analysis and to avoid pitfalls. The sources of data, given in the references, should be consulted directly. A number of excellent and comprehensive introductions to demographic analysis are now available (Cox 1976, Woods 1979a, Pollard, Yusuf, and Pollard 1981, Newell 1988). The last of these is particularly friendly to the user. For guidance on UK sources of population data and the best methods to analyse them, Benjamin's recent survey (1989) is the most comprehensive. Other sources cover more specific areas, for example statistics on family planning (Selman 1989) and the topics covered in censuses (OPCS/GRO Scotland 1977).

The pioneer work from the seventeenth century of John Graunt, William Petty, Edmund Halley, Gregory King (see Glass 1964, 1965a, and Kreager 1988) and their nineteenth century successors Robert Malthus, William Farr, and T. H. C. Stevenson, gives Britain a strong claim to be the homeland of modern demography and its application to practical problems (even if, like so many British inventions it is now better developed abroad). British official demographic data, except those relating to migration, are among the best in the world. However they do suffer a unique flaw, which will be evident throughout the book. As a consequence of the history of the United Kingdom, and the need to consider regional sensibilities, there is not one Registrar-General for the UK but three: for England and Wales, Scotland, and Northern Ireland. Data are therefore published and analysed separately for England and Wales, Scotland, Northern Ireland, Great Britain, and the United Kingdom.

The most comprehensive demographic analysis and commentary are given by the Office of Population Censuses and Surveys, until 1973 the

General Register Office, for the data it collects on England and Wales. A list of its annual series of official population statistics is given in the Appendix. The General Register Offices for Scotland and Northern Ireland command fewer resources. The level of the analysis of demographic statistics in their Annual Reports is correspondingly lower; the publications for Northern Ireland in particular retain a charming period air (see Registrar-General for Scotland 1990, Registrar-General for Northern Ireland 1990). There is no official medium for demographic commentary on Scotland or Northern Ireland comparable to *Population Trends* although that journal does occasionally publish articles on Scottish or Irish matters and contains summary statistics on Scotland and Northern Ireland. However, since the middle 1980s it has become more routine for OPCS annual statistics, at least on mortality, to include comparable data for all the countries of the United Kingdom, as does the annual official report *Social Trends*. The annual General Household Survey, widely used in this book, reports most of its data for Great Britain. The reader is urged to look carefully at the headings of tables and figures to note the geographical level to which they refer.

Other aspects of official demographic publication have also changed. One of the joys of nineteenth- and early twentieth-century censuses was the wide-ranging, erudite if sometimes idiosyncratic comment on census results, and the elegant literary style in which they were presented in the General Reports (e.g. Registrar-General 1904). The last such census report relates to 1951. Since then the reports have confined themselves to statistical housekeeping and to such dreary if essential topics as representativeness and error. No longer are there critical analyses of the social or economic impact of population trends, trenchant discussions of their bearing on the ideas of Malthus and other theorists, or quotations from Shakespeare. The Reports which comprised Part III of the annual Registrar-General's Statistical Reviews, which also commented on selected aspects of the trends in births, deaths, marriages, and so on, became extinct in 1973 along with the Quarterly Returns (see OPCS 1987a). The annual data are now published in the annual volumes listed in the Appendix. Annual and quarterly data are also published in the quarterly OPCS journal *Population Trends*, together with analysis by OPCS staff and outsiders. These articles, based on direct access to official data not all directly available to outsiders, form a huge corpus of detailed analysis of all aspects of British population. They were used extensively for this book.

In general, journals are by far the most important medium of communication in demography, as in most fast-moving subjects. On the whole, demographers seldom write books except on historical demography and on closely defined or technical subjects. None the less, the authors hope that this book will serve as a preliminary guide to this expanding literature. In some areas the authors have provided more references than can adequately be discussed in the text. This is deliberate. Some areas of population study, for example differential mortality, are politically controversial. Others involve technical problems or arguments which cannot be explored in appropriate detail in a general book. The interested reader can follow up his interest through the bibliography.

Thanks and acknowledgements

Thanks are due to many people for help with this book. Richard Doll, Robin Flowerdew, Peter Jackson, Jim Johnson, Kathleen Kiernan, Philip Kreager, John Simons, Tony Wrigley, all read various chapters of the book and made helpful suggestions for their improvement. John Haskey has helped in response to many queries. He and Alan Holmans kindly commented on a précis of the book which appeared earlier (in Halsey 1988). Elizabeth Whitmore and Nicholas Dimsdale provided data and graphs, Robert Bradbrook maps and diagrams. Mr D. N. O'Sullivan and his colleagues at the MoD Historical Branches provided unpublished military casualty figures. William Parry-Jones, Richard Smith, Malcolm Potts, and Peter Diggory located or provided many useful references. Numerous colleagues acted as sounding boards at various stages. The staff in the Longitudinal Study programme at the City University gave permission to cite data from their Working Papers, which are Crown Copyright. The OPCS permitted the use of some unpublished tabulations from the General Household Survey. All errors remain our own.

The tolerance extended by our spouses and children during the chronic dereliction of domestic duties involved in writing this book is a standing proof of the strength of the modern family.

DAVID COLEMAN
JOHN SALT

Oxford
Pinner

Acknowledgements

The authors and publishers wish to thank the following who have kindly given permission for the use of copyright material:

Edward Arnold (Publishers) Ltd. for data (Figs. 2.1, 2.7, 2.8) and graphs (Figs. 1.1, 1.2, 1.4, 1.7, 1.8, 2.2, 2.3) from *The Population History of England* by E. A. Wrigley and R. S. Schofield; and two maps from *Changing Places* by A. G. Champion, *et al.* (Figs. 3.4, 9.3).

The Board of Deputies Community Research Unit for a graph from *British Jewry in the Eighties* (Fig. 12.3).

The Brewers' Society for data from the *Brewers' Society Handbook*, 1989 (Fig. 7.10).

British Medical Journal for two diagrams from article 'Smoking and drinking by middle-aged British men' by Cummins, Shaper, Walker and Wale in vol. 288, 5 Dec., 1981 (Fig. 8.6).

The Controller of Her Majesty's Stationery Office for a Department of the Environment map (Fig. 10.2) and statistical projections (Figs. 6.4, 13.4); two diagrams from Home Office statistics (Figs. 11.2, 11.3); extracts from the *Employment Gazette* (Figs. 9.1, 9.2, 9.5); extracts from *Social Trends*, vols. 17, 18, and 19 (Figs. 5.8, 13.7, 13.10); and data and extracts from *Population Trends*, Working Papers and publications issued by the Office of Population Censuses and Surveys, *Population Trends* (Figs. 2.4, 2.5, 2.6, 4.6, 4.9, 4.15, 5.6, 5.7, 6.1, 6.3, 7.1, 7.3, 7.8, 7.9, 11.1, 12.1, 12.2, 12.4, 13.2, 13.5); Publications (Figs. 4.1, 4.4, 4.5, 4.7, 4.10, 4.11, 4.12, 4.13, 4.14, 5.1, 5.2a, 5.2b, 5.3, 5.9, 5.10, 5.11, 5.12a, 5.12b, 5.12c, 5.13, 6.2, 7.5, 8.1, 8.2, 8.3, 8.4, 8.7, 8.8, 9.3, 13.6).

Harvester-Wheatsheaf and The Johns Hopkins University Press for two sets of data from *The European Demographic Systems, 1500–1820* by M. W. Flinn (Figs. 1.5, 1.6).

The Institute of British Geographers for two maps by A. M. Warnes and C. M. Law, 1984 (Figs. 3.1, 3.2); map by A. E. Green, 1986 (Figs. 9.6), and diagram by P. H. Rees, 1986 (Fig. 10.1).

Pergamon Press PLC for diagrams from *British Cities: An Analysis of Urban Change* by N. Spence, *et al.* (Figs. 3.6, 3.7).

Routledge for two maps from *Regional Demographic Development* edited by J. Hobcraft and P. Rees, published by Croom Helm (Figs. 2.9, 2.10).

Tobacco Advisory Council for research figures (Fig. 7.4).

Unwin Hyman Ltd. for an extract from *Political Arithmetic: A Symposium of Population Studies* edited by Lancelot Hogben (Fig. 13.1).

Weidenfeld (Publishers) Ltd. for a diagram from *The U.K. Space: Resources, Environment and the Future*, 2nd edn., edited by J. W. House (Fig. 3.5).

Every effort has been made to trace all the copyright holders, but if any have been inadvertently overlooked the publishers will be pleased to make the necessary arrangement at the first opportunity.

Contents

List of Figures

List of Tables

Abbreviations

ASFR	age-specific fertility rates
ASTMS	Association of Scientific, Technical, and Managerial Staffs
BSPS	British Society for Population Studies
CDR	crude death-rate
CEPR	Centre for Economic Policy Research
CNS	central nervous system
COMA	Committee on Medical Aspects of food policy
CPS	Centre for Population Studies, London School of Hygiene and Tropical Medicine
CURDS	Centre for Urban and Regional Development Studies
DE	Department of Employment
DES	Department of Education and Science
DHSS	Department of Health and Social Security
DoE	Department of the Environment
ESRC	Economic and Social Research Council
GHS	General Household Survey
GRO	General Register Office
HSE	Health and Safety Executive
ICD	International Classification of Causes of Death
IHD	ischaemic heart disease
ILO	International Labour Organization
IMR	infant mortality rate
IMS	Institute of Manpower Studies
LFS	Labour Force Survey
LLMA	Local Labour Market Area
MELA	Metropolitan Economic Labour Area
MLH	minimum list heading
MRC	Medical Research Council
MSD	Migrant Services Division
NCC	Nature Conservancy Council
NCWP	New Commonwealth and Pakistan
NRPB	National Radiological Protection Board
OPCS	Office of Population Censuses and Surveys
RAWP	Resource Allocation Working Party
RGSR	Registrar-General's Statistical Review (now *Population Trends*)
SEG	socio-economic group
SIC	Standard Industrial Classification
SMLA	Standard Metropolitan Labour Area
SMR	standardized mortality ratio

STD   sexually transmitted disease
STICERD Suntory–Toyota International Centre for Economics and Related
              Disciplines, London School of Economics
TFR   total fertility rate
TPFR   total period fertility rate
WFS   World Fertility Survey

1 British Population: The Starting Point

1.1 Introduction

This book is about the population of contemporary Britain. Why begin by looking at its past? Historians insist that without knowing the past it is impossible to understand the present. So it is with demography. People live a long time. Populations have enormous inertia. Today's age structure, fertility, and mortality are created by people born from the present back to the 1880s. Most of the people who will constitute the population of Britain in 2030 are already alive. Our urban and regional population distribution is a legacy of past economic and social conditions.

More generally, demography is but a measure of the risks and chances involved in belonging to a particular society. Demographic differences reflect differences in national attitudes and habits as well as circumstances. These can change, but they usually change slowly. And they change more readily between generations than within the minds of individuals. British attitudes and circumstances, although in the mainstream of Western European development, have had a distinctive effect on demographic risk, and this will be one of the themes of the book.

It is also necessary to dispel imaginary pasts, conjured by theoreticians for their own purposes. University students still learn that Britain once had a society, like that of the contemporary Third World, of extended families and kin support for dependants; that before the industrial revolution marriage was early and universal; or even that Victorian values prevented the elderly living on their own. All false.

Only a historical perspective can show population in action over the decades or centuries that are needed to unfold its processes; to show how its growth and decline work in relation to changes in economy and environment, and how it can, and has, changed them in turn to produce the social and geographical setting in which we live today.

Major themes: growth and stagnation

This chapter is not intended to give a detailed history of population in the past. Thanks to the efflorescence of historical demography in the last two decades the reader can choose between several excellent accounts (e.g. Flinn 1981, Laslett 1983, Coale and Watkins 1986). More specialist works are given throughout the text for further reference, even when there is no space to discuss their contents. Instead this chapter's aim is to show how we arrived at our present position, to emphasize the distinctive features of British demographic experience, and what is similar, and what different, between today and the past.

For the population as a whole, the highlights are three episodes of rapid growth in the thirteenth, sixteenth, and from the eighteenth to the twentieth centuries. Two ended in crisis or at best stagnation; those in the early fourteenth century and the later seventeenth century. Then the positive checks of increased mortality, and in the latter case the more developed preventive check of deferred marriage and consequent lower fertility, reversed the upward trend of population growth (figure 1.1). The first of these demographic punctuations was made more severe and protracted by the advent of plague. The third burst of growth, from 1750 to the present, has succeeded. The achievement of

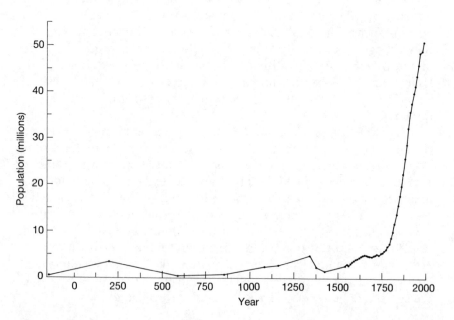

Note: After 1801 data refer to England and Wales, before 1801 to England only. Before 1541 data are highly conjectural.

Sources: See tables 1.1, 1.2. OPCS Monitor PP1 89/1 (revised mid-1988 population estimates for England and Wales). Census 1981, Historical Tables 1801–1981 England and Wales.

FIG. 1.1. Population Growth, 150 BC–1990

agricultural surplus and the new industrial mode of production freed the population from subsistence checks on population growth, so that population increased tenfold from 1695 to 1990.

Major themes: moderation

The demography of Britain stands out even in the unique setting of North-Western Europe as a paradigm of restraint (see Flinn 1981). Fertility and mortality have been lower than elsewhere and more uniform, both in time and space. In England the people may have been emancipated earlier than elsewhere in Europe from the restrictions of classical peasant life by markets in labour, land, and food of considerable demographic and social importance (Macfarlane 1978). The West European late and variable pattern of marriage kept fertility generally low and made it more adaptive to economic trends. Hence population growth was characteristically modest, creating a 'low-pressure' demographic regime. In England population density and mortality were lower, and crises less frequent, than on the Continent— a pattern helped by the diversity of agriculture and economy.

Britain, almost alone in Europe, has been relatively free from civil strife and invasion for 900 years. Few countries have enjoyed the ethnic and religious homogeneity characteristic of England at least until recently, and the consequent freedom from civil wars fuelled by ideological or racial hatreds. Some historians (e.g. Macfarlane 1986) suggest these advantages are not unconnected with the avoidance of the more absolute forms of autocracy and the grosser forms of inequality, the early rise of constitutional government, security of property, protection from the Counter-Reformation and from the spread of Roman law (Jones 1987).

The preventive check of marriage, not the positive check of mortality, has been the characteristic regulator of numbers at least since the sixteenth century (Wrigley and Schofield 1981). Household formation rules, still partly observed, kept production of children in relation to available resources. Marriage created a new household, and marriage could not take place unless that new, separate, household could be supported (Hajnal 1982). A fundamental influence of the Western Christian church has been invoked to explain the unusual 'diverging devolution' form of inheritance prevalent in the West. This system permits inheritance of property to children of either sex, rather than preserving it within descent groups or lineages. It implies the absence of a dowry. Without dowries, marriage was neither supported nor controlled by parents, but it had to be correspondingly delayed

(Goody 1983). The Anglo-Saxon common-law tradition of individual ownership and property rights, together with the concentration of inheritance of land on the first-born son (as opposed to partition among all children) helped underline the independence of households and made it worthwhile to wait. Other customs particularly emphasized in Britain, such as the boarding-out of young people as 'servants' (see Kussmaul 1981), assisted the flexibility of the labour force and the delay of marriage. Such a household was impermanent and constantly changing its age structure. It required a welfare system for its support (see R. M. Smith 1986), a major preoccupation of British economy, society, and politics since Elizabethan times. This in turn has helped domestic consensus.

A summary of population trends from the earliest times to 1550

In this account, population history begins in the sixteenth century.The insoluble fascinations of the medieval period and before are passed over with regret, thanks to lack of space in a volume primarily devoted to the present. Conjectures on earlier population size (table 1.1) and on birth and death rates are based on archaeological and ecological evidence (Darby 1973a, Renfrew 1987) and anthropological comparisons. Theoretical demography generates population models which show the limited options open to simple societies (Ward and Weiss 1976) given knowledge of their environment, agriculture, and technology (Coleman 1986) and puts at least an upper bound on population estimates.

Nothing remains of Roman censuses of Britannia, although more recent estimates point to a population of at least two million and possibly five million or more (Salway 1981). Apart from crude Saxon population estimates based on crude Saxon tax returns, demography of a very tentative kind (Krause 1957) begins with the 1086 Domesday inventory of feudal holdings, which put English population at 1–2 million (McEvedy and Jones 1978). Occasional further benchmarks like the 1377 poll tax give a basis for subsequent total population estimates (table 1.1). More continuous local evidence comes from the manor court rolls (records of local courts from about 1250—Razi 1980), feudal dues on inheritance and land use (heriots and entry fines), and legal proceedings (Inquisitiones Post Mortem).

Ecclesiastical records and manorial accounts of tenancies, incomes, and rents give indirect evidence of changes in local population (Titow 1969; Helleiner 1965) and of population pressure on land (Thirsk 1959; Donkin 1973). Their interpretation is usually controversial (see Harvey

Table 1.1. Population estimates for England up to 1801

Date	Period/People	Estimate	
10000 BC	Upper Palaeolithic: late glacial hunter/gatherers	2,000[a]. 250 over-wintering (S + E only)	
7500 BC	Mesolithic: hunters, gatherers, fishers	3,000–4,000[a]	
3000 BC	Neolithic cultivators and pastoralists: 'Windmill Hill'	20,000[a]	
2000 BC	Bronze Age: 'Beaker' people	30,000–40,000[a]	
510–250 BC	Iron Age: Halstatt/La Tène culture	250,000[a]	
150 BC	Belgae (in south and east)	300,000–600,000[a]	
AD 43–410	Roman occupation	400,000–800,000[b] 1–2 million, 5–6 million[c]	
450	Saxon–British conflict	300,000[b]	
590	Saxons and British (tribal hidage)	440,000[b]	
856	Anglo–Saxons (Peter's Pence)	750,000–850,000[b]	
1086	Domesday	1,750,000[b], 1.1–2.6m[i]	
1164	Peter's Pence	2.9m[i]	
1340	1377 Poll Tax and plague mortality	4–6m[f]	
1377	Poll Tax	2.2–2.8m[f]	
1421	Inquests post-mortem	1.6m[g]	
1430	Inquests post-mortem	2.1m[h]	
1545	Muster Rolls	2.8m[i]	2.8m[k]
1603	Ecclesiastical Census	4.1m[h]	4.1m
1650	Hearth Tax	5.0m[i]	5.2m
1695	Hearth Tax (Gregory King's estimate)	5.2m[f,j]	5.1m
1750	Parish Register back-projection	6.3m	5.8m
1801	Census	9.2m[j]	8.7m

[a] Clarke (1966).
[b] Russell (1948).
[c] Frere (1974); Salway (1981).
[d] Postan (1972); McEvedy and Jones (1978).
[e] Glass (1965a).
[f] Grigg (1980).
[g] Hollingsworth (1976).
[h] Cornwall (1967).
[i] Atsatt (n.d.).
[j] Includes Wales.
[k] Wrigley and Schofield's (1981) estimate for years ending −01 and −51 (except 1546).

1966). None of them was intended for demographic purposes, but with imagination give us some idea of individual survival and of the trend in population, if not its absolute level. Russell's great work (1948, 1985) analyses these sparse sources exhaustively, although sometimes with a daring artistry which few would care to follow.

The disturbed early years of the Norman succession were replaced in the thirteenth century with a rapid population growth (figure 1.1) of almost 1 per cent per year for a century (Hatcher 1977, Grigg 1980). By about 1300 there may have been more than five million people in England; a population not rivalled until the time of the Tudors (Postan 1966) or even until the eighteenth century (Smith 1990). By the beginning of the fourteenth century Britain and much of the rest of Europe shows signs interpreted by many economic historians as symptoms of over-population—rising death-rates, sky-high rents, falling wages, many holdings below the subsistence level of about 4 hectares (10 acres) on a three-field system for a family of 4–5 people (Titow 1969, Postan 1972, Hallam 1961, 1972). On top of that, a substantial deterioration of climate began in the fourteenth century (Lamb 1982, Goudie 1983) and lasted until the eighteenth, lowering the carrying capacity of an already overstretched agricultural system. Other economic historians dispute this interpretation (Harvey 1966). In the absence of national totals, it is difficult to be certain that population had already started to fall before the Black Death of 1348 (Smith 1990). Once bubonic plague was established in Western Europe (Bradley 1977), it became the dominant influence in mortality for three centuries, killing, in the view of all but a few dissenters (Bean 1963, Shrewsbury 1970) about a third of the population in the first few epidemics: the greatest recorded disaster in history (see Ziegler 1968; Morris 1971; McNeill 1977; Tuchman 1979). Plague mortality is not much influenced by population density or living conditions. Population was held down by this external force for more than a century (for medical details see Wright and Baird 1971; Biraben 1977).

Perhaps predictably, historians cannot agree when population began to recover (see Saltmarsh 1941, Bean 1963, Hatcher 1977). Plague is an acute disease which kills but does not maim. It may have helped European populations to escape the Malthusian trap whereby population tends to increase up to the level of subsistence so that population growth chokes on the restricted food supply and low wages which it helps create. The century after the arrival of the plague is sometimes known as the 'golden age of the peasant'. Because of the shortage of labour, social and economic conditions moved in favour of the labourer and villein. Real wages rose to values not rivalled until the eighteenth century (Postan 1966, Grigg 1980), an unprecedented combination of high mortality with relatively high living standards (Bridbury 1981, 1986).

By this time some important characteristic features of the British demographic scene had already become established: a free market in land, labour, and food (Macfarlane 1978); freedom from feudal pressures to marry and remarry (Macfarlane 1986), more than on the Continent (a claim the Continentals deny). This prevented a classical peasant economy developing and encouraged geographical mobility and later marriage (Helleiner 1967). These are the origins of a 'low pressure' demographic system, with lower density—dependent mortality balanced by low fertility to the advantage of individual surplus and economic growth (Wrigley 1972).

In the Tudor period where we begin, it is clear that population is at last climbing away from its medieval nadir. The inquisitive fact-gathering needs of a more intrusive state, with a greater surplus at its disposal from a richer, diverse economy, leave for the first time traces of total population size and records of vital events (Hollingsworth 1977, Laslett 1983). Using them, historians can agree more often on the demographic reconstruction of population and of individual and family life.

1.2 Data for Population History

Muster rolls (for military purposes, see Rich 1950), lay subsidy rolls (for head taxes like the poll tax), and religious 'censuses' give some clues to total size (Thirsk 1959; Cornwall 1967; Russell 1948; Smith 1978). The institution of parish registers in 1538, following the establishment of the new national church in 1534, gives a wholly new coverage of births, deaths, and marriages in so far as they were recorded as baptisms, burials, and religious solemnizations of marriage. These new records are no coincidence. They represent new inquiries by a modernizing mercantilist state into its own resources and security, made possible by the growth of literacy and numeracy, and a more settled social and political order.

The parish registers

The parish registers are the most useful of these new sources. Some parishes already recorded the baptisms, burials, and marriages of parishioners, but the records were erratic and unstandardized. The earliest are for Burgundy, beginning in 1334. Records of baptisms, marriage, and burial were important to the new State Church as well as to individuals as proof of legitimacy, parenthood, marriage, and inheritance. The emphasis on publication after the Reformation is associated with Protestant denial of the strictly sacramental quality of marriage based on mutual consent of the partners, and the re-emphasis of the need for parental consent. Thomas Cromwell, Lord Privy Seal, required all parish incumbents in the 10,000 parishes of England to record these religious events in standard form from 1538 onwards. Registration in Scotland began in 1557 (births and marriages) and 1565 (burials) but they were poorly kept and worse preserved (see Flinn *et al.* 1977). Registers in Ireland have been even less studied (Goldstrom and Clarkson 1981).

Parish records are useful only as far as the religious facts of Anglican baptism and burial correspond to demographic facts of birth and death. This depends on the efficiency of the incumbent and his vestry, and the denominational structure of the country. Extraordinary efforts have been made since the nineteenth century to determine the size and trend of these errors, because of the immense potential value of the material. No definitive answer is ever likely to be achieved, but it seems agreed that the registers were more accurate in the sixteenth and seventeenth centuries than later on, that records of burials are a better surrogate for deaths than are baptisms for births and that urban parishes present particular problems (Griffith 1926, Krause 1965, Hollingsworth 1977, Wrigley 1968, Wrigley and Schofield 1981).

Accuracy of the registers

In the early period, plurality of livings and other abuses had not yet arisen, there were few Dissenters and fewer Papists. The large urban populations of the eighteenth and nineteenth centuries, with their secular burial grounds, were still far off. Births were less well recorded than deaths partly because so many new-born babies died before baptism, and their deaths might not be recorded either. Religious opposition to early child baptism in the sixteenth and seventeenth centuries increased the proportion of unregistered births. The known relation between the risks of early and late infant death (Bourgeois-Pichat 1951), permits some statistical estimation of deaths of missing, unbaptized infants. Dissenters might often baptize in their own chapels or homes, but the possession of a burial ground might be beyond their resources so their deaths, but not births, would find a place in Anglican parish records.

Aggregated statistics

Parish records are exploited in two chief ways; by 'aggregation' and 'family reconstitution'. In the former, the totals of vital events in one or several parishes are added together for each week, month, and year to form a time-series. Unfortunately these are numerators without denominators. Without an estimate of population they cannot be turned into death- or birth-rates, and long-term increases or declines cannot be interpreted without further information. However in the short run the population base is unlikely to change fast so the totals of baptisms, burials, and marriages themselves are interpreted directly as population responses to epidemics and economic crises and to show whether the local, and by extension the national, population is growing or declining (figure 1.2).

Family reconstitution

By linking the recurrence of the same name at baptism, marriage, baptism of children, and eventual burial, a dated life course of individuals and families can be reconstructed. This 'family reconstitution' technique was first developed in France (Fleury and Henry 1956; see also Hollingsworth 1957, 1964, Wrigley 1966*a*). Although immensely laborious—only about 26 parishes have been thoroughly analysed in this way since Wrigley's pioneer study of Colyton (Wrigley 1966*b*)—it yields unique information on expectation of life, age at marriage, family size, and the spacing and timing of births unobtainable from aggregate methods (Wrigley and Schofield 1983; Wilson 1984). It broke the log-jam in which aggregative studies had been wedged, especially by enabling vital rates to be estimated without the need for population estimates as a denominator. It depends to some extent on the assumption of geographical immobility of the population—which tends to be exaggerated (Coleman 1984) and on the representative nature of the 10 per cent of baptisms which can be traced to their burial (Hollingsworth 1977).

The Bills of Mortality

The Bills of Mortality, published from 1629 to 1849, were weekly and yearly summaries of deaths and births published by the Worshipful Company of Parish Clerks (a secular institution), first in London, then in provincial cities, as also, for similar reasons, in many European cities. The Company employed 'searchers' to investigate the deaths reported to them and to record the cause of death in so far as it could be

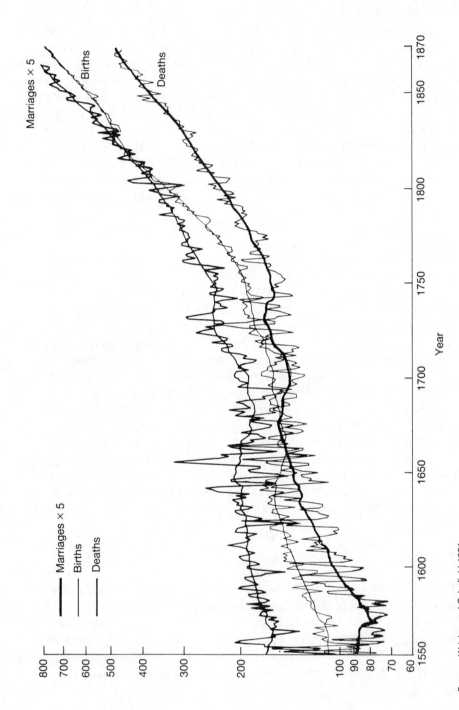

Source: Wrigley and Schofield 1981.

Fig. 1.2. Baptisms, marriages, and burials, 1541–1871

determined. The aim was to give advance warning of rising levels of mortality that heralded a new epidemic, especially of the plague. (The Registrar-General's Weekly Return and other series still have a similar function to screen for unusual trends in deaths or malformations). Causes of death listed in the Bills are often symptomatic or circumstantial: 'headache', 'teeth and worms', 'sudden', 'apoplex', 'frighted' are listed together with more useful diagnoses: 'consumption', 'plague', 'pox' (figure 1.3). The more distinctive of these diseases are thought to be useful as evidence of patterns and trends (Galloway 1985, Landers 1987). They were used as the data source for the world's first book on demography, John Graunt's *Natural and Political Observations upon the Bills of Mortality* (1660, see Glass 1963, Kreager 1988). They are published already aggregated, but they are ostensibly complete, with Nonconformists, Dissenters and all—though not in practice (Glass 1973).

Population estimates

John Rickman, Controller-General of the first four Censuses was the first (1802, 1843) to attempt to project back the population into the demographic unknown of the eighteenth century and earlier, using the yearly totals of baptisms and burials (Farr 1863, Brownlee 1916, Griffith 1926, Glass 1964). The unknown national totals have to be grossed up from a sample of parishes. Rickman required parish incumbents to return the totals of baptisms and burials for selected past years at the first four censuses. Migration has to be estimated too, of course, with hardly any direct data.

The most ambitious attempt to reconstruct past population—and one of the largest demographic enquiries ever made—is a back projection based on data collected mostly by amateur historians from no less than 404 parishes, to reconstruct English population history from 1541 to 1871 (Wrigley and Schofield 1981), using essentially aggregate-based methods with some help from selected reconstitution data. While not exactly representative of the 10,000 ancient parishes (there are none from London) and although few are continuous over the whole period, the prodigious checks on the data ensure that it is the best treatment that we are likely to get (Hollingsworth 1982; Flinn 1982). These estimates of population, and the vital rates derived from them, will be referred to throughout this account (figure 1.4).

The starting point is 1871, an accurate census preceded by other fairly accurate censuses, which enable the results to be checked. Births

A generall Bill for this prefent year,

ending the 19 of *December* 1665. according to
the Report made to the KINGS moft Excellent Majefty.

By the Company of Parifh Clerks of *London*, &c.

	Buried	Pla.		Buried	Pla.		Buried	Pla.		Burie	Pla.
St A'bans Woodftreet	200	121	St Clements Eaftcheap	28	20	St Margaret Mofes	38	25	St Michael Cornhill	104	52
St Alhallowes Barking	514	330	St Dionis Back-church	78	27	St Margaret Newfifhft	114	66	St Michael Crookedla	179	133
St Alhallowes Breadft	35	16	St Dunftans Eaft	265	150	St Margaret Pattons	49	24	St Michael Queenhit	203	122
St Alhallowes Great	455	426	St Edmunds Lumbard	70	36	St Mary Abchurch	99	54	St Michael Que ne	44	18
St Alhallowes Honila	10	5	St Ethelborough	195	106	St Mary Aldermanbury	181	109	St Michael Royall	152	116
St Alhallowes Leffe	239	175	St Faiths	104	70	St Mary Aldermary	105	75	St Michael Woodftreet	122	62
St Alball. Lumbardftr.	90	52	St Fofters	144	105	St Mary le Bow	64	36	St Mildred Breadftreet	59	26
St Alhallowes Staining	185	112	St Gabriel Fen-church	69	39	St Mary Bothaw	55	30	St Mildred Poultrey	68	46
St Alhallowes the Wall	500	356	St George Botolphlane	41	27	St Mary Colechurch	17	6	St Nicholas Acons	46	28
St Alphage	271	115	St Gregories by Pauls	375	232	St Mary Hill	94	64	St Nicholas Coleabby	125	91
St Andrew Hubbard	71	25	St Hexens	108	75	St Mary Mounthaw	56	37	St Nicholas Olaues	90	62
St Andrew Vnderfhaft	274	189	St James Dukes place	262	190	St Mary Summerfet	342	262	St Olaves Hartftreet	237	100
St Andrew Wardrobe	476	303	St James Garlickhithe	189	118	St Mary Stayning	47	27	St Olaves Iewry	54	32
St Anne Alderfgate	282	197	St John Baptift	138	83	St Mary Woolchurch	65	33	St Olaves Silverftreet	250	132
St Anne Blacke-Friers	652	467	St John Euangelift	9		St Mary Woolnoth	75	38	St Pancras Soperlane	30	15
St Antholins Parifh	58	33	St Iohn Zacharie	85	54	St Martins Iremonger	21	11	St Peters Cheape	61	35
St Auftins Parifh	43	40	St Katherine Coleman	299	213	St Martins Ludgate	196	128	St Peters Cornehill	136	76
St Barthol. Exchange	53	51	St Katherine Creechu	335	231	St Martins Orgars	110	71	St Peters Pauls Wharfe	114	86
St Bennet Fynch	47	12	St Lawrence Iewry	94	48	St Martins Outwitch	60	34	St Peters Poore	79	47
St Bent. Grace-church	57	41	St Lawrence Pountney	214	140	St Martins Vintrey	417	349	St Sievens Colmanft	160	391
St Bennet Pauls Wharf	355	172	St Leonard Eaftcheap	42	27	St Matthew Fridayftr.	24	6	St Stevens Walbr. oke	34	17
St Bennet Sherehog	11	1	St Leonard Fofterlane	335	255	St Maudlins Milkftreet	44	22	St Swithins	93	56
St Botolph Billingfgate	83	50	St Magnus Parifh	103	60	St Maudlins Oldfifhftr.	176	121	St Thomas Apoftle	63	110
Chrifts Church	653	467	St Margaret Lothbury	100	66	St Michael Baffifhaw	253	164	Trinitie Parifh	115	79
St Chriftophers	60	17									

Buried in the 97 *Parifhes within the walls,* —— 15207   *Whereof of the Plague* —— 9887

	Buried	Pla.		Buried	Pla.		Buried	Pla.
St Andrew Holborne	3958	3103	Bridewell Precinct	230	179	St Dunftans Weft	958	665	St Saviours Southwark	1230	1446
St Bartholmew Grea	493	344	St Botolph Alderfga.	997	755	St George Southwark	1613	1260	St Sepulchres Parifh	4509	2746
St Bartholmew Leffe	193	139	St Botolph Alſgate	4926	4051	St Giles Cripplegate	8069	4838	St Thomas Southwark	475	371
St Bridges	2111	1427	St Botolph Bifhopfg	3464	2500	St Olaves Southwark	4793	2785	Trinity Minories	168	123
									At the Pefthouſe	159	156

Buried in the 16 *Parifhes without the walls* —— 41351   *Whereof, of the Plague* —— 28888

	Buried	Pla.		Buried	Pla.		Buried	Pla.
St Giles in the Fields	4457	3216	St Katherines Tower	956	601	St Magdalen Bermon	1943	1362	St Mary Whitechappel	4766	3855
Hackney Parifh	232	132	Lambeth Parifh	798	537	St Mary Newington	1272	1004	Rearifhe Parifh	304	210
St James Clarkeawel	1863	1377	St Leonard Shordicch	2669	1949	St Mary Iflington	696	593	Stepney Parifh	8598	6583

Buried in the 12 *out-Parifhes, in Middlefex and Surrey* : 18554 *Whereof, of the Plague* —— 21420

	Buried	Pla.		Buried	Pla.	
St Clement Danes	1969	1319	St Mary Savoy	303	198	*The Total of all the Chriftnings.* —— 9967
St Paul Covent Garden	408	261	St Margaret Weftminft.	4710	3742	*The Total of all the Burials this year* — 97306
St Martins in the Fields	4304	2883	*bevreof at the Pefthouſe* —— 156			*Whereof, of the Plague* —— 68596
Buried in the 5 *Parifhes in the City and Liberties of Weftminfter* — 12194						
Whereof, of the Plague —— 8403						

The Difeafes and Cafualties this year.

A Bortive and Stilborne —— 617
Aged —— 1545
Ague and Feaver —— 5257
Appoplex and Suddenly —— 116
Bedrid —— 10
Blafted —— 5
Bleeding —— 16
Bloody Flux, Scowring & Flux 185
Burnt and Scalded —— 8
Calenture —— 3
Cancer, Gangrene and Fiftula 56
Canker, and Thrufh —— 111
Childbed —— 625
Chrifomes and Infants —— 1258
Cold and Cough —— 68
Collick and Winde —— 134
Confumption and Tiffick —4808
Convulfion and Mother —— 2036
Diftracted —— 5
Dropfie and Timpany —— 1478
Drowned —— 50

Executed —— 21
Flox and Small Pox —— 655
Found dead in ftreets, fields, &c. 20
French Pox —— 86
Frighted —— 23
Gout and Sciatica —— 27
Grief —— 46
Griping in the Guts —— 1288
Hangd & made away themfelves 7
Headmouldfhot & Mouldfallen 14
Jaundies —— 110
Impoftume —— 227
Kild by feverall accidents —— 46
Kings Evill —— 86
Leprofie —— 2
Lethargy —— 14
Livergrown —— 20
Meagrom and Headach —— 12
Measles —— 7
Murthered and Shot —— 9
Overlaid & Starved —— 45

Palfie —— 30
Plague —— 68596
Planner —— 6
Plurifie —— 15
Poyfoned —— 1
Quinfie —— 35
Rickets —— 557
Rifing of the Lights —— 397
Rupture —— 34
Scurvy —— 105
Shingles and Swine pox —— 2
Sores, Ulcers, broken and bruifed Limbs —— 82
Spleen —— 14
Spotted Feaver and Purples 1929
Stopping of the ftomack —— 332
Stone and Strangury —— 98
Surfet —— 1251
Teeth and Worms —— 2614
Vomiting —— 51
VVenn —— 8

Chriftned { Males —— 5114, Females —— 4853, In all —— 9967 }
Buried { Males —— 48569, Females —— 48737, In all —— 97306 } Of the Plague —— 68596

Increafed in the Burials in the 130 Parifhes and at the Peft-houfe this year —— 79009
Increafed of the Plague in the 130 Parifhes and at the Peft-houfe this year —— 68596

Source: Glass 1973: 22.

FIG. 1.3. Bill of Mortality, 1665

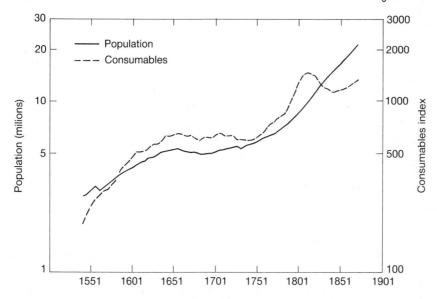

Note: The consumables index represents a 25-year moving average of the index figures centred on the dates shown.

Source: Wrigley and Schofield 1981, fig. 10.1.

FIG. 1.4. Population estimates from back-projections, 1541–1871, compared to an index of prices

and deaths of the preceding five years, produced by a reverse survival technique, initially independent of the parish register data, generate the preceding age structure. Deaths are distributed by age according to a set of model life tables based on the English Life Table No. 3 of 1838–54. Net migration is estimated by a precarious method using fixed age-specific migration rates (ignoring the few scraps of empirical data which exist) which are essentially based on migration filling in the gap between the estimated births and observed births. Iterative recalculations of the estimates adjust the balance between migration and mortality, and generate a set of estimates consistent both with demographic principles and with the parish register data.

1.3 A Demographic Picture of the Early Modern Period

These new sources of data emphasize that Western Europe's population starts from a point different from that of the developing world, and that the demographic regime in Britain is exceptional even in the context of Europe (see Macfarlane 1978; Flinn 1981).

Households

Households then were typically large compared to today's average of 2.6—about 4.7 persons on average, varying within narrow limits from the late sixteenth to the early twentieth century (Laslett 1969; Wall 1979; R. M. Smith 1981; see Chapter 6). But they seldom contained family members outside the nuclear family. This distinguishes them from the full-scale extended family typical of the modern developing world (Hajnal 1982) and especially of tropical Africa. Neither vertical extension with three generations present at once, nor lateral extension with several closely related people living with their wives as one family were common. Even then many old people lived on their own. From the mid-seventeenth to the early nineteenth century, only 5–7 per cent of households embraced three generations (Wall 1983).

Predominance of the nuclear family was a matter of choice. Seventeenth-century mortality would have permitted more than 40 per cent of families at any time to have been 'stem' families, that is, with at least three generations cohabiting, while in fact less than 20 per cent did so (Wachter, Hammel, and Laslett 1977). Then as now, the children would leave home on marriage and the new husband would be head of a new household. One of the major constraints on marriage was the difficulty of marrying until a separate establishment could be maintained. Marriage, and consequently fertility, followed economic trends as measured by real wage indices. 'It was the initiation of new households that powered the demographic motor in early modern England' (R. M. Smith 1981).

Households were made diverse by lodgers and 'servants' (Hajnal 1982). Over this period, about 30 per cent of households included servants (resident household or farm workers (Kussmaul 1981), not predominantly personal servants). They were unmarried boys and girls, aged 15–30, boarded out from other families. This common experience was rare outside North-West Europe, especially as girls as well as boys took part in the system. Up to three quarters of boys, and a half of girls, entered service at some time in their lives, and at any one time about a third of the 15–25 age-group would be in service. Service made the British population unusually geographically mobile (Schofield 1970) and made it easier to delay marriage if circumstances were unfavourable (Smith 1978). Individuals could remain as servants for longer and so servants would become more numerous (from 10 per cent to 20 per cent of the population over age 15). Marriage rates, and so fertility, would decline; and *vice-versa* when circumstances became more favourable.

Table 1.2. Average age at first marriage and proportions never married, England, 1600–1849

Marriage cohort	Average age at first marriage[a]		Proportion never married (%)[b]	Marriage cohort
	Men	Women		
			6.3	1556–71
1600–1649	28.0	26.0	24.1	1601–6
1650–1699	27.8	26.5	27.0	1651–6
1700–1749	27.5	26.2	11.2	1704–6
1750–1799	26.4	24.9	4.9	1751–6
1800–1849	25.3	23.4	9.6	1801–6

[a] Wrigley and Schofield (1981), mean of 12 reconstitution studies, t. 7.26.
[b] Wrigley and Schofield (1981) (men and women together), t. 7.28.

The West European marriage pattern

In these ways marriage was the key to household formation, family size, and population growth in pre-industrial Europe. A unique pattern of late marriage (26–7 for men, 23–4 for women) (Hajnal 1965) and of a high proportion remaining celibate throughout life (10–15 per cent of men, and more women, still unmarried by age 50) was general throughout Western Europe by the sixteenth century; earlier in some places (Anderson 1980; Dupaquier *et al.* 1981). The medieval aristocracy retained a 'non-European' pattern, marrying younger than commoners, but by 1575–99 their mean age at marriage for men was 26, for women 21. It is a pattern clearly apparent in the parish registers as soon as these come into existence. By the end of the seventeenth century, mean age at first marriage in England was 28 for men, 26 for women (table 1.2). More than 25 per cent never married at all around that time: an all-time high. Ordinary people may have married late even in the fourteenth century (Smith 1990*a*); in line with the relatively modern state of British medieval society in general (Macfarlane 1978).

By themselves, nuclear families encounter difficulties in remaining self-sufficient at all stages of their development and in protecting themselves from risk and the demands of old age. Consequently, in the absence of an extended family, substantial external systems of welfare have a long history in Western Europe to provide relief. The manor, Guilds, the Church through the parish and the monasteries, the rich through private charity were all involved (Webb and Webb 1927).

After the Reformation in the sixteenth century and the dissolution of the monasteries from 1536 the first Poor Law of 1601 marked the beginning of a more codified welfare state, initially based on the parish (see Wales 1984). For example in the parish of Aldenham, Hertfordshire at any one time from 1641 to 1701 about 43 per cent of the population was paying for welfare (through the parish rates), about 27 per cent was receiving it, and about 30 per cent was untouched by it either way (Neuman Brown 1986). Relatives were also obliged by law to help certain categories of dependants, but children do not seem to have been looked upon as a necessary form of old-age security, or as important assets for work or protection against risk. The contrast between Western, and especially British domestic strategies for risk management, and the different responses found elsewhere, is full of insights for the way that developing societies may be changing (R. M. Smith 1986, 1988).

Marriage and fertility

Late marriage depresses final family size and hence population growth. Through its responsiveness to trends in subsistence and economy, variable marriage enables population growth to adjust so as to minimize subsistence crises. This is the essential mechanism of the preventive check described by Malthus (Wrigley 1986, Winch 1987). Accordingly family size was relatively small throughout Western Europe (an average of 5–6 children born to each married woman surviving to the end of her fertile life) even though fertility ran at the 'natural' level after marriage (table 1.3). Because many women did not marry, the average per woman was seldom as high as five. With earlier and universal marriage, average completed family size per woman would have been nearer the 7–8 children typical of many areas of tropical Africa today; in fact the spacing of births was shorter than in African populations. Generally in Western Europe less than 5 per cent of births occurred outside marriage.

At this time 'natural' fertility levels seem to have prevailed within marriage. 'Natural' fertility is the term given to fertility unimpeded by attempts to limit family size to a given number of children through contraception or abortion, although numbers may be limited, for example, by long birth spacing arising from protracted breast-feeding, or by late marriage. The concept enables the fertility of 'non-contracepting' populations to be compared, and the intensity of contraception to be inferred once it has started (Henry 1961, Leridon and Menken 1982). Although techniques such as coitus interruptus

Table 1.3. Fertility in England, 1600–1799

Period	TFR[a]	% illegiti- mate	Legitimate TFR	% never married	Estimated completed family size[b]	Reconstituted completed family size[c]
1600–49	4.31	2.4	4.21	20.5	5.30	5.22
1650–99	4.22	1.9	4.14	22.9	5.37	5.00
1700–49	4.61	2.3	4.50	11.6	5.09	5.14
1750–99	5.35	4.4	5.11	5.9	5.43	5.61

[a] From back-projection estimates.
[b] Calculated from:
$$\frac{\text{legitimate TFR} \times 100}{100 - (\text{per cent never married})}$$
[c] From family reconstitution estimates. For details of comparability see source.
Source: Wrigley and Schofield 1983, t. 12.

were known in the Middle Ages, there is no good evidence for widespread family limitation within marriage in Britain before the mid-nineteenth century, although it began earlier elsewhere (Chapter 2). Women who did marry at about age 20 had more than seven children in their lifetime (Wilson 1984). Most women married later, producing an average of five children in the late sixteenth century if they survived to the end of their fertile life, fewer in the late seventeenth when marriage was even later (Wrigley and Schofield 1983). Ignoring pre-marital conceptions (inferred from a birth within eight months of marriage) by excluding the first age-group in each case, women marrying at age 15–19 would have 6.2 children, at 20–4 5.0 children and at 25–9 3.6 (Wrigley and Schofield 1983). Pre-marital conception was, however, quite common—about 20 per cent of first births before 1750, and 35–7 per cent from 1750 to 1820 (Flinn 1981). After the promises of betrothal, it would be normal to begin sexual relations although the marriage would occur well before the birth. Pregnancy might determine the timing of the wedding when sexual relations had begun before betrothal, and the child might then be christened shortly after marriage.

The English 'low pressure' regime

English fertility was uniformly low, lacking the regional differences characteristic of many Continental countries. Given changes in age at marriage, fertility within marriage varied remarkably little over two centuries, remaining at about 67 per cent of the maximum natural

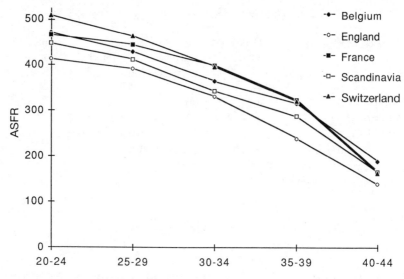

Source: Data from Flinn 1981.

Fig. 1.5. Age-specific fertility rates, selected European countries before 1750

fertility which could have been realized (by comparison with the Hutterites, the benchmark population for high human fertility). English fertility within marriage seems to have been, in parishes from widely scattered areas, consistently lower than in other countries of Europe (figure 1.5), with birth intervals after the first considerably longer (Flinn 1981, Wrigley and Schofield 1983, Wilson 1984). This is likely to be due to long and near-universal breast-feeding, which would space children at longer intervals, but which was by no means the rule in all Continental areas especially in some where Roman Catholicism predominated (Fildes 1988). Breast-feeding would tend to moderate mortality of infants by keeping family size more modest and birth spacing more generous, and in general by lowering population pressure. Infant mortality in England seems to have been lower than elsewhere (figure 1.6).

Late marriage, low fertility, and relatively high mobility in a social setting where land and labour could be bought, and where acquisition of landholding or wealth was a prerequisite for marriage, helped the development of a new economy. Savings and market forces became more important, rather than the unmonetized subsistence and self-sufficiency of a peasant economy. Low fertility produced a relatively favourable age structure with about one third of the population under age 15. Such a 'low pressure' demographic regime makes it easier to

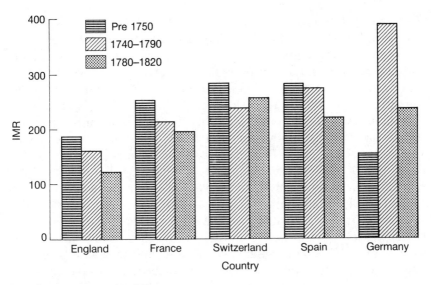

Note: Germany: suspect data 1750.

Source: Data from Flinn 1981, t. 6.9 (reconstitution data).

Fig. 1.6. Infant mortality rates, selected European countries up to 1820

develop and accumulate a surplus over and above the output necessary for subsistence. These are circumstances favourable to economic growth and diversity, especially outside the agricultural sector, and to the growth of cities.

Mortality

Exogenous high mortality?

Up to the seventeenth century, European aristocrats, ruling families, Jesuit priests, and other privileged groups do not seem to have enjoyed longer lives than anyone else (Livi-Bacci 1983, Hatcher 1986). British aristocrats suffered higher infant mortality, and high adult mortality from violence, which gave them lower expectations of life (38) than the contemporary rural commons (40 or more) (Hollingsworth 1977). This is taken to be strong evidence for the 'exogenous' nature of many mortality risks at that time, especially those associated with contaminated water, plague, and risks to infants. Despite their protection from want, peers seemed no more immune than anyone else from the prevailing high environmental risks of infectious disease. On top of that they suffered high risks of death in battle or execution after unsuccessful treason: 46 per cent of peers died violently from 1330 to

1479, and even 10 per cent of the 1680–1729 birth cohort—though by then as often on the hunting field as on the field of battle. In the eighteenth century they enjoyed a 10 per cent improvement in child survival and a 20 per cent reduction in adult mortality (Hollingsworth 1964). Expectation of life among peers born in 1730–79 improved from 35 years to 46; a longer life than European ruling families (Peller 1965).

In the early modern period mortality fluctuated violently from one year to the next, primarily from epidemics, much less from crises of subsistence (figure 1.2). Out of every 1,000 infants born in country areas, 160–90 died before their first birthday, another 100 more by their fifth. No more than 70–5 per cent of births survived to age 15 (table 1.4). The expectation of life at birth was about 35 years, the crude death-rate (CDR) about 30 deaths per 1,000 population per year. There was a constant heavy burden of deaths due to ill-recorded diseases of childhood and infancy, especially diarrhoea and dysentery, measles and other fevers, as well as more spectacular epidemics. In urban areas, especially London, only about 50–60 per cent of births survived to age 15 (Finlay 1981). Other diseases (to which infants were also susceptible) were more catastrophic or periodic, especially in rural areas (Landers 1987). Smallpox in rural areas, plague, and influenza are of this epidemic type. These were the prime causes of 'crisis mortality'.

Crisis mortality may be defined as a year where the overall death-rate was 10 per cent higher than average. In the twentieth century this would be an unprecedented disaster; for Britain the Second World War would only just qualify. There were forty-five national crisis years of such mortality from 1541 to 1871—one year in seven (Wrigley and Schofield 1981). The worst periods are 1557–8, 1558–9 (CDR 47 and 65), 1625–6 (CDR 36), 1657–8 (CDR 39), 1728–9 (CDR 43), 1727–8 (CDR 42). These are all well-known periods of crisis; influenza in the mid-sixteenth century, disastrous harvests in the early seventeenth. Some regions and parishes were much more prone to crises than others (Schofield 1972). Taking now a crisis year as one where mortality is double the average, a sample of 54 parishes from 1538 to 1809 had on average one crisis every 46 years. But 26 of them had 3 or less, while 7 had 10 or more over the same period.

Crises of subsistence were relatively infrequent compared to Continental countries, especially France, where agriculture was more intensive and specialized (Wrigley 1966a, Appleby 1979, Flinn 1981). The English diet appears to have been varied; the prominence of meat was commented upon by foreign visitors (Drummond and Wilbraham 1938). Montesquieu observed in 1729: 'The people of London eat much

Table 1.4. Infant mortality

(a) Infant mortality in the early modern period, England

	Aristocracy[a]	National population[b]	
		Males	Females
1550–99	—	143	127
1600–49	—	142	123
1650–74	210⎱	154[c]	133[c]
1675–99	196⎰		
1700–24	169⎱	168[d]	148[d]
1725–49	166⎰		
1750–74	102⎱	135[e]	122[e]
1775–99	85⎰		
1800–24	82	—	—

(b) Contrast between neonatal and overall infant mortality[f]

	IMR	Neonatal	Neonatal as a percentage of total infant mortality
1680–9	204	88	43
1730–9	181	74	41
1780–9	165	51	31
1840–9	150	23	15
1875 'healthy rural'	103	21	20
1875 Liverpool	234	23	10

[a] Hollingsworth (1964).
[b] Wrigley and Schofield (1981).
[c] Covers period 1650–99.
[d] Covers period 1700–49.
[e] Covers period 1750–99.
[f] Fildes (1980).

meat, which makes them very vigorous, but at the age of 40 to 45 years, they die.' England escaped to some extent the Europe-wide subsistence problems of the 1690s and 1720s—evidence of the tightening grip of adverse weather—as a result of its more diverse and market-based agriculture. It also escaped the periodic removal of its means of subsistence by marauding armies. Unlike France, there were few villages depending primarily on specialized non-agricultural activity (such as silk weaving).

Plague

Medicine in Tudor and Stuart times could cure nothing and prevent nothing. The rising knowledge and professionalism of medicine and the empirical enquiries into anatomy and physiology have left us rather better descriptions of diseases, but the mortality rate from these diseases did not decline.

Bubonic plague was one of the most important single causes of death, at least of adults, from the fourteenth century to the seventeenth. Human populations have never adapted to it: untreated case–fatality rates remain about 80–100 per cent. High proportions of those who remained in towns risked infection—between 35 and 80 per cent in Tuscan towns in the 1630s, 56 per cent in eighteenth century Provence (Benedictow 1987). Plague accounts for 24 per cent of all recorded deaths in some sixteenth century London parishes, and 13 per cent of all deaths in London from 1609 to 1636 (Finlay 1981). In London the plague continued to kill large numbers of people up to the time of its last appearance in 1679. There were major epidemics in 1603, 1625, and especially 1665 when at least 95,000 out of the 400,000 inhabitants of London died of it (Sutherland 1972).

Its decline, still not adequately explained (Appleby 1980*a*), helped the gradual recovery of population from the sixteenth century onwards. The withdrawal of plague first from northern and country areas, its isolation in the great towns and finally in London, is evidence for the effectiveness of quarantine and other empirical public-health measures in preventing its spread (Slack 1985). It had gone from Scotland by 1649. Effective imposition of quarantine at seaports became possible as the State's power and efficiency improved; although the measure would only be effective if there was no endemic focus for the disease in native animals. If quarantine were responsible for suppressing plague, it would be the first effective public-health measure and one of the most important.

Tuberculosis

Tuberculosis (especially pulmonary tuberculosis) was also among the most important causes of death after infancy and became paramount until the late nineteenth century, helped by urbanization. A slow-acting disease spread by droplet infection (pulmonary) and contaminated milk (bovine) its prevalence is strongly influenced by nutritional standards (which help to determine the strength of immune response against it) and by overcrowding (which aids its dissemination from one person to another) in the country as well as in town. Records in one Shropshire parish attribute between 16 and 28 per cent of deaths to tuberculosis from 1750 to 1780, and in the London Bills of Mortality it claims 20 per cent of deaths in 1629–35, rising to a peak of 24 per cent in 1801–10 (Greenwood 1935, Galloway 1985). More will be said of TB in Chapter 2.

Smallpox

Smallpox ranked third as a cause of death after plague and TB, accounting for up to 18 per cent of deaths in London in epidemic years, but more usually 5 per cent (Creighton 1891). Most children in London caught it; in rural areas it was more epidemic and even more feared. In the Bills of Mortality of provincial towns, between 10 and 19 per cent of deaths are attributed to smallpox in the mid-eighteenth century (Razzell 1977). It may be a relatively recent disease in England (Gale 1959), arriving maybe no earlier than the reign of James I (1603–25). The constant acquisition of new diseases should cause no surprise; rapid growth of trade links and overseas empires open up many new opportunities for the exchange of previously provincial pestilences (McNeill 1977). The burden of mortality from smallpox among the majority of the population living in the countryside is more difficult to determine, but other European countries experienced heavy rural mortality from smallpox in the eighteenth century, for example 14 per cent of deaths in rural parishes in Finland (Mercer 1985).

Malaria

Deaths from 'ague' or marsh fever were common in low-lying areas. This was almost certainly vivax malaria (Dobson 1980). Death-rates in low-lying parishes in Kent and Essex from 1551 to 1750 were between 46 and 71 per 1,000 per year compared to 30 or so in nearby rural parishes which were not marshy—a major deterrent to settlement and prosperity. New drainage techniques, developed in the Low Countries, were introduced by progressive landowners to drain marshlands around the Wash and the Humber, with considerable effects on the mortality rates of low-lying parishes by the eighteenth century.

Warfare and political mortality

Mortality from warfare is difficult to measure; records and record keeping perish with the victims of disorder. In Britain 1066 marked the beginning of the end of the depopulating invasion, conflict, and genocide which, apart from the *Pax Romana*, had characterized the preceding millenia, and of which the iron-age hill forts are a lasting memorial. Thus the British experience differs from that of most other European countries. Except for three civil wars, all British conflicts since then have been away matches. Nothing is known of the demographic effect of the eighteen-year conflict between Stephen and Matilda's forces from 1135 to 1153. In the Wars of the Roses from 1455 to 1471 most of the mortality seems to have been inflicted by the aristocracy and their retainers on each other.

In the Civil War of 1642–6 armies were tiny even though the casualties might be proportionately heavy; 7,500 Royalists fought 13,500 Parliamentarians at Naseby in 1645. England was not much afflicted by the atrocities and massacres which were the order of the day in the contemporary Continental religious wars—a difference commented on at the time. Ireland was not so lucky. Scottish raiding may have prevented the northern English counties reaching their full settlement until the union of the Crowns in 1603. The Stuart insurrections of 1715 and 1745, especially the latter, depopulated the Highlands through subsequent expropriation, enclosure, and emigration.

Most soldiers and sailors serving abroad died there. 135,000 out of 185,000 (73 per cent) sailors recruited for the Seven Years War (1756 to 1763) died of disease (Keegan 1985). Tropical diseases such as falciparan malaria and yellow fever made casualties in tropical theatres of war particularly horrendous; penalties of the British 'blue water' maritime strategy (Barnett 1970). Scarcely one in ten of those embarked returned from the failed expedition to Cartagena in 1739, for example; 23,000 died of disease, compared with 217 killed in action, in the expedition to the Dutch island of Walcheren in 1809. In Continental campaigns the mortality caused by the diseases and malnutrition which followed armies everywhere could be an enormous burden on the civilian population (see Flinn 1981, Zinsser 1935).

Apart from epidemics of typhus, expropriation of food from the civilian population caused widespread starvation, especially the unprecedentedly large armies raised by Louis XIV (395,000 by 1696) and subsequently by his enemies. The demographic effect on the rural populations that supplied most recruits could be crippling—93 per cent of the peasants in one North Swedish village raised to fight Gustavus Adolphus's wars from 1621 were dead by 1639, by which time the male population of the village had fallen 40 per cent (Parker 1988). Even in peacetime the attrition of trained troops was about a quarter per year. At a time when most taxation was raised for war, prolonged campaigns could impoverish the whole country and provoke crises of subsistence or even revolution. However, if wars caused hardship, many evidently enlisted to escape impossible conditions in civilian life (conscription was rare). This raises unsolved questions about the relationship of warfare and 'surplus' population (Coleman 1986).

Unlike the Thirty Years War in Germany, the Great Northern War for Sweden, or the Napoleonic Wars for France, no British campaigns were demographically crippling. Britain deployed fewer men in all against Napoleon (400,000, including 140,000 in the Navy in 1806) than Napoleon lost in his 1812 campaign against Russia, from which just 1 in 20 returned. Marlborough and Wellington were noted for the care they gave to the organized subsistence of their armies. But it was not until the First World War that casualties from disease were fewer than casualties in action, and even then only on the Western Front.

The importance of climate

There is evidence for a sharp deterioration of climate in the late sixteenth century; the winters of 1693 and 1709 were so bad that they damaged the economy of all Europe (Appleby 1980*b*, Lamb 1982). Climatic change may have had a pervasive exogenous influence on long-term trends in mortality and population, as well as precipitating short-term crises, by reducing the carrying capacity of the land. The population stagnation of the late seventeenth century and the decline after the medieval peak (even before the plague) may owe something to these trends. The reduction in carrying capacity which this implies raises a question mark over the more conventional Malthusian economic analysis of medieval and seventeenth-century population pressure.

Geographical mobility

The parish registers, records of apprenticeships, and other material show that the population was surprisingly mobile. The rural population of Britain was not one of peasants bound to the land. Instead, individual (saleable) property rights, the absence of 'family' property, marriage, and the market in labour kept the population on the move. The boarding-out of adolescent children as servants gave them knowledge of other places and a chance to save money and marry away from home (Schofield 1970). The larger towns recruited apprentices over great regions of the country (Patten 1973), and court records show the cosmopolitan origins of town populations (Clark 1972). Parish registers apparently show that about 84 per cent of men in a sample of eighteen mostly rural parishes married within their own parish (Coleman 1984). But marriage records strongly underestimate the true extent of geographical mobility (Pain and Smith 1984), partly because the requirements of obtaining settlement under the poor law encouraged claims to previous local residence. Generally in parish registers, only a third of

Table 1.5. Mobility of the rural population in the early modern period: Some estimates of population mobility or turnover from surnames, all causes

Parish	Source	Period	Surnames in common (%)	Duration of period (years)	Author
Horringer (Suff.)	Baptisms	1575–1850	42	25	Buckatzsch 1951
Shap (Westmld.)	Baptisms	1600–1799	63	25	Buckatzsch 1951
Warkworth (Northbld.)	Baptisms	1750–79	60	30	Dobson & Roberts 1970
Felton (Northbld.)	Baptisms	1750–79	52	30	Dobson & Roberts 1970
Vale of Trent	Baptisms/burials	18th C.	50–60	c.30	Chambers 1957
Colyton (Devon)	Marriages/burials	1538–1624	66	c.20	Wrigley 1968
Earls Colne (Essex)	Baptisms/burials	1560–1750	33	c.30	MacFarlane 1978
Kirkby Lonsdale (Cumbria)	Baptisms/parish listing	1660/9–95	30	30	MacFarlane 1978
Wigston Magna (Leics.)	Manor	1570–1670	44	100	Hoskins 1963
Earls Colne (Essex)	Manor	1549–1589	28	40	MacFarlane 1978
Godalming Hundred (Surrey)	Muster Rolls	1575/7–83	53	7	Rich 1950
Cogenhoe and Clayworth (Northants)	Muster Rolls/census	17th C.	50	10	Laslett and Harrison 1963
Northamptonshire 15 parishes	Lay Subsidy Rolls	1625–8	40% freeholders 73% non-freeholders	30	Rich 1950
North Clay (Notts.)	Lay Subsidy Rolls	1544–1641	0–27% names	97	Peyton 1915
Leightonstone Hundred (Essex)	Lay Subsidy Rolls	1611–28	36% names	17	
Corby Hundred (Northants.)	Lay Subsidy Rolls	1611–28	37% names	17	
Bedfordshire	Lay Subsidy Rolls	1545–1671	0–100% name survival	126	Marshall 1934

Note: 'Surnames in common, %' refers to the proportion of surnames noted in the registers or records of the parish in question, present both at the beginning and the end of period of time in the adjacent column.

Source: Coleman 1983 t. 4.

people baptized are recorded as being buried in the same place. Analyses of population turnover using surnames show that only 30–60 per cent of surnames in a sample of parishes are found both at the beginning and at the end of a 30-year period, confirming Buckatzsch's comment (1951) that 'it seems to be untrue that at any time between 1650 and 1850 more than a very small minority of the inhabitants of this village were descendants of men who had been living there a hundred years before' (table 1.5). The geographical catchment areas for apprenticeships, lawsuits, pilgrimage, and the rest was surprisingly large in London (Cressey 1970; Finlay 1981) and other towns (Sheffield, Lincoln, Canterbury). For example, only a quarter of York freemen were born in the town, only half even came from Yorkshire (Patten 1973). Only a quarter of witnesses in some Kentish towns in 1585–1640 were born there (Clark 1972) although there was also much return migration (Cornwall 1967). As the death-rate in towns could easily exceed the birth-rate, migration was essential for their growth.

Urban living

London became pre-eminent in Britain and in Europe by the end of the seventeenth century. In the past the proportion of population living in towns and cities (often defined as places with more than 5,000 people) seldom exceeded about 5 per cent. By 1600, England had moved away from this classic pattern. Up to 20 per cent of the population was already urbanized, although Finlay (1981) suggests just 8 per cent. In England London is, and has been for centuries, hugely bigger than any other city; the only world city in an otherwise provincial scene. In 1600 and 1700, London comprised more than 60 per cent of the entire estimated urban population. It increased from 50,000 in 1500 to 200,000 in 1600 and to a prodigious 575,000 in 1700 (table 1.6). London's inhabitants were highly cosmopolitan (Stone 1966). Sixteenth–seventeenth century court records suggest that only 15 per cent had been born in London, and more than two-thirds came from at least fifty miles away (Cressey 1970). About a seventh of each cohort which survived to adulthood may have lived in London at some time in their lives (Wrigley 1967). After London the next town was Norwich, with about 15,000 inhabitants. Four other provincial capitals had populations of 10,000 or over: York, Bristol, Newcastle, and Exeter; and ten others with about 5,000, 30 of about 3,000. Contemporary accounts list about 605 market towns; many would have less than 1,000 inhabitants (Emery 1973).

The rise of towns had implications for the death-rate. Dense populations encouraged crowd diseases such as smallpox and measles (Slack

Table 1.6. Population estimates, London,
1500–1800

Year	Population[a]	Per cent of English total[b]
1500	50,000	2
1550	70,000	2
1600	200,000	5
1650	400,000	8
1700	575,000	11
1750	675,000	12
1800	900,000	10
1986	6,775,000	14

[a] Finlay 1981 t. 3.1.
[b] Derived from Wrigley and Schofield 1981, t. 7.8.

1982). These were endemic infections in larger towns—often afflicting children—but epidemic (intermittently present) in the countryside. Cramped urban living conditions would encourage tuberculosis and typhus, although the rural poor also lived in cramped and overcrowded hovels even if their aggregate population density was low. In the absence of any effective urban sewage system, opportunities for the contamination of drinking water in wells and rivers were unrivalled.

1.4 Population Trends 1500–1750

Tudor population recovery and seventeenth century stagnation

By the time of the Tudors both economy and population were moving upwards again. Prices rose to match (Postan 1966) (figure 1.4). At the beginning of the sixteenth century, contemporaries complained of the thin population of the realm, and proposed pronatalist remedies of the kind later implemented in France by Colbert. By its end, voices were raised against over-population, wages had fallen to a low level, and land hunger was a major problem for the first time since the early fourteenth century. By the late seventeenth century the population boom of the Elizabethan and early Stuart periods had turned to demographic stagnation and decline, as population slowly recovered to a density approaching that reached before the calamitous fourteenth century. Mortality rose, though not catastrophically (figure 1.7). Fertility fell, in response to unprecedented delays in marriage and its

Note: Five-point moving averages. The data are centred on the years indicated (each reading covers a 25-year period).

Source: Wrigley and Schofield 1981, fig. 7.8.

FIG. 1.7. The trend of expectation of life at birth, 1551–1861

frequent avoidance. But the seventeenth century was not the same world as the fourteenth; economic and social advances had created much bigger towns than had existed during the Middle Ages. Over 20 per cent of the population now lived in towns where higher mortality, until reversed, would have a damping effect on national population (Helleiner 1967).

By 1620 agricultural day-labourers' wages had fallen to half their real value in the late fourteenth century, in terms of grain prices, as population growth raised the price of food relative to other commodities. Wool, for which so much land had been enclosed in the previous century, became unprofitable as grain prices recovered and rents rose. Many sheep areas were deparked and put under the plough again. The trend towards fewer, larger farms and more very small farms continued the transformation of the rural work-force into land-less labourers: the early demographer Gregory King estimated the labouring (i.e. landless) population at 47 per cent in 1695. By about 1650 most land had already been enclosed; open fields remained predominant only in the traditional grain-growing areas of the Midlands (Rackham 1985).

Renewed interest in marginal land is another sign of over-population, as it was in the late thirteenth century. The sixteenth century saw the draining of fen and swamp, the recultivation of abandoned land, the deparking of sheep grazing, further encroachment into forest in the Weald and into moorland in Yorkshire, with new farming settlements at high altitudes in Dartmoor and elsewhere. No radical improvements in agriculture came into general use until the eighteenth century, so output could only be improved by increasing the area of cultivated land or by applying existing methods more intensively.

Sidestepping the crisis: economic diversification

The fall in population was mild compared to that of the fourteenth century. Although mortality rose the population responded to difficulty by delaying marriage and used other avenues to escape or sidestep the crisis, not available in the earlier period. Now people could expand into the more diversified economy by taking up non-agricultural work in the countryside or by migrating to the towns. Country life became much diversified by cottage industry associated with woollen, hemp, and linen textiles, leather working, and mining: 25–30 per cent of adult males may have worked in mining and manufacturing by the late seventeenth century. Labourers' probate inventories from as early as 1540–1640 suggest that 60 per cent had some other form of employment. A Muster Roll from Gloucestershire in 1608 showed that only 50 per cent of the rural population worked in agriculture (Grigg 1980). These are interpreted as responses to rural over-population and landlessness. By the end of the eighteenth century the British economy was so developed and diversified that less than one half of the population still worked on the land (table 1.7). This was a very different starting point from the developing economies of today's Third World (Spengler 1972).

Agricultural improvement

Many of the innovations whose widespread use was to improve eighteenth century output were known locally at earlier times (Darby 1973*b*). Ley farming, the ploughing up of pasture while arable was left to rest under grass, thereby preserving fertility, was widespread by 1650. Nitrogenizing legumes such as peas, vetches, and lentils were used on the fallow, with clover and other techniques borrowed from the Low Countries to follow later. Carrots were grown from 1600 in the south and west, turnips in the south-east half a century later, with cabbages by 1700. The potato was known in Lancashire before 1700, but was not widely grown until the nineteenth century. Roots were particularly important because they enabled herds to be preserved over winter, giving more milk and meat throughout the year, and improving

Table 1.7. Occupational distribution of the population, 1700–1951 (%)

Year	Proportion of work-force engaged in:				
	Agriculture, fisheries, forestry	Manufacture, mining, building	Trade and transport	Domestic, personal	Public, professional, other
1700[a]	40–5		33–7	—	—
1801	35.9	29.7	11.2	11.5	11.8
1821	28.4	38.4	12.1	12.7	8.5
1841	22.2	40.5	14.2	14.5	8.5
1861	18.7	43.6	16.6	14.3	6.9
1881	12.6	43.5	21.3	15.4	7.3
1901	8.7	46.3	21.4	14.1	9.6
1921	7.1	47.6	20.3	6.9	18.1
1951	5.0	49.1	21.8	2.2	21.9

[a] Approximate estimates only for years before 1801 census. For detailed notes see source.
Source: Deane and Cole, 1969, t. 30.

the output of manure. Natural manures were at least discussed in books from the sixteenth century, noting the merits of chalk and lime in breaking up clay soil, and of marl (chalky clay) to give structure and fertility to thin sandy soils. The absence of a chemical industry prevented much further progress. No effective farm machinery came into use until Jethro Tull's (1674–1741) seed drill (1700, which sowed seeds in even rows without waste, spaced to prevent crowding and to permit hoeing) and the all-iron Rotherham triangular plough, based on a Dutch design and patented in 1730. With this plough, two horses and one man replaced the four or more oxen and two men needed by the traditional design.

Migration

Migration to London and to overseas colonies absorbed some of the population, a response not available to meet the population crisis of the fourteenth century. Seventeenth-century London may have absorbed about half the nation's natural increase (Wrigley 1967). Its endemically high mortality (40/1,000 per year) would tend to suppress population growth (Landers 1987). From 1630 to 1700 half a million people may have been lost to emigration to Ireland, North America and the West Indies. This accounts for over half the late seventeenth century population decline (Smith 1990*b*). Many emigrants were townsmen or richer farmers; then, as later, the rural poor could seldom afford such mobility without assistance—which the Poor Law provided after 1834. No statistics on emigration were collected at the time, although data from the colonies can help. Wrigley and Schofield's indirect estimate (1981), subject to their 'strong reservations', suggests that net outflow increased unevenly from about 20,000 persons a year in the mid-sixteenth century up to a peak of about 60,000 a year in the mid-seventeenth century, declining again to 20,000–30,000 until the early nineteenth century, after which it increased fast to over 100,000 a year by 1851. By then the residual calculation is much more accurate, being based on census and vital registration. These figures correspond to 1.3, 2.4, 0.6, and 1.4 per thousand of the total population, respectively, compared to a crude death-rate (for example) of about 30 per thousand in the earlier period, and a rate of natural increase of between zero and 10 per thousand per year. Net migration was always outward; a characteristic feature of English demography into the twentieth century.

1.5 A Working Model of Population

A homoeostatic population system?

One of the major questions in demography is whether the population worked as a homoeostatic system—i.e. whether long-term swings in population growth and demand for labour (expressed as real wages) are connected. Malthus claimed that marriage, births, population growth, and prices were all connected in a feedback system (figure 1.8) where mortality played a minor role: 'In almost all the more improved countries of modern Europe the principal check which at present keeps the population down to the level of the actual means of subsistence is the prudential restraint on marriage' (Malthus 1830). With rising real wages, more people could marry and marry earlier, because the conditions for setting up an independent household were more easily achieved. The birth-rate would then increase, absorbing much of the new economic surplus. Population would increase until the growth of labour supply started to drive down real wages (if population growth were over 0.1–0.5 per cent, Lee 1986), and reserves of additional cultivable land were exhausted. Accordingly marriage would be delayed or avoided and the death-rate might also rise, reducing the rate of population growth and possibly diminishing population size.

Wrigley and Schofield's analysis over three centuries appears to show

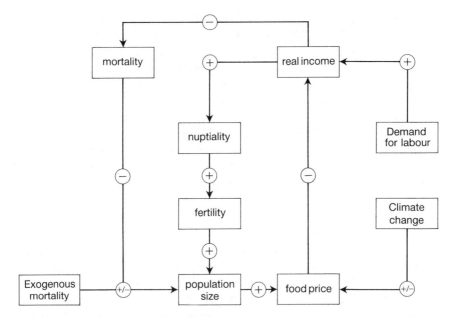

Source: Adapted from Wrigley and Schofield 1981.

FIG. 1.8. A model of population homoeostasis

that, up to the industrial revolution, which broke the link between agricultural capacity and population, Malthus was generally right and there was at least a system of 'dilatory homoeostasis'. There were major long-term variations in marital fertility. This was due to changes in the timing and popularity of marriage. Fertility changes had about twice the numerical effect upon changes in population growth rate than mortality: Malthus's preventive check was more important than the positive check. Marriage rates and birth-rates are strongly positively correlated with changes in real wages; death-rates only weakly so. Most English mortality crises were exogenous; not related to falls in real wages (Walter and Schofield 1989), and only about 16 per cent of variation in short-term death-rates can be accounted for by changes in the wheat price (Wrigley and Schofield 1981).

Wrigley and Schofield's grand analysis has its flaws (Hollingsworth 1982, Flinn 1982). The Phelps Brown and Hopkins long-term index of wages and prices they are obliged to use is far from perfect. The forty-year lag in the response of fertility to real wages is difficult to explain. Three centuries barely provide time for two complete cycles of the kind they describe. The ultimate driving force remains in dispute; whether generated by the system itself and the underlying power of human reproduction, or a long-run increase in the demand for labour responding to improvements in technology and social organization (Lee 1986). The apparent disconnection between population growth, wages, fertility, and domestic agricultural capacity, achieved around 1800, is the most striking difference between twentieth-century population systems and those of the early modern period, although the Netherlands may have escaped even earlier from Malthusian constraints through urbanization and foreign trade (de Vries 1986). Whether this disconnection can be maintained permanently has been doubted (Thomas 1986). It is at the root of contemporary concern about resources and environment (see Chapters 2 and 13).

Into the eighteenth century

On the eve of its demographic take-off in the eighteenth century, described in Chapter 2, England was relatively thinly populated, with low fertility balanced by low mortality and a tradition of emigration. Its family and household patterns, its property law and traditions were remote from peasant custom. Its economy was dominated by markets in labour, land, and produce, and was already substantially emancipated from dependence on agriculture. Its capital was rapidly growing to be the largest city in the world, far ahead of any other English urban settlement, a testimony to the efficiency of agriculture (Wrigley 1985). It was about to begin the extraordinary episode of population growth (Wrigley 1983) that would take it from being one of the small states of Europe, with just five million people in 1700, less than half that of Germany and Italy and a quarter that of France, to the demographic equivalence of today.

2 Into the Twentieth Century

2.1 From the Eighteenth Century to the Present

The eighteenth century marks a turning point in British population history. It begins just after Gregory King's population estimate in 1695 of 5.3 million (Glass 1965a); possibly no more than the medieval peak. At its end, the first census of 1801 recorded the unprecedented population of 9.2 million; a decisive break with the past. From about 1750, population increased yearly for the next 226 years (figure 2.1). Britain became the most urbanized country in the world, with the fastest growing population, and the first to establish the primacy of the industrial mode of production. By the end of the century industrialization uncoupled fertility and population growth from its Malthusian connection with the price of grain and real wages. Fertility could remain high and mortality continue to decline without population growth being stifled by a fall in wages and increases in the cost of subsistence. (figures 1.4, 2.2). Substitution of manufactured exports for domestic grain imports permitted the population to be fed for a century, beyond the capacity of domestic agriculture, without a reduction in fertility or a rise in mortality. The new factory system made earlier marriage easier by the end of the eighteenth century and larger family size correspondingly more common, although these trends were reversed by the the early nineteenth century. New prosperity did not raise fertility to new heights. Instead, by the mid-nineteenth century family limitation within marriage first appeared.

New sources of data

Compulsory civil registration of births and deaths replaced the defective parish registers from 1837 (OPCS 1987a). It puts discussion of the nineteenth-century mortality and fertility trends on a different footing from the uncertainties of previous centuries, where perpetual controversy flourishes in the dark. It included the medical certification of cause of death and the age, sex, and occupation of the deceased. Parish registers of baptisms were increasingly incomplete, of declining value as proof of ancestry and statistically inadequate, a source of annoyance to officials and derision by foreigners. At first, registration

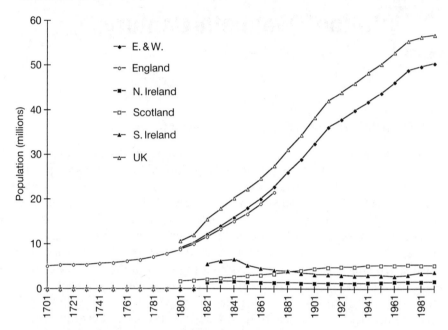

Sources: England 1701–1801: Data from Wrigley and Schofield 1981, t. A3.1. Other data: Census 1981, Historical Tables, Census 1981, Scotland and Northern Ireland.

Fɪɢ. 2.1. Population growth, 1701–1991, United Kingdom and constituent countries

of births was only about 95 per cent complete. Mothers were not asked questions about their previous children and the date of their marriage until the Population (Statistics) Act of 1938, so earlier analysis is rather thin (Werner 1987). After a contentious and abortive attempt to set up a population register in 1753, a Bill for a Census was finally passed without fuss in 1800 (Glass 1973). The population base is known from 1801 (with initial under-enumeration, see Wrigley and Schofield 1981) and in more detail from the first household-based census of 1841. The 1911 Census was the first to ask detailed questions about fertility, child survival, and occupation (Craig 1987) and to use a form of classification of social class (Szreter 1984). However, individual census household schedules are kept secret by the hundred-year rule, and it is impossible to use civil registers to reconstruct individual life histories and family formation. In these respects the demography of the nineteenth century is less easy to explore than that of the parish-register period.

Controversies

These new data have made for better informed controversies but have not resolved them all. The reasons for the declines of mortal-

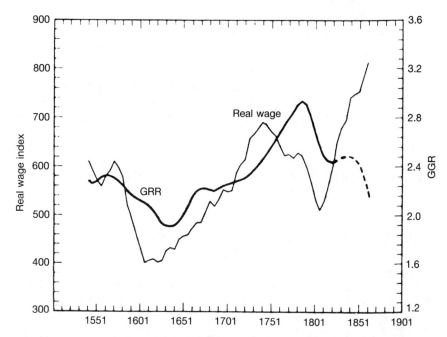

Notes: The cohort GRR graph represents the fertility of generations born in the 5-year period preceding the years shown. The real-wage graph is a 25-year moving average centring on the years shown. Since the cohort GRRs are very closely similar in level to a 5-point moving average of the current GRRs 30 years later, the directly calculated set of cohort GRRs has been extended using appropriate values from the set of current GRRs supplemented by Glass's estimates of the current GRR for 1881, 1891, and 1901 suitably adjusted to remove the 'jump' between his series and that produced by back projection. The estimated cohort GRRs are shown by a broken line.

Source: Wrigley and Schofield 1981, fig. 10.7.

FIG. 2.2. Trend in Gross Reproduction Rate and real wages, 1541–1861

ity and fertility are still not agreed; nor the relative impact on mortality decline of the conquest of smallpox, the agricultural revolution, or environmental improvement (Woods and Hinde 1987); why infant mortality fell in the eighteenth century but not in the nineteenth; economic versus cultural explanations for the decline in fertility. There is yet no general explanation for the fertility decline (Cleland and Wilson 1987); it is now clear that the transition began within the space of a few decades throughout Western Europe, from Trieste to Tromso, in a wide variety of countries (Coale and Watkins 1986). There is still argument about the primacy of trends in birth- or death-rates in generating population growth. Malthus (1830) and Habakkuk (1953) argued that fertility change (regulated through marriage) was primary. The population reconstructions of Wrigley and Schofield (1981) support them and indicate that from the sixteenth to the nineteenth centuries fertility change was about twice as important as mortality in accounting for variations in population growth, and that declines in mortality were modest until the mid-nineteenth century. McKeown (1976) and Hollingsworth (1982) insist that mortality response was the key to understanding the beginning of the demographic transition, particularly its continued decline despite the rapid population growth and urbanization of the nineteenth century, which might have been expected to raise the death rate.

2.2 The Decline of Mortality from the Eighteenth century

General trends

The pattern of mortality decline changes substantially across the two centuries. Infant survival improved considerably in the eighteenth century, then showed no further improvement until the first decade of the twentieth. Improvements in public sanitation and the consequent fall of cholera and typhoid, and also of tuberculosis, belong wholly to the later nineteenth century. Mortality fell only erratically and modestly

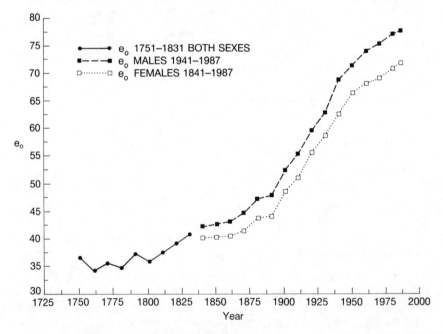

Sources: 1751–1841 England only, Wrigley and Schofield 1981, t. A3.1; 1841–1987: OPCS (1987*k*)

Fig. 2.3 Expectation of life at birth (e_0), 1751–1987

during the eighteenth century. The most significant development is the gradual disappearance of crisis mortality (Schofield 1972), clearly graphed in the burial totals (figure 1.4). Family reconstitution work and later vital registration shows the improvement of expectation of life (figure 2.3), also noted at the time from early life insurance and annuity schemes. The reports of the Select Committee on the Laws respecting Friendly Societies (1825–7) show improvements of 20–35 per cent from the early eighteenth to the early nineteenth century. Assurance against death began in the late seventeenth century; properly funded schemes based on actuarial principles were available from 1762 (Ogborn 1962), a product of the advance of science and of financial services.

Improvements in expectation of life are slight in the eighteenth century. It only increased from about 37 in 1801 to 42 by 1842 (Farr's First English Life Table based on census and vital registration). About seven more years had been added to expectation of life up to 1901, after which the pace accelerated sharply. Lower infant mortality may have contributed to the eighteenth-century fall. From the 1840s child and young adult mortality contributed most of the decline. Infant mortality remained unremittingly high at about 150/1,000 from 1840 until about 1900, although this apparent stability may have been in part an artefact of the extension of birth registration to the least healthy groups of the population, and of a shift in the social class composition of births. Further declines in infant mortality and substantial declines in mortality of older adults had to await the twentieth century, where the former was substantially responsible for the improved trend in expectation of life (see Woods and Hinde 1987). Improvements in the survival of the elderly were modest (figure 2.4).

The first national life tables (1842) already show that women enjoyed better survival than men at all ages, and their lead in expectation of life has expanded from two to six years. Improvement in female mortality is particularly striking in young adult life as childbirth became safer— and, after 1870, less frequent. Because tuberculosis affects women more than men, the gradual decline of that disease benefited female survival. Female advantage in life expectation is not universal. Where the status of women is low, female mortality may exceed that of males: in Pakistan and some states of North India today, and, because of the prevalence of TB, in Ireland up to the beginning of this century (Coleman forthcoming *a*).

Social and geographical contrasts

There are substantial social and geographical differences in mortality at this time. By the early nineteenth century some areas and classes had

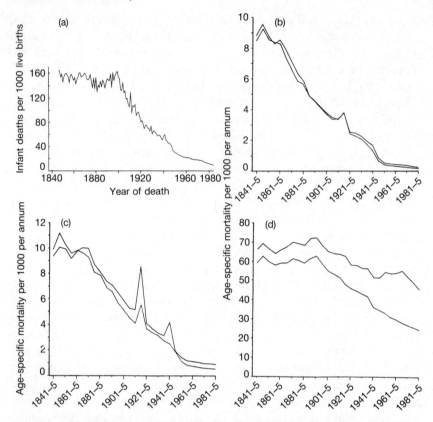

Note: Civilian mortality only in 1915–20 both sexes, and 3 Sept. 1939–31 Dec. 1949 for males, 1 June 1941–31 Dec. 1949 for females (but perhaps the World Wars nevertheless had an impact on the rates for young adults in fig. 2.4*c*).

Sources: Swerdlow 1987; OPCS Monitor, DH3 85/3, 'Infant and Perinatal Mortality 1984'.

FIG. 2.4. Trends in age-specific mortality, England and Wales, 1841–1985

already achieved levels of survival not enjoyed by the country as a whole until about 1900. The improvement of mortality from the nineteenth century is to a considerable degree the improvement of the risks in the worst favoured classes and areas (Woods and Hinde 1987). National improvement in mortality faltered as a result of the mass movement of people to the unhealthy towns. Perhaps the most remarkable aspect of mortality during early industrialization, accelerating population growth, and the Napoleonic Wars is that it did not worsen. Instead expectation of life rose from 36.8 years in 1796–1800 to 40.2 in 1836–40 (Wrigley and Schofield 1981); these correspond to CDRs of 25.1 and 21.7 respectively.

Table 2.1 Urban and rural populations in England and Wales, 1801–1911

	Population (in millions)			Percentage	
	Total	Urban	Rural	Urban	Rural
1801	8.9	3.1	5.8	34.8	65.2
1811	10.2	3.7	6.4	36.4	63.6
1821	12.0	4.7	7.3	39.2	60.8
1831	13.9	5.9	8.0	42.5	57.5
1841	15.9	7.3	8.6	45.9	54.1
1851	17.9	9.0	8.9	50.2	49.8
1861	20.1	11.0	9.1	54.6	45.4
1871	22.7	14.0	8.7	61.8	38.2
1881	26.0	17.6	8.3	67.9	32.1
1891	29.0	20.9	8.1	72.0	28.0
1901	32.5	25.1	7.5	77.0	23.0
1911	36.1	28.2	7.9	78.1	21.9

Source: Lawton (1967).

Industrial towns and mining villages grew fast through migration and their own natural increase (table 2.1). By 1850 half the population lived in cities of over 10,000 inhabitants, far ahead of any other European country. Urbanization went hand in hand with a rapid change in the distribution of the work-force towards manufacturing (table 1.7). Much of the housing rapidly thrown up to accommodate the workers was overcrowded and insanitary (see Ferguson 1964). Contemporary criticism of these deplorable urban conditions (notably Chadwick's Report of 1842, see Flinn 1965) eventually led, after long delays, to national improvements in sewage and water systems, building regulations, and local government. There were sharp differences between different areas and classes in the same towns (table 2.2). In 1831–9, Farr (1840) estimated that the death-rate in the country areas was 18/1,000 compared to 26 in the towns. A survey of Manchester in 1840 (Flinn 1965) shows that crude death-rates varied from 16 in the suburbs to 35 in the poor urban areas. Professional families in Liverpool had about the same age at death as labourers in Wiltshire (table 2.2).

As late as 1861, expectation of life at birth for males in Liverpool was 26; in Okehampton, Devon, it was 57; as big a difference as the national difference between 1840 and 1960 (Woods 1982). In general, expectation of life in rural areas in the south, south-west, and Wales

Table 2.2. Mortality differences by rural/urban residence and social class: average age at death, 1837–1840

Class	Wiltshire	Rutland	Whitechapel	Manchester	Liverpool
A	50	52	45	38	35
B	48	41	27	20	22
C	33	38	22	17	15

A = 'Gentlemen, professional persons and their families'.
B = 'Tradesmen and their families'.
C = 'Mechanics, labourers and their families'.

Note: These data are not the same as 'expectation of life at birth'; they are slightly lower than expectation of life, to the extent that the population was growing.

Source: Chadwick 1842 (ed. Flinn 1965).

was over 50, and under 30 in urban Lancashire, Yorkshire, and the north-east. Infant mortality in Leicester, Preston, Manchester, and other large towns in 1871–80 was over 200 per 1,000 births per year when nationally it was about 150 and under 100 in favoured rural areas (Woods and Hinde 1987). Social and geographical differences in mortality are still with us and are still contentious issues (Chapter 8); but these very severe differences have gone, and the convergence of mortality is one of the major factors behind the faster improvement of mortality from the end of the nineteenth century. Arguments about what caused the decline in mortality shift between eighteenth- and later nineteenth-century changes. The slight improvements in the eighteenth century are important because they mark the beginning of the downward trend. Because of the weakness of data it is difficult to come to definite conclusions. Later causes of decline are clearly different, and do not relate to the same age-groups or causes of death, and there are better data to argue over. Contending explanations include the adoption of new ways of caring for infants, the rise of medical science including the attack on smallpox, improvements in diet and general living standards, and improvements in urban sanitary conditions, especially drinking water and sewage disposal. The first two are particularly relevant to the eighteenth century.

2.3 Infant Mortality and the New World of Children

In the parishes studied by Wrigley and Schofield, IMR declined from about 160 in the first half to about 130 in the latter half of the eighteenth century. Mortality of the babies of aristocrats fell from about 160 to about 100 at the same time. In a group of Shropshire villages, infant mortality fell from about 200 in 1661–1710 to about 100 in 1761–1810 (Jones 1980). Brownlee (1925) used the London Bills of Mortality to show that the death-rate of children under 2 fell by 40 per cent from 1730 to 1800. Infant survival improved during the eighteenth century, but it is not obvious why.

Many historians believe that 'there is a tremendous change in attitudes towards children from the 17th to the 18th centuries' (Plumb 1976). Historians themselves have 'rediscovered childhood' in the last three decades (Aries 1962). Before the eighteenth century, literature, diaries, monuments, art, and law indicate a coolness towards children (Stone 1977). Many early child-rearing practices were barbarous by modern standards. Children were swaddled shortly after birth, to keep them out of mother's way. Medical opinion believed that early breast milk (antigen-rich colostrum) was harmful, and that feeding should be delayed until the passage of the first stools. Early medications and purges were recommended, and unsuitable solids for early weaning, not to mention spirits and laundanum to keep the infant quiet (Fildes 1980). Medical advice, like wet-nursing, was only followed by the wealthy, and may explain their inferior infant mortality rates.

Breast-feeding

Breast-fed babies usually survive better than artificially fed babies (see Chapter 7) (Beaver 1973). In modern societies living in a healthy environment, the difference is slight. But in developing societies, as in Victorian times, the difference in death-rates can be up to threefold (Knodel and van de Walle 1967). Furthermore, the contraceptive effect of lactation doubles the interval between babies in women not practising birth control (Bongaarts and Potter 1983), contributing further to child survival. In the eighteenth century educated women became more likely to breast-feed their babies. By the century's end it was fashionable to breast-feed, often in an ostentatious way, as now (Stone 1977). The Dispensaries made breast-feeding one of the main planks in their platform for reform. By the latter half of the century, the majority of books on child care—which were enjoying a tremendous popularity—strongly recommended breast-feeding and described it as the normal practice (Fildes 1980). In the mid-seventeenth century no text recommended early breast-feeding with colostrum; by 1800 all did. These apparently autonomous changes in attitude, with their powerful demographic consequences, are difficult to account for (Stone 1977). But they were accompanied by other changes indicating greater interest in childhood as a unique stage in development. More was spent on children and produced for them. Previously they had few books or toys. By the eighteenth century toy windmills, printing presses, farms, alphabet cards, and jigsaw puzzles were to be found in the nurseries of the better-off. After the 1740s children's books included part works for the children of the poor.

Foundlings and infanticide

But there was a darker side in attitudes to children. Unwanted babies were frequently abandoned in the streets, particularly in the great towns. Many but not all the mothers were unmarried: prostitutes and servant girls made pregnant by their masters. Overlaying, often re-corded in the Bills of Mortality, was a cover for infanticide. Babies were often sent away to be nursed in rural parishes where they were ill fed, overcrowded, and quieted with opiates (see Fildes 1988). Few re-turned, as their parents would well know. In England the practice was not nearly as widespread as in France (Langer 1972), where 'only the middling poor, probably a substantial proportion of rural society, . . . nursed all their own infants' (Flinn 1982). Legislation to control baby farms in Britain was not introduced until 1872.

Thomas Coram's revulsion at the infant corpses in London gutters led him to campaign for a hospital for foundlings, established in 1741. It proved impossible to find enough wet nurses for the thousands of babies left at the hospital. Mortality rates at this and similar institutions were astonishingly high: only 4,400 of the 15,000 admitted in the first four years lived to adolescence. This movement was more developed in other great European cities, especially in France where the mother of an illegitimate child had no legal recourse to the father and no access to poor relief (Fuchs 1987). For example, the Hospice des Enfants-Trouvés in Paris, founded 1670, was admitting several thousand babies a year by the 1770s, equivalent to over 20 per cent of the yearly baptisms in Paris, although almost half came from outside the city, and 13 per cent into the nineteenth century. Most of these babies, put out to wet nurses, failed to survive infancy. In the country areas in England the Overseers of the Poor Law assigned foundlings to paid nurses. Of about half a million foundlings christened in workhouses after 1728, only 40 per cent survived to their second birthday.

The adoption of contraception was one response: illegitimate births began to decline from about 1850 throughout Europe (Shorter *et al.* 1971). Abortion was another; abortifacients, some of them potentially effective like ergot and savin, were advertised from the eighteenth cen-tury onwards in journals and handbills (Potts, Diggory, and Peel 1977).

Infanticide became a major and much discussed social problem, with about 1,000 recorded cases each year (Sauer 1978). These pressures against infant survival can be seen as early indications that fertility was an increasing burden in a changing society.

2.4 The Irrelevant Rise of Scientific Medicine

In the enlightenment of the sixteenth and seventeenth centuries, scientific medicine finally struggled out from beneath the dead hand of classical authority. Armed with the new empirical understanding of the human body and its function from Vesalius, Harvey, Malpighi, Hooke, Baillie, and others, respect for medicine grew and the profession expanded, although London and Edinburgh remained the only British medical schools. Altogether twenty-five provincial hospitals were established in the eighteenth century, usually by individual benevolence, as in John Radcliffe's Oxford Infirmary of 1770, and several more in London to join the medieval foundations of Bart's and St. Thomas's and the specialist Bethlem and Bridewell. In view of this heightened activity it is hardly surprising that medicine should be given credit for the decline in mortality (e.g. Griffith 1926). But it has been long established (Habakkuk 1953, McKeown and Brown 1955) that medical knowledge of the time could not cure any important cause of death, could prevent only smallpox, and with a few exceptions remained impotent until the present century.

Hospitals and midwifery

McKeown and his colleagues blame the general hospitals for killing their patients more often than relieving them, at least until the 1875 Public Health Act. Fever patients were admitted to general wards. Hospital nutrition was bad and standards of cleanliness worse: dysentery and louse-borne typhus, known as 'hospital fever' were common. Nursing, without the continent's religious orders, was uninformed by training, devotion, or honesty until Miss Nightingale's reforms in the 1860s. But in the eighteenth century McKeown's criticisms may be on less secure ground (Woodward 1974). Some hospital charters forbade the admission of infectious diseases such as smallpox. From the eighteenth to the early nineteenth century between 4 and 14 per cent of in-patients died in hospital (Cherry 1972, Woodward 1974). 90 per cent are listed as cured or relieved at York from 1740 to 1783 (Sigsworth 1972). But these in-patients were a selected group; the treatment may not have brought the 'relief'. Institutional delivery of babies was uncommon before the middle of the eighteenth century. In 1749 the London Lying-in Hospital was founded, followed by Queen Charlotte's and three others in 1765, in response to poor standards of midwifery. But hospitals without hygiene helped the transmission of puerperal sepsis (childbed fever, a streptococcal infection). None the less, the London Bills of Mortality suggest that maternal mortality halved from 1700 to 1800. Hospitals in the eighteenth century may not have made national mortality worse (Cherry 1980), but they were too few to improve the national health.

Surgery and drugs

Effective treatment was restricted to general nursing, setting simple fractures, lancing abcesses (common in an age of poor nutrition and hygiene), amputations, trephining, operations for cataract, and 'cutting for stone' (lithotomy), apparently more common in an age of high cheese consumption and stoneground bread.

Post-operative death varied from 4 to 14 per cent by the mid-nineteenth century. But later in the nineteenth century operative technique greatly improved and the advent of anaesthesia (1800 for nitrous oxide, 1848 for chloroform) made surgeons more adventurous. Despite brilliantly successful surgery, the patient still died. Without antiseptic practice, post-operative mortality at University College Hospital in the 1870s was 35–50 per cent in general and 90 per cent for some operations. The eighteenth century pharmacopoeia was none too impressive. Laudanum (opiates) was a painkiller then, as now, expensive and addictive. Mercury, itself poisonous, was used against syphilis, which was never demographically important. Digitalis, effective against congestive heart failure (dropsy) was no use against the major coronary diseases. Cinchona, the rare and valuable 'Jesuit bark' from South America, is the source of quinine and a specific against malaria. But malaria was only regionally important and the drug too expensive to give in sufficient dosage (McKeown and Brown 1955, Hobhouse 1985).

The attack on smallpox

Smallpox may be an exception. Crude inoculation (immunization) was introduced against smallpox in the eighteenth century. It may have helped reduce eighteenth-century mortality (see Chapter 1). It can be effective where it does not kill the patient. Material from a smallpox pustule is introduced into the body of the person to be protected, by a light scratch. The patient should then receive a light dose of smallpox, with only a dozen or so pox, and lifetime active immunity. The process works (sometimes) because the immune system can cope with small numbers of viruses, although this was unknown in immunological terms at the time.

Lady Mary Wortley Montagu, wife of the Ambassador to the Sublime Porte in Constantinople, was so impressed with the results of this folk practice by the Sultan's Greek subjects that she had her children treated and introduced fashionable society to its advantages in 1721; as much for the protection of complexion as for the preservation of health. But in the hands of the medical profession the original crude jab became elaborated into a less safe deep incision followed by expensive treatments (Razzell 1977). This confined the treatment to the well-off and to demographic insignificance until in the 1760s the Sutton family popularized their cheaper method which was closer to the original simple practice and devoid of expensive medical encrustations. The new method may have been widely used, especially is country areas, by doctors and by itinerant inoculators. Smallpox mortality is claimed to have fallen correspondingly (Razzell 1977), a view support by the Bills of Mortality in provincial towns. In the latter half of the eighteenth century parish vestries (the local 'council') were often prepared to order general inoculations when smallpox was abroad locally, and the Poor Law Overseers paid the fees of paupers (up to a third of the village). This eighteenth-century controversy may be insoluble as it is so difficult to determine the extent of rural inoculation, and the proportion of deaths attributable to smallpox in country areas.

Edward Jenner was himself a keen inoculator, but he was impressed by the apparently safer prophylactic effects of the mild natural disease of cowpox; a zoonosis often caught by milkmaids which apparently protected them from smallpox, as he demonstrated in his paper of 1798. The practice of vaccination spread fast at home and abroad. It was made compulsory in Denmark, Norway, and Sweden around 1810. We now know that the viruses of vaccinia (cowpox) and of variola (smallpox) are antigenically similar. A fierce and often unscrupulous controversy arose over the relative merits of vaccination and inoculation, which persists to this day in demography journals. The vaccinators triumphed, securing the legal prohibition of inoculation. Vaccination was made free in 1840, made compulsory in 1851, and enforced in 1867. By then the disease was no longer a major public health menace. Similar measures (including inoculation) had also controlled smallpox in Western Europe and the USA (Mercer 1985). The last epidemic in Britain was in 1900–5; 1935 was the first year without a smallpox death, by 1941 there were no cases. Major smallpox may have become extinct in Britain since the First World War, with all subsequent cases imported (Gale 1959). Outside a few laboratories smallpox became extinct worldwide in 1977.

2.5 Agriculture, Diet, and the Death-Rate

Demographic and economic consequences of agricultural reform

Agriculture coped with the demands of the growing population with almost no recourse to imports. Food output increased considerably from 1700 to 1800, accommodating the needs of a 60 per cent rise in population with, in most years, a small surplus to export. Despite the increase in numbers 'there was no very great change in the overall relationship between the consumption of cereals and the total population over the 18th century as a whole' (Deane and Coale 1969). By the early nineteenth century the Malthusian links between rising population and fertility and rising domestic wages, food output, and prices were broken by industrialization (figure 2.1). For the first time population could increase with a declining grain price and a less than commensurate food output, subsisting on grain imports paid for by manufactures; 'It is one of the most striking ironies of intellectual history that Malthus should have fashioned his analysis just at the time when it was about to cease to be applicable to the country in which he lived' (Wrigley 1986).

The surpluses increasingly generated by eighteenth century agriculture were turned by the cash economy into increased consumption of non-agricultural produce, providing savings and capital for non-agricultural demand and investment, as Malthus observed (1836). The good harvests of 1715–45 cheapened the costs of some of industry's raw materials and generated a surplus for consumption of new cheap textiles and cheap gin made from the grain surplus. Later on, the relation was reversed—the growing town population increased the demand for grain and raised its price, putting a premium on agricultural efficiency and enclosure (Deane 1979). Price as well as quality of food is of the essence; food was by far the biggest item in the wage-labourer's budget. In 1790–6, labourers spent 40 per cent of their income on bread and flour, 20 per cent on animal products (e.g. bacon), 9 per cent on sugar, tea, beer—70 per cent in all (Gilboy 1936).

Improved agriculture and enlightened landowners

Eighteenth-century agricultural improvement has been credited with beginning the downturn of the death-rate (McKeown and Record 1972,

McKeown 1976*b*). But the primacy given to it depends on the belief that other explanations (including smallpox) have been excluded. It is difficult to show that individual diet, and consequently survival, had improved (Rotberg and Rabb 1985). It is true that new crops—turnips, parsnips, swedes, mangelwurzels—diversified the landscape and the food supply, especially by keeping herds alive over winter. The potato was not widely used directly as food in England until the nineteenth century, although its capacity to sustain a family on very little land has been credited with the rapid Irish population growth from the late eighteenth century (Connell 1950*a*, Langer 1975). Clovers helped remove the fallow stage from cultivation, effectively bringing more land into use—as in the 'Norfolk Four Course' (wheat, turnips, barley, and clover) advocated but not invented by Viscount Townshend of Raynham ('Turnip' Townshend, 1674–1738). For the first time a technically competent farming literature was available to help the better educated farmers and landowners (e.g. Townshend and Thomas Coke of Holkham (1691–1755) who could drive their tenants to improve (Mathias 1972*a*). It is not easy to evaluate the spread of improvement. Turnips and clover, for example, may not have been really widely used until the nineteenth century, and the diffusion of knowledge across the countryside may not have exceeded a mile a year from the points of origin (Deane 1979). Crop rotations and equipment could not be exploited in some areas until enclosure removed the remaining open fields and increased farm size.

Enclosure

Only half the arable land was still open fields in 1700. By 1800 most had gone. Enclosure turned small or fragmented holdings and commons suitable for little more than subsistence agriculture into consolidated holdings able to support the new farming and generate capital for improvement. Half a million acres came newly under the plough between 1761 and 1792, one million more during the Napoleonic Wars. High grain prices encouraged the pace in the later eighteenth century. The holdings and rights of freeholders and tenants to common land were bought out after the survey and valuation of often hundreds of parcels of land and rearrangement of drainage, hedges, and roads (Rackham 1985), which increased demand for labour. Private Acts of Parliament could be used to overcome opposition; 472 between 1770 and 1779, 2000 in all (Darby 1973*b*), although it seems that more land was enclosed in the seventeenth than in the eighteenth century. The Enclosure Acts gave smaller farmers, freeholders, and copyholders consolidated allocations in return for lost common rights although they would have to pay for hedging and ditching. Many landless cottage labourers (cottagers) and rural squatters with only customary use of common land received compensation to buy small plots (Chambers 1953). The diet of the rural poor may have deteriorated towards the end of the century because they had lost their pasturage and could no longer collect firewood or game from the common land (Taylor 1975).

In the first half of the nineteenth century there was a 'second agricultural revolution'. As a result, urban populations, economically emancipated from the land, could still enjoy cheap bread. Potatoes became an important part of the national diet, grown on 40,000 acres in 1795 and 142,000 in 1851 (Salaman 1989). Machinery was not widely introduced until the latter half of the century, as wages rose due to migration to the towns. The new primacy of the urban interest was marked by the repeal of the Corn Laws in 1846, which reduced grain and bread prices. Tinned meat from 1860, cheap refrigerated meat from New Zealand from 1880, fish, packed in ice and moved rapidly by the new railway system; all became a cheap commonplace of working-class diet. Milk brought by rail from the country to the town enabled the atrociously insanitary urban dairies to be abolished from the 1870s. Milk remained a health hazard until compulsory pasteurization eliminated tubercle and diphtheria bacilli from it in 1922 (McKeown and Turner 1975, Beaver 1973) with beneficial effects on infant mortality. The common and often spectacular adulteration of food was not seriously tackled until the Food and Drugs Act 1875 (Burnett 1968).

The national diet

New techniques and organization of land may have led to a better diet. But there is only scattered evidence that it did until the later nineteenth century. The stature of children and age at menarche are fairly sensitive indicators of nutritional status and health (Tanner 1962, 1978). The records of the Marine Society, a charity which prepared poor London boys for a career at sea, show a slight increase in stature up to about 1790, a decline until about 1800 then a sharp increase up to 1830, correlated with London labourers' wages. These increases are attributed (Floud, Wachter, and Gregory 1990) to improvements in the diet of the London poor. Later in the century there is a further trend towards greater height and weight among both adults and children (Fogel *et al.* 1983). Age at menarche, almost the only indicator of sexual maturity of which we have any historical evidence, is also sensitive to nutritional status. It declines progressively from the high average of about 15 years in the middle of the century to about 12.5 today. Some of these high estimates for the nineteenth century, which put mean age at menarche higher than in previous periods, have been questioned (Bullough 1981). But most of the decline dates from the end of the nineteenth century. None the less, even at the time of the Boer War (1899–1902) about 38 per cent of recruits to the army were rejected as undersized or unfit, especially that growing proportion that lived in cities (Oddy 1982). This disturbing discovery encouraged further state intervention in child health and welfare in the following decade including school meals from 1906, medical inspection for schoolchildren from 1907 and the compulsory notification of tuberculosis in 1912.

Tea and sugar give clues about the ability of the working class to afford a reasonable diet. Tea is nutritionally worthless, however vital. Like sugar it was originally rare. But as both are imports, there are data on them. By the early nineteenth century both were becoming staples of working-class diet. Sugar consumption fell from 31 lbs/head in 1805 to 18 in 1833, but it started to rise from 1845 as did consumption of tea. By the 1750s, wheaten bread (as opposed to rye or barley) became almost universal, even in provincial towns. By 1800 most of it was white bread, bought from a baker, possible because coal drove the cost of fuel down.

The food thesis is attractive but unproven. Death directly by starvation in famines seems to have been rare in Britain, less so abroad (Walter and Schofield 1989). Improved diet would have reduced death rates primarily because well fed people are better able to fight off infectious disease. There is strong evidence that ill-fed people in modern industrial and Third World societies are more likely to develop some infections and succumb to them, primarily because their immune systems are less effective: the so-called 'synergistic' effect (Scrimshaw et al. 1968, Taylor 1983). In the earlier part of the period much mortality seems to have been exogenous, with little respect for social or nutritional status (Livi Bacci 1983), and crisis mortality is not well correlated with grain prices (Wrigley and Schofield 1981). However the departure of plague in the seventeenth century, the reduction of infant mortality, and the rise of tuberculosis, which is more sensitive to nutritional status, may have changed the situation. By the early nineteenth century, and probably much earlier, substantial social and geographical gradients in infectious-disease mortality exist which are plausibly associated with nutritional status as well as environmental factors (Rotberg and Rabb 1985).

Table 2.3. Causes of death, England and Wales, 1860 and 1880 (selected causes, both sexes)

Cause	1860		1880	
	Number	%	Number	%
All	442,721	100.0	528,624	100.0
Smallpox	2,713	0.6	648	0.1
Typhus[a]	13,012	2.9	530	0.1
Enteric fever	—	—	6,710	1.3
Cholera	327	0.1	797	0.2
Venereal diseases	1,244	0.3	2,441	0.5
Erysipelas	1,662	0.4	2,014	0.4
Premature birth	7,642	1.7	12,266	2.3
Congenital malformations	1,168	0.3	2,275	0.4
Croup	4,380	1.0	3,571	0.7
Convulsions	25,205	5.7	23,503	4.4
Non symptomatic	30,477	6.9	46,272	8.8
Diarrhoea, dysentery	10,858	2.5	30,185	5.7
Measles[b]	9,557	2.2	12,328	2.3
Scarlet fever[b]	9,681	2.2	17,404	3.3
Whooping cough[b]	8,555	1.9	13,662	2.6
Diphtheria	5,212	1.2	2,810	0.5
Puerperal sepsis	987	0.2	1,659	0.3
Childbirth	2,186	0.5	1,833	0.3
Phthisis (resp. TB)	51,024	11.5	48,201	9.1
Other TB	14,232	3.2	21,427	4.1
Respiratory	68,158	15.4	93,167	17.6
Rheumatic fever	1,998	0.4	3,354	0.6
Circulatory	19,034	4.3	35,390	6.7
Cancer	6,790	1.5	13,210	2.5
Old age	28,442	6.4	25,823	4.9
Accident, negligence	13,023	2.9	15,187	2.9
Homicide	377	0.1	310	0.1
Suicide	1,365	0.3	1,979	0.4
Ill-defined, unspecified	44,551	10.1	39,353	7.4

[a] Typhus and 'enteric fever' (typhoid) not distinguished until 1868.
[b] Epidemic diseases such as measles are highly variable from year to year. Comparisons are complicated by changes and improvements in diagnosis and reporting. 'Old age' is no longer an admissible cause. Note the reduction in 'ill-defined'. The population of England in 1860 was 18.8 million, in 1880 24.2 million. Only about 5% of the population was aged 65 or over.

Sources: Registrar-General (1885) t. 27.

2.6   Major Causes of Death and their Control in the Nineteenth Century

The causes of death

Tuberculosis (TB) retained its dominance well into the century (table 2.3). Because it affects primarily younger people, and in particular young women, it has a powerful effect upon expectation of life. In the eighteenth century the rise of towns enabled it to increase. The Bills of Mortality suggest that TB was at its maximum between 1780 and 1830; 30 per cent of deaths in London in 1796 (Brownlee 1916). Nationwide, 17.6 per cent of all deaths in 1839 were due to TB according to the Registrar-General's first national analysis of causes of death. From about 1850, it begins to decline at an increasing rate up to the present day (figure 2.5). 22 per cent of the overall decline in mortality from 1848 to 1971 have been attributed to the decline of TB in all its forms (McKeown 1976), and 45 per cent to 1900.

This decline—like that of most infectious diseases—took place despite the absence of any generally available cure or prevention. Apart from smallpox it was the first major infectious disease to decline. Koch identified the tubercle bacillus only in 1882. Effective cure with drugs

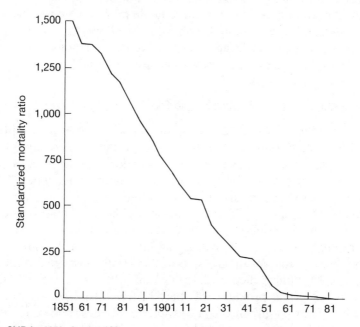

Note: SMR for 1950–2 set at 100.

Source: Swerdlow 1987, fig. 4.

FIG. 2.5. SMRs for tuberculosis, both sexes combined, England and Wales, 1851–1985 (1950–2 = 100)

(para-amino-salicylic acid or PAS, and isoniazid) and antibiotics (strep-tomycin) was not available until 1947. Immunization by BCG (Bacille Calmette Guerin) was not introduced until the 1950s. Pasteurization of milk, to destroy the bacteria of bovine TB and other parasites, was not introduced until 1922. Sanatoria, popular by the end of the century, were only for the better-off, apart from some charitable foundations, and in any case had little effect. There is no evidence of diminishing case–fatality rates among untreated patients, and therefore no evidence for the diminution of virulence favoured by some historians (see McKeown and Record 1963).

Instead the explanation may lie with better housing, which reduced the chance of transmission of the bacterium, and improved diet (discussed above). A reduction in shared bathrooms and kitchens reduces the contact between individuals and families. Adequate nutrition is particularly important because TB was an almost universal childhood infection and can be unusually long-lived. Depending on nutritional status, the disease will be eliminated or reduced to dormancy by the body's defences, to erupt again if the antibody level falls. As late as 1952, 56 per cent of Scottish 13-year-olds reacted positively to the tuberculin (Mantoux or Heaf) test, which indicates exposure.

Other important contributions to the fall in mortality up to 1900 arise from the decline in typhoid and typhus fevers (22 per cent of the total mortality reduction), scarlet fever (19 per cent), diarrhoea, dysentery, and cholera (8 per cent) (McKeown and Record 1962).

Diseases of infancy and childhood and their decline

Even at the end of the nineteenth century infant mortality still accounted for almost one death in five. Almost half of these were from diarrhoea and related gastro-enteric infections: dysentery, 'colic', 'convulsions', 'griping in the guts', infantile summer diarrhoea. Most deaths from diarrhoea occurred in the summer and early autumn, and this 'summer diarrhoea of infants' was one of the most notorious child health problems in London (Finlay 1981) and even worse in the great Northern cities. It rose to a peak in the latter years of the nineteenth century, the last survivor of 'crisis' mortality. In the last great outbreak in 1911, 32,000 infants died of diarrhoea and the infant mortality rate climbed to 130. The problem was particularly severe because of the inevitable fly-born contamination of food and babies' bottles in cities, poor households where food hygiene was difficult, and streets that received the dung from 250,000 horse-drawn vehicles. Severe seasonal crises went with the advent of motor transport, but the pasteurization of cows' milk fed to infants and the wider availability of clean drinking water were probably the main causes. In 1921, the ratio in summer of diarrhoeal deaths to all infant deaths was 1 : 6; in 1931 it was 1 : 10 and later fell much further. The epidemics of the hot, dry summers of the 1890s probably obscured an underlying decline in infant mortality which may already have begun by the 1880s. The improvement of women's education, particularly marked in the late nineteenth century, and the decline in the birth rate from the 1870s emerge as two of the most prominent factors correlated with the decline of infant mortality in the 1900s, while the rise in real wages had a surprisingly weak effect (Woods *et al.* 1989).

Diphtheria, scarlet fever, measles, and whooping cough attacked older children just when they seemed clear of the terrible hazards of infancy. Diphtheria is a congestive throat infection which kills by the effect of bacterial toxins upon the heart. 10,000 children died of it in 1859, and from the 1870s until the turn of the century there was little downward trend in deaths. Accordingly it became a relatively more important cause of death than scarlet fever, which declined fast from the 1860s (the two diseases have some symptoms in common and were not separated in death certification until 1858). As an infection carried on the air and in milk, diphtheria was not much affected by changes in living standards. It flourished in the playgrounds of the newly schooled child population and was disseminated in unsterilized milk. It is one of the few diseases which medicine could attack before the Second World War, by passive immunization. Von Behring's anti-toxin was widely available after 1896, though incidence remained almost unchanged until the 1940s. Scarlet fever is one of the few examples of a disease whose virulence has obviously declined. From the 1830s it became the single most important cause of the death of children, peaking at four deaths per thousand children per year aged under 15; at worst, 30,000 deaths a year in the 1860s. Then deaths declined steeply as mysteriously as they had increased. Other streptococcal diseases such as erysipelas and puerperal sepsis (childbed fever) declined less dramatically.

In the nineteenth century, measles infected nearly all children, especially between 6 months and 2 years of age, and killed about 1 in 2,000 every year. It is pre-eminently a 'crowd disease' (Greenwood 1935): fast moving, short-lived, needing a large population size to remain endemic. Its nineteenth-century decline in mortality went straight down from a peak in the 1860s to oblivion in the mid-1950s, although notifications remain high to the present day. Measles is particularly sensitive to the nutritional status of the victim; which helps explain its decline and also its marked social class gradient; in 1931 mortality from

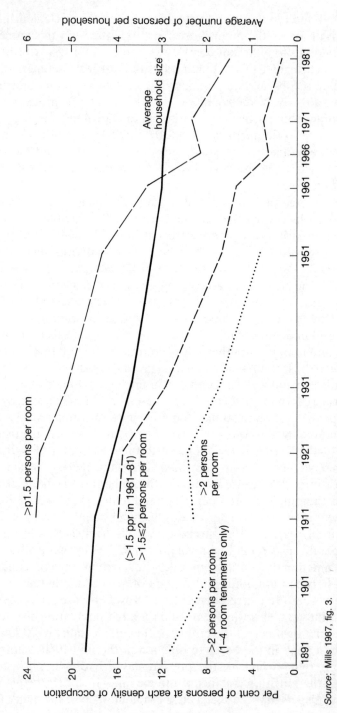

Average number of persons per household

Per cent of persons at each density of occupation

>p1.5 persons per room

(>1.5 ppr in 1961–81)
>1.5≤2 persons per room

Average
household size

>2 persons
per room

>2 persons per room
(1–4 room tenements only)

Source: Mills 1987, fig. 3.

Fig. 2.6. Trends in household size and overcrowding, England and Wales, 1891–1981

measles in social class V was 20 times that of children in social class I. The fall in family size probably helped the decline of this and other childhood diseases; fewer younger and vulnerable siblings would be infected at home by playground infections brought home by older children (Gale 1959).

Housing

The decline of tuberculosis mirrors the amelioration of living conditions in the later part of the nineteenth century, as its increase in the late eighteenth reflects the increasing proportion of the population moving to the insanitary towns. Later in the century, income figures, data on the number of persons per room from the census after 1891 (Hole and Pountney 1971; Benjamin 1964), public health reports, and nutritional surveys (Burnett 1968, Drummond and Wilbraham 1938) all show trends which are ecologically unfavourable to the spread of tuberculosis, especially trends in overcrowding (figure 2.6). National data on the proportion of households sharing kitchens, bathrooms, and other amenities have only been available from the census since 1951.

Overcrowding was not just an urban problem. We should not glamorize the overcrowded, insanitary rural cottages—scarcely adequate as holiday homes for a two-child family now—in which parents tried to raise five children, which were so strikingly condemned in Chadwick's 1842 Report on the Sanitary Condition of the Labouring Classes (Flinn 1965). In the towns, rapid urban growth (table 2.1) made it very difficult to build houses fast enough. Between 1831 and 1841 Glasgow's population increased by 37 per cent, Manchester and Salford by 47 per cent from 1821 to 1831, West Bromwich's by 60 per cent, and Bradford by 78 per cent. In the decade from 1831, the average occupancy per house in Liverpool increased from 6.4 to 6.9. Some local areas were much worse. Church Lane in St. Giles, London (a notorious 'rookery') had 655 people in its 27 houses, 4.9 to a room) according to a London Statistical Society survey of 1841, and in 1847, 1,095 or 8.1 to a room—an increase due partly to comprehensive redevelopment nearby, partly to renewed Irish immigration after the Famine of 1845–6.

Urban rents took 10–20 per cent of wages, compared to 5 per cent or so in the countryside. Back-to-back houses usually in a terrace, with a front door on each side, separated by a transverse party wall, could be particularly cramped, having no back yard or through ventilation, although later versions, still to be seen in Leeds and other northern cities, were no worse in this respect than modern flats. They were prohibited in the Metropolis by the series of Building Acts which had improved the capital's housing since 1667, notably that of 1774. But in Nottingham in 1840 7,000–8,000 of the 11,000 houses were of this type (see Burnett 1986). Many people, especially the Irish immigrants in Liverpool, lived in damp and ill-ventilated cellars (22 per cent in 1841) despite the attempts of local authorities to fill cellars with sand and gravel (Ferguson 1964). Evidence for the easing of overcrowding comes late in the century. By that time, higher real wages allowed ordinary families to rent more spacious and better equipped accommodation (95 per cent of households rented until after the First World War) and encouraged builders to improve quality. Almost all houses were equipped with their own privy or WC by the end of the century (outside was considered more hygienic), most from the medium size up had an internal bathroom. In terms of these amenities, and of rooms per household, Britain was ahead of other European countries.

Welfare and the Poor Law

For many poorer people food and housing depended on welfare. It had always been so (see Chapter 1). Welfare was local, paid out of parish rates. One system established by the magistrates of Speenhamland (Berkshire) in 1795 was widely copied until its abolition by the New Poor Law of 1834. According to Malthus, its fiercest critic, it depressed the wages paid by farmers by compensating wherever they fell below a scale set by the bread price and the number of the labourer's children in relation to his wage (Marshall 1968). It ensured that the unemployed earned as much as the labourer, reminiscent of the 'poverty trap' problems of today's welfare. Malthus claimed that its introduction encouraged improvident early marriage, although evidence for this is difficult to find (Digby 1983). The transfer payments of the Poor Law— finally abolished and transformed into the 'Welfare State' in 1948— were considered by many to be an intolerable burden. The indoor relief (workhouses) established by the New Poor Law was widely criticized, but the system as a whole provided a safety net for the poorest, and thereby helped mortality trends. From 1834 little change was made in the welfare system until the first decade of the twentieth century. Universal state old age pensions were introduced by the Old Age Pensions Act of 1908, workmen's insurance in 1911. Their contribution to further falls in mortality is difficult to estimate, but income and mortality is considered further in Chapter 8.

Civil engineering, vital statistics, and local government

Intervention by national and local government to reduce environmental risks had dramatic effects on urban death-rates. Typhoid and cholera were eliminated in the nineteenth century by engineering, epidemiology, and bureaucracy. Typhoid and cholera are different bacterial diseases which share a similar ecology; they are transmitted in food or water contaminated by the faeces of an infected person. They were ideally suited to town life before the spread of hygienic knowledge, readily distributed by polluted rivers, reservoirs, and wells. Their control merely requires the segregation of sewage from drinking water. Ordinances had been passed since medieval times to remove rubbish from streets (Howe 1972) with further Nuisances Removals Acts in 1855, 1860, 1863. But although closed sewers had been dug in larger towns in the eighteenth and earlier centuries to replace open ditches, because of their square cross-section and inadequate fall and water supply they endlessly blocked up. By leaking, like cesspits, they contaminated ground water. The water closet had been patented in 1775 but the widespread use of water carriage for sewage needed abundant water supply and good leakproof glazed drains. In 1850 most nightsoil was still collected—expensively and with much fallout—by cart. Drinking water was still taken from contaminated sources, so although pipes were laid to many individual houses and street stand-pipes by the 1840s, the water was impure (see Cruickshank and Burton 1990). Water companies were required to stop taking their water from tidal (most polluted) sources only by the Metropolis Water Act of 1852. The miasmatic theory of disease—favoured into the 1850s even by such luminaries as William Farr—hindered realization that the agents of disease might be present in water which looked quite drinkable.

The 'Great Stink' of 1858 (from untreated sewage in the Thames), which drove Parliament from the House of Commons, and the death of Albert, Prince Consort, in 1861 from typhoid contracted from Windsor's contaminated water, underlined the need for reform. Asiatic cholera, a new enteric disease, provided the spur to action. Endemic in Bengal for centuries, the first of four epidemics to attack the British population first appeared in Sunderland in 1831 (the others were in 1848, 1853, and 1866). It spread fast in the contaminated water of the great cities, killing in all four epidemics about 100,000 people. In 1854, Dr John Snow and William Farr assembled demographic statistics on the distribution of deaths from the new vital registration system to demonstrate beyond doubt, and contrary to received opinion, that the disease was water-borne and came from specific sources (Lewes 1983). The disease had been efficiently delivered to the homes of victims through the water pipes of the Southwark and Vauxhall Water Company from the contaminated tidal Thames. Customers of the rival Lambeth Water Company, which took its water from the upriver source of

Thames Ditton and which served houses in the same London streets, suffered only a sixth of their risk.

In London, and later in all major cities, new impervious trunk sewers were built on scientific principles to replace or intercept the old ducts and to ensure that all sewage was discharged downstream. Cesspits were filled in and nightsoil collection ended. Eventually sewage was treated before discharge in two enormous sites on each side of the lower Thames. The London works, capable of disposing of 400 million gallons of sewage a day and still in use, were finished in 1865 under the direction of Bazalgette (Daley and Benjamin 1964). By 1866, London's drinking water was taken from upstream or tributary sources, and later treated before distribution. Chlorine was first used to treat water after the Maidstone epidemic of 1897–8 when hop-pickers contaminated spring water. The incidence of typhoid collapsed. Cholera never returned after 1866. None of the subsequent pandemics, such as that of 1893, became established in Britain. Precise information on deaths dates only from 1868; before that typhoid was confused with the symptomatically similar but epidemiologically different disease, louse-borne typhus. Typhoid is more difficult to eliminate because symptomless 'carriers' can transmit the disease to others, although most of the few cases today are imported (see Chapter 7).

This was action by national government backed up by national statistical systems. At the local level, sanitary reform was at first hampered by the chaotic diversity of different local bodies (Flinn 1969). In response, the Public Health Act 1872 set up new local sanitary authorities to police legislation. Local authorities assumed something like their present form after the Local Government Act of 1888, which gave them greater powers to raise funds and pass by-laws. Local Medical Officers of Health had been established by the Public Health Act of 1845, but the Act was ineffectual and Chadwick's ideal was not approached until the 1875 Act. The officers' activities were spurred by the contemporary knowledge of mortality differences between town and country, different towns, and different areas in the same town (Woods 1982). Their role in the reduction of mortality was—and still is—to remove environmental risks to health, to encourage the building of proper sewage and water systems following the Metropolitan example, to enforce housing standards, to ensure that rubbish is collected, to organize health inspections of schoolchildren. Such local action may be a neglected dimension in the late nineteenth century/early twentieth century mortality reduction (Szreter 1986).

Most of the discussions above have centred upon specific factors particular to Britain. By the end of the nineteenth century, British mortality was still more favourable than in most other Western countries, despite the very high level of urbanization. Around 1900 expectation of life at birth for males was about 48 in Britain compared with 45 in Germany and France, 44 in Italy and 40 in Spain. However Denmark and the Netherlands had both exceeded 51. In Britain, babies were more likely to be breast fed, public health and sanitation were more advanced. Real wages were still higher than in most other countries except the USA and Germany. Nevertheless mortality had begun to fall in most Western countries only slightly later than in Britain, almost irrespective of the degree to which they had industrialized their economies, and with a similar diminution of particular causes of death (Preston 1975, 1976). Common factors were widespread education, rising incomes, sanitary reform, and effective government. Innovations such as vaccination could spread over Western Europe and North America within a decade; later the acceptance of the germ theory of disease spread even faster. A specifically formulated general explanation which meets all these circumstances is still awaited. This is true to an even greater extent of the fertility decline to which we now turn.

2.7 The Decline of Fertility

The pattern of fertility decline

Starting in the 1870s, average family size had declined from five or six children to today's two-child family within 60 years (figure 2.7). This transition was without precedent in history. It is almost certainly permanent. It has had the most profound effects on family life, on population growth, age structure, and the economy.

By the late eighteenth century, in a lagged response to higher and more reliable wages from industrialization and more prosperous farming, median age at marriage had fallen to 23 for men, 22 for women, compared to 26 and 24 in the century before. Only about 5 per cent of those generations never married—a very low proportion for Europe (see Chapter 1). In response to the marriage boom, fertility reached an all-time high at around 1800. It seemed that the industrial revolution was creating its own work-force. A trend to higher fertility is a temporary response to the earlier phases of modernization in recent developing societies too, although for different reasons. By the 1840s marriage returned to its former level and fertility consequently fell (figure 2.7). The post-war fall in food prices, together with the larger cohorts seeking work, depressed agricultural wages, but new average real wage levels were dominated by industrial employment and continued to rise

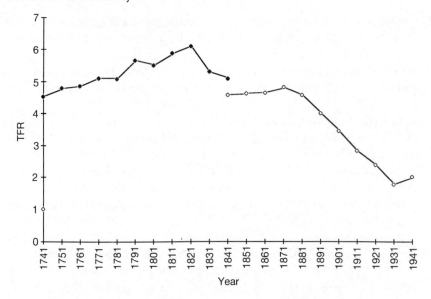

Sources: 1741–1841: data from Wrigley and Schofield 1981, t. A3.1 (England only); 1841– : OPCS 1987n, t. 1.4 (England and Wales).

FIG. 2.7. Trend in total fertility rate, 1741–1941

until the end of the nineteenth century. Throughout the nineteenth century fertility in Britain remained high. By the marriage cohorts of 1870 a decline in national marital fertility became apparent, unrelated to any major retreat from marriage. Unlike previous declines, it continued without interruption for sixty years, eventually embracing all sections of the population, until a completely new pattern of low fertility had been established by the 1930s, essentially that which we have today. That is in itself a problem, for nothing in the arguments to explain the decline suggests why the fall in fertility should stop at about a two-child family, rather than 'overshoot' and decline still further (Chapter 4).

Explaining fertility decline

This transformation from large to small family size, and the mortality decline which (in Britain) preceded it, is known as the demographic transition. All industrial countries have experienced such a transition from high to low birth- and death-rates in the last century, usually (except in France) with an intervening period of moderate population growth when the death-rate falls before the birth-rate. No simple agreed explanation is available; it remains a major problem in demography.

Proximate determinants

It is relatively easy to identify the immediate or 'proximate' reasons for the decline in births (Bongaarts and Potter 1983, see Chapter 4). Women can only have fewer babies if they have intercourse less often (because of delays in marriage or less frequent sex); begin practising contraception or suffer from declining physiological ability to conceive ('fecundity'); or prevent the gestation of conceptions by abortion.

As to these immediate causes, the choice is straightforward. Contemporary observers were quite clear that the modest decline in marriage around 1870 could not account for more than 10 per cent of the fall in births (Yule 1906). Setting aside fanciful notions that Western fecundity declined through a surfeit of meat eating or a failure of 'racial vitality' (Soloway 1982), there is no evidence for declining fecundity. The proximate cause of the decline in births was the adoption of contraceptive practices by the majority of married women and to a lesser extent (illegal) abortion. This is amply confirmed by analysis of the 1911 census (Matras 1965), by the enquiries on contraception begun by Dr. E. Lewis-Faning in connection with the 1946 Family Census (Lewis-Faning 1949, Glass and Grebenik 1954), and by all other surveys since, as well as by contemporary accounts (Fryer 1965).

But families do not just decide, for the first time in history, to adopt contraception out of the blue. Limitation of family size will not happen unless it can be done without trespassing on conscience and unless practicable means are available; and unless it is perceived to be in the families' interests to do so (Coale 1973). Why and how this happened are the more difficult questions.

Models of the demographic transition

The 'demographic transition model', first put forward sixty years ago (Thompson 1929, Davis 1945, Notestein 1945) is an attempt to answer these questions. At its least ambitious it is a description of a sequence of events in mortality and fertility decline in modernizing societies. At its most comprehensive it proposes an explanation of historical population trends and a forecast of trends in the developing world. Fertility falls because of the effects of industrialization and urbanization of the economy, and the concomitant modernization of society, upon the economic viability of large families and their support by traditional institutions and attitudes. In recent years micro-economic interpretations of fertility transition have been dominant (e.g. the 'New Home Eco-

nomics' of Becker (1981) and others, which emphasize the increased costs of children, and the competition of demand for children with demand for consumer goods previously not available. On this view high fertility is economically irrational, or at least is made so by the new circumstances.

Rational high fertility?

Under some circumstances high fertility may be rational (Caldwell 1982). In rural, agricultural society children cost little. They may not stop the wife's contribution to the household economy. They can bring in returns of their own. Large family size can help insure against risk of natural disaster or widowhood (Cain 1981; Smith 1986). If women enjoy low status they may need sons for prestige as well as protection. There may be no alternative institutional support. Modernization eventually takes away children's ability to earn and turns them into a cost as they need education to earn as adults. Only irrational 'props' to high fertility then remain; religion, tradition, and ignorance. A more educated, literate, and rational society weakens their effect; contraceptive knowledge and practice spreads first in the more educated classes, then to poorer people.

This outline does not fit the European experience very well, let alone that of developing countries. Even in developing societies children may bring little return or 'insurance' (Vlassoff 1982, Nugent 1985). Pre-transitional European fertility cannot be explained by the utility of children to their parents. Where a familial, labour-intensive mode of production is predominant, among peasant farmers and cottage industries, children might provide useful labour. This is less obviously true for wage-labourers; not at all for the middle class. In practice in Europe, the returns seem to have been slight, of a kind which could be met by resident servants (Smith 1981), and did not include automatic old-age support.

With high mortality rates even a large family size only just replaces the parents. The decline of infant mortality makes it easier to accept the idea of smaller family size. But clear declines in infant mortality in Britain and in Belgium only become apparent some time after the beginning of the fertility decline, and in France mortality and fertility declines begin at about the same time. Overall there is no correlation; both seem to be consequences of a more general modernization (van de Walle 1986).

International comparisons

European comparisons do not support the primacy of industrialization and urbanization in the fall in fertility. In France, fertility decline within marriage began a century earlier, in the 1780s (Wrigley 1983), without industrialization on the scale of Britain's. Furthermore the decline began in many rural areas at the same time as in towns. Migration and fertility decline are alternative escapes from population pressure in societies sufficiently developed for mortality to be declining (as in eighteenth century France) and can to some extent substitute for each other (Davis 1963, Friedlander 1983) to relieve population pressure (Woods and Smith 1983). High fertility in Ireland (by modern standards) depended upon the institutionalized pattern of high emigration which prevented population rising from the 1840s until the 1950s. But France had no industrial towns or suitable overseas colonies to migrate to (Grigg 1980). Despite lower British fertility levels, migration out of England exceeded 100,000 per year by 1870; 3–5 per 1,000 population, representing up to a third of natural increase (Baines 1985).

Education and ideas

Almost all the countries of Europe except Spain and Ireland started their fertility decline just a few decades after Britain, before the First World War (Coale and Watkins 1986), even though some (e.g. Scandinavia) remained dependent on agriculture, fishing, forestry, and other primary production. The modernization and the industrialization of a society need not be linked (Wrigley 1972). The spread of literacy and of universal education may be more crucial in precipitating fertility decline, even if it cannot occur without the development of a more market oriented economy, less based upon family and subsistence production, and a perception of real income growth. The spread of ideas and aspirations among literate and mobile populations is now given much more prominence as the key characteristic of 'modernization' which can explain fertility decline (Banks 1981, Cleland 1985, Cleland and Hobcraft 1987, Cleland and Wilson 1987). New ideas and a 'revolution of aspiration' through higher real wages around the 1850s may have persuaded populations that economic advancement was possible away from subsistence agriculture into manufactures, services, and cash agriculture and that large families stood in the way of it (Lesthaeghe 1983). Such changes must depend on the spread of education, which widened expectations and brought a more rational and secular mood inimical to the traditional values opposed to contraception. People had become disinclined to believe without doubting what was revealed to them. Such vague propositions need to rest on some testable factual basis. In England, literacy and educational level increase, church attendance and Communion figures fall markedly at the end of the century (Woods 1987). Throughout Europe, the rise of divorce from negligible levels and the doubling of suicide rates from 1875 to 1914 suggest that fertility decline goes hand in hand with other radical changes in attitudes and behaviour.

Cultural and religious contrasts

Cultural and linguistic boundaries seem to be important in accounting for regional differences in the onset of fertility decline in different parts of Europe (Lesthaeghe 1983). Areas which supported reformist social democrat political parties (as opposed to traditionalist Christian ones) had the fastest fertility decline. Those with a local culture, under attack by central secular government and re-enforced by identification with the Church, preserved high fertility longest (Ireland and Brittany). Catholic areas generally retained higher fertility than Protestant ones. Secular attitudes go with a low proportion of population engaged in family farming and agriculture and a high proportion of women working (Lesthaeghe 1983). Although difficult to measure, these differences cannot be accounted for simply by their accompanying economic differences. The ideological dimension favoured in the explanation of Continental fertility differences seems less applicable to Britain, which lacked major foci of religious or social dissent. The rural unrest of the early nineteenth century, the urban unrest of the Chartist and Gordon riots, the industrial turmoil of 1913 seem minor compared with the political and ideological upheavals and bloodshed abroad in the revolutions of 1789, 1815, 1830, 1848, and 1871. Partly perhaps as a legacy of the risk-sharing of the old Poor Law (R. M. Smith 1986), British society preserved a more common interest and aspiration, without political parties embracing specific faiths or revolutionary ideals.

Particulars of the British fertility decline

In Britain, fertility fell surprisingly uniformly over the different regions of the country (Brass and Kabir 1978) with only a few exceptions (Woods 1987). The prominent regional variations on the Continent revealed by the Princeton study (Coale and Watkins 1986) were minor in Britain, largely because regional linguistic and religious differences were minor. However, fertility was higher where areas had high Irish or Roman Catholic populations (Teitelbaum 1984); some parts of Wales, the Highlands of Scotland, and Ulster had later fertility declines (the rest of Ireland much later) and Wales and Scotland also retained distinctive marriage patterns.

However, people of different social status began to limit their families at quite different times. These differentials give us important clues about the motivation and causes of the fertility decline. Family limitation can first be inferred, primarily from the data of the 1911 census, among the families of professional men, particularly the clergy, doctors, and lawyers. After them, families with heads in occupations which would now be placed in social class II: civil servants, school teachers, accountants, and the like (table 2.4). In the middle classes, businessmen and farmers began to limit their families last (Innes 1938, Glass and Grebenik 1954, Matras 1965). In general, working-class families reduced their families later than the middle class, but among them there were some important differences. Skilled artisans adopted small family size before labourers; people in occupations where married women customarily worked (e.g. textiles) were also prompt to limit family size. Agricultural labourers and coal miners, despite the skills and high income of the latter, were the last to follow, preserving high fertility into the twentieth century.

Many of the classic economic and social indicators of fertility decline had been present for a long time in nineteenth-century Britain. In terms of the 'demographic transition' it is a great puzzle to explain why the response to them was so late in a relatively literate, urbanized, and industrialized society where returns from children do not seem to have been plausible for a long time (R. M. Smith 1981). The closer the inspection, the less like a 'classical' demographic transition the British record seems to be, and the more difficult it is to attribute its timing directly to the development of an urban-industrial society (Woods 1987). The question becomes; why did it take so long, not why did it happen at all.

Earlier—and still persuasive—analyses suggest that fertility decline was precipitated by a crisis in the ability to maintain rising standards of living (Banks 1954). By mid-century living standards were perceptibly improving in all classes (Taylor 1975). Large families began to threaten this prosperity because expectations of consumption kept rising while costs of children, especially for middle-class education, also rose. The education which accompanied—or indeed may have preceded the new economic order made family planning thinkable (Banks 1981). Marriage had always to be delayed until a suitable standing was achieved among middle-class and respectable poor (Macfarlane 1986). The possibility of marrying on £300 a year and preserving any pretentions to gentility was much discussed in agony columns (Banks 1954).

Servants were essential to run a large house and family, to free the middle-class mother for her prime role of managing her house, not

Table 2.4. Fertility by social status, Great Britain, 1890–1924[a]

Date of Marriage	Social Status Categories									All status groups
	(1) Professional	(2) Employers	(3) Own account	(4) Salaried employees	(5) Non-manual wage earners	(6) Manual wage earners	(7) Farmers and farm managers	(8) Agricultural workers	(9) Labourers	
Number of live births per woman										
1890–9	2.80	3.28	3.70	3.04	3.53	4.85	4.30	4.71	5.11	4.34
1900–9	2.33	2.64	2.96	2.37	2.89	3.96	3.50	3.88	4.45	3.53
1910–14	2.07	2.27	2.42	2.03	2.44	3.35	2.88	3.22	4.01	2.98
1915–19	1.85	1.97	2.11	1.80	2.17	2.92	2.55	2.79	3.58	2.61
1920–4	1.75	1.84	1.95	1.65	1.97	2.70	2.31	2.71	3.35	2.42
Ratios: All Status Groups = 100 (for each cohort)										
1890–9	65	76	85	70	81	112	99	109	118	100
1900–9	66	75	84	67	82	112	99	110	126	100
1910–14	69	76	81	68	82	112	97	108	135	100
1915–19	71	75	81	69	83	112	98	107	136	100
1920–4	72	76	81	68	81	112	95	112	138	100
Ratios: 1900–9 Cohort for Each Status Group = 100										
1890–9	120	124	125	128	122	122	123	121	115	123
1900–9	100	100	100	100	100	100	100	100	100	100
1910–14	89	86	82	86	84	85	82	83	90	84
1915–19	79	75	71	76	75	74	73	72	80	74
1920–4	75	70	66	70	68	68	66	70	75	69

[a] Women married under age 45 only.

Sources: Glass and Grebenik 1954; Part I, table 41.

labouring in it, and caring for her children's development. Domestic service was a commonplace of life before the First World War, even among the better paid working-class households. In 1871, 1,106,000 men and women were employed as servants, the biggest single employment group outside agriculture. Their wages increased by 30 per cent over the period through competition with industrial wages, to add to increases in costs from aspirations in housing, transport, social life, and many new conveniences, at a time when the general trend in prices was downwards (Deane and Cole 1969). The 'Great Depression' after 1873 is alleged to have forced a decision between children and consumption, or at least between their number and the quality of their upbringing. This 'Depression', unlike that of 1929, was a transient failure of the rate of growth. An already antiquated industrial economy was overtaken by newer and more competitive ones in export and domestic markets, particularly by German manufactures (Barnett 1972, Wiener 1981).

Education and the costs of children

Children's costs rose because traditional middle-class occupations and positions in the services, professions, and the civil service (now much expanded) required some evidence of ability, following reforms of medical education (1858) and selection for the army (1871) and civil service (1870). Education at a public school and university became essential (Banks 1981). School fees were about £50–£100 per year; three years at Oxbridge might cost £600. Girls' public schools began after 1870, and colleges after 1879. Preparatory schools proliferated to replace tuition at home and to provide a middle-class alternative to the Board Schools following compulsory education in 1870. Education was important too for the Pooters, if only to keep children out of manual work, even though the multitude of clerks' jobs were often less well paid—£70 per year—than much manual work. Generally speaking, but with some local exceptions as in Sheffield, people in lower middle-class occupations (shopkeepers, clerks, junior teachers, and businessmen) limited their families later than the professional classes—possibly more because of the greater hold of traditional and religious influences on their behaviour than because their need was any the less (Woods and Smith 1983).

Early in the century the upbringing and education of working-class children was inadequate but cheap and their employment could at least contribute to their keep. But the employment open to children and the age and the hours they could work were curtailed by legislation throughout the nineteenth century, beginning with the 1833 Factory Act. Such legislation was a response to liberal humanitarianism but it was made possible by the inevitable tendency of industrial processes to require more skilled labour. Education was encouraged by the General Education Act of 1870; and made compulsory in 1876 up to age 10 and to age 14 according to the Act of 1880. Until 1891 there was no state payment of the modest fees (see Smith 1931). Whatever may have happened before, wealth flowed decisively from parents to children in all households in Britain from then on. It is claimed that no society can maintain high fertility in the face of two generations of mass education, and that had been achieved in much of Western Europe by the end of the nineteenth century (Caldwell 1982). But it would not be difficult to construct *post hoc* explanations for fertility decline occurring earlier in the nineteenth century as well.

2.8 Thinking the Unthinkable: The Rise of Birth Control

The spread of family planning in Britain is the story of the spread of information and the change of attitudes. The supply of *matériel* was much less important. Much of the fertility decline was achieved without mechanical contraception and initially without professional advice (see Chapter 4).

The beginnings of birth control

Written knowledge of contraception and abortion, some of it potentially effective like coitus interruptus and vaginal sponges and spermicides, goes back at least two millenia (Himes 1936, McLaren 1990). The account below of the struggle to establish the knowledge of family planning and its moral acceptability derives mostly from Fryer (1965), McLaren (1978), Leathard (1980) and Soloway (1982). There is no good evidence for the widespread and effective use of any methods of family planning outside a few élite or urban groups until the end of the eighteenth century (Wilson 1984, Livi-Bacci 1986), and even then appliance methods do not become important for another century.

Robert Malthus brought the problems of excess fertility to the front of public discussion in 1798, yet he regarded contraception and abortion—which he alluded to only elliptically—as species of vice. His argument that excess fertility impeded the solution of poverty inspired less squeamish reformers to resolve the problems of poverty he described with a new 'neo-Malthusian' prescription of contraception, not deferred marriage. Utilitarians like Jeremy Bentham, uninhibited by Malthus's fear that contraception would remove a spur to industry, recommended contraceptive devices for the poor (sponges) in 1797.

The radical reformer Francis Place (1822, ed. Himes 1967) was foremost in this movement (Fryer 1965). His unsigned handbills addressed 'to the married of both sexes' both 'in Genteel life' and 'of the Working People', distributed from London to Manchester in 1823, constitute the first known birth control publicity. They specifically described and recommended the use of coitus interruptus and other contraceptive methods in marriage. Richard Carlile followed with the first book on contraception in 1826 (*Every Woman's Book*), followed by *Moral Physiology* by the American socialist Robert Dale Owen, 1830, and Dr Charles Knowlton's *Fruits of Philosophy* in New York in 1832.

The reformers accepted Malthus's analysis but not what they regarded as his negative attitude towards working-class behaviour. But their radical and often anti-clerical politics hampered the spread of their own ideas among the respectable middle class, who distrusted practices so reeking of unwed vice and its connotations of disease. The medical profession feared quasi-medical self-help. Working-class leaders—influenced by Marxist hostility to Malthus—disliked these individualistic appeals, although many of the socialite socialists of the Fabian Society, notably the Webbs (1907) were enthusiasts. Feminist opinion remained curiously muted, more concerned about defusing male sexuality and social dominance (Banks and Banks 1964).

In terms of the circulation of literature, birth control ideas made only modest progress before the 1870s. But there is inferential evidence for the early adoption of family planning. From the 1840s to 1900 the proportion of illegitimate births declined throughout Europe, from 7 per cent to less than 4 per cent, with no evidence that chastity outside marriage had become more popular. Those most in need of contraception were finding out how to do it (Shorter, Knodel, and van de Walle 1971). Indirect evidence from the 1911 census suggests that about 20 per cent of married women born in 1831–45 (and therefore marrying from the mid-1850s onwards) and over 40 per cent of those born 1861–70 were controlling their fertility (Matras 1965). More direct if understated evidence comes from the retrospective questions posed in the first official birth control enquiry in 1946 (Lewis-Faning 1949) (see Chapter 5).

Heroes and heroines of the birth control movement

The public profile of birth control was changed radically by the celebrated Bradlaugh/Besant trial of 1877. Charles Bradlaugh had founded the National Secular Society and edited the radical *National Reformer*, which often sought publicity for its views by courting prosecution. In

1877 they republished Knowlton's old pamphlet *The Fruits of Philo-sophy* and were prosecuted for obscenity—in the end unsuccessfully. But thanks to the newspapers, now circulating millions of copies in a population over 80 per cent literate, birth control was 'brought onto every Englishman's breakfast table' (Banks and Banks 1954). Sales of Knowlton's and other pamphlets soared, selling in millions over the next few years when previously they had sold in tens of thousands (Teitelbaum 1984).

Marie Stopes was the most prominent of the later campaigners. She was untainted by the radical politics of earlier reformers and wisely avoided the tendentious macro-economics of the Neo-Malthusians. An aggressive self-publicist, her inflamed prose brought her much notori-ety. Her books *Married Love* and *Wise Parenthood*, published with difficulty in 1917 and 1918, had sold a million copies by World War II. Although alienating some support by her excessive regard for the physiologically and morally uplifting properties of semen, she empha-sized the erotic, mystical, and fulfilling aspects of sexual relations and for these reasons rejected the use of coitus interruptus and the condom, recommending instead the use of the vaginal rubber cap and the quin-ine (spermicidal) pessary which she naïvely believed to be generally available in chemist's shops and which have never, in the event, proved to be very popular.

Under the banner of her Society for Constructive Birth Control and Racial Progress, Stopes's first 'mothers' clinic' in Holloway opened in 1921. The Malthusian League's Women's Welfare Centre opened in Walworth later that year. These pioneer clinics, which numbered only sixteen even by 1930, had treated only 21,000 women by that time. The great majority of women limiting their families did not attend clinics at all but learnt from their neighbours, friends, or literature. Family planning was in the air; newspapers and women's magazines were openly discussing family planning by the 1930s in a manner which would have been considered outrageous just ten years before.

Methods

Most of the fertility decline was achieved with coitus interruptus and the use of contraceptive vaginal sponges with spermicides such as vine-gar, alum, or lemon, together with illegal abortion, whose practitioners were known to every working-class street. Early condoms, intended to protect against disease, originally made of animal membranes and de-scribed by Johnson as a 'cuirass against pleasure and a cobweb against infection' were not really suitable. Their large-scale use had to await the vulcanization of rubber in the 1870s. Once again, the First World War marked a turning point. After a bitter debate between the rival proponents of cold baths and of condoms, and with the equivalent of two divisions out of action with venereal disease by 1917, the government eventually had to authorize the issue of condoms to the troops (Winter 1985). The 'Dutch Cap' was not introduced by the German physician Mensinga until the 1880s and was only ever used by a minority of women, despite its promotion by clinics. Manipulation of the womb by pessaries, stemmed and unstemmed, was a popular late nineteenth-century medical fad. These intra-uterine devices would have had a contraceptive effect and were relied on by some women for that purpose. Contraceptive IUDs as such were not developed until 1930 by Ohta in Japan, and were not made in a form suitable for mass use until after the Second World War.

Responses and reactions—religious, medical, and political

Individual need, private enterprise, advertising, and warfare effectively sidestepped medical and religious objections to contraceptive use. Doctors and clergymen were among the earliest birth controllers in the middle class. But their official bodies opposed family limitation. The Church of England, which in its 1908 Lambeth Conference had condemned family planning, changed its mind when it was clear that the faithful were simply ignoring its precepts. Although the 1920 Lambeth Conference took a hard line (not helped by Marie Stopes's literary, erotic, and religious excesses), the 'safe period' had been endorsed by 1913. More and more Anglican bishops broke ranks before the next Lambeth Conference in 1930, which emphasized motives rather than method and gave grudging acceptance to 'other methods' than abstinence, noting that Church opposition was rooted in tradition not in Scripture.

The Church of Rome, on the other hand, hardened its attitude against birth control. The refusal through contraception to reaffirm life during intercourse was—and is—regarded as a kind of Manichean heresy. There was little conflict with congregations because, in England anyway, Catholic congregations (mostly poor) started to adopt birth control considerably later than others (Teitelbaum 1984). The rhythm method had been approved by Catholic clergymen on the Birth-rate Commission as early as 1913 and in the 1930 Encyclical *Casti Connubii*. But the general hostility of the Roman Catholic Church to all other forms of family limitation and abortion and contraceptive sterilization were reaffirmed in 1951, in the Encyclical *Humanae Vitae* in 1968, and repeatedly by the present Pope John Paul II. None the less, higher Roman Catholic fertility has now disappeared in Britain (Chapter 12) as in the USA and most Western countries.

Medical reaction to family planning

The medical profession ignored family planning in the first half of the century, only speaking to condemn it. The British Medical Association refused to consider family planning at its meetings from 1912 to 1928, considering it to be tainted by association with vice and radicalism. Dr Henry Allbut was struck off the register in 1880 for publishing *The Wife's Handbook*, popularizing contraceptive knowledge. He claimed he was really being punished for making medical advice too cheap at 6*d*. Some doctors recognized the medical need for relief from child-bearing, others were concerned about the eugenic aspects of differ-ential birth-rates. But most medical writing—even up to the 1920s—displays unscientific ignorance of sexual matters: dire warnings of phy-sical and mental consequences of 'Onanism' or 'conjugal masturbation'; the consequences to women deprived of 'vital fluid' being especially severe. Breast-feeding was recommended to space births and the rhythm method was approved. Unfortunately, until well into the twentieth century, the safe period was assumed to be at mid-month.

But in 1921 the King's personal physician, Lord Dawson, stunned his profession alike and delighted the press by praising the morality of family limitation and warning Church leaders that they risked losing a whole generation by their unrealistic pronouncements; an example followed in 1925 when the next King's physician, Sir H. Rolliston, Regius Professor of Physick at Cambridge, became president of a new family-planning clinic. The medical profession was about to be ex-cluded by its ignorance from an almost universal practice. There was no instruction on contraception in medical school; many doctors knew less than their patients. Leadership had been abandoned to Marie Stopes, whose textbook *Contraception* appeared in 1923. The Eugenics Society set up in 1926 the first medical study on contraceptive experience, which reported benefits to health. In 1930 the Royal College of Public Health started the first family-planning courses for physicians.

The role of government

The government, unmoved by Continental fears of population decline (Teitelbaum and Winter 1985), did not follow the 1920 French example in making family-planning propaganda illegal (see Glass 1940). But the public health and welfare aspects of family planning went unrecognized by local or central government, despite pressure from some Medical Officers of Health. The Ministry of Health insisted that it was not the business of maternity centres to offer family-planning advice, and the new Labour government in 1924 specifically forbade welfare centres from disseminating it. The socialist position was hostile, an extension of Marxist anti-Malthusian analysis of poverty and its causes; and the Roman Catholic influence on the Labour Party was not negligible. More Tory (54) than Labour (28) MPs supported a 1926 Private Members' bill to enable local authority welfare centres to give family-planning advice to married women. The depression of the late 1920s and chronic unemployment appeared to confirm Malthusian pessimism. Local authorities, many Labour, e.g. Stepney, Shoreditch, Sheffield, and Bootle, overwhelmed with welfare problems, challenged the Ministry of Health ruling. Eventually a secretive 1930s Ministry memorandum enabled local authorities to give advice, initially on medical grounds only. By 1939 280 local authorities were providing family planning help, together with almost seventy private clinics. Most of the latter (except Stopes's five clinics) affiliated with the Family Planning Association which had been formed from the National Birth Control Association in 1939. By 1949 there were 500 clinics helping 150,000 women every year. Despite the Royal Commission's recommendations, their complete absorption by the National Health Service took a further twenty-six years.

2.9 Consequences: The Creation of a New Population

Population growth and structure

The gap between birth- and death-rates from the eighteenth century opened up an unparalleled new window for population growth. Population had not previously exceeded five million and growth had seldom exceeded 0.5 per cent per year, which may have been the maximum that the underlying economy could sustain (Lee 1986). Freed from previous restraints, British population reached 10.5 million by 1801 and 37 million by 1901 (figure 2.1). Growth was most rapid in percentage terms around 1831 when it reached 1.55 per cent per year and in absolute terms around 1870. This was small beer by the standards of today's Third World which (outside China) is growing at 2.5 per cent per year and in which some countries (Kenya, Zambia, Syria) approach 4 per cent. But it was still enough to double population every fifty years. From the beginning of the seventeenth century to the beginning of the nineteenth there had been relatively little change in the age-

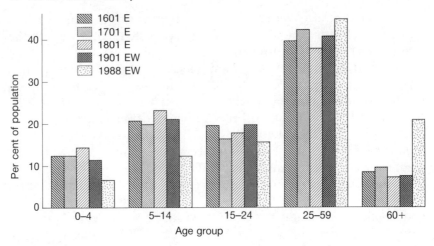

Sources: 1601–1801: data from Wrigley and Schofield 1981, t. A3.1; 1901– : OPCS Marriage and Divorce Statistics Series FM 2, t. 1.1, OPCS Monitor PP1 88/1.

Fɪɢ. 2.8. Age structure in broad age-groups, 1601–1988

distribution of the population. The growth which began in the eighteenth century had made the population more youthful by 1801; the normal consequence of any decline in mortality and increase in fertility (figure 2.8). The later fertility decline aged the population, a process already detectable by 1911 and marked by 1931 (figure 2.9) (Chapters 3 and 12). Throughout the nineteenth century the proportion of the over-65s in the population remained below 5 per cent. The enormous relative growth of older age-groups in the twentieth century is primarily due to the decline of fertility which began in the nineteenth (Chapters 6 and 13).

A new population map

The modernization and industrialization of nineteenth century Britain changed the population map. During the nineteenth century Britain became the world's first modern urbanized society. At the beginning of the century only about a third of the population lived in towns. On the eve of the First World War, about three-quarters did, not far from the balance today (table 2.1). Rural Britain had failed to hold onto its own natural increase, and had lost it to migration.

In the hundred years before 1851 rural population grew by only about 0.5 per cent per annum, compared with almost 2 per cent in the towns (Law 1967), despite the heavier urban mortality. Numbers living in rural areas more or less stood still until mid-century, falling by just

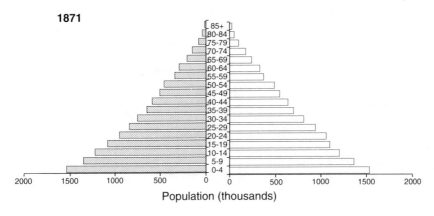

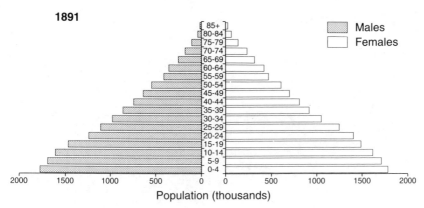

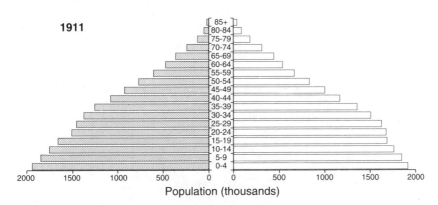

Sources: Censuses of England and Wales, 1871–1971.

FIG. 2.9. Age-structure of England and Wales in five-year age groups, 1871–1971

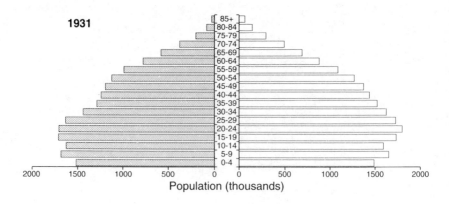

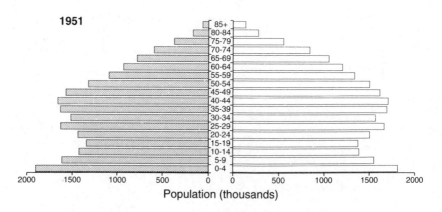

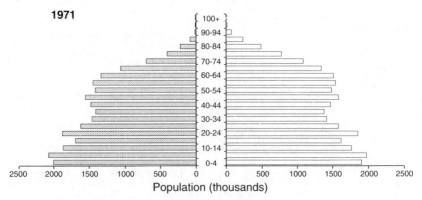

Table 2.5. Rate of loss by migration, Britain and Ireland, 1851–1939 (annual rate per 1,000 mean population)

	Wales	England	Scotland	Ireland		Sweden
				North	South	
1851–61	−28	−16	−101	−194		−7
1861–71	−47	−7	−44	−169		−37
1871–81	−35	−5	−28	−119	−127	−32
1881–91	−11	−23	−58	−108	−163	−74
1891–1901	−5	−2	−13	−55	−118	−37
1901–11	+45	−19	−57	−52	−82	−36
1911–21	−21	−16	−50	−47	−88	−11
1921–31	−102	+3	−80	−82	−56	−15
1931–39	−72	+24	−8	−5	−63	+9

Source: B. Thomas, The Welsh Economy: Studies in Expansion (Cardiff, 1962), p. 7.

half a million between 1831 and 1911. Losses reached a peak during the decade 1881–91 when the net figure approached 85,000 per annum, just as the whole population was growing at its maximum absolute rate (350,000 per annum). Emigration abroad was also high; a net loss of about 1.2 million between 1841 and 1911. But it was never so severe on the mainland as in Ireland (table 2.5). Rural areas beyond immediate urban influence did not all behave similarly. Loss rates may have varied according to the type of farming practised, depopulation being worse in heavier clay arable areas (Roxby 1912, Eversley 1907, Vince 1955).

Birthplace data from the 1841 census onwards show that only 40 per cent of those aged over 20 (the only people for whom data are available) had been born in the town they lived in. Some rural parishes also recorded relatively high adventitious populations. Over half of the population of Pinner, an agricultural village in 1851, were born elsewhere (Kirkman 1985). Despite the view that southern England must have been emptied by trekkers to the coalfields of the north, migrants did not travel far. South-easterners went to London; the coalfield towns were predominantly populated by nearby rural dwellers who brought with them high rates of natural increase. Half of Liverpool's immigrants in 1851 came from Lancashire and most of the rest from Ireland, which in terms of travel costs was nearer than southern England. New industrializing areas attracted migrants from the south to the north (and to South Wales) the reverse of 'drift to the south' which has preoccupied us this century. But the growth of these areas was also substantially due

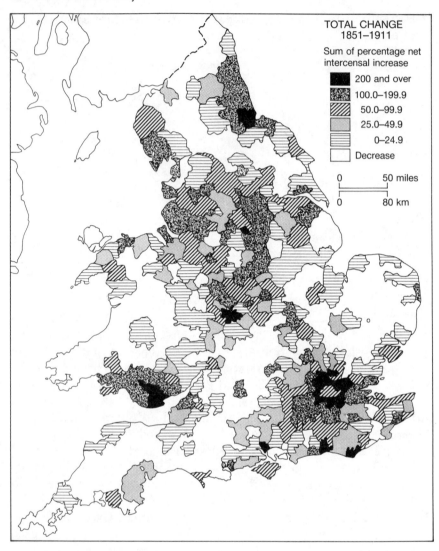

Sources: Lawton (1967).

Fig. 2.10. Population change in England and Wales, 1851–1911

to their higher fertility (see Chapter 9). Between 1801 and 1851 only limited areas were directly affected by urbanization, and high rates of increase still occurred in many rural areas, especially in the east and the south. The map for the later period (figure 2.10) shows a very different picture with a broad band of population decline across the country from East Anglia to the South-West which is the area of maximum growth today.

The role of migration in bringing about these rural changes was decisive. Growth from 1851 to 1911 was concentrated on the few urban industrial regions in which an increasing proportion of the population lived; these experienced both net immigration and natural increase. Most rural areas lost population. A few areas of early industrialization

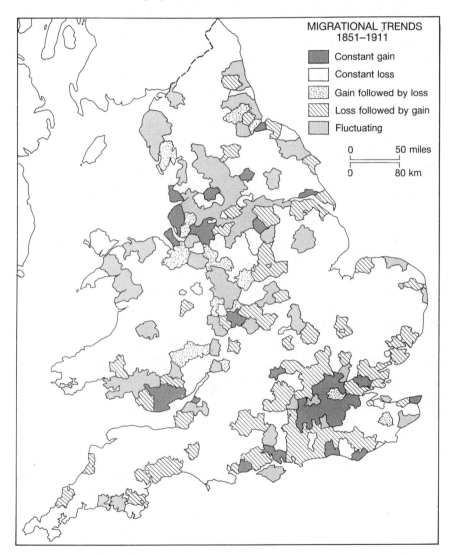

Note: The categories relate to the trends over the census decades 1851–1911, regardless of the amount of net migration involved.

Sources: Lawton 1967

Fig. 2.11. Trends in migration in England and Wales, 1851–1911

also suffered losses, in north-east Lancashire and West Yorkshire, where cramped sites based on water power were no longer economic. Only a few city regions and industrial areas gained constantly throughout the period (figure 2.11). The penetration of metropolitan influences into the Home Counties reversed early migration loss. In the centres of conurbations, natural gains were already partly offset by net out-migration: higher incomes and better building regulations resolved problems of overcrowding. Suburbanization became a powerful vehicle of population redistribution. Merchants no longer needed to live close to their businesses (e.g. in Manchester, Girouard 1985) and the railway network permitted businessmen to commute to work from new high-status outer suburbs, notably around London, and later on to create Metroland. Later in the century the development of 'workmen's trains' in London's unique network enabled many of London's workers to become commuters too.

More important, the repeal of the Corn Laws in 1846, following the triumph of Free Trade over Protection, reduced the price of grain with cheaper imports from North America, Russia, and later Australia (Deane and Cole 1969). The 'Golden Age' of English agriculture was over; after the 1860s it entered a period of decline from which it was not to recover until the Second World War. The introduction of labour-saving agricultural machinery to reduce wage costs began in earnest from the mid-nineteenth century. The Great Reform Bill of 1832 enabled the growing urban demography, reflected in urban voting power, to challenge the agricultural interest in high food prices with an urban interest in low prices. Temporary leadership in a world-wide free trade of manufactures enabled, for the first time, a population growing at between 200,000 and 350,000 people per year to be fed without dependence upon domestic food production. But this required a free trade in food. 'Those who had followed Peel with open eyes (to abolish protection and destroy his own party) . . . had done so because population was growing at the rate of 300,000 per annum. It had been a question of time, a race between life and food. To such men free trade was a need to be faced, not a treasure to be won' (Clapham 1932, cited in Grigg 1980).

3 The Changing Distribution of Population in the UK

3.1 Introduction

The last half century has seen the emergence of a number of trends in the changing distribution of the UK population. These include the 'drift to the south', rural decline and subsequent revitalization, planned urban overspill and decentralization from cities, small town growth, and now perhaps a halt to the decline of the major metropolitan centres. Two facts characterize these trends. First, though there have been some marginal changes, most notably in the steady trickle away from the north and west to the south and east, the main features of the regional distribution of population remain the same. Second, where change has occurred, particularly at the intraregional scale, migration has played the leading role.

The combination of census data with tried geographical techniques of cartographic analysis means we have been relatively well informed about the essentials of population distribution for over half a century. The planning maps of the Ministry of Housing and Local Government showed which local authorities were gaining or losing people up to and including 1961. A number of academics have used census data to plot details of changes in distribution in the inter-war and post-war periods (e.g. Willats and Newson 1953, Carter 1956, Moisley 1962, Champion 1976, Lawton 1977, Compton 1982). From the 1966 census, but with analyses pushing back to 1961, several major studies have attempted to use a wide range of census data grouped in new and more functional ways to depict the spatial characteristics of the British population. Most notable among these are the studies of Hall *et al.* (1973) for 1966, Spence *et al.* (1982) for 1971, and Champion *et al.* (1987) for 1981. More recently studies have combined decennial census data with annual population estimates supplied by the Registrar-General to enable more rapid updating of trends (Champion 1983, 1987). Census atlases of individual conurbations have also become more common, such as those for the West Midlands (Rosing and Wood 1971) and London (Shepherd *et al.* 1974). A corollary of these studies has been the classification of places in the UK according to their demographic, employment, and housing characteristics (Johnson, Salt, and Wood, 1974, Warnes and Law, 1984, Champion and Green, 1988).

This chapter will show the principal trends in population distribution since the inter-war period, focusing particularly on the last couple of decades. It will attempt to assess the overall stability of the pattern and discuss the underlying forces which affect it.

3.2 Sources of Data

Study of the distribution of the British population has to be based largely on the census, an amazingly rich and flexible source of data but capable of providing us with only occasional, if regular, views of what is happening. Filling in between times necessitates recourse to the mid-year estimates of the Registrar-General which provide details of the numbers of people in each local authority, together with a breakdown of annual changes by natural change and migration components.

The mid-year estimates are accurate for natural change, much less so for migration (see Chapter 10). The only direct counts of migration fed into them relate to military personnel and to the residents of some institutions (mainly prisons). The migration component has to be based on estimates gauged from a variety of sources like the Electoral Register, the NHS Central Register, the International Passenger Survey, and the migration patterns revealed by the last census. There may also be problems of boundary changes resulting either from major local-government reorganization or from more local adjustments. Despite these drawbacks the mid-year estimates undoubtedly provide an invaluable source and Champion (1987) concludes that for monitoring population change in England and Wales between 1971 and 1981 they may well be superior to the census; Scottish estimates, however, he considers less accurate because they were not revised in the light of 1981 census results. For the period since 1981 both sets have similar problems but advances in methodology, especially in handling migration, make them more useful than in the past.

3.3 Where do the British Live?

The general distribution pattern

The UK is one of the most densely populated countries in the world, with an average density in 1981 of 242 per square kilometre. There are, however, wide variations, ranging from densities of over 200 persons per hectare in some inner wards in London to virtually uninhabited

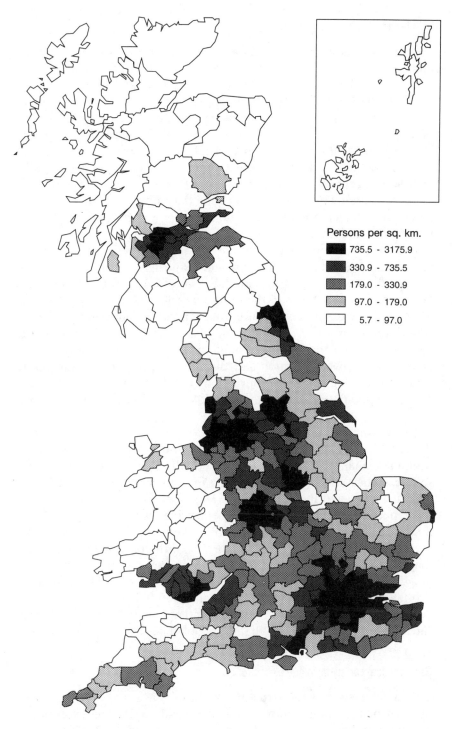

Persons per sq. km.

■ 735.5 - 3175.9
■ 330.9 - 735.5
▨ 179.0 - 330.9
▨ 97.0 - 179.0
□ 5.7 - 97.0

Source: CURDS 1984.

FIG. 3.1. Population density by local labour market areas, 1981

remote moorland areas in Scotland. A feature of most high density areas is that there has been a long-term decline in population and density since before the Second World War (Craig 1986).

The high overall density reflects the urbanized nature of the population. Even in 1911 over three-quarters of the British people lived in urban districts, the proportion being less in Northern Ireland where Belfast remains the only large industrial city. The proportion of urban dwellers has changed little during the present century, though in reality over 90 per cent of the population now effectively lives an urban form of existence. Few rural areas are beyond the ambit of a town or city and much of the increase of population in many parts of rural Britain reflects the underbounding of urban administrations.

The British people have chosen to dispose themselves unevenly across the national space. The present map (figure 3.1) shows an axis of high density extending broadly south-eastwards from the southern Pennines, where it takes in the industrial conurbations of Lancashire, Merseyside, and South Yorkshire, through the Midlands to the London conurbation. In the 1930s this zone was variously referred to as the 'axial belt', even the 'coffin', though in truth there was always a low-density gap between London and Birmingham, so perhaps 'doughnut' would have been more appropriate. It is interesting that the current growth of population in this empty middle is creating a proper axial belt for the first time.

Away from this are primary outliers of population concentration in the older industrial areas of South Wales, the North-East, and Central Scotland. Smaller, secondary foci include the Belfast area, parts of the southern coast of England, especially in the vicinity of the Solent, the Norwich area, and the banks of the Humber. Indeed, an almost cruciform pattern of high densities is emerging, with the North-West–South-East axis being crossed by one extending from South Wales, along the M4 corridor, passing to the north of London into East Anglia. In contrast to these areas of high density large parts of the kingdom remain 'empty'. These are particularly the upland areas of Scotland, northern Britain, Wales, and South-West England; however, more rural parts of Northern Ireland and the East Midlands (including the Fens) are still lightly peopled.

Geographical variations in age structure

The beehive-shaped age structure of the UK as a whole is replicated by each of the main countries but one (figure 3.2). The exception is Northern Ireland, whose age/sex pyramid is reminiscent of an earlier

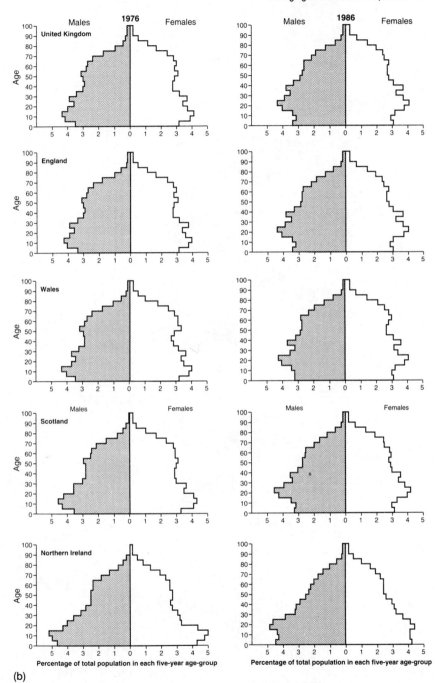

(b)

Source: Population Trends 51 (1988).

FIG. 3.2. Age structures in the constituent countries of the UK, 1976 and 1986

20.2–35.3%

(a)

Source: Warnes and Law 1984.

Fig. 3.3. Local authorities in Great Britain in the highest quintile by percentage of the population of pensionable age, 1981

phase of the demographic transition, with continuing high rates of fertility creating a much broader base. In Northern Ireland, too, the booms and busts of earlier generations are much less apparent than in England, Scotland, and Wales. For all countries the ten-year difference in the two sets of pyramids demonstrates how the excess births of one generation moves through the population, creating a successive need for new schools, jobs, houses and, ultimately, pensions. The implications of this ground swell are returned to in Chapter 13.

There is a considerable degree of variability in the age structure of different parts of the UK, owing to the age-selective nature of the migration process (Chapter 10). Particular interest attaches itself to the distribution of the elderly population, because of its implications for the provision of retirement accommodation and social services. Law and Warnes (1976, Warnes and Law 1984) have shown that the elderly are peripherally located, especially in coastal areas (figure 3.3). During the post-war period they have shown a quite stable distribution although in the 1970s the process of growing concentration in selected retirement areas, noticed in the 1960s, appeared to end. Instead a new trend seems to have manifested itself. This is for the proportions of the elderly to decline in the populations of some large, traditional retirement resorts, such as Bournemouth and Torquay, and to rise in adjacent and nearby local authorities. The elderly are themselves decentralizing, it seems, in consequence of the growing attraction of large south-coast towns for the population at large. This has pushed up housing costs and forced retirees with some capital but often on fixed incomes to seek out cheaper places.

The young, too, display their own distribution characteristics. Figure 3.4 shows the massive concentration of 25–44-year-olds to the north and west of London, in precisely those counties which have recently had substantial population increases and which are regarded as some of the most prosperous places in the country (Champion *et al.* 1987; Champion and Green 1988). The attractive power of this vibrant economic region for working-age people suggests its success will be long term.

3.4 Historical Patterns of Regional Change

Overall growth pattern

The basic regional distribution pattern has changed remarkably little since the beginning of the last century (table 3.1). The South-East has increased its pre-eminence in both absolute numbers and share of the

Table 3.1. Population at selected censuses, UK regions, 1801–1981[a]

(a)

Region	Population (1,000s)									
	1801	1851	1891	1911	1931	1951	1961	1971	1971[b]	1981[c]
N	634	1,161	2,215	2,815	3,038	3,137	3,250	3,296	3,137	3,118
YH	809	1,794	3,115	3,877	4,285	4,522	4,635	4,479	4,868	4,918
NW	885	2,531	4,714	5,796	6,197	6,447	6,567	6,743	6,602	6,460
EM	651	1,166	1,776	2,263	2,531	2,893	3,100	3,390	3,635	3,853
WM	854	1,705	2,664	3,277	3,743	4,423	4,758	5,110	5,121	6,186
EA	625	1,049	1,105	1,192	1,232	1,382	1,470	1,669	1,686	1,895
SE	2,499	5,102	9,171	11,744	13,539	15,127	16,271	17,230	16,994	17,011
SW	1,349	2,255	2,471	2,687	2,794	3,229	3,411	3,781	4,088	4,381
W	587	1,163	1,771	2,421	2,593	2,599	2,644	2,731	2,723	2,814
S	1,608	2,889	4,026	4,761	4,843	5,096	5,179	5,229	5,217	5,180
NI	(1,649)[d]	1,443	1,236	1,251	1,243	1,371	1,425	1,528	1,538	1,564
TOTAL UK	(20,183)[d]	22,259	34,264	42,082	46,038	50,225	52,709	55,507	55,610	56,379

(b)

Region	1801[e]	1851	1891	1911	1931	1951	1961	1971	1971[b]	1981[c]
	Shares of the UK population									
N	5.49	5.22	6.46	6.69	6.60	6.25	6.17	5.94	5.64	5.53
YH	7.02	8.06	9.09	9.21	9.31	9.00	8.79	8.65	8.75	8.72
NW	7.68	11.37	13.76	13.77	13.46	12.84	12.46	12.15	11.87	11.46
EM	5.65	5.24	5.18	5.38	5.50	5.76	5.88	6.11	6.54	6.83
WM	7.40	7.66	7.77	7.79	8.13	8.81	9.03	9.21	9.21	9.20
EA	5.42	4.71	3.22	2.83	2.68	2.75	2.79	3.01	3.03	3.36
SE	21.67	22.92	26.77	27.91	29.41	30.12	30.87	31.04	30.56	30.17
SW	11.70	10.13	7.21	6.39	6.07	6.43	6.47	6.81	7.35	7.77
W	5.09	5.22	5.17	5.75	5.63	5.10	5.02	4.92	4.90	4.99
S	13.95	12.98	11.75	11.31	10.52	10.15	9.83	9.42	9.38	9.19
NI	8.92	6.48	3.61	2.97	2.70	2.73	2.70	2.75	2.77	2.77
TOTAL UK	100.00	100.00	100.00	100.00	100.00	100.00	100.00	100.00	100.00	100.00

[a] The regions are the 'old' standard regions, current at the 1971 Census; The elements in each column of the table and the column totals were independently rounded from figures in the table source. In certain cases this may lead to a difference in the last figure between the sum of column elements and the column total given.
[b] These are the populations and shares of the 'new' standard regions (post 1 April 1974) as at mid-year 1971.
[c] Based on 1981 boundaries.
[d] These are 1841 populations.
[e] The shares of the United Kingdom are estimated for 1801.

Sources: Rees (1979) and Census.

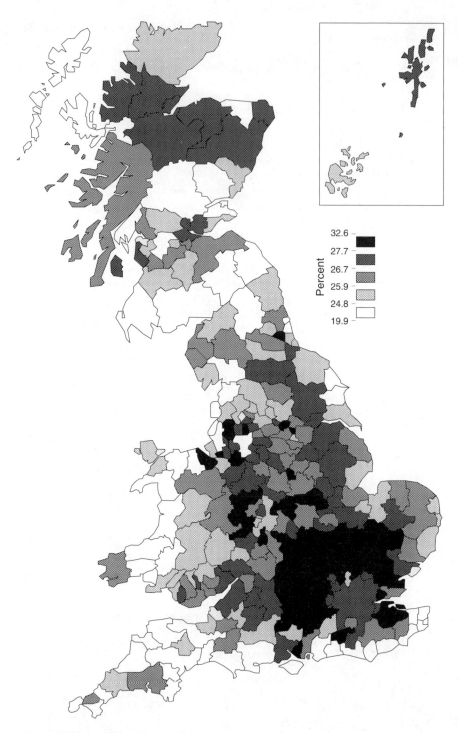

Source: Champion *et al.* 1987.

FIG. 3.4. Age structure by local labour market areas, 25–44-year-olds as per cent of total, 1981

national population but generally the regional batting order remains much as it was in the days of W. G. Grace. The older industrial regions of the North, North-West, and Yorkshire and Humberside enhanced their population shares during the nineteenth century then fell back in the twentieth. Scotland has steadily declined throughout; Northern Ireland fell steeply in the nineteenth century since when it has been relatively stable. Wales's share of the British population has fluctuated little. The more rural regions of East Anglia, the South-West and, to a lesser extent the East Midlands, lost out in the nineteenth century, but their fortunes have taken an upturn in recent decades.

Although there has been a generally stable long-term distribution pattern at the regional level, closer inspection reveals that since the industrial revolution growth has not been uniform across the country. Between 1841 and 1911 the most rapidly growing regions were South Wales and north-east England; the big cities also grew rapidly, especially London and Manchester (Craig 1987). Between 1911 and 1981 national growth was much slower and regional patterns differed from those earlier. The most rapidly growing counties were all in the South-East, largely ones that had experienced below average growth rates in the nineteenth century. Remote rural counties, such as those of mid and north Wales and Cornwall grew at below average rates over both periods until the middle 1970s, since when they have had above average growth. This latest period has, in fact, seen its slowest growth rates in those counties which grew most rapidly during the Industrial Revolution. Craig (1987) concludes that the trends are now back to the pre-industrialization pattern of population and that the '1911 type' may eventually turn out to have been exceptional.

The absolute size of population gains and losses gives a slightly different picture of regional change. From 1841 to 1911 the national increase was twenty million, over half of which took place in the metropolitan counties. In contrast, from 1911 to 1981 the national increase was only thirteen million, the metropolitan counties in aggregate took under one-tenth of this and, from 1961, actually lost population.

Inter-war distribution of population

The inter-war period was one in which the distribution of population began to come to terms with a range of structural economic and social changes. Competition from other industrial countries was already attacking the markets for traditional British manufactures before the turn of the century; the First World War meant that many overseas markets were lost or severely curtailed. At the same time new types of industry, demanding different locational requirements, were coming to the fore. In particular the new 'light' industry regions no longer needed to be near to coal. Electricity was flexible and clean, altogether a more congenial source of energy than steam. The internal combustion engine created a new mobility, for people and goods alike. New technologies meant that workers were no longer needed in such numbers, in many of the older industrial areas especially. Already in the 1930s government was having to cope with this decline, and ventures like the Team Valley Trading Estate at Gateshead and the new iron and steel works at Ebbw Vale were testament to the need for regional support. People's attitudes to where they wanted to live were also changing. Ebenezer Howard's 'garden city' movement was one man's attempt to express the desire for a more suburban type of existence, although this was only ever fully developed in Welwyn Garden City and Letchworth.

The new pattern shunned the old industrial areas and the conurbation centres. Employment and people alike began a southward drift, partially reversing the redistribution in favour of the coalfields that had characterized the Industrial Revolution. The South-East was particularly vibrant, increasing its share of the national population by 2 percentage points between 1911 and 1951.

During the 1920s the loss of population from rural parts of England and Wales was relatively gradual, only exceeding 5 per cent in upland Wales, northern England, and parts of Wiltshire and Suffolk. During the 1930s losses became more widespread and more acute in Wales, northern England, and Devon. It was at this time that regional experiences diverged: the eastern part of the country, especially Lincolnshire and East Anglia, was recovering from its period of maximum depopulation, while in the west and the north the period of heaviest losses occurred (Willats and Newson 1953). In general those rural areas experiencing persistent loss during the inter-war years were the uplands and other remote places (which in a generation or so would experience a surprising resurgence); in contrast, persistent increases occurred in rural places adjacent to the large urban areas. In some parts of Wales, south-west, and northern England small town populations increased because of a local retreat from rural areas where there was little employment apart from agriculture, much of which was in a depressed state.

Regional population change in the 1950s and 1960s

Even before the Second World War the planning problems resulting from population growth in southern Britain were apparent. Two major

Royal Commissions dealing with the issues produced reports in the early war years which were to provide the blueprints for post-war planning. The Barlow Report (Royal Commission 1940) highlighted the strategic disadvantages of so much of the nation's industry and population being concentrated in South-East England (and within range of enemy bombers). It recommended steps to prevent further growth there and to encourage dispersal of both people and jobs to other parts of the Kingdom. The Scott Report (Ministry of Works and Planning 1942) was more concerned with the land use implications of growth, proposing a set of planning controls to deal with the spread of urban Britain. Out of these two reports, and Abercrombie's proposals for the planning of London, came the dual strategy of containment (through Green Belts) and decentralization (through new and expanded towns) that have characterized post-war planning in metropolitan Britain.

In the regions where the drift to the south had its origins, new strategies were being adopted. Regional policies designed to promote employment sought to maintain population levels in the less prosperous areas by curbing voluntary out-migration. It may be argued that regional industrial policy in the UK in the late twentieth century has aimed to maintain—some might say fossilize—the population distribution created on the coalfields in the early nineteenth century. Despite these strategies, applied in both depressed and prosperous Britain, it cannot be argued that there is or ever has been a clearly defined national population-distribution policy in the UK. It is not hard to see why, since we are not in a position to evaluate the merits of different population distributions in any meaningful way.

It is in this light that we must view post-war regional population trends. Despite attempts to diminish the drain of people from the depressed areas the flow to the south continued. During the 1950s the population of the South-East went up by 1.13 million, with a net migration gain of 438,000. East Anglia and the South-West also grew, by 110,000 and 189,000 respectively, some of this being overspill from their megalopolitan neighbour. The West and East Midlands housed an additional 335,000 and 212,000 by the end of the decade. The 1960s saw the beginnings of a change. East Anglia and the South-West continued to grow, as did the South-East until 1966, then it experienced net loss owing to the massive haemorrhage from the capital. Migration losses from the more peripheral areas were stemmed, no doubt in response to the government's development-area assistance (Eversley 1971).

The patterns of aggregate change described here reflect the interplay of natural change and migration which is not the same in all parts of the country. Areas of high natural growth, like Merseyside, the coalfields of northern England and South Wales, and Northern Ireland, have traditionally exported surpluses of population arising from their high birth-rates. Many rural areas have acted in similar fashion. Lawton (1977) has summarized the interaction between components of change for the 1950s and 1960s (figure 3.5). Growth was widespread. The fastest growing areas (types 2 and 3) experienced both natural increase and migration gain, and included large areas of central England, the Welsh borders, north-east Yorkshire, and parts of central Scotland— all regions combining the traditionally high fertility of rural areas with the immigration of overspill populations from the conurbations. In more remote rural areas, such as northern England, parts of the Grampians, west Wales, and Northern Ireland, net migration loss was more than compensated for by high fertility (type 4). In contrast, many retirement areas, such as the coasts of north Wales, north-west England, and Sussex, grew by virtue of continued in-migration exceeding natural decrease, itself a consequence of unbalanced age structure (type 1). More widespread was natural increase exceeding migration loss (type 4), such areas including most of the conurbations and older industrial areas, together with some less remote rural regions in south Wales, northern England, and southern Scotland.

Areas of loss fell into two broad categories. In Greater London (where decline has recently reversed) and in some of the older industrial areas, together with some remote rural areas in highland Scotland and Wales, long-standing out-migration created a population growing older but not yet suffering natural decrease (type 5). Finally in north-east Lancashire net out-migration was compounded by natural decrease among the ageing population (type 6).

3.5 Population and the Urban System

Decentralization in the 1950s and 1960s

The urban nature of the British population was recognized in 1951 with the designation of six conurbations in England and Wales (London, Merseyside, South-East Lancashire, Tyneside, West Yorkshire, and the West Midlands) accounting for 38 per cent of the population, together with Clydeside, which held 35 per cent of Scotland's people. By 1971 the processes of urban decentralization and deconcentration had, despite some modest growth in absolute numbers, reduced these proportions to 33 per cent. Such relative losses of population by the conurbations were paralleled in most large towns of over 100,000

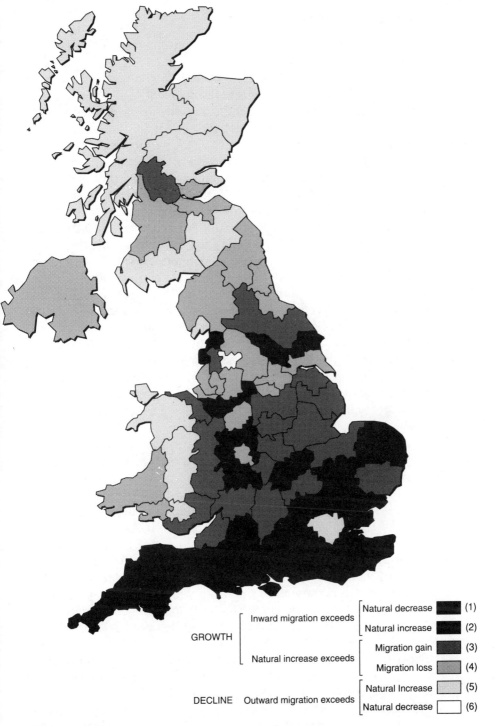

		Natural decrease	■	(1)
GROWTH	Inward migration exceeds	Natural increase	■	(2)
	Natural increase exceeds	Migration gain	▨	(3)
		Migration loss	▨	(4)
DECLINE	Outward migration exceeds	Natural Increase	▨	(5)
		Natural decrease	□	(6)

Source: Lawton 1977.

Fig. 3.5. Components of population change, UK economic planning sub-regions, 1951–1969

people: during the 1960s their growth was only one-third of the national average (Champion 1976).

Much of this loss of population was from the inner, high density areas of the large cities. Clearance and redevelopment took their toll in a planning system which decreed that the densities deemed acceptable by the Victorian house builders were not appropriate for the late twentieth century. Many rehousing schemes were on the peripheries of the conurbations, often in adjacent local authorities, some still designated as rural districts. Other inner-city inhabitants left for the suburbs of their own accord, trading a more pleasant environment for the often cramped, dirty, and increasing unsafe inner urban areas. The exchange was not always beneficial; migrants from the old inner areas often regretted the life they had left behind in the move to a more open plan or high-rise environment (Young and Wilmott 1954). They were encouraged by the first major decentralization of employment. The Location of Offices Bureau showed the way in South-East England; distances moved from central London were often modest but they did have the effect of prising population outward. Later it would become apparent that the decentralization of jobs was, in fact, following the drift outwards of the population and labour force. Manufacturing industries, too, were finding existing sites, many dating from the end of the last century or even the 1930s, becoming cramped. As their space requirements changed they sought more open greenfield sites away from the conurbation centres (Wood 1974).

Decentralization from the inner parts of cities accelerated from about 1960, affecting the largest places first and then spreading down through the urban hierarchy. Analysis of this process can best be done by dividing urban areas into their functional zones. The studies of Hall et al. (1973) and Spence et al. (1982) divided the urban system into Standard Metropolitan Labour Areas (SMLAs). According to their scheme each SMLA consists of an urban core together with a metropolitan ring comprising the local authority areas from which at least 15 per cent of the workers commute to the urban core, while beyond the SMLA is an outer commuting ring from which at least 1 per cent of workers travel daily to the core. The three areas together, core, ring, and outer ring, comprise a Metropolitan Economic Labour Area (MELA).

Between 1951 and 1971 Britain was urbanizing through an outward extension of commuter hinterlands, the populations of urban cores falling from 53.7 per cent of the national total to 47.9 per cent. In the 1950s the decline of the cores was relative, absolute numbers of people living there continuing to increase, but in the 1960s absolute numbers declined as well. In contrast, the metropolitan rings did well, as the

Inter-zonal migration within labour markets, 1966-71

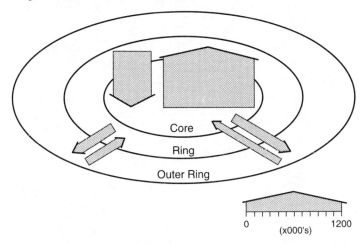

Source: Spence *et al.* (1982).

FIG. 3.6. Inter-zonal migration within labour markets, 1966–1971

flight of population to them accelerated in both decades (Spence *et al.* 1982).

Migration was the vital component of population redistribution between urban zones (figure 3.6). During the 1960s the cores lost about 2.5 million people from net out-migration. In aggregate, substantial gross flows occurred between all zones, although an inflow to an individual ring was not necessarily from its own core or outer ring. Especially in southern England, expansion in the metropolitan and outer rings of some MELAs originated from inflows from the cores and rings of other MELAs, frequently from other parts of the country (Kennett 1977).

The dynamism within the urban system is reflected in the performance of individual cities. New and expanded towns experienced the highest rates of population growth in the 1950s and 1960s, but in absolute terms it was the medium-sized cities, like Bristol, Leicester, and Southampton, which made the biggest contribution to overall population increase. Spence *et al.* (1982) have run their own 'British urban bumps race' to show the changing fortunes of individual places (figure 3.7). The new towns did well: Stevenage, for example, rose from 123rd in 1951 to 86th in 1971, Basildon from 122nd to 75th. Other southern cities did well, Slough from 43rd to 32nd, Oxford from 27th to 21st. But there were snakes as well as ladders. Rhondda slumped from 71st to 110th, Burnley from 64th to 87th.

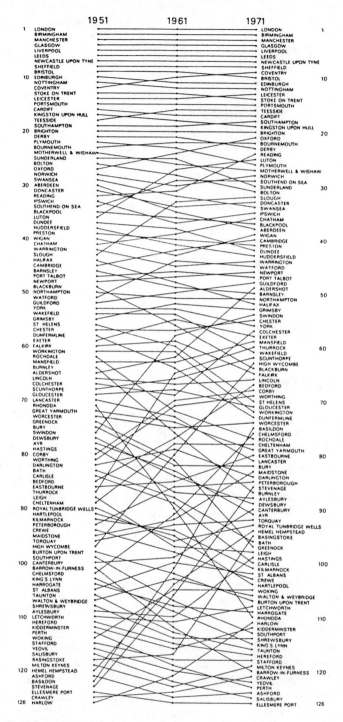

Source: Spence *et al.* 1982.

FIG. 3.7. Change in population rank order of SMLAs, 1951, 1961, and 1971

Table 3.2. Population distribution and change by SMLAs and MELAs, 1951–1971

	Population						% change	
	1951 '000s	%	1961 '000s	%	1971 '000s	%	1951–61	1961–71
Urban cores	26,077	53.4	26,577	51.8	25,858	47.9	1.9	−2.7
Metropolitan rings	12,584	25.8	14,292	27.9	16,795	31.1	13.6	17.5
SMLA total	38,661	79.2	40,869	79.7	42,653	79.0	5.7	4.4
Outer metropolitan rings	7,836	16.0	8,084	15.8	8,876	16.4	3.2	9.8
MELA total	46,497	95.2	48,953	95.5	51,529	95.5	5.3	5.3
Unclassified areas	2,357	4.8	2,331	4.5	2,450	4.5	−1.1	5.1
Great Britain total	48,854	100.0	51,284	100.0	53,979	100.0	5.0	5.3

Source: Compton (1982*b*).

The decentralization process operated in association with the urban hierarchy, beginning with the largest place then moving successively downwards (table 3.2). The capital was first in line. Already in the 1950s the core was losing heavily, and this worsened in the next decade. By the 1960s the London ring's increase had fallen and was no longer able to compensate for core losses, leading to a massive net loss in the SMLA as a whole. In Manchester, Glasgow, and Newcastle similar patterns of change occurred; elsewhere decentralization only became absolute in the 1960s, for example in Birmingham, Sheffield, Leeds, and Nottingham. Smaller cities, such as Peterborough, Ipswich, and Bedford were centralizing, absolutely and relatively, during the 1950s, but then entered a phase of relative decentralization.

The mainland pattern was also occurring in Northern Ireland (Compton 1982). Despite a natural increase of about 60,000, the Belfast Urban Area (population 612,000 in 1971) grew by only 3,000 between 1966 and 1971, indicating a high level of out-migration. The beneficiaries of this movement were the new and expanded towns around the city—Bangor, Newtownards, Ballymena, Antrim, and Craigavon. Within Belfast itself the inner city lost heavily, down from 417,000 to 340,000 between 1971 and 1978.

Decentralization in the 1970s

One major problems of 'custom made' urban functional regions like MELAs is that of comparability with time periods beyond the immediate study. A similar analysis for 1971–81 has to be based upon a different set of regions, this time devised by the Centre for Urban and Regional Development Studies (CURDS) at the University of Newcastle. The CURDS regions are again based on population and employment size and commuting patterns, but they use different thresholds and, unlike MELAs, they exhaust the UK space. In consequence the definitions used in table 3.3 are not directly comparable with their predecessors.

Despite decentralization, the British population remains highly concentrated in the urban cores (Champion *et al.* 1987). The main built-up areas at the hearts of the 228 functional regions recognized still account for 61.6 per cent of the total population, despite losing nearly 1.5 million people during the preceding ten years. Further evidence of the degree of concentration at this zonal scale is that 70 per cent of the rest of the population is housed in the rings. This share changed little during 1971–81 because all three types of zone outside the cores gained population roughly in proportion to their original shares, each growing

Table 3.3. Population distribution, by zone, 1971–1981

Zone	1971		1981		1971–81 change	
	'000s	%GB	'000s	%GB	'000s	%
Core	34,912	64.7	33,446	61.6	−1,466	−4.2
Ring	13,258	24.6	14,467	26.7	+1,208	+9.1
Outer Area	3,232	6.0	3,559	6.6	+327	+10.1
Rural Area	2,575	4.8	2,803	5.2	+228	+8.8
Great Britain	53,977	100.0	54,274	100.0	+296	+0.5

Source: CURDS (1984).

by about 9–10 per cent. The result is that in 1981 the cores and rings together accounted for nearly 9 out of 10 of the British population.

How the pattern changed among different types of urban area can be seen in table 3.4. London's rate of population loss in the 1970s was virtually the same as the average for the next five cities (Birmingham, Glasgow, Liverpool, Manchester, and Newcastle), so the relative gap between them changed little. In relation to the rest of the country, however, the share of the top six cities fell by 2.5 percentage points. Further down the hierarchy the proportion of the population living in Other Dominant cities (cities at the core of the twenty major urban regions excluding the top six—e.g. Nottingham, Edinburgh, Coventry, Brighton) fell marginally, that of Subdominants (medium-sized cities

Table 3.4. Population distribution, by type of functional region, 1971–1981

Type (and number) of functional region(s)	1971		1981		1971–81 change	
	'000s	%GB	'000s	%GB	'000s	%
London (1)	8,577	15.9	7,937	14.4	−740	−8.6
Conurbation dominants (5)	6,185	11.5	5,659	10.4	−526	−8.5
Other dominants (14)	6,186	11.5	6,073	11.2	−113	−1.8
Subdominants (93)	13,305	24.6	13,820	25.5	+515	+3.9
Freestanding (115)	19,161	35.5	20,279	37.4	+1,118	+5.8
Great Britain (228)	53,977	100.0	54,274	100.0	+296	+0.5

Note: Numbers may not sum to given totals because of rounding.
Source: CURDS (1984).

surrounding the Dominants) rose by one percentage point and that of Freestanding cities went up by nearly two percentage points. Hence, though change was taking place its pace has been slow, and it is unlikely there will be any fundamentally new pattern of population distribution in the urban hierarchy in the foreseeable future.

3.6   Regional Trends since 1971

The intercensal period of the 1970s was a decade of unprecedented decentralization in the UK, USA, and elsewhere, over more extensive geographical scales than hitherto (Champion 1983). The widespread nature of the process took people by surprise; it was assumed that metropolitan growth was a permanent feature of modern society. From the middle of the decade the idea developed that a 'clean break' with past patterns of urbanization had occurred (Berry 1976, Vining and Kontuly 1978). Elsewhere, decentralization was seen less as a clean break, more as a part of the natural cycle of urban growth and change (Hall 1981). Looking back from the late 1980s it seems that decentralization was not a clean break, nor was it a temporary aberration, since elements of both continue to exist side by side in the British settlement system.

Analysis of UK census data for 1981 do indeed show a country seemingly confirming the clean-break hypothesis (table 3.5). In the preceding decade London and other large metropolitan cities recorded massive population losses; medium-sized cities either lost people or

Table 3.5. Population change: urban and rural areas, England and Wales, 1961–1981

	1961–71	1971–81
Inner London	−13.2	−17.7
Outer London	−1.8	−5.0
Metropolitan counties		
Principal cities	−8.4	−10.0
Other metropolitan districts	+5.5	−2.0
Towns		
Population >100,000	+2.6	−1.6
Population 50,000–100,000	+9.4	+2.0
Population <50,000	+13.0	+5.5
Rural remainder	+17.9	−9.7
National change	+5.7	+0.5

experienced only slow growth. In contrast, small towns and rural areas were consistent gainers, with remoter rural areas increasing their rates of population growth between the 1960s and 1970s. What seemed to be happening was the spread of population growth out from the major urban centres where it had occurred in the nineteenth and early twentieth centuries progressively to the more rural periphery, leaving a population loss in its wake.

The picture we glean from a straight intercensal comparison is, however, misleading. Using annual-change figures Champion (1983, 1987) showed that the main decentralization process peaked in the early 1970s, and that by the time of the 1981 census the former pattern had to some extent reasserted itself. During the 1980s rural populations have grown more slowly then they did ten years earlier and some have declined; in contrast not only has there been a substantial slowdown in the rate of London's population decline (Britton 1986), but it has now gone into reverse in a small way.

The period since 1971 shows the cessation of the drift to the South-East, then its recovery. During the first half of the 1970s all three of the most heavily urbanized regions (South-East, North-West, West Midlands) had population growth below the national rate, suggesting that the urban–rural dichotomy had taken over from the north–south divide as the main feature of UK population change. The fastest growth rates during this time were in the three least urban regions of southern England: East Anglia, South-West, and East Midlands (table 3.6). The South–East and the North-West were, in fact, doing worse than the traditional problem regions of Scotland, the North, and Wales, the last of which was doing very well.

By the early 1980s the situation had changed. The South-East had improved considerably, its growth reasserted, and the north–south divide was re-established. The scale of the region's recovery is shown by an analysis of percentage-point shifts in regional performance between 1971–4 and 1981–4 (table 3.6). The South-East was the only region to record an upward shift in its growth rate during the period (Champion 1987).

The major part of these changes predate 1981. The South–East's improvement was a feature of the second half of the 1970s, the 1980s being years of consolidation. The relative deterioration experienced by other regions was likewise a child of the middle–late 1970s, especially in the cases of East Anglia and Wales. Scotland and the South-West have been exceptions, moving against the national trend since 1981 with an upturn in their population fortunes.

The story implicit in this description of the general pattern of re-

Table 3.6. Population change, by standard region, 1971–1984

Region	Change rate (% year)				Shift (% points)		
	1971–4	1974–8	1978–81	1981–4	1971–4 to 1981–4	1971–4 to 1978–81	1978–81 to 1981–4
East Anglia	1.65	0.99	0.96	0.80	−0.85	−0.69	−0.16
South West	0.96	0.49	0.52	0.61	−0.35	−0.44	+0.09
East Midlands	0.85	0.35	0.48	0.19	−0.66	−0.37	−0.29
Wales	0.55	0.17	0.11	−0.06	−0.61	−0.44	−0.17
West Midlands	0.27	−0.06	0.07	−0.07	−0.34	−0.20	−0.14
Yorkshire/Humb.	0.17	−0.04	−0.01	−0.10	−0.27	−0.18	−0.09
Scotland	0.06	−0.22	−0.28	−0.22	−0.28	−0.34	+0.06
Northern	0.02	−0.16	−0.18	−0.26	−0.28	−0.20	−0.08
South-East	−0.11	−0.19	0.14	0.20	+0.31	+0.25	+0.06
North-West	−0.17	−0.31	−0.30	−0.33	−0.16	−0.13	−0.03
Great Britain	0.20	−0.03	0.09	0.06	−0.14	−0.11	−0.03

Note: Regions ranked according to 1971–4 change rate.
Sources: Mid-year population estimates; Champion (1987).

gional change is reinforced by Champion's analysis at the more detailed county and district levels. Counties with some of the highest growth rates up to 1978 were in the rural extremities of southern England, Wales, and Scotland, a most unusual situation for the twentieth century. The Scottish Highlands went through something of a renaissance as English and Welsh moved there, often in semi-retirement, in search of a good and quieter life (Jones *et al.* 1986). From the end of the 1970s modern normality was restored with a shift of population back to the South-East at the expense of more peripheral areas. After 1981 the most rapid growth occurred in southern England, with the Wash–Severn axis emerging as a clear boundary. The industrial and mining counties of the north performed badly, and many of the less industrialized parts of the north were also doing relatively worse than their experience in the earlier period. Within the South-East divisions emerged, with western areas pulling ahead, along with adjacent parts of the South-West along the M4 corridor between London and Bristol. Further north the impact of urbanization again began to be seen as a positive stimulus to growth, leading Champion (1987) to conclude that the most outstanding aspect of population change there was the strong upward shift recorded by the main conurbation areas, with the metropolitan counties of the West Midlands, Merseyside, Greater Manchester, Tyne and Wear, and Strathclyde registering the strongest improvements.

The significance of the degree of urbanization in accounting for these changes can be seen at district level. Between 1971–8 and 1978–84 the largest upward shifts in rates of population change all occurred in Inner London boroughs. In Inner London as a whole the average level of population loss fell from 63,000 per year in the early 1970s to 14,000 per year a decade later. Absolute losses also fell in Outer London, from 26,000 to only 3,000 per year over the same period. All of the other large cities had trends in the same direction, albeit on a less dramatic scale. Southern coast seaside resorts also improved through their ability to attract a more balanced age structure. In contrast, new and expanded towns experienced the greatest declines in growth rate, confirming that the new towns are mostly no longer new nor are they so fertile. In non-metropolitan districts as a whole the rate of population growth in the first years of the 1980s was less than half what it had been a decade earlier, though again most of the fall preceded 1978. Never the less such places, including remoter rural areas, continued to grow; decentralization may have slowed but is not yet completely out of steam.

Analysis of components of change again demonstrates the import-

Table 3.7. Trends in natural change, by types of district in England and Wales, 1971–1984 (per 1,000 people per year)

District type	1971–8	1978–84	Shift	1978–81	1981–4	Shift
Greater London	1.0	2.0	+1.0	1.8	2.2	+0.4
Inner London	0.7	2.2	+1.5	1.8	2.8	+1.0
Outer London	1.2	1.8	+0.6	1.8	1.8	+0.1
Metropolitan districts	1.0	1.1	+0.1	1.1	1.1	0.0
Principal cities	−0.1	0.3	+0.4	0.0	0.6	+0.5
Other districts	1.6	1.5	−0.1	1.6	1.3	−0.3
Non-metropolitan districts	1.1	0.8	−0.3	1.0	0.6	−0.4
Large cities	0.7	1.2	+0.5	1.0	1.3	+0.3
Smaller cities	0.0	0.6	+0.6	0.6	0.6	−0.1
Industrial districts	2.2	2.1	−0.1	2.2	1.9	−0.3
Wales and North[a]	1.1	1.4	+0.3	1.4	1.4	0.0
Rest of England	3.5	2.8	−0.7	3.0	2.5	−0.5
Districts with new towns	5.0	5.1	+0.1	5.3	4.7	−0.6
Resort and retirement	−6.4	−5.9	+0.5	−5.8	−5.9	−0.1
Other urban	3.1	2.3	−0.8	2.6	2.0	−0.6
Outside South-East	2.6	1.5	−1.1	1.8	1.2	−0.6
Within South-East	3.4	2.8	−0.6	3.1	2.5	−0.6
Remoter, largely rural	−0.4	−1.0	−0.6	−0.6	−1.3	−0.7
England and Wales	1.0	1.0	0.0	1.2	1.0	−0.2

[a] North-West, Northern Region, and Yorkshire/Humberside.

Sources: Unpublished data provided by OPCS; Champion 1987.

Table 3.8. Trends in net migration, by types of district in England and Wales, 1971–1984 (per 1,000 people per year)

District type	1971–8	Shift	1978–84	1978–81	1981–4	Shift
Greater London	−12.0	+5.5	−6.5	−8.6	−4.6	3.9
Inner London	−19.5	+7.9	−11.6	−15.3	−8.2	7.2
Outer London	−7.0	+3.6	−3.4	−4.3	−2.5	1.9
Metropolitan districts	−5.6	+0.8	−4.8	−4.9	−4.7	0.2
Principal cities	−10.3	+4.0	−6.3	−7.1	−5.7	1.4
Other districts	−3.3	−0.8	−4.1	−3.9	−4.3	−0.3
Non-metropolitan districts	4.9	−1.6	3.3	4.0	2.6	−1.4
Large cities	−5.1	+1.0	−4.1	−3.8	−4.5	−0.7
Smaller cities	−1.7	−0.8	−2.5	−0.9	−4.0	−3.2
Industrial districts	1.6	−3.0	−1.4	0.2	−3.0	−3.2
Wales and North[a]	1.1	−3.6	−2.5	−0.7	−4.3	−3.6
Rest of England	2.2	−2.5	−0.3	1.1	−1.7	−2.8
Districts with new towns	10.7	−5.4	5.3	8.1	2.5	−5.6
Resort and retirement	12.6	−1.0	11.6	10.5	12.6	+2.1
Other urban	4.6	−0.3	4.3	4.7	3.7	−1.0
Outside South-East	7.0	−2.2	4.8	4.4	5.2	+0.9
Within South-East	2.9	+1.0	3.9	5.0	2.7	−2.2
Remoter, largely rural	11.7	−4.1	7.6	7.7	7.4	−0.3
England and Wales	−0.2	+0.2	0.0	0.1	−0.1	−0.2

[a] North-West, Northern Region, and Yorkshire/Humberside.

Sources: Unpublished data provided by OPCS; Champion 1987.

ance of migration in modifying the population distribution map (tables 3.7, 3.8). The recovery of births in the late 1970s helped London and other large cities to improve their population levels relative to smaller places. This may have been due to the tendency of the former to attract in young people, leading to net gains by migration among 15–24-year-olds (Chapter 10). Any subsequent slowdown in out-migration may thus lead to natural growth as this group remains in the city to start a family.

3.7 Processes of Change

While no radical shift in the distribution of the British people at the macro-regional scale has occurred during the present century, the settlement pattern has displayed a dynamism that has proved difficult to forecast. A number of writers have speculated on the underlying processes involved in counterurbanization (for example, Berry 1976, Hall and Hay 1980, Fielding 1982, Champion 1987). Much discussion has focused on whether or not it is a general phenomenon, related to a 'natural' cycle of urban change that will in time affect all developed countries, or whether there are specific national and/or regional circumstances which mean different trajectories.

In the British case, Champion (1987) has argued that explanations for decentralization and counterurbanization should be sought chiefly in the 1960s and that the circumstances of the 1970s should be used to explain the resurgence of growth in the more urban regions in the 1980s. At the same time he rightly argues that it is premature to conceive of a cycle of decentralization since that might 'presuppose the existence of one single major engine behind the process and suggest the possibility of the recurrence of a similar round of developments in the future' (pp. 35–6). We need to seek answers in the range of influences that guide migration decision making, particularly in those forces responsible for investment and thus employment, in changing residential preferences, and in the interaction between demographic change and the housing stock.

The role of investment

Massive changes have taken place in the location and scale of investment, especially in manufacturing, since the middle 1960s (Chapter 9). It has been argued that a new spatial division of labour has been created which has changed the relative attractiveness of locations (Massey and Meegan 1982, Massey 1984). At the same time the structure of corporate organization has changed with the growing importance of the multi-locational, often transnational company. Such employing organizations have sought out locations away from traditional ones in the large cities, seeking female and other non-unionized labour and sites with room for expansion. Many of these new locations, particularly in the 1960s, were in areas attracting regional industrial assistance from government, further reducing costs. Keeble (1980) and Fothergill and Gudgin (1982) have demonstrated the huge shift in manufacturing towards freestanding cities and smaller towns from the early 1960s onwards. This trend has been reinforced by new, high technology industries with small-scale employment, and by the growth of self-employment. Neither of these needs to be close to traditional large labour markets and their locations can pay greater attention to residential preferences.

Changes were taking place in rural economies too. Government attempts to relocate small industries in rural areas through the COSIRA scheme had some success. Other rural investments, in minerals (North Sea oil installations, for example), agriculture and service provision, had multiplier effects which increased the general desirability of living in more remote areas.

Residential preference

There is no doubt that the population at large has become more mobile in many ways. Travel is easier and we are continuously bombarded with information about distant places. For many, but not for all, there is a greater degree of choice about where we live, though, ironically, changing household lifestyles often introduces new constraints as more members go out to work.

It is in the USA that residential preference has been invoked most as an explanation for decentralization (Berry 1976), perhaps partly as a return to old ideas of the frontier and the rural idyll, as Champion (1987) suggests. In the UK, a much smaller land, nowhere is very far from 'civilization' and most small towns have a reasonable range of services. Retirement migration is the most commonly discussed example of movement away from large urban areas, and has increasingly affected younger retirees. As will be discussed in Chapter 10, the first big generation of owner-occupiers began to retire from the 1960s onwards. With capital to invest, the cheaper house prices and quietness to be found outside the large urban areas proved attractive to them. Such virtues were also likely to appeal to many people of working age, especially if employment could be found in the growing service industries that had themselves decentralized.

Demographic structure and housing

Changes in family structures since 1960 have coincided with changes in housing stock. The rise in birth-rate from the middle 1950s created new young households from the middle 1970s; higher divorce rates led to further fission; trends in retirement meant more elderly lived away from their families. At the same time home ownership became easier and the norm.

Meanwhile the housing stock was being changed. The search for an affordable home led many to leave the high priced housing markets of the cities (Salt and Flowerdew 1980). Within cities older and cheaper houses were disappearing. Slum clearance accelerated during the 1960s; elsewhere 'gentrification' removed the cheap end of the private rented sector. Other forces were at work too, including new attitudes to urban redevelopment after the Ronan Point collapse in 1974, and the general slowdown in local-authority building that resulted from the growing awareness of the disasters of tower-block living.

Hence, at a time when growing numbers were seeking houses the capacity of the cities to cope was being tested. It was not simply a question of equating total stock of houses with that of households, but with ensuring that individual aspirations could be satisfied. Often the only way for that to happen was for those already in the cities to move out and for those contemplating a move in not to come.

4 Fertility Trends

4.1 Introduction

The new fertility regime

This chapter will describe the course of fertility since the First World War, relate its trend to social and economic change, and discuss some of the differences in fertility within British society. Since the 1920s fertility in Britain has been a variation on a two-child family theme. Since the 1970s, in common with the rest of the industrial world, it has fallen to its lowest level ever recorded. Contraception within marriage is now nearly universal, so families can control the timing as well as the number of births to a degree new in history. As a consequence, fertility has been highly volatile. The annual number of births determines the age structure, and these twentieth-century fluctuations have created a new highly irregular outline (figures 2.9, 3.2). The power to make effective decisions on fertility, reached independently but simultaneously by millions of families, has had startling aggregate effects on our population, society, and economy, the consequences of which are discussed further in Chapter 13.

The measurement of fertility trends

The Total Fertility Rate (TFR) is a useful way of expressing movements in current fertility (figure 4.1). It is sometimes called the Total Period Fertility Rate (TPFR) or Total Fertility Ratio or Index, as it is not strictly a 'rate'. It shows the family size a woman would have if she experienced current age-specific fertility rates through her lifetime. It cuts out the effects of the age structure of the population which can confound simpler measures such as the crude birth-rate. But when changes in births are due to shifts in timing, the TFR exaggerates current trends in relation to the final future outcome of family size. The completed family size is also shown in figure 4.1 for real birth cohorts of women. Their family size is plotted on the graph at the year when they were aged 27—the generation length, or age at which they gave birth to their median child. As always with cohort measures, the data

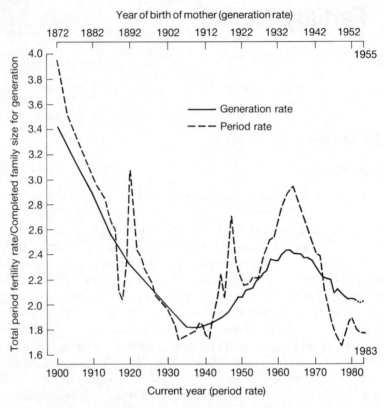

Source: OPCS Variant Population Projections 1983–2023, Series PP2 No. 14, 1986, fig. 1.

FIG. 4.1. Trends in period and generation fertility rates, England and Wales, 1900–1983

cannot be taken up to the present day without a considerable element of projection (broken line) of the generation rate.

More satisfactory measures of total fertility can be based on estimates of the chances of women going on to have first, second, third etc. births ('parity progression ratios'). True ratios need completed cohorts. But estimates can be made from period data e.g. the 'Total Quantum Fertility Index' (Brass 1989). Although it cannot be entirely free of period distortions, it shows more modest fluctuations in fertility than the TFR and in particular gives an estimate of fertility of over 2 children for most of the time since 1972, not the 1.8 or so given by the TFR. However the data needed for this index, especially parity data on illegitimate births, are not routinely available, and its calculation demands a number of assumptions.

Overall fertility trends in the twentieth century

Fertility declined steadily from the 1870s to a new low in the 1930s. Its downward trend was disturbed only by the uncertainty of the First World War and a sharp but transient post-war baby boom. The 1930s nadir is usually regarded as the final maturity of the new trend towards small family size which began in the marriage cohorts of the 1870s. In 1933 fertility was the lowest ever recorded until the 1970s. In that year the TFR was 1.72, corresponding to a Net Reproduction Rate of 0.74. None the less, women married for the first time in the 1930s actually had family sizes only just below replacement rate. Average family size after thirty years of marriage fell below 2.1 among women married in 1928, reached a low of 2.01 among women married in 1936, and rose to exceed 2.1 among women married from 1943 onwards. These figures exclude extra-marital births and births to remarried women.

Birth-rates recovered somewhat by the end of the 1930s (e.g. to 1.83 in 1939). It seems reasonable to suppose that they had been particularly depressed by the economic conditions of the inter-war period. Unemployment in the UK peaked at 17 per cent in 1932 but had fallen back to its 1920s level of 8 per cent by 1937. Births fell and employment and real wages worsened in almost all industrial economies in the early 1930s. It is important to remember that Britain fared less badly than the USA and some of its Continental neighbours, and that even adjusted for unemployment, real wages continued to increase on average until the early 1930s (figure 4.2, see Dimsdale 1984). In the UK the unemployment was strongly concentrated in Scotland, Wales, Northern regions, and rust-belt industries. Throughout Europe, these trends showed that population growth and even population replacement could no longer be taken for granted. They provoked a renaissance of national interest and public debate about demography (Reddaway 1938, Hogben 1938, Glass 1936, Charles 1936), which is discussed further in Chapter 13.

The Census of 1911 had asked new, detailed questions on past births as well as present children, some of which were repeated in 1921. The (private) National Birth Rate Commission was set up in 1913; the Eugenics Society established the Population Investigation Committee in 1935 to analyse the new trends. The Population (Statistics) Act of 1938 enabled more data to be collected at the registration of birth. The first and only Royal Commission on Population (1949), was set up in 1944 to see if Britain was indeed facing population decline and to

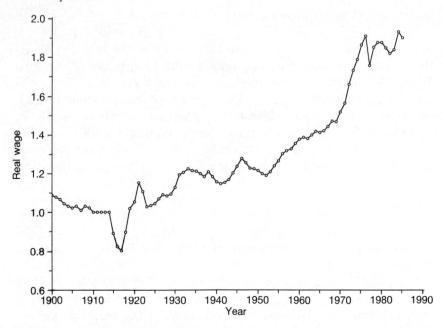

Note: The vertical scale is the real wage relative to the 1910–14 level set at 1.00. The weekly wage rate series was discontinued after 1983. Incomes after that date relate to earnings, not just wages.

Sources: Feinstein 1976, Statistical Tables of National Income, Expenditure and Output of the UK 1855–1965 Cambridge, Cambridge University Press (weekly wages to 1965 table 65 col. 11, retail prices to 1965 table 65 col. 3). Economic Trends Annual Supplement 1986 (weekly earnings 1965–83 table 110). Economic Trends Annual Supplement 1987 (weekly earnings 1983–5 table 111, retail prices 1965–85 table 114). Mr N.H. Dimsdale, Queen's College Oxford, kindly assembled and computed these data.

Fig. 4.2. Real wages adjusted for unemployment, 1900–1985

'consider what measures, if any, should be taken in the national interest to influence the future trend of population'. But it led to no official population policy, nor to real changes in government policy towards family support (see Chapter 13).

Even before the Second World War births were increasing again: imperceptibly in France (Ogden and Huss 1982), slowly in Britain from 1933, and most dramatically in Germany. It is only in Nazi Germany that population policies, general between the wars in Continental Europe, may have been effective in raising the birth-rate (Glass 1940, Bleuel 1976). The Second World War itself had an erratic effect on the tempo of British fertility. Wars generally suppress fertility, as families are separated, marriages delayed (after an initial precipitate rush), and the outlook for childbearing seems uncertain. But this effect was weaker in the Second World War than in the First. Unlike the earlier conflict, British armies were expelled from Europe for four years. This may be one reason why fertility recovered somewhat after its initial wartime decline, to reach a peak in 1944 (781,478 births), unmatched since 1923, only to fall again in late 1944 and 1945 as mass armies were once again able to operate overseas (see Registrar-General 1954).

Most recent wars have ended in a baby boom, even for the losers. Despite the unpromising post-war British economic scene, births sharply increased from 1946 to 1948 as servicemen returned home. The end of this demographic spike (smaller than that which followed the end of the First World War) brought a renewal of anxiety, expressed in the Royal Commission's Report (1949), lest renewed low fertility should revive the threat of population decline. Fertility languished at a low level into the early 1950s, seemingly appropriate to the austere circumstances and declining real wages of the time. But the flat or declining projections made then (Chapter 13) were soon confounded by a regular and sustained increase in fertility, shared with most Western countries. From 1953 to 1964 the total fertility rate in England and Wales rose from a nadir of 2.14 in 1951 to its zenith of 2.94 in 1964. The marriages of the late 1950s and early 1960s have produced an average of up to 2.4 babies. This is the famous 'baby boom', shared more or less by all Western industrial countries (not Eastern Europe or Japan), which has now produced almost as many books as it has people.

Earlier childbearing by women born in the 1940s was responsible for most of the baby boom of the 1960s. Absolute numbers of births increased from 667,811 in 1935 to 875,972 in 1964, an increase of 31 per cent. The total fertility rate went up from 2.22 to 2.94—an increase of 32 per cent. But the family sizes of women married in 1945 and in 1954 after 10 years' marriage were 1.79 and 1.96 children respectively—a difference of only 10 per cent. The most fertile birth cohort of women since the 1920s has been the women born around 1937, who would mostly have married by the early 1960s. By age 40 they had produced 2.4 children on average; a statistic which seems to have become famous.

From then onwards fertility has declined and remained low, gradually until 1971 (TFR 2.38)—when population growth was still sufficient to alarm the environmentally conscious (Taylor 1970, Brooks 1974)—then much more severely. Fertility fell below replacement level (TFR 2.1) in 1972; a new trough was reached in 1977 (TFR 1.7), a return to the position of fifty years earlier. Fertility has oscillated around 1.8 ever since. From the 1960s onwards, period fertility rates began to fall below the replacement level throughout Europe and the rest of the industrial

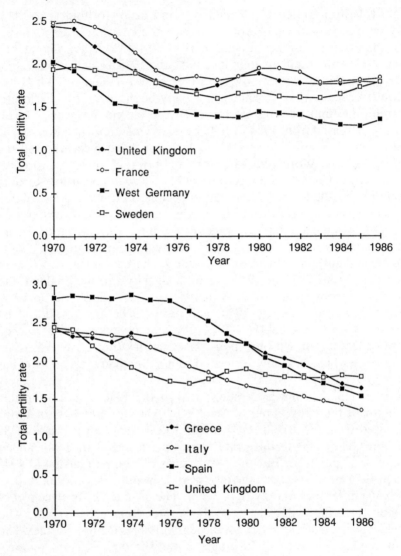

Sources: Council of Europe 1979, 1989.

FIG. 4.3. Total fertility rate (*a*) Western Europe, (*b*) Southern Europe and UK, 1970–1986

world, and have stayed there ever since. The coincidence of the timing of these changes is remarkable, and even Southern European countries with more rural populations and traditionally higher fertility have followed since the early 1980s (figure 4.3) (see Council of Europe 1989, Davis, Bernstam, and Ricardo-Campbell 1986).

In fact Britain in 1989 had one of the highest fertility rates in Europe;

Table 4.1. Family building of birth cohorts, 1923–1968

Women's year of birth	Mean number of children per woman achieved by successive exact ages reached before the end of 1987					
	20	25	30	35	40	45[a]
1923	0.07	0.67	1.36	1.80	2.03	2.10
1928	0.09	0.74	1.46	1.95	2.19	2.24
1933	0.11	0.81	1.66	2.18	2.36	2.38
1938	0.13	0.97	1.86	2.26	2.36	2.39
1943	0.19	1.06	1.83	2.12	2.22	2.24
1948	0.22	0.99	1.62	1.97	2.08	
1953	0.24	0.82	1.48	1.86		
1958	0.17	0.71	1.35			
1963	0.14	0.61				
1968	0.15					

[a] Includes births at ages 45 and over achieved up to the end of 1986.
Source: OPCS Birth Statistics 1987 Series FM1 No. 16, t. 10.2.

1.8, half a child higher than the astonishing 1.3 of Italy and West Germany, which are the lowest in world history. In Britain it is later childbearing, rather than the abandonment of parenthood, which caused most of this fall in annual births and period fertility measures. Recent cohorts will not match the 2.4 children per family of the baby boom years, but the total seems unlikely to fall much below 2 (table 4.1). This is discussed further below. Family size at longer durations of marriage has been rather stable in recent years; the similarity of family building of people born in the 1960s to that of the 1920s does not imply much reduction in family size. However West Germany and its neighbouring countries may be heading for a different pattern.

Fertility recovered a little from its 1977 low (figure 4.4) but by 1980 this recovery was spent, at a level still below that needed to replace the population in the long run. Up to 1989, TFR has not exceeded 1.8 in Britain. This transient revival, shared with other Western nations, was probably a 'technical rally' (Calot and Thompson 1981). It is impossible to postpone childbearing indefinitely without children being cancelled altogether. The baby bulge birth cohorts have been of an age to have children for some time. But they have not produced the expected increase in births. The postponement of first births by women born in the 1950s (mostly married in the early 70s) has made these births more 'spread-out' in time (Kiernan and Diamond 1982) and contrib-

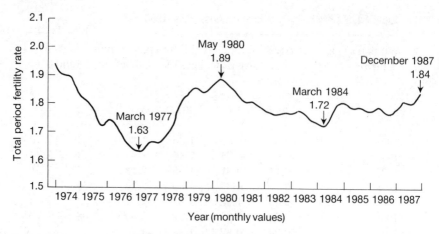

Source: OPCS Birth Statistics 1987 Series FMI No. 16, fig. 1.
FIG. 4.4. Recent trends in the total fertility rate, England and Wales, 1974–1987

uted to the trough in births observed in 1975–9. In the end, there is no guarantee that the 'natural' level of fertility in modern societies has to be at or above the replacement rate. Indeed no one yet knows what a 'natural' or 'equilibrium' level of fertility may be in such societies. We will return to that problem in a later section.

4.2 Explaining Fertility Trends: 'Proximate' Causes

Sex and fecundity

Fertility rates are the outcome of complex processes affecting each couple which lead to millions of individual decisions, accidents, failures, and results. In trying to account for overall trends it is helpful to start with the sequences of factors which control the immediate risks of fertility for the individual and without which births cannot occur: natural fecundity (the physiological capacity to conceive and bear children), exposure to intercourse within and outside marriage, and evasion of the consequences of intercourse through contraception and abortion. Changes in these immediate precursors of childbearing or 'proximate' variables provide one level of analysis and measurement (Bongaarts and Potter 1983) and point the way to the more remote social and economic factors, such as costs of children, desired family size, and their variation between social groups, which we will look at in section 4.3.

Fecundity and the frequency of intercourse are usually taken to be constant factors. Malthus assumed that the 'passion between the sexes' was constant; modern demographers seldom think of it at all in academic terms, leaving it to medicine and biology (Austin and Short 1980, Parkes 1976). But this may assume too much. For example, data from the United States suggests that the human sperm-count per ejaculation is about half its value of a quarter of a century ago (James 1980). In a number of Western countries including Britain the relative frequency of fraternal (dizygotic, non-identical) twins approximately halved from the 1950s and 1970s. In England and Wales, the sex ratio at birth has fallen from 106.3 in 1971–5 to 104.8 in 1988 (Shaw 1989). As the frequency of such twins, and the sex ratio, are thought to depend partly on the levels of female sex hormone, this has been taken as evidence for a general decline in Western fecundity (James 1980, 1982). But sexual intercourse seems to be becoming ever more popular. US evidence suggests a 20 per cent increase in coital frequency at all ages from 1965 to 1975 (Trussell and Westoff 1980). Sexual activity is certainly starting earlier (Mant *et al.* 1988). Since the late 1960s most women have had sex before marriage—increasing from at least a third of women who were married in the late 1950s to three-quarters of women married in the early 1970s (Dunnell 1979). Average fertility is so low today compared to the total number of children that might be conceived that factors affecting fecundity would be unlikely to influence final family size. But they might affect birth spacing.

A certain proportion of women and men are sterile or have difficulty having children. These difficulties can arise from sexual problems, infertility and pregnancy loss. The overall prevalence of involuntary childlessness is difficult to estimate. Demographic statistics include both the voluntarily and involuntarily childless. Within marriage, fluctuations in the proportions without children are due to changes in choice about childlessness, not changes in fecundity. In England and Wales the average proportion of each marriage cohort still without children after twenty years of marriage (all ages at marriage together) is between 10 and 15 per cent (e.g. 1951 13 per cent, 1956 10 per cent). The lowest proportion of any cohort of married women to remain childless by age 50 is about 7 per cent (see figure 4.10). Eight per cent of all women aged 40–4 (married or otherwise) had no liveborn children according to the 1987 General Household Survey. Apart from women sterilized for contraceptive purposes, 6 per cent of women aged 16–44 claimed it would be difficult or impossible for them to have children. In the United States in 1982, 8 per cent gave the same answer in a similar survey (US Dept of Health and Human Services 1987).

In 1976, 10 per cent of US married couples with wives aged 15–44 had been unable to conceive after a year. If married persons sterilized for non-contraceptive reasons are included, the proportion of the sub-fecund rises to 25 per cent (most non-contraceptive sterilizations are for conditions which would themselves cause sterility: McFalls and McFalls 1984). The proportion of women married below age 20 still childless after 20 years was about 2 per cent for women married in 1951, 3 per cent for women married in 1956. In 27 countries studied in the World Fertility Survey, the proportions of married women still childless by age 40–9 varied from 1.3 to 6.7 per cent, and historical data suggest that 3 per cent of couples are sterile from the beginning of reproductive life (*Population Reports* 1983, Bongaarts and Potter 1983).

The trend towards later marriage and childbearing, especially among career women, has sharpened interest in how far children can be deferred before running into seriously increasing risks of sterility. Historical data from non-contracepting European populations reinforces a view from contemporary data that the risk rises gradually from youth until after age 35—and then rises more steeply: 6 per cent of women aged 25 were sterile, 24 per cent at age 40, (Menken 1985, Trussell and Wilson 1985). Median age at menopause in contemporary Western society is about 51. Advances in medical science, surgery, and sex hormone therapy should tend to reduce involuntary childlessness. Up to 2,500 births a year in Britain result from artificial insemination by donor (Teper and Symonds 1985) and since the birth of the first 'test tube' baby in 1978 there have been several hundred such births in Britain alone (see Edwards 1983).

Contraception and abortion

It seems obvious to blame the fall in fertility from the mid-1960s on the pill and legal abortion. The contraceptive pill became available in Britain from about 1962. Contraception became freely available through the National Health Service on social grounds, for unmarried as well as married women, by the National Health Service (Family Planning) Act 1967 (see Leathard 1980). The grounds under which abortion could legally be carried out were greatly widened by the Abortion Act of 1967, although these stop short of the 'abortion on demand' available in several other countries. These are tempting explanations for fertility decline. The Germans have even called the post-1960s dent in their age structure 'Der Pillenknick'. But the implication is wrong.

This view assumes that people always want fewer babies than they actually have (because of inefficient family planning). Hence any improvement in efficiency or availability of contraception will always drive down the birth-rate. Such a simple view cannot accommodate increases in fertility at times when contraceptive knowledge and technique were generally increasing, as in the late 1930s and the post-war baby boom. Neither is it true that well-developed contraceptive techniques are necessary to achieve low fertility. Severe reductions in fertility, to low levels similar to today's, were achieved in the past with quite rudimentary means of contraception. The total fertility rate in the 1930s was reduced to 1.7 in 1933 from 2.4 ten years earlier (a 28 per cent reduction) and from 2.8 twenty years earlier (a 39 per cent reduction). This was achieved solely through the use of the condom, the cap, coitus interruptus, abstinence, with the help of illegal abortion.

Better contraception does not necessarily mean lower fertility, although it should mean less unwanted fertility. Planned pregnancies have declined much less than unplanned ones, especially in higher order births in Britain and in the USA (Westoff and Ryder 1977). Better contraception should be regarded as the means whereby desired family size, and short-term accommodation to economic circumstances, can be more efficiently accomplished. Fertility increases in Britain occurred in a modest way in the later 1930s and much more strikingly between the mid-1950s and 1960s. But contraceptive techniques were improving throughout this time and successive marriage cohorts were more likely to use contraception (table 4.2) and use it more effectively than before (Rowntree and Pierce 1961, Langford 1976, Cartwright 1978, Dunnell 1979).

Sterilization is becoming one of the most important methods of contraception among women of childbearing years, and the normal method of contraception for couples where the woman is aged over 30. In 1970 only 4 per cent of married women aged 18–44 were protected by contraceptive sterilization (i.e. either the husband or wife was sterilized). By 1987, 30 per cent of married or cohabiting women aged 16–49 were. It is not merely a final precaution taken by couples near the end of their fecund life. In 1987, 10 per cent of such women aged 25–9 were protected by sterilization, 24 per cent of women aged 30–4, 46 per cent aged 35–9. Eleven per cent were protected by sterilization after one birth, 35 per cent after two (GHS 1987). Such terminal sterilization, common among all social classes, is likely to depress high parity births still further, although its relative irreversibility is already causing problems for remarrying couples.

'Pill Scares' and Fertility

Fear of the risks of contraception may turn women towards apparently safer but less reliable barrier methods. This may increase unwanted

Table 4.2. Contraception: trends in ever-use by marriage cohort, 1941–1965

Year of marriage	% ever-use	Method used by ever-users (%)								
		Pill	IUD	Condom	Cap	Withdrawal	Safe period	Spermicide	Other
1941–50	84.6	6	<1	59	15	47	9	27	5
1951–60	90.2	22	2	65	22	47	12	29	4
1961–5	91.4	31	4	60	17	36	13	22	3
All	88.2	18	2	61	18	45	11	27	4

Source: Langford 1976, t. 4.1 (1967–8 Population Investigation Committee Survey).

Table 4.3. Contraception: trends in current use, 1970–1989 (% ever-married women aged 16–39/40)

Form of contraception	(1) 1970 England and Wales Family Planning Services survey	(2) 1976 Great Britain Family Formation survey	(3) 1983 General Household Survey	(4) 1989 General Household Survey
Pill	19	32	29	25
IUD	4	8	9	6
Condom	28	16	15	16
Cap	4	2	2	1
Withdrawal	14	5	4	4
Safe period	5	1	1	2
Abstinence	3	0	1	—
Other	—	1	1	1
At least one non-surgical	71	61	58	50
Female sterilization ⎫	4	8	12	11
Male sterilization ⎰		8	12	12
Total at least one	75	77	81	72
Not using any	25	23	19	28

Note: Figures for ever-use higher than for current use. People may use more than one method. Base samples: (1) 2,520; (2) 3,378; (3) 2,850; (4) 4,776. Data in column (4) refer to all women aged 18–44. 'Non-use' figure also inflated by new 'no sexual relationship' option in questionnaire.

Source: General Household Survey 1983, t. 5.5, OPCS Monitor SS 90/3, t. 17.

fertility. In the so-called 'pill scare' of 1977 attention was first drawn to the risks from thrombosis to older women on the pill (Vessey *et al.* 1977; Beral and Kay 1977). These researches showed that with the pills then in use, mortality from circulatory diseases among pill users was five times that of non-users, and ten times higher among women who used the pill for 15 years or more. Smokers had much higher risks. Overall mortality of users was raised by 40 per cent (in age-groups where mortality is low). Pill use declined, especially among older educated women, from 45 million courses in 1977 to 38 million in 1979. Some of the less educated women in Askham's (1975) Aberdeen study had given up the pill as a result of such articles in popular newspapers and had become pregnant in consequence. Births and abortion rates increased at about the same time. However, the increase in fertility seems to precede the publicity about the pill, and the fertility increase has other explanations (Bone 1982, Ermisch 1983). Fertility still remains low, despite lower pill use. Although use of the IUD and condom has increased, especially among educated women, the rise of sterilization is much more important as it marks an almost certain end to childbearing (table 4.3). Pill users have since been further worried by reports that early use of the pill can cause cancer of the breast (Pike *et al.* 1983) and that its prolonged use may increase the risk of cervical cancer (Vessey *et al.* 1983), although at the time the Medical Advisory Panel of the International Planned Parenthood Federation (IPPF) concluded that the evidence was insufficient to modify current medical practice. Despite many investigations, the evidence for these cancer risks is still not conclusive, although it is certainly disturbing (Vessey *et al.* 1989). Even a small increase in breast cancer is significant because it is already the most important cause of cancer death in women. The pill's more certain beneficial effects on benign breast disease and on cancer of the ovaries and of the uterus are less widely known. In the 1980s AIDS revived interest in the ancient protective properties of the condom.

Legal abortion

Legal abortion in Britain since 1967 came too late to explain the beginning of fertility decline. Furthermore, there were many illegal abortions before the Act. Estimates vary between 20,000 and 100,000 per year, with the most likely number probably around 60,000 (Leete 1976, James 1971, Goodheart 1973). Many illegal abortions which would have happened anyway could be performed legally after 1967. Since then, observed levels of legal abortion cannot be responsible for more than a fifth of the decline in legitimate fertility, although its impact

Sources: *Population Trends* 45, 55; Registrar-General's Supplement on Abortion, t. 2*a*. (various years)
OPCS Abortion Statistics 1988 Series AB No. 15 t. 3.

FIG. 4.5. Legal abortions, women resident in England and Wales, 1968–1989

on illegitimate births is greater. In 1988 there were 168,298 legal abortions on residents of England and Wales (figure 4.5). Legal abortions accounted for 39 per cent of all conceptions outside marriage in 1975, declining slightly to 37 per cent in 1985, and accounted for 8 to 7 per cent respectively of all conceptions known inside marriage from those two years (table 4.4). The ratio of abortions per 1,000 live births was 229 in 1987, compared with 180 in 1977. From 1967 to 1987 annual births dropped from 832,000 to 682,000. The difference is double the increase in the number of abortions, and one abortion cannot be considered to 'prevent' one live birth—a ratio of 3:1 is often assumed. From 1977 to 1987 births increased from 569,259 to 681,511, despite an increase of 53,514 in the annual total of abortions.

Legal abortion may have its greatest demographic impact in reducing pre-maritally conceived births and 'forced' marriages. Overall, 40 per cent of conceptions outside marriage to women of all ages were terminated in 1976, and 36 per cent in 1986 (OPCS 1989*c*). Unmarried teenagers and older unmarried women have the highest abortion rates, but the proportion changes little with age. In 1986 38 per cent of the 103,000 conceptions outside marriage to teenagers (under age 20) were aborted, declining to 32 per cent of the 25,000 such conceptions to women aged 30–4 and rising to 56 per cent of the 2,000 conceptions to unmarried women aged 40 and over. The abortion ratio for teenagers in England and Wales of about 500 per 1,000 live births is about the same as that of other industrial countries except for Japan, Denmark,

Table 4.4. Proportion of pregnancies terminated by legal abortion, England and Wales, 1969–1987 (%)

(*a*) *Conceptions outside marriage*

Year	under 16	under 20	20–4	25–9	30–4	35–9	40 and over	all ages
1969	26	14	19	22	21	24	27	17.2
1971	37	26	33	34	34	38	40	29.9
1973	45	33	40	40	39	45	51	36.8
1975	52	38	41	40	41	44	54	39.5
1977	53	39	39	38	40	47	59	39.4
1979	55	40	39	37	39	49	64	39.7
1981	57	41	39	37	39	48	62	40.2
1983	57	40	37	34	36	45	59	38.1
1985	56	39	36	34	34	42	59	37.0
1987	54	39	36	33	32	39	54	36.2

(*b*) *Conceptions within marriage*

Year	under 20	20–4	25–9	30–4	35–9	40 and over	all ages
1969	1	1	3	7	13	23	3.8
1971	2	3	5	12	23	38	6.6
1973	2	3	6	15	29	47	8.0
1975	3	4	6	14	31	51	8.1
1977	3	4	5	12	30	52	7.7
1979	4	4	5	11	28	51	7.8
1981	4	4	5	11	27	48	7.9
1983	3	4	5	10	23	44	7.4
1985	4	4	5	9	22	43	7.4
1987	5	5	5	9	20	42	7.6

Sources: OPCS Birth Statistics 1985 Series FM1 no. 12, t. 12.3, 12.5. OPCS Birth Statistics 1986 Series FM1 no. 13, t. 12.4, 12.5. OPCS Birth Statistics 1988 Series FM1 no. 17, t. 12.4, 12.5.

and Sweden where the ratio is about 1,500 per 1,000 live births (Clearie *et al.* 1985). However the actual number of teenage conceptions in Sweden is much lower than in Britain, thanks, it is believed, to comprehensive sex education.

Within marriage, abortions are uncommon: 7 per cent of all conceptions within marriage in 1986. The number of abortions performed on married women has remained at about 40,000 per year for the last fifteen years, while the number performed on single women, and divorced, separated, and widowed women has approximately doubled. Most abortions within marriage are carried out on women over age 30 (56% per cent in 1988). In 1986, only 4 per cent of conceptions to married women aged 20–4 were legally terminated compared to 43 per cent to married women aged over 40. Some are unwanted high parity conceptions; in addition a high proportion of abortions at this age are carried out because a congenital malformation has been diagnosed in the foetus. The risks of such abnormalities as Down's syndrome and spina bifida increase rapidly with maternal age from 1 in 2,700 births to mothers aged 25–9, to 1 in 170 to mothers aged over 45.

The proportion of these abortions to older married women is declining: 55 per cent of conceptions to married women over age 35 were aborted in 1975; 25 per cent in 1985. Part of the decline in abortion at this age is due to the greater number of wanted pregnancies from re-married women. The incidence of many congenital malformations has declined in the last decade thanks to advances in screening coverage (see Carter 1983, Royal College of Physicians 1989) and techniques, and wider knowledge of the availability of abortion. But some mal-formations cannot be diagnosed until late in pregnancy. Restriction of the gestation period within which abortion may legally be performed from the 28 weeks defined in the 1967 Act was frequently urged by abortion reformers, for example to 18 weeks in the failed 1988 Private Members Bill by David Alton MP. Such changes would be likely to increase the incidence of some of these conditions, as well as of births to women who do not report, or even discover, their unwanted pregnancies until late in gestation (see Royal College of Obstetricians and Gynaecologists 1984). These tend to be those least capable of caring for a child, or those bearing a foetus with malformations for which the diagnosis is time-consuming. In practice, the professional bodies concerned, e.g. the Royal College of Obstetricians and Gynaecologists, had already agreed to a limit of 24 weeks and in 1990 a Bill was passed to reduce the legal limit to 24 weeks.

Attitudes to childbearing and family size

Attitudes are not a 'proximate determinant' in the technical sense, but it is useful to discuss the issues in the context of family planning. A succession of opinion surveys strongly suggests that most people regard a family size of two children as ideal; this preference seems to have grown stronger over the years (Woolf 1971, Woolf and Pegden 1976, Dunnell 1979, General Household Survey, Jowell et al. 1986, 1987). Two or three children remain the ideal of 80 per cent, only 6 per cent think one or none is ideal (Gallup 1986). Average desired or intended family size is rather higher than the family size implicit in birth-rates since the 1970s. TFR has been below 2.1 since 1972. 'Ideal' family size in 1967 was about 2.4 and has only declined marginally since. 'Expected' family size, recorded in the General Household Survey, has varied from 2.28 to 2.24 (table 4.5). Women born before and during World War II expected (and duly produced) higher family size— 2.5 to 2.4 children. Women born in 1945–59 expected 2.27 children; women born in 1960–4 expect 2.33 on average. These are all substantially above replacement level and about a third greater than the fertility (1.8) implied by current rates. This is one of the reasons why fertility is expected to rise a little in official projections, to 2.0 (OPCS 1989*a*), although there are reasons for believing that these high expectations will not be matched by performance (Shaw 1989).

Demographers look on surveys of family intentions with mixed feelings, although according to one analysis 80 per cent of the women married in 1959 achieved their intended family size (Barrett and Brass

Table 4.5. Average number of children expected

(*a*) *Average number of children expected in all in present marriage, 1971–1987*

Year of interview	Year of present marriage				
	1960–4	1965–9	1970–4	1975–9	1980–84
1971	2.3	2.1	—	—	—
1973	2.3	2.1	—	—	—
1975	2.3	2.1	1.9	—	—
1977	2.4	2.0	1.9	1.1	—
1980	2.4	2.1	2.0	2.0	—
1981	2.4	2.2	2.0	2.0	—
1983	2.5	2.2	2.1	2.0	—
1987	—	2.2	2.1	2.1	2.1

(*b*) *Average number of children expected, including children born by previous marriage or outside marriage*

1982	2.4	2.3	2.2	2.2	—
1983	2.5	2.3	2.2	2.2	—
1987	—	2.3	2.2	2.2	2.3

Source: General Household Survey 1983, t. 4.27, 1987 t. 11.20.

1974). While they may often be approximately right in aggregate, these forecasts are often wrong in the individual family. Forecasts made by married couples of their personal family size seem to share many of the drawbacks of demographic forecasts made by demographers; especially too much dependence on current conditions (Westoff and Ryder 1977). There may be a general tendency to exaggerate; couples seem to be more willing to abandon expectations of a third child than they are to opt for a third child after stating an earlier preference for two.

Accidental and planned fertility

In a modern society where just two children are the norm, any birth is a major event, every birth has major consequences for the mother's material circumstances and future. This is especially true for the unmarried and the poor. Why, then, are there still so many unwanted births among people with less favourable circumstances? In some cases the birth, however objectively undesirable, may make circumstances less unfavourable. Pregnancies of single mothers may have been made less unfavourable by housing legislation (Ineichen 1972). Fewer single mothers are employed, contrary to the trend among married mothers and among single mothers overseas. This may reflect the welfare benefits available to some single mothers compared to their low earning power (Campbell 1984). Girls with unsatisfactory parenting may crave a baby of their own to provide the affection lacking in their own upbringing; but then themselves repeat the problems which they are trying to get away from (Kiernan 1980*b*). Unemployed single teenagers are particularly likely to have children; it has been suggested as a 'short cut' to adult status (Penhale 1989).

Teenage fertility

Teenage fertility—both legitimate and illegitimate—brings together many of the problems of poor knowledge and planning, the harmful consequences of unwanted fertility, and its transmission across generations. Teenage mothers are least able to cope with motherhood, being often themselves emotionally immature and sometimes physically immature (Russell 1981). Often they possess no resources or accommodation of their own. They are twice as likely to live in council housing, twice as likely to be supported by someone in class V (if at all) than in any other class (Werner 1984). Their pregnancies are likely to be troublesome and repetitive. In a Newcastle study, more than 70 per cent of first illegitimate pregnancies were followed by another.

   The earlier the pregnancy, the worse the circumstances. Girls who become pregnant by their 16th birthday are likely to have parents who are divorced, separated, alcoholic, or in gaol, or to have been themselves in care or in a special school. In one survey, 83 per cent of the younger girls never used contraception or used it sporadically. Only 51 per cent of the girls over 16 had attempted to avoid pregnancy; others thought that they could not become pregnant because they were too young or had sex too infrequently. Although just over half of a sample of teenage mothers in 1979–80 had had some kind of family planning lesson at school, only a quarter had attempted to use contraception around the time they conceived. Others replied: 'it just happened', 'it didn't cross my mind', 'you don't think you are going to get caught'. Only 30 per cent considered having an abortion.

Teenage mothers often copy their parents' experience (Madge 1988), especially 'conventional' teenage mothers of legitimate births who conceive within marriage (Kiernan 1980b). Parents of teenage mothers usually married young themselves, had primary education only, were mostly in manual occupations, and came from large families. The teenage mothers like their parents had little ambition and worse prospects for anything except further childbearing (Cartwright 1978). Teenagers who conceived pre-maritally were five times as likely as the average to have been conceived pre-maritally themselves. More than half teenage marriages are likely to end in divorce by twenty-five years' duration at risks current in 1979–82 (Haskey 1984). Teenage marriage and pregnancy have comprehensively gloomy outcomes. Their discouragement should be a prime aim of public policy.

Psychological aspects

Many births are unambiguously described as 'unwanted' by parents in response to survey questions. It is a considerable puzzle to know why they are still so common. Several studies on the differences between those who do and do not effectively plan their fertility emphasize the importance of belief in the possibility of control, and its connection with material or occupational circumstances (e.g. Askham's 1975 study in Aberdeen). Unfavourable circumstances encouraged strong orientation towards the present, not the future: a feeling of lack of control over events and a tendency to accept them passively. In a national survey, 'forward planners' in all classes had lower fertility (and family size clustered more tightly around an average of two children), and were more likely to use effective methods of contraception. Considerably more women in the higher social classes had a 'forward planning' outlook which assumed control over their futures (Dunnell 1979).

These differences in attitude and personality are crucial for control of fertility. It is not known if they are acquired through upbringing or inheritance or acquired later through experience. Their effects on life chances in general, not just fertility, are a prominent feature of classic sociological accounts of the British class system (Klein 1965). The most important question seems to be how far individuals believe they are in control of their own environment and can control what happens to them. Such problems are studied by psychologists under the general rubric of 'locus of control': whether control of life's events lies outside the individual or within his power. 'Internal' locus of control is associated with higher education and income, occupational position, and success. Although the connection between these psychological ideas and sociological observations is highly suggestive, it has only occasionally been studied in the context of fertility and marriage (see Coleman 1990). Other psychological attributes with a bearing on fertility trends, concerned more with ideas than with personal adequacy, are discussed below.

The 'perfect contraceptive' population

It has been estimated that in the UK in 1981 about 54 per cent of married women aged 15–44 wanted no more births. About 42 per cent of unwanted pregnancies resulted in live births and there were about 15 unwanted births per year per 1,000 married women who wanted no further births; almost 10 per cent of the marital fertility rate. A higher but unknown proportion of the 28 per cent of births now outside marriage are also likely to be unwanted. A so-called 'perfect contraceptive' birth-rate, perhaps 15 per cent lower than now, and lower population growth would result if all births were wanted. A wider use of existing methods of contraception among non-users—and a reduction in the use of the IUD, which has a high failure rate—would pull down the abortion rate 46 per cent. Even if non-users started to use the least effective contraceptive methods the abortion rate could fall by 30 per cent (Westoff, Hammerslough, and Paul 1987). Perfect contraceptive practice would be completely compatible with population growth, not decline, if desired family size remained at about its present level and was actually realized in achieved family size.

Marriage and illegitimacy

Over 70 per cent of births still occur within marriage, so the popularity of marriage and its timing remain important in the study of subsequent fertility. For this reason, and because it is the basis of most households, marriage is considered separately in Chapter 5. Where average family size is only about two children, it is perfectly possible for women to

Table 4.6. Relation of family size to age at marriage, England and Wales, 1925–1969[a]

Year of marriage	Age at marriage						
	<45	<20	20–4	25–9	30–4	35–9	40–4
(a) Actual data							
1925	1.72	2.38	1.93	1.48	1.28	0.79	0.39
1930	1.64	2.38	1.81	1.44	1.10	0.67	0.27
1935	1.60	2.31	1.76	1.42	1.10	0.54	0.27
1940	1.63	2.08	1.73	1.50	1.16	0.61	0.24
1945	1.79	2.22	1.85	1.69	1.33	0.73	0.25
1950	1.84	2.41	1.89	1.50	1.32	0.68	0.22
1955	1.99	2.45	2.00	1.83	1.40	0.74	0.23
1960	2.13	2.50	2.11	1.99	1.57	0.80	n/a
1965	1.97	2.19	1.95	1.84	1.49	0.78	n/a
1969	1.82	2.03	1.79	1.73	1.39	0.78	n/a
(b) Proportional data: 20–4 rates as 100							
1925	89	123	100	77	66	41	20
1930	91	131	100	80	61	37	15
1935	91	131	100	81	63	31	15
1940	94	120	100	87	67	35	14
1945	97	120	100	91	72	39	14
1950	97	128	100	79	70	36	12
1955	100	123	100	92	70	37	12
1960	101	118	100	94	74	38	n/a
1965	101	112	100	94	76	40	n/a
1969	102	113	100	97	78	44	n/a

[a] Average number of liveborn children per married woman. First marriages, marriage duration ten years.

Note: Comparable data are not available for more recent years.
Sources: OPCS Birth Statistics 1974 Series FM1, 1, t. 10.4, OPCS Birth Statistics 1980 Series FM1 No. 7, t. 10.4. Registrar-General's Statistical Review 1969 Part II, t. QQ(b), pp. 174–9.

delay marriage quite late—until their mid-30s—and still complete a family at or even above the average size. But in general later marriages still produce fewer children (table 4.6).

Trends in marriage

In the late 1930s a new pattern of earlier marriage began to emerge which had not been seen in the West for centuries. Hitherto, marriage in Britain had been late (average age at first marriage about 25 for women, 28 for men). Up to 15 per cent of women and 10 per cent of

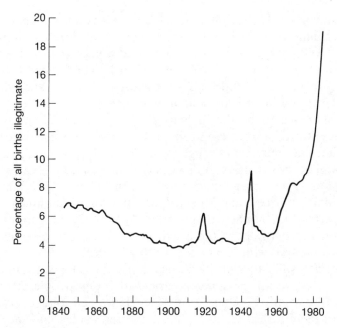

Source: Werner 1987, fig. 3.

FIG. 4.6. Percentage of all births illegitimate, England and Wales, 1838–1985

men avoided it altogether. The advance in age at marriage, and in its popularity, accounted for about 30 per cent of the increase in annual fertility rates from the 1930s to the 1950s which comprised the 'baby boom'. As a later chapter will emphasize, birth-rates do not 'blindly' follow marriage. The desire for children may determine the timing of marriage, rather than the desire for marriage determining the arrival of children. Marriage is often a sign that a couple is prepared to accept children, so fertility intentions drive marriage rates as well as the other way round.

Illegitimacy

Over one in four births now occur outside marriage. This is quite new. Illegitimacy was relatively rare until the 1960s. Illegitimate births declined from mid-Victorian times in most countries in Western Europe, and except for huge wartime increases (see Registrar-General 1954), remained relatively low until the 1950s (figure 4.6). In the past, delayed marriage and low illegitimacy both followed the inhibition of sexual behaviour by strong social controls, including religion. Then, pre-marital sexual intercourse tended to occur during courtship shortly before marriage. Even if marriage was not intended, the almost inevitable pregnancy would precipitate it. Therefore, the later the marriage, and its preliminary courtship, the lower the rate of illegitimate births in relation to the larger number of unmarried women (Crafts 1982). In the 1930s and the 1950s over 96 per cent of births were legitimate, even more than in the 'good old days' of Victorian Britain—and without its high levels of infanticide and unregistered births. In retrospect this period seems to be the 'golden age' of respectable behaviour. Illegitimacy started to increase again in the 1960s; later marriage since 1972 has been accompanied by higher, not lower, levels of illegitimacy.

As unwanted pregnancies can so easily be avoided by abortion and contraception, why is illegitimacy now so high? There are still important contraints on access and knowledge. Abortion is still much easier in some parts of the country than others. In 1987, 31 per cent of conceptions outside marriage in the North-West were terminated by legal abortion, compared with 45 per cent in the South-East. Contraceptive techniques are still far from ideal, especially for romantic, ignorant, or embarrassed youth. Sexually experienced young people often use effective contraception—80 per cent of single women using contraception are on the pill. But younger, inexperienced adolescents may not. Effective sex education needs to be attuned to the realities of sexual behaviour when the average age at first intercourse is now between 16 and 17 (Mant *et al.* 1988).

The contrast between Sweden and the USA is instructive. In Sweden intensive and early sex education is geared to family planning. In the USA sex education is forbidden in many schools, despite the permissive attitudes of the society outside. In Sweden, the ratio of abortions to births among teenagers is high but teenage conceptions and births are low and declining. In the USA teenage births are the highest in the Western world despite a relatively high abortion ratio: 347 per 1,000 live births; 696 for girls aged 15–19 (National Center for Health Statistics 1989).

Even so, in England and Wales most illegitimate babies are born to women in their 20s, not to teenagers: in 1988, 44,642 illegitimate babies were born to teenagers, 68,151 to women aged 20–4, 38,168 to women aged 25–9, 26,391 to older women: overall (177,352) three times the number in 1978. It is unmarried women in their late 20s who have the highest risk of illegitimate birth. Accidental and unwanted births are a high proportion of this total. But the picture is changing. In the early 1970s the normal response to a pre-marital conception was marriage; abortion or illegitimate birth were less favoured alternatives. In the 1980s abortion or illegitimate birth have been the most likely outcomes.

Most of the increase in illegitimate births has been to women who are

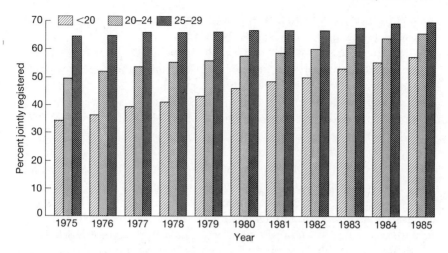

Sources: OPCS Birth Statistics Series FM1 1983 No. 12, t. 3.9, 1987 No. 16, t. 39.

Fig. 4.7. Illegitimate births: percentage jointly registered by age of mother, England and Wales, 1975–1985

in some kind of informal union, not living on their own holding the baby. This is inferred from the increase in the joint registration of illegitimate births by parents who give the same address, published since 1983. Couples who register their births together are likely to be living together (Werner 1982, Haskey and Coleman 1986). About 68 per cent of illegitimate births were jointly registered in the names of both parents in 1987 compared to 53 per cent in 1977, and in 1987, 70 per cent of such parents gave the same address. Between 1977 and 1987 illegitimate births increased from 55,400 to 158,400; 76 per cent of this increase was in jointly registered births. The increase is particularly striking among younger women (figure 4.7). Eight per cent of women aged 18–49 were cohabiting in 1988, and over 20 per cent of those had never been married (see Chapter 5). Cohabitation before marriage is becoming normal: 50 per cent before first marriage, 58 per cent before all marriages (Haskey and Kiernan 1989). Partly because it is not routinely recorded, relatively little is known about cohabitation and the extent to which it may become an ordinary setting for childbearing before or instead of marriage. It is discussed further in Chapter 5.

4.3 Explaining Fertility Trends: The Underlying Causes

It is easy to see how fertility has been kept low since the middle of the twentieth century, and how the control over its timing given by contraception could permit a new pattern of fertility fluctuation. But the means do not explain the motivation. Two major problems dominate further enquiry into today's fertility patterns and trends in Britain and the whole industrial world. First: why have there been such strong fluctuations in fertility in the last half-century, and are they likely to continue? Second and more fundamental: is there nowadays any normal average level of fertility to which post-industrial societies are tending? Is a two-child average here to stay? Might the current TFR of 1.8, or even less, become the norm? Or even no children at all? At the moment there are no complete answers to these questions. In modern society there are no economic advantages for the individual in having children, and the personal compensations may be less attractive than they were. The apparent rise of voluntary childlessness suggests that many have reached this conclusion. Prediction is a good scientific test of any quantified theory. Since the Second World War, most theories of fertility have failed it (see Ryder 1979).

Classical Malthusian ideas

These questions are common to all developed countries. Let us look first at the easier one—explaining variations in fertility. Fertility used to march in step with the economy. When real wages rose or unemployment fell, marriage and then fertility increased, and vice versa, roughly as Malthus claimed it would. This seems to work both in short-term fluctuations and in long-term trends (Habakkuk 1971), although with an awkward time lag in the latter (Wrigley and Schofield 1981). This connection between economic performance, marriage, and fertility, perhaps the best known empirical association in social science, then worked through the 'valve' of marriage: delaying marriage or avoiding it was the only practical way of controlling births. When times were good, men married earlier and some were able to marry who otherwise could not have married at all—and vice versa. This system depends on most fertility being marital fertility and on marriage being late, avoidable, and variable in age—until recently the unique property of Western European societies.

Well into the twentieth century there was a simple correlation between economic indicators, such as unemployment, and marriage rates (Glass 1938, Galbraith and Thomas 1941, Kirk 1942), even though by 1870 the birth-rate had begun its decline within marriage. The great increase in the popularity of marriage and the baby boom which it partly caused accompanied the post-war economic growth of the 1950s. This may be regarded as the last fling of this relationship.

The British and most other Western economies sustained acceptable growth rates in their economies and real wages into the 1970s (see figure 4.2) and beyond. Yet fertility throughout Europe and the industrial world began its post-war decline from the mid-60s. By the time Western economies suffered the severe shock of the quadrupling of oil prices in 1973, and subsequent further increases in 1979, the baby boom was already long over, although marriage continued to become more popular until 1972. In the UK the depression of the early 1980s was mainly a failure of growth of individual incomes of those who remained in employment. Incomes are 'sticky downwards'; most of the decline in income has been borne by the unemployed. But fertility has not fallen accordingly—its nadir was in 1977. Since 1982 real incomes in the UK have been growing fast, about 4–5 per cent per year, and from 1986 to 1989 unemployment fell. None of this has produced a rise in fertility. Economic facts since the 1960s no longer fit the demographic trends expected from the traditional theory, which predicts a positive relationship between birth-rates and the performance of the economy.

Cohort size and population cycles

Conventional ideas about prosperity and fertility fit the upward slope of the baby boom but not its decline. Many new circumstances might account for the new relationship—the movement of married women into the work-force, unprecedented economic security, the decline of religious feeling. These new circumstances require a new model, but there is still disagreement on its form. The American economist and demographer, Richard Easterlin, has suggested (1961, 1968, 1980) that population and economy are linked in a perpetual series of fluctuations, powered by income expectations, alternations in cohort size, and autonomous cycles in the economy itself.

There is nothing new in the idea of population cycles, or in the suggestion that they may influence the business cycle (Losch 1937). Easterlin's ideas emphasize the importance of cohort size on life chances. His model consists of a set of hypotheses. First, that economic aspirations of cohorts of adults are fixed in adolescence through their experience of the household in which they were brought up. Second, that fertility of these cohorts depends on the extent to which they can match these aspirations in their subsequent adult life, any shortfall in 'relative income' being met with responses to limit fertility through deferred marriage or smaller family size. Third, that the economic opportunities available to large and small cohorts of births are quite different. Members of larger cohorts experience fiercer competition throughout their lives for places in schools, university, employment, and promotion. Their incomes and standards of living relative (with allowances for rising expectations) to those of their parents will seem unsatisfactory.

To preserve expected standards as far as possible, marriage will be delayed and family size kept small. Wage growth will be low, unemployment high, with consequent feedback effects on the economy. But their children, born into small cohorts, will themselves experience comparatively favourable opportunities for promotion, recruitment, and wage increase. Their income relative to their parents will be correspondingly higher, their fertility will be high, and so the cycle will continue. As a result of these disadvantages, members of large cohorts are also claimed to suffer—and generate—higher crime rates and other indicators of social discontent (Easterlin 1978). The last two components of the model are classical Malthusian approaches, applied to cohorts rather than to whole populations. In the USA, income in the largest post-war cohorts is indeed about 15 per cent less than in smaller cohorts (Easterlin 1980) and their scholastic education scores have been lower. In part, the model is excellent.

But it is difficult to get numerical estimates for 'relative income', a concept much attacked by critics. Relative cohort size (the ratio of men 35–64 to those below 34) may be used (Easterlin and Conron 1976), to see if high ratios are associated, as expected, with high birth rates. The model fits variations in US fertility trends reasonably well, although not necessarily much better than conventional economic variables (D. P. Smith 1981). It fails to predict the downturn in fertility in the UK and in West Germany (Ermisch 1979, Eversley and Köllmann 1982). Furthermore, cohort studies in Britain show that the relation between a woman's family size and the family size in which she is brought up is positive, although not very strong: childless women are more likely to be single children themselves, mothers of large families tend to come from larger than average families themselves, even when other influences are controlled for statistically (Kiernan 1989*a*).

Women's work and the 'New Home Economics'

The problems endured and created by large cohorts seem considerable and there is no reason why Easterlin effects should not be recognized and incorporated into other models. But a more promising line of enquiry emphasizes the demographic importance of working wives, which Easterlin's original model neglects (Oppenheimer 1976). There are now two kinds of household: a minority where the wife does not work, and may have no intention of returning to work, to which the old expectations apply, and a rising majority of households with work-

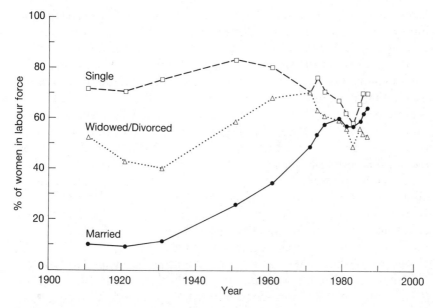

Sources: Price and Bain 1988, t. 4.4, t. 4.5; General Household Survey 1987 t. 9.4.

FIG. 4.8. Female labour force participation rates, 1911–1987

ing wives for which the economics of childbearing have been reversed. For most women, working and childbearing are alternatives, at least for a few years. When a wife's income forms an important part of the family income, rising wage levels make children a less attractive option.

The movement into the work-force by married women has been one of the most startling and far-reaching social changes since the Second World War. In 1911 just 9 per cent of married women worked, by 1966 38 per cent, and in 1988 66 per cent of married women aged 16–59 were working (figure 4.8). At recent rates about 80 per cent of married women can expect to work at some time in their married lifetime (Martin and Roberts 1984). By contrast, the proportion of single women and of divorced women in the work-force has remained more constant over that time; about 70 and 55 per cent respectively. In recent years an increasing proportion of married women even with pre-school children have taken on part-time work. This matters because married women who work have fewer children than married women who do not (Dunnell 1979, Jones 1981). Employed married women tend to delay their first and second child, compress their childbearing into their late 20s and the second five years of their married life, and avoid third and subsequent births (compared to housewives) (ni Bhrölchain 1986b).

This revolution in the labour force has affected almost all industrial economies. It has contributed much more to labour force growth than immigration, and will be the main source of its growth for the rest of this century (DE 1987). In Eastern European countries, where labour productivity is chronically low, women's labour force participation is correspondingly even higher—89 per cent in the Soviet Union. It is not hard to find reasons why married women now go out to work. In fact it is more of a puzzle to work out why it took so many decades to become established (Hatton 1986). In part, it is a consequence of the completion of the demographic transition. Since the 1920s women have been free of the burden of high fertility which previously would have given them young children to cope with for more than two decades of their adult life. Two World Wars have helped to break traditional restrictions and change attitudes and laws concerning the work that women could do. So has the parallel progress of women's education, giving them at least in theory the same job opportunities as men.

Recent legislation in most industrial countries has helped to turn this into reality. In Britain the Equal Pay Act became law in 1970. In 1984 it had to be amended further to follow the Euro-notion of 'equal pay for work of equal value' whereby the pay of women occupying jobs without immediate male comparison is set equal to men's through the opinion of a judge rather than the operation of market forces. The demand for labour from the 1950s and, later, rising relative wages compared to men has tempted many married women to stay in the work-force or to return to it. The shake-out of labour after 1979 affected women's employment less than men's, both here and abroad. The advantages of work appear to keep women in the work-force even when circumstances subsequently become less favourable (Joshi and Owen 1985). High divorce rates (and public awareness of them) encourage women to preserve their independence both financially and socially (Willmot 1976, Ermisch 1981). These changes in society seem irreversible, especially when the household's standard of living comes to depend more on the wife's income in dual earner households (60 per cent of all households with two adults under retirement age in 1987, compared with 52 per cent in 1973).

The 'New Home Economics' model relates family finance and decision making to individual behaviour, especially family formation and employment. It represents a revival of interest in the factors of the family budget and their effect upon life chances such as cohabitation, marriage, childbearing, and divorce (see Becker 1981, Willis 1973). In the past, other things being equal, improvement in a man's income removed obstacles to marriage. With the rise of family limitation, it would also remove the need to delay children within marriage. But the relation of fertility to women's employment and income is quite different. Babies deprive women of the opportunity to earn money through the expanding opportunities for full- and part-time work now available.

These market and legal changes have imposed an 'opportunity cost' on childbearing which previously did not exist. The cost in foregone earnings of bearing two children has been estimated at £119,000 if they are born when the mother is in her early 20s to £121,000 if they are born when the mother is in her mid-30s (Joshi 1987a). Other calculations based on similar data yield an estimate of £135,000 (Roll 1986). Discounting the cost at present value, to give a more realistic estimate of the loss at the time decisions are made, emphasizes the importance of deferring births: earlier childbearing leads to a loss of £84,000; having the two children later loses £62,000 (quite apart from the career implications). These estimates assume eight years out of work altogether and twelve years' part-time work subsequently. Lost hours of work, and lower rates of pay from missed experience, contribute approximately equally to loss of income (Joshi 1987a). So if the overriding aim is to minimize loss of earnings, it is economically rational for working women to delay or avoid marriage when it is no longer necessary for their financial security (Ermisch 1981). On economic grounds it is also prudent for both husband and wife to delay and limit childbearing within marriage, and compress the period devoted to childbearing. For many couples children clearly remain the first consideration. In 1987, 36 per cent of married women of working age were not at work. But enough couples respond to economic motivations for the theory to describe 'average' behaviour quite well since the 1960s (ni Bhrólchain 1986b).

Data from other countries point to a similar penalty on childbearing. In the USA in the 1970s a middle-class child raised through four years at college cost $74,000 and $145,000 if the wife's opportunity costs were included as well (Espenshade 1980). These US estimates tend to emphasize direct rather than opportunity costs, partly reflecting the lower level of welfare support especially for the higher education of children. The opportunity costs of two children to a white mother in the 1970s have been estimated at $50,000 (Calhoun and Espenshade 1988). The correlation between fertility trends and relative wages and work-force participation works well over time within particular countries. But there is considerable variation between countries and the differences do not correlate well with current fertility. For example, West Germany and the Netherlands both have lower female work-force participation than Britain but also have considerably lower fertility; while Japan, with a period fertility level about the same as Britain's has a relatively low work-force participation by married women.

Such a model assumes that the fertility in families with and without employed wives responds to wage changes quite differently. The crucial factors are the relative opportunity costs and the ratio of men's to women's earnings. These increases in women's relative wage rates, from about 65 per cent of men's in the 1960s to 75 per cent by 1975, can be shown to have substantially reduced the number of births during the 1970s—by 130,000—and made their timing more volatile (de Cooman, Ermisch, and Joshi 1987, 1988). However the effect is not always negative. The anticipation of future employment by women may bring births forward. In the 1950s and 1960s the movement of women into the work-force, or its anticipation, appears to have accelerated the pace of childbearing temporarily, especially of first and second births, reinforcing the positive economic effect through men's income (ni Bhrölchain 1986*a*, 1986*b*).

When applied to British fertility trends, the correlation (elasticity) between fertility and women's real wages increases over time because of the rise of the real wages of women and their increasing tendency to work. The model correctly predicts a downturn in fertility around 1964. Further change reinforced by acceleration of women's real wage growth led to a further decline after 1970. The effect of the sharp rise of the ratio of women's to men's wages in 1972 is evident in the graph (Ermisch 1979). Housing may also be an important component as its relative cost increased in Britain from 1955 to 1975. In the public sector, scarcity is more important than price. In the 1950s and 1960s supply improved as a result of policies to build large numbers of council houses, especially in Scotland and major cities in the North of England. Since 1979, public sector housing has been severely curtailed. It is discussed further below.

All this has upset the applecart of the relation of fertility to prosperity. It may even have reversed it (Butz and Ward 1979) so that the short-term effects of economic growth in modern societies may be further to reduce fertility, not increase it. As wage rates rise, more women will enter the work-force, so the opportunity costs of childbearing will increase and fertility decline—and vice versa. But in the relatively short-run experience so far, women have not in fact left the work-force when conditions have been less favourable.

Forecasting fertility

These changes are so recent that it is difficult to know if we are beginning a series of cyclical changes or a once-for-all transition to a new, low fertility regime. The latter seems more likely. Mass movement of women into the work-force dates only from the Second World War—especially from 1960—and the improvement of women's wage rates relative to men's happened only since 1970. Women have been attracted into the work-force by wages. They have been enabled to enter the workforce by their prior control over fertility. There are many reasons for supposing that the small family is here to stay. Families may become dependent for their living standards upon two incomes. This dependence may increase, not decline, if wage rates deteriorate in real terms. Unemployment may force the husband, not the wife, out of work. High fluctuations in fertility, characteristic of the period from the 1920s to the 1960s, are therefore likely to be a thing of the past. On this analysis, the 1950s–60s fertility boom can be regarded as a once-for-all anachronism. Established birth control and resulting low fertility permitted a unique advance in marriage at a time when married women were not yet committed to the work-force. That permitted a last Malthusian response to the then unprecedented economic growth and prosperity which followed the Second World War. A relaxed attitude to family size and the timing of births then cost little. But the economic trends which helped created the baby boom have subsequently ensured that it would have no successors, by drawing married women permanently into the work-force.

Forecasting future fertility is the most difficult task in demography, and seldom successfully attempted. The econometric models described above can derive current fertility from current socio-economic indicators. Whether they can predict the future remains to be seen. Short-range time-series projections of fertility are reported to be promising (de Cooman, Ermisch, and Joshi 1988). But it is notoriously difficult to predict the economic trends by which the models estimate fertility. Other factors may also be important: the mild upturn in fertility and its rapid failure evident after 1977 were forecast on other grounds: the impossibility of deferring children indefinitely; the new contribution to fertility from remarriages. None the less, some things do seem clear: the unlikelihood of more baby booms, except for weaker echoes of the present one, and a generally lower level of fertility. The balance of influence between husband's and wife's income, in aggregate, keeps fertility low. But each has different effects at different ages so the balance is sensitive to changes in age structure (de Cooman, Ermisch, and Joshi 1987, 1988). Analysis of current fertility by parity, and the responses to attitude surveys, have persuaded official statisticians and some demographers (OPCS 1989, Shaw 1989, Brass 1989) that fertility in Britain is likely to return to a higher, if not replacement level.

At what level, if any, will it stabilize? Is there any reason to suppose that individual decisions on family size will result in an average which happens to be the replacement rate? The models described above relate economic change to fertility change. They do not tell us why the level is set at its current average rather than some much higher or lower figure. There are good family economic reasons for believing that fertility will not become high. There are none which tell us why it should not become zero. For that we must rely more on the intentions and attitudes of potential parents, and the importance of children for parents, and cast our ideas rather wider, beyond economic trends and family finance.

Fertility, intentions, and ideology

Parents in modern society seldom receive material benefits from their children and do not, except in Japan, usually live with their children in old age. Instead, they receive benefits from their own parents. But as family size may not be tending to zero, it is evident that income and material benefits are not the only considerations in determining family size. The difficulty of accounting for the historical demographic transition by conventional economic measures (Cleland and Wilson 1987), and the fall of fertility even in some Third World countries with little economic progress today (Cleland 1985), has revived interest in non-material motivations for childbearing.

Children can be regarded as a 'consumption good' bringing non-material satisfactions. The belief that they do so, and compete for household spending with the costs of other 'consumer durables' until an acceptable living standard is achieved, is one of the underlying assumptions of the 'New Home Economics' approach to the economic analysis of family size variation, although one which has been strongly attacked (Blake 1968).

The analysis of these non-material motivations, to explain why family size is not zero in modern societies, is one of the most difficult problems confronting demography. Prestige, honour, loyalty to norms of society or religion, or apathy, may transcend material calculations, especially when the chances of improving material comforts are weak or unimaginable. Such considerations are far from the traditional preoccupations of demography. But if they can be measured they may help us relate fertility decisions to the values, meanings, or signs which people use to make sense of the world and which motivate or justify their actions.

Childbearing can be regarded as a confirmation that the parents feel at one with the nation and culture in which they live (Simons 1986a).

Statements from couples concerning family size and childbearing often have a strong normative or quasi-religious quality stressing niceness, decency, responsibility, and so on (Busfield and Paddon 1977, Askham 1975). The lack of reaffirmation of their society thought to be implicit in the low fertility current in the Federal Republic of Germany is worrying some members of that society, quite apart from the obvious material consequences. British attitudes to fertility, judged by actual behaviour in relation to fertility and marriage, and by the values stated in surveys, seem more conservative (Simons 1986b).

In some societies (e.g. Hutterites and other fundamentalists, Shi'ite Islam and the Wahhabi school of Sunni Islam, Puritan sects, Mormons, the Irish form of ultramontane Catholicism) reproductive behaviour has a 'sacred' role, whatever the cost, manifested either as an obligation to have as many children as possible or to avoid the means of limiting them (Simons 1982). Some ethnic minorities emphasize the duty of procreation and in-marriage to preserve their society from assimilation, alongside a generally rigid control over behaviour (Siegel 1970). Most religions take a more pragmatic attitude (e.g. French Catholicism, the Church of England and other mainline Christian Churches, and less fundamentalist (Sunni, Ismaeli) Islamic sects). These admit various ways of accommodating the sacred to the profane; i.e. behaving more or less like a rational economic man.

This contrast between 'fundamentalist' and 'pragmatic' attitudes is not specifically religious but can be generalized to describe the range of attitudes within a society and the direction in which they are changing. According to this notion, fertility decline since the war can be interpreted partly in terms of concomitant swings in public attitude, irrespective of formal religious affiliation, between the fundamentalist and the pragmatic pole (Simons 1982). On this view, by the end of the 1960s parents raised under the more fundamental, disciplined 1930s had been replaced in the childbearing years by those brought up with more material security and freedom, both moral and legal, from traditional restrictions. The trends in number of Easter Communicants, of conversion to the Roman Catholic Church, or the National Secular Society, are regarded as indicators of a switching of ideological allegiance. There is some similarity in these trends with those of fertility from 1900 to 1975.

This model has much in common with the dichotomy between 'post-material' versus 'traditional' attitudes much debated on the Continent (van de Kaa 1987). 'Post-material' attitudes emphasize egalitarian, non-material hedonistic attitudes which welcome novelty and ignore the past, contrasting with more 'bourgeois' values which emphasize the importance of family, country, traditions, security, duty, and altruism. The former values tolerate childlessness, cohabitation, and liberal sexual attitudes. They tend to depose the 'child king' (Aries 1983) and lead to a weaker level of 'familism': that is, supportive feelings towards marriage and childbearing (Lesthaeghe and Meekers 1986, Lesthaeghe and Surkyn 1988). International differences in these attitudes can be correlated with differences in the birth-rate. The high fertility countries (UK, France, Ireland) tend to be more conservative or nationalistic compared to their lower-fertility neighbours (Simons 1986b). It must be said that continental discussions of some of these ideas read rather strangely, at least to the authors of this book. They present as a major force in society attitudes and tastes which would be regarded as rather eccentric and marginal in Britain. One of the most important unsolved questions here is the extent to which changes in ideas and attitudes are really autonomous. For example, responses to questions on attitudes change with economic conditions—the worse the inflation, the more traditional the responses (van de Kaa 1987). Ideas and values seem to be rather fragile props for the permanence of any particular level of fertility. Other societies have adopted, or are adopting, different behaviour and values; we may do the same.

Voluntary childlessness

Perhaps 5 per cent of married couples choose to be childless. There has been much speculation whether this proportion is likely to grow substantially in industrial societies. The trend in successive cohorts suggests it is. The proportion of women still childless by age 25–9 doubled from 20 per cent in 1961 to 40 per cent in 1981. In Britain 34 per cent of women of that age were childless in 1964, and 47 per cent in 1984; levels not seen since early this century. Many of these women may still start families in their late 20s or 30s. Only 10 per cent of the 1940–4 birth cohort of women (now aged 45–50) remained childless; this figure is expected to rise to at least 15 per cent and possibly 20 per cent for the 1960–4 birth cohort (Werner 1986, OPCS 1989a, figure 4.9). Such high levels of childlessness do not fit the consistent response to questions in the General Household Survey that only about 5–7 per cent of women intend to remain childless; but up to 20 per cent of women have failed to reply to this question, although fewer in more recent surveys. This uncertainty makes it particularly interesting to know whether intentionally childless women are different in personality or attitudes from those who wish to have children, and whether these attitudes could readily become more widespread. The research on this subject so far gives a mixed answer (Campbell 1985, Baum and Cope 1980, Kiernan

(a) Average numbers of children achieved (from birth registration data)

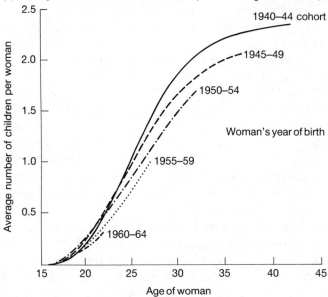

(b) Per cent of woman childless by given age

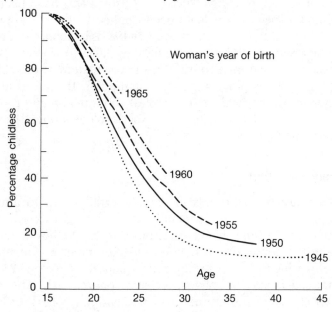

Source: Werner 1986: 21.

Fig. 4.9. Average number of children born by 1985 to women born 1940–1964, and percentage remaining childless

1989*a*). Childlessness increased strongly with age at first marriage, even at ages where fecundity is usually still high. Motives for remaining childless were mixed: hedonistic, ideological, and medical. No particular personality type seemed to predominate. The intentionally childless married woman was likely to be well educated, employed in a high status occupation, married to a husband in a professional or managerial job. Childless men, especially those with a broken marriage, were more likely to be ambitious, highly educated professionals. While most of those who were delaying children cited economic reasons first (70 per cent), only 41 per cent of those who intended to remain childless mentioned the costs. The most important consideration was freedom of action; an understandable response, as childbearing may be regarded as equivalent to a fifteen-year sentence of partial house arrest, without remission for good behaviour.

So far these problems have hardly been explored from the viewpoint of psychology or sociobiology. The interpersonal dynamics of a two-child family, especially two children of opposite sexes, may be especially rewarding for parents and insufficiently increased by the prospect of a third child to warrant further disruption to domestic economy. Biological explanations of fertility based on principles of maximizing a broadly defined reproductive success (Wilson 1975) have been useful in non-human species and have been applied to human populations with natural fertility (Borgerhoff-Mulder 1987), in an attempt to relate reproductive success with the resources available to women. But such models seem to have little to offer in the elucidation of the behaviour of complex societies practising family limitation. If there is any long-term tendency to produce a family size of about two, then the explanation may lie in social psychology or sociobiology rather than in the realm of economics.

4.4 Family Formation

To make sense of the trends in overall fertility, and to attempt to answer questions about future family size, we need to know more of the 'components' of the changes in annual births. Do they depend upon changes in the popularity of families of different sizes ('quantum') or the pace at which parents produce their children ('tempo')? Has fertility changed mostly because successive cohorts each grow up with their own characteristic attitude to childbearing ('cohort' effects), or do families respond in a more opportunistic way to the economic and social opportunities or problems of the moment ('period' effects)? With enough data, fertility trends can be separated into the components due to period and to cohort effects (Hobcraft, Menken, and Preston 1982, Ryder 1980). In general, period effects seem to be more important than used to be supposed in determining fertility (Brass 1974). Almost 60 per cent of the annual fertility rate change in the upturn and in the downturn of the US baby boom were due to tempo changes rather than changes in final family size (Ryder 1980). Final family size is strongly affected by the timing of the first birth (Brass 1974). Women who start having babies early end up with more babies than average, and this is the single most important statistical determinant of final family size (Kiernan 1987). For example, in the 1946 birth cohort, women who had their first child at age 15–19 went on to produce an average of 2.8 by age 36, compared to 1.9 children in all for mothers who had their first child between ages 28–30. So the socioeconomic factors affecting the timing of the first birth (see Thompson 1980) are important determinants of future fertility.

Fertility and age at maternity

In Victorian times, women frequently continued producing their large families into their 30s and even early 40s. Average age at last birth is about 40 years in populations not practising birth control. The fall in family size made childbearing a more youthful activity and the reduction in age at marriage from the late 1930s reduced the average age at first birth even further so that it reached a minimum of 23.8 from 1968 to 1970. Earlier marriage meant a great increase in teenage births in the 1960s, up to the time when average age at marriage increased (after 1972), when legitimate births to teenagers began to fall as well. Women giving birth at over age 30 began to be regarded by the medical profession as something of a curiosity. When marriage trends went into reverse from 1972, so did the pattern of fertility by age. Childbearing after age 40 is now almost extinct (1.31 per cent of births in 1988). But the 30s have become once again more popular for motherhood (figure 4.10).

Several factors have encouraged the fertility of women over age 30. Most married women now work. Professional women in particular need to establish their career before having children; a disproportionate number of mothers aged over 30 are in social class I or II. One in four marriages of women are remarriages, and these women (and their new husbands) often wish to start a family of their own. In 1988 only 8 per cent of legitimate children were born to remarried women, but they contributed 13 per cent of births to women aged 30–4 and 22 per cent of births to women aged 35–9.

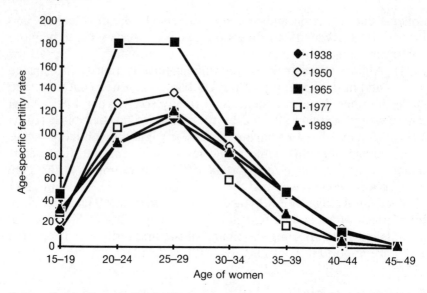

Sources: Registrar-General's Statistical Review 1938, 1950, 1965 Part II, t. EE(G); OPCS Birth Statistics Series FM1, t. 3.1*b*; *Population Trends*, 62, t. 9.

Fɪɢ. 4.10. Age-specific fertility rates, England and Wales, 1938–1989 (selected years)

As well as marrying later, women have been starting their families later in marriage. Family size has been 'squeezed' from both extremes of the age range: at older ages as a continuation of long-term trends away from large families; and more recently at younger ages as women have married, and started families, later in life. From the 1930s to about 1970 the median interval from marriage to first birth remained 20 months. In 1978 it had risen to 31 months, from which it has now declined a little, to 27 months in 1986 (see Werner 1988). The result has been a compression of childbearing into ages 22–30 to a degree never seen before; about two-thirds of all births (figure 4.10). Couples married in the 1930s took six years from the birth of their first child to the birth of their second, and almost ten years from the birth of their first to the birth of their third. Couples married in the early 1950s produced the same family sizes in 4 years and 7.4 years respectively (table 4.7).

Consequently, childbearing is concentrated within the first decade of married life (84 per cent of births within marriage in 1956–60, 92 per cent in 1976), and especially in the second half of the decade—33 per cent of births occurred in the fifth to the ninth years of marriage in 1976 compared to 26 per cent in 1951–5 (figure 4.11). The most popular time for a first child is the third year of marriage (41 per cent). Only 5 per

Table 4.7. Interval between marriage and last birth, and first and last birth, England and Wales, 1931–1960 (years)[a]

Year of marriage	2 children born by 1971		3 children born by 1971	
	marriage/ last birth	first birth/ last birth	marriage/ last birth	first birth/ last birth
1931–5	8.6	6.0	11.5	9.8
1936–40	8.1	5.0	10.9	8.7
1941–5	7.5	4.6	10.6	8.4
1946–50	7.1	4.5	10.2	8.2
1951–5	7.0	4.0	9.5	7.4
1956–60	6.1	3.4	7.8	6.0

[a] Women under 45, married once only.

Source: OPCS (1983*a*) 1971 Census fertility report, t. 7.3.

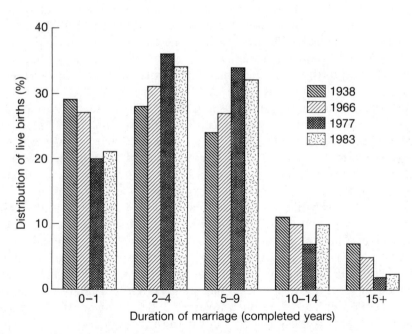

Note: Scale changes from years 5 to 9

Sources: OPCS Series Birth Statistics FM1 No. 13, t. 5.1, t. 5.5a.

Fig. 4.11. Live births by duration of marriage, England and Wales 1938–1985 (selected years)

cent of women want a child within the first year, and 12 per cent prefer to wait until after the fifth year of marriage. So there is still scope for further delay.

Pre-marital conceptions

Births in the first seven months of marriage are assumed to be pre-maritally conceived. Pre-marital conception is nothing new. Perhaps a third of first births in Victorian times were so conceived. In 1967, 26 per cent of first births were premaritally conceived. By 1976 this had fallen to 16 per cent where it remained without significant change up to 1986. Conceptions which in the 1960s might have precipitated a 'forced' marriage now either lead to abortion or, increasingly, to births in non-marital unions, concerning which more will be said later. More babies conceived pre-maritally are also being born to remarried women. Looking now at all legitimate births, not just first births, remarried women contributed 7 per cent of the 40,231 pre-maritally conceived births in 1976, 18 per cent of the 41,250 in 1986.

Over the last twenty years, trends in pre-marital conceptions, and the fate of those conceptions, have been complex. In the 1960s the number of pre-maritally conceived live births increased—not surprisingly at a time when sexual inhibitions were being cast off (Bone 1986). From 1964 to their peak in 1968 pre-marital conceptions increased 10 per cent (to 74,531) to comprise more than 10 per cent of legitimate births, even though total births were declining. The Abortion Act of 1967 changed that pattern and made it more useful to consider all the known conceptions outside marriage to observe their changing fate (figure 4.12). In 1970 there were 185,900 conceptions outside marriage—21.2 per cent of the total known. Then the most likely outcome (40 per cent) was a legitimate birth following the marriage of the parents. Twenty-four per cent were legally aborted, 36 per cent led to an illegitimate birth (OPCS 1984a). Since then extra-marital conceptions have increased sharply while all conceptions, and all births, have fallen. In 1987 40 per cent (337,100) of all conceptions occurred outside marriage. The proportion of such conceptions ending in illegitimate births (especially jointly registered) has greatly increased; up from 36 per cent in 1977 to about half (51 per cent) in 1987. Thirty-six per cent ended in legal abortion—less than in 1977. Only a minority (12 per cent) ended in legitimate birth (Werner 1982) following the marriage of the parents (OPCS 1987b)—down from 25 per cent in 1975. Pre-marital conception leads to larger than average family size, even when other factors are taken into consideration: 2.6 children compared with 2.3 in the 1946 cohort.

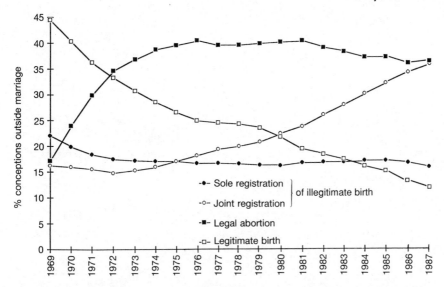

Sources: OPCS Birth Statistics Series FM1 No. 13, t. 12.5; OPCS Monitor FM1 87/2, t. 1.

FIG. 4.12. Conceptions outside marriage: percentage leading to maternities or abortions, 1969–1987

Parity and the distribution of family size

In the long run, the replacement or growth of population depends on the number of women who go on to have third or further babies. There is therefore considerable interest in the decision to have a third child. But final family size cannot be known until women are in their late 30s or well into their second decade of marriage. Seventy-four per cent of women who were married in 1900–9 who reached two children went on to have a third or more. By the marriages of 1925–9, this figure was halved. Birth-rates by the number of previous children (parity) are not routinely available because the appropriate denominators—the number of women by age and number of previous children—are not known without appropriate questions in the census (as in 1911, 1951, 1961, and 1971). But much can be inferred from statistics of births in any year to women who already have 0, 1, 2, etc. children (figure 4.13). The number of births to married women each year according to their parity is known, but not for unmarried women. The chances of going on to an additional baby from a given family size ('parity progression ratios') can be calculated from past data for women who have completed their families. They can only be estimated, with difficulty, from current data, as described in an earlier section (see Brass 1989).

Second babies have been least affected by the squeeze on fertility—

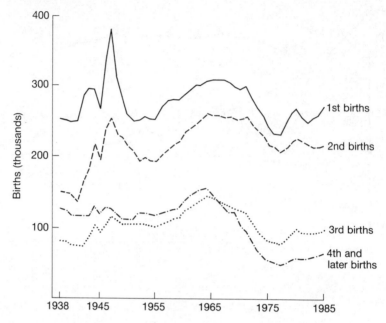

Note: These data refer to all births, not just births to married women. For details see source.

Source: OPCS (1987) Period and Cohort British Order Statistics Series FM1, No. 14, fig. 1.

Fig. 4.13. Live births by parity, all women, England and Wales, 1938–1985

the two-child family is more popular than ever. Between 1966 and 1976 34 per cent fewer babies were born. Births to women with 4 or 5 previous children fell by a precipitous 77 per cent and even third and further births were down by almost half (49 per cent). First births declined by less than average—26 per cent, while second births fell least of all, just 19 per cent. The large family becomes ever scarcer. But once families are committed to at least one child and all the disruptions of career and household which inevitably follow, they are then inclined to have the second child that most expect, and are expected, to produce.

The modest increase in births from 1977 to the late 1980s (11 per cent overall) has favoured first births and births of higher order (parity). Second births, having declined little, also recovered little, increasing by just 6 per cent. But third births increased by almost a quarter, and higher order births by 18 per cent. This indicates that some of the previous reduction was a slowing in tempo: a postponement, rather than an absolute decline, in family size. Many women have been delaying births for years. But births cannot be delayed forever—postponed births will eventually become cancellations. Some women decided to have their babies before they or their marriage became too old to begin or continue childbearing, as Eversley (1980) correctly forecast. Remarried women contributed a third to that increase in births. In 1977 13 per cent of births to women married once only were third births, but among remarried women 24 per cent of births were third births. Because of the increase in low parity births to remarried women, these proportions had converged by 1987, to 15 per cent and 16 per cent respectively. The high fertility of mothers born in the New Commonwealth also contributes particularly to higher order births (see Chapter 12).

These trends have concentrated family size on two children. In 1938 66 per cent of births were first or second births and 80 per cent were first to third. In the peak fertility years of 1961–5 the figures were very similar: 67 and 83 per cent respectively, even though 1938 was a period of 'low' fertility, 1961–5 of 'high' fertility. This shows the importance of timing of births in year-to-year marital fertility change rather than the final number. But by 1977 the shift towards lower order births was much more apparent; 81 per cent were first or second births, 94 per cent including third births. That year was the high point of the concentration of marital fertility on first and second births.

Despite the two-child family becoming the average this century, most women married since 1930 have not had two children: three-quarters had at least one child more or less than the average. This was particularly true of marriages earlier in the century (Glass and Grebenik 1954). Even in 1971, with one-child and large families more scarce, only 44 per cent of families were two-child families. It is only now, in the late 1980s, that half of all completed families will be two-child families (table 4.8). By the time they had reached age 36, with their fertility almost complete, 52 per cent of the mothers in the 1946 cohort of births had two children, 16 per cent just one, and 32 per cent three or more (Kiernan 1989c).

4.5   Socio-Economic Differentials and Trends in Fertility

Historical Background

So far we have discussed average fertility, ignoring differences of social class, education, and race. Social differentials in fertility which have emerged in the last century have powerful implications for population growth, social welfare, and political power. Ethnic differences are so striking that they are described separately in Chapter 12, although there are a few references in the text below. The censuses of 1911,

Table 4.8. Distribution of family size by year of marriage, England and Wales, 1911–1965

Year of marriage	Number of children								Total
	0	1	2	3	4	5	6	7 or more	
1911–15	139	193	224	159	102	64	42	77	1,000
1921–5	178	252	245	139	76	43	26	41	1,000
1931–5	175	270	266	143	70	35	18	23	1,000
1941–5	97	258	331	167	77	34	18	18	1,000
1951–5	112	179	334	197	100	42	20	16	1,000
1961–5	113	205	444	175	48	11	3	1	1,000

Note: Family size of some women married 1961–5 would not be completed by 1971.
Source: OPCS (1983*a*) Fertility report from the 1971 Census, t. 4.7 (p. 36).

1951, 1961, and 1971 are basic sources on social class patterns of fertility. More recently, information from the registration of births can be related to estimates of the social class distribution in the population derived from the General Household Survey and the Labour Force Survey. Before the rise of the West European marriage pattern the aristocracy married earlier and therefore had more children than others. But little is known about differentials within the commons. In many (but not all) traditional societies outside Western Europe where family planning is not practised, for example Bangladesh (Stoeckel and Chowdhury 1980) higher status rural women have more children than others. The underlying pattern in modern societies may be of this kind too (Becker 1981). According to this view, the preponderance of large families among the poor and ill-educated only persists today because their demographic transition is not yet complete, their higher fertility being due to unwanted births from poor family planning.

Social class and family planning

The early adoption of family planning by some groups of society before others in the nineteenth century created a gradient of family size by social class whereby lower social groups had higher average family size. This has come to be regarded as normal but it is now looking rather transient. Before the First World War there were big differences between social classes in the proportions of those who planned their families (see Chapter 2). But they were disappearing even before the

Table 4.9. Socio-economic group and family planning, Great Britain, 1983

Current methods of contraception usually used	All women aged 18–44, percentage using specified method Socio-Economic Group[a]							
	Professional	Employers, managers	Intermediate non-manual	Junior non-manual	Skilled/own account	Semi-skilled/personal service	Unskilled	All women
Pill	21	21	35	36	25	33	22	28
IUD	5	8	5	5	7	6	8	6
Condom	21	19	14	8	14	9	10	13
Cap	6	3	3	1	0	0	—	2
Withdrawal	2	3	4	3	6	4	5	5
Safe period	2	2	2	1	1	1	1	1
Go without, only method	1	1	1	4	1	2	1	2
Go without, and others	1	0	0	1	0	1	—	0
Foam etc.	1	1	0	0	1	0	—	1
Other	1	0	0	—	0	—	—	0
% using unreliable method[b]	7	7	7	9	9	8	5	8
% using at least one method	58	55	60	56	54	54	44	55

[a] Husband's SEG or own SEG if unmarried
[b] 'unreliable method' = any except pill, IUD, condom, cap.

Note: 0 = less than 0.5%; — = 0.

Source: General Household Survey 1983 (unpublished table FP 8B).

Second World War. Family planning is now general throughout society, although there are marked social differences in the popularity of different methods (table 4.9). Fertility is still not uniform. There remain some class differences in the proportion who take a more casual or a more planned approach to family building, and in the reliability of the methods which they use, and therefore in the proportion of unintended pregnancies. On top of that, there are class differences in desired, as well as in actual family size.

By the late 1960s 56 per cent of managerial and 52 per cent of other non-manual workers' wives then used reliable methods of contraception, while only 45 per cent of skilled manual workers' wives and 38 per cent of other manual workers' wives did so. 20 per cent of the wives of non-manual workers used less reliable methods (mostly withdrawal but also douching, the use of cap, or spermicide, only) compared with 26–30 per cent of the wives of manual workers. Since the 1960s pill use has changed radically. In 1967 only 13 per cent of the wives of unskilled workers used the pill. By 1973 this proportion had risen to 43 per cent. But over the same time the proportion of women in professional families using it remained steady. So by the 1970s the most effective method was used more by working-class wives (47 per cent of wives of skilled manual workers, 41 per cent of unskilled workers) than by the wives of non-manual workers (32 per cent of professionals, 44 per cent of skilled non-manual workers) (Cartwright 1978). By then many women in social class I (45 per cent) had given up the pill, compared to 39 per cent in class II and 28 per cent of the others. They were more likely to be aware of, or be deterred by, the health risks discussed earlier. Barrier methods such as the sheath came to be used more, not less, by wives with husbands in the professional and intermediate class (34 and 32 per cent) compared to skilled and unskilled manual (25–21 per cent).

Of the other contraceptive methods, the cap has remained almost exclusively a middle-class contraceptive, withdrawal predominantly a working-class practice, although now little used. The IUD and safe period are about equally unpopular in all classes. In Britain, as elsewhere, sterilization is becoming the most important means of family limitation among all classes. Male sterilization is more normal among middle-class couples; among working-class couples it is more the wives' responsibility (General Household Survey 1984). Despite this growing equality of method of contraception, in the 1970s about 20 per cent of the wives of non-manual workers, 27 per cent of the wives of skilled manual workers, and 47 per cent of the wives of unskilled manual workers said their last pregnancy was unintended (Dunnell 1979).

More recent data of this type are not available, as Dunnell's was the most recent major survey of family formation.

Askham's study in Aberdeen (1975) showed that much of the high fertility of parents of larger than average families (four plus children) was unwanted. The higher the social class (from V to IIIM) the more likely the extra children were to be described as being unwanted. The parents of small families knew much more about sex, contraception, and family building and had talked much more about them before marriage. The large families in class V were born of ignorance and fear of sex and contraception, and of reluctance to discuss them by parents. Disapproval of contraception too, and not just ignorance, was a powerful factor. Attitudes were different: high fertility families were less concerned for the future, had little faith in their ability to control their own life, and little ambition.

Material circumstances seemed to condition these responses. High fertility families in social class V enjoyed much less financial security than the low fertility families in class III. They had less secure and frequently changing employment, more marital problems, and less adequate accommodation. The low fertility families in social class III had courted for a long time, decided carefully about marriage, moved house seldom, and tended to be upwardly mobile in their jobs.

The present pattern of family size by social class

For some decades now the lowest average fertility has been found, not at the top of the social scale, but among families where the husband is in social class IIIN (clerical workers, clerks, salesmen). On each side of the class scale, fertility then rises. Even in the census of 1951 average family size where the husband was in social class I was 1.57 children compared to 1.48 for social class II. But 1961 social class II fertility was almost as high as that of class III, while that of IV and V—semi-skilled and unskilled workers—had fallen by a tenth or more. By 1971 this J-shaped curve was long established (table 4.10), with fertility lowest in social class IIIN and still highest in social class V. As might be expected, fertility is related to social class based on women's own occupation in more linear fashion. Average family size at age 36 among the 1946 birth cohort of women was 2.0 among women in social class I increasing to 2.7 among women in social class V. During the declining fertility of the 1970s, social classes I and V moved even closer together, as fertility of the latter fell faster (Pearce and Britton 1977, Werner 1985). In the aggregate, social class differences in fertility are

Table 4.10. Social class differences in average fertility, 1971

Period of marriage	Husband's social class						
	I	II	IIIN	IIIM	IV	V	All
1941–5	2.04	1.99	1.86	2.20	2.24	2.47	2.14
1946–50	2.11	2.02	1.90	2.24	2.29	2.57	2.19
1951–5	2.25	2.17	2.00	2.34	2.36	2.66	2.29
1956–60	2.23	2.12	2.00	2.29	2.31	2.58	2.25
1961–5	1.80	1.76	1.66	1.89	1.93	2.14	1.85
1966–70	0.60	0.66	0.62	0.85	0.92	1.05	0.79
All periods	1.75	1.81	1.62	1.95	2.03	2.26	1.91
All periods, by woman's class	1.45	1.61	1.35	1.65	1.95	2.39	1.70

Note: Fertility of recent marriage cohorts, especially 1966–70, is incomplete at 1971. 'Inadequately described' and 'others' omitted from table.

Sources: OPCS (1983*a*) Fertility Report from the 1971 Census OPCS Series DS no. 5, t. 5.7, t. 5.30. OPCS (1979) Census 1971 Fertility Tables, vol. ii, t. 24.

diminishing. In the 1946 birth cohort, their effects were mediated mostly through differences in timing of first birth, the significance of which was underlined above (Kiernan 1987). It is important to remember that we are talking about averages; families of all sizes can be found in all social classes, but in different proportions.

The shape of families is determined by parents' decisions to start, space, and stop their childbearing. Patterns of starting and spacing, and of the distribution of family size, differ more by social class than does the simple average. Despite lower average fertility and a later start, fewer women in social class I and II end up childless than in class IV and V, and one-child families are least common in these two highest classes (figure 4.14). Higher fertility in class I and II than in IIIN is therefore due to the relative rarity of families with just one child or none. Family size in class I and II is concentrated on two- and three-child families more than in any other class. The two-child 'norm' is a middle-class norm. Families above three children, and less than two, are more frequent in the manual social classes, especially class V. Manual workers have higher average fertility because they are more likely to have big families, not because they avoid having really small ones. Forty-one per cent of wives of manual workers married in 1955–60 have at least four children compared to 29 per cent in the non-manual group.

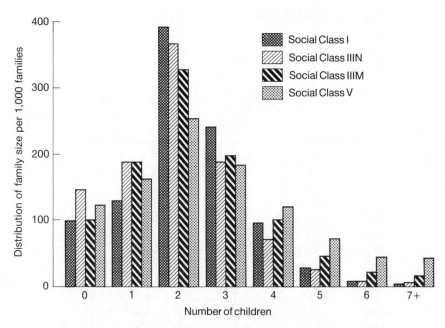

Sources: OPCS 1983*a*, Fertility Report from the 1971 Census, Series DS No. 5, t. 5.11.

Fig. 4.14. Distribution of family size per 1,000 by social class of husband 1971

Social class differences in age at marriage and timing of births

Middle-class couples marry 2–3 years later than working-class couples (see Chapter 5). They also start their families two years later after marriage. As a consequence wives in social class I and II in 1986 produced their first child when they were more than four years older than wives in social class IV and V. From the 1930s until the 1970s the average couple's first baby arrived about twenty months after their marriage. But from 1971 to 1979 the gap widened to thirty months. Brides with husbands in social class I had their first baby on average thirty-two months after marriage in 1971, but waited a full year later (to forty-four months) in 1979, a delay of 38 per cent (table 4.11). In 1975, women with husbands in social class V gave birth for the first time a mere nine months after marriage, as at most times in the past. A high proportion of these births were pre-maritally conceived, also as at most times in the past. Now this interval has increased to thirteen months.

Much of this shift is due to the reduction in pre-marital conceptions, which used to be a major precipitating factor in marriage (Britton 1980). In 1971 47 per cent of first births in social class V, compared with

Table 4.11. Social class differences in median birth intervals, 1970–1987

Year of birth	Social class of father				
	All social classes	I and II	IIIN	IIIM	IV and V
Median interval from first marriage to first birth (months)					
1970	19	29	26	19	13
1973	24	33	30	22	15
1977	29	40	36	27	19
1980	29	41	37	25	18
1983	29	39	34	27	20
1987	27	35	31	25	18
Mean age of mothers at any legitimate birth (years)					
1970	26.5	28.1	26.3		25.7
1973	26.4	28.0	26.9	25.9	25.5
1977	26.8	28.7	27.5	26.2	25.5
1980	27.1	29.1	27.6	26.4	25.5
1983	27.5	29.5	28.0	26.8	26.0
1987	28.1	29.9	28.4	27.4	26.5
Mean age of mothers at first legitimate birth (years)					
1970	23.9	25.9	23.7		22.6
1973	24.3	26.3	25.3	23.7	22.7
1977	25.0	27.2	25.9	24.2	23.2
1980	25.2	27.5	26.0	24.4	23.1
1983	25.6	27.9	26.2	24.8	23.7
1987	26.5	28.4	27.0	25.8	24.5

Notes: Social classes IIIN and IIIM not separated in 1970.
Sources: Werner 1985, t. 6; OPCS Birth Statistics 1987 Series FM1 no. 16, t. 11.3, 11.4.

7 per cent in class I, were pre-maritally conceived. This difference is now smaller—in 1988 10.2 per cent of first marital births to women with fathers in class I and II were pre-maritally conceived, compared with 24.1 per cent in class IV and V. Ten per cent of all births in 1988 in classes I and II, and 30 per cent to classes IV and V occurred illegitimately but within informal unions (as inferred from the joint registration of their birth) (see Werner 1985). If pre-marital conceptions are eliminated from the calculation, the social class gradient in the duration of time from marriage to first birth is only half as steep as before, from forty-five months in social class I to twenty-four months in class V. In

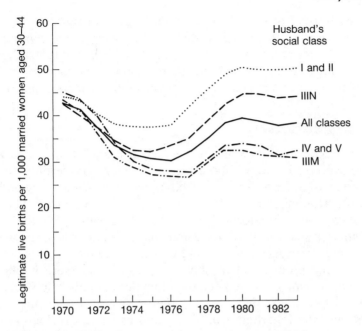

Sources: Werner 1985, fig. 3, p. 9.

Fig. 4.15. Legitimate fertility rates age 30 and over by social class of husband, England and Wales, 1970–1983

these respects, as in many others, there seems to be a sharp difference between the behaviour of social class V and the rest of the population.

Young age at marriage powerfully increases the fertility of working-class women, but it has less effect on the fertility of middle-class women. In 1971 social class I women who married under age 20 had on average 1.96 children, declining to 1.23 (63 per cent of the average for teenage marriage) for women married at age 30–44. Outside class I and II the fertility gradient with age at marriage is steeper; more like a natural fertility decline. In class IIIM the equivalent decline by age is from 2.33 to 1.00 (43 per cent), and in class V 2.69 to 1.11 (41 per cent). Social class differences in fertility are little evident in women who marry between ages 25 to 29. Among women married over age 30, women in class I and II have more babies than the average. In the 1980s, age-specific fertility rates in class I over age 25 were the highest of any group (figure 4.15).

The average number of children being born to middle-class couples has held up much more than in working-class families, and these children are now also born consistently later in marriage. Women in middle-class occupations have more qualifications to acquire and more of a career structure to protect than women in manual or routine jobs. It is more important for them to defer their childbearing and to compress it into a short space of time in their married life. This means that although fewer remain childless in the end, more non-manual couples are still childless compared to manual workers even after ten years of marriage.

The social origins of children

Victorian eugenists and biometricians such as Francis Galton and Karl Pearson expressed concern about higher working-class fertility and its supposed consequences for social welfare and national average ability. The Royal Commission (1949, Chapter 15) while uncertain that the trend of 'national intelligence' really was downwards, felt that 'it is clearly undesirable for the welfare and cultural standards of the nation that our social arrangements should be such as to induce those in the higher income groups and the better educated and more intelligent within each income group to keep their families not only below replacement level but below the level of others'. Arguments on the measurement and the inheritance of ability and its social distribution (see Mascie-Taylor 1990) remained hot issues in the 1950s and 1960s. Sir Keith Joseph, when Secretary of State for the Social Services, revived the controversy in 1972 by attributing the persistence of some social problems to the high fertility of least educated girls.

At least one of the trends behind the argument is now reversed. Annual data on the social class origin of births, routinely available since 1970, have highlighted a startling shift in the relative contribution which each social class has made to each birth cohort and therefore to each future generation (table 4.12). In 1970 only 22 per cent of births within marriage occurred in social class I or II families. By 1982, the proportion had reached 32 per cent, in 1988 it was the same (32 per cent). This trend has been driven both by shifts in fertility and in the distribution of occupations. There has been a long-term move away from manual and less skilled occupations towards skilled, service, and professional jobs (Werner 1985, Boston 1984, Routh 1987). Its implications are explored further in Chapter 13. During the fall in fertility in the 1970s, all legitimate births fell by 24 per cent between 1970 and 1975, and a further 3.4 per cent by 1985. Births in manual workers' families, particularly to women in class IV and V, fell by a third. Births to routine non-manual workers families (IIIN) fell by roughly the national average. But women with husbands in class I and II did not share in this decline at all.

This shift in the distribution of births between classes ceased in

Table 4.12. Social class differences in numbers of legitimate births, 1970–1986

(*a*) *Thousands*

Year	I & II	IIIN	IIIM	IV & V	Other	All
1971	154.7	75.3	297.9	160.1	29.5	717.5
1976	140.8	55.5	204.6	110.2	19.4	530.5
1981	163.3	60.4	198.2	111.4	20.1	553.5
1986	160.1	55.2	179.5	101.1	23.8	519.7
1986[a]	13.3	5.8	38.3	31.8	—	89.1

(*b*) *Figures expressed as a percentage of all legitimate births in each year (omitting 'other')*

Year	I & II	IIIN	IIIM	IV & V	All
1971	22	11	43	23	100
1976	28	11	40	22	100
1981	31	11	37	21	100
1986	32	11	36	20	100
1986[a]	15	7	43	36	100

[a] Jointly registered illegitimate births in 1986.

Note: The 1981 and 1986 figures are based on different occupation definitions and thus are not strictly comparable with the earlier figures. Percentages may not sum to 100 because of rounding.

Sources: OPCS Birth Statistics 1977, Series FM1 No. 4; OPCS Birth Statistics 1988, Series FM1 No. 15.

the 1980s. But it had already made a difference in the balance of class origins of future generations. In 1971, for example, there were about 224,000 births to fathers in non-manual groups, compared to 469,000 to 'manual' fathers—a ratio of 1 : 2.1. But by 1980, 'non-manual births' remained almost the same—226,000; 'manual' births had fallen to 333,000—a ratio of 1 : 1.5. In 1988 the respective numbers were 222,500 and 269,000—a ratio of 1 : 1.2 (OPCS 1990). It must be remembered that these statistics refer to legitimate births and omit the 26 per cent (in 1988) of births which are illegitimate. In a high proportion of these cases the occupation of father or mother's chief economic supporter, where known, is manual (particularly social class V). In 1983, 76 per cent of the 61,000 illegitimate births which were jointly registered by both parents had fathers in manual occupations; 34 per cent were in social class V (see Werner 1985). If allowance is made for such births, the proportion of births in 1986 with fathers in social classes I and II falls to 29.6 per cent. Births registered by the mother only cannot be assigned to a social class, but the Longitudinal Study showed that 73 per cent of teenage illegitimate births in 1970–4 occurred to women where the 'chief economic supporter' (usually father) was a manual worker; 13 per cent in social class V (Werner 1989).

The shifts in legitimate fertility by social class match shifts in family intentions. In the 1940s and 1950s working-class women expected to have more babies than middle-class women. These preferences and expectations are now reversed (table 4.4), and seem to offer further evidence in support of Becker's view that the better-off will eventually have more children than others. Social class patterns of 'ideal' family size were rather uniform in the 1960s (Woolf 1971). But when couples were asked how many children they were likely to have in reality, bigger social class differences became apparent. Manual workers' expectations of family size had fallen, managerial workers' expectations had risen since 1945. Women born in 1935–9 with 'non-manual' fathers expected 2.10 children compared to 2.52 for women with 'manual' fathers. Women born in 1955–9 with non-manual fathers expected rather more children (2.44 to 2.12) than women from manual backgrounds, and the new difference is maintained in the most recent cohorts (General Household Survey).

Married women at work

Aid with child care may be essential to help women combine work with childrearing. Access to it varies by social class. Pre-school facilities in general are mostly used by children of middle-class parents. The cheap care provided by childminders is mostly patronized by poorer mothers, especially African and West Indian mothers. In a sample of 5-year-olds in 1975, only 8 per cent of children with fathers in class I had no pre-school experience, compared to 43 per cent of children with fathers in class V. In 1980 there were places in all these institutions, plus childminders, for only 4 per cent of the 0–4 age-group. Up to a third of mothers using such facilities have no job, except for day nurseries where 60–70 per cent of the mothers are employed (Osborn, Butler, and Morris 1984). Only the relatively few places at these institutions provide full-time care, particularly for single mothers.

Full-time employment may be less of a deterrent to childbearing if mothers can pay for personal child care. Only women in class II and (especially) class I are likely to have the accommodation, income, and confidence to employ any kind of residential domestic service: au pairs, housekeepers, or nannies. Their services may not be essential to the ability of school teachers to combine children with employment; they may be to business women and barristers, and more so to divorced or single working women. At high income levels, the ability to buy child care may make women more, not less likely to have more children as their income rises still further (Ermisch 1988). Whatever the truth of it, mean family size by class of employed women varies more than men's. Women who are themselves in professional jobs (class I) have lower fertility than women with jobs in class II, whereas the wives of men in social class I have higher fertility than the wives of men in social class II. Perhaps the remarkable thing is that married women who are professionals in their own right have any children at all; a high proportion certainly stay unmarried. The general importance of child care in supporting the fertility of married women is recognized by those countries which have policies to encourage fertility. In Britain the government has allowed tax relief for child care provided by employers, to encourage women to return to the work-force to compensate for the missing teenagers of the 1990s (Chapter 13).

Education and fertility

In general, people with more education have fewer children, partly because they marry later. The two censuses of 1951 and 1961 both asked the age at which education had been completed ('terminal age of education'). This question was not repeated in 1971; it has the drawback that most of the population give the minimum age, which itself has changed over time. But since 1961 a question has been asked to list all educational qualifications, and the General Household Survey and the cohort studies now provide additional information.

As might be expected women who left school at the minimum age had the largest families, but the best educated were next in line. Furthermore, between 1951 and 1961 the fertility of better educated women increased relative to the less educated, amidst a general decline of family size, in parallel with the social class changes. The trend according to educational qualifications from 1961 to 1971 shows a similiar pattern. In the 1970s the average family size of graduate women at the time of interview (1.53) was considerably lower than the fertility of women with no further education (2.04) (Cartwright 1978) and they were likely to be childless.

But when graduate women do marry, beyond age 20 their fertility is higher than that of other women—in 1971 5 per cent higher among graduate women married at age 20–2 ½ rising irregularly to 41 per cent higher for graduates married at age 35–9. Graduates are least likely to have just one child or four children and over. Graduate husbands are less likely to be childless in their marriages than are graduate wives.

This apparent paradox arises because 52 per cent of graduate wives have graduate husbands, while only 31 per cent of graduate husbands have graduate wives. Dual graduate couples have the highest fertility of all, if family size up to four children only is considered. As with social class, the effects of the wife's education predominate over those of the husband (OPCS 1983*a*).

The cohort studies underline how far qualifications, ability, and family history determine the age at which childbearing starts (Kiernan and Diamond 1982). In the 1946 cohort the less able (measured at age 11) and women with no qualifications start having babies earlier and are also more likely to go on to have third and higher order births and have them at shorter intervals. At the other extreme, women still child-less at age 32 were more likely to be from a professional background with few brothers or sisters, and with mothers who themselves married late, and to have more than average personal ambition and parental interest. Educated women have fewer unwanted babies; they are more likely to use family planning methods. Even by the 1970s, fewer university educated women took the contraceptive pill—just 21 per cent compared to 43 per cent of other women. Forty-eight per cent of university educated women used the sheath compared to 27 per cent of the rest. Graduates were better aware of the health hazards associated with the pill—even though the alternatives they had taken up were less reliable.

Fertility and housing tenure

The fertility difference between council tenants and owner-occupiers is one of the biggest of any between major social groups (table 4.13). In the 1976 Family Formation survey, family size of council tenants was almost one child (0.84) more than owner-occupiers (Murphy and Sullivan 1985). The distribution of the fertility of council tenants was different: three times as many—almost a third in all—had four children or more, higher than the average manual working-class pattern. A higher proportion also had only one child, but that is primarily due to the very high proportion of divorced women in this tenure (in the 1946 birth cohort, 32 per cent of women who were council tenants were divorced by age 36). Almost half the girls married in their teens and who were occupying council houses in their mid-20s had conceived their first birth before marriage (47 per cent), compared to 30 per cent of owner-occupiers, 14 per cent renting privately, and 9 per cent who were still living with parents (Kiernan 1980*b*). In that cohort, council tenants have their first child much sooner after marriage than

Table 4.13. Fertility and housing tenure, Great Britain, 1977

(*a*) *Average number of live births in current marriage to married women aged 40–4 in 1977*

	Housing Tenure				
	Owner-occupied	Local authority	Private furnished	Private unfurnished	All
Women in first marriage	2.11	2.95	(1.67)	2.26	2.37
Remarried women	0.75	0.78	(0.50)	(0.13)	0.67
All married women	2.02	2.71	(1.20)	1.95	2.22

Note: ( ) = sample size less than 10.

(*b*) *Family size distribution of married women aged 40–4*

Live births	Owner-occupied (%)	Local Authority (%)	Private rented (%)
0	13	10	22
1	17	13	22
2	38	26	20
3	23	22	25
4 or more	9	29	12

(*c*) *Birth interval ever-married women aged 40–9*

Housing tenure	Interval marriage—first birth (months)	Average number of live births	Average age at marriage
Owner-occupied	27	2.29	23.4
Local authority	17	2.89	21.7
Private rented	24	2.51	22.2

Source: Murphy and Sullivan 1985, t. 2.3.

owner occupiers (median interval thirteen months compared with thirty months) and also have their third births much sooner after their second.

It is not just a question of social class. All social classes are to be found in all tenure groups, although to a very unequal degree, and tenure differences still hold within social classes and categories of education (Murphy and Sullivan 1985). Owner-occupiers in different social classes have similar achieved family size and intended family size, although among council tenants, family size differs more according to social class (Cartwright 1976).

Tenure brings together many influences under one roof. It combines together the effects of both parents' social class, occupation, and attitudes, in a common physical and social environment. It divides the population into just three substantial, although unequal sections—in 1989 66 per cent of households were owner-occupiers, 24 per cent rented from a local authority, 6 per cent rented privately, 2 per cent from a housing association.

Many tenure effects are selective—many council tenants have no other choice of home. The elderly, unemployed, the less skilled, single-parent families, larger families are all concentrated in council tenure because it is the only form of tenure to which they may have easy access. Partners who divorce are more likely to end up as local authority tenants even if they were previously owner-occupiers (Holmans, Nandy, and Brown 1987).

However, the concentration of people with particular demographic characteristics is clearly not just a selective effect. For example, fertility differences persist within each tenure after the initial selection effects, partly independently of social class (Fox 1982). Council tenants are also more likely to become divorced. The housing itself is unlikely to provide the reason. There are more physical constraints in council housing than in owner-occupied housing in terms of bedrooms and size, but these are minor compared to the restrictions in the private rented sector. The physical difference between average (purpose built) local authority houses (not flats) and owner-occupied houses is small; private rented accommodation is much more likely, and owner-occupied housing slightly more likely, to be sub-standard. Twenty per cent of council properties (mostly flats) lack gardens and a high proportion are three floors or more from the ground, which is rare in private accommodation. But most of these factors might be expected to depress, not to enhance, fertility. More council households have no earner at all, or three or more earners. There are many fewer two-earner households, so the 'housewife effect' may be important. Clustering of high fertility families, and geographical and social isolation of some estates, may be important too. The ethnic factor was relatively unimportant as until recently immigrants have been under-represented in local authority accommodation. West Indians now comprise an increasing proportion of tenants in urban estates.

Instead, the strategies suitable for obtaining housing of different tenures appear to encourage differences in family formation, especially early fertility or its postponement. Owner-occupiers tend to delay childbearing because they face heavy housing costs at the beginning of their marriage. They may have to save before they marry, and both may need to stay in work for as long as possible. Council tenants (or intending council tenants) do not face such a cost problem because rents are low (1988 average with rates £20) and may be paid in part or whole by Housing Benefit (65 per cent of tenants). Instead they face a rationing problem, where priority is awarded according to assess- ment of 'need'. Accordingly they may marry early and begin a family quickly; that will increase their chances of being allocated a council house through the points system, even though it reduces their chances of buying or renting privately (Ineichen 1979a).

The 1977 Housing (Homeless Persons) Act (now consolidated in the 1985 Housing Act) responds to pregnancy of single women by giving them priority for rehousing by the local authority. Previously those living with their parents would have been expected to continue living there. Fourteen per cent of those accepted as statutorily homeless in 1989 were pregnant women (DoE 1990). The proportion of unmarried mothers living with their parents declined from 49 per cent in 1973–5 to 30 per cent in 1983–4, with a corresponding increase in those living in their own home from 36 to 59 per cent over the same period. This is believed to be a consequence of the legislation (Kiernan 1989b). Some small-scale surveys suggest that some young girls do indeed become or remain pregnant with this in mind, but the impact at the national level is not known (see Murphy 1989).

Tenure differences may also reflect differences in lifestyle and at- titudes. Family 'clans' could develop on old-established estates (Young and Willmott 1954) and help with mutual support with children and a consolidation of lifestyle. These close contacts in urban working-class life may have been a twentieth-century creation of local authority tenure (Anderson 1983). It has often been claimed that especially in large, newer urban estates, residents have little ability to control their personal environment, the state of repair of their flat or its surround- ings (Power 1988). Some urban estates, partly as a result of allocation policies, are effectively one-class areas with few examples of success, clearly labelled by their architecture and appearance as distinct from the rest of society. Their residents are heavily dependent upon others in most aspects of their lives and unaccustomed to taking action to change their own condition or to the belief that it is possible. Some communal aspects of the design make these problems worse (Coleman 1985). The importance of apathy and fatalism behind high fertility has been mentioned earlier, but in the absence of specific research, any connection between attitudes on council estates and fertility must remain speculative.

Tenure differences may become sharper in time as the proportion of households in each tenure changes. The privately rented sector is declining fast, marginalized after seventy-five years of rent controls and other restrictions, although the present government seeks to change and revive it through partial deregulation. Just before the First World War over 90 per cent of households rented privately. In 1939 58 per cent were still doing so. By 1985 the figure was just 8 per cent. Council tenure, almost non-existent in 1914, grew to a maximum of 34 per cent of households in 1980 and has since declined to 24 per cent, plus 2 per cent of households which rent from housing associations. Government policy since 1979 has encouraged the sale of council homes to more than a million tenants (Daunton 1987). If these policies continue council tenure may decline to 20 per cent, or less if present government policy to transfer whole estates to other landlords or to their tenants succeeds. Seventy per cent home ownership by the end of the century seems inevitable (Morgan Grenfell Economics 1987). Councils may eventually cease to be major landlords (Coleman 1989a) and this dimension of fertility differences will have to be analysed in new ways. If the tenure effects are in part causal, not just selective, and if the new housing association or private landlords operate a different rent and allocation regime, then family formation patterns among tenants may change in consequence.

5 Marriage, Divorce, and Remarriage

5.1 Why Marriage Matters

New images of marriage

Three old images of marriage have became obsolete in the twentieth century. The first is that marriage confers on a woman a secure, settled income and a status and role based on children and housekeeping around which most of the rest of her life revolves. The second is that marriage lasts for the rest of an increasingly long life. The third is that marriage is the setting for almost all childbearing and sexual cohabitation. New ideas, new economic roles for women, new laws, and especially family planning have changed all that. Small family size has given decades of adult life back to women. Many have used it to go back to work. As a result they are more independent of men inside the home, and can compete with them on more even terms outside it. Now that contraception has taken the waiting out of wanting for sex, some of the other advantages of married life also seem less clear. Births outside marriage are more common than at any time in recent history. The welfare state has narrowed the gap between single and married states by assuming some of the financial role of the husband.

With or without childbearing, cohabitation is a common preliminary to marriage, especially to remarriage (Brown and Kiernan 1981) and is to some extent a replacement for it. Divorce is now threatening to end one marriage in three. It is a potent force behind the increase in the number of new households and homelessness. And although remarriage is retarded by cohabitation, younger divorced people have higher marriage rates than single people, indeed many divorce in order to remarry. Remarriage, now one wedding in three, is creating new patterns of family life and relationships between step-siblings and step-parents, now made complicated, unlike those of the past, by the presence of former partners. So our conventional picture of marriage and family life needs to be redrawn. This chapter will explore these trends and their implications.

Marriage and Ferility

Marriage is not a demographic fact like birth and death. Its paramount demographic importance follows from its being the chief setting for fertility. Malthus regarded the timing of marriage as the chief preventive check against excessive and untimely fertility, at a time when illegitimacy was for the most part avoided. On the whole Malthus was right, at least up to the nineteenth century, in believing that population movements were determined more by fertility than by mortality change, that fertility change was determined mostly by responses in the marriage rate, and that in turn these depended on prevailing economic circumstances, or those of the relatively recent past (Wrigley and Schofield 1981, see Chapter 1). Although new modes of industrial production weakened the link between population growth and marriage by the end of the nineteenth century (see Glass 1938), none the less late marriage, until the last years of that century, continued to moderate fertility for most families (see Chapter 2). The timing of marriage still has a powerful effect upon trends in fertility in industrial countries, even though family planning within marriage has been generally practised for half a century (table 4.6).

A two-child family was becoming normal by the 1930s. But couples did not take the opportunity which they could have done of marrying much earlier and delaying children within marriage. Instead, although age at marriage declined from the late 1930s, the average interval between marriage and first birth remained remarkably constant until the early 1970s (table 4.11). This is because marriage is not just a decision taken on its own merits, and on the balance of its own advantages. It carries the implication of imminent childbearing (Busfield and Paddon 1977). For most people marriage is a public declaration of intent to begin childbearing, or at least to accept the risk of it. Childbearing is not an accidental consequence of a marriage entered into for a variety of other reasons. Childlessness increases consistently with age at first marriage, surprisingly, even between teenagers and women marrying in their early 20s, where physiological factors are unlikely to be important. Factors associated with delayed marriage may be associated with a low inclination towards childbearing (Kiernan 1989a). In so far as that is true, the timing of marriage depends on the decision to accept childbearing, much as it used to in the pre-family planning era. This is what makes the increase in the interval between marriage and first birth, and the rise of cohabitation, so interesting. For while it is clear that some couples reject marriage but still have children, cohabitation in England, if not elsewhere, is still predominantly child free.

One birth in four now occurs outside marriage. If illegitimate births continue their rapid increase, marriage will become less central to the study of fertility trends. Up to 73 per cent of the illegitimate births of the 1980s were jointly registered, by parents who gave the same address and were inferred to be cohabiting (see Haskey and Coleman 1986, and Chapter 4). The term 'common law' marriage is sometimes applied to such households, as it was in the past (Laslett 1972). But the term has no meaning in law, although it has been argued in the courts that financial protection should be afforded to partners of cohabiting unions which are breaking up.

These illegitimate births clearly fall into a different social context from births occurring to single women with no relationship with the father. Many of the parents of such children subsequently marry. How many is not known, but 50 per cent of (previously unmarried) couples who were married in 1988 lived together before their marriage, and 74 per cent of couples marrying for a second time (GHS 1989). The legitimation of illegitimate births rose in the 1970s to about three-fifths of such births, although this rising trend has now stopped. Strictly speaking births within marriage where the father is not the husband are also illegitimate and a few are recorded as such every year. The great majority presumably pass unrecorded, although the much quoted figure (derived from blood typing in Sussex maternity wards), that a tenth of the babies there had blood groups incompatible with that of their fathers, is now put down to careless blood-typing procedures, rather than to careless sexual zeal in the south of England.

Divorce, remarriage, and fertility

Marriage has become much more interesting now that it is so likely to fail, not the least because of the effects of divorce on fertility. When divorce was relatively infrequent, occurred late in marriage, and might not easily be followed by a remarriage, it was assumed to reduce fertility compared with that of a marriage left intact. But frequent and early divorce and its succession by remarriage or cohabitation may be changing all that. When couples divorce and remarry in their late 20s and 30s they usually want to start a second family, in part to affirm their new relationship, and have what may often be a third or fourth child. A high and growing proportion of high-parity births now come from remarried women (Chapter 4). Large family size (four or more) may also make marriage breakdown more likely (Kiernan 1986). Modern divorce, here, in the USA, and West Germany may now have a posit-ive effect upon fertility, through the numbers of third births at pre-viously unfashionable ages over 30, when divorced people marry a new partner. And when couples divorce in their late 30s or 40s, they are likely to have already completed their families from their first marriage.

The cohort of births in 1946 being followed up by the MRC longitudinal study show strong effects of broken marriage on family size distribution. Women with broken marriages are much more likely to be childless, to stop at one child, or conversely go on to have three or more children by age 36. Thirty-eight per cent of women childless at that age, and a third of all the women who had stopped at one child, had broken marriages (and for the most part had not remarried). The result was that 52 per cent of teenage brides with intact marriages had two children compared with 32 per cent of teenage brides with broken marriages. Twenty-three per cent of the latter had only one child or no children compared with 11 per cent of the women in intact marriages, and 45 per cent had three or more compared with 37 per cent of those in intact marriages (Kiernan 1986). Average family size was 2.6 among women with broken marriages, compared with 2.3 for women in intact marriages. These women married in their teens. The fertility advantage will decline among women married at later ages. In the United States, such children themselves tend to marry sooner and have children sooner, following the model of their parents.

In some respects this is demographic *déjà vu*. In the eighteenth century marriages were almost as frequently broken: remarriage, a series of families, and a complexity of step-relationships were commonplace. But then it was mortality, not divorce that ended marriages. It was widows and widowers who remarried, often quite young, and gave step-parents to their children and step-children to their spouses (Laslett 1972). Not unreasonably, we are comparing our present to the recent past; to the golden 1930s and 1950s of secure marriage which was little threatened by high mortality or high divorce rates. But this period, far from being normal, may have been a transient conjuncture born of a unique combination of circumstances, an unrepeatable combination of late marriage, low illegitimacy, low fertility, and long survival of marriages (Anderson 1983). Remarriages of one or both parties now account for one in three marriages, and one in ten births. Less than seven children in ten start life with the 'normal' pattern of legitimate birth in a first marriage—and fewer still survive their childhood in that conventional state.

Marriage, household, and society

The social significance of marriage is immense: it is still the usual way in which adults of opposite sex live together, the foundation and origin of most households, and of much support between individuals across generations, including inheritance. Marital choice in an open society is

Table 5.1. Proportions ever-married, England and Wales 1901–1987 (per 1,000 of relevant age-group)

(a) Men

	16–19	20–4	25–9	30–4	35–9	40–4	45–9	50–4	55–9	60–4
1901	4	174	550	746	826	860	884	896	913	910
1921	5	178	555	769	837	863	876	885	894	900
1951	6	237	651	810	867	892	902	913	923	921
1961	13	309	706	826	868	892	904	912	915	920
1971	26	364	739	861	889	892	900	913	918	922
1981	12	251	654	830	886	906	910	906	909	920
1988	6	149	497	767	859	898	912	919	914	915

(b) Women

	16–19	20–4	25–9	30–4	35–9	40–4	45–9	50–4	55–9	60–4
1901	17	274	590	743	800	832	857	871	878	889
1921	22	273	590	740	796	821	833	841	845	848
1951	55	482	783	854	867	858	849	850	844	844
1961	82	580	844	890	902	903	895	877	862	857
1971	109	601	867	922	930	929	922	917	904	885
1981	57	455	802	911	940	947	943	935	927	921
1988	34	307	671	859	919	946	952	950	942	933

Sources: Census tables England and Wales 1901–81. OPCS Marriage and Divorce Statistics Series FM2 no. 15, t. 1.1b.

a definitive expression not just of personal taste but also of notions of eligibility and acceptability of individuals from different social classes, ethnic groups, and religious affiliations, and thereby of the structure of a society and its development. Its geographical extent is a measure of day-to-day mobility, of the individual's knowledge of his surroundings (Shannon and Nystuen 1972, Morrill and Pitts 1967) of the isolation of communities past and present (Ogden 1973, Dennis 1977) or even of their genetical structure (Coleman 1982). Marriage is one of the few ways of measuring society's internal boundaries. These may not all be demographic concerns, but demographic statistics can measure them.

5.2 Marriage

Trends in marriage

Victorian bachelors and spinsters married late–about 28 and 26 years of age respectively, as they had in previous centuries. About one in ten men and one in seven women never married at all (table 5.1). In the first half of this century, especially until the 1930s, young women's marriage chances suffered from a particularly unfavourable sex ratio (table 5.2) arising from heavy male emigration, a modest mortality advantage over men, and a constantly increasing number of births. The last always favours men's choice, as men usually marry women 2–3 years younger than themselves, who therefore have come from a more numerous cohort.

Table 5.2. Sex ratio, England and Wales, 1901–1988 (females per 1,000 males)

Year	All ages	At birth	5–9	20–4	30–4	60–4	80–4
1901	1,068	964	1,005	1,119	1,100	1,171	1,481
1911	1,068	962	1,001	1,113	1,091	1,138	1,556
1921	1,096	950	992	1,176	1,186	1,132	1,685
1931	1,088	953	980	1,057	1,132	1,130	1,690
1951	1,082	944	957	1,051	1,034	1,282	1,703
1961	1,067	942	953	1,007	987	1,243	1,956
1971	1,058	942	950	989	966	1,136	2,258
1981	1,059	948	947	975	993	1,118	2,310
1988	1,050	954	949	965	988	1,075	2,027

Sources: *Statistical Abstract of the United Kingdom* 1924–38. *Annual Abstract of Statistics*, 89 (1952), 122 (1986). OPCS Birth Statistics Series FM1 no. 1 (1974), no. 11 (1984). OPCS Monitor PP1 89/1 (revised) 'Mid-1988 population estimates for England and Wales', t. 2, London, OPCS.

The First World War made this disparity between the marriage chances of men and women even more severe. 720,000 men had died. Many women aged 20–30 in 1914 lost fiancés or never found husbands. In 1921, 26 per cent of women aged 30–4 had never married and of the survivors aged 40–4 ten years later 18 per cent were still spinsters. These were the old single women of the 1950s and 1960s; 16–17 per cent of women aged 75 or more in 1951 and in 1961 had never married. And these figures underestimate the extent to which their generation had been unable to marry, because survival rates for the single are worse than for the married.

But although extraordinary factors depressed marriage rates after the First War, none the less a great change in the West European marriage pattern, both in Britain and other industrial countries, began in the late 1930s. It was first apparent among the over-30s marrying after 1938 (Hajnal 1950,1953). Average age at marriage fell, propor-

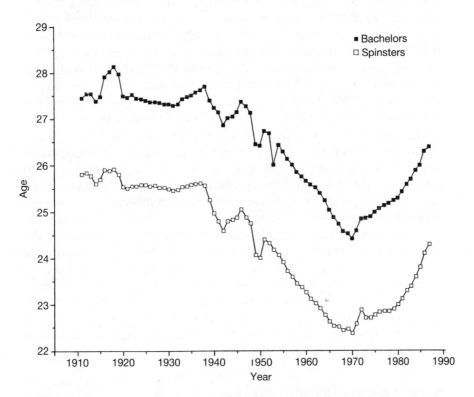

Sources: Registrar-General's Statistical Review Text 1929 t. 78, 1938 Part II Civil t. L, 1946 Part II, Civil, t. 1, 1969 Part II t. 2, OPCS Marriage and Divorce Statistics Series FM2 (various years), t. 3.5*b*.

FIG. 5.1. Mean age at marriage, bachelors and spinsters, 1911–1989

tions marrying increased, to levels not seen for centuries (table 5.1, figure 5.1). This trend continued without peacetime interruption until 1970, by which time mean age at marriage for bachelors had declined to 23.9 years, for spinsters 21.8 years, the lowest for centuries. Age differences between marriage partners narrowed from 2.6 to 2.1 years from 1951 to 1970. Almost all this reduction in bachelors' age at marriage occurred after 1963.

Inevitably, such a fall in age at marriage increases the proportions married at younger ages. It does not necessarily increase the final proportions marrying, although this happened too. By 1951, the proportion of men already married at age 30–4 (31 per cent) was the same as that achieved by men five years older in 1911. By 1972, when marriage was at its most popular, marriage patterns had moved downward by ten years: as many men in their early 30s were already married as men in their early 40s had been in 1921 (table 5.1). Women's experience was transformed much more—and earlier—than men's. Men born after 1925—those who married, that is, around 1950—were the first to leave previous trends behind. But women born even before 1920 had started to enjoy the new chances of marriage. In 1921, for example, 83 per cent of women alive at age 45–9 had married at some stage in their lives. In 1951 the proportion was almost the same—85 per cent. But by 1970 it had risen to 92 per cent. The proportion of women remaining unmarried all their lives had been halved in twenty years.

Changes in the sex ratio improved women's marriage chances and squeezed those of men instead. New cohorts healed the demographic damage of the First World War. Many emigrants (mostly male) returned in the 1930s after the recession bit deeper in the USA than it had in Britain, where at least the returning migrant could rely on some support from his family. After the Second World War, too, the old pattern of emigration changed. Whole families left the country for the Dominions and the USA, rather than the single men who had gone before. Ninety-two per cent of women born in 1925 (and 91 per cent of men) were married by age 50 compared with 85 per cent of women born in 1900. To begin with, the changes in marriage for men were more a matter of timing, whereas women experienced, at least up to the 1970s, not only earlier marriage, but also a much greater chance of marrying.

Measuring marriage and forecasting the future

Measuring marriage trends, and assessing their implications for the future, can be quite difficult. Merely relating the number of marriages

(a) Males

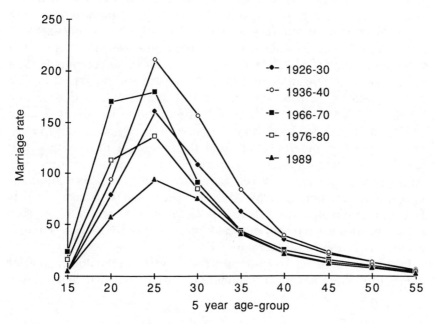

(b) Females

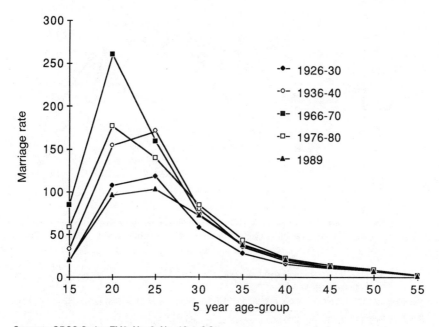

Sources: OPCS Series FM2, No. 2, No. 12, t. 3.3*a*.

FIG. 5.2. Age-specific first marriage rates, England and Wales, 1926–1989

to the total unmarried population is unsatisfactory. The rates look low and their variation unimpressive. The figures lack intuitive meaning. They are particularly vulnerable to changes in age structure because of the intense concentration of marriage—or at least first marriage—in the third decade of life. Age-specific rates are instructive but voluminous (figure 5.2). Total marriage rates can be computed in the same way as total fertility rates, cumulating age-specific rates to give a number representing the total number of marriages experienced in a lifetime (Shryock and Siegel 1976). For first marriages this number should, of course, be less than one. But in fact downward shifts in age at marriage can put the cumulated figure over a total of one first marriage per person; clearly impossible even in this adventurous age. And delayed marriage, as well as avoided marriage, can reduce the measure to an unreasonable degree. Total first marriage rates in England and Wales in 1970 were 0.92 for women and 0.87 for men (Coleman 1980*b*). By 1980 they had fallen to 0.76 for women and 0.74 for men (Eldridge and Kiernan 1985).

Life table methods avoid impossible answers and yield a figure for 'nuptiality'—representing the cumulative risk of marriage by any given

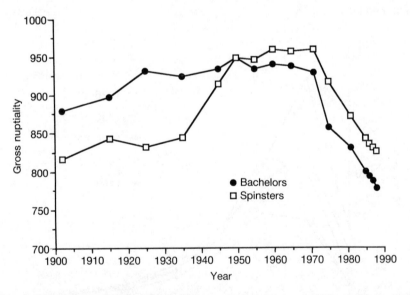

Note: Gross nuptiality is a life table estimate of the proportion likely to have married by age 50, at current marriage rates, ignoring the effects of mortality.

Sources: to 1971: Coleman 1980*b*, t. 3; then OPCS Marriage and Divorce Statistics Series FM2, t. 3.8.

Fɪɢ. **5.3.** Gross nuptiality, England and Wales, 1900–1988

age, given current marriage rates. The calculation of 'gross nuptiality' (figure 5.3) ignores the additional risk of dropping out of single status by death, which is rather small until about age 50. These calculations show that the male advantage in marriageability has been lost since 1946–50 following an extraordinary acceleration of female nuptiality in the 1930s, which has outstripped the more modest increase among men. They also show clearly the retreat from early marriage which has been in progress since about 1970.

The birth cohort of 1946 has the lowest proportion remaining single of any cohort for which we have data. By age 36 only 5 per cent of the women and 8 per cent of the men had never married (Kiernan 1989*b*). They have moved into middle age surrounded by married—or once married—colleagues. But since their peak age at marriage in the 1960s we have seen two decades of decline in proportions married at given ages (figure 5.4), a rise in average age at marriage, and growing uncertainty and speculation about the future of the institution. Mean age at marriage has risen by over two years for bachelors (24.4 in 1970 to 26.9 in 1989), and among spinsters (22.4 in 1970, 24.8 in 1989) (figure 5.1). Average age at marriage of all men marrying in 1987 (including remarriages) was over 30 (30.4), 27.8 for women—the highest this century.

These changes in the mean conceal even bigger changes in each

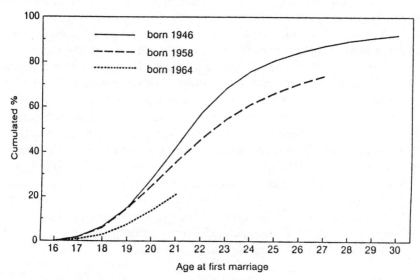

Source: Kiernan 1989*b*, fig. 3.1.

FIG. 5.4. Cumulated proportions ever-married by age: women born in 1946, 1958, and 1964

age-group, particularly ages 15–34. Teenage marriages have halved (table 5.1): the proportions ever-married in their early 20s in 1987 (15 per cent of men and 32 per cent of women) are now only 60 per cent of what they were a decade ago. Over age 30, marriage rates have held their own. As befits the scarcer sex, women's first marriage rates have held up rather better than men's. Teenage marriages were one of the talking points of the 1960s but despite the dispensation of teenage marriage from parental control following the Family Law Reform Act of 1969, whereby young people could marry without parental consent at age 18 instead of 21, teenage marriages have become less frequent. In 1970 more than 10 per cent of marriages were teenage marriages (for both partners); in 1980 the figure was down to 8 per cent. In 1988 11 per cent of women married for the first time in their teens, compared to 32 per cent in 1970. In general, these figures seem to indicate some return to the marriage rates of the previous period. At period rates current in 1988, about 22 per cent of men and 17 per cent of women will not marry at all—a reversal of the position at the beginning of the century, and OPCS projections expect that up to 20 per cent of recent birth cohorts will remain single (figure 4.9c).

There has been speculation—more in the US than here—that we may be heading for a new era of lifelong spinsters, as the attraction of careers displaces marriage. The movement of married women into the work-force has certainly upset many old patterns, but so far the data do not amount to a revolution against marriage, and it is easy to exaggerate the appeal of many of the jobs that women do (Pahl 1985, Osborn et al. 1984). First of all, there has been no great change in the expectations of young people. An enquiry carried out by the Study Commission on the Family (1982), an organization created by concern about the state of marriage and its future, showed that over 90 per cent of young people still expect to marry eventually. And most—up to 90 per cent depending on assumptions—of the reduction in the overall level of period marriage rates can still be attributed to backwards shifts in timing ('tempo'), not to any substantial reduction in the eventual likelihood of marriage ('quantum'). A comparison based on standardization suggests that in the 1970s about 60 per cent of men and women were delaying marriage, and about 40 per cent of them were marrying each year. If that continues, about 90 per cent of women born in 1964 will marry by age 50 (Eldridge and Kiernan 1985). There is no good evidence yet for the general rejection of marriage.

Cohabitation

The delay in marriage does not mark a return to the old West European marriage pattern. Sexual freedom, cohabitation, divorce, and remarriage are creating a new pattern. Cohabitation, rare in the 1950s, is now common. In 1988 about 8 per cent of women aged 18–49 were cohabiting, and 21 per cent of non-married women. About 900,000 people aged under 60 were estimated to be cohabiting in 1986–7. Only about one woman in twenty who was married in the 1950s reported having lived with her future spouse before marriage. The Family Formation Survey of 1976 marked a change in attitudes in more ways than one by being the first official enquiry to ask a question on pre-marital cohabitation (Dunnell 1979). Subsequently the General Household Survey (Brown and Kiernan 1981), revealed that one in four couples married in the late 1970s had cohabited, and almost two-thirds (62 per cent) of remarried couples. By the mid-1980s, 27 per cent of first marrying couples had lived together before marriage and 70 per cent of remarried couples (table 5.3). By the late 1980s this had risen even further to 50 per cent and 74 per cent respectively (General Household Survey 1988). In the 1970s, the average length of cohabitation before marriage was not long—about nine months—and the average effect in delaying marriage may be not more than three months. But by the 1980s the median duration had risen to 15 months

Table 5.3. Pre-marital cohabitation, Great Britain, 1960–1984 (women aged 16–49 who were under 35 at time of this marriage)

Age of woman at marriage	Percentage who cohabited before marriage[a]				
	1960–4	1965–9	1970–4	1975–9	1980–4
First marriage for both partners					
Under 25	2	2	7	15	24
25–34[b]	—	—	10	23	36
Total[b]	—	—	8	16	26
Second or subsequent marriage for one or both partners					
Under 25	17	28	39	53	62
25–34[b]	—	—	45	60	74
Total[b]	—	—	45	57	70
All marriages	—	—	12	25	37

[a] Data for the 1960–79 marriage cohorts are taken from the 1979, 1981, 1982, 1983, and 1984 surveys combined. Data for the 1979–84 cohort are from the 1983 and 1985 surveys only.
[b] Table excludes women married at ages 25–34 in the 1960s as some of them would have been aged over 50 when interviewed and so were not asked the Family Information section.
Source: General Household Survey 1985, t. 4.9.

which may be assumed to be displacing and delaying marriage for longer. About half the delay in marriage, and of the proportions remaining unmarried in their early 20s, can now be attributed to cohabitation before first marriage. In the late 1980s 12 per cent of unmarried men aged 16–59, and 14 per cent of women, were cohabiting so the proportions married underestimate conjugal households by a similar degree. In 1986–7, 11 per cent of single men and 18 per cent of single women aged 20–24 were cohabiting. These are more than half the proportions married at those ages (Haskey and Kiernan 1989). It is difficult to determine how many cohabitations do not end in marriage, how many either persist through life or end in equally unrecorded separation. By definition they appear on paper nowhere, but it may be as high as 50 per cent (Eldridge and Kiernan 1985). Single men and woman currently cohabiting when interviewed for the General Household Survery of 1986 and 1987 had already been cohabiting for a median 22 and 20 months respectively.

Although the recent trend is still upward (table 5.4), marriage in Britain is not yet being permanently displaced by cohabitation as it is to a marked degree in Sweden and Denmark (Eldridge and Kiernan 1985). There, more young people aged 20–4 are cohabiting than are

Table 5.4. Recent trends in cohabitation, Great Britain 1979–88 (women aged 18–49)

	Legal marital status of currently cohabiting women				All women excluding married	All women, including married
	Single	Widowed	Divorced	Separated		
1979	8	—	20	17	10.6	2.7
1980	8	6	20	17	10.8	2.9
1981	9	6	20	19	11.6	3.3
1982	10	3	21	18	12.6	3.8
1983	10	2	21	9	12.1	3.6
1984	12	[4]	20	17	13.7	4.2
1985	14	5	21	20	15.7	5.0
1986	15	[8]	27	7	16.6	5.5
1987	17	11	27	15	18.8	6.4
1988	20	5	28	16	21.0	8.0

Note: Percentages in brackets are based on less than five cases.

Sources: General Household Survey 1987 table 11.3; OPCS Monitor SS 89/1 General Household Survey: preliminary results for 1988, London OPCS.

married (Nilsson 1985) and about a half of babies are born outside marriage, most of them to couples rather than to single women. The development of fertility to couples living in 'stable' non-marital unions was documented in Chapter 4. (No one knows if these unions are at all 'stable' but the adjective is frequently used none the less). Up to 65 per cent of illegitimate births may now be born into such unions; perhaps 16 per cent of all births. Some of these unions may have been encouraged by quirks of the welfare or taxation system which encourage cohabitation rather than marriage. One of the most notorious of these was the provision that mortgage income tax relief was available to each joint purchaser of a house up to the limit of £30,000 for each person (£60,000 for a cohabiting couple, even more for a more complex ménage) but was limited to £30,000 in all for a married couple. As home ownership among young people in Britain is the highest in the world (35 per cent of 20–4 year-olds, 61 per cent of 25–9-year-olds in 1988) the potential effect of this rule was considerable. It will be interesting to see what impact its abolition in the Budget of March 1988 will make to figures on cohabitation. Perhaps surprisingly people of different social statuses and educational attainments are about equally likely to cohabit. However, there are substantial regional differences, in line with regional differences in remarriage and also in line with the geography of house prices (Hurst 1989). In the late 1980s about 16 per cent of unmarried people were cohabiting in the South-East and East Anglia compared with 9 per cent in Scotland and 8 per cent in Wales (Haskey and Kiernan 1989).

Sexual contact before marriage with the intended partner is nothing new—about 60 per cent of first births in Victorian times were pre-maritally conceived. But it is likely that pre-marital sexual activity for most people was confined to the period shortly before marriage. The evidence for a real and substantial change in pre-marital sexual activity from the 1960s onwards is very strong (see Laslett 1977, Schofield 1965, Bone 1986, Mant et al. 1988). Now birth control enables people to enjoy sex without conception and modern attitudes enable them to enjoy domesticity without marriage.

Cohabitation before remarriage is now the rule rather than the exception—70 per cent in recently remarried couples (table 5.4). Much of this high level of cohabitation may arise because couples had changed partners for their next marriage while still married to their original spouse. At least 10 per cent of currently cohabiting women in 1987 were still married to someone else. Adultery is cited as the main reason for divorce in about a third of divorce petitions. The age-specific adultery rate based upon petitions is at its highest (for men) at age

35–9. This must be an underestimate of the prevalence of extra-marital liaisons. Adultery may not be detected by the other partner and if detected, it may not necessarily be cited in a petition. Evidence from surveys, at home and abroad, suggests that a much higher proportion of men than that may deceive their wives during their marriage. As divorce by mutual consent requires two years to elapse before a decree absolute is given, some of these cohabitations may be of quite long standing, beginning before the divorce is finalized. Circumstances which may make it difficult for a couple to remarry may also prolong cohabitation: financial problems, housing problems (divorce is the quickest route out of owner-occupation and into a council house), or the reluctance of a former spouse to grant a divorce (Coleman 1989*b*).

Social differences in marriage

People in different social classes marry at different ages and different proportions of them remain unmarried (table 5.5). There is about three years between the average age at marriage in Social Class I and V; this difference is of long standing and has remained intact in the ups and downs of average age at marriage in the twentieth century. As a

Table 5.5. Median age at marriage, and proportions ever-marrying to age 40 at 1979 rates, by social class, England Wales, 1979

Social Class	Bachelors		Spinsters		
	Median age	% ever-marrying	Median age		% ever-marrying
I	25.8	93	26.0[a]	23.9[b]	86[c]
II	26.2	89	24.0	23.2	93
IIIN	24.5	84	21.6	22.0	87
IIIM	25.0	86	21.2	21.4	94
IV	23.2	81	20.4	20.8	86
V	23.5	74	22.0	21.0	98[d]
Armed Forces	23.0	—	—	20.7	—
All	24.5	85	21.7	21.7	91
No. in sample	870		832		

[a] By spinster's own class.
[b] By spouse's class.
[c] To age 35.
[d] To age 30.
Source: Haskey 1983*d*, t. 3, 6.

consequence young people in different social classes have very different chances of being married by any given age. This has considerable significance in relation to career structure, participation in higher education, and housing tenure. However, in the end most men in high status occupations get married while quite a high proportion of unskilled manual workers in class V stay single all their lives. This may follow in part from differences in their financial attractiveness and their capacity to set up separate households. Women's marriage chances are different. Professional women (in their own right) and graduate women (Kiernan 1989*a*) are most likely to remain single; almost all women in social class V eventually marry (Haskey 1983). Career contraints on professional women are severe; the marriage chances of women at the bottom end of the social scale are helped by the general tendency of marriage to be hypergamous—women tend to marry above their own social origins.

Similar differences in mean age at marriage are seen with respect to educational level. The longer the education, the later the marriage: each additional year spent in full-time education delayed marriage by 0.4 years in the MRC 1946 birth cohort sample. The effect is stronger on women than on men, partly because they tend to marry sooner after finishing their education. Graduate women are more likely than average to remain single, so are men and women who needed special education, for mental subnormality or other reasons. The advantages of delayed marriage to those with the chance of going on to higher education and the broader career opportunities which it opens up are obvious, given the difficulty of combining the two. More educated people are also more likely to have wider social horizons and be inclined to defer a final choice of partner. The MRC sample allows social class, education, and other variables to be analysed together. Education emerges as the real factor behind the social class differences (Kiernan 1987). Other, although less important, influences to emerge are personality and aspirations, and the educational level and age at marriage of parents, suggesting some transmission of values across generations.

One of the most prominent effects on age at marriage is associated with differences in housing tenure. Average age at marriage of people who move into council housing, and who are brought up in it, is considerably lower than that of couples who move into owner-occupation or who are brought up in it. As was discussed in Chapter 4 in relation to fertility, the costs of owner-occupation require that marriage and childbearing be delayed. This factor is absent in council housing. On the contrary, single people have a very low priority on council

allocation schemes and the chances of housing are greatly increased by becoming married and producing children quickly.

With the apparent increase in the number of people remaining single, the characteristics of single people become more important. It is evident that they are not a homogeneous group—people remain single for very different reasons. In general single people tend to to be more introverted and to have parents who married later than average. Not surprisingly, single women share many characteristics with childless women (see Chapter 4). Single women in the 1946 cohort are more likely to have high intelligence, education, and occupational status. Single men are more likely to have unskilled occupations. A significant minority of the single of both sexes are handicapped. There seem to be no substantial British data on the number of single people with homosexual or lesbian sexual inclinations although the Cox report estimated 4.5 per cent of adult males (Cox 1989, Rees 1990). If this proportion remains constant over time, such persons must comprise a greatly varying proportion of single people at different times, as single people have comprised between 5 to 15 per cent of different cohorts.

5.3 Divorce and Widowhood

Divorce and marital breakdown

Popular divorce is a twentieth-century innovation in industrial societies, although an institution of long standing in other cultures. Its study is complicated—unlike that of fertility, mortality, or marriage—by its control by law. The legislative response to popular pressure for easier divorce has turned upward trends into a series of leaps. For this reason, divorce rates are not the most sensitive indicator of marital breakdown or dissatisfaction. It has been suggested that the enormous rise in divorce rates need not mean that marital dissatisfaction was particularly less in the past. It is difficult to decide such questions; but the variety of choices available to women has greatly increased (women now petition in 72 per cent of divorces). There are other ways of ending a marriage but without the ability to remarry—e.g. separation. Judicial separations are rare: in 1965 there were 130 judicial separations compared to 37,000 divorces; in 1975 323 compared to 121,000 divorces. The number increased sharply to 1,640 in 1979. Applications for maintenance (i.e. of a woman still married but separated) were more common. In 1965 27,262 were granted. By 1975 this had fallen to 8,899, and by 1979 to 4,519. Some of these applications may have been preliminaries to divorce especially before 1973, but clearly they are no substitute for it. There has been a major upswing in genuine marital breakdown in the second half of the twentieth century. Legal changes have only facilitated and followed them, not caused them (Leete 1979).

Trends: popular pressures and legal change

Until the Divorce Act 1857, divorce required a complex process culminating in an individual Act of Parliament. It cost about £1,000 (Macfarlane 1986). This was an escape route only for wealthy noblemen. There were only 131 divorces in the 130 years from 1670 to 1799. After 1857, divorce might be granted legally on grounds of matrimonial fault—of adultery by the wife, or adultery and other aggravation: rape, bigamy, cruelty, by the husband. Those without standing or position in the community might not be able to appeal to Parliament, but had other means available to them such as desertion or even wife sales (Menefee 1981, Phillips 1988). Before the First World War, the incidence of divorce was negligible. Between 1876 and 1880, for example, there were only 2,301 petitions for dissolution and annulment (mostly the former), and only 60 per cent succeeded. The position changed little until 1914. Divorce was still considered a major scandal, confined by expense to the rich. The hasty marriages, the separations, and the adulteries of the First World War yielded a crop of divorces a few years later—petitions trebled from 5,167 in 1911–15 to 14,768 in 1916–20 (figure 5.5), 67 per cent filed by husbands compared to 45 per cent before and 41 per cent after (Registrar-General 1954). As in so many other things, the World Wars provoked radical social change. But even the higher number represents a mere two in 10,000 married couples divorcing per year. Divorce rates declined a little again once the wartime entanglements were sorted out, but to nothing like the previous low level. After 1923, wives were enabled to petition for divorce on the same footing as husbands.

Divorce became slowly more common during the 1930s, and was much discussed although socially still unacceptable in polite society. In this, the British position was similar to that of most of the rest of North-Western Europe, although the Americans as usual had forged further ahead in the matter. As time went on, petitions began to be more successful. Less than two-thirds succeeded at the beginning of the inter-war period, three-quarters at its end, 90 per cent by the late 1950s (Registrar-General 1963).

The marriages of the 1930s were some of the longest lived in history; preserved from termination by death by declining mortality, not yet threatened by the high divorce rates which lay in wait in the future. For

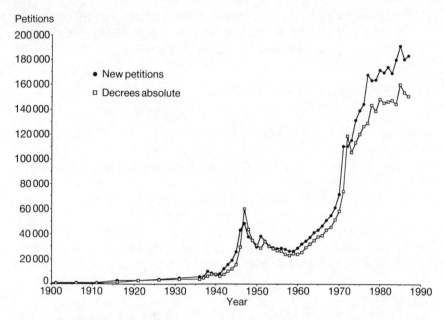

Petitions

Note: Data 1900–1935 are 5-year means.

Sources: Registrar-General's Annual Review Part II; OPCS Marriage and Divorce Statistics FM2, t. 4.1, t. 4.7.

FIG. 5.5 Trends in divorce, England and Wales, 1900–1987

example, only 0.5 per cent of the marriages in 1926 had ended in divorce after ten years of marriage, only 1.9 per cent after twenty years and 4 per cent after thirty years (i.e. by 1956). But of the marriages of 1936, 1 per cent had been dissolved after ten years and 8 per cent after thirty years. Divorce was not a realistic risk to the average marriage.

Marriage cohorts do not, it seems, take with them any lifelong immunity to divorce. Legal changes facilitated further dissolution: the Matrimonial Causes Act (1937, effective in 1938) doubled the number of petitions in a year to 10,233, and the decrees absolute granted per thousand population aged 20–49 increased from 0.77 (1937) to 1.22 (1939).

Once again, marriages celebrated in wartime proved much more fragile—four times as many wartime marriages ended in divorce after ten years than had the marriages of 1936 (see Rowntree and Carrier 1958). There were 194,503 petitions filed between 1946 and 1950, almost ten times the number in 1926–30; the 1947 level of petitions was seven times that of 1940. It was not just the wartime marriages that suffered. The marriages of the later 1930s also suffered severe casualties in the post-war period, more than any other peacetime

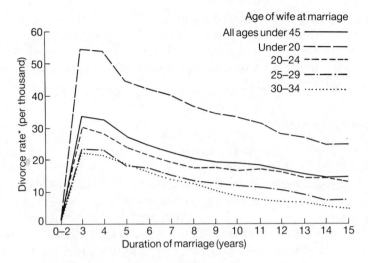

*Divorces per 100 estimated related marriages at risk in year and age-group concerned (for marriage durations over 10 years the denominators are approximations).

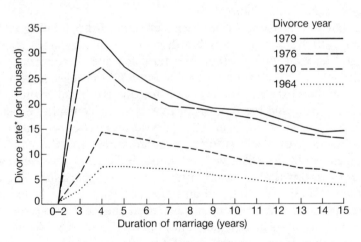

*Divorces (all ages of wife at marriage under 45) per 1000 estimated related marriages at risk in year concerned (for marriage durations over 10 years the denominators are approximations).

Source: Haskey 1982a, fig. 1.

FIG. 5.6. Distribution of divorce by duration of marriage, England and Wales 1979 (*a*) by age at marriage, (*b*) by year of divorce

cohort, possibly as a result of wartime liaisons coming to light on the soldiers' return. Fifty-six per cent of divorce petitions were filed by husbands in 1941–50, compared to 47 per cent before and 44 per cent after, and adultery was cited in over 70 per cent of petitions (Registrar-General 1954).

The recent rise in divorce

The marriages of the 1950s marked a return to the more tranquil marital scene (statistically at any rate) of the 1930s. Only 3 per cent of 1951 marriages were dissolved after ten years, 7.4 per cent after twenty years. The return to the golden age was short lived. By the end of the 1950s a strong upward trend in divorce was apparent once again. For example, in 1961 there were 3.9 decrees absolute per thousand married men aged 25–9 (the most vulnerable age), by 1971 12.5, by 1981 27.6. The increase was not restricted to recent marriages. It has affected to some degree all marriage cohorts and all ages and all durations of marriage. But because the lifespan of marriage has its highest risk of dissolution in the first five to ten years, it is inevitably the more recent cohorts which bear the weight of any secular increase, just like secular changes in mortality (figure 5.7).

The Divorce Reform Act of 1969 (effective from 1 January 1971), radically altered the grounds for dissolution of marriage, in a way comparable with many other Western European countries which reformed divorce law around the same time. By this legislation, instead of matrimonial offence, the criterion for divorce became the general one of 'irretrievable breakdown of marriage'. This could be deduced from a petition of adultery, cruelty, or desertion as before, but proof of these was not of itself sufficient. In addition, for the first time, marriages could be dissolved by mutual consent after two years' separation and without consent after five years' separation. The latter effectively eliminated the ground of 'desertion', which has since progressively declined. Women have used the new provisions more than men: husbands filed 40 per cent of petitions in 1965, 36 per cent in 1970, and their share declined rapidly to 30 per cent of all petitions in 1975. By 1987 the proportion of decrees absolute granted to husbands had fallen to the lowest ever—28 per cent (see Haskey 1986). This seems to be further evidence that women are less dependent upon marriage than they used to be.

While these new criteria added a new quantum to divorce—and precipitated the demise of many long dead marriages in the early 1970s which previously could not be legally ended—they only added to the

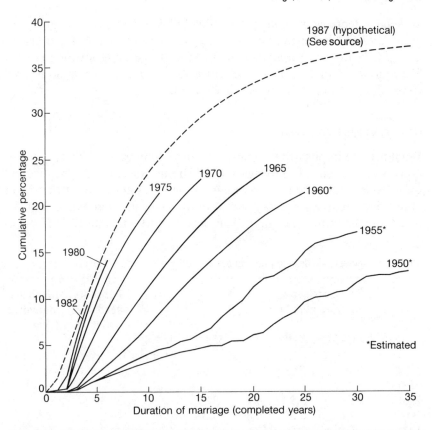

Note: 1950–82, actual marriage cohorts; 1987 experience of synthetic cohort based on risks current in 1987.

Source: Haskey 1989a, fig. 1.

Fig. 5.7. Proportion of marriages ending in divorce, England and Wales, 1950–1987

underlying strong upward trend (Leete 1979). They did not create it. After a brief relapse following the sudden bulge in the early 1970s divorce continued on its apparently inexorable upward trend. The latest legislative change, the Matrimonial and Family Proceedings Act 1984, allows divorce after a year, although in no circumstances before that. Once again, further legal liberalization provoked a flurry of divorces. Petitions filed increased to a peak 191,055 in 1985, compared to 179,976 in 1984 (figure 5.5, table 5.6), and declined to 180,398 in 1986 and 173,845 in 1987. These legal hiccups apart, the underlying trend in numbers of petitions has recently shown signs of flattening off (as in the USA and elsewhere). This may be accounted for by the decline since the early 1970s of divorce-prone early marriages, and especially teenage marriage. In 1988 152,633 decrees absolute were granted, 7,667 fewer than in 1985. In the 1980s the pace of increase in age-specific divorce rates slackened. After the jump following the 1984 Matrimonial and Family Proceedings Act, age-specific rates in 1989 were slightly lower than those of 1987 (table 5.6).

How many marriages will fail?

What are the implications of current rates of divorce for the survival of marriages, or that of marriage itself? The notion that one marriage in three ends in divorce is now widely quoted. It happens that there was about one divorce for every three weddings in the mid-1980s. But the figure means more than that. The best way to evaluate the effects of

Table 5.6. Age-specific divorce rates, England and Wales, 1961–1986

	Divorce decrees per 1,000 married population					Per cent aged under 35	Mean age at divorce (years)
	16–24	25–9	30–4	35–44	45 and over		
Males							
1961	1.4	3.9	4.1	3.1	1.1	38.3	—
1966	2.6	6.8	6.8	4.5	1.5	44.2	38.6
1971	5.0	12.5	11.8	7.9	3.1	44.8	39.4
1976	13.6	21.4	18.9	14.1	4.5	48.6	38.0
1981	17.7	27.6	22.8	17.0	4.8	48.6	37.7
1983	19.9	28.2	24.0	17.6	5.0	45.6	38.0
1985	31.7	32.9	24.8	18.2	5.2	47.5	37.4
1987	27.2	30.7	25.2	18.0	5.1	44.8	38.0
1989	24.2	30.4	26.0	18.3	5.2	43.8	38.3
Females							
1961	2.4	4.5	3.8	2.7	0.9	49.3	—
1966	4.1	7.6	6.1	3.9	1.2	54.7	35.8
1971	7.5	13.0	10.5	6.7	2.8	54.4	36.8
1976	14.5	20.4	18.3	12.6	4.0	56.6	36.0
1981	22.3	26.7	20.2	14.9	3.9	58.0	35.2
1983	23.6	27.1	21.1	15.5	4.0	55.0	35.4
1985	33.0	29.7	21.4	16.1	4.2	56.5	34.9
1987	28.3	28.3	22.4	15.7	4.1	54.5	35.5
1989	25.9	28.7	23.0	15.9	4.2	53.6	35.7

Source: Population Trends 51 (1988), t. 14, 62 (1990) t. 23.

divorce is a life table approach; to see what would happen to the average marriage if it were exposed to the current risks of divorce. Calculations of this kind show the implications of the extraordinary increase in divorce since the 1960s. In 1961, about 8 per cent of marriages would have ended in divorce by twenty-five years' duration. At the rates of 1971, about 22 per cent would have ended by the husband's fiftieth birthday and 35 per cent according to the rates of 1975 (Coleman 1980*b*).

These calculations ignore mortality, which is relatively insignificant up to about age 50. Finer calculations enable a net divorce table to be calculated showing the separate effects of death and divorce on marriage (Saveland and Glick 1969, Haskey 1982, 1989*a*). At 1979 risks, 32 per cent of marriages would end in divorce by twenty-five years' duration if mortality is ignored. At the risks current in 1987, the proportion ended by divorce after twenty-five years rises to 35 per cent. These proportions of failed marriages depend on current risks lasting a quarter of a century. They are not yet completely reflected in reality because no recent marriages have yet had time to experience the risks for long enough, and earlier marriages would have passed through their earlier years at lower levels of risk. But a third of some cohorts of teenage marriage and remarriage have already failed. At twenty years' duration 23 per cent of the marriages of 1965 have already ended in divorce. The accelerating rates at earlier durations of marriage (figure 5.7) suggest that the forecast will be comfortably realized. In 1989 these rates gave us the highest divorce risks in Western Europe, measured per 1,000 marriages. The example of the USA shows that there is no obvious reason why the risk to marriage should stall at one in three. There, according to similar calculations, more than one in two marriages will fail after twenty-five years' duration and almost two-thirds of those of blacks, teenagers, and previously divorced persons (Weed 1980). In fact the current British risks were already surpassed by those of California in the early 1970s (Schoen and Nelson 1974).

Although divorce is much more frequent now, some of its characteristics have changed less. Divorce ends marriages at only slightly shorter average durations: it was 12.9 years in 1964, 12.3 years in 1970; the median duration by the time of decree absolute in 1984 was 10.1 years, 9.7 in 1988. Mean age at divorce for men has fallen little: 39.1 years in 1964, 37.6 in 1970, 37.6 in 1980 and 38.3 in 1988. Women divorced in 1964 were aged on average 36.3, in 1970 34.8, in 1980 35.2, and 35.7 in 1988. Couples who have made a mistake usually find it out quickly and want to get out of it as soon as the law allows. The highest divorce rates occurred in the fourth year of marriage during 1964–70 when the legal minimum was three years; the 1971 legal provisions enabling marriages to end after two years permitted an earlier peak—just under three years (figure 5.6). The impact of the latest reform, the Matrimonial and Family Proceedings Act of 1984, which permits divorce after just one year, immediately shifted the mode down even further (Haskey 1986) to 0–2 years, especially among marriages where the wife was married at under age 25 and previously married partners, whose divorces increased 20 per cent between 1984 and 1985. Ten per cent of the divorces of 1987 ended marriages of less than 3 years' duration. There is no evidence from the divorce statistics of a seven-year itch, or of a later rise in divorce rates at about the time that children leave home.

Given the legal delay that is required between petition for divorce and the granting of a decree absolute, and the near impossibility until 1983 of getting a divorce before two years' marriage had been completed, it is evident that most marriages which break up must have the seeds of their destruction already present on the wedding day (Thornes and Collard 1979). Divorce statistics underestimate the speed at which marriages break down. There may be delay between the breakdown of feelings between the partners and the beginning of proceedings. Then there is a further delay until a decree absolute is granted. In the 1960s, almost three years elapsed between *de facto* breakdown and decree absolute (Chester 1971); but nowadays things move faster. In 1975, 50 per cent of all divorces were through within seven months of petition, couples with children taking rather longer (median 6.8 months) than the childless (5.6 months). None the less, 17,494 (15 per cent) had to wait more than a year and 1,057 (1 per cent) more than three years.

A lot is now known about what puts marriage at risk. Far the most important factor is age at marriage; the earlier, the worse (Murphy 1985). Forty-nine per cent of marriages where the wife was aged less than 20 would have failed after twenty-five years of marriage at 1980–1 divorce rates in England and Wales, three times the proportion of those who were married in their 30s. Remarriages of divorced persons are about twice as likely to fail as first marriages; at risks current in 1980–1, about 60 per cent are likely to fail before their twenty-fifth wedding anniversary (Haskey 1983*b*). Remarriages are accordingly featuring more and more in the divorce statistics. In 1961 and in 1971, only 7 per cent of divorces of men were divorces the second time round. By 1981 this had risen to 12 per cent, by 1986 to 17 per cent.

Evidence from different sources (Murphy 1985, Haskey 1984) does not tell quite the same story (table 5.7), but in general manual workers

Table 5.7. Risks of divorce by socio-economic group: alternative estimates

Socio-economic group		Census (1)	Haskey (2)	Murphy (3)
1&2	Employees and managers	72	130	108
3&4	Professional workers—all types	53	47	51
5	Intermediate non-manual	82	89	56
6	Junior non-manual	109	119	92
7	Personal service	237	365	235
8	Foremen and supervisors—manual	61	30	12
9	Skilled manual	102	112	92
10	Semi-skilled manual	110	115	103
11	Unskilled manual	177	241	176
12	Own-account non-professional	134	10	91
13&14	Farmers	48	65	59
15	Agricultural workers	56	82	67
16	Armed forces	73	270	112

Note: The overall figure is set to 100.
Source: Murphy 1985, t. 4.

(especially unskilled) have higher divorce risks than non-manual workers (especially professionals). Some particular occupations, for example in transport, which frequently separate husband and wife also carry high risks of divorce. In the unskilled working class, partners are often chosen from a limited social and geographical horizon (Ineichen 1979b). Couples who marry after a long courtship, and who marry in church, are also less likely to divorce. What little evidence there is does not clearly indicate whether previous cohabitation helps the stability of subsequent marriage, even though many young people apparently have this hope in mind (Eldridge and Kiernan 1985).

One of the few sociological comparisons of divorced and non-divorcing couples in this country showed that couples who divorced had known their partners for a shorter time before marriage, were less likely to have been formally engaged, were more prone to romantic illusions about marriage, and had enjoyed a less satisfactory sex life. Divorced couples had also much less satisfactory housing, often starting off as 'concealed households' with in-laws and then moving around more frequently. The early arrival of children, especially when money and housing were a problem, weakened marriages rather than re-inforced them. More than a third of the problems that eventually proved terminal had become apparent before the first wedding anniversary (Thornes and Collard 1979). Although pre-marital conception weakens marriages, divorces at most durations of marriage are more likely to occur between childless couples.

Widowhood

Every year, more than a quarter of a million marriages end in the death of partners. This is still about twice the number ended by divorce. Death progressively replaces divorce in ending marriages at longer durations. Even at twenty-five years' duration only 4 per cent of marriages are likely to have been ended by death. Beyond forty-five years of marriage the position becomes reversed. By the fiftieth anniversary 34 per cent have been ended by divorce, 43 per cent by death. At the death-rates of 1980–2, a man aged 30 and a woman aged 25 could expect to spend 41 years together, in the absence of divorce and separation. To this should be added a 'bonus' of 3 per cent (which increases with age) to take account of the higher expectation of life of married people, to make 42.5 (OPCS 1987d). Divorce holds our attention because it is avoidable and usually terminates marriages prematurely, and leaves young single parents with dependent children. Widowhood is important for other reasons. Sex differences in mortality ensure that widows greatly outnumber widowers. Beyond age 65–70, more women are widowed than remain married. As a consquence, a much higher proportion of a woman's life than a man's is spent on her own, without spouse or resident children and their support (Murphy 1983).

   In 1985, 3.7 per cent of men over 16 and 14.7 per cent of women were widowed. Almost all the increase in widowhood since the 1940s (when information first became available under the Population Statistics Act 1938) has arisen from the death of husbands—69 per cent by the early 1970s, reflecting the widening gap between the life expectations of women and men. Thanks to this changing gap, there are actually proportionately fewer widowed men in the population today than in 1901 (then 5.4 per cent of the male population over 16; widows were 11.1 per cent). The widening gap in remarriage rates between men and women as they grow older also contributes to the difference. Duration of life in the widowed state is quite different for men and women. Thanks to the differences in survival between the sexes, husbands are widowed later than wives and also live shorter lives from any given age. In 1987, median age at widowhood for men was 72, for women 67 (see OPCS 1989d). These are not life table expectations; they are affected by the age-distribution. At these ages, females can expect a further 15.5 years of life, males a further 9.1. This takes no account of the 44 and 25

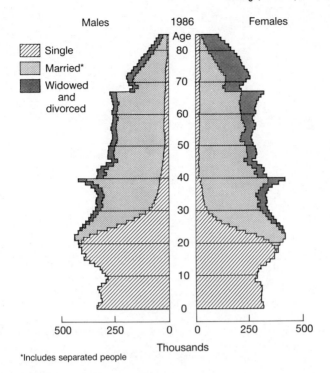

Males   1986   Females

*Includes separated people

Source: *Social Trends*, 19 (1989), fig. 1.4.

FIG. 5.8. Population by marital status, England and Wales, 1986

per cent excess mortality rates suffered by widowers and widows respectively, both at age 67, compared with married people (OPCS 1987*d*) (see Chapter 8).

5.4 Remarriage

Divorce and mortality free partners for remarriage. Early in this century as fewer and fewer people of an age likely to remarry lost their partners, remarriage became uniquely uncommon. But since the 1960s more and more people have remarried as more marriages are broken by divorce at relatively young ages. At younger ages only a few who have been widowed or divorced avoid remarriage. At older ages remarriage rates are much lower. So despite rocketing divorce rates, the number of currently divorced (and not remarried) people in the population remains surprisingly small and is not growing fast (figure 5.8) while the remarried population at the present varies from 1 per cent of all married people in the youngest age groups to 11 per cent at

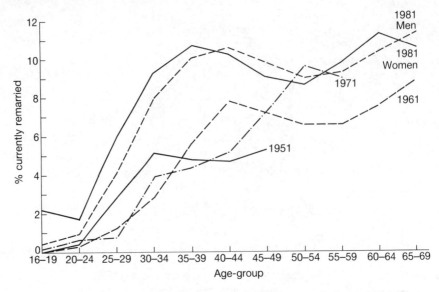

Sources: Census Fertility Reports or Tables 1951, 1961, 1971; Census Age, Sex, and Marital Status Tables 1981.

FIG. 5.9. Proportion of remarried women among all currently married women, England and Wales, 1951–1981, and men 1981

old age (figure 5.9). This proportion will increase substantially in the years ahead as the population catches up with the third of recent marriages which are remarriages.

Remarriage trends

In the 1980s, we returned to a high frequency of marital break-up, with its relict spouses, dependent children, and complexities of remarriage, last encountered in the eighteenth century. A remarriage here refers to a marriage where one or both partners had previously been married. Remarriage after widowhood was almost as common then as it is now after divorce. Modern divorce has been described as 'little more than a functional substitute for death' (Stone 1977). By prolonging the expected duration of marriage to unprecedented and possibly intolerable lengths, longer survival has required an alternative institutional escape hatch of divorce. Nowadays remarriage is more complicated. Often the former spouse is alive and well and living in society, maybe even in the same workplace, not safely confined to the churchyard. In 1860 18 per cent of marriages were remarriages. In 1901–5 (figure 5.10) only 12 per cent of marriages were remarriages, almost all involving

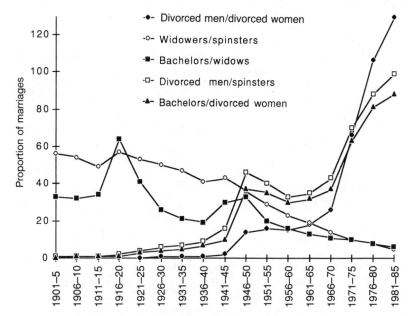

Note: Change of scale

Sources: OPCS Marriage and Divorce Statistics Series FM2, t. 3.2; Monitor FM2 87/1.

FIG. 5.10. Proportion of remarriages of different types, England and Wales, 1901–1986 per thousand of all marriages solemnized each other

widows. Only one in a thousand involved a divorced person. In the 1930s, first marriage dominated, with mortality and widowhood falling fast and divorce still a novelty. More marriages than ever before or since were first marriages, and these marriages lasted longer than ever before or since. In the last two decades divorce has displaced mortality as the cause of premature termination of marriage. Remarriages involving divorced people have outnumbered those of widows since the Second World War. By 1965 16 per cent of all weddings involved a previously married partner. By 1988, 37 per cent did. Ninety-one per cent of remarriages involved at least one divorced partner, 36 per cent of remarriages involved two divorced partners; 54 per cent involved one single partner, only 17 per cent involved at least one widowed person.

Contrasts by sex and previous marital status

Remarriage rates have not followed the rise and fall of first marriage documented earlier: they have remained more constant, though both

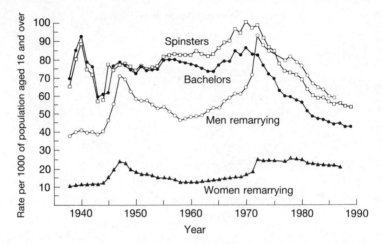

Note: Bachelors/spinsters: first marriage rates per 1,000 single aged 16 and over; widowed and divorced: remarriage rates per 1,000 widowed and divorced aged 16 and over.

Sources: Registrar-General's Statistical Review 1969 Part II, t. H1; OPCS Marriage and Divorce Statistics Series FM2, t. 2.1; *Population Trends* 62 (winter 1990), t. 21.

Fig. 5.11. Marriage rates by previous marital status, England and Wales, 1938–1989

are now declining (figure 5.11). The chances of remarriage depend on age, sex, and whether the first marriage was ended by divorce or widowhood. In the 1980s, remarriage rates among divorced men were about 50 per cent higher than among divorced women. The difference is particularly clear between ages 30 and 40, when most divorces occur. Remarriage chances are much higher for younger people. Thirty-one per cent of divorced men and 37 per cent of divorced women at ages 16–24 remarried in 1980, compared to 16 and 11 per cent respectively of the 35–44-year-olds. By 1988 divorced men were remarrying at average age 39.6, women 36.5. This does not help women who wish to remarry. Older men tend to marry women progressively younger than themselves, and older women thereby become less marriageable. In 1981 almost half—47 per cent—of divorced men and more than half—59 per cent—of divorced women who remarried did so under age 35.

Remarriage rates of divorced people shared in the general upsurge of marriage in the 1960s, increasing 40 per cent between 1961 and 1971 for men and 39 per cent for women, but since then they have fallen. By 1985 remarriage rates were below those of 1961 and men's rates were falling faster than women's (figure 5.11). The remarriage peak in the early 1970s, particularly evident in older people, was an artefact of the Divorce Reform Act (Haskey 1983*c*). The underlying trend in the

1970s has been slowly downwards; among people aged under 34 it was even apparent in the 1960s. So although the numbers of remarriages are increasing rapidly and remarriages are becoming an unprecedented proportion of all marriages, this is entirely a response to the enormously greater rate at which people are leaving first marriages at relatively young ages and forming new partnerships. Remarriage is not more popular, it is just that there are more people around to be remarried. The three graphs in figure 5.12 make this clear.

This suggests there is no general disillusionment with marriage, but possibly higher expectation. Most divorcees still remarry quite soon after divorcing and divorcees have not, on the whole, rejected marriage. Many have rejected their current partners because they could not enjoy a good marriage with them. And many divorce specifically to live with—if not to marry—another partner. Ideals and expectations of marriage still remain high, at least first time round.

(a) Proportions of males ever divorced or widowed by given exact ages, by year of birth

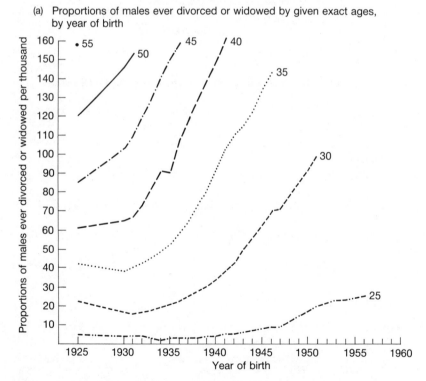

Sources: OPCS Marriage and Divorce Statistics Series FM2, No. 7, t. 3.9, t. 4.4, t. 5.3.

Fig. 5.12. Proportions ever divorced, widowed, and remarried, England and Wales birth cohorts, 1925–1955 (see over for parts 'b' and 'c')

(b) Proportions of males and females ever remarried by given exact ages, by year of birth

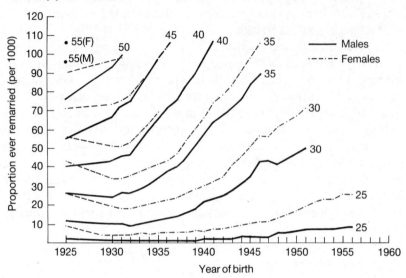

(c) Proportions of males ever divorced or remarried by given exact ages, who had remarried by that age, by year of birth

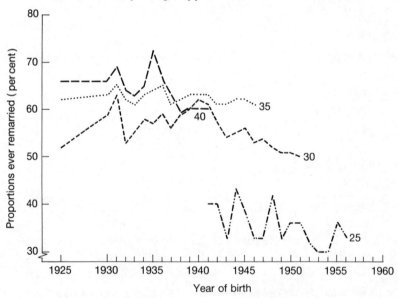

Fig. 5.12. (Continued)

Divorced people are much more likely to remarry than widows, at any age. Remarriage rates for divorced men aged 40–4, for example, are 22 per cent higher than those for widowed men of the same age; and for divorced women are 86 per cent higher than for widowed women in the same age group—which are about the same rate as divorcees ten years older. Differences in remarriage between the sexes are much sharper among the widowed than among divorcees. However remarriage rates for widowed people of each sex have held remarkably steady, while remarriage rates for divorced women have fallen. They have very likely been set back by the cohabitation which usually precedes remarriages, especially of divorced people, who unlike most widows will often have a replacement partner already waiting. There have been few changes in the circumstances of widows and widowers. Grieving widows may have no wish to forget their former spouse, or replace their lost partner—who may be more idealized as memories fade. Insurance, too, may take some of the pressure out of the need to remarry, especially for women.

Most widowed people eventually remarry, if they lose their spouse at a young enough age. Fifty-seven per cent of the 1930 male marriage cohort widowed by age 45 had remarried by that age. Except for the marriage cohorts affected by war, less than 40 per cent of widows had remarried by age 50—about half the proportion of widowers remarried by that age (Haskey 1982). But 86 per cent of widows from the 1915 birth cohort, widowed in World War II, had remarried by age 35 (i.e. by 1950). The chances of remarriage from divorce or widowhood can be summarized through a life table. At 1981 remarriage rates, life table calculations show that remarriage at age 20–30 is almost certain, declining to about 50 per cent for divorced women by their early 40s, and 50 per cent for divorced men by their early 50s. Divorced men are the most likely to remarry, widowed women the least (see Coleman 1989*b*). 'Multi-state' life table methods enable all relevant data to be used to estimate contemporary risks of marriage, divorce, remarriage and widowhood over a lifetime: Estimates have not yet been made for Britain but they have been calculated for (e.g.) California and Belgium (Schoen and Nelson 1974, Willekens *et al.* 1982).

The social class differences in chances of remarriage are even sharper than those which affect first marriage. Men in non-manual occupations are a third more likely (41 per cent) to remarry (within 2.5 years of divorce) than are men in manual occupations (31 per cent), but women whose husbands were in non-manual occupations are a third less likely (27 per cent) to remarry than women whose husbands were in manual occupations (35 per cent). Former wives of unskilled manual labourers were the least likely of all to remarry (Haskey 1987*a*). The presence of dependent children, perhaps surprisingly, increases women's chances of remarriages slightly—34 per cent with dependent children remarried within 3.5 years, compared to 31 per cent of divorced wives with no children. This was more true of women over age 35, and especially so among 'non-manual' women.

Cohabitation now precedes most remarriages (70 per cent of remarriages in the early 1980s). In the late 1980s, 32 per cent of currently divorced men aged 16–59, and 23 per cent of divorced women, were cohabiting, and these comprised 26 per cent and 31 per cent respectively of all men and women cohabiting (Haskey and Kiernan 1989). Cohabitation is particularly the rule among couples where both are remarrying, more than where one was previously single. This is depressing remarriage rates. Compared with an earlier linkage study in 1973, the proportions remarrying after any given time from divorce are about a quarter lower; for example the 20 per cent of husbands (48 per cent of those who remarried) remarried within two months of divorce (Leete and Anthony 1979). It is not known how many couples cohabit without ever remarrying. But at any one time, over half of all cohabiting couples include at least one formerly married person, or someone still currently married to someone else (see Coleman 1989*b*).

The interval to remarriage

An increasing number of people have a personal interest in knowing how long they may expect to stay unmarried after a marriage ends. It is difficult to give a complete answer. Surveys such as the General Household Survey ask retrospective questions of the duration to remarriage of those who have remarried. There are no routine sources which state the duration of divorce or widowhood on the registration of a new marriage. Information on the termination of widows' benefits from the DHSS shows that young widows are quick to remarry (Haskey 1982). Ninety-three per cent of the young widows (under age 40) had married again by ten years of widowhood and even 77 per cent of those remarrying at 55–9. The big difference seems to be between widows who remarry before and after age 45, which may have something to do with children.

Until recently, the subsequent marital career of divorced men and women could only be traced by tedious forward linkage studies to connect their record of divorce with that of subsequent remarriage.

This cannot yet be computerized because the key identifier used in the Longitudinal Study—date of birth—is not recorded on marriage certificates. So the time depth of these studies tends to be short, as the inspection must all be done by hand. A high proportion of divorced people remarry as soon as they legally may: 14 per cent of divorced men in a 1979 sample remarried within two months of their decree absolute. This is 41 per cent of all the men who remarried within the 2.5 years surveyed. The corresponding proportions of wives were 12 and 36 per cent. This early peak is not evident in the remarriages of the widowed; if it were it might attract the attention of the police. But it does suggest that a high proportion of divorced people have a new partner already arranged, and that the desire to marry them might have been the cause of the original divorce. The relatively low rate of re-marriage after this initial peak suggests that some partners who did not take this precaution, or who were taken unawares by the failure of their marriage, either do not have a strong desire to remarry or may find it difficult to do so. The General Household Survey shows that 58 per cent of men divorced in 1979–82 had remarried within ten years, and only 40 per cent of women.

The remarried state is clearly a varied and heterogeneous one, an 'incomplete institution' (Cherlin 1978). For many it may be a more complicated, sober, and financially difficult period than their first marriage, still entangled with financial and emotional burdens from the previous marriage, and for some made complicated by the strains of step-parenthood (Maddox 1975, Burgoyne and Clark 1981, Brown 1982). For others it may be a chance to see what a first marriage really could have been like. But for whatever reason, remarriages are twice as vulnerable to divorce as first marriages, other things being equal (Haskey 1983b), in England and Wales and in other industrial countries. Some who enter it may be divorce prone; repeating the same mistakes in partner choice and marriage management. Some data suggests this in the USA (McCarthy 1978); less is known about the UK. The characteristics of remarried couples are in many ways quite different from couples marrying for the first time. Remarried couples are more likely to be older and to have children already. In Britain, the partners in remarriages are closer to each other in terms of social class and of age at marriage, although not necessarily in terms of educational level (Coleman 1977a). They are more likely to have cohabited before marriage, to live further away from each other at the time that they met, both to be employed and to have met at work, and not to have met through any common links of friends or family (Coleman 1981).

5.5 Marriage and the Social Structure

Social groups and marital choice

The strength of social boundaries in our lives is reflected in the relative frequency of marriages within and across class, religious, and ethnic lines. And in turn the pattern of marriages across these boundaries will determine how strong they remain in future. No strong cultural differences can be successfully maintained for long against very high rates of out-marriage. For these reasons social scientists have long been interested in patterns of intermarriage between social, religious, ethnic, and racial groups. Ethnic intermarriage is considered further in Chapter 12.

Men and women are more likely to marry within their own class than into any other. Measuring these differences is troublesome (Coleman 1982). Men and women in the social classes in the middle of society—for example class IIIM—show the highest probability of marrying a partner in their own class (in-marriage or endogamy) while those at the opposite ends of the social spectrum (I and V) show the lowest. But high rates of in-marriage are most likely when the group itself is large; social class III is by far the largest. The social isolation of groups can be better shown in terms of the difference between their

Table 5.8. Social class of husband and wife in combination England and Wales, 1971: Ratio of observed marriages to those expected on the assumption of random marital choice with respect to social class. (10 per cent sample)

Social class of husband	Social class of wife						Inadequately described occupations
	I	II	IIIN	IIIM	IV	V	
I	7.24	2.06	1.30	0.36	0.34	0.14	0.81
II	2.24	2.23	1.15	0.47	0.52	0.25	0.87
IIIN	0.70	1.01	1.48	0.70	0.67	0.48	0.81
IIIM	0.23	0.56	0.93	1.33	1.19	1.20	0.97
IV	0.15	0.52	0.74	1.17	1.40	1.57	1.04
V	0.05	0.36	0.52	1.24	1.44	2.34	1.36
Inadequately described occupations	0.61	0.84	0.84	0.63	0.87	1.03	4.03

Note: These data relate to current marriages at the time of the 1971 Census

Source: OPCS (1983*a*) Fertility Report from the 1971 Census, Series DS no. 5, t. 5.33.

actual marriage patterns compared to the marriages which would occur if partner choice were random with respect to class, etc. (Table 5.8). Men in social class I marry women from that background seven times as often as if they chose irrespective of class; and so on. Women have a markedly different pattern of employment from men, with a high proportion in social classes II and IV, which tends to increase endogamy rates for men in those classes at the expense of others. There are still few women in professional occupations, and relatively few who are unskilled manual workers (see Haskey 1983*d*). It can still be useful to classify brides by their fathers' social class.

In Western society marriages are seldom arranged, nor have they been in recent history except for dynastic or royal marriages. Most marriages follow from initial accidental meetings in commonplace circumstances: for example in a local South-East sample in the 1970s 17 per cent of first married couples, 32 per cent of remarried couples had first met at work (Coleman 1979,1981). Non-manual workers are more likely to meet their future spouses at work, manual workers at dances and pubs or through simple proximity. Eighty seven per cent of the marriages originated in meetings which were quite fortuitous, between people most of whom did not know of each other's existence beforehand (63 per cent). About 60 per cent of the partners had friends in common before they met; about 30 per cent were introduced by friends. Only 2 per cent of the partners' parents had intervened to try to bring them together, 8 per cent of the brides' parents had tried to keep the couple apart (we do not know how many had tried and succeeded, of course). Less than 1 per cent were aware of being related. On average, two people taken at random from the British population are likely to be single fifth or sixth cousins (Coleman 1980*a*). But however important chance may be in bringing together a particular couple, marriage is far from random as far as the characteristics of the couple are concerned. People of remote social, religious, or racial origins (see Chapter 12) are much less likely to marry each other and are less likely to regard each other as eligible or attractive. Data on marriage within and between classes can be used to construct measures of 'nearness' of social groups; assuming, with some evidence, that marriage is a good proxy for other forms of social interaction (Coleman 1983).

The geography of marriage

Most marriages are between people who live in the same area. About 75 per cent marry a partner living in the same town—about 50 per cent for London boroughs and smaller towns (Coleman 1977*b*). A national sample of marriages in 1979 showed that the median distance between partners' homes at the time of marriage (excluding the 32 per cent who gave identical addresses) was 4.7 km. The most common distance was 1 km., 75 per cent lived within 14 km. of each other (Coleman and Haskey 1986). Middle-class people are much more likely to marry a partner who lives at some distance and who was born far away. Marriage horizons are therefore relatively limited spatially during courtship, although older people, up to about age 40, marry substantially further afield.

Most marriages connect families which originated from quite different areas. The distance between birthplaces of spouses in the 1970s was typically much greater than the distance between their homes at marriage, a median 47 km. Marriages at this range will tend to scramble any characteristic local or regional differences within a few generations. For example, about 50 per cent of the marriage cohort settling into the region around the Berkshire town of Reading in the 1970s were born outside it; almost as high a proportion of those born in it moved out at marriage. Berkshire is an area of high mobility. At this rate of exchange even the most extreme local differences of ancestry would become indistinguishable from the rest of the country within six generations assuming they did not affect migration or marital choice. This does not matter from a biological point of view, but it is an indication of how fast local culturally transmitted traditions, accents, attitudes, and tastes could be mingled by migration and intermarriage into a more national culture. Despite this it is clear that substantial regional differences in behaviour still persist especially in areas receiving little inward migration. Later chapters (8, 9, 13) will consider this further.

Studies of surnames, which became fixed around the fifteenth century (Lasker 1985), show that most of those surnames which are known to have a particular local origin have now diffused across the whole country, leaving little regional concentration. But some differences in ancestry remain. Early anthropologists (Beddoes 1885) claimed to be able to show average physical differences between British regional populations. The more reliable blood group data from the transfusion service still shows a concentration of the A group in the South and East, giving away to a higher O in the North and West, particularly Wales, Scotland, and Ireland. All populations have a mixture of A, B, and O, but high A is characteristic of the Scandinavian populations. Despite a millenium of migration and marriage the frequency of A is still higher in the old Danelaw (Roberts and Sunderland 1973). There are also still relatively sharp differences in blood group frequency in old boundary areas, for example between the traditional Welsh and

English parts of Pembroke, in rural Northumberland (Sunderland and Cartwright 1974, Sunderland and Murray 1978), and in particular between predominantly Protestant, and predominantly Catholic areas in Northern Ireland (Potts 1987). In these areas at least, marital choice has helped keep ancestries more separate than chance over many centuries.

6 Households and Families

6.1 Introduction

The importance of family and household

Ninety per cent of the population share their living arrangements with others, in the same household. For most people this is a dominant social experience; for a few their only social experience. The household provides support and refuge. Its size and structure defines the scale of intimate social life and the most constant examples for socialization. It is not surprising that trends in the size, composition, and stability of family and household have attracted so much attention in education, psychology, and social work as well as demography and history. Variables which affect everyone in the same household, such as housing tenure, are now attracting great interest. The influence of the household environment on the lives of children, and on the transmission of characteristics across generations, has been detailed in the longitudinal studies referred to in earlier chapters. Almost all the variables on the 'environment' side of the nature/nurture debate relate to the household of upbringing or its individual members. Household income, from the wife's as well as the husband's earnings, now dominates the economic analysis of fertility trends.

Definitions

Household is a wider definition than family. Household is defined as a person or persons living in a single dwelling unit and sharing meals and household costs (see OPCS 1982*b*). It is a definition which can be fuzzy at the edges; it suffers from an unusual degree of international variation and of change of definition between censuses (as recently in the USA), partly in reflection of changing social circumstances.

Not all households comprise or contain families. In 1981 73 per cent of households comprised one family; 4 per cent comprised one family with 'others'; for the remaining 69 per cent the family and the household were the same thing. An additional 1 per cent of households comprised two or more families (table 6.1). The small number of 'others' includes relatives such as grandparents and non-relatives such

Table 6.1. Private households, England and Wales, 1981 (10 per cent sample)

Type	Distribution of household type			
	Number of households	%	Number of persons	%
All households	1,770,699	100.0	4,780,807	100.0
No family	469,086	26.5	570,382	11.9
1 person	384,913	21.7	384,913	8.1
2 or more persons	84,173	4.8	185,469	3.9
Households with one family	1,286,158	72.6	4,120,295	86.2
Married couple, no children	458,363	25.9	945,265	19.8
without others	432,608	24.4	865,216	18.1
with others	25,755	1.5	80,049	1.7
Married couple with children	680,867	38.5	2,743,777	57.4
without others				
with dependent children	413,265	23.3	1,631,728	34.1
some children dependent	98,157	5.5	480,438	10.0
no children dependent	133,027	7.5	447,122	9.4
with others				
all children dependent	19,848	1.1	100,126	2.1
some children dependent	6,656	0.4	40,474	0.8
no children dependent	9,914	0.6	43,889	0.9
One-parent family	146,928	8.3	431,253	9.0
without others				
all children dependent	43,042	2.4	119,005	2.5
some children dependent	14,628	0.8	57,309	1.2
no children dependent	58,080	3.1	123,293	2.6
with others				
all children dependent	21,430	1.2	81,663	1.7
some children dependent	3,991	0.2	20,327	0.4
no children dependent	8,757	0.5	29,656	0.6
Households with two or more families	15,455	0.9	90,130	1.9
All children dependent	7,458	0.4	43,301	0.9
Some children dependent	4,691	0.3	31,715	0.7
No children dependent	1,591	0.1	7,959	0.2
No children	1,715	0.1	7,155	0.1

Source: 1981 Census Household and Family Composition England and Wales (t. 1), 1984.

as lodgers. In this respect a similar pattern is found elsewhere in the industrial world (except Japan); for example in the USA in 1988 72 per cent of households were 'family' households. For British census purposes a family is defined as 'a married couple living with or without their never-married children or a father or mother together with his or her never-married children or grandparents or a lone grandparent with their never-married grandchildren if there are no parents usually resident in the household'. Thus a family must comprise more than one person. It is usually based on reproduction although a married couple without children still constitutes a 'family' for the purposes of the census. Other related people living together (e.g. adult siblings) do not constitute a 'family'. In Britain in 1989 less than half (42 per cent) of the population was a member of a 'classic' family of a married—or even cohabiting—couple with dependent children, a further 34 per cent comprised a married or cohabiting couple with no children or non-dependent children; 9 per cent were lone parents and their children.

6.2 Problems of Studying the Family and Household

The demography of household and family is perhaps the most difficult of any part of population study. There are so many possible relationships to be specified, so many potential different kinds of family and household to be incorporated into any system or classification, and such radical changes over time in the composition of families and households. The cross-sectional distribution of different kinds of households in the population has changed over time. Each individual household changes its membership and has a beginning, a development, and an end. It is only the households containing the co-resident extended families of Third World societies, often including three generations, which are potentially immortal (see Brass 1983, and Overton and Ermisch 1984).

Little will be said about non-resident kin, which, whether co-resident or not, are the chief organizing factor in social life in many traditional societies. Kin outside the nuclear family are a minor component of Western households. With the possible exception of the dependence of married daughter on mothers living close at hand in traditional urban working-class society (Young and Willmott 1954, Klein 1965), kin are not primary in ordering social life and its rights and obligations. Numbers of kin (e.g. cousins, uncles, aunts) depend on sibship size (Hajnal 1964) and have fallen rapidly as family size has declined. A general adoption of a one-child family would, of course, extinguish them.

Analysis and classification

British censuses have traditionally described household relationships in terms of the standing of each member to the 'head of the household'. Such terms and concepts are less fashionable today but some kind of a 'marker' (who may be taken as the senior female—Brass 1983) is needed in longitudinal studies as a fixed point in a changing group of people, especially for the analysis of the demographic and other determinants of composition (see Bongaarts, Burch, and Wachter 1987). Nuclear families are subject to particularly radical changes in size, composition, and economic status. A couple marries, has children, the wife often leaves work to return later, the children grow up and leave an 'empty nest' behind, one spouse dies and the family is extinguished, the other spouse dies or goes into institutional care and the household is extinguished (see Grebenik, Höhn, and Mackensen 1989). This 'normal' sequence is now often preceded by cohabitation and inter- rupted and restarted by divorce and remarriage. Thus there are several such potential family life cycles, not just one (Kiernan 1983). And

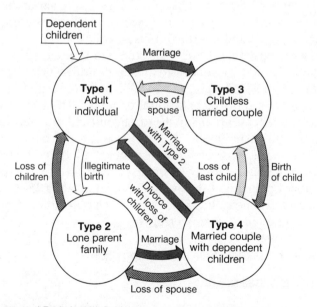

Source: Overton and Ermisch 1984, fig. 1.

Fig. 6.1. The minimal household unit family life cycle

although most households are based upon families (that is, a married couple and any co-resident children), many are not. There are many different kinds of non-family households (cohabiting couples, flatsharers, siblings living together) comprising in all 27 per cent of private households. The overwhelming majority are one-person households.

The volume of data needed for a complete description is usually daunting and seldom completely available, or adequately comparable between different countries (Wall 1984). In response, dynamic models of households have been developed (Brass 1983). To help the analysis of household formation these various different types have been grouped into four building blocks which by themselves or in combination comprise all possible households, just as different combinations of subatomic particles make up each type of atom. The four 'minimal household units' are non-married individuals, one-parent families with dependent children, married couples with and without dependent children. They correspond to the basic stages of the family life cycle (and can be ordered in several different ways) and defined kinds of transition lead from one to the other (Overton and Ermisch 1984; figure 6.1).

'Non-private' households

At the 1981 census 2.5 per cent of people (1,361,200, about the same as the total population of Northern Ireland) were present in 'non-private households'—hotels and boarding houses, colleges, military establishments, prisons, hospitals, hostels and the like (Pearce 1983). 657,000 were 'residents'; 140,000 were resident staff; and 565,000 were present but not normally resident (e.g. the 200,000 in non-psychiatric hospitals and homes; mostly short-term hospital patients). The largest numbers of (non-staff) residents are in homes for the old and disabled (201,000), psychiatric hospitals and homes (133,000), and defence establishments (77,000). The characteristics of these residents are quite different from the general population. Only a small proportion (13 per cent) are married. Only 1 per cent of the overall population aged 25–64 lives in a communal establishment, but 5 per cent of the population aged 75–84, and 19 per cent aged 85 and over do.

6.3 Trends in Household Size and Composition

Decline in average household size

This century family and household composition and average size in Britain, as in the rest of the industrial world, have been declining fast. Until the beginning of this century, average household size had been about 4.6 for hundreds of years (Laslett 1972). Since then it has

Table 6.2. Average household size, England and Wales 1901–1989

Year	Average household size	No. of private households ('000s)	Population[c] ('000)
1901	4.6	7,037[a]	32,528
1911	4.6	7,943	36,070
1921	4.5	8,739	37,887
1931	4.1	10,233	39,952
1939	3.5	12,000[b]	41,552
1951	3.4	13,118	43,758
1961	3.1	16,189	46,105
1971	2.9	18,317	48,759
1981	2.7	19,493	49,155
1989	2.5	—	50,563

[a] Modern household definition from 1911
[b] 'Potential' households
[c] Population includes a proportion not in private households

Sources: Census 1911 Preliminary Report t. A. Census 1951 Housing Report t. A. Census 1981 National Report t. G, t. 4. OPCS Monitor: General Household Survey: Preliminary Results for 1989, no. SS 90/3 t. 1. OPCS Monitor: Mid 1989 population estimates for England and Wales PP1 90/1 table 1. Holmans 1987, t. IV. 4 (1939 only). Census 1981 Historical Tables 1801–1981, England and Wales.

declined to 3.0 in 1961 and to 2.5 in 1989 (table 6.2). There are three main reasons for this. The most important is the modern decline in fertility from a five- or six-child to a two-child family, and the consequent rarity of very large families. This has had less impact on household size than might be supposed, because high infant and child mortality meant that the average family might expect to lose at least one of its children before maturity (Anderson 1983), and adult death-rates too were higher. Second, there are now many fewer non-related people living with families, such as servants and lodgers. Third, many more people, both young and old, now live on their own. Thanks to low fertility, Western societies now have 15–20 per cent of their populations over retirement age compared to 5 per cent in about 1900. This has tripled the proportion of the population in the elderly age-groups who are at risk of living by themselves or just with their spouse. The fertility changes were described in Chapter 4; the sections below describe some of the other changes in composition.

The departure of servants and lodgers

The modern household has become smaller, and more synonymous with the nuclear family, by the departure of the non-related domestic servants and lodgers who often lived with families in the past. In 1861, 14 per cent of households had at least one residential domestic servant; in 1951, just 1 per cent. In 1981 about 20,000 residential domestic servants (mostly women) were recorded in private households (see Wall and Penhale 1989), but this does not seem high enough to include transient resident help such as au pairs. This blank is unfortunate, because there is renewed interest in the role of residential help in permitting high-earning women to combine children with work (Ermisch 1988).

Lodgers ('boarders') are members of the household paying rent for substantial board as well as bed, and who consequently enjoy much more restricted tenancy rights than tenants with a resident landlord but with a separate household. Between 1650 and 1850 5–8 per cent of household members were unrelated lodgers. They still comprised 2 per cent in 1947 (a time of great housing shortage). No one knows how many lodgers there are today. The 1981 census recorded about 133,000; the equivalent of 1 lodger in 0.6 per cent of households (Wall and Penhale 1989), although the figure is likely to be an underestimate. Between them, unrelated servants and lodgers comprised up to 20 per cent of household members in the past (table 6.3); now, together they make up less than 1 per cent. It is the disappearance of these extras that principally distinguishes the households of today from those of the past (Wall 1988). And in pre-industrial times, it was their presence, rather than differences in size, which principally distinguished the Western European household from all others (Hajnal 1982).

Relatives in the household

The presence of relatives (beyond the nuclear family) in the household has become very light. In 1861, 15 per cent of households contained relatives of the household head, the same as in 1951, although this fell to 10 per cent in 1966. Today, relatives comprise about the same proportion of household membership as 200 years ago—about 4 per cent. There are about 250,000 (1.5 per cent) parents and parents-in-law—almost all elderly, four-fifths female. According to the Longitudinal Study, 12 per cent of men aged 85 and over and 19 per cent of women aged 85 and over lived in the household of one of their children (substantially more than recorded in the GHS). A slightly larger number of siblings also live with relatives. All other relatives together are less numerous—just about 150,000, under 1 per cent of households (see Wall and Penhale 1989). The proportion grew in the nineteenth and early twentieth century. In the nineteenth century this was a

Table 6.3. Composition of households 1650–1970. Distribution per 100 persons of household members according to their relationship to the household head

	England 1650–1749	England 1756–1821	England & Wales 1851	Great Britain 1947	Great Britain 1970
Head	22	21	22	27	34
Spouse	14	16	15	22	24
Child	40	43	44	37	37
Relative	4	5	7	12	4
Servant	14	11	5	1	} 1
Attached lodger	6	5	8	2	
Total	100	101	101	101	100
Mean household size	4.44	4.81	4.60	3.67	2.93

Source: Wall (1983), modified in Wall (1988) table 1.

consequence of the longer survival of the elderly. The peak in 1947 (table 6.3) followed the acute housing shortage caused by the destruction of 60,000 dwellings in the Second World War. Many young married couples had to stay with one or other parent as 'concealed households' until they could find a home of their own. This still happens today, especially in social classes V and IV (Grundy and Fox 1985), but as there is now a gross surplus of dwellings over households it is less common.

Changes in the distribution of household size

Twentieth century changes in fertility, survival, and behaviour have transformed the distribution of household sizes. There has been an enormous growth in elderly single-person households and to a lesser extent in young single people leaving home. In 1989 a quarter of households (25 per cent) comprised just one person, compared with 5 per cent in 1911 (figure 6.2). Then there were more unmarried adult men and (particularly) women. There were more widows at younger

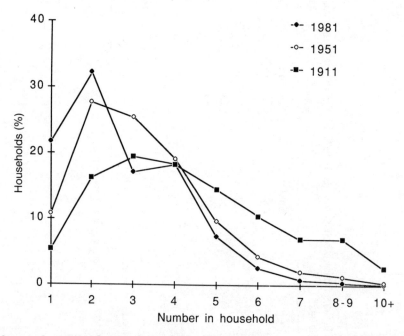

Sources: Census 1911 Summary Tables; Census 1951, Household Composition Tables; Census 1981, Household and Family Composition (10% sample).

FIG. 6.2. Distribution of household size, England and Wales, 1911, 1951, 1981

ages living alone, but almost no divorced persons. Now people are most likely to live alone in old age (mostly through widowhood) and to a lesser extent at younger ages. Only 7 per cent of single-person households are under age 35, about three-quarters are over 60 years of age. In 1981 5 per cent of people aged 25–44 lived alone, 29 per cent of people aged 65–74, and 47 per cent of those aged 75 and over. Beyond that age, an increasing proportion (19 per cent aged 85 and over) live in institutions. The immigrant populations since the Second World War have brought with them more diverse patterns of household considered further in Chapter 12.

The proportions living alone increase rapidly after about age 40, mainly due to marital breakdown (Haskey 1987). The 1.2 million single people in middle life in 1985 (between age 30 and 59) were a mixed group. Fifty-three per cent of the 660,000 men had remained single; 29 per cent were divorced and had not remarried or cohabited. Fewer (37 per cent) of the 510,000 women had not married, about the same proportion were divorced and not remarried (25 per cent) but a higher proportion (29 per cent) were widowed. Low rates of marriage and high rates of divorce are likely to increase the number of these households; at the rates of 1984, the proportion of men and women living alone up to age 45 is expected to double (Haskey 1987*b*). The other novelty is the growth of the one-parent family, now comprising 9 per cent of all households and continuing to increase at the expense of conventional families. This has been created by the two late twentieth-century novelties of high levels of divorce and illegitimacy, the former being the more important.

Most of the change in household size has followed from the growth in the numbers of one- and two-person households. At the other end of the scale, only 2 per cent of households included six or more people in 1989 (comprising 6 per cent of people); a decline from 6 per cent of households and 13 per cent in 1971. It is important, though, to remember that the picture looks different when analysed by people, not households (table 6.4). Almost half the population—42 per cent—lived in households of a married couple with dependent children, only 10 per cent of people of all ages lived by themselves.

6.4 The Life Cycle of the Household

Single young people

At some time in their early 20s most young people leave home to set up their own independent households; either by themselves, jointly with

Table 6.4. Composition of households, 1989

Type of household	Households (%)	People (%)
One person	25	10
Lone parent with children	9	9
Married or cohabiting couple with no children or non-dependent children	36	34
Married or cohabiting couple with dependent children	26	42
Other	4	5
TOTAL	100	100

Notes: Lone-parent and married-couple households may include other non-family individuals. 'Other' includes households containing two or more unrelated adults and households with two or more families. Figures may not sum to 100 because of rounding.

Sources: OPCS Monitor SS 90/3. General Household Survey: Preliminary Results for 1989, figure 2, OPCS.

others sharing a dwelling, or through marriage or cohabitation. According to the Longitudinal Study, more than 50 per cent of girls had left home by age 22, more than 50 per cent of boys by age 24 (Wall and Penhale 1989). In the past, children left home to join another household as a 'servant' or to form another household in marriage. Today the choices are more varied. British 20–4-year-olds are less prone than in many European countries to leave home to live by themselves. The proportion of single-person households where the occupants were under 35 was the lowest of the major European countries (Kiernan 1989*c*). In fact 8 per cent more 22-year-olds lived at home with their parents in 1981 than in 1971, partly because they were marrying later. This may follow from a shortage of easy access to rented housing. Housing supply can constrain household formation as well as respond to it (see Chapter 5). Rented housing is generally thought to be the ideal tenure for young single people given their mobility and lack of resources. But the private rented sector in Britain has shrunk after seventy years of rent controls to just 6.3 per cent of households in 1987—the smallest in the Western world—and is seldom an attractive first choice. Single people are not in general eligible for council housing. The consequences may include the unusually high proportion of 20–9-year-old owner-occupiers in Britain, the growth of single homelessness, and some of the increase in single parenthood, which accelerates access to council housing. If present government policies to revive private renting succeed they may accelerate household formation by young single people, increase housing benefit demand accordingly and make cohabitation easier.

Since the Second World War, too, the large numbers of concealed households created by a half million surplus of households over dwellings has diminished, so young married couples have less need to live with parents—and this has never been thought desirable. In 1985 there were estimated to be 275,000 concealed households; 109,000 married-couple households and 166,000 lone-parent households (DoE 1988*a*, 1988*b*). The possibility of concealed single-person households is not recognized. It is now common to precede first marriage with cohabitation, normal to do so before a remarriage, and some cohabit without ever marrying at all (see Chapters 4 and 5).

Married couple families

As a consequence of the reduction in family size and the departure of the 'extras', husband and wife dominate household membership—almost 60 per cent in 1970, compared with about 35 per cent in the past. But viewed another way, things have changed little. Despite the change in family size, in terms of composition 47 per cent of Victorian households in 1861 consisted of one or both parents with their children but no other relatives, exactly the same as in 1961 and 1966 (Hole and Pountney 1971) although somewhat higher than in 1985 (36 per cent). Even a hundred years ago, this 'classical' or 'normal' household type comprised less than half of all households. Partly thanks to the rapid growth of one-person households since the 1960s, married couples with dependent (under-16) children now constitute only 28 per cent of all households, although 45 per cent of people live in such households (table 6.4). Married-couple households without children, or without dependent children, have expanded at their expense, as childbearing within marriage has been delayed since the 1970s and completed within a shorter span of married life. Such households comprised 35 per cent of households in 1985, although only 32 per cent of people. The numbers of married-couple households visible to statistics have been eroded by the growth of cohabitation (Chapter 5). Because of the frequency of divorce and consequent remarriage, an increasing proportion of married-couple households are in fact remarried-couple households (figure 5.9). These are more heterogeneous than first-married households: there are more small and very large households (Chapter 5), a greater complexity of family relationships, sometimes more precarious financial circumstances (Coleman 1989*b*). About 7 per cent of all children aged under 16 already live with a step-parent. At the risks current in the early 1980s about one child in five (Haskey 1983*a*), and about one adult in four, could expect to spend some time in such a 'reconstituted' family.

The 'empty nest'

The earlier departure of children and the longer survival of parents has opened up a new phase in the family life cycle in all developed societies which scarcely existed at the beginning of the century (Glick 1977, Kiernan 1989*c*). This 'empty nest' phase, where parents are still active and working but children have left, begins for some families when the husband is in his 40s. In 1981 over 35 per cent of couples with the husband aged 50–4 had no dependent children still living with them. This new freedom for parents has attracted much attention from psychologists and market researchers. Contrary to earlier suppositions (McAuley and Nutty 1985), it seems that this is a particularly satisfying period of married life (although only reasonably content couples will have stayed married that long). Whether the thankful parents will find their empty nest newly refilled with returning divorced children, or with their own elderly and increasingly dependent parents, remains to be seen.

Single-parent families

In 1986 just over one million households (8 per cent) were one-parent families with dependent children (see Haskey 1989). The rise of divorce and illegitimacy together have increased the number of such families in Britain from 367,000 in 1961 (2.3 per cent), to 516,000 in 1971 (4 per cent), and 916,000 in 1981. Non-census estimates are slightly higher (Haskey 1986*a*). By 1986 they comprised 14 per cent of all families with dependent children (1,010,000 families), compared with 8 per cent in 1971. Most of these households are headed by lone mothers (90 per cent in 1986). The growth of one-parent families has caused much concern but so far no policy response except for proposals announced in 1990 to trace absent fathers and recover maintenance from them. The material welfare of the children and the effect on their future of their being brought up by only one parent is one source of worry. Another is the cost of their dependency as almost all receive welfare benefits: in 1986 58 per cent received One-Parent Benefit, an overlapping 59 per cent received Supplementary Benefit (now Income Support); 25 per cent received both. In 1990 welfare support for one-

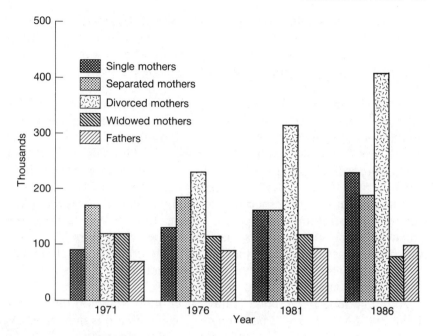

Source: Haskey 1989*b*, t. 4.

FIG. 6.3. One-parent families, by type of family, 1971–1986

parent families was estimated to cost £1,850 million. The absent fathers provided £155 million. In addition the majority of those 52 per cent who were tenants would be eligible for Housing Benefit. Forty per cent of such families rent from local authorities; some of the divorced parents would formerly have been owner-occupiers (Holmans, Nandy and Brown 1987).

The majority of one-parent families are the creation of divorce, not of illegitimacy (figure 6.3). In 1986 25 per cent of lone mothers were unmarried, 66 per cent divorced or separated, 8 per cent widowed. From 1971 to 1986 unmarried mothers increased from 18 per cent of all sole mothers to 25 per cent, divorced and separated mothers from 51 per cent to 58 per cent. Widowed single mothers have declined correspondingly in absolute and relative terms. More children in one-parent families lack a parent through divorce and separation (1,451,000) rather than illegitimacy (423,000). The average family size of divorced and separated women with dependent children in 1986 was about the same (1.8) as that of married couples with dependent children, although a higher proportion of divorcing couples at any age, compared to couples in continuing marriages, have no children at all.

Widows have a smaller average family size (1.4), single (i.e. never-married) parents have an average of 1.3. A minority of single parents evidently make single parenthood something of a way of life; 12 per cent of illegitimate births are second births or higher; 5 per cent are third or higher.

The social and financial situations of the two types of lone parent are different. Illegitimacy, even of the new cohabiting kind, is concentrated among mothers whose chief economic supporter or father is in social class IV or V, and also among West Indians. In the 1980s, about 49 per cent of births in England and Wales to West Indian born mothers have been illegitimate. Because of the spatial concentration of social classes and immigrant groups, especially on urban estates, there is a marked spatial concentration of one-parent families too. Divorce is also more frequent among the manual social classes, especially class V, but the difference is not nearly as strong. Remarriage prevents these numbers being much higher; the presence of dependent children does not seem to handicap remarriage chances.

Although lone parenthood is now much more common than in the 1950s and 1960s, it would be wrong to imagine that it is quite new. As far as comparable data exist, lone-parent families were just as frequent in the sixteenth and seventeenth centuries as they are now, declining in the nineteenth and early twentieth centuries before increasing to their present level (Wall 1988). Then, many families were broken by widow-hood and the children left without a parent, usually the father—and in many more cases, orphaned (Laslett 1972). Fewer children now lose a parent before they are 16, although in 1972–4 there were still more single mothers from this cause than from illegitimacy. As mortality declines and childbearing is earlier, widowhood is becoming an uncommon cause of lone parenthood. In 1986, 9 per cent of lone parents were widowed mothers.

The elderly and their households

By the 1960s in Great Britain, the proportions of people over 65 living by themselves or just with their spouse had doubled compared with the previous century to 58 per cent of men and 53 per cent of women. By the 1980s the proportion had increased almost as much again, to 77 per cent of men and 77 per cent of women. In Britain, as in most countries of Western Europe (but not, for example, in Poland or Ireland) about one half of women over age 65 live by themselves. Why have these radical changes occurred, even in the last twenty years? Smaller family size and an earlier end to childbearing (to 30 from 40 years of age) have meant that older people will seldom have young, dependent adult children still living with them, especially as, until the 1970s, average age at marriage had fallen by 3–4 years (Kiernan 1983). Until the 1930s up to 15 per cent of each generation of women remained unmarried, and at least potentially able to live as an adult with ageing parents. Since then, such women have become rare. Only 5 per cent of women in the 1940s birth cohorts remain unmarried.

The proportions of elderly people living by themselves are increasing partly because of changes in living habits and mobility, partly through underlying demographic movements. Their absolute numbers and also their proportion of the whole population increased subtantially from the beginning of the century until the 1970s, and will do so again early next century (Chapters 3, 13). In 1901 there were 1.52 million people aged 65 and over in England and Wales, comprising 4.7 per cent of the total. By 1981 the number had grown to 7.27 million, 15 per cent of the total. This growth in numbers is a consequence of last century's high fertility and to a lesser extent of the improvement in survival. The growth in the proportion is mostly a consequence of this century's declining fertility, such that successive birth cohorts are no bigger than their predecessors, and are often smaller. Recently continued improvement in the survival of the elderly is making a bigger contribution to their numbers. Until after the turn of the century change in the overall number and proportion of people over 65 will be modest because of the small number of births in the 1920s and 1930s, although within that age-group the numbers of people over 75 and 85 will increase rapidly. Next century, from the 2020s, the whole age-group will expand fast as the baby boom matures into old age.

An increasing number of the elderly—about a quarter of a million—now live in institutions rather than private households. In 1981 187,000 people aged 65 and over lived in institutions for the elderly (65 per cent local authority and 35 per cent private). In 1985 this had risen to 223,000 (46 per cent private). However, despite a very substantial increase in numbers this represents about the same proportion of the age-group (3.0 per cent) that lived in public institutions —mostly workhouses—in 1900 (25,000 people, 2.8 per cent). These figures include sheltered housing and 'care in the community' outside private houses. People aged over 75 (about 5 per cent) and especially over 85 (about 20 per cent) are much more likely to need sheltered or full institutional housing on grounds of infirmity. Because of high birth-rates up to the 1920s and the low birth-rates afterwards, the very old are a growing proportion of the elderly.

The household arrangements of the elderly have received much attention from public policy makers. The policy of 'care in the community' attempts to maintain the elderly in their own households, in those of relatives, or in small semi-private establishments such as sheltered flats. It is a response to the wishes of many older people to remain independent in their own household for as long as possible, to disturbingly poor conditions in some large residential institutions, and the costs of residential care. But 'Care in the Community' is not a cheap option. Most of the elderly who enter institutions need substantial care. The modern two-earner household is an unlikely place for the care of the elderly. The dwellings in which most families now live cannot easily accommodate an extra adult household member. The strains involved may not be manageable. The compensation or outside help offered may not be adequate especially if working women feel threatened by the risk of being called upon to care for the parent or parent-in-law when they become infirm. The problems presented by this growing population are discussed further in Chapter 13.

Such policies have been hailed as a return to 'Victorian values' of domestic care of the elderly. In fact most households in the past did not contain relatives outside the nuclear family, although demographically they 'could' have done (Wachter, Hammel, and Laslett 1978). However, relatively few of the elderly lived alone, and quite a high proportion lived with their children. This apparent paradox is accounted for by the small proportion (4 per cent) of the population aged over 65, and by considering who is the head of the household in question. In the seventeenth to the nineteenth centuries about 7 per cent of elderly (over 65) men and 15 per cent of elderly women lived alone, another 27 per cent and 14 per cent lived just with their spouse; 40 per cent and 15 per cent respectively lived with their spouse and their children, 27 per cent and 56 per cent respectively with their children or other relatives (table 6.5). The great differences between men and women reflects the great differences in their survival—women were, and remain, much more likely to be left widowed. It must also be remembered that women did not stop childbearing until average age 40, so with late ages at marriage (28 for men, 25 for women) it would be quite normal for young adults still to live at home with their parents, when their parents were past today's retirement age. The father would still be the head of the household, and the children would not yet have married. It is not necessarily a case of large numbers of children 'taking in' their elderly parents, although that too happened. These proportions were enhanced by Poor Law regulations of long standing, but only intermittently enforced, whereby the Poor Law Officers required younger people able to support their relatives to do so (although not

Table 6.5. Households with elderly person,[a] 1684–1980

Type of co-resident	Males			Females		
	England 1684–1796	Great Britain 1962	Great Britain 1980/1	England 1684–1796	Great Britain 1962	Great Britain 1980/1
(Alone)	7	11	17	15	30	45
Spouse only	27	47	60	14	23	32
Spouse and others	40	23	14	15	11	5
Child (with/without others)	18	12	4	39	24	10
Other relatives (with/without others)	9	4	3	17	9	5
Non-relatives only		2	2		3	2
TOTAL	101	99	100	100	100	99

[a] Persons 65 or over.

Note: Figures show distribution (%) of persons aged 65 and over according to other co-residents in the same household. Some columns do not sum to 100 because of rounding errors

Source: Wall 1984: 487 (in Wall 1988: t .4).

necessarily in the same house). Institutional care in the workhouse, begun by the new Poor Law of 1834, took in mostly elderly people with no close relatives. In all, workhouses accommodated 209,000 people in 1901 (Pearce 1983).

6.5 Households in the Future

These changes have meant that during this century growth in the number of households has been faster than the growth in population (table 6.2) in Britain and in all industrial countries. This is the other side of the decline in average household size. Households must be forecast separately from population. It is a precarious activity. Much anxiety on investment, housing, countryside protection, and political prospects depend on its results. This is because demand for housing and other services and for different sorts of housing, and therefore for land, depends on household growth and planning for it depends on its forecasting. Population can grow slowly, while households continue to increase fast through age-structure changes, such as the maturation of the baby boom, and through changes in living habits, such as the rise and fall of early marriage and divorce. Official household projections have great interest for local authorities and housebuilders because of their quasi-judicial status as a benchmark of future housing demand, and therefore of the need to release land for housing. For this reason only one 'variant' is published. It would be impossible to base or modify local authority Structure Plans or appeal against them if there were a variety of official projected totals to choose from and therefore no fixed criterion against which to judge the adequacy of proposals. This may be regarded as a triumph of bureaucracy over science, but it is necessarily so as long as the planning system remains in being.

Construction of household projections

Official household projections in Britain are made on the basis of the OPCS central variant of population projections, the latest being those based on 1985 and projected in detail to 2025 (DoE 1988*a*). These are turned into projection of households by the application of 'headship rates' to the population totals in each age-group separately by sex, taking into account the projections of marital status produced by the Government Actuary's Department. These projections assume, for example, continued delay and decline of marriage rates, stabilization of divorce rates at their 1984/5 levels and modest declines in remarriage (Haskey 1988). A 'headship rate' is the proportion of any category of the population which heads a household. Thus the 'headship rate' for the whole British population is the inverse of the household size, namely 1/2.56 in 1985 or 0.39. Headship rates are high for (say) males aged 35–40, low for females of the same age, zero for children of dependent age-groups. They are estimated from the last four censuses and subsequent Labour Force Surveys, with these trends extrapolated into the future. These projections are inevitably highly sensitive to variations in the projected distributions of age, sex, and marital status, as well as the underlying population totals. The most difficult technical task is to reconcile the numbers of married-couple, etc. households with the available numbers of people of each sex and age-group. Like their parent population projections, their projected totals have jumped in successive issues, to the dismay of the planners who depend on them. The 1987-based projections are likely to include further increases because they assume the continuation of net immigration from abroad.

The DoE approach has been criticized on a number of grounds (King 1986) for being too mechanistic, insufficiently explicit in its assumptions, and incapable of incorporating variant assumptions and showing their impact. The mechanical forecasting of the headship rates are perhaps their weakest element. They are not based on any dynamic model of household generation and dissolution, neither do they allow alternative scenarios to be explored. Instead headship rates are projected from present trends on a curve-fitting basis without explicit consideration of the sociological or demographic plausibility of the outcome of these trends. For example, the household projections take at face value an extrapolation which implies that about 20 per cent of future generations of married women will remain single throughout their lives, instead of the 10 per cent which seems more likely (Chapter 4). The household projections incorporate only formally married couples, as officially documented, and although the rise of cohabitation is recognized, it is not put into a separate category which can be combined with 'married'.

Only four types of household are projected by the DoE, and households consisting of an unmarried couple of opposite sex, with or without children or other unmarried adults, is classified as 'other' as long as the male is head of the household. The household projections may therefore understate the 'actual' number of 'married' households by up to five points (7 per cent) (see DoE 1988b). The DoE projections estimate 175,000 concealed households in 1985 and assume their future decline. The implications of the recent DoE projections have caused much alarm among protectors of the green belt; they have been used in justification for proposed housing development including private sector

Table 6.6. 1983- and 1985-based household projections for England, 1986–2001 ('000s)

Type of household	Base	1986	1991	1996	2001	1986–2001 change	% change
Married	1983	10,641	10,689	10,767	10,746	106	1.0
Couple	1985	10,724	10,559	10,449	10,350	−374	−3.5
Lone Parent	1983	1,587	1,728	1,802	1,832	245	15.4
	1985	1,661	1,868	2,013	2,074	413	24.9
Other multi-	1983	1,179	1,272	1,281	1,250	61	5.2
person	1985	1,206	1,378	1,465	1,475	269	22.3
One person	1983	4,473	4,971	5,355	5,653	1,180	26.4
	1985	4,452	5,099	5,691	6,184	1,732	38.9
All	1983	17,879	18,661	19,205	19,481	1,602	9.0
households	1985	18,044	18,903	19,617	20,083	2,039	11.3

Note: Figures may not sum due to rounding.

Sources: 1983-Based Estimates of Numbers of Households in England 1983–2001. London, Department of the Environment, 1986. 1985-Based Estimates of Numbers of Households in England, the Regions, Counties, Metropolitan Districts and London Boroughs 1985–2001. London, Department of Environment 1988.

new towns in the South-East. Alternative estimates based on the need for more housing, including replacement of existing stock, can be much higher. One, based in part upon notions of 'housing need' including 'concealed households', waiting list, and homelessness figures, estimates existing need of up to two million and projects further growth of between 2.2 and 3m. households (National Housing Forum 1989).

Projected increases in household types

The 1985-based household projections show a substantial increase (table 6.6) in the total number of households forecast for 2001, much more than population growth. In fact they forecast 490,000 households more than the number projected two years before from the 1983-based projections. The increase is entirely in single-person, single-parents, and 'other' households, which are projected to grow much faster than married-couple households. The latter are projected to decline slightly in numbers overall, most particularly in the youngest age-group. A decline in numbers of married couple households aged 30–44 is inevitable from trends in the age structure; likewise a modest increase in those aged 45–64. The substantial increases in lone-parent

Source: Department of the Environment (1988*a*), t. 2, t. 3.

FIG. 6.4. Projected percentage change in households of different types, England and Wales, 1986–2001

and single-person households in the 30–44 age-group follow from the expected continuation of delayed marriage and high levels of illegitimacy and divorce in the large baby boom cohorts (figure 6.4). The much more modest increases in these categories of household in the younger 15–29 age-group follow from the much smaller numbers in these cohorts. The decline in all households, especially married-couple households aged 15–29, follows almost inevitably from changes in the age structure. It may be the herald of a long-term slackening of demand for housing. In the short run, however, there has been much excitement about the projected further increase of 290,000 households in the South-East (4 per cent of the 1983 total), which comprises 48 per cent of the total projected increase for England. This increase is entirely in single-person, single-parent, and 'other' households, whose housing requirements may be quite different from married couples. These problems are considered further in Chapter 13.

7 Mortality: Trends and Patterns

7.0 Introduction

This chapter will look at this century's trends in risks and causes of death, the decline of infectious disease, and the rise of chronic diseases, the likely causes of the trends, and prospects for the future. A following chapter will look in more detail at the differentials in mortality and their causes.

7.1 The Decline of Mortality in the Twentieth Century

Overall trends

Most of the improvement in human survival since the eighteenth century has occurred within living memory (figure 7.1). Survival to early middle age is almost certain. Most people now die in old age (in 1985, 79 per cent of deaths occurred to persons aged over 64). Expectation of life at birth in 1985–7 was 72.1 for men, 77.8 for women. Infectious diseases (except AIDS) are being pushed into a smaller and smaller corner. The diseases (circulatory disease, cancer, chronic bronchitis) which now cause most deaths act late in life. They have no ultimate simple cause like a micro-organism, but depend on long-term environmental influences and on fundamental and irreversible processes of ageing.

Trends in mortality have become less exciting since the mid-nineteenth century. Crisis mortality from epidemics has been left behind; it is fertility which now has the erratic graph. None the less, progress has been far from even. The advent of the NHS did not bring a sharp fall in mortality, except perhaps in infant mortality. By the 1960s, mortality decline in most Western countries seemed to have come to a dead-end and even suffered some reverses (Preston 1976) due to worsening rates of circulatory disease and lung cancer, especially among men. This hiatus was mostly due to the epidemic of smoking, which has moved through most industrial countries this century, slowing mortality decline everywhere. But now improvement has resumed. Heart disease rates have declined in many countries (including, at last, the UK) and lung cancer rates have already peaked, at least among men (Council of

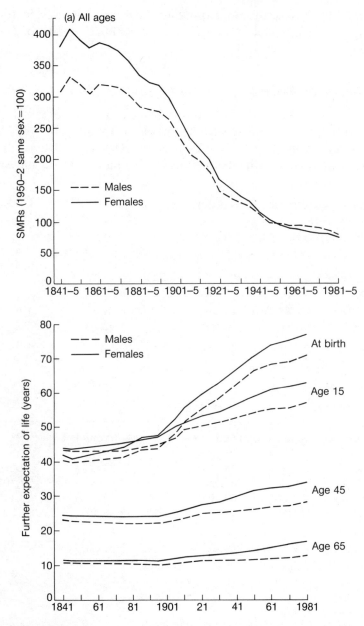

Source: Swerdlow 1987.

Fig. 7.1. Standardized Mortality Ratios and expectation of life England and Wales, 1841–1981

Europe 1982). But the unfavourable old trends continue in Eastern Europe and the Soviet Union (Davis and Feshbach 1980, Jozan 1986, Anderson and Silver 1989).

The impact of the World Wars

This century, two World Wars have disrupted the demographic trends of most industrial countries. In the First World War (1914–18) 723,000 British servicemen lost their lives in action. This appears to be the best of several possible estimates (Winter 1976; table 7.1). In the Second

Table 7.1. Casualties suffered by British forces, 1914–1982
(a) 1914–1918

Service	Served	Died	% died	% wounded	% casualties (incl. PoW)
Army	5,215,162	673,375	12.9	31.5	47.4
Royal Navy	640,237	43,244	6.8	4.0	11.6
RFC/RAF	291,175	6,166	2.1	2.5	5.7
TOTAL	6,146,574	722,785	11.8	27.3	41.7

Source: Winter 1985, t. 3.3

(b) 1939–1945

Service	Intake	Died	Missing[a]	Wounded	PoW
Army	—	144,079	33,771	239,575	152,076
Royal Navy	—	50,758	820	14,663	7,401
RAF	—	69,606	6,736	22,839	13,115
ARMED FORCES TOTAL[b]	4,748,500	264,443	41,327	277,077	172,592
Women's Auxiliary Services		624	98	744	20
Merchant Navy		30,248	4,654	4,701	5,720

[a] 'Missing' includes 244 still missing at 28 Feb. 1946 and 39,835 who rejoined their units.
[b] Includes men from overseas serving in the UK forces, in particular from Newfoundland and Southern Rhodesia.
Source: Central Statistical Office 1951, t. 14

(c) Korean War 1950–1953

Service	Died[a]	Wounded	PoW
Army	865	2,589	955
Royal Navy	75[b]	85[c]	24
RAF	27	—	1
ARMED FORCES TOTAL	967	2,674	980

[a] Includes killed in action, died of wounds, died in captivity.
[b] Includes 29 Royal Marines; 2 Merchant Seamen not included.
[c] Includes 66 Royal Marines.

Source: Ministry of Defence Historical Branches.

(d) Falklands War 1982

Service	Died	Wounded
Army	123	307
Royal Marines[a]	26	112
Royal Navy	89	127
RAF	1	4
ARMED FORCES TOTAL	239	550
Royal Fleet Auxiliary[b]	10	18
Merchant Service	6	—

[a] Royal Marines listed separately because they were a large proportion of the land fighting force.
[b] RFA are civilians.

Sources: Ministry of Defence Historical Branches.

(1939–45) 274,000 servicemen were killed, and 30,000 merchant seamen and 77,000 other civilians, 30,000 of them women (Central Statistical Office 1951). British losses were therefore considerably lighter in the Second World War than in the First. Despite the population being larger in 1939 than in 1914, rather fewer served in the armed forces (4,749,000 compared with 6,147,000); 5.6 per cent of these were killed compared with 11.8 per cent in the First World War. The demographic impact of these losses depends to some extent on what they are compared with. Each year this century there have been about 500,000–550,000 deaths from natural causes. But the extra wartime deaths were concentrated in narrow age groups from 20 to 40 (37 per cent of deaths were at age 20–4) with substantial consequences for marriage (see Chapter 5) and employment. Particular groups suffered much higher risks (Keegan 1976), especially pilots and machine-gunners. Junior officers really did suffer higher proportionate casualties than other ranks. About one in five graduates of Oxford and Cambridge universities who joined up in the First World War were killed, almost double the average (Winter 1985).

Despite these losses Britain suffered less than most combatant nations. In the First World War Germany lost 2.0 million military casualties, France 1.3 million, Russia 1.8 million. Serbia lost about 6 per cent of its entire population (UK 1.6 per cent). The US managed to win the war with only 114,000 dead. For most countries the Second World War was even worse than the first. Germany lost 3.25 million military dead, 600,000 in bombing, 3 million more civilians killed or missing fleeing from the East, and gained over ten million refugees.

The only 'political' mortality which Britain has suffered this century has been murders by Irish republican and other terrorists. Other countries have had to endure terrorism by their own governments; the most outstanding example being the murder of about six million Jews by the Nazis. About ten million peasants died of famine, disease, and the effects of deportation in the 1930s during Stalin's forced collectivization of landholdings (Nove 1990). KGB figures released in 1990 stated that 3.5 million people had been executed or died in camps since 1917, including those executed as a result of the 'terror' instituted in 1936 and during collectivization (*The Times*, 27 April 1990, Conquest 1970, 1990).

Wartime conditions improved civilian health in some respects. Deaths from TB went up in the First World War and until 1941 in the Second through temporary overcrowding and housing shortages. But concern about the adequacy of diet ensured that, even though many foodstuffs were rationed, the balance became more satisfactory in terms of vitamins, fat, and fibre content (Southgate *et al.* 1979). As a consequence of these efforts, sharpened by pre-war concerns, infant mortality continued to improve during both wars. Deaths from childhood diseases except measles were much lower in 1945 than in 1939. Overall civilian mortality did not deteriorate in the First and improved during the Second faster than in peacetime, even if this was a consequence of the nation living off its capital instead of its income (Central Statistical Office 1951, Winter 1988).

Trends by age

Death-rates at different ages have not changed uniformly. Infants, children, and the middle-aged of both sexes have gained most, because their heavy mortality was caused by infectious disease. A third of the overall mortality reduction since the turn of the century comes from improvements in mortality in the first year of life (figure 2.3), 15 per cent in older childhood and younger adulthood together (McKeown *et al.* 1975; OPCS 1978*a*). Infant mortality rates (8/1,000 in 1989) were less than a tenth of the level in 1900 (138/1,000) (see Chapter 2).

After infancy and childhood, the younger middle-aged of both sexes (25–44) have enjoyed the most improvement, following by adolescents and young adults aged 15–24. Since the 1950s some of this impetus has been exhausted. Mortality of young men aged 15–24 has hardly improved in thirty years; their mortality rates are now similar to those of women fifteen years older (figure 2.2). Most deaths of men at this age occur on the roads; exposure to this risk has grown with motor traffic. In the USA, death-rates of young men have actually increased at this age: homicide (unlike in the UK) has become demographically significant, as more recently has AIDS, which is becoming the leading cause of death of young men in some US cities. Death-rates for children aged 5–14 declined fast from 1931 to 1951. Children of this age have the lowest death-rate of all, and survival from beginning to end of this age-group is almost now complete (99.8 per cent OPCS 1987*d*); so there is little further scope for improvement. Apart from young adults, men aged 65 or over have enjoyed the smallest improvement in survival. A man aged 65 in 1985–7 had an expectation of life of 13.5 years; a woman 17.4 years, 1.8 and 3.1 years respectively more than in 1950–2. Only 4 per cent of the increase in expectation of life has come from improved mortality beyond age 65.

The quality of data

There is only one physiological way in which life begins, but the World Health Organization's International Classification of Causes of Death (ICD) recognizes 999 ways in which it can end (see OPCS 1983*e*). The clinical and epidemiological analysis of the cause of death and their correlates is one of the most powerful weapons in the fight against disease. Therefore much depends on their accurate identification by the medical profession (Heasman and Lipworth 1966, McKeown 1978). There are often serious intrinsic difficulties in determining the cause of death in the very young or the very old. Elderly people often suffer from several conditions which may contribute to their death and it may be difficult to decide which is the underlying cause. (OPCS has coded all causes mentioned on the death certificate since 1985). In 1967, only

28 per cent of men's death certificates listed one cause of death, 61 per cent listed two or three, 1.5 per cent listed six or more. Which one is chosen as the underlying cause may depend on the sex of the deceased (Registrar-General 1970, 1971 OPCS 1981*a*).

Only one death certificate in three is issued after an autopsy by a coroner. Only 20–30 per cent of the rest are followed by autopsy; and the cause of death as certified by a doctor is only fully confirmed in half the cases where an autopsy is held. In 15 per cent of cases, the different diagnosis might have affected the patient's treatment. Two out of three deaths now occur in hospital (compared to one in ten twenty-five years ago). Change in hospital practice can produce apparent trends in disease, for example, in the sharp rise of bronchial pneumonia deaths (not lobar pneumonia) over age 65 from the 1950s to the 1970s. This trend, at variance with declining trends in younger people and in other forms of respiratory illness, was probably due to the increasing practice in NHS hospitals of attributing deaths of the very old to pneumonia rather than to heart disease (OPCS 1981*a*).

New cancer cases have been voluntarily (but still incompletely) registered since 1969. Ischaemic heart disease is not registered in this way although, together with other circulatory disorders, it accounts for one death in two. Its synonyms were not all classified together until 1968 (8th revision of the ICD) and the picture has been complicated by changes in diagnostic fashion: 'ischaemic heart disease' has replaced obsolete entries such as 'myocardial degeneration' in the registration of deaths, possibly disguising the real trends in heart disease even into the 1970s.

International comparisons of risk can be complicated by national differences in registration of the causes of deaths, despite the ICD. Studies of immigrants, who tend to keep the real risks of their country of origin (their children do not) can help here. French immigrants dying in Britain (therefore certified in Britain) have an overall SMR of 95, about the same as the average for England and Wales (100). For ischaemic heart disease (IHD) the rates are much lower: 76 for men, 64 for women (England and Wales = 100). The SMR of 29 for French-men dying in France of IHD is too low as a real comparison with English rates. None the less the comparison of deaths of Frenchmen in England shows that there is a real and substantial difference (Marmot, Adelstein, and Bulusu 1983). International differences in defining live and still births creates substantial difference in infant mortality rates. This is one reason for the emphasis on the Perinatal Mortality Rate, which takes together still-births and early neonatal deaths. (Macfarlane and Mugford 1980)

Table 7.2. Deaths by cause, England and Wales, 1985 (selected causes)

Cause	ICD No.	Males		Females	
		Number	[%]	Number	[%]
All causes	1–999	292,327	100.0	298,407	100.0
Circulatory system	390–459	139,903	47.9	147,151	49.3
Ischaemic heart disease	410–14	91,627	31.3	71,478	24.0
Acute myocardial infarct	410	61,099	20.9	45,227	15.2
Cerebro-vascular disease	430–8	27,590	9.4	45,629	15.3
Neoplasms	140–239	74,324	25.4	67,294	22.6
Trachea, bronchus, lung	162	25,994	8.9	9,798	3.3
Female breast	174	—	—	13,513	4.5
Cervix uteri	180	—	—	1,957	0.7
Other uterus	179, 182	—	—	1,535	0.5
Ovary	183	—	—	3,810	1.3
Prostate	185	6,628	2.2	—	—
Bladder	188	3,251	1.1	1,331	0.4
Lymphatic (leukaemias)	200–8	4,716	1.6	4,322	1.4
Stomach	151	5,922	2.0	4,049	1.4
Respiratory system	460–519	34,065	11.7	30,542	10.2
Pneumonia	480–6	10,403	3.6	17,528	5.9
Influenza	487	212	0.1	450	0.2
Injury and poisoning	800–999	11,301	3.9	7,708	2.6
Motor vehicle traffic acc.	E810–19	3,379	1.2	1,453	0.5
Suicide	E950–9	2,949	1.0	1,470	0.5
Homicide	E960–9	188	0.1	156	0.1
Undetermined	E980–9	1,061	0.4	700	0.2
Infectious diseases	001–139	1,200	0.4	1,181	0.4
Tuberculosis (all forms)	010–18	324	0.1	199	0.1
TB (late effects)	137	145	<0.1	106	<0.1
Septicaemia	038	228	0.1	322	0.1
Meningococcal infection	036	47	<0.1	50	<0.1

Note: E980–9 refers to deaths 'undetermined as to whether accidentally or purposefully inflicted', many are suicides.

Source: OPCS Mortality Statistics 1985, Series DH 2 No. 12, Deaths by Cause, t. 2.

The replacement of infectious by degenerative disease

Nowadays, almost half of all deaths (table 7.2) in the United Kingdom are caused by failure of the circulatory system (heart and blood vessels), including one in four from strokes (blockage or rupture of blood vessels in the brain). Forty-five per cent of men can expect to show symptoms of ischaemic heart disease by age 65, 18 per cent with heart attacks and 27 per cent with other symptoms such as angina (Silman 1981). Cancers cause nearly one in four deaths; at present registration rates 30 per cent of men will acquire some kind of cancer in their lifetime, two-thirds of them at ages over 60. One in eleven men will develop lung cancer, one woman in fifteen will develop breast cancer (OPCS 1983*f*). Histological evidence from post-mortems suggests that about 80 per cent of 80-year-old men have developed cancer of the prostate (even though this would not normally have been the cause of death). Infectious and parasitic diseases, the dominant causes of death in all previous centuries, have been so suppressed that they account for only one death in 200 (Chapter 2). This figure does not include the 9 per cent of deaths (mostly in very old age) from pneumonia (see OPCS 1978*a*). In the 1980s the rise of AIDS reversed the trend towards the elimination of mortality from infectious disease for the first time.

7.2 The End of Infectious Disease?

The old enemies depart

The old infectious diseases have been reduced to a footnote in mortality statistics (Chapter 2). In 1988 there were 16 deaths from measles, none from whooping cough. 1984 and 1985 were free of typhoid deaths. In 1978 there were no notifications of diphtheria for the first time on record; there have only been two deaths since 1975. Tuberculosis (TB) retains a stronger presence: in 1988 382 people died of pulmonary TB, 96 from other forms, 240 from 'late effects', mostly older latent cases (see OPCS 1990*c*, Adelstein 1977). Pneumonia still commonly ends the lives of the very old, but no longer at younger ages. Around 1910, acute bronchitis and pneumonia were the first cause of death to children under 5. Pneumonia was a major complication in the great influenza pandemic of 1918 (157,000 deaths 1918–19, the last great epidemic before polio and AIDS).

Some of these diseases remain relatively common even though they cause few deaths. There is concern that unless they are eliminated, then declining rates of immunization may permit their recovery. Tuberculosis as a chronic disease has been reduced to the least incidence. In the 1950s there were still about 40,000 notifications annually, declining fast after BCG vaccination in the 1950s to 5,164 in 1988 (all forms). But there is a countervailing trend: TB among adult immigrants from the Indian subcontinent is about forty times as frequent as among the white population (Innes 1981); cases have also increased among young

Indians (Galbraith, Forbes, and Mayon-White 1980). After nineteenth-century sanitary reform typhoid, paratyphoid, and food poisoning became epidemic rather than endemic as water supplies and sewage became more strictly separated (Ferguson 1964). Symptomless carriers, immigration of infected people, and contaminated imported food make the final elimination of typhoid very difficult. 500 people in Scotland in 1964 caught the disease from contaminated corned beef; in 1978 there were cases from Chinese frozen eggs and desiccated coconut. About 250 cases a year are notified in Britain (174 typhoid, 180 paratyphoid in 1988), about 87 per cent contracted abroad (see OPCS 1990d).

As late as 1941 there were still 50,000 diphtheria notifications and 1,622 deaths in Britain. A nationwide campaign for the universal immunization of children to eliminate diphtheria, instituted by Sir William Jameson, the Chief Medical Officer of the Ministry of Health, reduced deaths and incidence to negligible levels in a decade: but immunization is still only 70 per cent complete, and declining as the disease passes from public concern. The case–fatality rate of scarlet fever declined of its own accord. It is still a relatively common disease—5,949 cases in 1988. But only one of the patients died. Measles mortality fell straight from a peak in the 1860s to oblivion in the mid-1950s. Notifications, though, remained at the same level from 1940 to the mid-1950s (307,408 in the 1970 epidemic year). Measles, being a viral disease, cannot be directly treated even now. After the large scale immunization against measles in 1968 notifications dropped but by 1980 the vaccination rate had fallen to 50 per cent. So after falling to a lowest ever figure of 55,502 cases in 1976, notifications recovered to 173,361 in 1977 and fell to 86,001 in 1988—there is a cyclical epidemic pattern. New measures to secure its elimination in the UK have recently been announced, late compared to other countries (e.g. the US). Whooping cough, as a bacterial disease, is curable, although it is more difficult to vaccinate against as it strikes those under a year old. After the national immunization policy in 1957 notifications fell sharply from 17,000 in 1968 to 2,069 in 1972. But as the threat receded many parents neglected to have their children immunized—or were influenced by publicity about the risk of immunization itself. By 1978 a new epidemic had driven notifications back to 1950s levels (65,957), falling again 5,117 in 1988. Over 80 per cent of each cohort would need to be vaccinated for the disease to be eliminated (Grenfell and Anderson 1988).

Unsolved problems

Gastro-intestinal diseases such as diarrhoea and food poisoning are undoubtedly increasing. They are caused by a wide variety of microorganisms, including at least twenty species of Salmonella, *Escherichia coli*, four species of Shigella, as well as sundry other bacteria and viruses. Nowadays few of these infections are fatal (163 in 1988; mostly infants and—especially—the elderly). The strong summer peaks of diarrhoea diminished after the First World War, but it continued to be a major cause of post-neonatal infant death until well after the Second, when new drugs could control it. Better living standards, education, and food storage—especially refrigerators—help to keep bacteria away from babies. Breast-feeding is always the first line of defence in protecting infants from such diseases. But the trend in breast-feeding in the post-war period was unfavourable until the 1970s. In 1985 39 infants died from all forms of intestinal infectious disease, out of 6,141 infant deaths from all causes.

Altogether about 14,000 identifications per year are made of the specific pathogens. These are cases referred to the medical profession and then referred onwards to the laboratory; the figure must greatly underestimate the incidence of the diseases. Dysentery declined from 1960 (40,000 notifications) to 1980 (2,709). But by 1984 notifications had risen to 6,844 (OPCS 1987*i*) although by 1988 they had fallen again to 3,692. A number of institutional outbreaks have followed defective kitchen hygiene, with serious consequences for elderly patients with low resistance to infections: 28 died in the worst epidemic at a Shrewsbury hospital in 1984. Notifications of *Salmonella* increased from 5,000 in 1972 to 10,315 in 1980 and 13,142 in 1985. All known cases of food poisoning doubled from 7,933 in 1977 to 14,253 in 1982 and trebled to 39,713 in 1988 (see OPCS 1989, 1990*d*).

New threats

As well as old problems persisting, some serious new threats to public health have arisen, such as poliomyelitis and legionnaire's disease (Communicable Disease Surveillance Centre 1988). The suppression of poliomyelitis is one of the success stories. The virus spreads through droplet infection or through faecally contaminated food, water, or milk. It is still endemic in the Third World, usually as a mild enteric disease of children. Among older children or adults, catching it late in more hygienic surroundings, the central nervous system is more vulnerable to infection, causing paralysis. Previously rare, by 1955 there were 4,000 notifications of paralytic polio. Mass immunization from 1956 and public health measures controlled it fast; by 1960 there were only 257 notifications, 3 in 1980, 3 in 1987. The widespread use of antibiotics and other drugs against bacteria has encouraged the spread through natural selection of drug-resistant strains of bacteria and made necessary a pharmaceutical arms race against them. For example, methicillin-resistant *Staphylococcus aureus* (MRSA), a cause of staphylococcal preumonia and septicaemia, has become difficult to contain in post-operative care and in intensive-care wards, and has become a worldwide problem (Maple *et al.* 1989).

Disease is casting a longer shadow over ordinary pleasures, particularly sex and travel (Nicholson and Wiselka 1989). Holiday-makers, and increased travel to and from the Indian subcontinent, have brought back new dangerous salmonellas and malaria and may introduce rabies. For example, hepatitis B (59 deaths in 1988) is often caught on holiday in exotic places, and increased at home in the early 1980s because of its strong association with the intravenous injection of drugs with shared needles and with anal intercourse. Sexually transmitted diseases (STD) are now the most common infectious diseases in the UK, as in most other Western countries. The clinic-based contact system has preserved us from even worse increases experienced abroad and antenatal screening keeps congenital syphilis at a low level. In 1986 there were 702,223 new clinic attendances in the UK for all forms of sexually transmitted disease (including 154,076 not requiring treatment and 175,112 'non-specific genital infections') compared with 457,637 in 1979 (Communicable Disease Surveillance Centre 1986). In the 1950s venereal disease levels reached the lowest ever recorded, after their post-war peak in 1946. But their incidence more than doubled from 1960 to a new record of 65,997 new cases in 1973, since then declining to 45,817 in 1986. The details are consistent with a change in the sexual habits of homosexuals. The decline started before knowledge of AIDS. Syphilis remains more common among men than women (2,594 new cases among men— mostly homosexuals—in 1984 compared with 713 among women). Among men gonorrhea increased less than 50 per cent over the period, from 27,000 to 36,000 new cases—but trebled among women from 7,000 to 21,000 new cases. Non-specific disease, mostly caused by the protozoan *Chlamydia*, has increased most, from 22,004 in 1960 to 123,860 in 1985. Genital infection by the *Herpes simplex* virus was the new sexual fright of the 1970s, increasing from 9,576 new cases in 1979 to 20,315 in 1986. Although (like all these diseases) not usually fatal, and not always very incommoding, it has the dismal characteristic of being a lifelong infection. Genital warts caused by the human papilloma virus have also increased (27,654 new cases in 1979, 75,995 in 1984) although it is not the same type that is believed to be the causal agent of cancer of the cervix. The rise in reports of herpes and warts may be due in part to generally raised fears about STD.

AIDS

The rise of the Acquired Immune Deficiency Syndrome (AIDS) has put all these worries in the shade. The disease is caused by the Human Immunodeficiency Virus (HIV) which attacks the immune system itself and makes the body much more vulnerable to infections like *Pneumocystis carinii* pneumonia and rare cancers e.g. non-Hodgkin's lymphoma, which it could otherwise reject. The disease was only identified (in the USA) in 1981 but is now known world-wide. Its chief centres are Central Africa, where it probably originated by mutation from a monkey virus, and the United States, particularly New York. Much is still unknown about the disease. Neither vaccine nor cure are yet in sight. Hopes for its containment rest with epidemiological knowledge and the modification of human behaviour. As is now well known, the fragile virus is relatively difficult to transmit and can only be caught through the exchange of body fluids: blood, saliva, semen.

It is therefore a disease often transmitted by sexual contact, especially where tissue damage is likely to occur as in the recipients of anal intercourse, and by drug abuse where needles are shared. Like syphilis, it can be congenital. About a fifth of Britain's haemophiliacs, who need the blood-clotting Factor 8 derived from large volumes of blood from many donors, are infected with HIV thanks to the use by the NHS of inadequately screened and treated blood from the US (which is sold, not given, often by derelicts and drug addicts).

On the basis of just a few years' experience it now seems likely that at least 20 per cent and possibly most of those who are positive for the HIV virus will contract AIDS or the AIDS related complex, and that a high proportion of those who contract AIDS will die of it. No cases are known yet of complete regression. The transmission risk appears to be about 0.1 per partner per year. The average number of partners per year in high risk groups is about 10. Both figures have high variance. Expectation of life in the infected (and infectious) state is from seven to ten years, but only about one year after the actual diagnosis of AIDS. We know least of all about the transmission risks and about sexual behaviour. The latter is crucial because the extent to which individuals from high risk groups also have sexual contact with low risk groups will determine the progress of the epidemic (Anderson and May, 1988).

At any point in time, the cumulated number of deaths is about half the number of known cases (figure 7.2). In Britain by June 1991 there had been 4,835 known cases and 2,787 deaths, both probably underestimates. Officially registered deaths from AIDS may under-

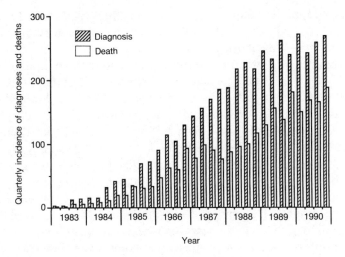

Note: 14 cases were recorded up to 1982, of which 13 have died.

Source: Public Health Laboratory Service 1991, unpublished data at 5 Aug. 1991.

FIG. 7.2. UK AIDS cases and deaths, 1983–1990

estimate by about half the total mortality from the effects of the HIV virus (McCormick 1989). In Britain most deaths (89 per cent to 1987 including homosexual drug abusers) had been of homosexual males aged between 20 and 50 (Public Health Laboratory Service 1988). A minority are drug abusers (1 per cent) and haemophiliacs (6 per cent), with so far a small number of congenital cases and heterosexual cases (3 per cent), although only a few with no known drug, foreign, or bisexual contact. Because of its causes, the disease is concentrated in major urban centres; particularly among homosexuals in London, also drug abusers in Edinburgh (see OHE 1988). The pattern differs by country; in the USA and Italy drug abuse is a more important route (17 per cent and 61 per cent of deaths respectively). In the US a growing proportion of births to Hispanic and black mothers in New York are infected. In Central Africa, where homosexual intercourse or intravenous drug abuse are rare practices, the sex ratio of victims is much more equal, and the disease is evidently spread there by vaginal intercourse, possibly because of the high incidence of genital sores, and, increasingly, congenitally. Some hospitals in Uganda record up to 15 per cent of hospital admissions for other causes as HIV-positive, suggesting a disaster of unparalleled magnitude in the making (Anderson, May, and McLean, 1988) with up to 2.5 million African adults infected by 1987 (Bongaarts and Way 1989).

US estimates suggest that the ratio of HIV infected people to AIDS cases may be 50–80 to 1. Applied to British case numbers this yields between 35,000 and 55,000 infected persons in Britain by 1987 (Doll 1987, Cox 1988). Other estimates have ranged from 30,000 to over 100,000 (Rees 1987). In the USA, 1.75 million people are thought to have the virus and deaths have exceeded 10,000 per year since 1986. The UK's unusually vigorous and blunt official message against AIDS, delivered to every household, has tried to emphasize that no group should consider itself free of risk. Most of the public understand the basic facts about AIDS, though few young people admit to a change in their sexual habits. None the less, the rates of notification of gonorrhea and hepatitis B, indices of promiscuous homosexual behaviour, have declined sharply since 1985, possibly because homosexuals have changed their habits (Johnson and Gill 1989). The absolute number of new cases is declining. It is uncertain how fast AIDS is moving into the hetero-sexual population. Once there it may become permanently established.

Whether it does so will determine the size of the future epidemic. Because there are so many unknowns, forecasting this is very difficult (May and Anderson 1987). It seems certain to overtake such hazards as cervical cancer in the near future. Rees (1989) extrapolated AIDS deaths to a peak in 2001 with up to 240,000 deaths in all by that time. Official population projections restricting deaths to males only based on the estimates by Cox (1988) suggest 100,000 deaths by 2001 (OPCS 1989a) with a further 100,000 deaths next century. One forecast, assuming restriction to homosexuals and intravenous drug users, pre-dicts a peak in 1994 with 63,000 AIDS cases and 48,000 dying. Another, assuming substantial heterosexual involvement, forecasts between 120,000 and 240,000 AIDS cases in 1994 with 12 million infected by HIV (OHE 1988). More recent estimates suggest a lighter mortality, peaking at about 10,000 deaths per year in the mid-1990s and then declining (Cox et al. 1989). This is about a 30 per cent reduction from the 1988 estimates by Cox. However, even these earlier estimates have been criticized for a deficient methodology which has substantially underestimated the prevalence of HIV infection (Rees 1990), so there is yet no consensus. Previously new lethal tropical viruses out of Africa —such as Lassa fever (first recognized in Nigeria in 1969) and Marburg virus or green monkey disease (first recognized in 1967)—have been contained by strict precautions or quarantine, reporting, and treat-ment. AIDS has broken out because it is chronic, diagnosed late, and is transmitted by two popular but private human activities. Until AIDS, new epidemic crises remained within the realm of science fiction.

7.3 The Rise of 'Diseases of Affluence'

The degenerative 'Western' diseases (Trowell and Burkitt 1981, McKeown 1988), or 'diseases of affluence' which have replaced infectious disease as major causes of death mostly affect older people. Some have been uncovered as major causes as infectious diseases were rolled back and more people survived to older age. Cancers, for example (except lung cancer) have changed relatively little as age-specific risks this century. Other risks, especially from circulatory disease, have increased, however they are measured—it is not just a question of more people surviving to older ages. Peptic ulcer and appendicitis have risen and fallen in a century. Changes in diagnosis can explain only a little of the movement.

Diseases such as cancer, circulatory disease, and chronic bronchitis have always existed in human populations. They have been regarded (Macfarlane Burnet 1980) as inevitable genetic consequences of the degeneration of physiological function with age, or 'senescence'. Some such changes undoubtedly do occur as a function of age, and they present some of the most interesting problems in biology (Kirkwood and Holliday 1986). Vital processes, such as respiratory capacity decline; so do DNA and cell repair mechanisms (Bittles and Sambuy 1986) where the fundamental ageing process probably resides. The inevitable consequences include the cumulative loss of non-dividing cells (such as brain cells) and the failing vigour of cell lines which must divide fast to do their job (the cells making cartilage and above all those which provide the immune system which guards against infections and cancers). But most practical interest is centred on the striking changes in the incidence of degenerative diseases this century, and on the marked difference between populations (Chapter 8). These suggest strong environmental influences. Epidemiological knowledge offers the most practicable hope for avoiding these diseases, in the absence of effective cures. The changing epidemiology cannot be understood without knowledge of their clinical development in the individual.

Circulatory disease

Atherosclerosis

Circulatory disease is primarily a disease of middle and old age, not of childhood or adolescence. This group of diseases includes ischaemic heart disease, cerebrovascular disease (stroke), haemorrhage, and embolism (blood clot). Many have in common such predisposing factors as high blood pressure and high blood cholesterol levels. An important underlying process associated with many of these diseases is atherosclerosis—sometimes called arteriosclerosis. This is a progressive degeneration of the interior lining of arteries, for example of the heart (coronary) and the brain (cerebral), leading to their obstruction by fatty growths called atheromatous plaques. These porridgy lumps are cholesterol-rich outgrowths within the arterial wall, not depositions on it. They may become sclerosed and calcified (hence 'hardening of the arteries'). Their inflexibility can drive up blood pressure, with consequent risk of heart overload or of catastrophic rupture (haemorrhage). However high blood pressure often arises quite independently of atherosclerosis.

Ischaemic heart disease (IHD)

When the bore or lumen of the artery is progressively restricted by atherosclerosis, blood supply to the tissues it serves becomes inadequate. Tissues thus deprived of sufficient oxygen or nutrients may cease to function. Degeneration in the arteries of the heart itself (the coronary arteries) leads to a progressive deterioration of heart function and finally heart failure (153,084 deaths in 1988). If there is no major myocardial infarction (see below), this is known as chronic ischaemic heart disease (IHD) or coronary heart disease (CHD) or coronary artery disease (CAD). IHD will be used here. The pain which the obstruction of the blood vessels causes in the heart, when overloaded by exercise or even after a heavy meal, is angina pectoris, or more usually just 'angina'. It was once regarded as a disease in its own right, but it is now regarded more as a symptom of heart disease (although 115 deaths were still attributed to it in 1987).

A major life-threatening crisis arises when a blood clot or thrombus forms or becomes lodged in such a restricted artery, shutting off circulation to the tissues beyond it. Such crises may be provoked by unusual demands on the heart associated with exercise, cold weather, or strong emotion. This is acute ischaemic heart disease, a 'heart attack' or 'coronary thrombosis' (97,199 deaths in 1988). If the vessel is important enough, like a major coronary vessel, the heart will stop pumping regularly (dysrhythmia) and the patient may drop dead on the spot. Acute IHD is by far the most important cause of sudden death, and of deaths outside hospital or the victim's own bed (about 30,000 such deaths a year)—although such sudden deaths in other people's beds are not unknown. Most deaths from acute IHD are within an hour of the attack. Patients who recover will have a permanently damaged or dead area which had been deprived of oxygen for too long: a 'myocardial infarct'. The term 'myocardial infarction' is often used to denote the event as well.

The extent and position of the infarct(s), the lost function which the surviving heart muscle must try to replace, will determine the survivor's handicap. This crippling effect on survivors is a serious aspect of the disease. These crises therefore depend on (i) the tendency for arteries to become narrowed with atherosclerosis; and (ii) the tendency of the circulating blood to clot spontaneously.

Similar problems can occur in vessels in any organ. In major arteries feeding the leg it causes the pain of 'intermittent claudication' and can eventually lead to gangrene and the amputation of all or part of the limb. In the brain, it causes cerebral infarction, one of the causes of stroke or cerebrovascular disease (CVD), which can be lethal or lead to permanent or temporary brain damage, usually one-sided (68,599 deaths in 1988). Strokes, like heart failure, can also be caused by haemorrhages of blood vessels as well—that is, rupture of the vessel with massive loss of blood and damage to surrounding tissue. Accurate diagnosis of the various forms of stroke is not easy—about one death in five is not specified—but despite confusing changes in classification (Acheson and Sanderson 1978) there has been a clear downward trend in most forms of cerebrovascular disease since the 1950s. Although people in their twenties and thirties can suffer the form of stroke known as 'subarachnoid haemorrhage', in general stroke victims tend to be older than IHD sufferers. Partly as a consequence, more victims are women. High blood pressure is a more important risk factor than atherosclerosis.

Causes of circulatory disease

There is no simple cause of circulatory disease. Part of the process may be cumulative DNA errors in ageing cells. The human genome has 100,000 genes with a total of about 3,000 million base pairs, and about 7,000 of these fall apart in the average cell every day. Not all are re-paired. The view of atheromatous plaques as benign neoplasms has been reinforced by the observation that the plaques contain active oncogenes (cancer-producing genes) (Scott 1987). This may be an underlying problem, but it cannot explain the considerable differences in risk between people with contrasting lifestyles and diet: Japanese versus Scots, social class I compared to social class V—or the marked trends over time. There is obviously a strong familial, i.e. genetical element in risk, and modern methods of recombinant DNA analysis and other techniques of 'genetic engineering' have made some progress in locating the genes concerned, especially in severe congenital cases of high cholesterol levels in the blood ('hypercholesterolaemia') which affects about 5 per cent of victims.

Physiological differences between people and habits of diet, smoking, and stress seem to be important. People living in simple societies are mostly free of it, suggesting that present high levels in the industrial countries may be avoidable. Most research, therefore, is concentrated on factors which relate to the environment and to lifestyle (Marmot 1980), which could be changed to prevent disease. Poor infant or maternal health may put infants on the wrong track for life, with higher blood pressure and an inability to cope with high fat diets (Barker *et al.* 1989). A small set of independent physiological and behavioural conditions—the 'risk factors'—appear to hasten directly the onset of the disease. The 'risk factors' account for about half the variation of the disease in the population—so much is still unexplained.

Risk factors in ischaemic heart disease

Three major 'risk factors' have been identified: high levels of plasma cholesterol (say over 200 mg/ml) and other low density lipoproteins; high blood pressure (above 120 mm Hg systolic); and any level of cigarette smoking—the more, the worse (Royal College of Physicians 1986). The risk of IHD from smoking is much more severe (4–8 times) in younger than in older men. Obesity and lack of exercise, for example, are not in themselves risk factors; they are problems in so far as fat and sedentary people are more likely to develop high blood pressure and high cholesterol levels (WHO 1982, Shephard 1981, Leon *et al.* 1979, Thelle *et al.* 1983).

High blood pressure (hypertension) is not a disease in itself. The underlying cause is unknown. There is a strong familial element (Sever 1981) and possibly even a racial element. In Western societies, blood pressure increases with age, but in people living a traditional way of life in simple societies it does not unless they move to live in towns (Sever 1981; Sever *et al.* 1980). There has been much research (Harrison and Gibson 1976) and even more excitement about the effects on high blood pressure of the 'stresses' of modern life and of urban living, but with little guidance for evasive action. Blood pressure can be kept low or reduced by low salt diets, by avoiding obesity, and by drugs.

Smoking can, at least in principle, be avoided completely, but it may not be easy to reduce the other factors to optimum levels. High cholesterol and high blood pressure are associated with lack of exercise, urbanization, 'stress', diet, drinking, and other commonplaces of life in complicated ways. High levels of cholesterol in the diet should certainly be avoided, but the body manufactures it from other fats and it is only really common in eggs. Because of the complexity of the human diet, genetical differences in individual physiology and the difficulty of arranging controlled or intervention trials, it has been difficult to demonstrate unequivocally the harmful effects of saturated fats (meat, cheese, milk) or the protective effects claimed from poly-unsaturated fats (vegetable oils, fish, special margarines, and especially mono-unsaturated olive oil). As research accumulates, blood cholesterol emerges as the most important risk factor and, less certainly, fat in diet as the biggest avoidable cause (Doll 1987, Smil 1989). In Western societies and most others, the higher the proportion of fat in the diet the worse the level of IHD (Marmot 1984). Over half the difference in international IHD levels can be accounted for by differences in the amount of fat consumed and the ratio between saturated and unsaturated fat. Low fat diet, especially in combination with a high intake of dietary fibre (e.g. bran) significantly lowers cholesterol levels in men who change their eating habits (Lewis *et al.* 1981). Fat provides about 40 per cent of energy intake in the UK diet, which is at the top of the world fat-eating league, compared to about 37 per cent, in the US, 27 per cent in Southern Europe and even less in Japan (DHSS 1974*a*; Royal College of Physicians 1976; WHO 1982, US Surgeon General 1988).

Risk factors are multiplicative and may be further magnified by personality type (Rosenman *et al.* 1970). People who score highly for the 'type A' personality: impatient, time-conscious, ambitious, unwilling to foreclose options (but not for these reasons necessarily more successful than others), have twice the risk of IHD than those who do not (see Wood 1981). Risk factors can account for only about half of the variation in IHD within some populations (Reid *et al.* 1976) and are poor predictors of its onset. Bereavement or anxiety, overwork, or over-arousal, which pushes people beyond their capacity to respond, and absence of a supportive family and friends, all precipitate adverse physiological changes and may provoke heart attacks and impede recovery in survivors. So can stress at work (Cooper 1980). There is now renewed interest in behavioural management of lifestyle and attitudes (Wood 1984) both in avoidance and recovery—a return, in some ways, to earlier attitudes to the disease (Nixon 1982).

Cancer

Cancer is a failure of control of cell growth and division, leading to uncontrolled growth of abnormal tissue. Cancer (neoplasm) can arise in any organ but in some much more frequently than others—especially those involved in rapid division (bone marrow) or physiological activity (liver), or exposed to the environment (skin, gut). Malignant cancers can spread secondary cancers—metastases—throughout the body. 'Benign' neoplasms do not have this property but can still be lethal (465 deaths in 1987) through, for example, pressure on vital organs. Cancers kill about one person in four in Britain (table 7.2) and in most industrial countries, rather more in Japan. Cancer in each system has its own characteristic pattern of epidemiology and etiology. Fundamentally there is a common problem of loss of control over the growth and function of cells. Age-dependent failure to replicate DNA correctly and to eliminate errors in it may be important, but more interest has been in environmental insults which set susceptible cells onto a cancerous path: substances in food, cigarette smoke, environmental pollutants of various kinds, radiation, and viruses (Doll and Peto 1981, Kinlen 1981). On this view the apparent effect of age on cancer incidence is a by-product of the fundamental effects of length of exposure to carcinogens, acting over years or decades to initiate cells into a pre-cancerous state and then to promote the cancer itself.

The rise of twentieth century degenerative diseases

All this suggests that high mortality from 'Western' diseases is not inevitable and should be regarded more as a consequence of environmental factors, diet, smoking, and work habits, and inadequate income and education among the poorer sections of the populations. The declining incidence of lung cancer, stomach cancer, stroke, heart disease when Western incomes are growing by at least 3 per cent per year makes it difficult to label them 'diseases of affluence'. None the less it has been suggested that their epidemiology points to three groups (Barker 1989): 'affluent' diseases which have increased steeply (stones, breast, prostate, and ovarian cancer); 'deprivation' diseases which are becoming less common (chronic bronchitis, stroke, stomach cancer); 'mobile' diseases initially linked to affluence, now to poverty (IHD, stomach ulcers). This classification will be questioned, but at least it recognizes that some of these diseases have declined as well as increased.

Answering the question whether modern living has actually increased risks over the last century is complicated by the relatively recent clinical definition of some 'degenerative' causes of death. For example, although angina pectoris was described in 1768, coronary thrombosis was not clearly described until 1786 and it was not recognized as a disease from which recovery was possible until 1912. It was not until the 8th revision of the Inernational Classification of Diseases in 1968 that all the terms which doctors are likely to use to describe deaths from IHD were put into one group (Doll 1987). This makes it difficult to establish a baseline for the 'pre-affluent' level of the disease. But putting together all likely synonyms for deaths from IHD, including 'angina' and 'myocardial degeneration' shows that it was still infrequent as late as 1920 and has since shown an extraordinary fifty-fold increase, peaking in the 1970s; a picture confirmed by contemporary medical and epidemiological accounts (Mackinnon 1987, Doll 1987).

Lung cancer, although long recognized, was regarded as a rare disease until after the First World War. Its strong upward trend is confused by improved diagnosis from chest X-rays and other techniques. After the 1930s drugs could cure the concomitant infections and allow the cancer to grow more distinctively in survivors. But the baseline can be defined because cigarette smoking is the only important cause, and on that basis the level before the cigarette era will not have been greater than the contemporary level in non-smokers—about fifty deaths per million per year—compared to about 1,000 deaths per million men per year at its peak in the early 1970s (figure 7.3)—at least a twenty-fold increase, responsible for at least one million premature deaths (Doll 1987). Pipes and latterly cigars have been with us for centuries, but they are less hazardous than cigarettes. Their stronger alkaline smoke delivers its nicotine in the mouth and is not usually inhaled. Smoking began as an upper-class fashion at the beginning of the twentieth century and became a popular habit among men after the First World War, and among women after the Second (figure 7.4). At the peak of cigarette consumption in 1973, the average adult was smoking almost ten cigarettes per day (see Alford 1973, Tobacco Advisory Council 1983). Lung cancer is now clearly in retreat among men. Its decline is primarily due to wider public knowledge of the high risks of smoking, and its consequent abandonment (Doll and Peto 1976).

There are few other unequivocal examples of increases. Breast cancer is becoming slowly more frequent; leukaemia more rapidly. Cancer of the oesophagus and testicular cancer, now the most important cancer affecting men aged 25–34, have increased since the war. The former may be a consequence of the trend of alcohol consumption (before the war both trends were downwards). For the latter speculation has blamed tighter dress, central heating, and sedentary work combining to overheat the scrotum. It is one of the few cancers (breast cancer is another) to have a positive correlation with social class (see

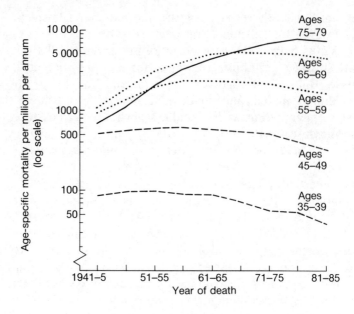

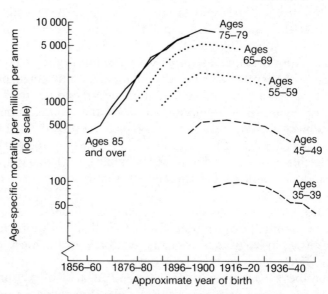

Note: The points at the graph are average rates over 5 year periods. 'Lung cancer' defined as ICD5 47b, ICD6 162–4, ICD7 162–4, ICD8 162–3, ICD9 162–4.

Sources: Swerdlow 1987, figs. 6, 7.

Fig. 7.3. Trend of lung cancer deaths among males by age and birth cohort, England and Wales

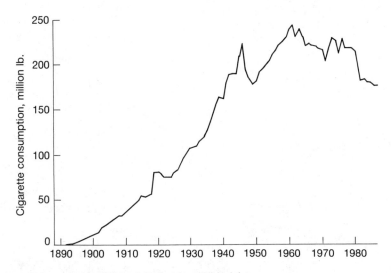

Sources: Tobacco Research Council 1983 and unpublished data.

FIG. 7.4. Cigarette consumption in the UK, 1888–1987

Chapter 8). New industrial processes can create new risks, usually highly specific and hence epidemiologically detectable. Bladder cancer's occupational epidemic is on the decline as exposure to industrial amines has been controlled. Deaths from mesothelioma will decline in the future now that the risk from asbestos is recognized. Most other causes of death—stroke, stomach cancer, duodenal ulcer, accidents— have been declining, not increasing, since at least the Second World War although many were previously increasing. Cancer death rates are declining in each sex in each successive generation born from 1900 (men) and 1925 (women) (except for lung cancer, declining in men born after 1920 but still increasing among women; and cervical cancer, increasing from the 1930s to the 1950s cohorts of women) (OPCS 1978*a*). Apart from lung cancer, there is no cancer epidemic.

As fashions move through society so the diseases they cause follow them. The middle classes are usually the first to satisfy needs and to know about and be able to pay for new luxuries (most notably cigarettes). Other desires which do no harm in societies where most people do manual work and are underfed, and which are desirable goals under those circumstances (e.g. heavy diets), cannot safely be continued by sedentary well-fed workers. The ability of rich and technically capable nations to turn luxuries into commonplaces (sugar and refined flour for example)—introduce new and unrecognized risks (e.g. diabetes, obesity, and bowel cancer). But societies which can

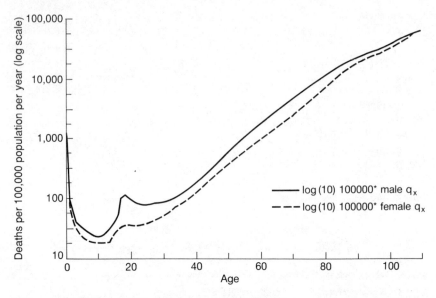

Note: q_x represents the probability of dying during the next year of life from any given exact age x. The q_x (which are decimal fractions varying from .00024 for males at age 10 to .61896 for males at age 108)) here are multiplied by 100,000 and then transformed to their logarithms.

Source: Data from OPCS 1987*d*, table 14.1.

FIG. 7.5. Life tuble death rates (q_x) England and Wales, 1980–1982

master their economic environments to change diets and gratify tastes in ways which may bring new hazards, are also societies with educated populations which can recognize and avoid hazards, given freedom of information and representative government. The increasing concentration of some modern diseases in the lower social classes may be more readily attributed to educational 'deprivation' rather than want of sustenance. And it is only in Eastern Europe that the increase of 'diseases of affluence', and of industrial and environmental hazards, has substantially reversed the downward trend of the death-rate.

7.4 Mortality Risks through the Life Cycle

The risks of death, and the causes of death, are radically different at different ages. Figure 7.5 shows the huge differences in mortality risk with age; a species-specific pattern the shape of which looks similar in all human societies even though the absolute levels of risk can differ by a factor of ten or more. In 1988, circulatory disease accounted for 47 per cent of deaths, cancer 25 per cent, respiratory diseases 11 per cent

Table 7.3. Main causes of death in each age-group, England and Wales, 1988

Age-group	All causes totals	Rank Order of causes of deaths, with total numbers		
		First	Second	Third
28 days–14 yrs	13,593	1,441 Signs, symptoms and ill defined[a]	759 Congenital malformations	684 Accidents
15–24	4,273	1,677 Accidents	537 Suicide	508 Cancer
25–34	5,037	1,119 Accidents	1,061 Cancer	718 Suicide
35–44	9,880	3,518 Cancer	1,440 IHD	940 Accidents
45–54	22,149	9,061 Cancer	5,935 IHD	1,175 Stroke
55–64	63,895	25,228 Cancer	19,963 IHD	4,162 Respiratory
65–74	137,446	44,863 Cancer	43,210 IHD	13,017 Stroke
75 and over	320,156	82,321 IHD	59,625 Cancer	49,840 Stroke

[a] Mostly 'cot deaths' between age 0 and 1. Total includes deaths up to age 28 days.

Note: Underlying cause can no longer be given for deaths up to age 28 days. Since 1980 cancer has displaced IHD from first place in the 55–64 and 65–74 age-groups.

Source: OPCS Monitor DH2 89/2 Deaths by Cause: 1988 Registrations, t. 2.

(table 7.2). But these causes are dominated by deaths in old age. The hazards faced as the individual ages through infancy, childhood, and adulthood are quite different (table 7.3), and avoidable to a different degree. We will therefore look at them separately.

Infants

Eight babies in a thousand died before their first birthday in 1989, 43 per cent in the first seven days of life. The day of birth is the second most dangerous day of life. Of the 6,141 infant deaths in England and Wales in 1985, one in three (2,293) was attributable to 'perinatal' causes. The most important are breathing difficulties arising from the immaturity of the infant's respiratory system: 'hyaline membrane disease' or 'respiratory distress syndrome' (608 deaths), strongly associated with short pregnancy and low birthweight. Placental problems leading to inadequate oxygen supply to the infant are still relatively common (308 deaths) especially in working mothers or very young, or older mothers. These and other difficulties can cause death shortly before birth as well as during or just after it; partly for this reason 'Perinatal Mortality Rates' (8.3 per 1,000 total births in 1989) are defined which include still births (babies born dead after twenty-eight weeks' gestation; 3,236 in 1989) as well as babies born alive which die within a week of birth ('early neonatal' deaths).

Low weight babies—below 2,500 grams or 5 lb. 8 oz.—have the highest risks. Most infant deaths occur to low weight babies (figure 7.6). Low birthweight can be due to pre-term birth (less than twenty-seven weeks' gestation) or to growth retardation in the uterus of babies born at the expected time ('small for dates'), or to both. Cigarette smoking by the mother during pregnancy is an important cause of growth retardation. Only 38 per cent of British babies are born in the best weight range for survival (3,500–3,999 grams; 7 lb. 11 oz. to 8 lb. 13 oz.), where perinatal mortality in 1985 was just 1.8 per 1,000. In 1985 65 per cent of perinatal deaths occurred to the 6.5 per cent of babies under 2,500 grams; 38 per cent to the 0.7 per cent of babies weighing less than 1,500 grams. Ninety-one per cent of deaths from respiratory distress syndrome occurred to underweight babies in 1985. (OPCS 1987e). Since the introduction of a new neonatal death certificate in 1986 it is no longer possible to assign an underlying cause of death for deaths occurring under 28 days of age. The new categories give equal weight to main conditions arising in the foetus and in the mother (see OPCS 1989e, 1988d).

Perinatal mortality depends on the physiological state of mother and

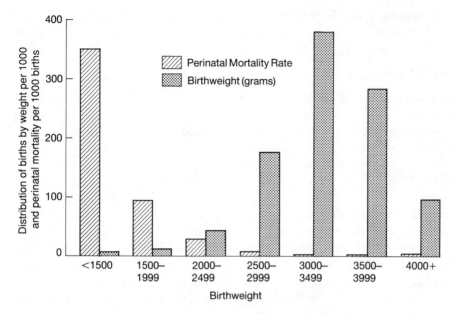

Sources: OPCS Monitor DH3 87/1 Infant and Perinatal mortality 1985; Birthweight

Fig. 7.6. Perinatal mortality rate and birthweight, England and Wales, 1985

infant and on the quality of medical care available (Beard 1981). The respiratory distress syndrome, for example, can be overcome with mechanical ventilation in specially equipped intensive care baby units. Such units, whose distribution is still rather inadequate and patchy, can halve mortality rates in underweight babies (House of Commons Social Services Committee 1980; the 'Short Report'). Other perinatal problems are more difficult to deal with. Perinatal mortality would improve greatly if more babies were born nearer the optimum weight. This could happen if mothers were healthier, gave up smoking and drinking during their pregnancy, and planned their childbearing for optimal ages. The UK Health Departments' report (1977) encouraged early and frequent antenatal visits to screen for problems (e.g. blood pressure and diabetes); but the benefit of general screening is still uncertain (see Chalmers 1989). Perinatal mortality goes on improving regardless. Babies brought through crises can survive handicapped with spastic disabilities (Diggory 1981); at a rough estimate, 30,000 a year (Loring and Holland 1978) of which about 2,000 have cerebral palsy or spastic disability. Most cases of cerebral palsy appear to be unconnected with perinatal events (Bryce *et al.* 1989). Despite more intense management of childbirth, the prevalence of cerebral palsy is increasing in the UK (Pharaoh *et al.* 1987) and elsewhere in Europe. Mortality rates alone are not necessarily the best measure of perinatal problems or perinatal care (Chalmers 1981).

Congenital malformations

A quarter of all infant deaths (1,600 in 1985) are due to congenital malformations. These are defects present at birth due to abnormal genes or chromosomes or to some environmental effect, such as radiation, infection of the mother by rubella (German measles), excess alcohol or harmful drugs, which induce errors in development (Bradshaw, Weale, and Weatherall 1980). Seventy per cent of these deaths occur in the neonatal period. Since 1964 all congenital malformations apparent at birth have been notified (a response to the thalidomide disaster) in order to detect and respond to trends (Weatherall and Haskey 1976). Altogether 13,020 were recorded in 1988 (OPCS 1990*a*), affecting about 2.2 per cent of all births. Some conditions like anencephalus are never compatible with life; Albinism, club foot, and harelip are seldom deadly; mild neural tube defects, e.g. spina bifida, can be surgically corrected, and some enzyme defects like phenylketonuria have become less severe now that their effects can be controlled by dietary management. The most radical malformations are not compatible even with life in the womb. At least 50 per cent and probably three-quarters of human conceptions are spontaneously aborted (mostly in the first month of pregnancy, therefore not noticed). Most of these early abortions have chromosome defects (Lauritsen 1982).

Survival of babies with central nervous system (CNS) malformations varies. In 1958, 23 per cent of those notified survived one year; in 1969, 56 per cent. In 1980, survival to 1 year had stabilized at about 40 per cent (Monitor MB3 82/5). Enthusiasm for attempted treatment in the 1960s and 1970s waned when the strain of caring for surviving handicapped and often permanently incontinent children in families became apparent (Armytage and Peel 1978). Antenatal screening and therapeutic abortion have reduced the incidence of some congenital malformations and infant deaths from them. All chromosome defects, neural tube defects, and many inborn errors of metabolism are now detectable by amniocentesis (tests on the amniotic fluid) and blood tests (Royal College of Physicians 1989). In some hospital regions tests are standard for mothers over age 35 or with previous malformed children. In 1989 1,667 abortions were performed on UK residents on the grounds of substantial risk of serious handicap. Although the registration scheme only started in 1969 and did not become complete until the mid-1970s, notified CNS malformations have declined since then, from

2,553 in 1973 to 1,016 in 1982; a reduction from 37 per 10,000 births to 16. Anencephalus rates in 1985 were about one-tenth of the 1971 level (OPCS 1988a). But the overall rate of notified malformations is unchanged due to increases in malformations of the cardiovascular system, external genitalia, and limbs. The Down's syndrome ('mongolism') notification rate has hardly changed since 1971 (428 births in 1988). Congenital rubella (German measles) is highly disabling for the foetus when not lethal. Vaccine has been available since 1970 but the UK vaccination rate is only 50 per cent and a scheme for the elimination of the disease, as in Sweden and North America (Dudgeon 1983), has only recently been announced.

Post-neonatal mortality and 'cot deaths'

Later infant deaths which occur after the first month have a different distribution of causes. Respiratory and other infections are much more frequent. Unlike neonatal and infant mortality as a whole, there has been no downward trend in the 1980s (Rodrigues and Botting 1989) although this is partly due to deferred deaths from conditions arising around the time of birth. In 1986, an increase in post-neonatal mortality raised the whole IMR for that year. 'Cot deaths' are the most important of the unsolved problems of post-neonatal infant death. A child, usually around six months old, suddenly dies shortly after being seen in apparently perfect health: this is the 'sudden infant death syndrome' (SIDS). This accounts for 22 per cent of all infant deaths (1,390 in 1988), 49 per cent of all post-neonatal mortality. These tragedies must have occurred in the past as well, but the SID syndrome was only introduced into the classification of deaths in 1971, creating an apparent rapid increase, resumed in the mid-1980s, partly at the expense of deaths attributed to respiratory diseases, which may indeed contribute to some SIDS deaths. Deaths are almost twice as frequent in the March as in the September quarter. Previously, smothering by bedclothes or pillows ('overlaying'), parental negligence, or foul play were also blamed. Accordingly, deaths from 'accidental mechanical suffocation' have fallen from 259 in 1970 to 131 in 1978 and to 7 in 1988. Most grieving parents are innocent. None the less, much the same group of infants is at risk of 'non-accidental injury' (baby battering) as of sudden death (Murphy et al. 1982). Siblings of 'abused' children have three times the death-rate of others (Roberts et al. 1980). It has been claimed that up to 10 per cent of victims of cot deaths have in fact been smothered (Meadow 1989). These tragedies can occur in all kinds of families. Young, unemployed mothers in poor families of low social class, living in poor areas, who have had a number of children already, who smoke but do not breast-feed and are careless about attendance at antenatal clinics are more likely to lose their babies in this way (Murphy *et al.* 1982). Defining the causes of cot death and effective guidelines for reducing its incidence remain major unsolved paediatric problems for the 1990s. Many theories compete to account for cot deaths: fear response, over-heating, congenital respiratory control defects, metabolic disorders, biochemical deficiencies of the lining of the lung. All may contribute to what may be a heterogeneous syndrome (Milner 1987).

Mortality from childhood to early middle age

Childhood from 1 to 14 is the safest period of life. The risks of childbirth are over; the dangers of cars and motor bikes, cancer and heart disease are still in the future. Deaths at these ages are mostly due to accidents, and remain so until the mid-30s. But from adolescence onwards mortality starts to get inexorably worse. Initially this is mostly due to accidents, cancer, and suicide.

Accidents

Although accidental swallowing of medicines and other poisons is the single most important reason for admitting young children to hospital, hardly any die of poisoning until after 15 years of age—less than ten a year in each age-group. Unlike infants and older children, children aged 1–4 are most at risk from fires at home (48 in 1988) and from drowning and murder. Although there are few recorded murders of children each year, the NSPCC has estimated that each week there are about 4 deaths to children aged up to 15 caused by or contributed to by abuse or neglect (Creighton 1988). Accidents become the single most important cause of death (one in three) of people between 15 and 35, mostly road accidents. In all there were 5,052 accidental deaths of road users in 1988 compared with 6,831 in 1978. Men are much more at risk than young women, because they are more likely to drive cars and motor cycles and to drive aggressively and when drunk. Motor cycles are by far the most dangerous vehicles. There are three times as many motor cycle deaths as car deaths among teenagers, while by age 25–9 the position is reversed. Once drivers have survived their 30s, they are much less likely to die on the roads. Pedestrians on the other hand, are safest in their 30s. Road deaths keep male mortality much higher than female at this age: the proportion at risk keeps growing as vehicle ownership increases.

Legislation in 1983 requiring drivers and front-seat passengers to wear seat belts was claimed to have saved 500 lives in its first year, apparently without causing any corresponding increase in non-fatal accidents by encouraging overconfidence, which has been noted elsewhere (Scott and Willis 1985, Adams 1985). However, the decline in road traffic deaths has been even more to the benefit of motorcyclists and pedestrians (McCarthy 1989). In 1988 deaths of car drivers (1,280) and car passengers (862) were still below their 1982 figure (1,472 and 971 respectively). The UK road death rate of 92 per million in 1988 was only 77 per cent of the 1978 rate. Measured as deaths per 10,000 road vehicles, at 2.4 the UK had the lowest rate in the industrial world except for Norway, Sweden, and Japan in 1988. (Dept. of Transport 1989). Road deaths per vehicle decline substantially as the number of vehicles increases. The most dangerous time to drive on the roads was in the 1930s (peak year 1934) before any driving test became compulsory, and more pedestrians were killed on the roads in 1927 (2779) than in 1987 (1703) (see Adams 1985). Radical improvements in emergency techniques for resuscitation and repair of previously hopeless accident cases have reduced deaths substantially. Despite this progress it is claimed that at least 1,000 road accident deaths (about one in five) could be averted by better emergency diagnosis and treatment (Royal College of Surgeons 1989).

Early cancer

Cancer is not just a disease of old age (figure 7.7). Some specific primitive cancers strike early in life, mostly in the eye and brain (retinoblastoma, neuroblastoma, CNS tumours) and in the tissues that produce the cells of the immune system and blood (leukaemia, including Hodgkin's disease). In 1988, leukaemia and related cancers accounted for 39 per cent of the 396 cancer deaths of children aged under 15, a much higher proportion than later in life. Modern treatment has revolutionized the outlook for many of the less common cancers. Up to 90 per cent of sufferers from Hodgkin's disease now survive at least five years, although the rate remains about 40 per cent for victims of CNS tumours (Draper, Birch *et al.* 1982). Treatment has greatly improved the outlook for breast cancer but has had little impact on most other common cancers. Over the last few decades, incidence and death-rates from leukaemias have increased considerably (OPCS 1987*j*, 1987*k*). These cancers are a particular hazard of exposure to radiation. The overenthusiastic medical use of X-rays for diagnosis may be responsible. Fallout from nuclear weapons, and leaks from nuclear plant make only a minor contribution to radiation exposure (see below).

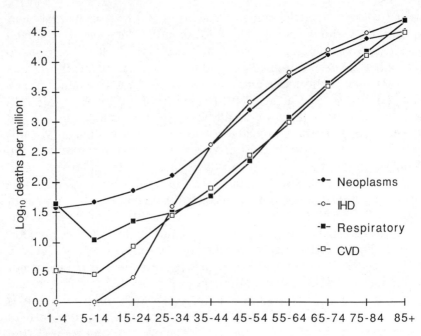

Note: logarithmic scale of death-rate.

Source: OPCS 1987*m*, t. 13.

FIG. 7.7. Age-specific death-rates, males, selected causes, England, 1985

Beyond age 30, cancers more typical of older life begin to make an appearance—in the digestive system, lungs, genito-urinary organs, and the female breast. Some cancers become numerous at young ages simply because they are even more numerous at older adult ages, like cancer of the lung and of the gut. Others are especially common among younger people, like cancer of the female breast and the uterine cervix. Almost a third (29 per cent) of all deaths from cancer of the cervix occur to women aged under 35, compared to only 1.4 per cent of all female cancer victims (table 7.4). It may be caused by some types of the human papilloma virus. It has become much more common in recent decades and is generally believed to be a consequence of the larger number of sexual partners enjoyed by women, or by their promiscuous male partners.

Smoking is now thought to increase the risk of this cancer. It is more common among women using the contraceptive pill, which has been available since 1962 (Vessey 1988, Chapter 4). But the extra risk which is claimed, even if correct, is not enough to account for the upward trend. Cancer of the cervix is eminently curable if caught at an early

Table 7.4. Cancer registrations, deaths, and five-year survival, most commonly registered sites, England and Wales, 1984, 1985.

Rank Site	ICD No.	Registrations	%	Deaths	%	5-year survival (%)
Males						
All	—	105,519	100.0	74,324	100.0	33.5
1 Lung	162	26,203	24.8	25,994	35.0	5.0
2 Skin (not m.m.)	173	11,678	11.1	263	0.4	—
3 Prostate	185	9,524	9.0	6,628	8.9	49.3
4 Stomach	151	6,788	6.4	5,922	8.0	9.8
5 Bladder	188	6,886	6.5	3,251	4.4	66.9
6 Colon	153	6,648	6.3	4,929	6.6	37.0
7 Rectum, etc	154	5,269	5.0	3,289	4.4	39.4
8 Pancreas	157	2,926	2.8	3,063	4.1	3.0
9 Oesophagus	150	2,437	2.3	2,719	3.7	8.2
10 Kidney & urinary	189	1,994	1.9	1,331	1.9	36.4
11 Other	—	25,166	23.8	16,935	22.8	—
Females						
All	—	112,263	100.0	67,294	100.0	46.3
1 Breast	174	21,363	19.0	13,513	20.1	62.8
2 Skin (not m.m.)	173	10,576	9.4	199	0.3	98.3
3 Lung	162	9,840	8.8	9,798	14.6	9.4
4 Colon	153	8,192	7.3	6,364	9.5	38.9
5 Stomach	151	4,465	4.0	4,049	6.0	11.8
6 Ovary, etc.	183	4,539	4.0	3,810	5.7	24.8
7 Rectum, etc.	154	4,308	3.8	2,751	4.1	39.7
8 Cervix uteri	180	4,043	3.6	1,957	2.9	54.3
9 Body of uterus	179, 182	3,759	3.3	4,535	6.7	77.2
10 Pancreas	157	2,772	2.5	3,014	4.5	4.0
11 Other	—	38,406	34.2	17,304	25.7	—

Note: Registrations refer to 1985. Deaths refer to 1984. Survival is the relative percentage (allowing for life table mortality) surviving five years from registration, registrations of 1979–81. Deaths in one year may exceed registrations in the previous year. Data on skin cancer exclude malignant melanoma.

Sources: OPCS Cancer Statistics 1984. Registrations. Series MB1 no. 16 1988, t. 2. OPCS Mortality Statistics, Cause, 1985 Series DH2 no. 12, t. 2 1987. OPCS Monitor MB1 86/2 Cancer Survival 1979–81 Registrations.

stage. Screening may reduce mortality from the disease in future, although it has not been very successful since its introduction in 1966. Half the cases now being treated were never screened (Acheson 1989). In 1988 the government began a campaign to contact every woman over age 35 to arrange for a test.

Suicide and murder

Suicide is one of the discoveries of adolescence. From then on, suicide is a relatively constant risk throughout life, increasing towards old age. But because risks from other causes are so low in early adult life, suicide then ranks third among the causes of death. In 1981 one in nine of all deaths aged 15–34 were from suicide. These figures are probably an underestimate: coroners may wish to spare the feelings of bereaved relatives (see Adelstein and Mardon 1975). In 1988, for example, 2,108 deaths at all ages were recorded, if only temporarily, as being caused by 'injury undetermined whether accidentally or purposefully inflicted'. A few may be successfully concealed murders: perhaps 150 are eventually reclassified as such, but most are suicides. If so, suicide would account for one in six deaths in this age-group. The trend in suicide, down during most of the 1970s, up during the 1980s, is difficult to interpret according to any simple hypothesis (Bulusu and Alderson 1984).

Murder is demographically unimportant in Britain. In England and Wales in 1988 there were 645 homicides, including manslaughter and infanticide (Home Office 1989). In Northern Ireland there were 54 homicides connected with terrorism in 1985; the peak year was 245 in 1976 (*Social Trends* 17). In the United States, by contrast, there were 22,190 deaths by 'homicide and legal intervention' in 1988, the fourth most important cause of death of men aged 25–44, and the most important cause in New York City until recently overtaken by AIDS. The risk of being killed by another is about a tenth the risk of being killed by oneself. The risk of murder is relatively high in infancy, falls in childhood, and then rises sharply with puberty by a factor of about three as young people become more likely to be involved in adult fights and crime or become attractive to sexual attack. Murder associated with rape accounts for not more than one in five murders of women of any age. Homicide is one of the few causes of death where risk declines after early adulthood.

Mortality from middle age to the end of life

Adolescence and early adult life marks a watershed between the mortality risks of development and immaturity and the mortality risks

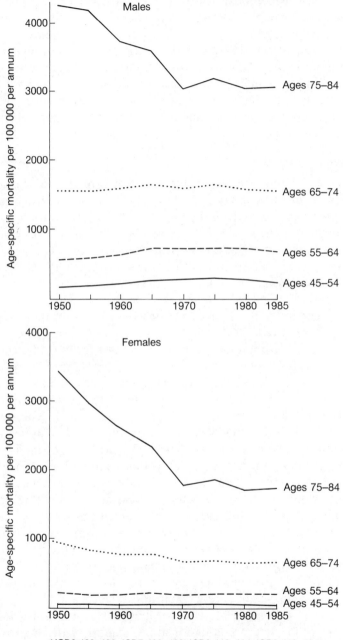

* ICD6 420–422; ICD7 420–422; ICD8 410–414; ICD9 410–414
† For simplicity every fifth year is plotted here

Notes: The points in the graph are average rates over 5-year period.

Sources: Swerdlow 1987

FIG. 7.8. Age-specific death-rates from ischaemic heart disease, England and Wales, 1950–1985

of senescence, when most deaths now occur (figure 7.5). Most deaths from circulatory disease occur at the oldest ages, unlike cancer when mortality peaks earlier (figure 7.7). Circulatory problems, especially heart disease, affect men more than women. Women appear to be protected until after the menopause. Beyond age 74 almost three times as many female as male deaths occur from stroke (and about 30 per cent more female than male deaths from ischaemic heart disease). Surviving men still have the higher risk because women greatly out-number men at these ages.

Trends and prevention

In most of the Western world, the trend of cardiovascular disease is downwards; in the US since the late 1950s, subsequently in most of Western Europe, recently in the UK. In the US IHD mortality used to be the highest in the world. It has now gone down by 25 per cent since its peak around 1957. But no one knows exactly why. There are fewer heart attacks and more people are surviving them (Stallones 1980, Goldman and Cook 1984, Epstein 1984). About 40 per cent of the decline in the US in 1968–76 seems to be due to improved treatment and the remainder to changes in lifestyle (smoking, diet, exercise) (Goldman and Cook 1984). The US Surgeon-General (1988) has re-cently insisted that these deaths can be reduced further, blaming over-fatty diet for as many as 1.5 million of the annual 2.5 million deaths.

In Britain, the decline in coronary artery disease (figure 7.8) first became apparent among doctors (Doll and Peto 1976), social classes I and II generally (Marmot, Adelstein, *et al.* 1978) in younger men (OPCS 1978*a*). It has now become more general although death-rates remain stubbornly high in social classes IV and V. As in the USA, the decline owes more to changes in habits than to medicine although IHD death-rates have not responded as much as lung cancer to the decline in smoking, which may have accounted for no more than 20 per cent of deaths at their peak (Doll 1987). The result of this relatively late and slow decline is that UK rates of mortality from coronary artery disease are the worst in the Western world (table 7.5). Northern Ireland and Scotland have worse rates than England and Wales. Direct medical intervention—drugs, beta-blockers, and anticoagulants, drug therapy to control low-density lipid (e.g. cholesterol) levels and blood pressure, and surgery to bypass the affected coronary arteries—has helped to an increasing extent and accounts for about a third of the improvement (Beaglehole 1986).

Favourable general trends have masked the effects of specific preventive measures. The enormous American Multiple Risk Factor

Table 7.5. International comparisons of mortality of men aged 55–64, 1980, selected causes (deaths per 100,000)

	Circulatory system	Neoplasms	Respiratory system	Injury, Poisoning	All causes
Scotland	1,152	633	176	91	2,220
N. Ireland	1,248	513	170	109	2,192
Finland	1,133	506	113	182	2,093
England/Wales	946	562	147	59	1,829
Denmark	774	546	93	116	1,756
Belgium	663	597	136	107	1,745
West Germany	729	505	79	89	1,673
France	428	621	68	138	1,604
Norway	774	393	58	98	1,531
Netherlands	669	550	53	57	1,514
Sweden	721	372	54	108	1,414
Greece	503	457	62	72	1,307

Note: Countries are arranged in descending order of all cause mortality.
Source: Catford and Ford (1984), t. 11.

Intervention Trial—'MR FIT'—identified 12,896 high-risk men and allocated half to an intervention programme over seven years to reduce their risks of heart disease: to stop cigarette smoking, reduce blood pressure (with drugs), and alter diet in order to reduce cholesterol levels, at a cost of $115 million. Half stopped smoking, mean diastolic pressure fell by 11 per cent, cholesterol level fell by 5 per cent. But the 'control' group who were left alone also reduced all these risk factors to a lesser extent. The study could find no significant difference in mortality. Both had got better (MR FIT Research Group 1982); Mr Fit ended up little better off than Mr Slob (Oliver 1982). A five-year Finnish study (Puska *et al.* 1979) was also baffled by the decline of risk factors and of heart disease in their controls and in their intervention group. A few years ago it could be said that 'much as we might like to think otherwise, it is not yet possible to prevent coronary heart disease in the community—let alone in an individual' (Oliver 1982). Other intervention trials (Hjermann *et al.* 1981) have managed to bring down risk factors by control of diet and smoking. Blood fat fell 20 per cent more than controls, smoking 48 per cent, heart attacks 47 per cent. Overall experience of twenty trials now gives a favourable outlook for prevention and shows that a 10 per cent reduction of blood cholesterol reduces risk by a sixth within two years (Doll 1987).

Patterns and trends in cancer mortality

More women than men die of cancer from age 25 to age 54; cancer of the cervix and female breast have no real male equivalent. From then on their relative risk is lower than men's. Heavy excess male mortality from cancer beyond the mid-50s is due particularly to lung cancer which kills more than three times as many men as women. As most smokers start smoking in their early adult life, and as the smoke is not highly carcinogenic, lung cancer deaths reflect smoking patterns of the previous decade or two. Male lung cancer deaths are now declining at all ages and in all cohorts of men (figure 7.3) reflecting the rise and fall of male smoking habits. In general the female trend is still upwards because women took up the habit later and have been slow to abandon it. Their lung cancer death-rates will accordingly increase; but breast cancer still remains the most important cancer among women. Here the trends are not favourable (figure 7.9) with an increase evident in age-specific death-rates for women over 50 from the 1950s onwards. The timing and age-concentration shows that the pill cannot be blamed for much of this increase, and it is not easy to interpret the date in terms of later first pregnancy or breast-feeding trends although the former is suspected of being a major factor. Because of the trends in lung and breast cancer, women's cancer deaths were 1.5 per cent higher in 1989

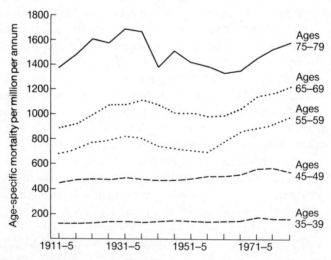

Notes: The points on the graph are average rates over 5-year periods. ICD2 43, ICD3 47, ICD4 50, ICD5 50, ICD6 and 7 170, ICD8 and 9 174. Females only.

Sources: OPCS 1987; *Population Trends*, 48.

Fig. 7.9. Age-specific death-rates from breast cancer, England and Wales, 1911–1985

than in 1988 while those of men fell slightly. Some cancers strike late in life: cancer of the prostate in men is particularly late—half of all the deaths occurring to men aged over 75. The reason is unknown, although it may follow the gradual withdrawal of some protective effect from testosterone.

Respiratory Disease

In most industrial countries, respiratory disease is the third most important cause of death (11 per cent of all deaths in Britain). Almost all the 26,424 pneumonia and 285 influenza deaths in 1988 were elderly. At the end of life, people become more vulnerable to respiratory infections, especially pneumonia, which when younger they could easily have shrugged off. At age 15–24 only 3 per cent of deaths (1988) are due to it. But over age 85 it is responsible for 17 per cent. Influenza is an epidemic disease. From time to time (1969–70, 1972–3, 1976, and 1989–90) there are substantial increases in influenza deaths. In the latest epidemic during the winter of 1989–90, 2,508 more deaths were attributed to influenza than in the previous winter. However it seems likely that the epidemic was actually responsible, directly or indirectly, for up to 25,000 excess deaths, 82 per cent of them among persons aged 75 and over (Curwen *et al.* 1990).

Bronchitis, emphysema, and asthma are now grouped together as 'chronic obstructive pulmonary disease', although the causes and trends of asthma are different from the other two. Together they accounted for 28,749 deaths in 1988, 18,817 of them male. Chronic bronchitis is a deteriorating airway obstruction, originally brought on by smoking or atmospheric pollution, although often complicated by infections. The threat to life comes from inadequate lung ventilation and consequent strain on the heart. It is caused or made worse by smoking or atmospheric pollution, like emphysema, and is associated with childhood poverty. Like heart disease, its crippling effects can incapacitate its victims for years, reducing their mobility and independence. Risk increases with age only gradually. The trend has been downwards from the early 1950s. Among older cohorts of men, exposed to a lifetime of heavy smoking and atmospheric pollution in their youth, there is no change in death-rates, while death-rates among older women have halved (OPCS 1981*a*). In general, men are twice as much at risk as are women. Emphysema is an erosion of the alveolar wall, leading to conflation of the alveoli, reduction of their surface area, and inadequate lung function. It is difficult to differentiate from chronic bronchitis except at autopsy. Preference for one diagnosis rather than another is to some extent a question of medical fashion: 'emphysema' is more favoured in the United States, 'bronchitis' in the UK.

Asthma is a muscular paroxysmal allergic condition, leading to temporary narrowing of the bronchi and consequent difficulty in breathing, especially breathing out. Acute attacks may need immediate pharmacological treatment and can be fatal. Chronic asthma can lead to severe lung damage as well as characteristic changes in the rib cage and in posture. It is often set off by breathing in organic material; pollen, animal dander, house dust, etc. It is demographically much less significant than bronchitis or emphysema, although it is relatively common among young people (2,006 deaths in 1988, 12 per cent of them under age 40 compared to 1 per cent for all chronic pulmonary disease). Mortality and handicap have been eased by modern chemical bronchodilators such as salbutamol ('Ventolin') and sodium chromo-glycate ('Intal') and other means of controlling bronchial spasm. Despite this deaths from asthma are slowly increasing—50 per cent from 1974–84, in Britain as in many countries. It is not possible to account for this by artefacts of diagnosis; the condition is becoming more common (Burrey 1988). It has been suggested that asthma, as a form of auto-immune disease, may increase as external challenges to the immune system from parasites diminish in a healthier environment.

In the 1960s deaths from asthma showed an alarming increase: by 1967 mortality was three times the 1960 level. In all, there were 3,500 deaths in the decade. This was a medical disaster, caused by the in-correct use of new aerosols (bronchodilators) to relieve asthma symptoms; especially those containing isoprenaline, orciprenaline, and adrenaline, whose sales graph closely matches the rise and fall of mortality. Women's death-rates fell to their previous level by 1969 and men's by the early 1970s (Inman and Adelstein 1969, OPCSa 1981) although there was a further, smaller epidemic in the 1980s. This is by far the heaviest mortality from medical mistreatment this century, but it has attacted much less attention than the much smaller mortality caused by treatment of premature babies with pure oxygen in the 1940s and 1950s, Thalidomide (1961–4), Opren, or the Dalkon Shield IUD.

7.5 Some Factors behind the Mortality Trends

The Role of medicine

Before the mid-1930s, there was little doctors could do to save lives from infectious or degenerative diseases which had already taken hold of the patient (Chapter 2). Surgery in the case of accidents and some acute illnesses like appendicitis were, and to some extent remain, an outstanding exception. This conclusion (McKeown 1976a) is supported by the timetable of effective medical innovations this century which makes it impossible for more than 17 per cent of the overall reduction in the twentieth century to be due to specific medical intervention (McKeown and Turner 1975).

The denigration of medicine can be overstated. When we are feeling ill we do not call for a medical historian. None the less it has received 'experimental' support from the astonishing lack of change in death statistics during or after a 17-week partial doctors' strike in Jerusalem in 1983 (Slater and Ever-Hadani 1983) and from the absence in uniform of 60 per cent of the medical profession during the Great War, without notable effect on civilian mortality (Winter 1985). By the 1950s preventive treatments were available against almost all serious infectious diseases, and cures were available for almost all those caused by bacteria. The capacity of acute surgical and life-support treatment to save lives in crisis has also expanded beyond recognition in saving the lives of underweight babies, accident victims, and victims of appendicitis and internal haemorrhage, in which progress is continually being made. However despite decades of work with interferon and other substances there is still no means of curing most viral diseases. Medicine became much more useful after the realization that rigorous experimental designs, notably the 'randomized controlled trial' introduced by Austin Bradford Hill (1937), were needed to see if new medical practice did more good than harm.

The powers of curative medicine—or at least its capacity to arrest disease—are now having an impact in degenerative diseases. Some kinds of cancer, of the stomach, pancreas, and lung for example, remain relatively unresponsive to modern treatment. But others such as cancer of the breast, colon, cervix, testis, and especially some cancers of childhood (e.g. Hodgkins disease) are no longer the death sentence they once were, thanks to advances in early diagnosis, surgery, drugs, and radiation therapy. Drugs such as streptokinase and ordinary aspirin, and coronary bypass surgery can greatly improve survival for victims of ischaemic heart disease, accounting for perhaps a third of the improvement. The contribution of medicine to alleviating suffering and saving lives has not been bought without risk (Adelstein and Loy 1979), especially in some of the more daring procedures which can now save hopeless cases. For example, in 1988 11 patients died from the drugs administered to them, 47 died from 'misadventure' (i.e. actionable errors) during surgery or medical care, 137 from 'abnormal reactions' to medicine or surgery. Analysis of differences between hospitals in death-rates following or during comparable operations suggests that up to 1,000 lives a year may be lost as a result of variations in surgical practice or skill—out of three million operations (Nuffield Provincial Hospitals Trust 1987).

Cigarette smoking: a twentieth century hazard

Smoking is the biggest avoidable health hazard in the Western world. The whole trend of twentieth century mortality has been bent upwards by the rise of cigarette smoking (Ravenholt 1990). In all, cigarettes may kill 100,000 people a year prematurely (Royal College of Physicians 1983)—one in six of all deaths (most of the 35,000 yearly lung cancer deaths, about 40,000 premature deaths from cardiovascular disease, most of the 20,000 deaths from chronic bronchitis). Cigarette consumption peaked in the early 1960s (figure 7.4) and has now declined to the level of the late 1930s, with lung cancer rates in men following it down.

Risks of smoking

Studies all over the world have established the dangers of smoking beyond even unreasonable doubt. Doll and Peto, for example (1976), followed most of the British medical profession (34,440 doctors) over twenty years. In general, death-rates in men under 70 years who smoked were twice those of non-smokers. Between one in two and one in three smokers died prematurely because of the habit. Smoking caused directly the excess mortality among smokers from cancer of the lung, oesophagus, and other respiratory sites, chronic bronchitis, emphysema, and pulmonary heart disease. Excess mortality from IHD, aortic aneurysm, cerebral thrombosis, respiratory TB, peptic ulcer, bladder cancer, and other cancers were thought to be wholly or partly attributable to smoking.

According to this research, smokers suffer particularly elevated risks below age 45: fifteen times the risk of non-smokers of dying from IHD compared with three times the risk at age 45–54 and twice the risk at age 55–64. Lung cancer risks too are much worse among heavier smokers: up to 14 cigarettes a day multiplies the risk eight times; 15–24 a day thirteen times, more than 25 a day twenty-five times. Cancer risks fall for up to fifteen years after smoking is abandoned. Lung damage through bronchitis caused by smoking can never be made good, although the rate of loss with age becomes normal once smoking stops. After this statistical battering, most doctors have given up smoking with a corresponding fall in some, but not all, smoking-related diseases. Other studies such as that of 18,403 male civil servants over five years (Reid *et al.* 1976) confirmed the special, independent risks from ischaemic heart disease caused by cigarette smoking. Studies overseas tell the same story (e.g. US Surgeon-General 1982, 1983).

Non-smokers cannot always avoid cigarette smoke. The sidestream smoke, not inhaled and therefore not filtered by a smoker's lungs, is a potent source of nicotine to others, also of the 20 different carcinogens and 4,000 other chemicals in tobacco smoke (nicotine, though poisonous, is not a carcinogen), notably nitrosamines (Shephard 1982). Non-smokers exposed to smoke breathe in the equivalent of about three cigarettes a day (Feyerabend *et al.* 1982), causing equivalent lung damage (White and Froeb 1980). The non-smoking spouses of smokers are about 50 per cent more likely to die of lung cancer than spouses of non-smokers (Wald *et al.* 1986). Children whose parents are just moderate smokers (10 per day) suffer a 40 per cent higher chance of bronchitis (Somerville *et al.* 1988). As long ago as 1958 a perinatal mortality survey suggested that 1,500 babies were lost each year because their mothers smoked: up to a 30 per cent higher risk than among non-smoking mothers and one of the biggest avoidable causes of perinatal mortality (Spastics Society 1982).

Drink

Heavy drinking is also a serious health problem (DHSS 1981, Royal College of Physicians 1987*a*). Alcohol consumption has doubled since the 1950s, especially among young people and women, after a marked

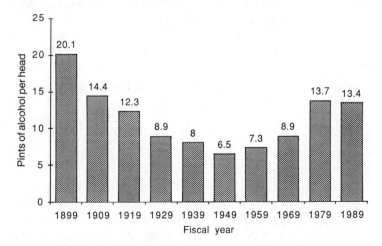

Source: Brewers' Society 1989, t. D2.

Fig. 7.10. Trend of alcohol consumption, UK, 1899–1989

fall since the beginning of the century. But it did not increase in the 1980s (figure 7.10). Cirrhosis, alcoholism, and drunkenness have all risen accordingly (Haskey, Balarajan, and Donnan 1983). Cirrhosis of the liver, the scourge of innkeepers, barmen, and waiters, killed 2,209 people in England and Wales in 1981, 3,023 in 1989. It also predisposes to liver cancer. Alcohol's direct effect as a carcinogen is not properly understood. It seems to help other substances, like cigarette smoke, to set off cancers. Heavy smokers are likely to be heavy drinkers (Cummins, Shaper et al. 1981). Drinking by itself leads to higher blood pressure (Shaper, Pocock, et al. 1981), to a higher risk of IHD (Dyer et al. 1977) and many other diseases (Taylor 1981; Edwards et al. 1977). The foetal alcohol syndrome—babies born deformed and underweight because of excess alcohol in their mothers' bloodstream (Jones and Smith 1973)—in its extreme form is still uncommon in the UK.

Deaths from all alcohol related diseases increased from about 1,600 in the UK in 1964 to 2,300 in 1978 and 3,222 (England and Wales) in 1985. As in most other countries, deaths attributed to alcoholism (now called the 'alcohol dependence syndrome') have increased fourfold in the same period (Sherlock 1983). The DHSS (1976) estimated from cirrhosis figures that there were half a million people in Britain with a serious drink problem, but estimates of dependence vary from 70,000 to 240,000 (DHSS 1981). There is evidence that severe alcohol dependence can partly be attributed to genetic factors (Gordis et al. 1990). The death toll is increased (to over 5,000) by accidental deaths attributed to drink; at home and at work as well as on the roads. One in five road deaths (i.e. about 1,300) is associated with excessive drinking. Up to a quarter of pedestrians killed on roads have excess alcohol in their bloodstream (one half in Scotland), and many serious crimes (including murder) are committed under the influence of drink (DHSS 1981). Between 15 and 30 per cent of men admitted to general medical, orthopaedic, and casualty departments in the UK are problem drinkers or dependent on alcohol. Overall, alcohol abuse is estimated to cause about 28,000 excess deaths per year in England and Wales among people aged 15–74 (Anderson 1988).

The Royal College of Psychiatrists (1979) suggested a generous safe maximum intake of four pints of beer or its equivalent per day (eight glasses of wine, or four single measures of spirits) but have now reduced it substantially to 20 'units' per week for men (i.e. 1½ pints per day) and 15 units for women. One 'unit' is approximately 8 grams of alcohol, equivalent to half a pint of beer, a glass of wine or sherry, or a single whisky (see Medical Council on Alcoholism 1987). Liver damage is likely over 80 grams of alcohol a day (8 pints of beer or its equivalent); but the level for women is much lower, both for intoxication and liver damage—as little as 20 grams per day (Sherlock 1983). Moderate drinkers used to be consoled by the belief that low levels of drinking—two pints, or four glasses of wine—might reduce risks from circulatory disease by raising high-density lipoprotein (HDL) levels (Marmot *et al.* 1981*b*). The higher death-rate of non-drinkers compared to moderate drinkers is well established. But it is accounted for by the high death-rate of non-drinkers who have given up previous heavy drinking because it was already affecting their health (Shaper 1988).

The UK has one of the lowest rates of alcohol consumption in Europe (about 7 litres/head in 1988) (Brewers' Society 1989). France has the highest consumption (double that of the UK) and the highest cirrhosis death-rate. Going on binges, favoured in Scandinavia, Scotland, and Northern Ireland, makes the indirect effects worse. In the Soviet Union and Eastern Europe, the immense consumption of alcohol, until recent severe cutbacks growing at ten times the rate of population growth, is thought to be partly responsible for the deteriorating male expectation of life (Davis and Feshbach 1980, Jozan 1986). Everywhere, the consequences of alcohol abuse and its control are complicated by its harmlessness in small doses and its central role in social life. Dependence on drugs other than alcohol (e.g. heroin) accounted for 127 deaths in 1985; the problem here is the incapacity of the large number of addicts and the huge criminal involvement in supply.

Food

Smoking and alcohol have relatively straightforward effects on disease; currently plausible estimates are that they are responsible for 30 per cent and 3 per cent of cancer deaths respectively. Diet is different. It has so many components: absolute amount, fibre content, fat content, protein, carbohydrate, sugar, and additives, that a clear picture of effects on health is difficult to find. None the less, international comparisons and laboratory work on animals show that to reduce mortality we should eat less fat (especially saturated fat), less salt, and more fibre. Doll and Peto (1981), for example, reckoned that 35 per cent of cancers might be avoidable by dietary choice—but their range of error went from 70 per cent to 10 per cent. Earlier this century, inadequate diet was still a major health problem. Data on food intake, the increase in the height and weight of children and adults, and the youthful trend of menarche show that most people now get at least enough food

(Tanner 1978, Floud *et al.* 1990). Instead, the most important problems are overeating, obesity, and the high fat content of our diet.
Weight consciousness now supports a substantial slimming industry,
which hardly existed thirty years ago. Overweight is strongly associated
with high blood levels of cholesterol, a major IHD risk factor (Thelle *et
al.* 1983, Royal College of Physicians 1983), diabetes, and other life-
threatening conditions. It is difficult to know if we are now eating less.
The National Food Survey (table 7.6) shows a 14 per cent decline in
average daily domestic food intake, but this may be accounted for by
the larger number of meals eaten out (now 3.5/week) (Rayner 1989).

Today's risk of an unbalanced diet is a penalty of our emancipation
from the habits of our hunting and gathering ancestors. Their lives were
brutish and short, probably nasty too, but their diets, judging from
modern ethnological and archaeological evidence, were varied and
flexible, if unpalatable (Howell 1986). They had not yet invented the
unnatural dietary monotony of intensive cultivation and the refinement
of food which early mass affluence has made possible, and which
mature affluence is now recognizing: the problems of low fibre, excess
fat, sugar, additives, and the like, especially when combined with a
sedentary life.

Dietary fibre

Dietary fibre includes plant carbohydrates such as lignin, cellulose, and
all the complex sugars (polysaccharides) in the diet not broken down by
the gut, mostly found in the outer covering of grain, or 'bran'. High
fibre levels protect against cancer of the lower bowel, diverticulosis,
and heart disease, possibly by speeding the passage of harmful meta-
bolites through the gut (including carcinogenic derivatives of bile
acids); by retarding the absorption of harmful food substances by the
body or by preserving the gut flora from harmful changes. People in
simple societies who eat bread from coarse unrefined flour, or other
whole cereals, suffer about one-tenth of our mortality from such
causes. Constipation, almost unknown in such societies, is a minor
inconvenience in modern living, much joked about. But large floppy
stools characteristic of Third World digestions (four times the weight,
with food transit of 30 hours rather than 80 hours) may seriously protect health (Burkitt 1971). Preferences for white flour (e.g. 80 per cent
extraction), white rice, etc. reduce fibre intake.

Since 1880 intake of dietary fibre has declined slowly—except in
wartime because of the need to use 85 per cent extraction flour. The
wartime diet seems to have had much to commend it (Southgate *et al.*
1979). 1985 fibre intake on a broader definition was about 21.4

grams/day. Pentose consumption, the most important component from bread and cereal, is about a tenth of that. The fashion for wholemeal bread, etc., may initially appeal only to those educated to its merits and accustomed to its flavour; but it may have affected the pattern of social class mortality. Large bowel cancer used to be more common in social classes I and II, but by 1971 these differences had vanished (Logan 1981). Overall the trend in fibre consumption (average 12.5 grams/day in 1988) remains unfavourable to health (National Food Survey Committee 1989).

Meat and fat

A high fat diet is known to predispose to circulatory disease (Lewis *et al.* 1981), gall bladder cancer, and ovarian cancer in women (Peto 1980) and is now suspected of causing breast cancer. Because of its high energy content it also predisposes to obesity (Royal College of Physicians 1983*b*). All enquiries have recommended a substantial reduction in the fat content of Western diet (WHO 1982; Royal College of Physicians 1976). DHSS has established a target of 35 per cent of energy intake from fat (COMA 1986). More recently the US National Academy of Sciences (1989) has recommended not more than 30 per cent of energy intake from fat; not more than 10 per cent from saturated fat, and not more than 6 grams of meat per day per kilogram body weight. High meat diets are suspected of promoting circulatory disease and bowel cancer; but some groups of people in the UK who live on low meat diets (e.g. certain orders of nuns) gain no corresponding relief from these diseases (Kinlen 1982).

Britain has a tradition of heavy meat eating (Drummond and Wilbraham 1938) compared with our European neighbours, although many of them have now overtaken us. Meat is a touchstone of welfare in Britain. Families unable to afford their daily meat and at least a weekly joint regard themselves as poverty stricken and deprived, and are so considered by the poverty lobby. High meat diets, even lean meat diets, usually mean high fat diets, although chicken has a much lower fat content than most other meat. Fish is full of unsaturated oils instead of saturated fat. National specialities such as pork crackling, Yorkshire puddings, chips, and roast potatoes all help to maximize fat input. In Japan, which enjoys the lowest IHD mortality of any industrialized country, fat comprises only 27 per cent of the energy content of food—compared to over 40 per cent in Britain—and the Japanese derive the industrial world's highest proportion of protein intake from fish (40 per cent).

Until recently meat and fat consumption increased substantially this century; one of the most obvious signs of higher living standards spreading throughout the community and one of the chief suspects for the concomitant rise of circulatory disease. The National Food Survey which began in 1950 (National Food Survey Committee 1989) shows that despite rapidly increasing personal wealth, domestic per capita fat consumption has declined about 13 per cent (to just over 90 grams/ person/day) from its peak of 111 grams around 1973. Unfortunately this drop may be made up from the larger number of meals eaten outside the home: chip consumption has doubled in ten years, meat eaten outside the home has increased by a quarter. Because total domestic energy intake has also declined, the proportion of energy from fat remains stubbornly constant at about 42 per cent. There are some clearly favourable trends: the rise in the ratio of polyunsaturated to saturated fat from about 0.22 to 0.35 over the same period (table 7.6); the decline of meat (but not meat products) as a percentage of domestic energy input, a sharp increase in the substitution of skimmed for full cream milk. This dietary change must have helped the modest downward trend of heart disease.

Table 7.6. Trends in fat consumption and energy intake, 1973–1986

Year	Total fat	Satur-ated fat	Polyunsatur-ated fat	Total energy	Fat ratio P : S	% fat in total energy
1973	111	51.5	11.5	2,400	0.22	41.6
1974	106	50.7	10.6	2,320	0.21	41.1
1975	107	51.7	10.1	2,290	0.20	42.0
1976	105	50.1	10.5	2,280	0.20	41.4
1977	105	47.5	10.4	2,260	0.22	41.8
1978	106	47.2	10.6	2,260	0.22	42.2
1979	106	47.8	10.7	2,250	0.22	42.4
1980	106	46.8	11.3	2,230	0.24	42.8
1981	104	45.6	11.4	2,210	0.25	42.3
1982	103	44.4	12.1	2,180	0.27	42.5
1983	101	44.5	12.8	2,140	0.29	42.5
1984	97	41.9	12.7	2,060	0.30	42.3
1985	96	40.6	13.1	2,020	0.32	42.6
1986	98	40.6	14.3	2,070	0.35	42.6
1988	93	38.3	14.2	1,998	0.37	42.0

Note: Fat intake is in grams per person per day. Total energy intake is in Kcal per person per day from food. In 1986 other sources included soft drinks 28, alcoholic drinks 157, sweets 139: total 2,390. These data do *not* include meals taken outside the home.

Sources: National Food Survey Committee Report 1989 and earlier: Household Food Consumption and Expenditure Annual Report 1988, t. 4.1, 4.3, 4.4.

Vegetables and vitamins

Frank vitamin deficiency diseases, such as rickets and osteomalacia (lack of vitamin D), once common among the children of the poor, have been almost unknown for many years in Britain except among Asian immigrants whose dietary inadequacy of vitamin D became apparent under certain circumstances (Hunt *et al.* 1976). Fresh fruit and vegetables, and any form of potato other than chips, still tend to be neglected in the UK diet, especially in the North and among manual workers. The only green thing in most hamburger takeaways is the paint. This is unfortunate, as carrots and other sources of vitamin A and C may offer protection against cancer, both of the stomach and of other sites (Kinlen 1981). Vitamin C is found only in fresh fruit and vegetables. Wholemeal bread is a particularly rich source of B vitamins. Fruit and vegetables are also a secondary source of dietary fibre (see Passmore and Eastwood 1986).

Food additives

Artifical food additives—especially preservatives, dyes, and artifical sweeteners—have become a natural target for the health reformers. But there is not much evidence that they do harm. Preservatives, notably nitrates and nitrites, are much used in tinned food, junk food, and instant TV dinners and their use has certainly been increasing until recently. They may cause problems because the body can turn them into nitrosamines, which are known carcinogens. Artifically 'smoked' food—cheese, ham, kippers or haddock—has more. Genuinely smoked food is also rich in nitrosamines together with other carcinogens from smoke, such as benzpyrenes; so is food charred by grilling or on a hotplate, such as overdone hamburgers and toast. But Doll and Peto (1981), for example, reckoned that less than 1 per cent of cancers could be blamed on food additives. By stopping the toxins and carcinogens of natural food decay as well as minimizing food wastage, they may well do some good. Preservatives have been credited with some of the substantial decline in stomach cancer throughout the industrial world since the last World War. Their withdrawal from food supplied in more health conscious outlets (including some supermarket chains) may have helped the recent increase in (mostly non-lethal) food poisoning. Commonplace salt and sugar may do more damage than high-tech novelties.

Sugar and salt

In Britain the average person consumes about a hundredweight of sugar every year. Not a grain of it is nutritionally necessary. It is a classic example of an expensive attractive exotic rarity which has become cheap and commonplace through affluence and international trade (Hobhouse 1985). In 1840 consumption was about 35 grams/head/day. By 1910 it had reached about 100 grams, by 1960 140 grams, since then declining a little (National Food Survey Committee 1989; DHSS 1974a). No one doubts its importance in rotting teeth (a problem now in full retreat thanks to the fluoridization of water). Its fiercest critics, notably Yudkin (1972), have overstepped the mark in labelling sugar a major health threat. It does have a specific effect on diabetes, it contributes to obesity and to high blood pressure, and hence IHD. It is alleged to cause some severe behavioural disorders, including heightened aggression in children. There is nothing more fattening about sugar than any other carbohydrate; but disorders may follow from its rapid absorption into the bloodstream and consequent violent effects on insulin response (especially on an empty stomach, whence it is blamed for some early-morning traffic accidents) Cumulative long term damage to body proteins may be a serious consequence of excess sugar consumption, especially of sweets and snacks between meals (Furth and Harding 1989).

Average salt intake is about 10 grams/day—well over the recommended 5 grams—about half added at table, a third added in cooking. None of the extra is needed. Much is added to manufactured food; ironically, high fibre bran cereals often have a lot of added salt. Savoury foods (crisps, cocktail snacks) boost salt intake and the salt content of one take-away Chinese meal can supply a week's dietary requirement. High salt diets can be a problem because they make high blood pressure worse (Frise 1976), and may set off other diseases: highly salted foods may cause stomach cancer (Kinlen 1982). A campaign to reduce salt consumption in Northern Japan, where highly salted food and stomach cancer are both common, has succeeded in bringing down death-rates. Even traditional societies with high salt intake have high blood pressure (Gleibermann 1973). In Britain reduction of salt intake to a third of average levels (3 grams/day) can reduce mild essential hypertension as effectively as drug therapy. Reduction to 5 grams/day is practicable by avoiding added salt. Reduction to 3 grams requires the avoidance of salted bread (almost all shop bread) and almost all eating out (MacGregor et al. 1989).

The physical environment: pollution, climate, radiation

Atmospheric pollution

The dense fog which covered London without lifting between 5 and 8 December 1952 killed more people than any other peacetime disaster in Britain this century; and it was only one among many in a long history of air pollution, without which no dramatization of Victorian London is complete. It was the right smog at the right time to spur action. In the following week there were 4,703 deaths in London compared to 1,852 in the same week a year before—an increase of 250 per cent. Bronchitis deaths rose nine times, deaths from heart disease trebled, deaths from pneumonia doubled. Mortality did not fall to normal levels for a month. Smoke and sulphur dioxide concentrations (mostly from domestic coal fires) trapped by cold air as smog were the culprits (Ministry of Health 1954).

The Clean Air Act 1956 was the response to this disaster. It was the first effective legislation to stop air pollution in a series of attempts which date from 1247. The immense growth of London after the eighteenth century, and the universal use of coal fires, had made the problem acute, but until this century the lack of suitable smokeless fuel prevented any practical response. The measurement of the mortality effects of air pollution is complicated by the concentration of cigarette smokers in cities (Gardner *et al.* 1983) but it is clear that since the Act and because of the Act air pollution and mortality from chronic lung disease has declined, including its seasonal variation (Stuart-Harris 1980). For example, average urban concentrations of sulphur dioxide in 1987 were less than a quarter of their level in 1963, and urban smoke concentrations were down to about a tenth (Department of the Environment 1989).

Atmospheric pollution is worse in winter as most domestic fuel is burnt then. This contributes to excess mortality through respiratory disease, although circulatory deaths which are provoked more by cold weather predominate in the overall excess. The seasonality ratio (the ratio of deaths in January to March to the yearly rate) deteriorated during the nineteenth century; from 110 in 1841–50 to 128 in 1920–30. Since then, the quarterly ratio has improved to 116 in 1971–80. In Europe, excess winter deaths are far fewer. Taking January as the worst month from 1968 to 1972, England and Wales had a ratio of 130, Scotland 131, compared to USA 114, Belgium 118, Sweden 111 (OPCS 1981*a*). By 1989, central heating was installed in 78 per cent of houses in Britain compared with 10 per cent in 1964. It emits less smoke pollution and protects against hypothermia (McDowall 1981). Excess winter mortality from respiratory disease declined 69 per cent from 1964 to 1984. But up to 1984 there was no corresponding decline in the seasonality of deaths from circulatory disease, which is believed to be more related to outdoor than to indoor cold stress (Keating *et al.* 1989).

Concern about acid rain from acid gases from large plant and fossil fuel power stations is justified more by its adverse effects on trees lakes, and buildings, rather than by known effects on human health. Neither is there direct evidence yet of harmful effects from street levels of vehicle exhausts in Britain despite their poisonous content and offensive impact. But there is concern that small particles in diesel exhaust ('particulates') may be carcinogenic. In London streets, levels of nitrogen oxides (NO_x) often exceed WHO guidelines (Royal Commission on Environmental Pollution 1984). NO_x and unburnt exhaust hydrocarbons can react under the influence of sunlight to form ozone, a powerful destroyer of vegetation, in photochemical smogs. Britain's weak sunlight does not generate photochemical smogs on the scale of Los Angeles, Tokyo, Athens, or Mexico City, but large areas around London are affected in the summer. Britain is implementing better controls on vehicle emissions intended to reduce or limit emissions of hydrocarbons and NO_x by the 1990s (DoE 1990). There is little evidence of deaths or illness caused by environmental lead, nor of intellectual impairment in children. Lead from petrol contributes not more than 20 per cent of average intake of lead in adults (Royal Commission on Environmental Pollution 1983).

Water and weather

In the British Regional Heart Study's examination of 253 towns (Shaper *et al.* 1981), five independent factors accounted for three-quarters of the geographical differences in ischaemic heart disease mortality: water hardness, percentage of days with rain, average daily temperature, percentage of manual workers, and extent of car ownership (a measure of poverty) (Pocock *et al.* 1980). Water hardness depends on the concentration of natural calcium and other salts. These produce boiler scales in kettles, scum in bath water, and lower rates of heart disease. The harder the water, the lower the risk—up to about average hardness (1.7 mol/l. or 170 mg/l.). The mechanism of protection is unknown. Most towns with soft water are in the North-West upland zone of acidic igneous and metamorphic rocks, while most of the harder waters are in the South-East, over younger calcareous sedimentary rocks. Nitrate in water has been suspected as a cause of stomach cancer. Some nitrate is natural, but modern intensive subsidy-driven farming techniques have increased levels sixfold since 1900 and doubled them since the 1970s (DoE 1986). The cancer connection seems unlikely, as stomach cancer rates have fallen, and both individual and regional nitrate intakes are inversely related to cancer risk (Beresford 1985, Forman *et al.* 1985).

Cold and wet areas have worse heart disease rates. Cold weather inhibits adequate ventilation, encourages smog and respiratory infections, and reduces physical activity. Mild surface cooling, even of the face alone, increases blood pressure, viscosity, and platelet count (Keatinge *et al.* 1984) which provoke heart attacks and strokes. This is probably the most important route through which cold weather raises mortality. Coronary and cerebrovascular disease account for 54 per cent (1984) of the total excess winter mortality. Temperature and humidity are known to affect IHD rates in the USA and Finland. In 1985 567 people died of 'excessive cold', some outdoors in freak weather, 438 from 'hypothermia' in the strict sense. Many of these hypothermia cases are already ill or immobile for other reasons (Collins 1987). Residents of sheltered housing suffer as much as other elderly people; brief excursions outdoors rather than low indoor temperatures appear to be responsible for most excess circulatory deaths in winter (Keatinge *et al.* 1989).

Sunlight and Radiation

High energy electromagnetic radiation (ultraviolet, X, and gamma), or irradiation by nuclear or subatomic particles (α and β radiation) destroys proteins and DNA in cells. The 'softest' form is the ultra-violet radiation in sunlight—the more harmful part of the sun's radia-tion spectrum is filtered out by the atmosphere, especially its ozone layer. Geographical differences in exposure to sunlight cause a mild North–South cline in mostly non-lethal skin cancers (epitheliomas), primarily among outdoor workers; sailors, farm workers, builders (see Royal College of Physicians 1987). Harder radiation causes cancers, especially leukaemia and genetic changes (mutations) in sex cells which can show up in future generations. The average annual radiation dose in the UK of about 2.15 milliSieverts (mSv) is probably responsible for about 2,500 cancer deaths per year. Eighty-seven per cent of this radiation is from natural sources (NRPB 1986): cosmic rays 14 per cent, γ-radiation from rock and soil 19 per cent, radon decay products 37 per cent, the human body itself 17 per cent, mostly natural potassium-40 from food.

A milliSievert (1 mSv = 0.1 rem in the old measure) is a measure of effective dose equivalent; i.e. a measure of radiation dose weighted for the harmfulness of each type of radiation and the sensitivity of different tissues in the body. Domestic exposure to the natural radioactive gas radon and the radioactive 'daughters' which it generates from its own decay is the largest single source of radiation exposure (37 per cent). It has only recently been perceived as a domestic threat. Percolating up through the soil and the sub-floor space, it accumulates in the ground floor of houses and may cause about 1,500 lung cancer deaths per year

(O'Riordan, 1988, see Chapter 8). Remedial measures and future building regulations should contain the problem with floor membranes and better underfloor and room ventilation—although at a cost to heat efficiency. Most artificial exposure is medical (11.5 per cent of the total dose), mostly X-rays equivalent to 250–300 cancer deaths per year. All other artificial sources are very small: weapons-test fallout 0.5 per cent, average occupational exposure 0.4 per cent (1.4 mSv to radiation workers in medicine, radiography and nuclear power), radioactive discharges (mostly from reprocessing) 0.1 per cent on average (1 mSv to the most exposed individuals). The Chernobyl disaster of 1986 added under 0.1 mSv (3 per cent) to the average dose (Hughes *et al.* 1989).

Fears over radiation from nuclear plant seem a little out of proportion to the immediate risk. More people died at Chappaquiddick than at Three Mile Island, and many more died in the Mexico City liquid petroleum gas explosion in 1984 than died at Chernobyl in 1986. It is the long-term consequences that are serious, especially as these are difficult to assess. Radiation exposure from Chernobyl will come primarily from the long-lasting radionuclides, caesium 127 and 134. It has been estimated that the radiation exposure to the average European outside the USSR will amount to the equivalent of an extra two months exposure to natural background radiation over 50 years, and that even in hot spot areas it is very unlikely that individuals will receive doses in excess of the IAEA guideline limits (Ap Simon *et al.* 1989). Consequences within the USSR will be serious: possibly an extra 600,000 cancer cases. Nuclear industry discharges in the UK are equivalent to two cancer deaths per year—about the same as the annual lightning casualties (Fremlin 1987). None the less clusters of leukaemias are found in various parts of the UK near nuclear plants, although other clusters are not. Some research suggests that cancer mortality is not overly increased near nuclear installations compared to controls (Cook-Mozaffari *et al.* 1987), others suggest it is. Estimates of Sellafield's radiation are 250 times too low to account for the four extra deaths actually recorded in the immediate population at risk of 1,225 children and young people (Stather, Dionian *et al.* 1986). Such a disparity is apparent in all the other studies, which seems to rule out a direct connection between radiation doses to the public and the leukaemias. Attention is now being directed to radiation exposure to children's parents who have been workers in the plant, and transmission of leukaemia to children by defective genes. It has now been shown that the radiation dose received by fathers during employment at Sellafield, before the conception of their children, is associated with the risk of developing leukaemia among those children. This accounts for the excess cases observed (Gardner *et al.* 1990). This is the first time that such transmission of risk across generations has been observed in human populations. It is bound to lead to a reduction in the maximum permitted annual dose for radiation workers from 50 mSv (established in 1965 by the International Commission on Radiological Protection) to the 15 mSv recommended in 1987 by the NRPB, or to an even lower figure.

The human environment: mortality and housing

Bad housing and poverty go together and it is difficult to untangle their effects on mortality. In the past, health was the main driving force behind reform of housing standards (see Burnett 1986). Today, poor housing in Britain is concentrated in a small and declining minority of households (figure 2.4). In 1987 only 1 per cent of households lacked an inside WC, 2 per cent lacked sole access to a bathroom. On average the British people are among the best provided in Europe in such facilities and in living space in terms of number of rooms, although not in terms of total living area. At the time of the 1981 census only 0.4 per cent of households were overcrowded in the (rather generous) statutory sense. More widespread physical housing problems which may affect health are dampness and inadequate heating. Disrepair, or bad design inducing dampness, is concentrated in local authority and private rented housing. Overcrowding, damp, poor ventilation, and families sharing facilities have long been known to increase mortality rates (Chadwick 1842, in Flinn 1965; Stevenson 1923; Stocks 1934; Titmuss 1943; Preston 1978), primarily by helping to spread infectious disease, especially tuberculosis and diarrhoeal disease. Nowadays many fewer people are at risk. The twofold difference in infant mortality from infectious disease between town and country of the 1930s is greatly diminished (Cheeseman, Martin, and Russell 1938). But post-neonatal infant mortality (mostly from infections, cot deaths, and accidents) is still much higher in overcrowded conditions, especially in households lacking amenities or sharing them (Fox and Goldblatt 1982, Royal College of General Practitioners 1982). Excess mortality is especially severe for respiratory disease. Young married couples who have only just set up house are most likely to suffer deficient accommodation and financial problems, so young children tend to live in the most crowded households (Fox 1978, Fox and Goldblatt 1982). Children who share the use of a bath with other families are even more at risk than those who do not have the use of one at all. Babies in large families are most at risk (Bradshaw *et al.* 1982). Factors such as these could account for three-quarters of variation in perinatal mortality and four-fifths of variation in low birthweight in the late 1960s (Ashford *et al.* 1973).

Housing tenure is becoming particularly important as a new variable in the attempt to pin down the causes of excess mortality. In general, council tenants suffer worse sickness and mortality compared to owner-occupiers, after allowing for age structure and social class (Fox and Goldblatt 1982, 1990). Modern purpose-built council housing compares well with average owner-occupied property, thanks to the Parker-Morris standards imposed on local authorities in 1964, in terms of space and amenity. One of the aims of municipal housing, from its beginnings with the 'Cross Acts' of 1875–90 (Cross was Home Secretary in Disraeli's Cabinet) was to solve problems of ill health associated with housing. The health problems associated with council tenure owe more to the characteristics of people who find themselves in council tenure, although it is true that the experimental designs uniquely inflicted on council tenants have brought a heavy burden of dampness problems. Council tenants include high proportions of one-parent families and large families. Early childbearing is more common than among other tenures (see Chapter 5). A high proportion are unemployed or on low income. The effects upon health and behaviour, including mental health, of the physical and social environment of some of the larger council estates, and their physical and social isolation, should not be ignored (Freeman 1984).

Income

Throughout this account, upward trends in income have been assumed to have automatically favourable effects upon mortality. Where the average income is only sufficient for subsistence, improvement in real income means a more secure provision of the necessities of life. For most of the twentieth century increases in income must have improved the health and survival of the poor because they could thereby afford to be better fed, housed, and warmed. Titmuss and his school argued from the evidence of high death-rates and mortality differentials, for greater equality of income, and public expenditure on welfare to raise everyone above the minimum level. Since the 'rediscovery' of poverty in Britain in the 1960s, death-rates have again become more widely quoted in league tables as examples of relative national failure; social class differentials have been produced as evidence of deprivation and the need for more equality of income (Wilkinson 1986, Keynes, Coleman, and Dimsdale 1988).

Personal income is not the only way the economy affects death-rates.

Some of the effects of economic growth are manifested in public, not private goods: changes in the disease environment deliberately or inadvertently brought about by public action. Public health works segregating sewage from drinking water are one example. Income support of the poor, developing into the comprehensive systems of the NHS, the Welfare State, and mass council housing after 1946, is another. This has brought us to a position where the social security system cost £45.9bn. in 1988–9, 10 per cent of GDP; the health service and personal social services cost £23.6bn., 5 per cent of GDP; not counting private health care and insurance. One household in four receives Housing Benefit, mostly on top of subsidized rent.

It is not clear that there is always a simple relation between income growth (at a constant distribution of inequality) and improvements in mortality. At certain times in the past general trends in mortality depended more on the external disease environment, little affected by the actions or wealth of individuals. Today most people are adequately fed and housed. Trends in income may affect directly the mortality risks only of a minority. In recent decades correlations between income trends and death-rates have been weak. The rise of 'diseases of affluence' in the middle of the twentieth century suggests that high proportions of modern populations can overshoot in food consumption and spend some of their income surplus on harmful extras—namely drink and cigarettes. This focuses attention on income inequality and the position of the very poor, and on the adequacy of health and welfare systems (Chapter 8). Further improvement for the majority may depend more on education and changes in tastes rather than increases in spending power.

7.6 International Trends and Comparisons

Most of the downward trends in mortality discussed above are shared with the rest of the industrial world. Britain does not distinguish itself in the international league table (table 7.5), and some lessons can be learned from international comparison (Fox 1989). In Europe, geography rather than national income differences seems a better predictor of mortality. The United Kingdom per capita GNP of $12,800 buys an expectation of life of 75. Some richer countries, such as Sweden (average per capita GNP $19,150), also enjoy a longer life expectation (both sexes together 77). Others do not, for example the USA ($19,780 and 75 years) and West Germany ($18,530 and 76 years) (1988 per capita GNP). Some Mediterranean countries, notably Greece, have lower death-rates than Northern Europe, despite being relatively poor. Spain and Greece enjoy the same expectation of life (77) but with per capita incomes of $7,740 and $4,790 respectively. Mediterranean diet (low meat, more fish and cheese, cooking with olive oil not fat) may help to avert heart disease. Japanese mortality is the lowest in the world. Japan combines high income, modest levels of inequality, and a diet sparse in meat and fat. Heart disease remains relatively insignificant even though fat consumption is increasing from its original low level, while stomach cancer and stroke are more important than in Europe.

The deterioration of mortality throughout Eastern Europe (except East Germany), and especially in Poland, Hungary, and the Soviet Union until recently (Davis and Feshbach 1980, Dutton 1979, Jozan 1986, Compton 1985, Blum and Pressat 1987, Blum 1989) shows how industrialized society can take wrong turnings in dealing with disease. Some of the increase in Soviet infant mortality may be an artefact of the extension of birth registration to high mortality Muslim populations (Anderson and Silver 1986) and some of the adult increase may be due to the maturation of war-damaged male cohorts (Dinkel 1985). But part is real. Potential causes are not hard to find: untramelled and unstructured rapid urbanization, the poor status and low quality of medical care (despite an abundance of doctors), heavy and rising consumption of high-tar cigarettes, extensive alcohol abuse, heavy industrialization with little control on environmental pollution (Cooper 1981, 1982, Komarov 1978).

These societies seem to be stuck in a stage of health development where any advantages of rural living have been lost, and where the hazards from smoking, drinking, fatty diet, and occupational disease and pollution are still increasing, unchecked by social or political feedback and legislation, despite near-equality of income, free housing and medical care, and almost free bread. Child care is not helped by the world record of 89 per cent of women aged 15–54 in the work-force; a necessity throughout Eastern Europe given the difficulties of increasing productivity in centrally planned, non-market economies. Cigarette consumption—mostly of high-tar brands—has risen fast to Western levels in the Soviet Union and cigarette production is a profitable state monopoly. Alcohol consumption there was rapidly increasing until a clampdown began in1986. Male death-rates from heart disease, cancer, cirrhosis, and accidents have all shown corresponding increases, although the position improved in the late 1980s. As death-rates—and official embarrassment—have risen, the volume of data diminished. This has made detailed analysis of underlying causes difficult until recently (Anderson and Silver 1989).

7.7 Future Progress against Mortality

Individual behaviour and social trends

At the beginning of the century, Britain was the most proletarian society in the world (Halsey 1987). Now manual work is being left behind (Boston 1984, Routh 1987). In 1984 29 per cent of an adult sample thought they had moved up a social class compared to their parents, only 9 per cent thought they had moved downwards (Jowell and Airey 1986). Risk-avoiding behaviour seems to go with middle-class lifestyles to which most people aspire. The trend away from smoking seems likely to continue in a favourable direction. But there has been little recent decline in smoking among women aged 20–50 (OPCS 1990). Favourable changes in food habits will continue the decline in circulatory disease and some cancer. If dietary changes brought down blood cholesterol to Chinese levels then the risk of heart disease would be reduced by about five-sixths (Doll 1987), but a real Chinese diet might encounter market resistance. Exercise is getting more popular, but it does not seem to reduce risk very much and the sections of the population that need it most do it least. The decline in fertility, its deferment, and its shifting class distribution will have favourable effects on infant mortality, although the births to immigrant mothers may continue a contrary pressure (Chapter 12). AIDS seems to be the only forseeable major infectious threat. Breast cancer is increasing. Higher risk from breast cancer may be a permanent penalty of smaller family size and delayed childbearing despite earlier maturation, with a debatable contribution from the contraceptive pill, whose use is declining. The popularity of sunbathing is thought to have caused the 37 per cent rise in malignant melanoma.

Public action

The most obvious public lever on health trends is the NHS. But most debate on the NHS has concentrated on funding, staffing, conditions of work, the direct care of patients, and waiting lists for operations; inputs often determined by employees, rather than performance indicators based on outputs for patients (Goldacre and Griffin 1983) such as lower death-rates. More recently, however, the reports of the Chief Medical Officer have discussed the need for performance indicators using mortality and other 'hard' data (DHSS 1988). In fact the demographic effects of cuts or increases in NHS spending are difficult to establish. Some expensive treatments offer no improvement in outcome (coronary care units) but others do (special baby units which can halve PMR rates in underweight babies, Pearce 1981, Chalmers *et al.* 1990). If social factors are allowed for, then some local authorities have higher—and lower—death-rates than their local characteristics would warrant. The mortality differences that remain (the 'residuals'), may indicate the scope for local NHS improvement (Charlton *et al.* 1983). Newspaper comment claimed that this represented a holocaust of 20,000 preventable deaths and 10,500 preventable premature babies. But the study assumed that regional differences are only due to local NHS performance (Chapter 8), and the final pattern made no obvious sense in terms of resource allocation. In Britain and in most EC countries, recent studies suggest that regional differences in 'avoidable' mortality do not substantially reflect inequalities in the supply of medical care (Carr-Hill *et al.* 1987, Kunst *et al.* 1988).

International comparisons of causes of death in relation to birthweight had suggested that 50 per cent of perinatal deaths were preventable (according to the Committee on Child Health Services 1976, HC Social Services Committee 1980, Spastics Society 1982). But the DHSS insisted that the figure could not be more than ten per cent; that more expenditure was not necessarily the answer, and to reduce PMR to Japanese levels would require a Japanese lifestyle, not just better services; and many of those saved would be handicapped. In 1989, for the first time, the Government asked health authorities to set targets to reduce infant mortality, although this does not go as far as a House of Commons Social Services Committee Report of 1988 which asked for target dates for reducing the IMR below 8 per 1000.

The Black Report (Working Group on Inequalities in Health 1980) and the Health Education Council report (Whitehead 1987, also Townsend and Davidson 1982), which repeats its conclusions, have continued the Titmuss tradition of emphasizing public expenditure as the road to better health. Commissioned by the (Labour) Secretary of State for Health and Social Services (Mr D. Ennals) in 1977, reporting to the (Conservative) Secretary of State for Health and Social Services (Mr P. Jenkin) the Black Report is concerned more with inequalities than overall trends. Its emphasis on the need to encourage child health to safeguard adult health is far-sighted. It reviews thoroughly all possible causes and theories. But its recommendations do not follow the weight of evidence it presents. It emphasizes the mortality directly attributable to working conditions, irrespective of its minor demographic impact, and gives insufficient weight to class differences in smoking, drinking, and other habits with potentially substantial mortality effects. In the end, without making a specific case for the results on mortality, it recommends a general policy of income redistribution and increased public expenditure.

Some of its recommendations were uncontentious. But the proposed shift of resources to community care seemed to threaten acute services (Acheson 1988). It also alarmed the government, which would have to find £4.8 billion (Hansard 27 October 1980, 6 December 1982, 31 July 1981) for free school milk and meals, doubled child benefit, more local authority housing expenditure, and the 'abolition of poverty'. The present (1990) government insists that spending on the NHS is already increasing at a high rate (45 per cent since 1979) and as demand for more services appears to be insatiable, other means, including private ones, must be found to increase health expenditure in a way more responsive to costs so that priorities are more effectively reallocated. Recent debate has highlighted the lower level of GNP spent on health in the UK (about 5 per cent) compared to most other industrial countries (8 per cent), but has also highlighted how much of that extra spent abroad is wasted on redundant doctors (as in Germany) or on lawyers and indemnity insurance (as in the USA). Mortality usually enters this debate in the context of inequalities. Meanwhile the overall death-rate continues to improve.

The most obvious target for priorities, apart from infant mortality, is the premature deaths of middle-aged adults, where British rates are relatively high (see King Edward Hospital's Fund for London, 1989). The benefit to be gained by preventing premature mortality from various sources can be gauged by calculating the years of life lost from the excess death-rates. Circulatory disease is the most important contributor to life lost among males between age 15 and 64 (246,000 years in 1987 or 125 per 10,000 population) but cancer is more important for women (table 7.7). Accidents are prominent because their youthful victims lose correspondingly more years of potential life, at a cost to the nation of up to £500,000 for each life lost, according to the Department of Transport. The advantages of prevention rather than cure are highlighted by the £500 millon/year costs of ischaemic heart disease to the NHS (National Audit Office 1989) and by the official estimate that heart disease costs £1.5 billion per year in lost production (Nicholls 1989).

To take preventive medicine further through health education, tobacco advertising, smoking in public places, and cigarette price increases are all obvious measures. But apart from the civil liberties questions, no government will abruptly imperil the £4 billion from tobacco revenues (equivalent to fifteen per cent of NHS costs) without securing an alternative source of tax, or jeopardize the jobs of

Table 7.7. Life-years lost between ages 15 and 64, England and Wales, 1985, selected causes

	Men			Women		
	No. (1000s)	Rate (per 10,000)	Mean age at death	No. (1000s)	Rate (per 10,000)	Mean age at death
All causes	1,029	482	70.4	627	299	76.4
Circulatory disease	265	124	72.4	94	45	79.6
IHD	195	92	71.1	43	20	78.3
Cancer—all forms	191	90	70.0	206	98	70.7
Lung	49	23	70.1	21	10	69.9
Female breast	—	—	—	60	29	67.9
Accidents—all causes	157	73	41.6	47	22	72.8
Motor vehicle	97	46	37.7	28	13	49.8
Perinatal (ICD 760–99)	67	32	0.5	47	23	0.6
Congenital anomalies	59	28	16.8	55	26	18.6
Suicide	57	27	47.5	18	9	55.9
Respiratory	50	24	75.8	36	17	80.4

Note: Major causes arranged in declining order for male years of life lost.

Source: OPCS Mortality Statistics 1985 Series DH1 No. 17 t.24.

thousands of tobacco workers. Attempts to abolish alcohol (USA) or to restrict its use severely have been counter-productive (Sweden, Finland). As the real price of alcohol has fallen significantly since the war, significant increases in duty are widely proposed to cut consumption, although this might fall foul of EC pressure to drink up the EC wine lake. Up to 20 per cent of respondents in a survey did not know how much drink was harmful to health; one in ten thought there was no limit to the amount of wine which could safely be drunk (OPCS 1983*g*). There was little change from 1978 to 1982 in public perceptions of the ill-health caused by alcohol, as recorded by the General Household Survey. But from 1982 to 1988, the proportion of respondents who agreed that alcohol damaged health rose from 38 per cent to 50 per cent.

According to a 1981 Health Education Council survey, most people in Britain in the early 1980s still had no idea that smoking, blood pressure, and obesity could give them heart disease. However recent surveys show that 75 per cent of people claim to be aware of the link between blood cholesterol levels and heart disease, and 95 per cent claim they would change their diets if their levels were too high. Rational choice on diet is still made difficult by the inadequate labelling of food contents. 1985 legislation has only obliged manufacturers to list ingredients in order of importance without proportions. Consumers might choose differently if they knew what percentage of fat, and what kind of fat, there was in mince, sausages, pies, and biscuits. Britain's agriculture and food industry have been geared until recently to gratify more traditional tastes. The Ministry of Agriculture, Fisheries and Food (MAFF) has sometimes seemed more concerned with the needs of the producers that it sponsors rather than the consumer. The Committee on the Medical Aspects of food policy (COMA 1984) recommended that our crucial dietary problem was the high proportion of energy derived from fat (especially saturated fat). This should be reduced from 42 per cent to 35 per cent of energy, and that we should eat less salt, sugar, and more fibre: a more vegetarian, wholefood diet cooked with oil not fat, including much more fresh fruit and vegetables; recommendations echoed by every other report. If these messages did change behaviour, recent research suggests that mortality trends would greatly benefit. But in the Health and Lifestyle Survey only half the respondents claimed to be taking any of these steps to improve health—in the USA almost everyone claims to do so (Cox *et al.* 1987).

Further prevention of accidents may be difficult, but quick medical response to accidents and heart emergencies from better equipped and trained ambulance services and trauma centres has cut death-rates abroad and could do so here (National Audit Office 1989). Perhaps the most effective specific legal interventions have been the succession of acts to restrict particular industrial hazards. For example, new regulations—common within the EC—will prohibit or phase out asbestos, except in a few applications, in five years. Further improvements of this kind may be difficult to find, as most of these problems were a product of earlier phases of industrial and chemical processes when science, monitoring, and health consciousness were less developed. But future measures must address real problems. Past legislation on Health and Safety at Work enforced expenditure on problems which are trivial from a health point of view. For example, Oxford University, which has not experienced an accidental death by fire since the fifteenth century, has been forced to spend £1.5 million on fire precautions at a time of financial cuts.

The complete elimination by vaccination of old diseases (measles, whooping cough), control of diseases imported from endemic areas abroad (TB, malaria), vaccination against respiratory diseases which kill the elderly (influenza, pneumonia) should all be within reach. The virus which causes cancer of the cervix uteri is also a prime target. Universal measles vaccination is coming, and the screening of all women against cervical cancer.

Gene mapping and the listing of the DNA sequences of specific genes will make it possible to identify many foetuses affected with major single gene defects (Wald 1983, Carter 1983). Such techniques as gene mapping and genetical fingerprinting will make it possible to identifying genotypes prone to cancer or heart disease before symptoms develop. Individuals could then be counselled to avoid their higher risks. Further in the future, genetical engineering techniques should enable specific harmful genes of this type (e.g. for hypercholesterolaemia) to be removed or switched off.

Screening of the population is likely to be most effective for common serious problems which can be cured if caught early enough: testing for high blood pressure every five years after age 16 to warn against IHD (Tudor Hart 1984), for breast cancer annually between ages 50 and 59, a cervical smear from sexually active women every three years, testing faeces for blood (for colorectal cancer) every year after age 45, and tests for incapacity after age 65 (Doll 1982). At present it would be difficult to operate a screening system for blood cholesterol similar to that in the USA. On US guidelines, 80 per cent of middle-aged men and all middle-aged women in the UK are over the US warning level of 6.2 millimoles per litre and would require detailed dietary advice or drug therapy (Tunstall-Pedoe *et al.* 1989).

We are entering a new period when substantial reductions in chronic disease can be secured by preventive treatment and cure. An aspirin a day reduced acute ischaemic heart disease by 47 per cent in a controlled trial of 11,000 US doctors, protects against stroke, and relieves attacks. Trials of an injected enzyme which dissolves blood clots (streptokinase or 'Eminase') are claimed to reduce deaths in heart attacks by almost 50 per cent (ISIS-2 1988).

It seems impossible that all the research which has gone into finding a magic bullet like interferon against viruses, to act as penicillin does against bacteria, will finally fail. Even more radically, the development of artificial designer antibodies—'monoclonal' antibodies of precisely known, genetically engineered molecular structure, may enable cancers and atheromatous plaques to be picked off without harming the patient. New knowledge of the immunology of cancer cell surfaces, and the identification of the cancer cells through their oncogenes, may enable them to be selectively destroyed.

Projecting future mortality

Official figures for the UK project a continued modest improvement in survival to an expectation of life of 75.7 for men and 80.5 for women by 2026–7 compared to 72.4 and 78.0 in 1987–8. (OPCS 1989a). This represents an extra 2.2 year of life at age 65 for men, an extra 1.7 for women. These projections incorporate assumptions about AIDS in men for the first time. Even though 1.6 per cent of the 1960 male birth cohort is assumed to die of the disease, overall death-rates are no worse than in the previous projection. Other projections of mortality by cause among people aged 60–84 included assumptions of up to 40 per cent reductions from 1981–4 to 2021–5 in IHD death-rates, and a halving or more of lung cancer and bronchitis death-rates (Alderson and Ashwood 1985) for men. In the most optimistic of the illustrative projections made before AIDS (Benjamin and Overton 1981), infant deaths will decline by 75 per cent. Smoking is assumed to become negligible, so 90 per cent of lung cancer deaths are avoided, 30 per cent of deaths from IHD below age 65 (the ages where IHD is most responsive to smoking), remaining deaths from these causes being deferred by medical advances. For the same reason, together with environmental improvements, all deaths from bronchitis, emphysema, and asthma are prevented (and redistributed). All cancer deaths are avoided by new therapies, and deaths from unspecified causes deferred ten years. Accidental deaths and from TB and diabetes remain undiminished. These improve expectations of life at birth to more than 81 for men, 87 for women (an increase of nine years). People retiring at age 65 could look forward to another quarter century of life—but the rest of the population would have to find some way of looking after aged dependants who would number almost one in three of the total (27 per cent, compared to 15 per cent now). These figures are not regarded as fantasy (Alderson 1982). We do not know what the final ultimate lifespan of the human species might be, and how far the survival curve can be made rectangular. There are certainly good reasons for supposing that it cannot be extended indefinitely (Kirkwood and Holliday 1986); a final average of 85 and an ultimate limit of 115 have been suggested (Fries 1980). But current expectations of life at birth for women in Sweden and in Japan already exceed 80 years. People in Britain have lived to 114, and the world record is 124 (in Canada and Japan).

8 Differentials in Mortality

8.0 Introduction

This chapter is about differentials in mortality. In Britain there are striking social and geographical inequalities in patterns of disease and death. A man in Wigan is twice as likely to die of bronchitis as one living in Oxfordshire. Bus conductors have twice the risk of dying of heart disease as university teachers. A baby born into a labourer's family is twice as likely never to see its first birthday as an executive's child. Furthermore, the social and geographical patterns are substantially independent of each other (OPCS 1978*b*, 1981*c*; Cummins, Shaper *et al.* 1981).

Studied epidemiologically, these differences in risk can show how modern diseases work and how they can best be avoided. If anything, the importance of epidemiology has increased, rather than diminished, with the rise of chronic diseases of complex aetiology which cannot yet be attacked in ways appropriate to parasitic diseases. For many years, social class and regional differences in mortality have been held up by reformers (e.g. Titmuss 1943) as evidence for the unacceptability of the living conditions and incomes of the poor, for the inadequacy of welfare spending and of the social and political system behind them, and for the need to redistribute income (Townsend and Davidson 1982, Whitfield 1987, Townsend *et al.* 1988, Wilkinson 1986). The existence of differentials is taken as prima-facie evidence for scope for improvement in average conditions, until all reach the level of the best. Occupation forms the basis of the social class classification. It also provides some of the least ambiguous examples of mortality differentials. So it is helpful to begin there.

8.1 Mortality and Occupation

Occupational hazards

It has been known for centuries that some occupations are more dangerous than others. In the sixteenth century, Agricola and Paracelsus first wrote on the special risks to miners. Ramazzini wrote the first treatise on occupational medicine in 1700. Some dangers are obvious—fishermen are shipwrecked; miners and quarrymen are killed

Table 8.1. SMR by occupation, England and Wales, around 1971, 1981

Code 1981	Code 1971	Occupational Unit Group	1971 SMR men 15–64	1981 SMR men 15–64	1971 SMR wives 15–64	1981 Single women 20–59	SMR men standardized for social class 1971
160[a]	097	Bricklayers' labourers	273	(243)	241	—	240[c]
148	116	Deck, etc. ratings	233	(304)	186	—	216[c]
032.03	115	Deck, etc, officers	175	(150)	112	—	148[c]
082	001	Fishermen	171	(234)	177	—	151[c]
127	034	Steel erectors, riggers	164	180	159	—	158[c]
109	109	Foundries/furnacemen	160	119	162	—	116[c]
—	008	Coal miners—above ground	160	—	136	—	143[c]
085.02	061	Shoemakers	156	157	116	—	145[c]
039.02	154	Publicans	155	152	139	55	190[c]
116.02	049	Watchmakers	154	111	101	—	144[c]
—	221	Armed forces	147	123	150	—	—
098.02	080	Brewers, wine-makers	143	152	144	—	134[c]
(145)[b]	007	Coal miners—underground	141	104	164	—	132[c]
—	011	Furnace-makers, coal gas, coke ovens	125	—	107	—	111

016	183	Nurses	112	115	114	80	138[c]
077	003	Agricultural workers	101	112	120	89	90
105.02	056	Cabinet-makers	99	85	106	—	93
019	206	Authors, journalists	94	87	90	62	116[c]
001	214	Judges, barristers, solicitors	93	74	98	33	120[c]
015.01	181	Medical practitioners	81	65	92	79	105
040	002	Farmers	81	72	96	65	100
003	178	Personnel managers	80	66	80	52	—
024.03/01	205	Physicists, biological scientists	76	38/80	99	33/112	101
014	213	Clergy	76	70	76	129	96
013	215	Social workers	69	74	84	57	85
011	193	Primary, secondary schoolteachers	66	61	80	57	82
—	173	Ministers of the Crown	61	—	72	—	—
009.01	210	Company secretaries, registrars	60	64	56	89	76
010.01	192	University academic staff	49	48	67	35	64

[a] Refers to 'general labourers'.

[b] Refers to 007 and 008 'Face trained'.

[c] Indicates statistically significant differences from expected SMR according to social class.

Notes: The classification of occupations 1970 and 1980 are not entirely compatible. '1971' and '1981' have been used as convenient central years for the periods 1970–2 and 1979–80 and 1982–3 covered by the two decennial supplements. Some occupations omitted in 1981 because classifications did not correspond with 1971.

Sources: OPCS (1978b) Series DS, No. 1, Appendix 2, table A, table 5M; (1986c) series DS, No. 6, Appendix IV.

by rock-falls and explosions; painters, steel erectors, builders, and steeplejacks fall off ladders (109 deaths in 1987) (table 8.1). The dangers of other occupations are more insidious, from infection, poisons, or carcinogens. Dairymaids used to contract cowpox, a zoonosis of cattle. Brucellosis and tetanus are still risks for agricultural workers. Farmers, veterinary workers, and sewermen risk catching Weil's disease (leptospirosis). Upholsterers used to risk contracting anthrax, the spores of which can live for years in horsehair (Hunter 1969). The most recently reported (non-fatal) case was in 1978. Publicans have high mortality from cirrhosis. So do doctors, who also have high death-rates from suicide—partly, it is believed, because they have easy access to the means. Lead, mercury, cadmium, uranium, and chromium, for example, used to cause chronic poisoning to painters and chemical workers, although there have been no deaths from lead poisoning since 1977. Hard insoluble dust causes chronic lung damage to miners and quarrymen (silicosis and pneumoconiosis; 234 deaths), ceramic workers, forge and foundrymen and—with cotton fibres—cotton workers (byssinosis). We are now in the middle of an epidemic of a particularly lethal form of lung cancer—mesothelioma–mostly found among asbestos workers and processors and its users (614 deaths in 1985). Most of these deaths today follow from exposure fifteen, twenty, or more years ago.

Most of the thousands of organic chemicals now widely used in industry were known fifty or even twenty-five years ago. Many are poisonous or carcinogenic or both, especially vinyl chloride, benzene, and benzidene, which are involved in the manufacture of dye, rubber, and the by-products of coal gas manufacture. Their effects may take years to become apparent. There are also chemical risks for workers in more traditional materials—asphalters and roofers, workers in hardwoods and leather, although in the latter cases the causal agents are still unknown (Doll and Peto 1981). Many of these specific occupational hazards are past history thanks to their identification by epidemiological detective work and appropriate legal responses and technical improvements. Some sedentary manual jobs (watchmaking, shoe repairing, table 8.1) have higher than expected mortality because people with handicaps can easily perform them and they can be done while smoking.

Statistics of occupational mortality

Identification of such hazards was one of the major arguments advanced by Farr and others in 1837 (OPCS 1985*b*) for a proper system of civil registration of deaths. The census first started asking detailed questions on occupation in 1831; since 1851 the Registrar General has produced a decennial report on occupational mortality (Registrar General 1885, OPCS 1978*b*, 1988*c*) which remains the most comprehensive in the world (See Fox 1989). For this purpose, William Farr developed the first classification of occupations and industries, and of causes of death, used in a much modified form to the present day (OPCS 1980*b*; McDowell 1983).

Indirectly standardized death-rates (Standardized Mortality Ratios, SMRs), calculated since the 1931 census, enable mortality trends and patterns to be compared unambiguously, showing the mortality of each group in relation to the national average set at 100 (see Alderson 1976) without the complication of age-structure effects. SMRs for any subpopulation or for any particular cause of death strictly only have meaning when compared with the standard population (see OPCS 1986c, Chapter 3). For example, SMRs are determined separately for each sex. A male SMR for a sub-group which is lower than a female SMR does not tell us that the male death-rate is absolutely lower than the female rate. It means that the male rate is lower, compared to the male average, than is the women's rate compared to the women's average in that class, region, or group.

A more general problem is that death-rates by occupation use census data on the population by occupation during life for their denominator and deaths by occupation from vital registration as the numerator (Chapter 7). They are not linked to individuals, except through the Longitudinal Study. And a person may be classified at death according to a final occupation only held for a short time. In fact only 53 per cent of a sample of deaths after the 1971 census, when linked with the same individuals recorded in the census, showed exactly the same occupation, although most were close (OPCS 1978*b*). The jobs recorded at death through the registration system are often much more vaguely worded than those recorded at the time of the census. This means that too many deaths are attributed to such residual categories as 'other labourer, not elsewhere classified' (see table 8.1) and 'other metal and electrical process workers' or 'machine tool operators' where otherwise unspecified engineers are recorded. Thus 'electrical engineers, so described' acquire an absurdly high SMR of 332. Machine tool operators have an SMR of 154 according to the census data, but only 112 according to the Longitudinal Study, which avoids this problem (OPCS 1986c). A similar problem has confounded intercensal comparisons of social class V mortality, of which the catch-all category of 'labourers, not elsewhere classified' now comprises a high proportion.

Longitudinal studies of individuals are needed because people change their job and there may be long latent periods between exposure and disease. Farr himself recognized this problem (Fox and Goldblatt 1982) but without modern data handling he was powerless to resolve it. The Longitudinal Study, based on a 1 per cent sample from the 1971 and 1981 censuses, is bridging these gaps by linking individuals recorded in the census, and all their associated data, with their subsequent registration of births, cancers, and deaths (OPCS 1988b). Other longitudinal surveys (see Blaxter 1986) have been useful in showing the long-term influence of the environment on disease patterns of national cohorts of children born in 1946 (The MRC National Survey of Health and Development, Wadsworth 1987) in 1958 (The National Child Development Study, Fogelman 1983) and 1970 (Child Health and Education Study, Butler et al. 1986), together with shorter-term longitudinal studies on more narrowly defined groups such as doctors (Doll and Peto 1976) and civil servants (Reid et al. 1976).

The demographic impact of occupational mortality

The demographic effects of some occupational risks are obvious. In 1985 there were 382 fatal injuries at work, a death-rate of 2 per 100,000 employees; including 102 in manufacturing, 95 in construction, 53 in mining and quarrying, and 20 in agriculture. The death-rate from fatal injuries in all industries declined from 4.5 per 100,000 employees in 1971 to 2.0 in 1985, but there was little improvement in the 1980s (449 deaths in 1981; 382 in 1985) despite the new regulations on building sites which are everywhere apparent (Health and Safety Executive 1987). Another measure is the number of deaths resulting in an award of an industrial death benefit—1,011 in 1985. But because of the subtle nature of other occupational hazards, it is not easy to make a total estimate of the overall demographic impact of occupational mortality in Britain. For example, stress in jobs (usually low-status routine jobs where the pace of work is not under the control of the worker) may be a contributor to heart disease (Marmot and Theorell 1989) and cancer (Karasek et al. 1982), and jobs with low levels of responsibility tend to shift the perceived locus of control of events away from the individual. Furthermore, mortality risks from the workplace can be brought home to the family. Fears that wives of asbestos workers might suffer raised cervical cancer risks now appear not to be well founded. The elevated risks of leukaemia in the children of radiation workers (Gardner et al. 1990) were discussed in Chapter 7.

In the USA (Doll and Peto 1981) it has been estimated that about

17,000 out of 400,000 cancer deaths (4 per cent) had occupational causes. These included 12,000 lung cancer deaths, 1,000 leukaemias, 1,000 bladder cancer deaths, and a small number of other types. 90 per cent of mesotheliomas are caused by asbestos (see Hodgson and Jones 1986), 1 per cent of cancers in all. The register maintained by the Health and Safety Executive (HSE) records 6,000 asbestos-related deaths in Britain since 1967. Preventive measures were instituted in the 1960s but because of the long (up to forty years) latent period new cases will continue to arise for some years to come. Mesothelioma deaths have risen in Britain from 269 in 1975 to 614 in 1985. Asbestos also causes a form of pneumoconiosis (asbestosis; 128 deaths in 1985) and 'conventional' lung cancer, at about four or five times the frequency of mesothelioma; so asbestos may have killed 25,000 people in all so far and the final toll may be double that (Doll 1987).

Estimates by the American Occupational Safety and Health Administration (OSHA), accepted by the US government and the International Labour Office (Peto 1980) claim that occupationally related cancers comprise at least 23 per cent of all cancers, asbestos alone causing between 13 per cent and 18 per cent and that about half of lung cancer deaths are due to asbestos (Epstein 1980, Epstein and Swartz 1981). Asbestos exposure is nothing like widespread enough to support such figures for lung cancer, for which cause we need look no further than smoking. Doll and Peto (1981) conclude: 'whoever wrote the OSHA paper did so for political rather than scientific purposes . . . and it will undoubtedly continue in the future as in the past to be used for political purposes by those who wish to emphasise the importance of occupational factors. Furthermore, any suggestions that 20–40 per cent of cancer deaths are or will be due to occupational factors should be dismissed.' These statistics quickly crossed the Atlantic. A publication from a major trade union (ASTMS 1980), using the OSHA data, claimed that 20–40 per cent of UK cancer deaths are from occupational carcinogens, by no means the highest claim (Doyal et al. 1983). Occupational mortality statistics, their importance heightened by the Health and Safety at Work Act 1974, have become weapons in industrial conflict.

8.2 Mortality according to Social Class and Geographical Area

Putting people into classes

Farr noted that specifically occupational causes cannot account for most mortality differences, especially in non-manual occupations (table

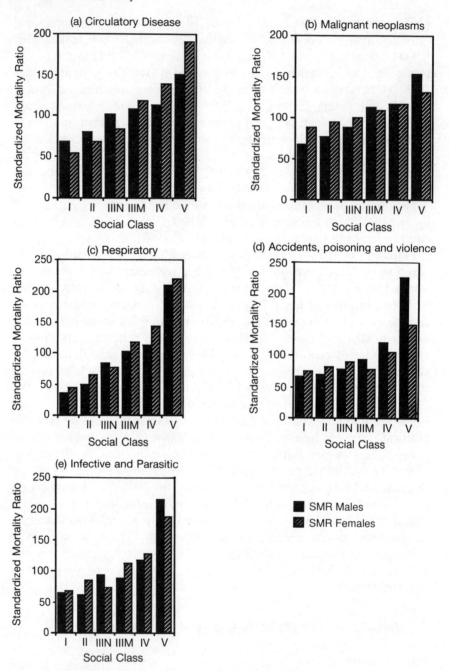

Note: SMRs can only be compared between classes within each sex.

Source: OPCS 1986*c*.

Fig. 8.1. SMR by social class, men and married women (by husband's occupation), selected causes, England and Wales, around 1981

8.1): wives of the workers in apparently high-risk jobs also suffer higher death-rates. Accordingly he grouped occupations into six classes in a way that reflected their general similarity, especially in social standing, according to economic and social criteria (Farr 1875; McDowall 1983). In this analysis, wives—whose occupation status as 'housewives' Farr recognized—often showed similar levels of mortality to their husbands (except in a few cases of obvious occupational risk), despite the fact that they either had no formal occupation at all or had quite different jobs from their spouse (figure 8.1). Some causes of death appeared to have no relation to the kind of employment. All this suggested the importance of general factors of shared household environment, life-style, and quality of health care as major determinants of survival. Big differences in mortality according to social status have been apparent since the first Registrar-General's Occupational Analysis of 1851, and have persisted into the late twentieth century (table 8.2).

For the 1911 Census, a classification of occupations was used which, belatedly following Farr's lead, was intended to reflect their prestige and general standing in the community. Stevenson (1923) developed this into the now familiar fivefold Registrar-General's Social Class scale, primarily for the analysis of mortality (Leete and Fox 1977, Szreter 1984). The modern scale (OPCS 1980b) lists more than 25,000 different jobs grouped into 404 different occupations, then condensed to 161. Social class is assigned by reference to this job ('unit group') and to occupational status; that is, whether employee, self-employed, or an employer of specified numbers of persons. A more detailed seventeen-fold classification by socio-economic group (SEG) is based more on the sector of economic activity. Mortality differentials are not too sensitive to the scale used (Fox, Goldblatt, and Jones 1986).

This social class scale usefully accounts for much of the variability of many social and demographic phenomena, and its widespread use more than compensates for its inevitable crudeness and its lack of empirical validation (Goldthorpe and Hope 1974; Szreter 1984, Mascie-Taylor 1990, Fox and Leon 1988, Goldblatt 1990). But because job and class movement is now considerable, similar occupations may no longer imply as similar a lifestyle as they used to (Ineichen 1972). For example, while many retired men in Bradford had remained in just one social class in their lives, the average lifetime movement was 2.3 'classes' (Cartwright 1980). Among parents of the 17,000 babies followed since 1957, 16 per cent of their parents had crossed social class lines in four years, 6 per cent of them from manual to non-manual classes (Fogelman 1983). Some detailed small-scale studies (e.g. in Aberdeen, see Illsley 1986) have shown that social mobility—movement between

Table 8.2. SMR by social class, England and Wales, around 1931 to around 1981

Social Class	(1) 1930–2 Males 15–64	(2) 1949–53 Males 15–64	(3) 1959–63 Males 15–64	(4) 1970–72 Males 15–64	(5) 1976–81 Males 15–64	(6) 1979–80, 1982–83 Males 20–64	(7) 1979–80, 1982–83 Females 20–59
I	90	86	76	77	66	66	69
II	94	92	81	81	77	76	78
IIIN	} 97	} 101	} 100	99	105	94	87
IIIM				106	96	116	110
IV	102	104	103	114	109	116	110
V	111	118	143	137	124	165	134
All	100	100	100	100	100	100	100

Sources: (1)–(3) Registrar-General (1971a) Decennial Supplement 1961; (4) OPCS (1978b) t. 4.1; (5) Longitudinal Study, in OPCS (1986c) t. 4.8; (6) and (7) OPCS (1986c) t. 3.3, Appendix IV.

social classes—is selective with respect to health and health-related behaviour. The much larger but less detailed Longitudinal Study, however, makes it clear that selection cannot be the main reason for social class differences. There is a general diminution of unskilled manual work and a growth of professional, managerial, and other white-collar occupations. Hence the need for the Longitudinal Study. The majority of married women—about 65 per cent—now work, so the analysis of women's mortality according to their 'own' social class, as opposed to the traditional use of their father's or husband's own, has become important. But there is less variation in mortality by women's social class in their own right (OPCS 1986c) than according to the husbands' (table 8.3). Partly because many married women do not work, and because of the concentration of much women's employment into few occupations, there are difficulties in the social analysis of women's mortality (see Chapter 4, Roberts and Barker 1987). Housing tenure differences (Chapter 4, 7) account for a high proportion of mortality variation and are to some extent displacing social class in the mortality analysis from the Longitudinal Study (Leon 1988).

8.3 Mortality Differentials by Social Class

Patterns and trends

A negative gradient in mortality according to social class has been evident ever since the system of classification has been used. Generally speaking the variation ranges from a mortality level (SMR) about 25 per cent less than average for social class I to 25 per cent or more above average for social class V (unskilled manual workers) (table 8.2). These are equivalent to a difference of expectation of life at age 20 of about five years betwen class I and II, and IV and V (figure 8.2). Mortality in all classes has fallen throughout the century, although life table indices suggest no improvement for social class IV and V from 1971 to 1981 (Haberman and Bloomfield 1987) while other analyses suggest only modest improvements of 7 per cent for class V and 14 per cent for class IV. Social differentials have been maintained or increased since SMRs were first introduced in the 1931 Report (Working Group on Inequalities in Health 1980, Marmot and McDowall 1986, Wilkinson 1986).

Particular interest has arisen about the apparent expansion of differentials from 1971 to 1981, and the marked relative deterioration of the SMR for social class V from 1971 to 1981 from 137 (compared to the 1971 average of 100) to 165 (compared to the 1981 average of 100).

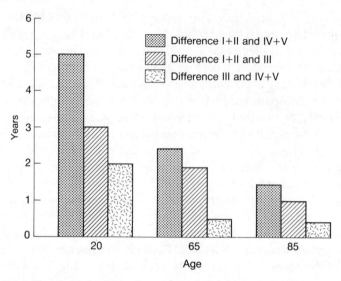

Source: Data from Haberman and Bloomfield 1987, t. 3, 4 (LS)
FIG. 8.2. Differences in expectation of life by social class at age 20, 65, and 85 around 1981

There are serious technical difficulties in evaluating how much of this expansion is real or artefactual. Analysis based on age of death variation over the whole population suggests there has been a continuous fall in inequality since 1921 and that changes of the size and composition of the classes and other statistical problems are responsible for the apparent expansion (Illsley and Le Grand 1987), although later analysis suggests that size changes are unlikely to have major effects (Goldblatt 1988, 1990). Different treatment of the occupations of the long-term sick and the substantial changes in the classification of occupations from 1970 to 1980 have caused serious problems of comparability. The latter appears to have artificially expanded the range of mortality, and the strong trend shown by the Decennial Supplements is not confirmed by the Longitudinal Study, which is not subject to the same statistical problems (Fox and Goldblatt 1986).

One reason for the poor relative performance of class V may be its progressive diminution over the last few decades, to become a numerically smaller and more negatively selected grouping as social mobility promotes more and more of its former members. The increasing domination of social class V by unskilled labourers 'not elsewhere classified' creates the numerator/denominator biases mentioned above (OPCS 1986c). Recent analysis suggests that most of the expansion in variability is real (Goldblatt 1989, 1990). Because of these problems social class analysis is little employed in the 1981-based occupational mortality supplement (but not its volume on child mortality: OPCS 1986c, 1988c), only being mentioned with nervous disclaimers. It is alleged that social class analysis is to be dropped entirely from the 1991-based Decennial Supplement (Delamothe 1989); a retrograde step if true. To other analysts social class seems no less relevant than in the past, and amalgamation of class IV and V appears to remove at least some of the technical objections (Marmot and McDowall 1986).

Mortality differentials according to social class are widely used partly because they are so readily available. In fact they comprise almost all the evidence for social distinctions in mortality risk. There are problems in this over-reliance. Overemphasis on differences between the averages of categories may obscure the real causes of inequality of risk between individuals. Emphasis on social class reifies a researcher's tool into a permanent entity. It has distracted attention from the substantial differences within social classes. Consequently insufficient research has been done to analyse behaviour and micro-environment to show how inequalities of risk are created and sustained in individual's lives (Illsley 1986). There is increasing interest in finding alternatives to social class, such as housing tenure, which identify high risk groups more efficiently.

Table 8.3. SMR of women aged 20–59 by social class, 1979–1983

Social class	All women own occupation[a] SMR	Single women own occupation[b] SMR	Married women husband's occupation[b] SMR
I	101	72	76
II	79	69	84
IIIN	77	80	93
IIIM	97	110	110
IV	98	105	125
V	87	121	157
Unoccupied	116	208	49
All	100	100	100

[a] Longitudinal Study.
[b] Registrar-General's Occupational Mortality Supplement, 1979–80, 1982–3
Source: OPCS (1986c) Series DS no. 6, t. 3.3.

Infant and perinatal mortality

Infant and child mortality in social class V is over twice that in class I (table 8.4). These social class differentials have survived the substantial improvement in infant mortality this century, despite the National Health Service (Pamuk 1988). In Scotland, though, differentials have shrunk as Scottish IMR has fallen below English levels since the 1970s. In 1946–50, for example, class V IMR (69) was three times that of class I. By 1981 (13) it was only 63 per cent higher. In England social differences in post-neonatal mortality, but not perinatal, have diminished substantially despite a lack of overall improvement (table 8.4, see Macfarlane and Chalmers 1982, Rodrigues and Botting 1989). Trends in perinatal mortality cannot be considered in isolation; lives saved in the perinatal period may be deaths deferred until later in infancy (Macfarlane 1982).

The infant's health risks are dominated by domestic environmental circumstances in post-neonatal mortality, by the mother's health and

Table 8.4. Mortality of children under age 15 by social class, England and Wales, around 1981 (per 100,000 population)

Sex and Social Class	Early neonatal	Post-neonatal	Infant	1–4	5–9	10–14
Males						
I	460	310	867	33	24	21
II	510	327	964	34	19	22
IIIN	573	323	1,008	41	23	20
IIIM	599	419	1,153	53	26	26
IV	759	575	1,510	64	32	30
V	870	759	1,815	112	50	36
Ratio V : I	1.89	2.45	2.09	3.38	2.07	1.77
Females						
I	350	254	684	33	17	15
II	393	272	762	31	15	15
IIIN	427	279	817	36	18	14
IIIM	460	331	902	42	18	19
IV	570	450	1,171	52	23	17
V	602	588	1,326	86	31	24
Ratio V : I	1.72	2.31	1.94	2.58	1.85	1.58

Note: legitimate births only.

Source: OPCS (1988c) Occupational Mortality Supplement (Childhood), Series DS no. 8, t. 2.6.

behaviour in perinatal mortality. Babies born to mothers in households headed by manual workers are more likely to be dangerously underweight. But even within each birthweight category, children born to such mothers (especially in class V) are more likely to die than the offspring of middle-class mothers (especially class I). Under 1,500 grams, births in social class 1 in 1985 suffered a perinatal mortality rate (PMR) of 283 compared to 389 for class V (37 per cent worse) but with no consistent gradient within the rest of the class scale. In the safest 3,500–3,999 gram group, class V mortality was 108 per cent worse. (OPCS 1987*e*). Post-neonatal mortality (respiratory disease, cot deaths, and accidents) was three times worse in class V than I, but the difference has narrowed substantially in the 1980s (Rodrigues and Botting 1989). These are associated with poor maternal care, large families, bad housing, and poor hygiene. Mortality from congenital malformation was more socially uniform from class I (93) to IV (102). But it rose strongly to 173 in class V (1974–9 data). The social class effect is independent of age of childbearing (OPCS 1982*a*).

Mortality differentials by social class are even higher among children aged 1–4 than among infants, and more so for boys than girls, partly because accidents become a more important cause of death (Chapter 7). Around 1981 in this age-group the death-rate in children in class V families was over three times that in class I, as against twice the class I rate in infancy. In older childhood social class differentials diminish, especially among girls, and are only substantial between social classes I and V. The absolute death-rates at these ages are very low, and cancer mortality, which has little class variation among children, is an important cause of death. But the accidental component of childhood deaths remains strongly class related.

8.4 Regional Differences in Mortality

Introduction

The effects of airs, waters, and places on health have fascinated medical science since the time of Aristotle and Galen and they are still important in modern Britain. For example, people in Wales, the North-West, and the North are 40 per cent more likely to die of stomach cancers than residents of the South-East (see Gardner *et al.* 1983). Bootle, Hartlepool, Stoke-on-Trent, and Salford seem to be cancer black-spots: all have 50 per cent worse rates for stomach cancer for men compared to the rest of the country (Chilvers and Adelstein 1978). Stroke, heart disease, bronchitis, and other major risks also

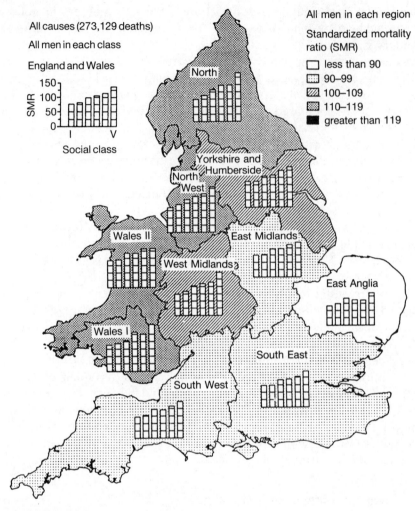

All causes (273,129 deaths)

All men in each class

England and Wales

All men in each region

Standardized mortality ratio (SMR)

☐ less than 90
▦ 90–99
▨ 100–109
▩ 110–119
■ greater than 119

Source: OPCS 1978*b*, fig. 8.7.

FIG. 8.3. Mortality by social class and region, males aged 15–64, England and Wales, 1970–1972

vary greatly by area. In general, regional differences in death-rates cannot be accounted for by social class differences between the regions (figure 8.3).

National and Regional variation within the UK

Many of these differences are of long standing; they excited the interest of William Farr (McDowell 1983) and have been analysed in the

Registrar-General's Decennial Supplement on Regional Mortality (OPCS 1979*a*, Britton 1990) since 1851 and in intercensal periods (see OPCS 1987*h*). Death registrations cumulated over a long period enable hazards in particular local areas to be pinpointed (Gardner, Winter, and Acheson 1982), although problems are difficult to establish with certainty in small areas (parishes or wards, or areas near nuclear plant) because of the fluctuation inevitable in small samples.

Death-rates in Northern Ireland (SMR from all causes 111 in 1987 for males and 110 for females), Scotland (SMRs 116 and 113), and Wales (SMRs 103 and 101) are generally worse than in England (SMR 98) (figure 8.4). Northern Ireland and Scotland are world leaders in mortality from heart attack and stroke. In 1987 SMRs for ischaemic heart disease for males were 118 in Northern Ireland, 121 in Scotland, 97 in England, and for stroke 110, 127, and 97 respectively. Scotland is worst for lung cancer (SMR 123). Northern Ireland suffers the highest mortality from respiratory diseases (159) especially pneumonia (277). This is suspiciously high when chronic obstructive pulmonary disease (bronchitis, SMR 78) is so surprisingly low. Northern Ireland enjoys an advantage over the rest of the UK in the death-rate for breast cancer (SMR 89), the most important cause of cancer in women, and cervix uteri (74). This may be a result of more child bearing but less fornication. Apart from that, its record is fairly dismal. But these national disparities were considerably greater around 1971 than a decade later (see OPCS 1989*g* and earlier issues).

Within England, the South and East enjoy the lowest mortality. Male mortality in the South-West, East Anglia, and the South-East outside London was only 90 per cent, 92 and 93 per cent respectively of the national average in 1987 (figure 8.4). By contrast, the North-West, North, and South Wales have death-rate risks which are up to 13 per cent worse than average. Around 1971 men living in East Anglia or Oxford Regional Health Authorities could expect to live for almost 3.5 years longer than residents of the North-West. Regional variation seems to affect the lives of women rather less. The maximum regional difference in expectation of life of women was only 2.6 years (Gardner and Donnan 1977; OPCS 1981*c*).

These regional differentials have proved durable over time, despite substantial improvements in mortality in all areas. The differences evident in 1951 and 1961 were about the same as those in 1971 (OPCS 1981*c*): Lancashire has the worst figures now and had the worst mortality in the first regional analysis undertaken by the Registrar-General for 1838–44 (Registrar-General 1849). But at least now—unlike in the past—towns are no longer startlingly less healthy than the

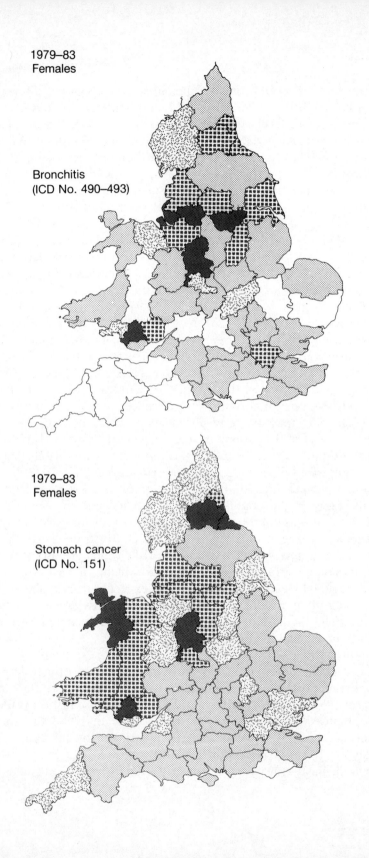

1979–83
Females

Bronchitis
(ICD No. 490–493)

1979–83
Females

Stomach cancer
(ICD No. 151)

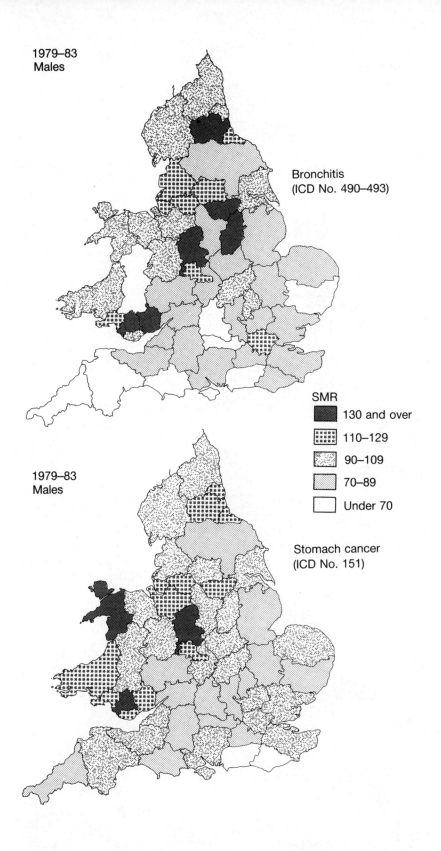

1979–83
Males

Bronchitis
(ICD No. 490–493)

SMR

■ 130 and over

▦ 110–129

▨ 90–109

▤ 70–89

□ Under 70

1979–83
Males

Stomach cancer
(ICD No. 151)

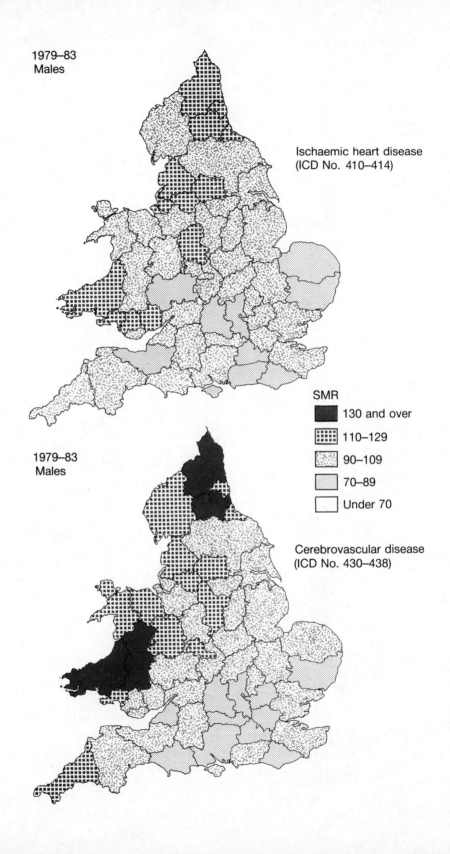

1979–83
Males

Ischaemic heart disease
(ICD No. 410–414)

SMR

■	130 and over
▦	110–129
▨	90–109
▦	70–89
□	Under 70

1979–83
Males

Cerebrovascular disease
(ICD No. 430–438)

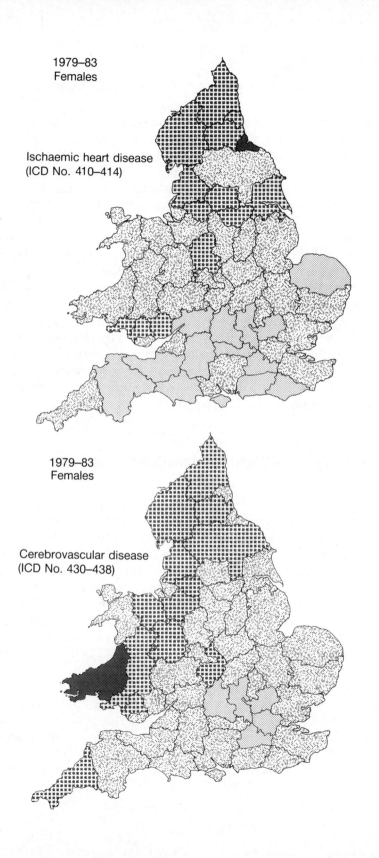

1979–83
Females

Ischaemic heart disease
(ICD No. 410–414)

1979–83
Females

Cerebrovascular disease
(ICD No. 430–438)

countryside (see Ferguson 1964): in 1971 urban male SMR was 110 to 86 in the country.

Infant mortality differences are relatively small. Around 1971, the North and North-West had the worst infant mortality; 16 per cent (males) and 13 per cent (females) more than the national average. The best area was East Anglia (89 and 84 per cent of the national average for boys and girls respectively). This neat picture has since disappeared. In 1988 the North-West, and the West Midlands RHAs had the worst rates (both 10.2). The lowest rates were in the North, Mersey, Wales, NE and NW Thames, while East Anglia had the lowest of all (6.9) (OPCS 1990*h*, Britton 1990). There have been considerable improvements in infant mortality over the period; the change in pattern may indicate the importance of intensive medical care in saving the lives of babies at risk, and the change in the geographical distribution of hospital resources. Respiratory diseases of infants—mostly post-neonatal—show the biggest differences. West Yorkshire was worst in 1985 (SMR 155, 148) together with other areas with bad mortality patterns for adults from the same causes. City-born babies are almost twice as likely as country babies to die of respiratory disease (SMRs 120 compared to 69 for males, 127 compared to 74 for females).

8.5 Specific Causes of Death: Social and Geographical Patterns

Social class patterns of circulatory disease

Early this century it seemed obvious that the affluent were much more prone to heart attacks and other circulatory diseases than manual workers, although the class gradient was exaggerated by differences in diagnostic practice between the kinds of doctors patronized by the rich and the poor. By 1931 there was little social class difference for all heart diseases: social class I SMR was 98, social class V 109. SMR for hypertensive disease was 123 for class I in 1949–53 against 83 for class IV and 101 for V. Now the peak of risk has clearly moved onto manual workers. (table 8.5). For circulatory disease around 1971, SMRs varied from 86 among the professionals in class I to 118 among the labourers and unskilled workers in class V. Around 1981 the SMRs for circulatory disease among social class I and V were 69 and 151 respectively.

Self-employed professionals (e.g. most barristers), have lower rates of IHD (SMR 82) than professional employees (most solicitors, scientists, doctors SMR 90). But in social class II, employers (i.e. mostly businessmen with their own companies, but including shopkeep-

Table 8.5. Social class patterns of circulatory disease, 1930–1983

Social class	Men aged 15–64						
	1930–2 All heart disease	1949–53 HT disease	1970–2				1979–80; 1982–3
			HT disease	IHD	CVD	All circulatory disease	IHD
I	98	123	71	88	80	86	70
II	101	106	85	91	86	89	82
IIIM	95	103	104	114	98	110	104
IIIM	102	103	104	107	106	106	109
IV	102	83	112	108	111	110	112
V	109	101	141	111	136	118	144
All classes	100	100	100	100	100	100	100

Notes: 'All Heart disease' causes of death amalgamated because of difficulties of certification in the 1930s. See OPCS 1978*b*, text. HT = hypertensive disease. IHD = Ischaemic Heart Disease. CVD = Cerebrovascular Disease (stroke).

Sources: OPCS 1978*b*, table 4B; OPCS (1986*c*), microfiche table GD 28.

ers) have higher mortality (SMR 108) than managers and executives (SMR 93). Among skilled manual workers, self-employed men have substantially lower mortality (SMR 80) than employees (SMR 112). Being in control of the pace and conditions of work may be important for health, and is an important component of that elusive problem of 'stress' (Cooper 1980, Karasek *et al.* 1982, Marmot and Theorell 1989). Women suffer a similar social gradient of risk in circulatory disease; worse if classed according to their husband's job. But the social class gradient is hardly apparent at all in older women aged 65–74. Even among men working in the same institution and the same place, all doing sedentary work, like the civil servants studied by Reid and his colleagues (1976), men in the lowest grade suffered almost four times the mortality from IHD as the administrators at the top. Social class accounted for more of the difference in mortality than did the conventional 'risk factors', which also varied considerably by employment grade. There is more to class differences in IHD mortality than risk factors alone (Marmot, Rose, Shipley, and Hamilton 1978). The class gradient from stroke (cerebrovascular disease) is steeper and more regular (from SMR 80 in class I to SMR 136 in class V), as is often the case in diseases which are clearly in decline. Employers again do worse than managers (118 against 78)—and foremen again do better than ordinary employees (74 against 113).

Regional patterns of circulatory disease

Recent regional differences in circulatory disease have diminished since 1971 and are now rather less than social class differences (unlike the position at the time of the 1971 census). Within England and Wales, circulatory disease follows the classic pattern of higher mortality north and west of the line from the Humber to the Severn (figure 8.4).

This excess is most marked for IHD and stroke. The North (1987 male SMR 116), North-West (116), Yorkshire and Humberside (112), and Wales (111) are worst for ischaemic heart disease. The South East had the lowest SMR in 1987: 88 for men, 87 for women (OPCS 1989*i*). Rural areas have lower SMRs than urban districts. Some Northern boroughs have spectacularly bad death-rates from this cause. Halifax was worst for both sexes in 1985 (SMRs 147,155), Dewsbury second. Aortic aneurysm (a ballooning out of the arterial wall) and venous thrombosis and embolism (blockage) are some of the few conditions which are worst in the South-East (119 for men, 117 for women). Regional differences in certification practice cannot (Diehl and Gau 1982) explain why towns like Bath, Hastings, and Oxford are at the top of the mortality league from these causes (SMR for males in 1971 172, 169, 155) rubbing shoulders with Hackney (155) and other poor areas. There is little obvious rural–urban gradient in deaths from hypertension; perhaps our rural areas are 'urbanized' already with respect to the causes of high blood pressure. Areas of high cardiovascular mortality are also areas of high maternal and infant mortality and low birthweight sixty or seventy years ago (Barker *et al.* 1989). The hypothesis that early physical stress disposes to much later cardiac disease is further supported by the fact that men who migrate from these mostly Northern areas take their risk with them (Britton 1990), although it does not easily fit the earlier social class gradient.

Social class patterns of cancer

Manual workers now suffer most from cancers. But this excess has only arisen since the 1930s (Logan 1982). Most of the overload comes from the two most common cancers of the lung and stomach (figure 8.5). In 1911 there were no class differences in lung cancer mortality. In 1931 medical practitioners had much higher than average death-rates from lung cancer (SMR 140). By 1951 a negative socio-economic gradient

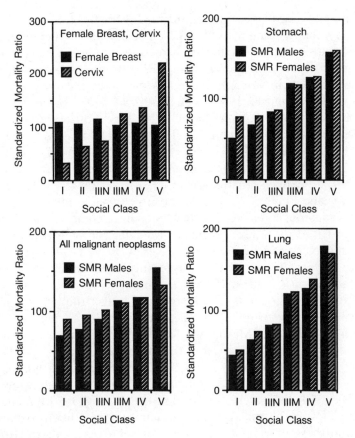

Source: OPCS 1986c.

FIG. 8.5. Mortality by social class and cancer site: men and women aged 15–64, around 1981

first became evident for lung cancer, a pattern which around that time became normal throughout the industrial world. By 1971 the lung cancer SMR of medical practitioners had fallen to 35. By 1981 lung cancer for males showed the largest differences of any major site: SMR 43 and 178 in social class I and IV respectively (Leon 1988). Other elevated middle-class risks in 1911—cancer of the large intestine and cancer of the brain—had disappeared by 1971 and the excess deaths from leukaemia and Hodgkin's disease are now slight. But there still remain positive gradients for cancer of the colon and testis and melanoma; for cancer of the breast and ovary among women. Before the war skin cancers were more frequent among outdoor manual workers. Now that suntans, foreign holidays, and artificial tanning and sunbeds are fashionable the gradients have been reversed.

In general, cancer risks among married women differ much less by social class than among men. The gradient is steeper when defined by the husband's occupation (showing a relative middle-class excess) than according to their own (see Logan 1982). Breast cancer is the most important cancer in women, and has been increasing since the 1960s after a decline from the 1930s. The death-rate is one of the few to be worse in high-status women. In 1931, the positive class gradient was quite severe—SMR 138 in class I, declining to 82 in class V. By 1971 this had evened out to 117 in class I, 92 in class V (married women) and by 1981 to 109 and 104 respectively. The gradient between owner-occupiers and council tenants was more severe: 106 to 78 (Kogevinas, Goldblatt, and Pugh 1989). Similar positive social gradients are found in other industrial countries. Single women have higher rates (SMR 116 in the Longitudinal Study). Women who delay (or avoid) childbearing have a higher risk of breast cancer (Kelsey 1979, Kvale *et al.* 1987). Fertility patterns by social class, especially later childbearing among higher social class women (Chapter 4) may account for the positive class and tenure gradient. Breast-feeding is also thought to protect against breast cancer but social class patterns of breast-feeding do not fit this hypothesis (see Martin and Monk 1982). There is an excess of middle-class deaths from cancer of the ovary (SMR 118 in class I, 93 in class V in 1971). Negative social class differentials for lung cancer became apparent for married women by 1961 and for single women by 1971. By 1981 they were almost as severe as those of men. The widening of women's social differentials in smoking is likely to maintain or expand these mortality differences for some years; these are even more striking by housing tenure than by social class (Pugh, Power, and Goldblatt 1989) (figure 8.6).

Cancer of the cervix has the strongest social class gradient of any cancer: among married women around 1981 SMR was 33 for social class I, 220 for V. The excess among women of manual origins has been evident ever since data have been available and is found in other industrial countries. Women who are council tenants have much higher rates than owner-occupiers. The supposed viral cause of cervical cancer fits the known social differences in sexual behaviour: manual workers begin sexual activity earlier than others. It particularly affects the wives of men in occupations which keep them away from home. SMRs vary from 12 for the wives of clergymen to 263 for the wives of seamen. Wives of aircraft pilots (class II) and policemen (class IIIM) also have high levels (150 and 138), while others in the same social classes have much lower risks (wives of teachers in class II SMR 5, printers in class IIIM SMR 21). Nuns have the lowest rate of all.

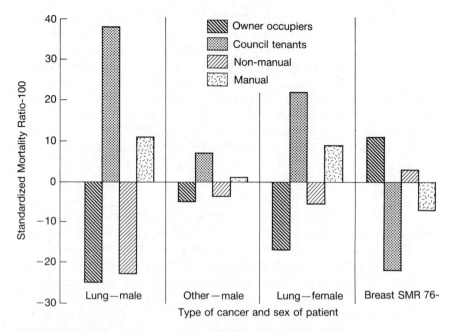

Sources: Data from Kogevinas *et al.* 1988, t. 1; Kogevinas *et al.* 1989, t. 1.

FIG. 8.6. Cancer rates by housing tenure and social class, 1971–1981

In the most important of these cancers; lung, stomach, and cervix, the biggest contrast of all is between owner-occupiers in the South and East (low) and council tenants in the North and West (Leon 1988). Most of the other cancers: e.g. rectum, pancreas, body of uterus, and prostate do not vary much by social class.

Regional patterns of cancer

In England, the risk of lung cancer is highest in the North-West (118 in 1987) and the North (123), and lowest in East Anglia (86) and the South-West (78) (figure 8.4). Rural areas have an SMR averaging 79 for men compared to 118 in conurbations: this obviously contributes to the regional differences. Some Northern industrial towns—Liverpool, Salford, Jarrow, Oldham, and Hartlepool—have cancer rates double the national average. This dismal list recurs for most causes of death. Some of the new towns outside London, especially Stevenage and Harlow, have much higher lung cancer rates for men than expected in the South-East, and worst rates for breast and prostate cancers (Gardner *et al.* 1983). Some boroughs have particularly high rates of cervical cancer, for example, South Shields (156), Dewsbury (213), Preston (202), Stoke (143), Islington (137), Brighton (142), and Swansea (151). Although some, but not all of the areas, include red-light areas like King's Cross, it is not easy to make sense of such figures in terms of sexual habits or the prevalence of prostitution, or availability of screening and treatment. In Wales, as in Durham, rural mortality is worse than urban (SMRs 121 and 115 respectively for men, 172 and 129 for women). Bracken may offer a solution to this puzzle. Toxins present in immature bracken fronds are thought to cause stomach cancer in Japan, where bracken is a culinary delicacy. Cows on wet Welsh hillsides may be eating a lot of bracken and transmitting the toxin through the milk, or water supplies may be contaminated (Galpin *et al.* 1990). People with blood group A, which is known to be regionally variable have a somewhat higher risk, but in fact the worst affected areas have lower 'A' than average, not higher.

The strong geographical concentration of some cancers in men has drawn attention to their industrial causes. High mortality from pleural mesothelioma is found only in towns where asbestos is or was recently made (e.g. Wigan, Rochdale, Leeds, Watford, and Barking) or used in dockyards for ships' boiler-room insulation (e.g. Barrow-in-Furness, Plymouth, Portsmouth, and Southampton). Bladder cancer is high in towns in the North of England and in London boroughs with rubber and dyeing industries and precision engineering (possibly because of the effects of cutting oils): Huddersfield (161), Barrow (160), Tower Hamlets (165), Islington (161). But there is no obvious explanation for the high incidence of cancers of the colon and ovary, and peritoneal mesothelioma, in towns such as Weymouth (Gardner *et al.* 1982, 1983).

Respiratory disease

Around 1981, unskilled manual workers were five times as likely (SMR 210) to die of respiratory disease than were professionals (SMR 36), although as usual there is a big step in risk between class IV (SMR 112), and unskilled men. Together with accidents, poisoning and violence, this is the highest relative social class V mortality risk. Wives of men in these different groups suffer almost the same as their husbands. But there is little class gradient in asthma deaths, which has an endogenous autoimmune cause. Some social class IIIM workers (miners, quarry-men, cotton spinners) have specialist occupational hazards (e.g. silicosis, anthracosis, byssinosis) but compared to the excess mortality from smoking, and to a lesser extent from air pollution, they are relatively minor. The extra risks in working-class households are already apparent in childhood, with a higher relative risk among girls (SMR 150) in class V households than boys (136)—although boys in class I have a worse death-rate than in class II (SMR 101 and 66 respectively) mostly due to asthma and acute bronchitis. Girls in working-class households lose their mortality advantage for some of these diseases, possibly because they stay close to mother in fumey kitchens with high NO_2 concentrations from gas cookers (Melia *et al.* 1977).

Respiratory disease flourishes in cold, damp areas, encouraged by smoking, air pollution, industrial dust, and infections by viruses, as well as genetical factors; but none the less the regional variation is small compared to the different social class risks. Northern Ireland has the worst mortality for all forms of respiratory disease (153, 177 in 1987). Within England, chronic bronchitis is much worse in the North, North-West, and South Wales. These diseases are particularly common in areas where most households burn coal, or did so until recently. Children born in such areas are at risk from birth, especially in social classes IV and V. They carry the disability through life with them, irrespective of later smoking habits (Stuart-Harris 1980, Colley and Reid 1970). But this does not explain Scottish SMRs. Bronchitis in Glasgow (116) is worse than in the Highlands (81), but no worse than rural Ayrshire and Arran (116) and better than Fife (133). There is a strong rural–urban difference (76–117 for men, 77–122 for women). Greater London rates (114, 117) are higher than those of the South-East in general, which may explain why mortality in the South-East—demographically dominated by Greater London—is relatively high. Some of the London boroughs (Tower Hamlets and Southwark) are well up with the North-Western blackspots—Salford (294), Oldham (203), and Barnsley (192). Oldham has the highest female SMR (311), with Salford, Burnley, and Dewsbury close behind. A few rural areas have high SMRs, particularly Durham and Glamorgan where coal is, or was, an almost universal fuel.

Accidents, poisoning, and violence

Working-class men suffer three times the risk of middle-class people of death from accidents and violence. The SMR around 1981 for men in social class I was 67, compared with 226 for class V. Their wives suffer a less severe gradient; from 75 to 150. Deaths rise steeply even from class IV to V. Some of these differentials are occupational. Hardly any non-manual workers die in accidents at work. But the same gradient also applies at home, from falls and other causes, and for transport accidents (SMR 67–177 in social classes I and V respectively around 1981). Motor cycle ownership, risks as pedestrians, and possibly driving habits more than compensate for lower car ownership in working-class households. Children suffer particularly: unskilled manual workers' families suffer about four times the mortality of children of class I and have almost double the risk for class IV. This applies especially to accidental falls (eight times) and accidental fires (almost ten times). Murder is definitely a working-class risk (SMR 34 in class I, 339 in class V around 1971)—and so is suicide (SMR 89 in class I, 198 in class V around 1981).

SMRs suggest that town roads are safer than country roads (SMR 87 in conurbations, 124 in rural areas) although this may just reflect the greater mobility necessary in the countryside. The worst areas are the most rural: North Wales (129) and East Anglia (119); Highland SMRs are 233 compared to 95 in Glasgow. Northern Ireland is worst of all. North of the Trent deaths from accidental falls seem particularly common (the North 139 for men, 145 for women; the South-East, 76 and 68). The usual blackspots seem to be exceptionally risky places for dying after falling as well; for example, female SMRs in Bootle are 305, in Liverpool 232, in Sunderland 231: fifteen times the risk for women in Wandsworth (SMR 19) or Harrow (SMR 23). The reason is not obvious. Town dwellers are three times as likely to be murdered as countrymen. The bigger the city, the worse it is. Westminster, Hammersmith, Lambeth, Manchester, and Bradford are places especially to avoid.

Infectious and parasitic disease

Infectious disease has the steepest class differentials of any major causes of death—from SMR 65 in class I to 215 in class V, tenfold for respiratory TB (SMR 32 in class I to 279 in class V around 1981). Most of the remaining deaths from infectious disease are deaths of children, especially babies in the post-neonatal period, which are considered separately below. Death-rates from infectious and parasitic disease are also the most variable of all causes between regions. Scotland is worst (SMR 122 for men, 118 for women in 1985) with Northern Ireland apparently much better off (74, 62). The Scottish excess is mostly due to TB (138, 130). Northern Ireland also has a high TB death-rate for men (123) and women (160), and even worse for its late effects, which throws some doubt on the overall figure. Some boroughs have twice the national mortality from infectious and parasitic causes: Tower Hamlets (220 for males), Manchester (205), Westminster (193), Lambeth (184),

Camden (183), Nottingham (177). Not surprisingly mortality seems particularly high in areas of high overcrowding.

8.6 Infant Mortality

Demographically defined risks

Differentials in infant mortality rates illustrate the complexity of analysing causes and suggesting remedies. Some of the extra risks to manual workers' babies can be inferred from the demography of childbearing. Women whose fathers or husbands are manual workers, especially in social class V, are more likely to have illegitimate babies, to be pregnant at marriage, to bear children before age 20, to have large families. All these characteristics are associated with additional risk to the infant (Adelstein, Davies, *et al.* 1980, OPCS 1988*d*); although the problem of these late births may have been exaggerated by late and risky births to the infecund or those prone to miscarriage (Chalmers 1981). Average family size, mean age at childbearing, and the social class distribution of births have all been changing in ways favourable to infant survival (Chapter 4) and have accounted for a quarter of the improvement in perinatal mortality from 1950 to 1973 (Hellier 1977), although for only 6 per cent of the improvement in Scottish perinatal mortality from 1970 to 1979 (Forbes *et al.* 1982). Most of that improvement seems due to new obstetric practice and clinical management and has been achieved despite the low Scottish level of breast-feeding.

Low birthweight

Babies born to wives of manual workers are more likely than average to be light for date. Intra-uterine growth retardation (Roberts and Thomson 1976) may be brought on by heavy smoking (babies of smokers are 100–200 grams lighter than average—Spastics Society (1982)), heavy drinking (Pratt 1981), unsuitable nutrition, or staying longer at work when pregnant. These attributes are more frequently found among women with manual worker husbands (GHS 1982; Fox and Goldblatt 1982). On top of that, infant mortality, especially within social class V is higher than others even for babies of the same weight. Wives of manual workers are more likely to suffer subclinical or worse vitamin and mineral deficiencies as a result of a defective diet too low in fresh vegetables and fruit. Subclinical multivitamin deficiencies, especially of folic acid, are suspected of being responsible for the high incidence of neural tube defects in children of social class V mothers and also in the North-West of England and Northern Ireland (Wald 1984). Inadequate maternal nutrition has been blamed not only for higher infant mortality but also for the later vulnerability to chronic disease of the children when adults (Barker 1989). Social class differences in adult height are also adduced as evidence of inadequate interuterine growth or nutrition in early life.

Women at work

Wives of manual workers are prone to stay at work until shortly before delivery, no doubt because they need to maximize income. The longer women stay at work, the worse the risk to their unborn children, although the picture is confused by the high mortality of pre-term babies, whose premature arrival naturally shortens the time between quitting work and delivery (Chamberlain and Garcia 1983). These babies are at risk from perinatal causes to do with birth injury, immaturity and anoxia, possibly due to the lower gestational age of the babies. Council tenure compounds the risk. Middle-class mothers who work when pregnant may nullify the advantages of their class. Infant mortality to 'non-manual' mothers who work is higher than that of non-working mothers with husbands in manual occupations.

Breast-feeding

Babies who are breast-fed survive better than those who are not. The worse the economic or environmental conditions, the bigger the difference (Cunningham 1980, Winikoff 1983; see Chapter 2). Even in the favourable conditions of modern Britain, babies who are breast-fed for 13 weeks or more suffer only a quarter of the gastro-intestinal infections of bottle-fed or early weaned infants (Howie *et al.* 1990). In 1980 just over half of least-educated women breast-fed their babies compared with 90 per cent of the most educated; there was a similar gradient between classes V and IV. Women in manual households who breast-feed do so for a shorter time. Only half of Scottish mothers, and even fewer in the North of England, breast-fed their babies compared with about three-quarters in the South-East. Until recently there was a trend away from breast-feeding in developed societies such as Britain (Langford 1978). In 1975, only half the mothers had attempted to breast-feed their babies; by 1980, two-thirds had done so, and the educational, class and regional contrasts have diminished (Martin 1978,

Martin and Monk 1982). The encouragement of breast-feeding by maternity hospitals, the medical profession, the Health Education Council, and perhaps fashion in women's magazines, seems to have paid off.

Regional variation

In the 1970s perinatal mortality in the worst Area Health Authorities was twice as bad as the best (Mallet and Knox 1979) even after standardization for birthweight and for social factors such as tenure, proportion of unskilled workers, and home ownership (Charlton *et al.* 1983). In the 1980s regional variation has become less pronounced. Infant mortality tends to be higher among immigrant mothers: 14.8 per 1,000 babies born to mothers from Pakistan compared with the national average of 9.4 in 1986 (OPCS 1988*d*, Chapter 12). The worst infant mortality at District Health Authority level in 1986 was in Bradford (18.1/1,000, 90 per cent higher than average), followed by Central Manchester and West Lambeth (50 per cent higher)—all areas of high proportions of births to immigrant mothers (27 per cent in Bradford). But infant mortality is also high in the North-Western towns without many immigrant births: Burnley (13.6), Preston (13.3), Rochdale (12.7) (OPCS 1987*h*).

8.7 Underlying Causes of Social and Regional Mortality Differences

Competing hypotheses

There is still no consensus about the ultimate causes of these social and regional differences in mortality. They are blamed on many different factors: on low income and poor housing, on unequal NHS provision and efficiency, on differences in smoking, drinking, and eating, and additionally on environmental effects: atmospheric pollution, temperature and humidity, hardness of water. All can be shown to play a role. The problem is to decide which matters most and which can be changed most readily. The majority view (Working Group on Inequalities in Health 1982, Whitehead 1987, Wilkinson 1987, Townsend *et al.* 1988) is that relative material deprivation, particularly income, is more important than 'lifestyle' differences in the maintainance of social class and regional differentials.

No statistical analysis has yet apportioned the responsibility between the different possible factors. Neither the Black Report nor its successors have done so, and this book does not pretend to. But substantial progress has been made, for example, on the geographical and social distribution of risk factors in heart disease (Cummins, Shaper *et al.* 1981); and there has been an attempt to unscramble the effects of various socio-economic factors on cancer (Leon 1988), which showed a mutually reinforcing effect of class, tenure, education, marital status, but with a different balance in different types of cancer. A limitation of analysis in Britain is the general lack of income data from the census and most official surveys linked to health. Social class affiliation appears to have an important independent effect even when relevant variables such as income and housing tenure can be taken into account (Cox *et al.* 1987).

Risk factors for survival from cancers and heart disease may be different from those affecting initial incidence. Access to medical care may be more important in the latter, although little evidence has been collected. Routine voluntary registration of cancer diagnosis permits incidence and survival rates to be known through the Longitudinal Study. In the more serious ones such as lung cancer and breast cancer, there is little or no socio-economic difference in case fatality rates, while for rectal cancer survival of council tenants was about 10 per cent worse. The reasons are unknown (Kogevinas, Marmot, and Fox 1988) but overall it is incidence rather than case fatality which creates the social differences. No such linkage is possible for heart disease, but some overseas studies suggest that differences in case fatality rates may be more important (Leon and Wilkinson 1985).

Other analyses have started from considerations of what people do rather than what class they belong to, for example the longitudinal study of health and lifestyle in Alameda County, California in 1965–74 (Berkman and Breslow 1983). The county is a fairly typical urban and suburban area including the cities of Oakland and Berkeley. The study focused on physical, mental, and social dimensions of well-being. It concluded that the most important 'high-risk health practices' independently associated with mortality were: cigarette smoking; excessive alcohol consumption; physical inactivity; being obese or underweight; and sleeping fewer than seven or more than eight hours a night. The findings were not disturbed by people who began the study with health problems and were independent of socio-economic status or race.

Avoiding each of the five high-risk factors was scored as 1. High-risk men (score 0–2) aged 30–49 had 8.4 times the mortality of the low scorers (score 4–5); and men aged 50–9 and 60–9 2.4 and 1.7 times respectively. Marriage and the support of friends and relatives helped substantially to reduce mortality risk: unmarried or socially isolated men and women had about 75 per cent and 30 per cent higher mortality than those who were married or lived in a strong social network. Those who scored highly on indicators of psychological well-being also had a substantial mortality advantage. In an earlier study, Belloc and Breslow (1972) established seven 'rules of behaviour', including eating breakfast and avoiding eating between meals, and claimed (Belloc 1973) an eleven-year advantage in expectation of life at age 45 for people who followed six or seven of their rules compared with those who followed less than three.

International comparisons

International comparisons let us see how wider ranges of incomes and wealth relate to each other, while taking care to avoid the 'ecological fallacy' into which one may easily fall when correlating aggregated data relating to different regions or groups without reference to individuals (see Bulmer 1986).

At any time richer countries tend to have better mortality levels than poorer ones. But some poorer countries with more egalitarian income distribution, educated populations, and broad if simple medical coverage tend to have better mortality figures than expected from their low average income (for example, China, Ceylon, some of the Southern states of India, Cuba). Egalitarian income distributions, socialized medicine, and universal welfare did not give favourable mortality to the industrial economies of communist Eastern Europe or the Soviet Union—quite the reverse (Chapter 7); and there are still substantial socio-economic mortality differences (e.g. for Hungary, Jozan 1986). Systems needed to deliver income control and a total welfare system may prevent economic growth and preclude individual choice in consumption and popular democratic feedback concerning expenditure priorities.

Substantial social and geographical mortality differentials persist in Western countries with unusually flat income distributions and generous welfare cover, including Sweden (National Board for Health and Welfare 1980) as well as countries with marked income inequalities (e.g. France: Desplanques 1976, USA: Milham 1983, see CICRED 1984, Fox 1989) and in Japan, which has modest income inequalities but meagre public welfare cover (Marmot *et al.* 1989). As they are all based on a different system of class or occupational or income classification it is difficult to say which are the most variable. A preliminary comparison has placed the UK in the lowest third of countries with respect to mortality inequality, superior to Japan, Norway, France, Germany, the US, and most of the Eastern Bloc (Le

Grand 1987). Within these countries equality of income is correlated with equality of survival, but so is decreasing per caput spending on medical care. Japan, with the world's lowest mortality, may point to a particularly favourable combination of a basically egalitarian meritocratic culture where group support is important, where personal discipline is strong, where almost everyone describes themselves as middle class, with an obsessive interest in education operating within a free market economy (Reischauer 1981).

Income differences

Income differences have been suggested as the key to mortality differences. Mortality variation among pensioners has been related to variation in state pension level, the convergence of post-neonatal mortality in the 1970s to the relative increase in manual workers' incomes (Wilkinson 1986), although the convergence continued in the 1980s (Rodrigues and Botting 1989) after wage inflation had been stopped. A comparison of eighty occupations gives a correlation of about 0.5 between their income and mortality around 1970, from which beneficial mortality consequences of income redistribution are inferred. Looked at in other ways, average income differences between classes may seem to count for little by themselves (table 8.6, OPCS 1978). There are major overlaps and inconsistencies between and within classes. Doctors in social class I whose incomes on average are about twice those of university lecturers (also I) and schoolteachers (II), and perhaps three times those of clergymen (I), none the less have substantially higher mortality. The last might benefit from the efficacy of prayer although only Galton (1885) seems to have looked at that statistically. Similar inconsistencies can be identified throughout most of the social scale; there is considerable overlap in the social class distribution of incomes. Attention therefore inevitably focuses on people at the bottom of the social and income scale, among whom the mortality disadvantage is marked and where purchasing power might make the most crucial difference.

Housing costs and income

What is it that poor individuals or families could buy to improve their mortality risks if their income were higher? In the nineteenth century the answer was obvious (Chapter 2)—more food, drier, warmer, accommodation for their exclusive use, more medical care. But in a

Table 8.6. Relation of income to mortality, England and Wales, 1970–1973 (males aged 15–64)

(*a*)

Social class	SMR	Mean income of median unit (£)
I	77	44.14
II	81	34.02
IIIN	99	24.12
IIIM	106	27.05
IV	114	22.46
V	137	22.09

(*b*)

Mean weekly income (£)	SMR	SMR standardized for social class
40 or more	77	97
30–39	88	95
20–29	122	102
10–19	105	96
less than 10	98	77

Note: Median unit = median occupational unit in each social class. Low wages groups in t. 8.6*b* do not take into account tips, accommodation, income in kind, which can be important in these groups (waiters, barmen, housekeepers etc.)

Source: OPCS 1978*b* Series DS no. 1 p. 151.

welfare state where basic material needs are satisfied, if necessary free of charge, the answer may be more difficult. Only a small minority of the British population pays anything for medical care through private insurance, and for the most part the treatments paid for are for convenience, not life-saving or preventive. Many poor households pay nothing for their housing. Sixty-five per cent of council tenants receive Housing Benefit to pay part or all their (already subsidized) rent (average before rebates £20 per week in 1988), as do 70 per cent of housing association tenants (3 per cent of households, average rent before rebates £20 per week) and 45 per cent of private tenants (6 per cent of households). As a consequence the proportion of income as well as the absolute amount spent on housing diminishes at the bottom of the income scale, so that, for example, families on the bottom third of the

Table 8.7. Pattern of household expenditure: by household type and income level, 1985[a]

	Percentage of all households	Percentage of reported expenditure									Average total expenditure (£s per week) (= 100 %)
		Food	Housing	Fuel and light	Alcohol	Tobacco	Clothing and footwear	Durable household goods	Transport and vehicles	Other goods, services, miscellaneous	
Pensioner households[b]											
Low income	7	32.7	11.0	16.1	2.4	3.2	6.1	3.9	4.2	20.4	46.51
Other	4	27.3	16.4	11.9	3.6	3.9	6.5	3.3	5.5	21.7	65.01
One-parent households											
Low income	2	32.1	5.9	13.8	2.3	6.6	9.7	5.1	5.9	18.6	66.84
Other	1	21.0	17.4	6.8	2.1	2.3	11.7	5.3	11.9	21.5	125.61
Other households with children											
Low income	5	30.0	9.7	9.7	4.1	6.0	9.1	5.4	9.8	16.1	119.73
Middle income	22	22.0	15.4	5.6	4.6	2.8	8.2	7.7	14.5	19.1	199.08
High income	4	15.6	15.5	4.4	4.1	1.0	8.6	9.1	15.6	26.2	341.24
Other households without children											
Low income	6	25.7	15.7	10.0	5.3	5.2	5.9	4.6	10.8	16.7	80.03
Middle income	33	20.0	17.2	6.3	5.4	3.0	7.0	6.5	15.5	19.1	150.18
High income	16	15.5	17.4	4.5	5.4	1.8	6.4	8.1	18.8	22.0	226.15
All households	100	20.2	16.1	6.1	4.9	2.7	7.4	7.2	15.2	20.2	161.87
Low income	20	29.4	11.6	11.5	4.0	5.2	7.5	4.8	8.6	17.4	76.58
Middle income	60	21.1	16.3	6.2	5.0	2.9	7.5	6.9	14.8	19.2	161.88
High income	20	15.5	16.9	4.5	5.1	1.6	7.0	8.4	18.0	23.1	246.74

[a] The income distribution used is that of equivalent normal net household income, low income is defined here as the lowest 20 per cent of this income distribution, middle income as the next 60 per cent, and high income the highest 20 per cent. See source Appendix, Part 6: Equivalent income.
[b] Pensioner households are defined as those households solely containing one or two persons of pensionable age.

Source: Social Trends 1985, no 17, t. 6.11 London, HMSO.

income distribution spend more on cigarettes and alcohol than on housing (table 8.7).

Overcrowding and shared amenities in housing are strongly associated with higher mortality (Fox and Goldblatt 1982) but now only affect a small and diminishing proportion of the population. Almost all houses have the standard amenities (Dept. of the Environment 1988) and very few households now have to share. In fact in council tenure, the most important social factor among those studied by Leon (1988) in the incidence of lung cancer and cervical cancer, the provision of amenities and space is the most complete of any tenure; better than that of owner-occupied housing. The problems of council estates have little to do with the provision of hot water, adequate space, or exclusive use of bathrooms. Material inadequacy and disrepair is most apparent in the private rented sector, where chronic under-investment has followed forty years of rent control. Despite this, private tenants have lower mortality than council tenants (Fox and Goldblatt 1982, Leon 1988).

8.8 Behavioural Factors in Mortality Differentials

The medical causes of excess mortality can be estimated by subtracting from the observed deaths the number expected on the basis of national average mortality (see OPCS 1986c). For social class V around 1981, 25 per cent of this excess of 14,444 deaths were due to IHD, 7 per cent to stroke, 14 per cent to lung cancer, and 5 per cent to chronic bronchitis. The prominence of these causes, which are related to cigarette smoking and unsuitable diet, suggest that behavioural differences are important here. Accidents, poisoning, and violence accounted for 16 per cent. Some of this must be occupational, but 3 per cent were road deaths (professional drivers are not classed in social class V) and 4 per cent suicide.

Smoking and drinking

Smoking is the biggest single cause of premature death (Chapter 7). It has a substantial negative association with social class. It is now generally declining; since the early 1980s only a minority in each socio-economic group have been smokers (OPCS 1990). It is becoming more and more a manual workers' habit: almost three times as common in class V as in Class I (table 8.8). In the British Regional Heart study, 43 per cent of the middle-aged urban men in social class I had never smoked as against only 17 per cent of the men in social class V

Table 8.8. Cigarette smoking by social class, Great Britain, 1972, 1988

Socio-Economic Group / Occupations	Code no.	% smoking cigarettes				Ex-regular smokers (%)		Cigarettes/week/smoker			
		1972		1988		1988		1972		1988	
		M	F	M	F	M	F	M	F	M	F
Professional	3,4	33	33	16	17	35	23	102	75	109	90
Employers, Managers	1,2,13	44	38	26	26	39	23	126	86	132	101
Intermediate & junior non-manual	5,6	45	38	25	27	30	16	114	81	113	88
Skilled manual, own account	8,9,12,14	57	47	39	35	31	20	124	93	122	104
Semi-skilled manual, personal service	7,10,15	57	42	40	37	30	17	119	85	117	102
Unskilled manual	11	64	42	43	39	24	18	111	87	111	104
All	—	52	42	33	31	32	19	120	87	120	99

Sources: General Household Survey 1972, t. 11.2, t. 11.3; OPCS Monitor SS 90/2 Cigarette smoking 1972 to 1988, t.3, 4, 6.

(Cummins, Shaper *et al.* 1981). Smokers in all social classes smoke close to the average of 120 cigarettes per week (men) and 99 (women) (GHS 1988). This represents an average expenditure for men of over £8 per week or £420 per year.

Men have been giving up smoking faster than women, among whom the habit started later. In social class I and II, almost as many women as men now smoke, although the trend in both is downwards. The decline in class V men has been sharp since 1972 but it has only been matched by a corresponding downward trend in class V women since 1982. Accordingly the gap between the smoking habits of men and women is narrowing (OPCS 1990). Recent evidence suggests that while adults may be giving up smoking, schoolchildren and young people are still taking up smoking, and that young women are responding to advertising campaigns directed specifically at them (Dobbs and Marsh 1985).

Regional differences in smoking are less sharp. Scots smoke the most: in 1982, 45 per cent were 'heavy smokers' (figure 8.7) and 39 per cent of women smoked, with the North next highest (43 per cent men, 38 per cent women). The area around Glasgow has the highest lung cancer death rate in the world (World Health Organisation 1986) and in 1984 smoking-related cancers accounted for 54 per cent of all male cancer deaths there. However the relationship of lung cancer with number of cigarettes smoked is weaker than in other studies and some other regional factor may also contribute to the high mortality (Gills *et al.* 1988). The very low local consumption of fresh fruit and vegetables, which appear to have a general protective effect against cancers, may be responsible. In all other regions less than 40 per cent smoke. The residents of the East Midlands, the South-West, East Anglia, and the Outer Metropolitan area smoke least of all (35 per cent of men; the last two have the lowest score for women too—25 per cent and 29 per cent respectively) (GHS and unpublished OPCS) (figure 8.7). The 14 per cent reduction in smoking from 1972 to 1982 was very uneven regionally. The decline was least in three of the heaviest smoking areas: North 9 points, Scotland 8 points, the North-West 7 points (OPCS unpublished data).

Alcohol consumption has a complex relation with social class. Most people drink at least some alcohol. But the proportion of 'moderate' and 'heavy' drinkers rises substantially with lower social class. In 1978 9 per cent of professionals admitted to being 'heavy' drinkers, compared with 34 per cent of unskilled manual workers (table 8.9). Hardly any women admit to being 'heavy' drinkers. The proportion of abstainers doubles from the top to the bottom of the social scale. 9 per cent of unskilled male workers, and 18 per cent of female, are non-drinkers. However a high proportion of such non-drinkers have

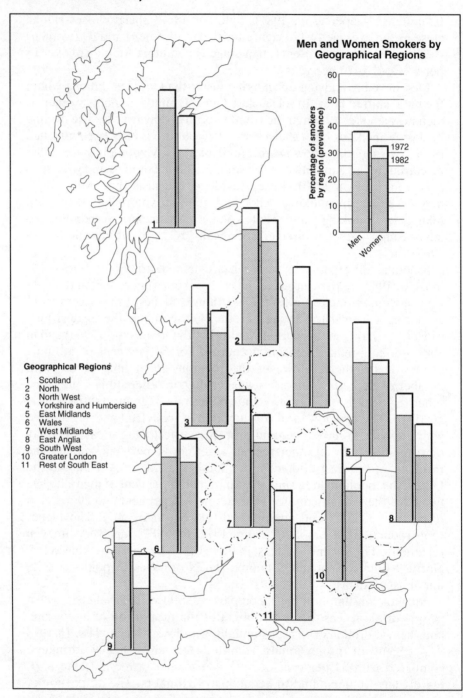

Source: GHS unpublished

FIG. 8.7. Regional differences in cigarette smoking, Great Britain, 1972 and 1982

Table 8.9. Type of drinker by sex and socio-economic group, standardized for age, Great Britain, persons aged 18 or over (%)

Socio-economic group	Male				Female			
	Abstainer		Heavy		Abstainer		Heavy	
	1978	1984	1978	1984	1978	1984	1978	1984
Professional	5	5	9	8	9	9	0	1
Employers and managers	4	4	15	12	9	7	1	1
Intermediate/ junior non-manual	4	5	15	15	9	9	1	2
Skilled manual/ own account non-professional	5	7	33	25	11	12	2	2
Semi-skilled/ manual/service	6	9	32	24	14	18	3	2
Unskilled manual	9	14	34	26	18	21	2	1
All	5	7	25	20	11	13	2	2

Sources: General Household Survey 1978, t. 8.18*b*; General Household Survey 1984, t. 11.4.

given up because previous heavy drinking has already made adverse effects upon their health (Shaper *et al.* 1988). In the mid-1980s fewer men claimed to be heavy drinkers, and social class differences diminished compared with the 1970s.

In England Northerners drink more than Southerners (GHS 1978, 1984) and even more than the Scots. South-east of a line from the Wash to the Bristol Channel, less than one in five are 'heavy drinkers', north of a line from Scunthorpe to the Bristol Channel about a third or more are; the North scoring highest (42 per cent) with Wales and the North-West next, and Scotland trailing after (29 per cent) (figure 8.8). In Scotland a disproportionate amount of alcohol is consumed by a small minority many of whom live in boarding houses, or are homeless, or in institutions (in a Scottish survey, 3 per cent of respondents accounted for 30 per cent of the drink—Dight 1976. Only about half the alcohol known from excise data to be consumed is accounted for in such surveys.) Scottish moderation may in part arise from the great difficulty of interviewing such heavy drinkers because of their patterns of residence.

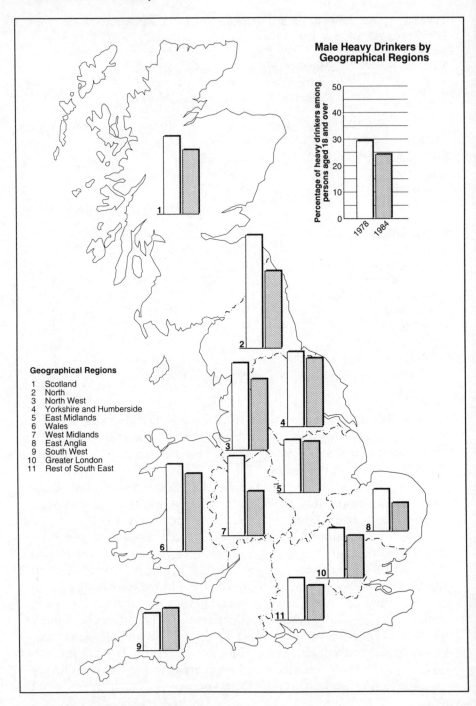

Male Heavy Drinkers by Geographical Regions

Percentage of heavy drinkers among persons aged 18 and over

Geographical Regions

1 Scotland
2 North
3 North West
4 Yorkshire and Humberside
5 East Midlands
6 Wales
7 West Midlands
8 East Anglia
9 South West
10 Greater London
11 Rest of South East

Sources: GHS 1978, t. 8.19*a*, *b*; GHS 1984, t. 11.13.

FIG. 8.8. Alcohol consumption by geographical region, Great Britain, 1978, 1984

Admissions to psychiatric hospitals for alcoholism and related disorders are highest in Northern Ireland (about 290 per 100,000 per year) and Scotland (160) is well ahead of England (50) (*Social Trends* 17, 1987). Cirrhosis mortality is also highest in Scotland. The very high figure for Greater London (156) may be accounted for by heavy drinkers living in central London hostels. Scotland is on a par with the North-West for expenditure on drink, and convictions for drunkenness. But expenditure on drink in Northern Ireland is lower than average in

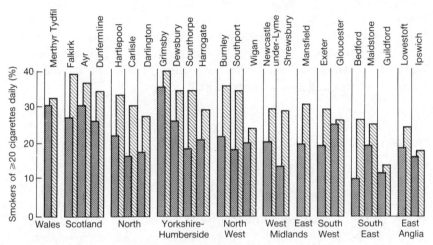

Percentage of men smoking 20 or more cigarettes a day by town, region, and social class

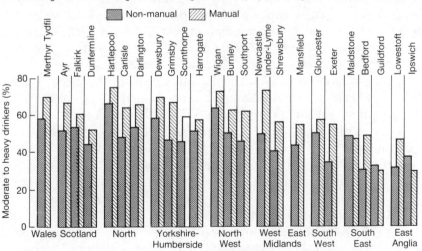

Percentage of men classified as moderate to heavy drinkers by town, region, and social class

Sources: Cummins, Shaper, *et al.* 1981, figs. 5, 6.

FIG. 8.9. Smoking and drinking habits: men aged 40–59, 24 British towns, 1970s

the UK; it has the highest proportion of teetotallers. In North Britain more drinking is done outside the home, and is concentrated at certain times of the week (Haskey, Balarajan, and Donnan 1983). Binges tend to magnify the impact of alcohol on liver and behaviour.

Differences between towns in smoking and drinking habits do not depend on social class; and social class differences in smoking persist in each town. For example, non-manual workers in Merthyr Tydfil, Ayr, and Grimsby smoked twice as much as non-manual workers in Carlisle, Shrewsbury, Gloucester, Guildford, and Bedford: indeed, they smoked twice as much as manual workers in those towns (Cummins, Shaper *et al.* 1981, figure 8.9). Manual workers in Hartlepool were two and a half times as likely to be 'moderate' drinkers as manual workers in Guildford. In general, towns in the West and the North tend to show heavier drinking than in the South and East, irrespective of class and socio-economic group.

Diet

There are substantial social class and regional differences in diet, most of them potentially unfavourable to manual workers and to residents of the North, Scotland, Wales, and Northern Ireland. Like smoking, the class pattern has changed in the course of the century. Data on expenditure per person on food is more readily available in relation to income rather than to class and is relatively inelastic with respect to income. The average expenditure per person per week for all households for domestic food consumption was £10.77 in 1988. Over the income range under £85 to £395 and above in households with at least one earner, per caput expenditure ranged from £9.24 to £11.83—a 28 per cent difference. Households without an earner and pensioner households all spent more than the average (table 8.10) on domestic consumption, but eat out less (National Food Survey Committee 1989).

As far as nutritional content is concerned, there was no clear relation between per caput domestic energy intake and income level, except that the low earners below £100 per week consume 1.5 per cent less than the national average (2,020 Kcal). The highest income bracket were markedly below the average; people with high incomes eat out much more than average. Unfortunately these figures are not standardized for household composition, but the lowest expenditure per head (£6.35) was among low income families with three children. There were no important differences in the protein or fat composition of the diet by income. All income groups consumed less (10 per cent) than recom-

Table 8.10. Food consumption by household income, Great Britain 1983 (ounces per week), selected foodstuffs

	Gross weekly income of head of household						No earner		
	A1 £320+	A2 £250–320	All A £250+	B £135–250	C £80–135	D <£80	E1 £80+	E2 <£80	OAP
Total expenditure (£)	9.33	9.08	9.19	8.70	8.17	7.15	10.08	8.56	9.43
Convenience food	2.54	2.46	2.49	2.57	2.38	2.10	2.37	2.32	2.10
canned food	0.46	0.50	0.49	0.54	0.54	0.51	0.47	0.57	0.50
Cheese	4.73	4.83	4.81	4.32	3.80	3.19	4.89	3.36	3.86
Meat	35.82	36.23	36.10	38.43	38.21	34.06	41.58	38.66	41.92
other products[a]	9.66	10.94	10.48	13.14	14.52	14.09	11.80	15.08	12.61
Fat	7.74	9.01	8.60	10.44	10.53	10.40	12.26	11.57	13.52
lard etc.[b]	0.39	0.87	0.70	1.50	1.94	1.96	0.97	2.10	2.36
Sugar etc.[c]	8.14	8.71	8.61	10.21	11.70	12.41	13.36	15.26	18.44
sugar alone	6.40	6.67	6.67	8.28	9.92	10.89	10.58	12.94	14.85
Vegetables	71.47	73.70	73.04	81.18	85.18	86.04	86.04	92.65	89.00
potatoes	27.16	28.68	28.13	36.51	42.60	47.03	34.65	46.47	44.41
fresh greens	11.07	11.00	11.03	10.37	9.83	7.73	16.98	11.53	15.71
processed	8.69	9.89	9.50	12.63	13.83	14.92	7.25	13.64	8.49
Fruit	42.67	41.19	41.77	30.83	23.62	16.85	48.31	26.60	31.11
fresh	27.02	26.73	26.92	20.52	16.32	12.30	35.27	18.91	22.44
Bread	21.64	23.30	22.75	29.11	32.85	34.39	26.60	34.00	33.15
wholemeal	3.86	3.55	3.64	2.86	2.18	1.58	5.36	2.39	3.51

[a] Other products: processed meat and meat products
[b] Lard etc.: lard and other hard cooking fat
[c] Sugar etc.: sugar, jam, confectionery
Source: National Food Survey Committee 1985, t. 14.

mended calorie intake; eating out will account for most of this, but it may reflect genuine deficiency among the poorest. As well as omitting meals out these figures do not include sweets consumed outside the house or alcohol—perhaps another 300 Kcal per person per day. Overall, in Britain, as in most other Western countries, daily per capita energy intake from all sources is almost 3,000 Kcal, between 10 and 20 per cent above the dietary requirement (in Preston 1982). Vitamin C intake is at least 50 per cent above recommended levels in all income groups. It is the only important food constituent which rises substantially with income; a result of higher consumption of fresh vegetables and fruit.

The poorest group of households spend slightly less on meat and milk and vegetables, much less on fish and cheese and fruit, cereals, flour, cakes, and biscuits, more on bread and sugar. These data on broad groupings of income make it difficult to sustain the view that much of the variation in mortality can be due to gross deficiency of diet that may be confined to a smaller group than routine statistics can identify. There are also differences by housing tenure. On average households owning their house outright in 1985 spent most per head (£11.35) and council tenants least (£9.21 per head). The tenants, however spend more on meat, bread, processed, and other categories of food than those owning with a mortgage, but less on milk, cheese, vegetables, fruit, and cereals. On the whole, other tenants of unfurnished property have consumption patterns nearer to the owner-occupiers than to the council tenants (National Food Survey Committee 1988). These averages per head are not corrected for age, and it must be remembered that 39 per cent of households renting from local authorities in 1987 were headed by persons aged 65 or over.

One of the biggest of these gradients is in sugar consumption. Expenditure on sugar is 50 per cent higher in the poorest than in the richest homes, and 30 per cent more in council households than mortgage-holders. There are also regional differences, though less striking ones—about 20 per cent greater in most Northern and Midlands regions than in the South and East Anglia (National Food Survey Committee 1985). This may help to explain social and regional patterns of tooth decay and obesity. Fat consumption is about 15 per cent higher in poorer than in richer households. A more significant difference is in the consumption of saturated fat for cooking, like lard, which is almost five times higher in the poorest compared to the richest households, and particularly in pensioner households. The latter may reflect a generation gap in taste and knowledge. Expenditure on fresh green vegetables is 40 per cent higher in the better-off households, that on fresh fruit 120 per cent higher. Expenditure on bread is 60 per cent higher in poorer households, but on wholemeal bread it is 140 per cent higher in the richer households.

There is little difference between income groups in the money spent per head upon domestic convenience (pre-cooked) food, except that the poorest earner households spent about 20 per cent less than all the others. It is generally supposed that working-class households eat more convenience food. Such foods tend to be higher in fat, sugar, and salt and lower on fibre and vitamins compared with fresh food and are unlikely to contribute to good health, and being partly processed they are inevitably more expensive than equivalent fresh food. This has led to some adverse comments on working-class cooking habits and skills, for which little evidence has been presented. These comments seem, therefore, to be based on a false premiss. However these figure do not include takeaway or meals eaten out. Market surveys show that hamburger takeaways and fish and chip shops, where the food lacks fresh fruit and vegetables and has a high fat content, are predominantly patronized by manual workers' families. A small-scale survey comparing mothers in Lambeth and Hampstead showed that the Lambeth mothers ate more takeaway food and less fresh vegetables and fish than the others, a diet deficient in essential (polyunsaturated) fatty acids and calories. This was blamed for their high proportion of underweight babies (Crawford *et al.* 1986).

Anthropological studies by intrepid participant observers (Douglas 1972) and other surveys show that foods such as salads or meals low on meat may be rejected as inappropriate, boring, or unmanly in working class (and other) households where traditional attitudes prevail. Real men don't eat lettuce. On average we eat 3.5 meals a week outside the home; many men, and increasingly women too, eat all their lunches out. Diets of many working men may be conditioned not so much by the home but by their works canteen and by workmen's cafés few of which appear to provide healthy food. Most provide fried, fatty, and fibre-free food; slabs of meat, tinned vegetables and potatoes, sugary puddings, chips with everything. In such one-class outlets alternatives are unlikely to be available: but the trend towards unified canteens for all staff may be broadening dietary horizons (Industrial Society 1989). School lunches may serve to prepare children for this kind of institutional diet later in life; despite changes many still seem designed to meet the needs of the hungry 1930s rather than today's problems of excess and imbalance. In 1983, the average school child took half its lunches at school and brought half from home. The contents of the lunch boxes are often a nutritionist's nightmare; crisps, chocolate,

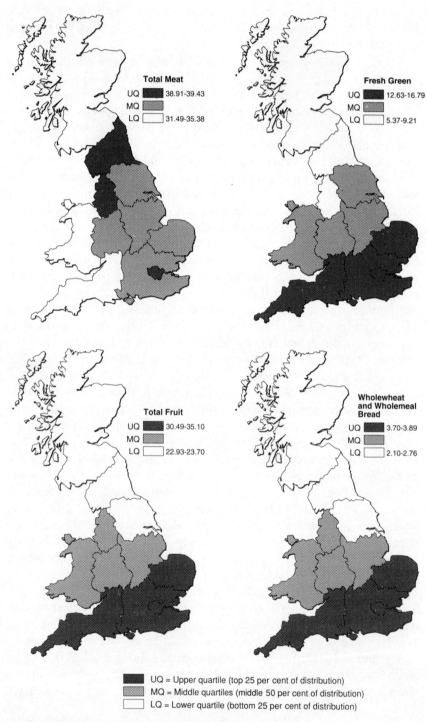

UQ = Upper quartile (top 25 per cent of distribution)
MQ = Middle quartiles (middle 50 per cent of distribution)
LQ = Lower quartile (bottom 25 per cent of distribution)

Note: Food bought for home consumption only, ounces/person/week.

Sources: National Food Survey Committee 1985, t. 7, t. 12.

Fig. 8.10 Regional variations in food consumption, Great Britain, 1983

and biscuits predominantly. Quite young children can develop the early signs of atherosclerosis.

Regional differences in diet

There does seem to be a North–South divide in eating habits (figure 8.10). Although total fat consumption varies rather little over the country, people in the North and the West Midlands consume about twice the amount of lard and similar hard fats than residents of the South-East. Northerners eat about a third more eggs than Southerners. But they eat about a quarter less fresh vegetables than Southerners, and about half the amount of fresh fruit, fresh green vegetables, and wholemeal bread. Scots' consumption of green vegetables is only about 40 per cent that of the South-East. Consumption of potatoes in Scotland, Wales, and the North generally is much higher than elsewhere. In Wales and the northern regions, cheese consumption is much lower, and relatively more processed than fresh meat is consumed. Consumption of other kinds of food varies little between regions, for example milk, fish, total meat intake, sugar, and convenience foods.

Obesity

Obesity is an indicator of excess nutrition, associated with bad health. There is a clear positive gradient of height with class; and a rather less clear negative gradient of overweight with class. Men in social class IIIM and women in all manual groups are most prone to be obese (OPCS 1981*d*). Maximum adult height is fixed by about age 18 and tends to reflect nutritional conditions in childhood, not adult life. Obesity, while it can be established in childhood, can be acquired (and lost) at any time. However, fat children tend to grow up into fat adults, and fat parents tend to bring up fat offspring (Whitelaw 1971, Royal College of Physicians 1983). Genetical differences account for some of the variation in adult height but little of the variation in weight or obesity (see Mascie-Taylor 1990). The present class relation with obesity, especially in children, may be quite recent. By the 1960s among Londoners half the women in classes IV and V were 30 per cent or more heavier than the ideal for their height compared with 20 per cent in class I. Older women are more likely to be obese than older men (Silverstone 1968). In the 1950s children of manual workers were less likely than average to be overweight (Hammond 1955). A recent study which confirmed the tendency for working-class people to be more obese (Rona and Morris 1982) found no social class effects in children under 11 years (Rona and Chinn 1982). Most of the poor have crossed the threshhold of nutritional adequacy. Deficient education and choice may have replaced deficient calories as the main influence on weight.

Attitudes to health

Social class differences

People in lower socio-economic groups and social classes suffer worse health than professionals and other non-manual workers. In particular they report much more long-standing illness (table 8.11). This is known from responses to General Household Survey and from general practitioners' and hospital records (Royal College of General Practitioners *et al.* 1982, OPCS 1987*e*). The social differences are prominent among younger adults, especially in social class V. Over age 65 there is little difference between the social classes (except for professionals). In general, however, social class differences in the frequency of medical consultation, when standardized for age, are not as great as the social class differences in SMR.

Despite this heavier burden of illness, manual workers and their families seek less medical advice than do non-manual workers for prevention or for cure (figure 8.11). They are less likely to attend

Table 8.11. Reported illness by socio-economic group, Great Britain, 1984 (%)

SEG	Limiting long-standing illness (not acute)				Persons consulting doctor in 14 days before interview			
	Age 16–44		Age 65+		Age 16–44		Age 65+	
	M	F	M	F	M	F	M	F
Professional	6	7	25	(13)	8	17	11	(2)
Employers and managers	7	10	34	44	7	16	13	18
Intermediate	9	9	35	38	7	16	16	18
Skilled manual, own account	10	11	43	43	8	17	18	14
Semi-skilled manual, personal services	12	13	44	47	7	18	17	20
Unskilled	14	18	48	47	8	24	25	25
All	10	11	40	44	7	17	7	19

Source: General Household Survey 1984, t. 8.17*b*, t. 8.26.

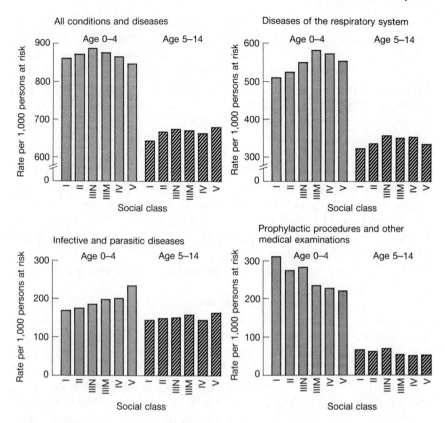

Source: Royal College of General Practitioners, OPCS, DHSS 1982.

FIG. 8.11. Patient consulting ratios for children, by parent's social class, England and Wales, around 1971

ante-natal clinics, or undergo routine examinations for cervical or breast cancer and mass radiography. They are less likely to take their young children for examination, vaccinations, and other preventive measures. Children under 14 from manual backgrounds, and especially under 4, are taken to consult doctors for respiratory and infectious diseases more than children from non-manual backgrounds, and their burden of illness and mortality from these causes is certainly higher. But for all conditions together, children in the middle of the social scale are taken to the doctor most often (figure 8.11). At older ages people in social classes IV and V consult their doctors more frequently than average, though not in proportion to their higher burden of disease and mortality (Royal College of General Practitioners 1982).

Free medical care was meant to have eliminated these differences and enabled access to medicine to reflect need. People in non-manual

occupations are likely to have easier opportunities for medical con-
sultations because their jobs offer more flexible working hours. Fewer
middle-class mothers work. But non-manual workers finish work
earlier in time for attendance at evening surgeries. Everyone except for
the small minority with private insurance has to wait in the same NHS
queue, at a higher opportunity cost for the higher paid. Preventive
measures can be planned well in advance and dealt with on Saturdays.

Some of these differences in access to medicine may follow from
differences in communication skills. Communication itself may be
difficult because of problems of language and jargon, embarrassment
and taboos, forcefulness or reticence. A fifth of Oxford doctors in a
recent survey mentioned that diagnosis and treatment were complicated by problems of communication with the patient. No class analysis
was given, but it would be surprising if the middle class were not more
effective at dealing with the medical profession, complaining about
poor service and meaningless appointment times, and getting past
doctors' receptionists.

Knowledge and attitudes towards disease and its causes may also be
important. If a connection is not seen between certain actions and
certain consequences, or if there is little faith in pre-emptive action,
then nothing will be done. The connection between smoking and
drinking and health is now generally known in all classes and in some
respects people are changing their behaviour, as the trend in smoking
and drinking shows. Manual workers, especially unskilled manual
workers, are less likely to know about, or believe, the connection
between smoking and disease.

There are considerable social differences in the degree to which
people believe themselves to be in charge of their own circumstances
and fate (the position of the 'locus of control', Lefcourt 1983). The
higher the social position, the more likely a belief in the power to
influence life events (see Chapter 4). A more 'internal' locus of control
gives people a wider variety and adaptability of responses to stress.
This apparently helps them to avoid mental illness (Pearlin and
Schooler 1978, Seeman and Seeman 1983, Turner and Noh 1983).
Although a link has been established with the use of contraception, the
connections with physical ill health and the use of preventive medicine
or more general risk-avoiding behaviour have not been studied. The
Health and Lifestyle survey (Cox *et al.* 1987) put little emphasis on the
'locus of control' dimension or on attitudes, and more on income and
social class. It reported a general belief in individual responsibility for
health, putting behaviour in front of environment.

Other evidence suggests a difference in social class attitudes to risk

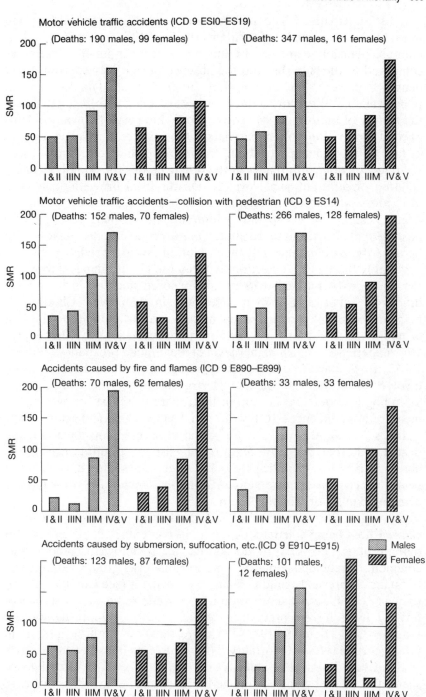

Source: OPCS 1988*c*, fig. 2.2

FIG. 8.12. Child mortality by parent's social class, selected external causes, around 1981

and its anticipation. The children of manual workers suffer high mortality from all causes of accidents (figure 8.12). The traffic accident data are plausibly explained by the heavy traffic in inner urban areas compared to the suburbs, and the absence of safe play space in high-density high-rise urban estates, although appropriate data do not seem to be available. But many council estates are low-rise cottage estates on the fringes of built-up areas. Tower blocks have well-known problems of child supervision from higher flats but the estates themselves are free of fast traffic. Flats apart (about one in five council dwellings), there seem few obvious differences in the opportunities for safe play among children of different social origins. Deaths from drowning can have little to do with access to telephones or to safe play space. Some fire deaths, caused by cheap but inhererently more dangerous paraffin heating appliances, can be attributed to poverty. But other deaths arise because the parents have left their children unsupervised.

Possibly there is a connection between the greater dangers to which the children of manual workers are exposed and the lack of inhibitions or supervision evident elsewhere in their lives. Children of manual workers experience sexual intercourse earlier than the children of non-manual workers and are also more precocious in other areas. Girls experience a much higher level of illegitimate pregnancy (Werner 1984). Boys start smoking and drinking earlier and become more involved in crime (Wilson and Herrnstein 1985) (the peak age for offending is about 15). On top of that, there is a negative gradient of measured intelligence (IQ) with social class (Mascie-Taylor 1990). Perhaps one of the reasons for social class gradients in accidental deaths and other causes of death is the existence of differences in the ability to perceive or anticipate risk. Other values—for the esteem of peers, which may require active risk-taking—may take priority over avoiding danger or trouble (Klein 1965).

To suggest this is to open a Pandora's box of controversy on social class without being able to close it with its contents in better order. But perhaps it is necessary to do so. Earlier sociologists made robust comments on the behaviour of some working-class groups with respect to financial foresight, child care and employment (see Coleman 1990); today an emphasis on deprivation is preferred. Some cohort studies of fertility have linked premature fertility to the IQ of the mother (Kiernan and Diamond 1982) but there seems to be little interest in intelligence in terms of mortality. For example the Health and Lifestyle study included no test of ability (Cox *et al.* 1987). Higher intelligence seems to be an obvious advantage in the successful avoidance of risk. But at present it is not on the agenda for analysis.

Social class factors and income may operate through the education received and expected by children of different social origins, the influence of housing tenure, especially on large single-class estates, and the control adults can expect over their lives. Educational reform, diversification of tenure and residence, and a weakening of work-force demarcations should join more direct welfare measures in health reform. Income and social class differences in risk may work indirectly, not necessarily through simple material deprivation.

Unemployment and ill health

It has been surprisingly difficult to establish a causal connection between unemployment and excess mortality. It seems obvious that unemployment should lead to ill health, given the pre-eminence of work in income and self-esteem. Unemployment ranks high, just below divorce and widowhood, on psychological scales of stressful life events (Holmes and Rahe 1967). The difficulty arises partly because prior ill health is a handicap in getting or keeping a job (e.g. Stern 1983). Cross-sectional and time-series studies fail to disentangle these effects. For example, claims that mortality of adults or of children worsened during the depression years in the 1930s do not appear to be statistically well founded (Brenner 1979, Winter 1984). Neither is there time-series evidence for a mortality response to more recent unemployment. The Longitudinal Study has overcome some of these problems. It has established that the excess mortality cannot be explained just by previous health or social status, and that the unemployment effect is likely to be causal. Mortality of unemployed men seeking work in 1971 and in 1981 was 30–47 per cent higher than average at three points in time after the appropriate census, and was more elevated in the regions outside the South and East where long-term unemployment has been higher and more persistent. Wives also suffered higher mortality (Moser, Jones, Fox, and Goldblatt 1986, Moser, Fox, Goldblatt, and Jones 1987).

Deaths by accidents and violence were particularly raised, notably suicide on which unemployment is likely to have a direct effect through its adverse psychological consequences (R. Smith 1987). However the most substantial increases in any causes of death, and numerically the most important, were in lung cancer and respiratory disease. Circulatory disease, perhaps surprisingly in view of its link with emotional state, was less elevated. Smoking is the only important cause of lung cancer, which suggests that the unemployed smoke more or resume smoking.

Marriage and social support

That married people enjoy better health than the single and widowed has been known for some time. Part of it may be selective, in that people with poor health may be less likely to marry or stay married. The advantage is about 20 per cent on mortality rates. It is often said that men get more from marriage than women; their mortality advantage when married is certainly greater. The Alameda County study reported 75 per cent higher mortality rates among single men than married men, 30 per cent higher rates among single women. The extra high death-rates of widowers within six months of bereavement, especially from ischaemic heart disease (Jones and Goldblatt 1987), reflect physical response to acute grief. They emphasize the greater dependence upon marriage of men than of women as well as the importance of the married state for health. But the health handicap never goes away unless removed by remarriage.

Divorced men and women also acquire higher health risks, notably from lung cancer (SMR 187, 314). This cannot entirely be explained by the concentration of divorced men in council housing and the manual social classes (Leon 1988). Breast cancer is higher among single women compared with married women (SMR 116). There may be a straightforward physiological explanation as they are not protected by childbearing. On the other hand single women have only half (SMR 49) the cervical cancer death-rates of married women, who in turn have much lower rates than divorced women (SMR 227). Single women in council tenure however, have high rates (SMR 157) compared to single women in owner-occupation (SMR 23) (see Chapter 7).

The same kind of life support can also be provided by friends and relatives (see House *et al.* 1988). The dependence of psychological well-being on the support of friends and relatives has been recognized for a long time (Argyle and Henderson 1985) and was commented on by Charles Darwin. The seven-year Alameda study of lifestyle and mortality (Berkman and Breslow 1983) demonstrated for the first time systematic advantages in death-rates among people with a broad range of friends. Socially isolated people were much more likely to die or develop life-threatening conditions.

Such findings may have implications for social class mortality differences (Marmot 1986). Marriage and divorce vary considerably by social class (Chapter 5). Middle-aged unskilled manual workers are the most frequent residents of bedsitters and boarding houses, prone to social isolation, living in physically restricted and often unsatisfactory accommodation, and often drinking a great deal. Within marriage divorce is more likely among manual workers (Chapter 5). Outside marriage, social networks tend to be wider and more supportive, possibly more materially useful, higher up the social scale, and also better integrated into home life and not just based on work (Willmott 1986).

Regional differences: from Bucks Fizz to Ulster Fry

Most data available for analysing regional contrasts in mortality describe the material rather than behavioural differences. Allocation of NHS resources has caused particular controversy, following the realization that the southern part of the country enjoyed more than its fair share (on various demographic criteria—see Hobcraft 1989) of medical facilities. The allocation of NHS resources between the regions of the country is now meant to be equalized according to need, taking into account the level of sickness and the prevalence of high-risk sections of the population, through the formula devised by the Resources Allocation Working Party (RAWP 1976). Since the 1970s the RAWP formula has reallocated resources away from those areas in favour of the North. But this has not yet reduced regional mortality differences, and would not be expected to do so if the influence of medicine on death-rates is relatively marginal (Kunset *et al* 1988). Long-standing extra NHS benefits enjoyed by Northern Ireland and Scotland have not rectified their poor mortality record (except for infant mortality in Scotland). Around 1980, for example, Scotland enjoyed about 20 per cent more doctors per thousand population, and Northern Ireland about 10 per cent more, than England. Both have about 45 per cent more available hospital bed space per 1,000 population.

Variability of NHS care in different parts of the country cannot easily be related to sickness or mortality levels. The worst areas, even after correction for social factors, tend to be towns in the North-West such as Rochdale, although Townsend *et al.* (1988) have also focused on the high mortality areas in Cumbria, Northumberland, and Durham, especially in the Newcastle conurbation. There seem to be considerable regional differences in attitudes to health. One example is the regional variation in immunization of children. In 1981, for example, immunization against whooping cough was under 44 per cent in all Regional Health Authorities in the North, North-West, West Midlands, and Wales (also North-East Thames), and over 50 per cent in Oxford, East Anglia, Trent, and South-West Thames RHAs (OPCS Monitor MB2 83/2). There are also regional differences in the proportion of pregnancies to single mothers which end in abortion, with the lowest proportions in the North, Yorkshire and Humberside, and North-West (30 per cent or less in 1986) and the highest in the South-East (44 per cent in 1986). That is allegedly due to regional differences in attitudes of medical staff and management, influenced perhaps by Roman Catholic views.

The regional contrasts in drinking and smoking and diet, which hold good within each social class, argue for strong differences in attitudes, values, and tastes which owe little to poverty. Like some of the social class differences, these may be better understood under the heading of culture. It is difficult to interpret differences in cooking under income or material heads. Generous Northern breakfasts are a revelation to Southerners increasingly used to insipid muesli, and the traditional 'Ulster Fry' looks like a particularly defiant rejection of nutritional rationality.

Attitude differences in Northern Ireland, Scotland, and northern England may survive partly because of migration patterns. Throughout the whole of the twentieth century the net movement of people has been away from these regions. The south and especially the South-East is now peopled with individuals from all over the country who are exposed to a wide variety of opinions and habits, not to a regional cultural homogeneity. Within the southern regions households are much more mobile than in the north and have been for most of this century (Chapter 10, Coleman 1981). Southerners are much more likely to travel long distances to work. In Northern Ireland and Scotland personal mobility and social mixing is especially inhibited by the majority of the population living in public housing (a higher proportion than in much of Eastern Europe), which has the lowest mobility beyond the local area of any tenure. The more traditional qualities of northern regional life may offer many advantages over the allegedly impersonal regime in the south, but permeability to new attitudes which promote health may not be one of them.

9 The British at Work

9.1 Introduction

One of the biggest problems confronting successive British governments since the end of the First World War has been the provision
of employment for all who want to work. During the 1930s a succession
of measures was aimed at alleviating the distress of the depressed areas,
but it was really the Second World War that finally put the nation back
to work. For a time the application of Keynesian economics seemed to
be the answer. The honeymoon lasted until the late 1960s, after which
unemployment rose again, seemingly inexorably. The 1980s have seen
numbers without jobs at an all-time high throughout the developed
world, though national variations in rates of unemployment have been
considerable. During the peak of 1986 in the United Kingdom the rate
reached 11.6 per cent, lower than Belgium (16.5 per cent), Italy (14.3
per cent), and Spain (21.5 per cent), the same as France, but higher
than Australia (9.1 per cent), West Germany (8.6 per cent), and the
USA (6.9 per cent) (DE 1987).

In the UK prolonged recession from the late 1970s to the mid-1980s
reduced demand; a new international division of labour favoured
investment overseas in the Newly Industralized Countries, like South
Korea, Singapore, and Brazil; the full job impact of new technology
still threatens to cut a swathe through existing job practices. At the
same time the basic facts of demography have dictated that the number
of people of working age has been increasing, fuelling demand for
work. The type of work performed has been changing—out of the
workshop and behind the desk especially. People retire earlier than
their parents and grandparents. New, more flexible forms of
employment are being introduced and experimented with; the growth
of part-time employment is particularly noticeable.

It is the intention of this chapter to review the main contemporary
features of the demand for both work and workers. It explores the main
links between demography and labour supply, the changing pattern of
labour demand, and the mismatches (between what employers want
and who is available) that produce unemployment.

9.2 The Supply of Labour: The Work-Force

The demography of the work-force

In the years since the Second World War the UK labour force has grown gradually, fluctuating according to economic conditions, but ultimately responding to the dictates of demography and willingness to participate. During the 1970s the increment was, on average, 130,000 per year (a growth rate of 0.5 per cent), but a surge occurred in 1976–7, with a growth of 401,000 reflecting the change in school leaving age, followed by a check during 1977–9 (DE 1984). In the later 1970s and early 1980s movements in the labour force have been dominated by two opposing tendencies: a rapid increase in the population of working age, and a fall particularly in male participation rates brought on by early retirements and a declining tendency for men to work after retirement age. Female participation rates, which had been rising steadily, levelled off and between 1977 and 1981 the female labour force grew only slowly. The net result was that in the fifteen years from 1971 the female labour force grew by about 1.7 million while that of males remained roughly constant (DE 1987). The most recent national projections from 1990 to 2001, indicate an almost unchanged male civilian labour force at around 15,900,000, with a rise of about 700,000 among females to a total of 12,900,000. These estimates are based on the assumption that unemployment rates will fall. A fall of 200,000 in the level of unemployment is reckoned to lead to an increase in the labour force of 100,000 as workers are encouraged to enter it as unemployment falls (DE 1990).

These demographic and participation rate trends are important influences in labour market planning. Low birth-rates during the First World War have meant fewer men reaching retirement age in recent years. The succeeding baby boom means a flurry of men leaving the labour force in the late 1980s, followed by a gradual decline, reflecting 1920s birth-rates (there is a similar pattern for women, but five years earlier because of their lower retirement age). The numbers entering the working population in the last decade or so are affected by the very high birth-rates of the 1960s, augmented by the children of immigrants who entered in the late 1950s and early 1960s. Although numbers of school leavers peaked in 1980–1, the numbers of both men and women reaching working age continued to exceed exits until the late 1980s, from when the situation will become fairly stable until the end of the century. Thus, in the absence of any change in participation rates, population growth alone increased the labour force by half a million men and a third of a million women between 1981 and 1988.

The potential future work-force is already fairly well defined. All of it—bar migrants—has been born for the next sixteen years. Projections show that we are coming to the end of a period of large numbers of entrants to the labour force. The peak of the 1960s baby boom is already past, and the future entrants, following the numbers of births, will decline until 1996 when the position will stabilize. In the decade to 1986 the population of working age grew by 200,000 per year. The future looks quite different, with increases of only 50,000 a year to the mid-1990s (DE 1988). This is because of the smaller numbers of young people who will be available: by 1995 there will be a million fewer 16–19-year-olds than ten years earlier. As well as a declining flow of youths on to the labour market, the stock of 16–19-year-olds is also set to fall, by 16 per cent between 1987 and 1995, a much higher decline than that of 20–4-year-olds (down 6 per cent), and in contrast to a rise of 3 per cent for the labour force as a whole.

The recruitment strategies of companies wanting to employ young people will have to be adjusted in the light of this smaller pool. The impact of this decline in new entrants will depend on how many young people seek work when leaving school and how many enter higher education. Present government policies envisage an increase in the demand for degree and similar courses lasting three or more years.

The numbers who leave by retirement will decline in the 1990s just as the numbers of new pensioners will decline, then remain constant until the perturbation of the wartime era is reached in 2005 (figure 9.1). The immediate post-war baby boom depression will reduce the work-force temporarily; after the boom a long time decline will set in as the bulge of 1953–70 transfers itself into the retirement category. So although demographic forces by themselves can reasonably be blamed for part of the increase in unemployment of the last few years, they will also deserve some praise for any future falls in unemployment as the number of those seeking work gradually declines.

Future shortages in the labour force, both here and in other industrial countries, may lead to pressure to loosen present restrictive immigration policies maintained by most Western countries (Espenshade 1987, Employment and Immigration Canada 1987). The large numbers involved, however, well over 100,000 a year, make this course of action extremely unlikely. Present portents are for increasing numbers of highly skilled workers to be required rather than mass immigration, the numbers being measured only in terms of a few thousand each year.

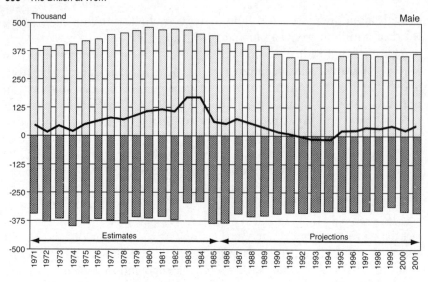

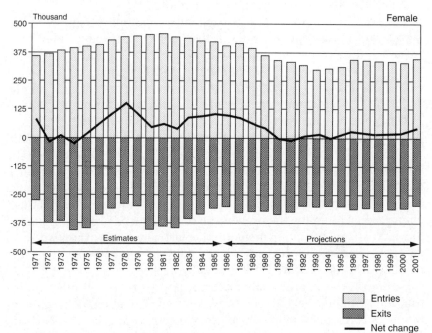

Entries

Exits

— Net change

Notes: Entries: those reaching the age of 16; exits: the residual change – mainly those reaching retirement age but also including net migration and deaths.

Source: *Employment Gazette*, May 1987.

FIG. 9.1. Changes in the population of working age

Participation rates

Males

Demographic parameters alone do not define the work-force. People can choose whether and when to work and retire. Male participation rates, which have generally declined in the past decade, have been nibbled at from both ends as a result of prolonged education and early retirement. In the late 1970s and early 1980s participation rates for older males, especially those aged 60–4, fell steeply, though rates for 20–54-year-olds held up remarkably well. About one-third of those in the pre-retirement group can be accounted for by the government's Job Release Scheme, but other major factors are shake-outs and early retirements under occupational pension schemes.

Females

Changes in work-force participation rates by women have been the most powerful determinant of changes in work-force size since the Second World War. The rates have changed quite a lot with age. They are low among teenagers (figure 9.2) because many are still in full-time education; they rise to a peak in the mid-20s and remain high until the mid-50s, and then fall off quickly thanks to early retirement or illness. Work-force participation rates of unmarried women—and also of the divorced and separated—are not that different from those of men, although they do very different jobs. Their participation, closely linked to childbearing, is less stable. In 1951 they peaked at 20–24, by 1975 the rates were lower overall in an almost flat curve from 20–54—much higher than in 1951 beyond age 34, possibly reflecting wartime experience (Martin and Monk 1982).

Women's participation rates are known to respond positively to higher real wages, as might be expected (Joshi 1985). At their new, higher level they proved quite tenacious in the face of the economic recession of the early 1980s, with no evidence of any shrinking of female labour supply when growth in demand stagnated (Joshi and Owen 1985), as was also true in the USA at the same time. This suggests strong non-economic motivations too, and deals a blow to some counter-cyclical models of fertility (Butz and Ward 1979).

Married women have changed their working habits most. There is a close, circular connection between married women's working habits and the timing of their childbearing. In fact, the return of married women to the work-force has probably had the biggest demographic impact of any social change in the mid-twentieth century, not just on

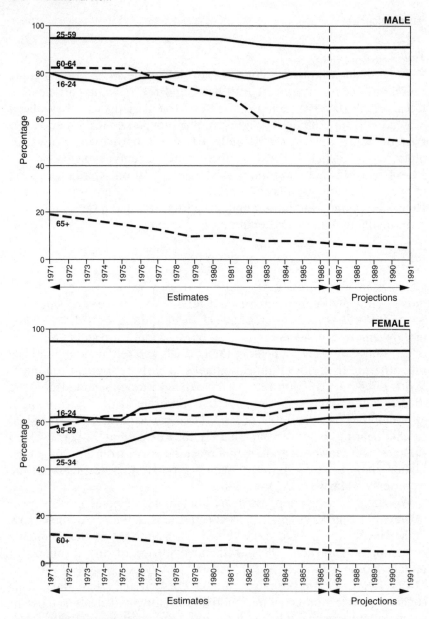

Source: Employment Gazette, May 1987.

FIG. 9.2. Activity rates by age-group

fertility but on marriage and divorce. Only 11 per cent of married women worked in 1931. By the late 1970s this had risen to about 50 per cent of all aged 16 and over, when it levelled off (table 9.1). About half this increase was achieved by 1961, since when change has been very rapid, especially in women aged 25–54. Small family size made this possible. The concentration of most childbearing before women are in their early 30s, or between the fifth and tenth year of marriage, has been encouraged by the attractions—or the need—to return to work (de Cooman, Ermisch, and Joshi 1987). As indicated in Chapter 4, it remains a major puzzle why, given that much of the reduction in family size had been achieved before the Second World War, it still took a few

Table 9.1. Economic activity rates, by age and sex (%)

	16–19	20–24	25–44	45–54/59	55–9/60–4	60/65+	All aged 16 or over
Married females							
1961	41.0	41.3	33.6	36.1	26.4	7.3	29.7
1971	41.6	45.7	46.4	57.0	45.5	14.2	42.2
1976	52.5	57.6	56.8	64.8	51.2	12.6	49.0
1979	50.9	57.8	58.7	65.6	52.1	10.1	49.6
1981	48.9	56.8	58.5	66.8	51.9	11.5	49.5
Non-married females							
1961	73.2	89.4	84.2	75.3	61.9	11.4	50.6
1971	57.2	81.2	80.4	78.1	67.2	11.0	43.7
1976	68.0	76.2	79.1	77.3	66.4	8.4	43.1
1979	65.9	78.1	78.4	76.7	63.8	5.3	42.8
1981	65.8	78.4	76.9	76.5	63.1	5.9	43.6
All females							
1961	71.1	62.0	40.8	44.0	37.1	9.7	37.4
1971	55.9	60.1	50.6	60.6	51.1	12.4	42.7
1976	66.6	65.7	59.9	66.9	55.0	10.2	46.9
1979	64.8	67.9	61.8	67.5	54.9	7.4	47.0
1981	64.5	68.0	61.6	68.5	54.7	8.3	47.2
All males							
1961	74.6	91.9	98.2	99.2	91.2	24.4	86.0
1971	60.9	89.9	97.9	96.8	86.6	19.4	81.4
1976	72.6	89.0	97.6	96.5	83.0	14.4	80.7
1979	70.7	88.3	97.4	95.2	75.8	10.2	78.6
1981	72.7	88.2	97.2	94.4	72.0	10.3	78.1

Source: OPCS (1984*a*)

decades more for the apparently natural response of moving into the work-force to become popular (Hatton 1986).

Regional labour force trends

Actual and projected change in regional labour participation rates for selected regions of the UK during 1971–91, based upon similar assumptions of unemployment and early retirement to those at national level, show that for both sexes there is a convergence of regional experience, though patterns are not uniform (DE 1984). For example, trends for men are downwards in the West Midlands but up in East Anglia and the South-West, where economic growth has been greater. Female rates show less variability in trend, though generally the direction is one of convergence. The consequences for regional labour forces are also variable. While the national labour force grew by nearly 4.5 per cent during the period 1981–8, those of the North and Greater London fell, the North-West remained static but substantial growth occurred in East Anglia, the South-West, and East Midlands (DE 1990b).

Although regional variations mainly reflect demographic conditions, trends in population and participation rate vary. In the North-West, for example, male participation rates fell more rapidly than in most other regions leading to a falling male labour force despite a rising population of working age. In Scotland, a substantial fall in male participation rate, together with a modest increase in that for females, failed to mitigate the effects of population increase well below the national average. Finally, although the population effect in the South-East was similar to the national average, a small fall in the male participation rate, but a large rise in the female, ensured that growth in the region's labour force was well above average.

What this means is that for almost all of the 1980s all regions in Britain, except for the North, experienced larger labour forces because demographic gains have offset reductions in participation. For women both demographic and participation rate effects have been positive in all regions, so their labour has grown universally. Projections to 2000 suggest that the regional pattern is likely to be more variable, with male labour forces in the more prosperous East Midlands, East Anglia, South-East, South-West, and Northern Ireland continuing to grow for demographic reasons, while those elsewhere decline. Female labour forces in all regions, are projected to grow up to 2000, largely because of higher participation rates. Hence at both national and regional levels during most of the 1990s the pattern is for participation pressures to outweigh a fairly flat demographic trend (DE 1990b).

Towards a more flexible work-force

Not every person who works wishes or is able to work full time and all the time. It suits many people, especially married women with young children, to tailor their hours of work to those of school. Others, again especially women, prefer or are forced into temporary employment. The incidence of both of these has been growing.

Part-time employment

The flexibility of part-time working appeals to many: according to one commentator its growth over the last fifteen years or so represents 'one of the most radical changes of employment structure this century' (Townsend 1986). By 1987 there were 5,000,000 part-time workers in Britain, 20 per cent of all recorded employees (DE 1990*a*). During the 1970s their numbers grew by over a million, an increase of 33 per cent compared with a reduction of 9 per cent among full-time workers. Since 1981 numbers have grown by about 120,000 per year. Most of them, about 4.3 million, are women; indeed, part-time working provides the majority of jobs for women over 30 (Martin and Roberts 1984).

The geographical pattern of part-time working to some extent confirms the traditional North–South and urban–rural dichotomies. The highest proportions are found in the 'Rest of the South-East' (the area excluding London) and in the non-metropolitan parts of Yorkshire and Humberside; the conurbations generally show below average rises in incidence (Townsend 1986). Many areas with high proportions of part-time working are coastal, although this does not appear to be due to seasonal factors, but to rising population totals which lead to a growth in demand for personal services. Hence part-time working is not found equally in all sectors. Medical and educational service provision accounted for a third of growth during the 1970s, with leisure industries such as hotels and catering also being very important. In contrast, more traditional services like railways, the post office, cinemas, and laundries reduced their numbers of part-time employees. It seems also that the growth of part-time working has led directly to some loss of full-time jobs, through a substitution effect (Townsend 1986).

Temporary workers

Since 1983 the Labour Force Survey has collected information on those taking temporary work, about 1.5 million in 1989 (1.6 million if those on government schemes are included). By comparison with permanent workers, those working temporarily are more likely to be women, and to be either younger or older workers. For about a third of temporary workers their status reflects a lack of choice. For the majority, though, temporary employment is the preferred option. In consequence, there is no clear regional relationship to rates of unemployment: London and the South-East, for example, have a higher incidence of temporary work. It would seem that in general a strong labour demand has the effect of drawing into the labour force those who would not otherwise be working and for whom temporary work provides flexibility. This is almost certainly related to the higher propensity of married women beyond their mid-20s to be in this form of work compared with their single sisters.

Table 9.2. Labour force industrial composition, 1911–1971 (%)

Order	Industry	1911	1931	1951	1971
I	Agriculture, etc.	8.4	6.1	5.0	2.7
II	Mining, etc.	6.3	5.7	3.8	1.6
III	Ceramics and glass, etc.	1.1	1.3	1.4	1.3
IV	Chemicals	0.8	1.2	2.0	2.1
V	Metal manufacture	2.8	2.6	2.6	2.3
VI	Engineering and shipbuilding	4.9	5.3	8.0	9.0
VII	Vehicles	1.6	2.0	4.5	3.3
VIII	Metal goods n.e.s.	1.8	2.2	2.8	3.1
IX	Instruments, jewellery, etc.	—	—		
X	Textiles	7.6	6.5	4.4	2.5
XI	Leather, etc.	0.5	0.4	0.4	0.1
XII	Clothing	6.5	4.3	3.2	2.0
XIII	Food, drink, and tobacco	3.1	3.5	3.4	3.1
XIV	Wood	1.5	1.6	1.5	1.3
XV	Paper and printing	1.9	2.4	2.3	2.6
XVI	Other manufactures	0.5	1.1	1.2	1.4
XVII	Building	5.3	5.5	6.4	7.0
XVIII	Gas, electricity, and water	0.6	1.2	1.6	1.5
XIX	Transport and communication	7.9	8.2	7.7	6.6
XX	Distributive trades	11.9	13.2	12.1	12.7
XXI	Finance	1.1	1.8	2.0	4.0
XXII	Public admin. and defence	3.9	4.9	7.7	6.6
XXIII	Professional services	4.4	5.2	6.9	12.2
XXIV	Miscellaneous services	15.5	14.0	9.3	9.9
	Primary	14.7	11.8	8.8	4.3
	Industrial	40.0	39.7	43.9	42.2
	Service	45.3	48.5	47.3	53.5

Source: Routh 1980.

9.3 The Demand for Labour: Jobs

The historical pattern

It was not until towards the middle of the nineteenth century that census data allowed the structure of employment to be identified, and even then it was necessary to use a hybrid of occupational and industrial classifications (Hatton 1984). The overall pattern of employment in the half century up to the First World War is fairly clear. Manufacturing's share of the total labour force remained relatively stable at around a third; agriculture declined and there were increases in mining. New services, like transport and distribution, made gains at the expense of domestic service—which never the less occupied 10 per cent of the labour force in 1911 (Feinstein 1972).

Changes from 1911 to 1971 are summarized in table 9.2, standardized on the 1948 Standard Industrial Classification (Routh 1980). The primary sector (agriculture and mining) declined, services grew, and manufacturing remained fairly stable. Within these major groups, however, there were marked variations between individual industries and services. Textiles declined, engineering expanded; financial and administrative services grew. Occupational composition changed too (table 9.3). Among the male labour force there was a strong upward trend in the share of professional, managerial, and supervisory grades. Women were different. Their proportional increases in higher socio-economic occupations were lower than for men. The share of skilled and semi-skilled groups in the female labour force as a whole declined, accompanied by rises in clerical and unskilled manual groups. These proportions are accompanied by sex segregation in the labour force: among professional and technical workers, for example, 91 per cent of nurses were women but less than 1 per cent of civil, municipal, and structural engineers (Hatton 1984). In recent years, however, sex segregation has been decreasing, a consequence of more women entering the labour force, of more in higher education, and of the trend towards sex equality in the work-place following the Equal Pay Act 1970 and the Sex Discrimination Act 1973 (Hakim 1978, Joseph 1983).

The 1970s saw almost universal employment decline in the primary, manufacturing, and construction sectors, with strong growth in a number of services—especially financial, professional, and some personal services in the miscellaneous category (table 9.4). Older industries, like textiles, clothing, metals, and shipbuilding continued their historic decline, while some of the newer growth industries of the post-war period also faltered. Among services the private sector grew more

Table 9.3. Labour force occupational composition, 1911–1971 (%)

	1911		1931		1951		1971	
	M	F	M	F	M	F	M	F
Higher professional	1.34	0.20	1.50	0.29	2.56	0.52	4.87	0.55
Lower professional	1.61	6.49	2.03	6.83	3.16	8.18	5.95	10.95
Employees and Proprietors	7.74	4.28	7.65	4.44	5.74	3.22	5.07	2.75
Managers and Administrators	3.91	2.30	4.54	1.60	6.78	2.73	10.91	3.51
Clerical Workers	5.48	3.30	5.53	10.34	6.35	20.41	6.38	27.00
Foremen, inspectors, supervisors	1.75	0.18	2.00	0.45	3.28	1.14	5.04	1.84
Skilled manual	32.99	24.78	29.96	19.09	30.36	12.75	29.08	8.48
Semi-skilled manual	33.63	53.42	28.85	49.51	27.92	43.12	20.82	32.90
Unskilled manual	11.55	5.05	17.92	7.45	13.84	7.94	11.89	12.02

Source: Routh 1980.

Table 9.4. Employment change by industry, 1971–1981

Sector and SIC (1968) order	Employed 1971 ('000s)	Percentage change		
		1971–8	1978–81	1971–81
Primary production	812	−11.1	−6.2	−16.6
I Agriculture, forestry, and fishing	419	−11.1	−8.3	−18.4
II Mining and quarrying	393	−11.2	−4.0	−14.7
Manufacturing industry	7,886	−9.7	−16.2	−14.7
III Food, drink, and tobacco	744	−8.1	−7.6	−15.0
IV Coal and petroleum products	44	−13.9	−4.3	−17.6
V Chemicals and allied industries	435	0.7	−11.1	−10.5
VI Metal manufacture	556	−16.4	−31.7	−42.9
VII Mechanical engineering	1,038	−11.5	−11.5	−21.7
VIII Instrument engineering	164	−9.6	−9.0	−17.8
IX Electrical engineering	799	−6.0	−10.0	−15.4
X Shipbuilding and marine engineering	183	−6.0	−18.6	−23.5
XI Vehicles	807	−7.4	−18.9	−24.9
XII Other metal goods NES	572	−6.2	−21.6	−26.4
XIII Textiles	581	−21.3	−29.7	−44.7
XIV Leather, leather goods, and fur	46	−18.9	−16.0	−31.9
XV Clothing and footwear	429	−16.3	−24.8	−37.0
XVI Bricks, pottery, glass, and cement	301	−14.1	−17.9	−29.5
XVII Timber, furniture, etc.	264	−4.8	−15.1	−19.2
XVIII Paper, printing, and publishing	589	−8.6	−7.4	−15.3
XIX Other manufacturing	331	−3.2	−21.2	−23.7
Construction (Order XX)	1,222	−0.1	−8.0	−8.1

Table 9.4. (Cont.)

Sector and SIC (1968) order	Employed 1971 ('000s)	Percentage change		
		1971–8	1978–81	1971–81
Service Industries	11,718	12.3	1.0	13.4
XXI Gas, electricity, and water	369	−10.5	2.4	−8.3
XXII Transport and communication	1,545	−5.7	−3.0	−8.6
XXIII Distributive trades	2,555	6.3	−1.2	5.1
XXIV Insurance, banking, etc.	963	23.0	9.6	34.9
XXV Professional and scientific services	2,916	22.8	2.6	26.0
XXVI Miscellaneous services	1,906	23.2	6.3	31.0
XXVII Public administration and defence	1,465	5.4	−9.9	−5.0
Great Britain	21,638	2.7	−5.1	−2.5

Source: Census of Employment.

Table 9.5. Employment change in Great Britain, 1971–1983 ('000s)

Year	Total	Percentage change	Manu-facturing	Percentage change	Services	Percentage change
1971	21,648		7,910		11,361	
1972	21,650	0.0	7,640	−3.4	11,641	2.5
1973	22,182	2.5	7,693	0.7	12,069	3.7
1974	22,297	0.5	7,737	0.6	12,217	1.2
1975	22,213	−0.4	7,365	−4.8	12,524	2.5
1976	22,048	−0.7	7,131	−3.2	12,604	0.6
1977	22,126	0.4	7,183	0.8	12,679	0.6
1978	22,274	0.7	7,147	−0.5	12,877	1.6
1979[a]	22,639	1.6	7,113	−0.5	13,239	2.8
1980[a]	22,458	−0.8	6,804	−4.3	13,370	1.0
1981[b]	21,314	−5.1	6,057	−11.0	13,101	−2.0
1982[a]	20,945	−1.7	5,790	−4.4	13,110	0.0
1983[a]	20,615	−1.6	5,560	−4.6	13,146	0.3

[a] Estimates
[b] Month for this year is September; all others are June
Source: *Employment Gazette*, May 1984.

slowly than the public sector before 1978, after which roles were reversed (Champion *et al.* 1987). During the 1980s these trends have continued, the main growth being in the 'producer services' whose main clients are other businesses rather than the general public (Marshall 1988).

The aggregate effect of these changes was that between 1971 and 1983 there was an overall decline of 334,000 jobs in Britain, though the rate of loss fluctuated (table 9.5). Until 1979 there was a general increase, but in the ensuing two years not only were 1,324,000 jobs lost, but the level of employment in 1981 was estimated to be over two million less than in 1979. There was also a substantial sectoral shift of employment, with manufacturing losing 800,000 jobs between 1971 and 1979 and over a million more by 1981. In contrast, service employment grew steadily until 1980, and managed an increment of 1,740,000 new jobs over the decade as a whole.

The geography of employment change

The overall spatial pattern

These changes had a distinctive spatial pattern (figure 9.3). In general terms, employment declined in the north and expanded in the South, the main exception being the rapid employment growth in northern Scotland owing to the oil industry. The conurbations and their satellite areas, with a dependence on manufacturing, suffered grievous job losses, while London lost jobs to areas within its metropolitan region. Heavy declines occurred in some formerly prosperous areas, most notably the West Midlands. In contrast considerable growth occurred in a belt stretching south-westwards from London, and in another including parts of the southern Midlands and East Anglia, containing the most successful new and expanding towns. Outside these belts some rural areas and service-based towns also grew.

It was the inner cities that suffered the worst job losses; suburban and fringe areas have experienced only small employment declines or even slight increases in numbers employed (Hasluck 1987). The length of this process is apparent in table 9.6. Outer city areas experienced a reduction in employment only during the decade 1971–81, and even then at a much lower rate than the inner areas. A similar, though smaller, reduction in employment afflicted the free-standing cities; small urban places and rural areas, in contrast, had continuous growth in jobs, a net increase of nearly 2.5 million in the thirty years after 1951.

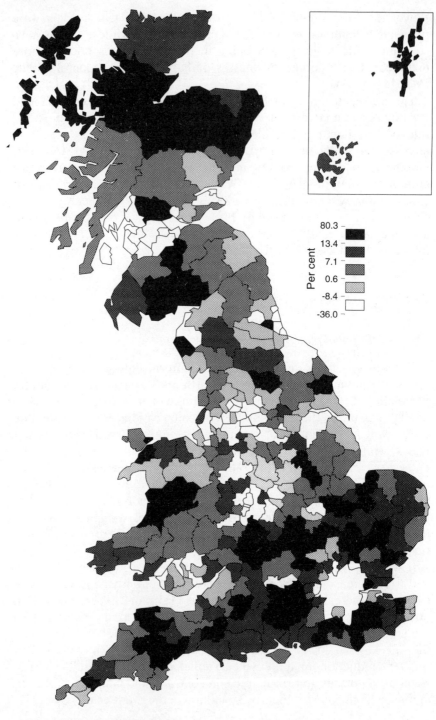

Source: Champion *et al.* (1987), fig. 5.2.

FIG. 9.3. Employment change by LLMA, 1971–1981

Table 9.6. Changes in employment, 1951–1981

	Inner cities		Outer cities		Free-standing cities		Small towns and rural areas		Great Britain	
	'000s	%	'000s	%	'000s	%	'000s	%	'000s	%
Manufacturing										
1951–61	−143	−8.0	+84	+5.0	−21	−2.0	+453	+14.0	+374	+5.0
1961–71	−428	−26.1	−217	−10.3	−93	−6.2	+489	+12.5	−255	−3.9
1971–81	−447	−36.8	−480	−32.6	−311	−28.6	−717	−17.2	−1929	−24.5
Private services										
1951–61	+192	+11.0	+110	+11.0	+128	+17.0	+514	+16.0	+944	+14.0
1961–71	−297	−15.3	+92	+8.1	−7	−0.8	+535	+14.5	+318	+4.2
1971–81	−105	−6.4	+170	+17.3	+91	+10.9	+805	+24.8	+958	+14.4
Public services										
1951–61	+13	+1.0	+54	+7.0	+38	+6.0	+200	+8.0	+302	+6.0
1961–71	+25	+2.0	+170	+21.6	+110	+17.7	+502	+17.3	+807	+14.5
1971–81	−78	−7.4	+102	+8.8	+53	+6.5	+456	+14.1	+488	+7.7
Total employment										
1951–61	+43	+1.0	+231	+6.0	+140	+6.0	+1060	+10.0	+1490	+7.0
1961–71	−643	−14.8	−19	+0.6	+54	+2.4	+1022	+8.5	+320	+1.3
1971–81	+538	−14.6	+236	−7.1	−150	+5.4	+404	+3.5	+590	−1.7

Source: Hasluk 1987.

Recession and redundancy

The pattern of redundancies which has led to these job losses has been charted for 1976–81 by Townsend (1982) and Peck (1984), using official data and information derived from other sources, including press announcements. Major job losses first occurred in peripheral regions; all areas had been affected by 1980, though South-East England and East Anglia were hit least. All sectors of the economy suffered. Between 1977 and 1979 widespread job losses occurred in steel, shipbuilding, vehicle manufacturing, mechanical engineering, textiles, leather, clothing, and footwear. By 1980 these and many other industries, including rubber, linoleum, watches and clocks, sound reproducers, and agricultural machinery were laying off staff: indeed all ten of the country's leading private corporations had announced redundancies.

Although the greatest losses were geographically concentrated on a small number of areas, especially those dependent on steel, Merseyside, Clydeside, and Tyne and Wear, the redundancy process had, by 1980, reached 'small town' England, often regarded as the principal new location of growth enterprise. Furthermore, in contrast to previous recessions, that of the early 1980s did not lead to the hoarding of skills (Gillespie and Owen 1981). Although manual workers were hardest hit, there was a tendency for all occupation types to be affected, with larger numbers of redundancies than before among professional and managerial workers.

Employment change in the 1980s

The middle years of the 1980s saw a substantial recovery in employment. From 1984 to 1987 the number of employees recorded in the Census of Employment grew by 2 per cent (425,000). Service sector employees increased by 6 per cent (793,000), while there were reductions of 4 per cent (219,000) in manufacturing (DE 1989). Regional estimates from the Department of Employment show that from September 1984 to March 1988 employment nationally increased by 2.9 per cent (table 9.7). The North-West, Wales, and Scotland fell back. The biggest increase was easily that of East Anglia, with the West and East Midlands both outstripping the South-East—where lower than average gains in London kept the regional total down.

The data confirm that the UK has become a service economy, at least in employment terms. The trend of employment away from manufacturing has continued, only East Anglia gaining, by a massive 12 per

Table 9.7. Regional employment change, 1984–1988 (%)

Region	Total employment	Manufacturing employment	Services employment
South-East	4.6	−9.0	9.7
Greater London	1.8	−11.0	5.3
East Anglia	14.8	12.1	19.2
South-West	1.2	−3.7	4.6
West Midlands	5.1	−2.8	11.7
East Midlands	5.0	−0.2	12.6
Yorkshire and Humberside	2.1	−8.6	11.0
North-West	−1.4	−10.5	3.8
North	3.4	−5.5	10.0
Wales	−2.3	−1.0	1.4
Scotland	−1.9	−10.9	3.4
Great Britain	2.9	−6.1	8.6

Source: *Employment Gazette* (various dates).

cent. There have been universal gains in service employment, which offset falls in manufacturing in most regions. East Anglia was again the economic leader, but the Midlands (East and West), Yorkshire, and Humberside and the North had double figure gains. The modest performance of the South-East—only just above the national rate—was largely due to the sluggish growth of London. Things were worst in Wales, Scotland, and the North-West, where growth in services has been too little to compensate for declines in manufacturing.

9.4 Unemployment: The Mismatch of Work-Force and Jobs

The post-war pattern

For a couple of decades after the Second World War it appeared that Keynesian economics (in the consensus form of 'Butskellism') had laid to rest the high levels of unemployment that had characterized the 1930s. Although the demand for labour continued to be weaker in the older industrial areas, where coal mining, textiles, and shipbuilding continued to rule, on the national scale unemployment levels remained low, generally between 1 and 2 per cent. Only in the 1952/3, 1958/9, and 1962/3 recessions did it rise above 2 per cent and it took the severe winter of 1963, on top of a recession, to bring the rate to over 3 per cent, with some 850,000 out of work.

Table 9.8. Unemployment rate in Great Britain, 1929–1963 (%)

(*a*)

Region	1929	1932	1937
London	4.9	13.2	5.8
South-East	4.0	13.4	5.2
South-West	7.0	16.6	6.5
Midlands	9.8	21.6	7.2
North-East	}12.7	}30.7	11.5
North			15.8
North-West	12.9	25.9	13.1
Scotland	11.2	28.8	16.3
Wales	18.5	38.8	19.9
Great Britain	9.7	22.7	10.0

(*b*)

Region	April 1949	April 1963
London and South-East	1.2	1.6
Eastern and Southern	1.3	1.9
South-West	1.5	2.1
Midland	0.7	2.1
North Midland	0.7	2.1
East and West Ridings	0.9	2.1
North-West	1.7	3.3
North	2.7	5.1
Scotland	3.1	5.2
Wales	4.0	3.9
Great Britain	1.6	2.7

Source: *Ministry of Labour Gazette* (various dates).

Despite full employment in Britain as a whole—but not in Northern Ireland—striking regional inequalities continued to exist (table 9.8), although rates were on nothing like the scale of those of the inter-war years. Nevertheless, in relative terms the depressed areas of the North and West continued to be as badly off compared with Southern England as they had been before the war. Throughout the late 1960s and 1970s national unemployment continued to rise. After each recession rates never fell to previous levels so each new surge started from a higher base (figure 9.4). The most rapid and sustained increase took place in the early 1980s, 1.8 million becoming unemployed

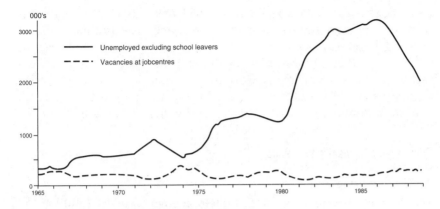

Note: 3-monthly moving average, seasonally adjusted.

Source: Salt 1985; Employment Gazette (various dates).

FIG. 9.4. Unemployment and vacancies in the UK, 1965–1988

between the end of 1979 and early in 1983. Numbers out of work continued to rise more slowly until spring 1986, peaking at over 3.3 million. Since then there has been a steady decline, to 1.6 million by the end of 1989, though strict comparisons over time are not possible owing to changes in counting procedures. It is likely that these figures understate the number of Britons without work. The Labour Force Survey in 1984 estimated that 870,000 people were seeking work but not claiming benefit, and hence were not included in the official unemployment count; perhaps half a million more were in government-funded temporary employment schemes. Conversely, it is known that a large though unspecified number of claimants are actually in work, so undercounting may not be as serious as was thought.

During the 1950s and 1960s unemployment was seen as essentially a regional problem, focused on the traditional depressed areas of the Northern coalfields. In the 1970s the emphasis switched to regarding unemployment as primarily an urban problem. Explanations were sought which stressed the structural characteristics of individuals (Metcalf 1975, Metcalf and Richardson 1978) and skills (Evans and Richardson 1980). During successive recessions a convergence of regional experience occurred as areas hitherto largely untouched by unemployment began to suffer. Even by 1973 warning bells were ringing for the West Midlands, and some more remote rural areas in East Anglia and the South-West became unemployment black spots (Salt 1975).

The rise in unemployment during the 1980s coincided with a fall in jobs of nearly two million between 1979 and 1983. Even when employment began to increase again from 1983 onwards it was insufficient to offset the increasing size of the work-force. The problem was the growing mismatch between the nature of new jobs created and the labour to fill them. The new employment of the middle 1980s has been especially for women, many working part-time, in service industries. Self-employment has also increased. In contrast, jobs lost in the recession were dominated by those occupied by men working full time.

British unemployment in the 1980s

Stocks and flows

By October 1990 total registered unemployment was 1.67 million (5.9 per cent), down by a million and a half on the high point of three years earlier. Because of its high population, and despite its prosperity, South-East England has the largest concentration of jobless (395,000 in October 1990, of whom 223,000 were in Greater London). Stocks are not static, though. In recent years about a third of a million have joined and left the register each month. These flow figures can be used to estimate the likelihood of citizens in different parts of the country becoming and ceasing to be unemployed. A clear regional division appears: people in South-East England (especially in London) and East Anglia have a below average likelihood of becoming unemployed and a high one of ceasing to be out of work, while the reverse is the case for those in the North of England and Wales (Green 1986).

Who are the British unemployed?

Some groups are more vulnerable to unemployment than others. Joblessness among men is half as high again as it is among women. Those aged under 20 are three times more likely to be out of work than those aged between 30 and 55. Young males suffer particularly badly, nearly three out of ten 18- and 19-year-olds were out of work in 1985. Most of those out of work previously had a job, 89 per cent in 1987 (DE 1988). Change to unemployment among men and single women is generally not their fault, the main reasons being redundancy (40 and 26 per cent respectively) and the ending of a temporary job (23 per cent for both). Among married women, however, family and personal reasons were most important (39 per cent).

High labour force status not surprisingly brings about a lower likelihood of being unemployed (table 9.9). Rates are clearly lower for those in non-manual occupations, highest for unskilled manual workers, with figures ranging from 3 per cent for professional and managerial groups to 21 per cent among general labourers. The level of qualifica-

Table 9.9. Unemployed[a] by occupation, Great Britain, Spring 1987 (%)

All aged 16 and over	Unemployment rate[b]			Occupation distribution of the unemployed[c]		
	Men	Women	All	Men	Women	All
All non-manual	3.7	5.0	4.4	14.3	30.6	20.9
Managerial and professional	3.2	3.6	3.3	9.0	8.6	8.8
Clerical and related	4.5	5.2	5.0	2.1	14.5	7.1
Other non-manual	5.9	7.9	7.0	3.2	7.6	5.0
All manual	9.7	8.3	9.3	46.9	27.1	39.0
Craft and similar	7.5	9.7	7.8	16.9	3.9	11.6
General labourers	21.3	20.3	21.2	2.6	0.3	1.7
Other manual	11.1	8.1	9.8	27.5	22.9	25.7
Never had a paid job	n/a	n/a	n/a	9.9	12.0	10.8
Left last job three or more years ago	n/a	n/a	n/a	28.7	30.1	29.3
All occupations	11.0	10.1	10.6	100	100	100
(thousands)				1,717	1,161	2,879

[a] ILO/OECD definition.
[b] Current or previous occupation.
[c] Previous occupation of those who left their last job less than three years ago.
n/a Not applicable.
Source: Labour Force Survey

tions held helps explain these variations. The better educated exhibit a much stronger labour force position (figure 9.5). The overall pattern of falling unemployment rates as qualifications increase broadly holds in all age-groups. Unqualified youths experience particular problems, their rates approaching a third. Time spent out of work is affected by qualifications too. The better educated spend shorter periods out of work: only 30 per cent of unemployed graduates or equivalent had been out of work for a year compared with over half of those unemployed who had no qualifications at all. Duration of unemployment is also related to age: only 11 per cent of 16–24-year-olds had been out of work for more than three years, rising to 35 per cent of the over-45s.

The geography of unemployment

Unemployment is very unevenly spread across the country (table 9.10). It is significant that over the period from 1976 to 1988 the ranking of

Table 9.10. Regional unemployment rates, 1976–1988

Region	1976			1984			1988		
	%	Rank	Ratio to nat. rate	%	Rank	Ratio to nat. rate	%	Rank	Ratio to nat. rate
North	7.2	2	1.31	18.1	2	1.38	12.3	2	1.46
Yorkshire and Humberside	5.3	8	0.96	14.3	7	1.09	9.8	6	1.17
East Midlands	4.5	10	0.82	12.1	8	0.92	7.5	8	0.89
East Anglia	4.7	9	0.85	10.1	10	0.77	5.0	11	0.59
South-East	4.0	11	0.73	9.6	11	0.73	5.4	10	0.65
South-West	6.2	6	1.13	11.5	9	0.88	6.3	9	0.75
West Midlands	5.5	7	1.00	15.2	5	1.16	9.0	7	1.07
North-West	6.7	4	1.22	16.0	4	1.22	10.9	4	1.30
Wales	7.1	3	1.29	16.2	3	1.24	10.6	5	1.26
Scotland	6.7	4	1.22	15.2	5	1.16	11.6	3	1.38
Northern Ireland	9.5	1	1.73	21.0	1	1.60	16.6	1	1.98
UK	5.5			13.1			8.4		

Source: Employment Gazette (various dates).

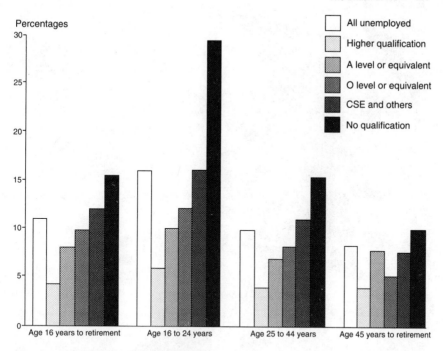

Note: Unemployment rates: ILO/OECD definition.

Source: Employment Gazette, Oct. 1988

FIG. 9.5. Unemployment rates by age and highest qualification in Great Britain, spring 1987

regional unemployment rates shows a basically stable pattern, despite all economic vicissitudes. Some trends are visible, though. Yorkshire and Humberside and the South-West have steadily deteriorated relative to other regions, East Anglia has steadily improved, by 1988 displacing the South-East as the region of lowest unemployment. Economic improvement during the four years since 1984 has seen the position of the West Midlands and Wales improve in terms of their unemployment rankings, while Scotland has got worse. Comparison of the ratio of regional with national rates shows evidence of the polarization nationally. Substantial relative improvements have occurred in East Anglia, the South-East, and the South-West, while the reverse is the case for the North, North-West Scotland, and especially Northern Ireland.

These regional totals hide considerable local variations in rates of unemployment (figure 9.6). People living in the traditional depressed areas are still at a disadvantage; in contrast, there is a broad belt of prosperity across southern England, interestingly the area of Britain that was traditionally the most populous and prosperous up to the

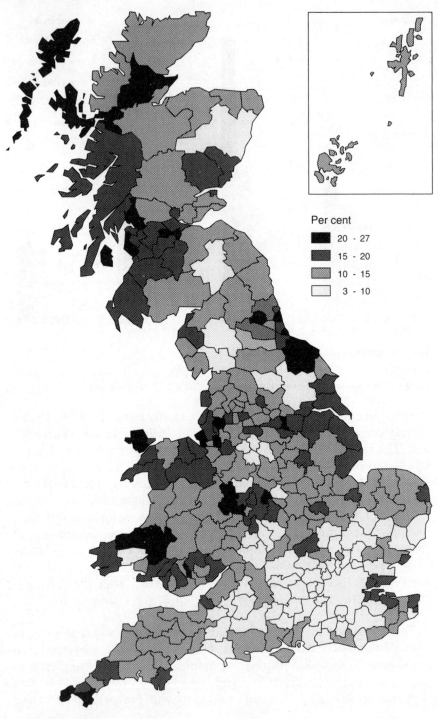

Source: Green 1986

FIG. 9.6. Annual average unemployment rate by LLMA, 1984

Industrial Revolution. The rural flanks of the Pennines and eastern Scotland have also done well, a comment on the economic as well as demographic rise of 'small town' Britain, and on the power of North Sea oil developments.

Cities have done less well, especially their inner areas. Census data show that at ward level unemployment rates may be two or three times higher for urban cores than for outer areas (DoE 1976, Evans and Eversley 1980, Hasluck 1987). However, quite large variations exist between the major conurbations in the proportions of their populations in the wards with the highest unemployment rates nationally. London easily fares the best; worst hit has been Liverpool, then Glasgow, with Birmingham, Manchester, and Newcastle intermediate (Owen, Gillespie and Coombes 1984). Clearly, as well as the familiar North–South geographical division, unemployment is also related to urban size and function.

Those in the South are again at an advantage over their more northern compatriots when it comes to time spent out of work. During 1979–83 the lowest proportions of long-term unemployed occurred in a belt to the south, west, and north of London, with an outlier in northern Scotland. High levels of long-term unemployment occur mostly north and west of a line from the Severn to the Wash, and the conurbations and their satellites in these regions have particularly suffered. Functionally it is in the largest cities (excluding London), together with many smaller places with a manufacturing focus, that the worst long-term problems have occurred, while peripheral rural areas, together with towns concentrating on service employment, have done better (Green 1984).

9.5 Work for Future Britons?

What happens in the future is conjectural, depending more than anything on the effect of employing new technologies. Jenkins and Sherman (1979) reckoned there would be five million unemployed by the end of the century, whether new technology was embraced or not. The Science Policy Research Unit at the University of Sussex thought that figure would be reached by 1990. Others are more optimistic, rejecting the view that new technologies will destroy jobs (Minford 1983). It is clear that much depends upon the speed at which new technologies are introduced, and the comparative rates of job loss in existing production and the development of new products (Central Policy Review Staff 1978; B. Jones 1982; Williams 1985; and many more).

What is clear is that the introduction of new technologies, in the form or robotics, automation, and word processing, has the power to do away with jobs. In France the Nora Report (Nora and Minc 1978), for example, concluded that the installation of new computer systems in banking would lead to 30 per cent reductions in personnel over ten years. Office activities generally are now thought to be undercapitalized, much of their activity being the sort of routine operations that can be computerized and word processed (Stonier 1982; Rowe 1986). Much of the loss of employment in manufacturing in recent years can be put down to new processes of production which have led to the 'vanishing middle' of the work-force. The introduction of high technology manufacturing has led to fewer skilled and semi-skilled manual workers, but more in the scientific, professional, and technical categories.

New industries based on new information technologies hold out some hope for job creation. But it has to be admitted that so far the prognostication is not promising. One Japanese study in 1979, quoted by B. Jones (1982), concluded that although computer software engineering would have annual growth rates of 15–35 per cent up to the mid-1980s, micro-electronics would reduce employmemt by up to half a million jobs. Markusen (1986) calculated for the USA that job increases in new high technology industries might create three million extra jobs 1980–90, but that figure would pale before the estimated 25 million jobs needed to compensate for those expected to be displaced by high technology.

Evidence from the UK is no more optimistic. Between 1971 and 1981 employment in new information technology producing industries (including radio, telecommunications, radar) fell by 12 per cent; older information technology industries, such as paper, printing, and publishing, fell by 14 per cent. Information technology service industries, such as computing and other information-related activities, in contrast, expanded by 17.5 per cent (table 9.11). Overall the employment-creating prospects of new information technology industries are unlikely to be great. During 1978–83 they managed a 35 per cent increase in output with a 16 per cent fall in employment (Preston *et al.* 1985). There is now growing evidence that during the 1960s growth of labour productivity 'caught up' with the growth of output. This seems also to be happening to new information technology industries. Up to 1970 their output growth averaged 7.2 per cent per year, while employment went up 3.7 per cent per year; during the 1970s output increased by 3.4 per cent per year but employment was virtually unchanged; from 1975 to 1981 output managed a 2.7 per cent gain each year but employment declined by an annual 4.2 per cent. New information technology

Table 9.11. Employment change in IT industrial sectors: total employees in employment, Great Britain, 1971–1981

	1971	1976	1981	1971–81 Change	% Employment Change 1971–81
New IT producing industries	561,497	512,683	492,632	−68,865	−12.26
Old IT producing industries	487,499	439,089	420,190	−67,309	−13.81
IT service industries					
New & Old IT producing industries & IT service industries	711,767	736.249	836,290	+124,523	+17.49
	1,760,763	1,688,021	1,749,112	−11,651	−0.56
Total employment in all industries in GB	21,637,883	22,037,268	21,092,016	−545,867	−2.52

Notes: Classified according to SIC68. 'New IT Producing Industries' = SIC 1968 MLHs 338, 351, 354, 363, 364, 365, 366, 367. 'Old IT Producing Industries' = SIC 1968 MLHs 481, 483, 495, 485, 486, 489. IT Service Industries = 1968 MLHs 708, 865, 881.

Source: Preston *et al.* (1985).

industries, which in earlier generations would have been seen as the driving force for manufacturing employment growth, now seem to have entered a period of 'jobless growth'.

What will happen in the 1990s and beyond is uncertain. Already some employers are complaining of shortages of skilled workers, but there is little sign of a surge in demand for a mass labour force of at best moderate skills. Even for highly skilled staff, most employers are able to recruit whom they need, though some complain about lack of choice (Salt 1990*a*). The demand that has occurred in the middle 1980s has been particularly for part-time workers, and the supply has been married women especially. The new international spatial division of labour favours new investment by multinational corporations in cheap-labour-rich newly industrialized countries, and not in those like the UK which are highly industrialized (Frobel *et al.* 1980). As it happens, the worst prognostications of the late 1970s have not yet been borne out, which is itself a measure of the degree of uncertainty with which we can plan the work future of the next generation.

10 Internal Migration

10.1 Introduction

We have already seen that over the last decade rates of natural increase in the UK have fallen to low levels. In these circumstances the role of internal migration in affecting regional and local population distributions and structures is enhanced.

The British people turn out to be more mobile than one might expect, though not so much as their American cousins. Rees (1979), using regional data for 1970–1, has calculated that during a lifetime each individual Briton is likely to make 7–11 migrations with 5–10 of these being within their region and only 1–2 between regions. These ranges reflect the higher mobility rates associated with some regions. East Anglians are the most mobile, the Welsh the least.

Long-distance movement between cities and regions is particularly significant in changing the population map. In so far as this involves members of the work-force and their families we may call it labour migration, defined as migration over distances long enough to involve a simultaneous change of both home and job location (Johnson, Salt, and Wood 1974).

Labour migration is intimately bound up with how much commuting people can stand. Generally speaking, workers will seek job and home locations with relatively easy access to each other. In reality the locations chosen represent a series of compromises; for example, between housing and commuting costs, between preference for centrality or serenity, between the divergent journeys to work or school of members of the same household. Various studies have shown changing patterns of journey to work since data became available in 1921 (Lawton 1968). Until 1961 commuting was very much tied in to the cores of major urban places but counter-urbanization in the 1970s created a more diffuse pattern with less emphasis on radial movement. By the late 1980s it seemed that, in southern England at any rate, commuting patterns may have undergone another sea change, related to astronomical house prices where jobs were available and to easier accessibility to cheaper housing areas through road and rail improvements. The 'Roseland' phenomenon extended way beyond the Home Counties (ROSE is planners' jargon for the Rest of the South-East).

But the collapse of the housing market in 1989, as well as higher rail fares for long-distance commuters, may well have changed the pattern yet again, perhaps encouraging some to relocate both their homes and jobs outside the South-East, others to stay put.

Commuting patterns have been used for a range of definitions of functional urban areas seen as constituting housing market and labour market areas (Chapter 3) and also containing within them the household's principal activity space for education, shopping, entertainment, and the like. Migration between such areas thus represents a move from one economic and social milieu to another and is likely to bring major changes to the household's activity pattern.

10.2 The Significance of Inter-Urban Migration

With little or no natural increase (Chapter 4) anything but equal exchanges of migrants must inevitably result in some areas losing people. Gross flows also have a regional impact through turnover. Where it is high there will be more housing and job vacancies and thus more choice for potential migrants. Service provision will also be affected. The British penchant for mobility means that population structures are affected by the selective nature of flows. Coastal resorts are well known as centres of retirement, though increasingly they are attracting a younger population. New towns have been associated with high birth-rates and young families because of their traditional attraction to couples in the most fertile age ranges, although the early new towns are now ageing places.

The effects of migration on both origin and destination areas manifest themselves in various ways. Local authority finance was affected by changes in numbers of ratepayers, as it is by those paying a community charge. Migration has had to be taken into account in the calculation of rate support grant from central government and in the allocation of funds to Regional Health Authorities. Service provision may need to adjust to variable numbers of children or elderly; one of the key determinants in forecasting primary school rolls, for example, is an estimate of the level of net migration of under-5s. Land-use planning policies are influenced by migration. Estimates of inter-regional migration in the OPCS population projections are incorporated into the official Household Projections by the Department of the Environment (DoE 1988), which have a key role in the structure plan and planning appeals process. The allocation of investment in housing is sensitive to migration flows, either locally within regions or between them (Congdon and Champion 1989). Hence, new pressures on land allocation may be created by migration growth areas such as the arc to the west and north of London. Prospectively too, labour migration may become potentially more important to cope with spatial mismatches in the employment market. Economic change in the 1980s has demonstrated that the locational requirements of new jobs do not match those lost so some spatial adjustment in the form of labour migration is necessary. Overheating of job and housing markets for some occupational and residential groups in Southern England is testament to this process.

10.3 Data Sources

There are many things we do not know about migration patterns and processes among the British people. Data sources are poor. There is no population registration system in the UK which might provide continuous detail, though the introduction of a community charge register will create one until its abolition in 1993.

The census

The census has become a useful source for internal migration study only comparatively recently. Before 1961 only birthplace and place of usual residence were recorded, making it possible to study only 'lifetime' movement. Since 1961 respondents have been asked to identify their place of residence one and five years earlier (only one year earlier in 1981 and 1991) making it possible for the first time to provide a reasonably accurate picture of movement. The use of census data is not without its pitfalls. For example, no account is taken of intermediate moves between the two recorded addresses, and there are omissions such as infants, those who have migrated and died, and those resident at the same address at each census but who have moved between. These problems are more likely to affect five-year than one-year data and the former are more likely to be devalued by recall failure among respondents. The periodicity of the census may also present a misleading picture of long-term trends, for example because of economic conditions at the time the census was taken.

The National Health Service central register

Since 1971 an additional published data source has become available from the National Health Service, based on re-registrations of patients moving between doctors in different Family Practitioner Committee areas. A 10 per cent sample of these is used to produce a matrix of interregional moves, disaggregated by age and sex since 1975. These figures provide an indication of internal migration flows within the UK which OPCS considers reliable, though there are some problems. There is no record of movers who do not register; some people may move short distances—even across regional boundaries—but keep the same doctor. There is also a lag, assumed to be three months, between moving and registering. Finally, the data are not accurate at much below the level of standard regions, though from 1984 information for metropolitan counties was provided until their abolition. Thus for inter-urban movement the census remains the sole published source. The NHS series fills a valuable role in indicating trends in volume and movement between regions (Ogilvy 1979, 1980, 1982; Stillwell 1983; Stillwell and Boden 1989). A comparison of migration data from the NHS register and the 1981 census shows the former to record 28 per cent more moves than the census for the twelve-month period, but that after adjustments the difference falls to only 3 per cent (Devis and Mills 1986).

Surveys

Although the census and NHS data provide some indication of migrant characteristics, though not at a local scale, the level of detail they come up with is partial. There is nothing on motivation or on migrant perceptions of gains and losses from movement. For information on these it is necessary to rely upon independent surveys characterized more than anything else by their thinness on the ground. Most survey data on migrants are, like the census, cross-sectional, recording mover characteristics at one time. Such information is extremely valuable but ultimately can only give us a partial view of the complex web of events surrounding the decision to go and the move itself. For recent years in particular, we are ill-served with even this information on the mobile British.

Migrant surveys in Britain fall into two main categories. The first obtains migrant information as a by-product of a survey for another purpose, the second sets out specifically to identify migrants and their characteristics but does not always specify the distance moved.

During the 1950s and 1960s data on migrants tended to come from surveys of housing conditions (Donnison et al. 1964; Cullingworth 1965; Woolf 1967) or of marriage patterns (Friedlander and Roshier 1966a, 1966b). By their nature such surveys fail to differentiate long and short distance movement, an important distinction when trying to assess motivation, which is known to be related to distance moved:

housing reasons, for example, are associated primarily with local residential moves, employment reasons for longer distance ones. Only three published surveys, two primarily of migrants, have allowed the nature of long-distance movers to be identified (Friedlander and Roshier, 1966a, 1966b; Harris and Clausen 1967; Johnson, Salt, and Wood 1974).

The first post-war survey of migrants related to the period 1953–63, and included a nationwide sample of 19,000. Its large size precluded much detail on migrant characteristics, motivation, and perception; most respondents were local movers and detail on inter-urban migrants was sketchy (Harris and Clausen 1967). As the 1980s drew to a close it was surprising that still the only detailed survey specifically of the characteristics and motives of inter-urban migrants was the Housing and Labour Mobility Study, carried out in 1972 (Johnson, Salt, and Wood 1974). Other studies have collected data on various aspects of inter-urban movement. Law and Warnes (1980, 1982) and Karn (1977) have looked at the retirement migration of the elderly in selected locations; Jones et al. (1986) have surveyed English and Welsh migrants to remote areas in Northern Scotland; Deakin and Ungerson (1977) studied migrants from inner London to Milton Keynes in the early 1970s while Mann (1973), Salt (1984, 1990b), and Atkinson (1987) have looked at aspects of employee transfers associated with corporate relocation. The characteristics of people moving in association with the government's Employment Transfer Scheme during the 1970s have been reported by Parker (1975) and for Scotland by Beaumont (1976).

Compiling a consistent picture of the nature of British internal migration from these surveys is not easy. A particular difficulty is in relating distance and motivation, as demonstrated by Gordon (1979) for example. The surveys lack comparability in sample size, design, questionnaire detail, timing, and aims and they vary in their spatial coverage. By their very nature they are expensive (finding labour migrants is difficult—see Johnson, Salt, and Wood (1974)). Unless specific local areas are sampled coverage is too thin for anything but macro-regional comparisons to be made, as demonstrated by the Harris and Clausen study. That rich local variations occur was clear from the Housing and Labour Migration Study which distinguished sharp differences in migrant characteristics, motivations, and perceptions in the four localities studied (Chatham, High Wycombe, Huddersfield, and Northampton).

The focus in most surveys on cross-section data restricts the use to be made of the information collected. It is difficult to put the move into some kind of temporal sequence despite the emphasis in much of the literature on life cycle and career paths, which imply a distinct time element. What is required is more longitudinal data which will allow migration to be placed in the context of a series of events. The general lack of longitudinal data is a major vacuum in understanding British migration yet the importance of this approach is apparent when we see that previous migration history is closely related to subsequent movement: those who have moved once are more likely to move again (Johnson, Salt, and Wood 1974; Gleave and Cordey-Hayes 1977).

Published sources providing biographical details which include migrations are minimal. The only such source in this country is for the clergy for whom *Crockford's Clerical Directory* provides enough information to establish the career and migration patterns of individuals. There is some hope that longitudinal migration studies will become more common. As the length of the Longitudinal Study set up by OPCS increases it should enable deeper insights into the processes at work, although at the moment it is still essentially a cross-section source on migrants. The longitudinal study being compiled by the National Children's Bureau, based on a 1946 birth cohort, may ultimately allow complete migration histories to be built up.

Thus far migration data have been discussed from the 'supply' side, and have related directly to migrants themselves. A source of data, used with profit in the Organizational Labour Migration Study, comes from the transfer records of large multi-location employers, the 'demand' side of the labour market (Salt 1984, 1990*b*). Most employers have records of their annual patterns of staff relocation. Their employee record cards usually contain details of all job changes, including geographical transfers, while working in the organization. The advantage of these data is that not only do they provide information on individual migrants but they allow analysis also of the work context in which migration occurs. This is a valuable perspective in a country where migration opportunities are, as we shall see, becoming increasingly polarized.

10.4 The Composition of Migrant Flows

General characteristics of migrants in Britain

The selective nature of the migration process means that at any one time migrants in Britain are different from the population as a whole. Additionally, migrants differ from each other in their motivation and distance moved. In consequence migration does not always have similar effects on origin and destination communities and areas.

At the risk of over-simplifying we can divide the mobile British into those whose moves are associated with life-cycle changes and those whose moves are dominated by career circumstances. Life-cycle migration is related to attributes of the household, including marital status, age, size, and composition. These change over time, bringing about conditions in which propensity to migrate increases. Cullingworth (1965) related the life cycle of a family to its housing circumstances; migration occurs in response to changing dwelling needs as households expand and then contract in size, beginning with fission from the parental household and ending with retirement. That most Britons move short distances shows how much migration follows the housing cycle: why move to a new environment just to get a bigger house? Career migration is a response to the occupational structure of migrants, including education, skill, income, type of employer, and the nature of the work being performed. As individuals proceed from job to job geographical career mobility may occur. Younger workers are generally more mobile while seniority tends to reduce movement, though much depends on career development and planning.

Limited information from the census and NHS register, together with details from surveys, gives us a passable picture of the sort of Britons who have been on the move in the last quarter century. Migrants over all distances are more likely to be younger than older, conforming to a migration rate/age schedule which shows a declining propensity to move during childhood followed by an increase, normally peaking in the late 20s, then a steady decline, perhaps interrupted by retirement migration in the 60s (Stillwell 1983). Census and NHS data show that 1966–71 and 1975–83 total movement was dominated by the 15–29 age-group which, on a proportional basis, had more than its share. The recession of the early 1980s had some effect on the age structure of migrants: between 1975/6 and 1982/3 mobility among the 0–14 age-group fell by over a quarter, the next largest falls being among the late middle-aged (45–64). Age-groups between these two fluctuated in mobility rates except for the 15–25s, who showed a consistent rise (Stillwell and Boden 1989).

With whom we live also affects our mobility. Larger households are more likely to be mobile than smaller ones, though this relationship is less clear for those moving long distances (Cullingworth 1965; Woolf 1967). Johnson, Salt, and Wood (1974) found that young families, couples without children, and unmarried adults were the labour migrants with the highest movement rates. Household type and socio-economic group combine to affect migration propensity: large households headed by manual workers are less likely to be mobile between local authority areas than those headed by non-manual workers (Friedlander and Roshier 1966a, 1966b). Marriage seems to slow us up. Single people have a higher propensity to move over long distances than those married, while census evidence for 1971–81 suggests that declining mobility over all distances has been less marked among non-married or never-married people than among the population as a whole, a feature that may reflect the growing incidence of divorce (Johnson, Salt, and Wood 1974; OPCS 1983b).

More discriminating characteristics in long-distance movement are those of education and employment. Those who have spent longer before the blackboard seem more aware of opportunities elsewhere, and their academic achievements ease them into occupations whose labour markets are geographically more extensive. All surveys are agreed that the higher the educational level reached the greater the propensity to migrate. Friedlander and Roshier (1966a) found that the grammar school educated were twice as mobile as those who were not; 71 per cent of those with a university education in Harris and Clausen's (1967) sample had moved in the previous ten years compared with less than 50 per cent of those with no higher education; Johnson, Salt, and Wood (1974) showed that labour migrants were far better qualified than the rest of the population.

From education flows wealth. It follows that level of education reached is closely related to employment and income. All surveys have demonstrated that higher socio-economic groups are over-represented among migrants and that there is an increasing propensity to move with rising income (Willis 1970, Woolf 1967, Cullingworth 1965). In the Housing and Labour Mobility Study only 3 per cent of the sample of long-distance migrants had been unemployed before moving and professional, managerial, and other non-manual workers were more strongly represented among migrants than in the population as a whole. Self-employed professional workers were the exception, probably the result of non-transportable 'capital' like clients. Labour migrants also earn more than the population as a whole. Wealthier households moving between cities move longer distances than poorer ones, a fact consistent with the location of high-paying occupations in large employment nodes at some distance from one another. The employment characteristics of migrants in recent decades thus suggest that they are well-off, work in high status occupations, and are not unemployed, features that seem likely to continue in the 1990s as will be seen below.

These characteristics are bolstered by job information systems that facilitate movement among the better-off. Employment search and recruitment methods vary significantly between occupation, industry,

and gender groups (Mackay *et al.* 1971), and there is a strong relationship between the vacancy advertising policies of employers and
migration to fill them (Saunders 1985). Those who are most mobile,
higher paid salaried workers, take part in national information systems
which put them into contact with job vacancies in other parts of the
country. In contrast, lower status occupational vacancies are advertised
only locally and attract applications almost entirely from the immediate
environs.

Other characteristics of migrants have been found to relate to migration propensity beyond the local area. Someone who has moved once is
more likely to move again, so that students leaving home to enter
higher education may be embarking on a more migratory life history
than those attending a local institution. In a different context, Taylor
(1969) found that in Durham mining communities out-migrants were
more likely to have prior mobility than those left behind. In a very real
sense, therefore, migration breeds migration, creating in the British
population a mobile élite which is superimposed on a large and generally immobile mass. Evidence suggests that this dichotomy is tending
to become more pronounced as employers increasingly subsidize the
moves of those staff they transfer around the country (Salt 1990*b*).

Characteristics of migrants within the urban system

A number of studies, mainly during the 1970s, focused on the migration
process within the urban system and especially on its relationship to
the decentralization of population, discussed in Chapter 3. Migration
was found to be a potent force in changing the character of urban
places, due to its highly selective nature. Its overall effect was to reduce
the proportion of upper SEGs in cities, leaving behind an urban core
population characterized by below average income and with relatively
high proportions of both young and old.

During 1965–6 and 1970–1 many big cities lost a lot of children and
those aged 30–65 while expanding their proportions of elderly and
15–29-year-olds (Redcliff-Maud 1969, Hall *et al.* 1973, DoE 1976,
Gilje 1975, Dugmore 1975, Spence *et al.* 1982). In conurbations as a
whole, and in inner areas in particular, the 1960s trend was for the
working-age population to fall proportionately and absolutely in some
cases (DoE 1976). Decentralization was more a white-collar than a
manual-worker phenomenon (Dugmore 1975, DE 1977, Kennett and
Randolph 1978). However, a larger proportion of unskilled migrants
moved out of the conurbations than in, suggesting the greater significance of counter-flows for the more mobile groups. South-East

Table 10.1. Distances moved by migrants aged over 16 in Great Britain, 1980–1981

Km. moved	Number			Percentage		% of total pop.
	Male	Female	Total	Male	Female	
<20	139,890	148,064	287,954	75.8	77.6	76.7
(<5)	97,003	104,005	201,008	52.6	54.5	53.6
>20	44,575	42,764	87,339	24.2	22.4	23.3
(>80)	26,394	24,287	50,681	14.3	12.7	13.5
TOTAL	184,465	190,828	375,293			

Source: 1981 Census.

England acted as a magnet for migrants in white-collar occupations; even London lost proportionately fewer of them than might have been expected. In general the selective composition of inter-urban flows indicates that the South of Britain experienced disproportionate gains of white-collar workers.

Confirmatory evidence for this tendency comes from Deakin and Ungerson (1977), Mann (1973), and Salt and Flowerdew (1980), the last demonstrating the importance of housing reasons in the decentralization of manual workers. Among white-collar workers an interesting trend during 1966–71 was the attraction of the South-East, and especially of Greater London, for female professional workers, perhaps reflecting the early stirrings of the dual career household.

The socio-economic composition of migration in 1980–1

The most comprehensive view comes from the 1981 census which recorded that 4,980,866 people in Great Britain (9 per cent of the total) had changed their address during the previous year. Distance moved is available only for those aged over 16, about three-quarters of whom moved less than 20 kilometres (table 10.1). Over half went no more than 5 kilometers, a figure consistent with the four miles recorded by the Nationwide Building Society (1983). It can be assumed that those moving short distances do so for housing or other reasons not related to work, although it does not follow that all long-distance moves necessarily result from changes in employment. However, men are slightly more likely than women to move longer distances.

The propensity of different socio-economic groups to migrate is shown in table 10.2, which compares the number of migrants with the

Table 10.2. Migration rate by socio-economic group: British males, 1980–1981

SEG	Migrants: all distances		Migrants over 20 km.		Migrants over 80 km.	
	No.	Rate	No.	Rate	No.	Rate
Professional and managerial	33,828	11.1	11,400	3.7	6,456	2.1
Intermediate/ Junior non-manual	30,855	11.8	8,405	3.2	4,551	1.7
Manual	67,171	8.8	7,580	1.0	4,072	0.5
Others	26,936	12.2	9,826	4.5	6,943	3.2
TOTAL EMPLOYED	158,790	10.2	37,211	2.4	22,022	1.4
Unemployed	23,307	13.2	5,250	3.0	3,358	1.9

Note: Rates are the percentage of economically active who are migrants. SEG categories refer to economic activity after migration.
Source: 1981 census (10% sample).

total economically active population for males over 16. Over all distances moved the unemployed were the most likely to migrate (13.2 per cent), but interpretation of this figure is difficult because of the definition used in the census. It includes those who are not working at the time of the count, but pays no attention to their circumstances or likelihood of getting a job. Junior and intermediate non-manual workers had a slightly higher propensity to migrate (11.8 per cent) than professional and managerial people (11.1 per cent), with manual workers trailing at 8.8 per cent; junior and intermediate non-manual workers and the unemployed also had high propensities to move short distances. Over 20 and over 80 kilometres, professional and managerial workers had higher mobility rates than junior and intermediate non-manual and manual workers. A third of the former group moved over 20 kilometres. Among the 'other SEG' category, the high proportion moving over 20 and over 80 kilometres is accounted for by the inclusion of the military population. The propensity of the unemployed to move over 20 and over 80 kilometres is higher than average on these data—nearly four times as high as manual workers, for example, for moves over 80 kilometres. The explanation for this lies in the inclusion of students and retirees rather than in the tendency of the unemployed to be labour migrants.

The low propensity of the genuinely unemployed to move is evident

Table 10.3. Cross-tabulation of economic status of migrant by distance of move, 1980–1981

Type of move	Self-employed	Employed	Out of work	Inactive	Total
No move	8,580	80,153	8,953	61,158	159,204
	90.9[a]	90.2	83.8	92.4	90.7
Inter-district	407	4,772	895	2,722	8,796
	4.3[a]	5.4	8.4	4.1	5.0
Intraregion	293	2,478	402	1,266	4,439
	3.1[a]	2.8	3.8	1.9	2.5
Interregion	128	1,193	343	779	2,443
	1.4[a]	1.8	3.2	1.2	1.4
Eire	1	10	2	4	17
	0.0[a]	0.0	0.0	0.0	0.0
Rest of world	27	256	93	308	684
	0.3[a]	0.3	0.9	0.5	0.4
TOTAL	9,436	88,862	10,688	66,597	175,583
	5.4[b]	50.6	6.1	37.9	100.0

[a] Percentages of column totals.
[b] Percentages of row totals.
Source: 1981 Labour Force Survey & Green *et al.* (1985).

from table 10.3, which cross-tabulates economic status by type of move during 1980–1 for the sample of persons aged over 16 captured by the Labour Force Survey (Green *et al.* 1985). The bulk of migrants are in employment. A breakdown of similar data for Greater London showed that only a tiny minority of movers to and from the capital were unemployed and seeking work (Salt 1985). Only a small proportion of LFS-recorded migration was interregional, even amongst the most mobile groups: 4.1 per cent of professional and managerial workers moved interregionally during the year compared with 0.5 per cent of manual (Green *et al.* 1985).

The migration of special groups

Two groups in the population with individual migration patterns are the elderly and students. Their migrations are for specific reasons, to retire or to enter higher education, and the consequences of their actions are highly localized and frequently have important implications for social and political life in the areas to which they are attracted.

The elderly

The distribution of the elderly population was indicated in Chapter 3. Between 1951 and 1981 the geographical pattern was generally stable though it is clear that in some areas the proportion of elderly people was increasing more than in others, especially in surburban rings and on the coasts (Warnes and Law 1984).

More than most other groups the distribution of the elderly population reflects the selections inherent in migration processes. In the UK and in other advanced industrial countries the 1960s witnessed increasing movement by the over-60s both in numbers and distance. In 1970–1 about 60,000 people aged over 60 moved interregionally in England and Wales, 5.5 per cent of the age-group and 11 per cent up on 1965–6 (Law and Warnes 1982). Data for individual years of age from age 50 show a generally decreasing migration rate during 1970–1 except for a peaking around age 65–6, with short-distance movement declining more rapidly than long (Warnes 1983). Surveys by Karn (1977) and Law and Warnes (1982) show that the age distributions of those retiring have been fairly consistent over time, indicating that a general lowering of retirement age would shift the retirement migration profile to the left. In that event, retirement destinations could therefore expect flows of progressively younger incomers.

Retirement migrations exhibit distinctive geographical patterns. Their origins and destinations tend to be more concentrated than the rest of the population, especially in the big cities. Greater London has been the biggest source of retirement migration; northwards the rate of out-migration falls (Law and Warnes 1982). Favoured destinations are those most climatically and scenically attractive, accessible, and well serviced.

In some respects retirees are similar to other migrants. Propensity to move is positively related to previous mobility and negatively to the strength of family ties. Retirement migrants are also more likely to be from higher socio-economic groups. The strongest associations with retirement migration appear to be the frequency and distance of residential migration during working age, fondness for the pre-retirement house, infrequency of seeing children at the time of retirement, and whether or not retirement occurred at a relatively youthful age (Law and Warnes 1980).

Unlike labour migrants, for whom work location is a major consideration, the destination decision for those moving upon retirement reflects a new set of opportunities. Karn (1977) found that most of those going to Clacton and Bexhill not only wanted to be by the seaside but also had friends and/or relatives there and were familiar with the place from previous visits. Similar factors applied in Exmouth, though a subsidiary attractive factor was if one spouse was originally from Devon (Glyn-Jones 1975). Law and Warnes (1976) focused on the search procedures of those retiring to North Wales and Dorset, and found that the most important link with the eventual retirement area was earlier holidays, though having friends and relatives in the new area was also important. Search procedures were also related to age and second-home ownership. Young retirees searched more widely, while a second home meant that for many no other areas were considered. A third of their sample had not thought about retirement migration until within five years of the event and this tended to narrow down the area of search. Married couples were less constrained than single people, reflected in a willingness to search more widely.

A major social question now causing concern is how far migration is creating a spatial dissociation of the elderly from the rest of the population. Retirement migration may remove parents from proximity to children; alternatively children may move away, perhaps for employment-based reasons. Since adult children are always likely to be more mobile than their parents it is their moves and characteristics which will have most influence on mutual residential separation (Warnes 1983). Not surprisingly, therefore, non-manual children are more likely than manual to live long distances from their parents. This spatial dissociation has important social consequences. Warnes found a very strong relationship between distance and frequency of visiting and one in five retired people in his sample wanted to live nearer their children.

Students

In any year a lot of students are on the move to and from centres of higher education. Because of the tradition of leaving home, especially among those going to universities, the geography of student migration differs from that of other groups. Unfortunately there is little information on detailed patterns. In the most comprehensive study, Rees (1986) found the average distance moved by a sample of 69,631 university students leaving home was 193 km.

The geography of student migration reflects the regional level of demand, itself a response to the size of the recruitment age-group and social class. Supply side factors include course availability and reputation, supply of places, university and locality attractiveness, individual perception, grant availability, and so on. The pattern of flows from home to university region shows a high level of migration of the recruit-

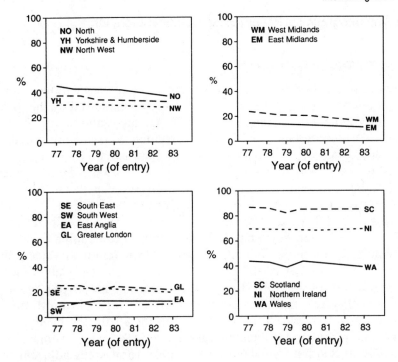

Source: Rees 1986.

Fɪɢ. **10.1.** Percentages of accepted candidates entering universities in their own region

ment age-group. In figure 10.1 the percentage of accepted candidates entering universities in their own region is variable but generally low. Northern Ireland and Scotland have the highest rates of self-containment, around 70 per cent and 90 per cent respectively. In contrast, only 20 per cent or fewer of students from Greater London, the South-East, East Anglia, and the South-West receive their higher education locally. During 1977–83 there was a steadily increasing propensity to migrate to a distant rather than a local university. In consequence the average distance of migration increased and the frictional effect of distance fell for almost all origin and destination regions (Rees 1986).

The migratory tendency among large numbers of the nation's intellectual young has important implications for future migration. Propensity to migrate increases the more moves one makes. By getting onto the migration train at an early age, and by breaking many of the social ties with the home region, it becomes easier to contemplate and carry through subsequent movements. In this way the system of higher education as presently operated encourages labour mobility for certain kinds of people.

10.5 The Geographical Pattern of Interregional Migration

Interregional migration between the wars

Losses of population from the rural areas to the towns continued during the inter-war period, but migration was overshadowed by the drift from the coalfield industrial regions to the Midlands and South. South Wales, Northumberland, and Durham experienced decline in population while rates of growth in Clydeside, Lancashire, Cheshire, and Yorkshire were below the national average. In contrast, the Midlands and Southern England experienced much higher rates of growth, the South-East, for example, growing by 9.8 per cent during 1921–31 compared with 2–5.3 per cent for the other regions. Willats and Newson (1953) mapped migration gains and losses and concluded that between 1921 and 1951 continuous migration occurred from remote or high rural areas; from a number of the older industrial areas, especially South Wales and parts of the North-East; and from the inner areas of London, especially the East End. Though net migration losses in rural areas were more widespread in the 1930s than in the 1920s, the beginnings of a rural recovery through migration gain were already manifest especially in Southern England and in those rural areas adjacent to urban areas.

The pattern of migration clearly reflected economic conditions (Dennison 1939). Areas with the greatest net migration losses were those with the poorest employment prospects, the remoter rural areas and the older industrial towns. Between 1923 and 1936 mobility fluctuated with the trade cycle, with more interregional migration during periods of relative prosperity (Makower, Marschak, and Robinson 1939).

Even then the position of London was anomalous. The population of inner London (the old LCC area) peaked in 1901. By the beginning of the century inner London was sustaining heavy population losses: half a million between 1901 and 1911. At this time gains in the outer areas were not enough to compensate, showing that those who were leaving the inner areas were moving further afield, many overseas. From 1921 onwards immigration to outer London exceeded inner area losses, indicating a lot of movement from the rest of the country to the capital as a whole which, between 1921 and 1937, had a net gain of half a million people. These gains spread beyond the capital into the Home Counties which received a net increment by migration of another half million during this period, giving a total increase of one million in 16 years. Most of this movement was spontaneous. During 1932–7 when the Industrial Transference Scheme, designed to assist the unemployed move from coalfield areas, was at its height, only 6,109 of the national total of 64,540 transferees came to London and 26,370 to the Rest of the South-East.

The attraction of the great wen for these migrants was jobs. An analysis by the Ministry of Labour of the exchange of unemployment books in 1937 compared the region of issue with that of exchange. Of 3.1 million insured people in London and the South-East, 281,000 had come from other areas compared with only 85,000 going in the opposite direction. The main sources of the labour migrants were the North, Wales, North-West, Scotland, and the South-West. According to the Barlow Report (1940), industrial development was the underlying force: between 1932 and 1937 Greater London had two-fifths of all new factories opened but only one-fifth of the total population, and its unemployment rate in 1937 was 6.3 per cent compared with a national average of 10.6 per cent.

Migration in the post-war period

In Chapter 3 it was seen that changes in regional populations after the war were largely due to net migration trends. The main currents of migration since 1945 have taken people out of the conurbations into surrounding areas, with the result that centrifugal movements have come to dominate local patterns of population change (Champion 1976). During the 1950s and 1960s net shifts of population through migration occurred from large cities to smaller urban places and rural areas. Rural depopulation continued from more remote areas. In Scotland there was a retreat from the hills and crofting counties had net losses of population as the excess of births over deaths was tempered by out-migration. Even then, though, tourism was beginning to stem the haemorrhage (Moisley 1962, Turnock 1968).

The regional migration pattern suggested a continuation of the 'drift South' characteristic of the 1920s and 1930s. During the 1950s net migration losses occurred in the North, Yorkshire and Humberside, North-West, Scotland, Wales, and Northern Ireland. Initially the greatest gains from migration were in the South-East and West Midlands, but by the 1960s East Anglia, the South-West, and East Midlands had become the main beneficiaries, the change reflecting both planned moves to new and expanded towns and voluntary migration out of the Greater London and West Midland conurbations.

Attempts to explain this interregional pattern focus, as in the 1930s, on net migration and its relationship to regional economic health, influenced by regional policy considerations (Wood 1976). Oliver (1964) showed some association between net interregional migration and regional differences in unemployment rates, though his results were inconclusive because of the correlation between unemployment and other regional factors such as industrial composition and social infrastructure. More significant was Hart's (1970) analysis of gross flows for 1960–1 which showed the highest propensity to move was not from depressed to prosperous regions but between prosperous regions, suggesting that migrants were moving from positions of strength.

New towns and population redistribution

A highly visible element in the post-war redistribution of the British population has been planned decentralization into the new and expanded towns. This process is best exemplified in South-East England, following Abercrombie's Greater London Plan of 1944. In order to relieve housing and employment pressures in London he estimated that a million people would have to move out, 415,000 from Inner London alone. Of these, Abercrombie proposed that 383,000 should be housed in eight new towns around London, 261,000 in additions to existing towns close to London, 164,000 in towns outside the London region but within a 50-mile radius, and 1,000,000 beyond the influence of London (Abercrombie 1945).

During the immediate post-war years a second theme was introduced into the motives for establishing new towns, the provision of an environment for growth in regions where older industries were in decay. This resulted in the designation of Cwmbran, Cumbernauld, and Washington among others. The late 1950s saw the creation of another batch combining both original aims, including Skelmersdale and Runcorn around Liverpool, Redditch and Telford near Birmingham, and Irvine to help out Glasgow (figure 10.2). The surge in population growth from the mid-1950s led to a further wave of new towns in the 1960s, mainly to take pressure off the South-East. Northampton, Peterborough, and Milton Keynes belong to this era and others reached the drawing board—Ashford, Ipswich, Solent City, Newbury/Swindon, for example. By this time, however, the breeding habits of the British people had again changed, downwards this time, and so one by one the new generation of new towns was whittled down to little more than the first three above. Only Milton Keynes fulfilled most people's ideas of what a new town was, opening up a brave new world of new town design for the United Kingdom—a miniature Los Angeles in Buckinghamshire. It is unlikely to have any imitators, at least in this country.

Fig. 10.2. New and expanding towns

No public sector new towns are proposed; decentralization has gone out of fashion since politicians discovered the inner city problem in 1977. However, a new generation of private sector new towns is being proposed amidst fierce controversy in the South (see Chapter 13).

Concern at population losss in large cities, especially London, effectively wound up the new towns' programme in the mid-1970s. By then they accounted for a shift of over a million people.

The overall impact of the new towns on the pattern of migration nationally is hard to isolate. They have embraced only a small part of the migration associated with the large conurbations. During one of their major drawing periods, captured by the 1971 census, the twenty-eight new towns in Britain received only just over 12 per cent of the net migration loss from the seven official conurbations in the preceding five years. Only 8 per cent of the gross movement from the conurbations went to new towns during these five years, although the precise proportion varied from conurbation to conurbation (Champion 1987). By no stretch of the imagination can the new towns be said to have taken an abnormal role in attracting population away from the larger cities.

The evidence for selective migration to the new towns is likewise not conclusive. Ruddy's (1969) study of the Industrial Selection Scheme, which attempted to link housing need in London with new homes and jobs in the new towns, showed no great bias towards skilled workers and Gee (1972) came to a similar conclusion. Overall, the profile of migrants to the new towns around London was not very different from that found in Greater London as a whole. Certainly there were fewer unskilled manual migrants than in the population at large, but the similarities are much clearer than the dissimilarities (Deakin and Ungerson 1977, Johnson and Salt 1981).

Interregional migration in the 1980s

The figure of about five million people changing address during 1980–1 is a considerable fall from the 6.25 million, 11.8 per cent of the population, who had moved ten years earlier. Neither the geographical pattern for 1980–1 nor change over the decade were uniform. Some local authorities were much more 'mobile' than others, extremes being 21 per cent of the population of Kensington and Chelsea who moved compared with only 5 per cent of those living in Afan (West Glamorgan). There were also variations in mobility by age: 16 per cent of 16–24-year-olds moved but only 5 per cent of those over 50.

Although the fall in mobility was general throughout the 1970s, the annual average decrease being 1.6 per cent, some places and groups maintained their mobility. Districts in which population grew rapidly had generally higher than average migration; some of the highest rates were in inner London, new towns, and areas characterized by armed services personnel or by large numbers of students. In contrast many industrial towns, especially in South Wales, had low mobility levels. The biggest declines by age-group were among the 45–59s, while divorcees had a lower than average fall.

The decline in interregional movement observed during the 1970s appears to have reversed in the 1980s. From a low of 800,000 in 1981–2 the numbers moving between regions steadily increased to 1,049,000 in 1988, no doubt reflecting the improved performance of the national economy. At the same time, moves within Family Practitioner Committee areas also increased, from 1,757,000 in 1983–4 to 1,880,000 in 1988. These changes in absolute numbers represent a genuine increase in mobility, not simply in the population at risk: the rate of migration for England and Wales rose from 31 per thousand in 1983–4 to 37 per thousand in 1988, though the Scottish rate remained low on 16 per thousand.

Increased mobility affected all regions though some were clear gainers and others lost people. From 1984 to 1988 four regions had net gains: South-West 203,000, East Anglia 89,000, East Midlands 64,000, and Wales 43,000. In contrast, net losers were the South-East (within which the Rest of the South-East (i.e. excluding Greater London) had a net increase of 161,000 while the capital lost 288,000), the North-West (−97,000), Scotland (−61,000), West Midlands (−40,000), the North (−35,000), Yorkshire and Humberside (−21,000), Northern Ireland (−25,000).

These net changes are marginal compared with high gross flows. For example, the net loss to the North-West of 2,000 during 1987–8 was on a total flow of 209,000, giving a relatively low migration efficiency. The South-East fared similarly, with gross flows totalling 585,000 and a net change of −55,000. Elsewhere migration efficiency was greater: East Anglia had a net increase of 15,000 on gross migration of 124,000.

In general the regional pattern of net gain and loss has been consistent year by year during the 1980s. The North, Yorkshire and Humberside, West Midlands, North-West, Scotland, and Northern Ireland were consistent net losers; East Midlands, East Anglia, South-West, and Wales were consistent gainers; the South-East changed from a gainer to a net loser.

A comparison of regional rates of in and out movement shows greater variation for the former, from 35 per thousand to 4 per thousand. Out-migration rates were more evenly distributed, from a high of 24 per thousand down to 8 per thousand (Stillwell and Boden 1989). The rank orders of regions for in- and outflows was similar (r = 0.95) indicating that those regions with high rates on inflow were also ones of high outflow, confirmation that the pattern of recent years echoes that found a decade ago (Gleave and Cordey-Hayes 1977). The UK interregional migration pattern generally remains one of large-scale population exchange with marginal net gains and losses.

The geographical pattern of inter-urban migration

When we look at migration at the level of Standard Regions it is easy to miss much of the geographical detail as it affects individual house-holds and local economic and social structures. A scale of analysis is needed which captures longer-distance movement within as well as across regional boundaries. This can best be achieved through study of the inter-urban pattern, which has been analysed for 1965–6 (Johnson, Salt, and Wood 1974) and 1970–1 (Flowerdew and Salt 1979) using the concept of local labour markets (Standard Metropolitan Labour Areas) established by Hall *et al.* (1973). Alas, data at a similar level of aggrega-tion are not available to enable a comparative analysis for 1980–1, though there is no reason to think that major changes have occurred.

The overall pattern can be broken down into three principal ele-ments. The first is associated with London. Migration to and from the capital accounted for most of the largest flows in 1971 (figure 10.3). In both 1965–6 and 1970–1 there was a tendency for migration to London to come from a broader area than migration from London, suggesting a process of population redistribution operating through the capital. Of particular importance is distance moved: in general in-migrants to London travelled longer distances than out-migrants (Flowerdew and Salt 1979).

The second element in the pattern comprises large flows associated with the remaining large cities, although movement between them accounted for only 6.8 per cent of the total inter-SMLA migration for 1970–1. In fact, large cities are part of two networks: the first is in exchanges with other places of similar size while the second, greater in terms of total volume of movers, involves interactions with smaller local labour markets.

The third element can be discerned if the influence of London is excluded and inter-SMLA migration is standardized according to the contribution of individual flows to the total number of in- and out-migrants for SMLAs. A number of local systems of migration emerge

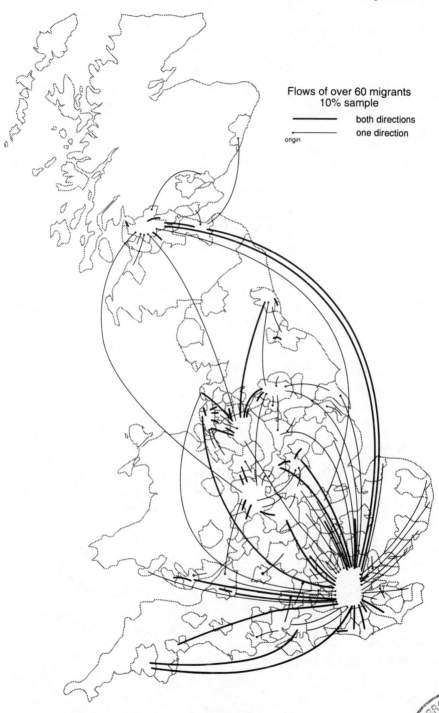

Flows of over 60 migrants
10% sample

⎯⎯⎯⎯⎯⎯ both directions
───────── one direction
origin

FIG. 10.3. Major migration flows between SMLAs, 1970–1971

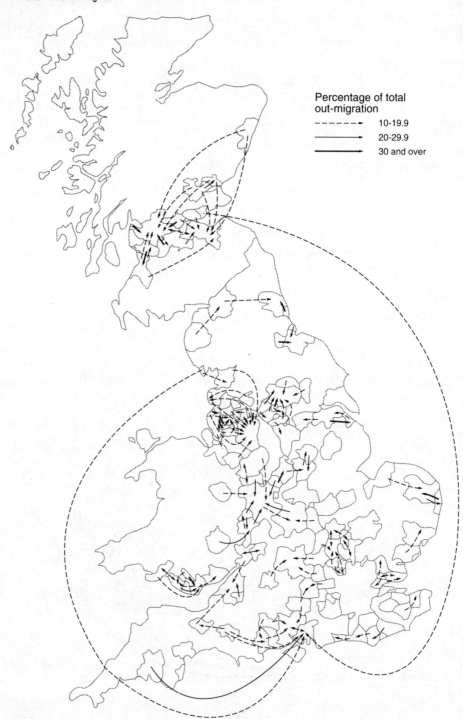

Percentage of total
out-migration

- - - - →   10–19.9

———→   20–29.9

━━━━━➤   30 and over

FIG. 10.4. Major destinations of out-migrants (excluding London), 1970–1971

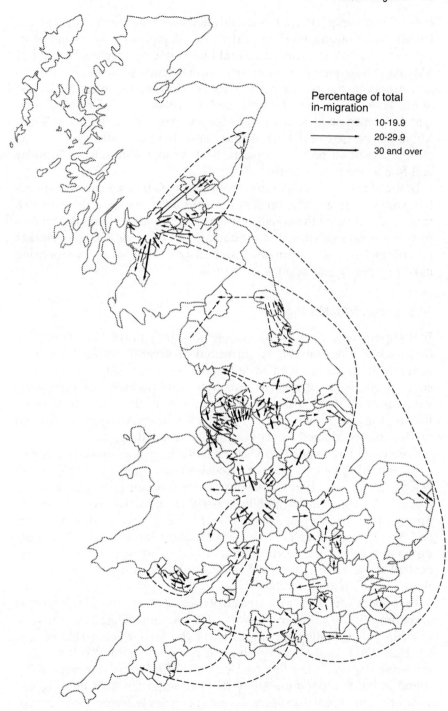

FIG. 10.5. Major origins of in-migrants (excluding London), 1970–1971

indicating the importance of local attraction and the creation of regional labour and housing markets with a fair degree of self-containment. Figures 10.4 and 10.5 reveal several interconnected regional groups of SMLAs. These include very clearly distinct Scottish and Welsh groups, and others in the North-West, West Yorkshire, the West Midlands, South Hampshire, the Chilterns, and the Bristol area. Smaller groups may be identified in South Essex, Surrey, parts of the East and South Midlands, Sussex and East Anglia, and there are other local inter-changes between pairs of adjacent SMLAs like Scunthorpe–Grimsby and Sunderland–Newcastle.

In the absence of comparable analyses for 1980–1 we can only specu-late whether or not this process has continued. Despite the evidence that in recent years the counterurbanization trend has slowed (Chapter 3) there is no evidence that interaction between local labour market groupings has not continued, especially in those areas experiencing most prosperity and population growth.

10.6 Reasons for Moving

It is superficially easy to ask people why they move. The trouble is that such a question can be answered at several different levels of generalization: terms such as 'job reasons' or 'housing reasons' may cover a multitude of diverse situations. Interpretation of survey an-swers must be done with care, especially as all the evidence suggests that reasons for moving form a complex weave. Attempts to consign motivation to selected categories may be misleading.

Problems of assessing reasons for moving have not stopped surveyors from enquiring and several consistencies have emerged. Cullingworth (1965), Donnison (1961), and Harris and Clausen (1967) each found that 17–18 per cent of mobile households gave job reasons as the primary ones for moving, though their studies refer to all households and not just to labour migrants. Harris and Clausen found that long-distance moves were more often ascribed to work reasons, 56.7 per cent of those moving over a hundred miles but only 8.5 per cent of those going less than ten miles.

Reasons given vary with the attributes of migrants. Single people seem more likely to move for work reasons, though age has little rela-tionship to motivation among those in the labour force (Harris and Clausen 1967). Higher socio-economic groups are more likely to move for work reasons according to Donnison (1961), and Simmie (1972) found in his Southampton study that the importance of housing and social reasons tended to increase for successively lower social groups as employment reasons decreased. Housing tenure may also be linked to motivation: Cullingworth (1965) found job reasons more likely to be given by those moving to privately rented furnished accommodation but less by those moving to council renting.

The Housing and Labour Mobility Study was specifically concerned with labour migrants and therefore employment reasons could be expected to dominate. They did, but not to the extent that might have been expected (table 10.4). In fact the survey identified a surprising range of unprompted reasons for labour migration in Britain. 'Return to a former area of residence', suggesting a range of social and sentimental ties, was the second most important primary reason, while housing reasons were relatively unimportant. The survey also showed that destination is affected by motives. The attraction of employment was significantly lower in Chatham than in the other three places; in contrast High Wycombe was relatively more attractive for those wanting to move for employment reasons or because they found the area attractive. Motivation was also found to be linked to changes in lifestyle consequent upon moving. Job motivated movers were more likely to improve their socio-economic position and their incomes (Johnson, Salt, and Wood 1974).

Good survey data on reasons for migration become scarcer as we approach the present, and tend to be related to specific groups. Building societies from time to time publish reasons for moving among those to whom they grant mortgages. One such survey of owner-occupiers found that 29.3 per cent moved for housing reasons, 20.4 per cent because of marriage, and 17.3 per cent for reasons of income or work (a figure remarkably consistent with those found two decades earlier and mentioned above) (Nationwide BS 1982). The National Mobility Scheme provides data on motivation for successful nominees. For 1986–7 only 29 per cent moved for job reasons (including 3 per cent who were unemployed before moving); most moved for a range of social reasons mainly concerned with the provision of support for a relative. This bias towards social rather than employment reasons has been consistent since the Scheme's inception in 1981.

10.7 The Role of Housing

For many years it has been accepted that housing constitutes a major barrier to the redistribution of the British population. Its exact influence remains elusive for its power to deter varies with individual circumstance. A good deal of the discussion about the role of housing has focused on tenure. Owner-occupation, privately rented fur

Table 10.4. Reasons for move to new labour markets

	Chatham		High Wycombe		Huddersfield		Northampton		Total	
	No.	%	No.	%	No.	%	No.	%	No.	%
Job reason	52	41.3	95	53.4	39	51.3	86	50.3	272	49.4
Setting up business	3	2.4	4	2.3	4	5.3	2	1.2	13	2.4
Housing reasons	19	15.1	9	5.1	3	4.0	31	18.1	62	11.3
'Home town'	21	16.7	18	10.1	16	21.1	19	11.1	74	13.4
'Liked area'	6	4.8	17	9.6	2	2.6	11	6.4	36	6.5
Personal reasons	10	7.9	10	5.6	6	7.9	7	4.1	33	6.0
Travelling time	15	11.9	22	12.4	3	4.0	14	8.2	54	9.8
Other	—	—	3	1.6	3	4.0	1	0.6	7	1.3
TOTAL	126		178		76		171		551	

Source: Johnson, Salt, and Wood (1974).

nished tenancies, and tied accommodation have been associated with higher degrees of labour migration, council housing and privately rented unfurnished tenancies with less (for example, Cullingworth 1969; Johnson, Salt, and Wood 1974; Robertson 1979; Hughes and McCormick 1981; Hamnett 1984). Trends in housing tenure may thus influence mobility.

The relationship between housing tenure and mobility rate has been documented for over twenty years. Cullingworth's (1965) study of mobility during 1960–2 showed significantly higher rates of movement in the privately rented furnished sector than in others. This sector also has a major lubricating role in providing temporary accommodation for labour migrants while a permanent dwelling in the new area is sought (Johnson, Salt, and Wood 1974). Data from the National Dwelling and Housing Survey further indicate the overall importance of the privately rented sector in aiding mobility: it accounted for 28 per cent of movers but only 14.4 per cent of households, with the furnished part of the sector having 16 per cent of movers but housing only 3.5 per cent of households (OPCS 1983*h*). The same theme is continued in the Labour Force Survey: in 1980–1 the annual mobility rate for the privately rented furnished sector was 51.4 per cent compared with 7.7 per cent among the owner-occupied, 9.2 per cent, 15.5 per cent, and 11.7 per cent respectively for those in council tenancies, housing association, and privately rented unfurnished dwellings.

Distance moved and motivation also seem to be related to tenure. Council tenants have been found to move shorter distances and to be less likely to move for employment reasons than other groups (Cullingworth 1965, Johnson, Salt, and Wood 1974). Using census data Minford *et al.* (1987) showed the importance of the privately rented sector for those moving long distances and seeking work; in contrast council tenants predominantly moved locally. The National Movers Survey of 1977–8 (OPCS 1983*h*) painted a similar picture. Only 11 per cent moving from a council tenancy and 6 per cent moving to one migrated over twenty miles, compared with 31 per cent and 27 per cent respectively for owner-occupiers and 17 per cent and 27 per cent for private renters. Council tenants were also less likely to move for job reasons: 8.6 per cent compared with 27.2 per cent of owner-occupiers and 25.5 per cent of private renters. Hughes and McCormick (1984) concluded that council tenancy inhibited mobility through its effect on the search process.

The effect of tenure legislation has been discussed by many commentators (see also Chapters 4, 7, and 13). Successive rent acts from 1915 have made access more difficult to the diminishing privately rented sector particularly for migrants. Together with economic changes, and the tax advantages of owner-occupation, traditional unfurnished private renting has become very unrewarding for private landlords and investors. Before 1914 over 90 per cent of households rented privately, usually unfurnished. By 1945, 45 per cent still did so. Now only 6 per cent of households rent privately (see Holmans 1987, Daunton 1987).

It has been argued that housing policies have drastically reduced the migration rates of a large segment of the population (Hughes and McCormick 1981). Cullingworth (1965) referred to a 'new law of settlement' being created by the residential qualifications imposed by local authorities and which deterred migrants between local authorities. The contradiction between government housing policies and mobility policies has been clear for some time. In general the former have operated to make it more difficult for poorer people and the unemployed to move about the country while the latter have attempted to encourage such people to move through the Employment Transfer Scheme (Johnson and Salt 1980b). However, the 1988 Housing Act has created new forms of private tenure in order to increase the supply of housing accessible to labour migrants. The polemical study of Minford et al. (1987) concludes that the 1974 Rent Act did not initially have much impact on mobility in the private rented sector. Licensing agreements which affected two-thirds of furnished lettings in London, 1980–4 (Grosskurth 1985) ensured that most privately rented furnished accommodation remained outside the machinery of the Act. Recent legal judgements, however, make the future of licensing unsure and Minford et al. argue that mobility will decline. Indeed, they suggest that falling mobility rates from the middle 1970s can ultimately be attributed to the 1974 Act, though this partial analysis does not seem to take into account the effect on mobility of economic recession, discussed above.

There is some evidence that the phenomenon of 'discouraged' movers occurs. The General Household Survey for 1976 suggested that 3.1 per cent of all households in England and Wales contained people who had seriously considered moving but had either given up or changed their minds, housing reasons being the main stumbling block. The National Consumer Council survey (1984) indicated that it was in the local authority sector that discouragement was highest, suggesting that it was not necessarily the rent acts that prevented people from migrating, although an alternative hypothesis is that the rent acts prevent people moving out of council housing by abolishing alternatives and institutionalizing a non-portable subsidy. More recently, Kitching (1990) has explained the immobility of council tenants in part to the existence of 'housing ladders' within the sector. Ascent of these depends upon a points system which may be maximized for the household by remaining in the local area.

The British have shown a remarkable willingness to forgo many of the fruits of income in pursuit of a home of their own. From 1971 to 1985 owner-occupation went up from 49 per cent to 61 per cent of households (table 10.5); council renting rose during the 1970s from 31 per cent to 34 per cent in 1981 but had slipped back to 28 per cent by 1985 and 24 per cent by 1989 in response to sales of council housing; private rented accommodation halved, to 6 per cent. The overall effect of these changes should be to ease the situation for better-off migrants while making it more difficult for others. There is as yet little empirical evidence of the extent to which this shift in housing tenure has differentially affected mobility. Congdon and Champion (1989) have concluded that inmigration into the South-East has not been in response to increases in owner-occupied stock there, and that new building has had only local effects.

Although owner-occupation has been associated with greater mobility, recent trends in house prices across the country may be changing that relationship in a strongly geographical way. The regional rank order of house prices has remained fairly constant in recent decades but in the last ten years or so the gap between top and bottom has widened (Nationwide Building Society 1987). Of particular importance has been the growing disparity, especially since 1984, between South-Eastern England (especially London) and the rest of the country, although latterly (1988–9) this has narrowed. For example, in 1975 prices in the capital averaged 57 per cent higher than in the Northern region; by 1987 they were 142 per cent higher. The ripple effect of rising house prices has extended beyond the South-East, often, it seems, following the motorways and upgraded railway lines. These pressures drive recent controversy over the adequacy of housing provision in county structure plans in the South-East.

Ultimately the limiting factor on house price increases is people's ability to buy their way on to the escalator in the first place. However, past relationships between property prices and incomes may be changing. Partly this is due to inherited wealth as the first big generation of owner-occupiers dies. Inheritances may then become available to first time owner-buyers, the children and grandchildren of those who have passed on, although there is evidence that it is the 40–60-year-olds, unlikely to be first-time buyers themselves, who mainly benefit (Morgan Grenfell Economics 1987). Others have been able to step on to the escalator in company, perhaps two or three people clubbing together to put down a deposit and share a mortgage, though tax changes in

Table 10.5. Housing tenure in Great Britain (%)

Tenure	1971	1973	1975	1977	1979	1981	1983	1985
Owner-occupied, owned outright	22	23	22	23	22	23	24	61
Owner-occupied, with mortgage	27	27	28	28	30	31	33	
Rented with job or business	5	4	3	3	3	2	2	2
Rented from local authority or new town	31	32	33	33	34	34	32	28
Rented from housing association or co-operative	1	1	1	1	1	2	2	2
Rented privately, unfurnished	12	11	10	8	8	6	5	5
Rented privately, furnished	3	3	3	3	2	2	2	2

Source: General Household Surveys.

1988 made this less attractive (Chapter 13). In the late 1980s mortgage finance was also more freely available, and from a wider range of sources than in the past. Home ownership therefore continues to grow, especially among young professionals who are in occupations which are geographically more mobile anyway.

Rises in house prices and growing regional differences affect labour migrants in several ways. They have an inhibiting effect on owner occupation, especially for young people. They also lead to price gradients too steep for many to climb. Owner-occupiers in Northern regions find their existing equity inadequate to purchase in the South-East; for potential migrants not already in owner-occupation buying in a high priced region becomes unthinkable. One response to this situation has been the growth of long-distance commuting on a Monday–Friday basis; one report in 1987 suggested there were as many as 10–15 long-distance commuters on every North-East bound coach leaving London on a Friday evening (Hogarth and Daniel 1988).

As house prices rise there is a knock-on effect for the costs of moving since agency and legal fees and stamp duty all change in line with house value. Hence removal costs between expensive houses are greater than those between cheaper ones. Other things being equal, it is more expensive to move house within Southern England. People in the best position are those for whom removal costs are paid, usually by employers. Particular problems arise when there is a steep price gradient between locations; in the recent past more and more employers, either transferring staff or recruiting new ones, have provided compensation for regional house price differences. There are signs, still largely anecdotal, that this practice is beginning to create its own migration fields in the South-East and East Anglia as companies prefer to recruit only from potential staff already living in the high price area, thus minimizing their outlay on relocation costs.

10.8 Relocation of Staff within Large Employing Organizations

The growing polarization between those who find it less difficult to move and those for whom the barriers to mobility seem insuperable is to a considerable extent related to corporate relocation of staff.

Volume of corporate relocation

It is little known that a high proportion of labour migrants about the country are company transferees, moving within the internal labour markets of large multi-locational organizations. They encounter fewer problems in moving than those who change firms; they do not have to search for a job in a new area; their moving costs are normally paid by their employer; local ties are often ephemeral due to repeated moves and are thus more easily broken; they usually know how the move is related to future career prospects.

There are few data on the scale of such transfers. About a third of labour migrants surveyed in the early 1970s did not change employer upon moving (Johnson, Salt, and Wood 1974). Analysis of a sample of sixty-two long-distance movers, handled by a network of estate agents between 1979 and 1981, showed 53 per cent were company transferees (73 per cent when those retiring were omitted). A survey in 1982 of seventeen large removal firms demonstrated clearly that company relocation, with the company paying the costs of removal, had been increasing and accounted for the bulk of removals beyond the local area, estimates suggesting a figure of 65–75 per cent (Salt 1984).

There is no official published source providing data on the volume of corporate relocation. However, unpublished Labour Force Survey data may be used to indicate the number of interregional movers aged over 16 who were working for the same employer before and after moving. The records distinguish between those employed both at the time of the survey and one year earlier and those who moved during the year but were not employed at one or both dates. Of 582,113 interregional movers during 1980–1 248,274 (42.7 per cent) were in employment at both dates (table 10.6). Among this second group 144,930 (58.4 per cent) were employed by the same organization before and after moving. Thus, in the context of the national pattern of labour migration, over half of all interregional movers from job to job were with the same employer and hence spared the hassle of searching for work in a new area. Similar percentages were found for 1974–5 and 1978–9. Proportions vary by region: almost three-quarters of labour migrants to Scotland were transferred, compared with only 41.5 per cent of those to East Anglia. In general, though, regional experience is similar, clustered fairly close to the average, indicating that transfer of staff is a national rather than a regionally differentiated phenomenon.

In the absence of official data, estimates of the overall volume of corporate relocation have to be based on survey. The Organizational Labour Migration Study, carried out in the early 1980s, analysed the practice in nearly a hundred multilocational organizations in the UK and suggested that 160,000–180,000 employees nationally were transferred annually (Salt 1990b). When household size was taken into account it was estimated that 370,000–400,000 people move home each year as a result of these transfers. Atkinson (1987) has suggested that

Table 10.6. Interregional migration, 1980–1981

Destination region	(a) All interregional movers	(b) Total employed both dates	(c) Worked for same organization	(d) b/a (%)	(e) c/b (%)	(f) c/a (%)
Northern	20,228	6,087	3,001	30.1	49.3	14.8
Yorkshire and Humberside	37,792	14,093	9,467	37.3	67.2	25.1
East Midlands	44,508	13,737	8,034	30.9	58.5	18.1
East Anglia	40,243	17,555	7,278	43.6	41.5	18.1
Greater London	95,325	42,131	25,515	44.2	60.6	26.8
Rest of South-East	159,094	76,726	46,068	48.2	60.0	29.0
South-West	63,037	27,946	16,069	44.3	57.5	25.5
West Midlands	33,034	14,152	7,366	42.8	52.0	22.3
North-West	36,800	14,784	7,805	40.2	52.8	31.2
Scotland	34,833	15,382	11,275	44.2	73.3	32.4
Wales	17,219	5,681	3,052	33.0	53.7	17.7
Great Britain	582,113	248,274	144,930	42.7	58.4	24.9

Source: Labour Force Survey, 1981.

there may be as many as a quarter of a million transfers each year, but it is not clear how the figure is derived. Most transferees are in managerial, professional, and senior technical grades, and are men. Their moves reflect a combination of career aspirations and the demands of the job.

Relocation costs

It was indicated earlier that the financial costs of moving can be considerable for the individual household, largely through house sale and purchase costs. Those who are transferred by their employers invariably move on a magic carpet, with most of their monetary costs covered by the company.

Many relocation assistance packages are long standing, others have been developed within the last decade; nearly all are subject to regular review. Their existence means that the costs of moving have been steadily transferred from the individual to the employer. Amounts paid vary with circumstances: the average cost in 1982–3 was around £10,000, the median £7,000. More recent evidence indicates that these figures have not changed much (Woolwich Building Society 1988). Hence a lot of money is made available to corporate movers. Increasingly too the use of relocation agencies by employers has further relieved the burden on corporate migrants. One consequence of all this is to widen further the gap between those who have the opportunity and the assistance in moving—generally the highly skilled and better off—and others who may wish to move but are less fortunate.

10.9 Government Policy towards Internal Migration

Successive British governments have failed to have a clear policy towards internal migration, particularly of labour. Ministerial exhortations from the Conservative government of the 1980s to migrate have not been accompanied by measures designed to achieve specific policy aims with regard to volume and direction of internal migration, nor were they ever intended to. Government philosophy is still largely epitomized by the concept of 'bikeism' introduced by Norman Tebbit in 1981, when he exhorted others to follow his father's example and cycle in search of a job.

Despite a verbal commitment early in its first term of office the Conservative government subsequently said and did little to encourage labour migration, adopting a *laissez-faire* attitude. Housing legislation, especially since 1988, has attempted to encourage labour migration by deregulating private renting and encouraging alternatives to council tenure. Measures to facilitate labour migration have barely featured in the Manpower Service Commission's programme and the 1986 budget abolished the Employment Transfer Scheme, designed to assist the unemployed to move to where work was available. Currently, the responsible government departments are engaged in no major studies of labour migration and, so far as one can tell, there is no clear policy aim as far as long-distance movement of the British population is concerned.

The National Mobility Scheme, set up in 1981, is now the main government-inspired attempt to aid mobility, though it is responsible for only a tiny part of long-distance migration. It is aimed mainly at tenants of local authorities, new towns, and housing associations, people high on their waiting lists, and others with a pressing need to move. They need to have sound employment or social reasons to move to somewhere beyond reasonable daily travelling distance from their present homes.

By 1986 a total of 41,931 had used the Scheme, mostly for moves between counties. The figure of 5,607 moves during 1985–6 needs to be placed in the context of 41,387 nominations for the year: clearly there is a massive and unsatisfied demand. Most of those who move do so for social rather than job reasons (table 10.7); for example, 32 per cent were elderly or handicapped people moving to receive support from relatives and friends (National Mobility Office 1987). The geography

Table 10.7. National Mobility Scheme: reasons for moving, 1985–1986 (%)

Reason	%
Employment	28
Moving to new job	11
To be near existing job	11
Currently unemployed	6
Social	72
To enable:	
Elderly/handicapped applicant to receive support.	32
Applicant to receive support from another person	15
Applicant to give support	7
Other social reasons	7
Not stated	11

Note: Total rehoused: 11,114.
Source: National Mobility Scheme, 1986.

of the Scheme shows a net positive demand for moves to Southern and Eastern England, losses elsewhere, and the actual pattern of movement confirms this trend. Hence the Scheme provides valuable help for those who are successful, but is clearly vastly oversubscribed.

Present government policy thus looks to individual choice and the market rather than to bureaucratic schemes in encouraging mobility. Lubrication is provided through some easing of planning controls in South-Eastern England, in attempts to make private renting more attractive, conferring the right to buy upon local authority tenants and trying to break council house monopolies by allowing transfers of tenancies to other landlords (Coleman 1989*a*). Migration and mobility feature prominently in the rhetoric used to justify these policies. However, the policies cannot be seen as migration policies *per se*; indeed, by emphasizing market forces the government lays itself open to the accusation that it is abdicating responsibility for the movements that occur. Furthermore, 'choice' is not neutral: those who are in the best position to move—through strength in housing and job markets—are not usually those in most need of a move.

11 International Migration

11.1 Introduction

Since the Second World War, new patterns of international migration have brought a whole new society, politics, and vocabulary to the UK. A multi-racial, multi-ethnic society has been created with far-reaching consequences, extending into the remote fastnesses of the social fabric and the wider realms of international political relations.

There are now 2.6 million non-white people living in the UK. There are 1.8 million foreign nationals, including some non-whites. About 56 per cent of non-white people are immigrants since the Second World War, the rest are their children. Before the 1950s the number of non-whites in the UK was negligible, perhaps 5,000–10,000 people. So this is a sensational demographic development by any standards, especially as the newcomers have highly distinctive patterns of fertility, marriage, custom, and social life. The picture is complicated further by the great differences between the diverse groups that make up the total ethnic minority population. Analysis and policy have been confused by the relative poverty of information on these distinctive new populations both in respect of their pattern of migration from overseas and their characteristics in this country.

The term 'immigrant' has become almost synonymous with the word 'coloured' in British popular perception, yet it is important to remember that the majority of the foreign-born in the UK are white (table 11.1). Throughout most of the post-war period Britain has lost population, not gained it, in its exchanges with the outside world. Except in the early 1960s and in 1973, which were the peaks of coloured immigration, and also since 1984, the departure of Britons from its shores has exceeded arrivals of people from the rest of the world, leading to a net loss of population (figure 11.1). These trends remind us that international migration is, in fact, a two-way process. A high proportion of intended migrants to Britain are of British nationality, coming home after a stay abroad. Many emigrants are foreigners or Commonwealth citizens going back to their own countries. Though it is tempting to see immigration and emigration as separate processes they are linked in a myriad of ways, socially and economically; too often, however, their connection is little explored.

Table 11.1. Population by ethnic group, country of birth, and nationality, Great Britain, 1984–1986 ('000s)

Ethnic group	Born UK	Born outside UK			All persons (including birthplace not stated)	% with British/UK nationality	
		British/UK nationals	Other nationals	Nationality not stated		Aged under 16	Aged 16 and over
White	49,120	865	928	10	51,107	98	97
All ethnic minority groups	1,038	728	584	11	2,432	88	64
West Indian or Guyanese	286	114	121	2	534	95	67
Indian, Pakistani, or Bangladeshi	473	493	245	3	1,260	89	69
Other ethnic minority	279	121	219	5	638	80	50
All groups (inc. not stated)	50,627	1,616	1,535	23	54,230	97	91

Source: Labour Force Survey.

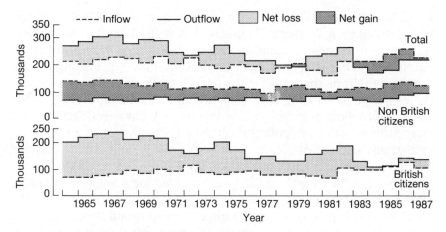

Source: *Population Trends*, 1989.

Fig. 11.1. International migrations, UK, 1964–1987

In fact, the UK today is the focal point of three different migration systems, defined on the basis of geography and motivation. The first is a 'settlement system' which strongly reflects old colonial ties and is centred on the Indian subcontinent at present. The second is a 'labour system' which has long been selective in the levels of skill of those involved but is now very much concerned with highly skilled workers often moving between advanced economies. Within this there is a subgroup, focused on the EC, between whose members free movement of people occurs, often unrecorded. Finally, there is a 'refugee system' which involves a small number of troubled countries sending an increasing number of asylum seekers who raise some tricky policy issues.

These three systems are not independent and as this chapter unfolds it will become apparent that they interact strongly, though their relationship may be seen to ebb and flow historically. At various times in the past the settlement and labour systems have been very closely related, for example, in attempts to recruit staff in the West Indies in the 1950s. Since 1986 the policy debate about refugees, and in 1989–90 about the people of Hong Kong, has tested the attitudes of politicians and populace to long-term migrant settlement generally and, in so far as economic motives are suspected for many would-be asylum seekers, to labour market conditions as well.

Most of the academic and political discussion about Britain's international migration has focused on settlement immigration, rightly it may be argued in view of the problems and perceptions it has engendered. This immigration has posed a number of major demographic questions which this chapter and the next will attempt to answer. What processes have created such an ethnically diverse UK in the 1990s? Is the present pattern of foreign settlement and ethnic diversity so very novel compared with the past? How demographically different are immigrant populations from the native British? What are the consequences of these migrations for geographical distribution, assimilation, and policy?

Flows of labour into and out of the country have received surprisingly little attention. Popular perceptions generally reflect attitudes to immigrants who are coming to settle permanently, and assume that the labour coming in is mainly of low skill level and status. Only slowly is it being grasped that highly skilled workers, the 'new nomads' (Findlay and Stewart 1985) and 'executive gypsies' (Marshall and Cooper 1976), are now more typical of foreign workers coming in and Britons moving abroad. What then are the patterns of international labour migration involving the UK in the late twentieth century?

Britain, along with other Western countries, has been justifiably proud of its open door policy towards refugees. But perceptions and attitudes forged in the aftermath of two European wars have been called into question by two parallel forces in recent years. The first is that the core of refugee creation is now far removed from Europe; places of first asylum tend to be likewise. The second is that the definition of refugee has become muddied by the concept of 'economic refugee', giving rise to fears in potential destinations like the UK that traditional humanitarian attitudes to genuine refugees would be taken advantage of by people seeking the old route from poverty through labour migration. What then are the trends in refugee admission to the UK? How should policy develop to cope with existing and anticipated pressures?

11.2 The Nature and Quality of the Data

When we review what we know about the UK international migration system as a whole it soon becomes clear that there are major gaps in our knowledge. We know little once they have arrived about immigrants given the right to settle here, or their offspring. Comments on immigrant demography easily become confused with the demography of ethnic groups. Our main sources of data are based on such small samples as to make estimates of exchanges with individual countries highly risky. The labour market impact of immigrant workers is uncertain: we are unsure about the specific skills coming in and leaving (especially where the EC is involved), where British skills go to, and from which parts of the country.

Our patchy picture of immigration and emigration reflects the topsy-like nature of data collection (Coleman 1987). Early attempts at collecting statistics, in the nineteenth century, were haphazard and reflected particular circumstances—the need to check human cargoes on emigrant ships and the waves of Jewish immigration that began around 1870. Not until after the Aliens Order of 1920 were data on all arrivals counted and published yearly by the Home Office according to purpose of stay, along with data on departures. Even then coverage was incomplete, omitting UK citizens, citizens of the dominions and colonies, and the Irish. British subjects or citizens of independent Commonwealth countries did not feature at all in Home Office statistics until after the 1962 Commonwealth Immigrants Act. Entry into the EC has introduced a new complication, for citizens of member countries may freely come and go without detailed enquiry for a stay of up to six months.

Since the 1950s the explosion of air travel has dramatically increased passenger movements, to 42.5 million arrivals in 1987, mostly short-stay visitors. By the 1970s counting by immigration officials of pass-engers coming in, and especially those going out, at points of greatest pressure, had become perfunctory in the extreme. Following the Moser Report in 1976 the collection and publication of outward movement ceased, abruptly ending the series of 'net balance' figures from the Home Office (Peach 1981).

From the nineteenth century the Board of Trade collected passenger statistics from shipping and airline companies, though the detail was slight. Faced with growing numbers coming in by air the Board set up a voluntary sample inquiry in 1961—the International Passenger Survey—primarily in order to collect tourist and exchange control data. After the Commonwealth Immigrants Act 1962 it acquired a wider function in estimating immigrants and emigrants, including those from the New Commonwealth for the first time. The sample generates about 250,000 interviews a year of which under 1 per cent are emigrants or immigrants, defined demographically as people intending to leave or stay in the country for at least a year, having been present or absent for at least a year.

The small sample size makes it nigh on impossible to say much about flows involving specific origins or destinations. For example, in 1985, gross flows with Jamaica of 1,931 people were based on only twenty-four interviews; four questionnaires from immigrants from Belgium were grossed up to 7,005 movements. Home Office data from the control of immigration are based on quite different principles but they do overlap, for example, with respect to dependants from the Indian subcontinent, sufficiently to allow the one to act as a check on the other (Population Statistics and Home Office 1979; OPCS 1982*b*; Coleman 1983, 1988).

The census has asked a question on birthplace since 1841 and intermittently questions on nationality too. These give some idea of the net end product of the different migration streams but they do not measure migration itself. Other census questions may refine the picture, for example, those on residence one and five years in the past and on date of entry into the UK, which were asked in 1971 but not 1981. No modern census has asked about nationality, but the 1991 census asked a question on ethnicity (see Chapter 12).

Migrant worker statistics come from three sources, and are mostly unpublished. The annual Labour Force Survey includes some details on foreign nationals living and working in the UK, and it is possible to estimate inflows. Because of sample size, data cells of less than 10,000 individuals are not released, so much detail is not available. The Department of Employment's Overseas Labour Section produces records of all work and trainee permits issued to foreigners (excluding EC citizens who do not need them). The data are an accurate record of those allowed in to work, initially for a period up to three years. A subsidiary but also unpublished source of annual data on foreign migrants coming to work in the UK is the Department of Social Security. Its statistics are derived from a 100 per cent sample of persons from abroad who register or re-register for National Insurance purposes during the year, but they are little used since they give no indication of the period worked. However, it is possible they provide a more accurate assessment of labour inflows than either the IPS or the LFS (Salt 1990*a*).

11.3 The Legal Framework for Immigration and Nationality

The pattern of contemporary international migration involving the UK has to be seen in the light of an evolving legislative framework governing entry, nationality, and right of abode. In fact, it is only immigration that is controlled; the UK has never had a policy designed to control emigration and no part of the legislative system deals with rights of exit, leaving those UK citizens with rights of abode to come and go as they please.

Immigration control in its present form is a child of the twentieth century. It began in 1905 with the passage of the Aliens Act, itself a response to the Jewish immigration of the preceding decades. Under the Act entry could be refused to individuals travelling steerage in large ships on grounds of disease, pauperism, criminal record, and other criteria; in reality it provided few barriers to most migrants. The war changed that. The Aliens Registration Acts of 1914 and 1919 extended control to all alien arrivals and, in the 1920 Aliens Order, defined Immigration Rules which governed the conditions under which they might be admitted. After 1920 foreign citizens, as aliens are now more gently called, might not land without leave of an immigration officer, and they were obliged to complete landing and embarkation cards.

All this legislation applied only to aliens, not to 'British subjects'. Under the Imperial Act (1914) every person born in a British colony or Dominion was deemed to be a British subject. So before 1948 UK citizenship did not really exist separately from the British subject status shared by residents of the dominions, colonies, and dependencies. All were free to enter without control. The British Nationality Act of 1948 preserved the 'British subject' status of citizens of newly independent states that remained within the Commonwealth. The Act created the new term of 'Commonwealth citizen', identical in its connotation with 'British subject'. British citizens were formally 'Citizens of the UK and Colonies', thereby sharing equivalent rights with colonial citizens in the UK. Because citizens of independent Commonwealth countries were not aliens, they were not subject to immigration control and were able to pass without hindrance. Such provisions applying to so many potential immigrants were unique to Britain. In most Western European countries citizens of former colonies are clearly defined as 'foreigners' and are enumerated through immigration control.

Debates on the desirability of controlling Commonwealth immigration continued throughout the 1950s, and may have been partly responsible for encouraging extra movement to 'beat the ban' while the door was still open (Peach 1968; Coleman 1987). Since 1950 Cabinet Committees had considered the need to control immigration. Finally, in 1962, the Commonwealth Immigrants Act was passed—amid considerable controversy—to limit the rights of entry to the UK of Commonwealth citizens. It limited the entry of Commonwealth subjects to holders of work vouchers, their dependants, and the dependants of those already settled in the UK. The problem of verifying the dependent status of migrants, especially from the Indian subcontinent, remained impossible to control. In 1968 a further crisis provoked action to check this and other loopholes. Many East African Asians had been given British passports on the independence of African countries. Political unrest led some of them to migrate to the UK. The 1968 Commonwealth Immigrants Act extended immigration control to them, despite their possession of passports, through a non-statutory quota system still in force. So just as the 1962 Act had taken away the automatic right of British subjects to enter the UK, the 1968 Act qualified the rights of some UK Passport Holders and introduced the notion of the 'patrial'. The subsequent Immigrant Appeals Act 1969 also required dependants to establish their entitlement to entry with British officials in the Indian subcontinent, before arrival in the UK.

Primary and secondary immigration continued despite these steps and the new government in 1970 promised further measures. The Immigration Act of 1971 put the control of Commonwealth citizens on essentially the same basis as the arrangements for foreign citizens. By the 1971 Act only persons who had right of abode in the UK (described as 'patrial') were not subject to immigration control, apart from Irish citizens. 'Patrials' are citizens of the UK and Colonies (since 1981 'British Citizens') who have that citizenship by birth, adoption, registration, or naturalization in the UK, or such a parent or grandparent, or who have been accepted for settlement and resided for five years, or Commonwealth citizens with a UK parent, and initially, spouses of patrials who were themselves Commonwealth citizens. The 1971 Act is supplemented by rules of practice (the Immigration Rules) which can be changed without further primary legislation but have to be laid before Parliament and are subject to parliamentary approval.

The period of rapid change in immigration control in the 1960s and early 1970s sat increasingly uneasily with the 1948 Nationality Act. It reflected a past reality—the UK as an imperial power which regarded, even into the late 1970s, some 950 million people throughout the world as British subjects. The British Nationality Act of 1981 created three types of British citizenship: British, British Dependent Territories (those connected with the existing dependencies), and British Overseas. Anyone who is a British citizen is exempt from immigration control. The other two have no automatic right of entry to the UK, but may qualify for admission in the same way as other Commonwealth citizens. The new Act did not adversely affect the position under UK immigration law of anyone already lawfully settled and such people are admissible as returning residents in the same ways as before. Nevertheless great concern about the legislation was generated leading to a surge of applications for citizenship just before the new Act came into force.

Despite a steady fall in settlement immigration during the 1980s it was felt that undue pressure was being put on the system by the need to verify rights of entry at ports of arrival. Illegal immigration was also becoming more of a problem. In 1986 an advance visa system was introduced for immigrants from India, Pakistan, Bangladesh, Nigeria, and Ghana—the major sources. It followed a similar system introduced for Sri Lankans the previous year to regulate large numbers of arrivals claiming to be refugees. The announcement—predictably—brought one of those rushes to 'beat the deadline' that British immigration control seems so good at precipitating. An estimated 4,000 visitors from the Indian subcontinent, especially from Bangladesh, are reckoned to have arrived at Heathrow airport in one day, completely swamping the abilities of an increased number of immigration officials to cope.

Under the Rules of the 1971 Act it was easier for a wife or fiancée to enter than a husband or fiancé. Test cases brought before the European Court of Human Rights ruled that treatment of the sexes should be the same. In consequence further amendments were made to the Rules in 1985 extending the rights of settlement to husbands of wives already settled in the UK and placing the sexes on the same footing. In 1988 a new Immigration Act was passed, designed to 'reinforce' the 1971 Act. It has tightened entry controls further, for example, by allowing in only one wife in the case of polygamous marriages and by making it mandatory for people seeking to enter the UK to establish the right of abode before arrival. Concern over the destabilizing effect of emigration from Hong Kong, in anticipation of its take-over by China in 1997, led in 1990 to the introduction of new legislation. The British Nationality (Hong Kong) Act will allow entry to the UK of 50,000 'key workers', together with their dependants, perhaps up to 250,000 people.

The legal framework for immigration is thus a complex one; its general tenor over the last quarter of a century has been towards greater restrictions on entry. Curtailing new settlement rather than controlling labour movement has been the dominant theme so that moves for employment purposes have responded to settlement legislation and controls—in contrast to many other Western European countries where the reverse has been the case. Underlying the erection of this legal framework has been the residue of Empire. Laws and Rules now seek to curb flows that evolved when the mother country and its colonies shared common citizenship. The main pressures for settlement today are from former Third World colonies. Any attempts to stem settlement from them must inevitably seem discriminatory, presenting acute political dilemmas. The overall impression remains, though, that in the long process of regulating human flows in and out of the country the UK government, whatever its political hue, has been reacting to events rather than seeking to control them from the outset. The debate in 1989–90 about the rights of Hong Kong citizens to migrate to the UK is an excellent illustration.

11.4 Trends in UK Migration in the Twentieth Century

Emigration from the UK

Since the beginning of the nineteenth century about 10 million Britons have moved overseas to settle, though in the peak years of population growth this huge movement still only accounted for about 10 per cent of natural increase. Most of the population of Australia and New Zealand is still of British descent, to a lesser extent in Canada. In the US census of 1980, 50 million people claimed English ancestry, 40 million Irish, and 10 million Scottish (US Department of Commerce, 1983). South America has small British colonies. In Asia British settlement was always limited, even at the height of the Raj. In Africa outside South Africa substantial settlement occurred only in Kenya and Rhodesia, now Zimbabwe.

Most of this movement has been spontaneous emigration, spurred on by the prospect of a more prosperous and open future in the English-speaking world overseas. The attitude of the UK government has been ambivalent. During the nineteenth century there was some encouragement to emigrate to ease poverty at home and settle the overseas dominions. Not until 1919 was there a general UK overseas settlement policy. The Free Passage Scheme set up in that year for ex-service men and their families accounted for 18 per cent of the migration from the UK to the Commonwealth in 1919–27. It led to the 1922 Empire Settlement Act which provided joint assistance to emigrants. But during the depression net migration went into reverse. After the Second World War the Overseas Migration Board, formed in 1953, took up the torch of re-establishing the migration tradition and satisfying the 'new and urgent needs for population in the Commonwealth countries overseas'. Assisted passage schemes were agreed with the governments of New Zealand, Southern Rhodesia, and, especially, Australia (the '£10 migrants').

Despite its fears of a declining home population the Royal Commission on Population in 1949 supported emigration to the Commonwealth as long as this did not provoke any excessive loss of skilled men. Non-economic consideration were paramount; the political and strategic advantages of a British-descended population in the Dominions and the USA led to a view that 'a large scale redistribution of manpower is desirable for the future of the Commonwealth' which was 'an important factor in maintaining world peace'. Declining average family size in territories overseas was commented upon, and it was felt that without immigration Canada, Australia, and New Zealand would remain sparsely populated.

These views have not stood the test of time in the UK, and encouragement of emigration now forms no part of British government policy. The dream of the decentralized British-descended Dominion Commonwealth has disappeared as Australia, New Zealand, and Canada have fallen more into the trading and cultural orbit of the USA and Asia, as their own national consciousness has grown, and as their immigrant populations have become more cosmopolitan. Neither Canada (since 1948) nor Australia now discriminate positively in favour of people of British origin. But migration to them has continued at a high level. Emigration exceeded immigration until it drifted below in 1984.

Since the mid-1980s the UK has entered a new phase in its exchanges of people with the rest of the world (Bulusu 1989). Until 1984 the pattern of net loss continued, but from then until 1987 the UK gained, and population projections (OPCS 1987c) had to be reviewed upwards accordingly. In 1987 though there was a steep fall in net immigration, and in 1988 net loss was reasserted. The old Dominions and the USA are still the favoured destinations of British emigrants, though New Zealand has been losing out: in 1985 only about 800 Britons emigrated there, while ten times that number went to Australia. Settlement emigration to tropical Africa has ceased. Direct emigration to South Africa continues, though since 1985 the net flow has been back to the UK. Overall, emigration to the Old Commonwealth has gone down sharply; that to the NCWP has also fallen, though more slowly. In contrast, migration to foreign countries has been rising (37,000 in 1988) and now comprises 58 per cent of all emigration from the UK. This trend indicates a further weakening of traditional migration ties with former colonies. In the mid-1980s non-Commonwealth countries were increasingly important origins for in-migrants, especially from Europe, and as with the emigration figures, immigration from non-Commonwealth sources accounted for a majority of movement. But as the UK fell into a net loss once more things changed. Hence, for 1988 the UK showed a net loss to the Old Commonwealth (26,000), USA (7,000), and EC (6,000) but net gains from NCWP (12,000), and 'other foreign' locations (4,000). British citizens continue to be well represented in flows, comprising 41 per cent of immigrants and 60 per cent of emigrants.

Immigration to the UK

The migration streams to Britain flow almost entirely independently of each other. Within the immigration settlement system different countries have predominated at different times and brought to the UK people of varied character. It therefore makes sense to look at each of these components separately. In popular perception immigration into the UK since the war has consisted mainly of poor non-white people from the New Commonwealth. While this is the most visible group it is not the only one and has provided the majority of migrants for relatively short periods of time; its members do not comprise the majority of the foreign-born. To correct this misapprehension the least visible migrants from outside the New Commonwealth, mostly from Ireland and Europe, will be considered first.

The Irish

The Irish have long been part of both the settlement and labour systems of the UK. The Potato Famine of the 1840s caused many Irish to settle on the mainland, creating chains of migration that have persisted to the present day. The diggers of canals and railway cuttings continue to have their modern counterparts on most big building sites in the UK, their numbers today reflecting the comparative states of the Irish and UK economies (Kirwan and Nairn 1983). Irish nurses, too, continue to play an important role in the NHS (Salt 1990*a*). Although periodic movement across the Irish Sea is common for many, the existence of substantial numbers of settlers, born in Ireland or with Irish ancestry is undeniable.

We still do not know how many Irish enter or leave the country every year. Migrants from Ireland are neither counted nor controlled. So it is necessary to turn to such sources as the census for information—both of Ireland and the UK—and the Labour Force Survey and National Insurance figures (Garvey 1985). Since the famine years in the 1840s the Irish-born presence in England and Wales has seldom gone below 400,000, the nadir being between 1911 and 1939. A surge in Irish immigration occurred in the 1950s leading to an Irish-born population of 900,000 by the end of the 1960s, almost 2 per cent of the the total. Since that time there has been a gradual decline, so that the 1981 census revealed just under 800,000 Irish born (1.6 per cent of the total). In 1987 the Labour Force Survey recorded 559,000 citizens of Eire living in the UK, 30 per cent of the total of 1,839,000 foreign nationals there (table 11.2).

Up to 1921 the figures relate, formally speaking, to UK internal migration. With the secession of the Irish Republic the data divide. In 1921 18 per cent of the Irish-born total in England and Wales came from Ulster; by 1981 this had grown to 26 per cent. In the past emigrants from Ulster have been mostly Roman Catholic, a fact which helped to counterbalance higher Roman Catholic fertility in the province and keep the numerical balance between the religious groups approximately constant. The return of terrorism in 1969 has since driven relatively more Protestants than Catholics out of the province.

British net passenger movements from 1921 fit the census totals only moderately. Data from the Irish Republic help to clarify some of the problems. These show a net return migration to Ireland during the 1970s as the Irish economy forged ahead, but a reassertion of the traditional net inflow to the UK in the 1980s (O'Grada 1985, Kirwan and Nairn 1984). The demographic characteristics of the Irish settled in Great Britain will be considered in Chapter 12.

Other Europeans and the US

Unlike the Irish, most other Europeans have come to the UK to work and then go home rather than to settle. The main exceptions are those who have come in as refugees or who remained in the UK at the end of the Second World War rather than return home. At first sight Britain

Table 11.2. Foreign nationals living in the UK, 1987 (thousands)

All nationalities	55,898
UK (incl Ch. Isles and IOM)	53,465
Foreign nationals	1,839
EC countries	809
EC countries (excl. Eire)	250
of which:	
Irish Republic	559
Belgium & Denmark	11
France	34
Italy	77
Netherlands	14
Germany (Fed. Rep.)	26
Germany (part not stated)	26
Greece	15
Portugal	19
Spain	28

Table 11.2. (Cont.)

USSR and Eastern Europe[a]	58
Northern Europe[b]	18
Central Europe[c]	14
Other Mediterranean Europe[d]	29
Northern Africa[e]	18
Eastern Africa[f]	31
Western Africa[g]	36
South Africa (Rep. of)	11
Turkey	24
Middle East[h]	64
Bangladesh	54
India	160
Pakistan	62
Sri Lanka	24
Malaysia	23
Philippines	11
Vietnam	10
China	21
Singapore & Japan	15
Other Asia[i]	10
Canada	27
USA	110
Jamaica	88
Other W. Indies/Caribbean and Guyana[j]	49
Central[k] & South America	10
Australia	33
New Zealand	12
Rest of World[l]/not stated/not known	602

[a] Albania, Bulgaria, Czechoslovakia, East Germany, Hungary, Poland, Romania, Yugoslavia.
[b] Finland, Iceland, Norway, Sweden.
[c] Austria, Switzerland.
[d] Malta, Gozo, Cyprus.
[e] Algeria, Egypt, Libya, Morocco, Sudan, Tunisia, Western Sahara, Gibraltar.
[f] Kenya, Malawi, Seychelles, Tanzania, Uganda, Zambia, Mauritius.
[g] Gambia, Ghana, Niger, Nigeria, Sierra Leone.
[l] Angola, Cameroon, Central African Republic, Chad, Congo, Equatorial Guinea, Gabon, Sao Tome and Principe, Zaïre.
[h] Bahrain, Iran, Iraq, Jordan, Kuwait, Lebanon, Oman, Qatar, Saudi Arabia, Syria, United Arab Emirates, North Yemen, South Yemen, Israel.
[i] Afghanistan, Bhutan, Brunei, Burma, East Timor, Indonesia, Kampuchea, North Korea, South Korea, Laos, Macao, Maldives, Mongolia, Nepal, Taiwan, Thailand, Hong Kong.
[j] Antigua and Barbuda, Bahamas, Cuba, Dominica, Dominican Republic, Grenada, Guadeloupe, Haiti, Martinique, Netherlands Antilles, Puerto Rico, St. Kitts-Nevis, Saint Lucia, St. Vincent and The Grenadines, Barbados, Trinidad and Tobago.
[k] Belize, Costa Rica, El Salvador, Guatemala, Honduras, Mexico, Nicaragua, Panama.

Source: Labour Force Survey (unpublished).

seems to be almost as powerful a magnet for labour as France and West Germany, but the comparison is misleading. Migration to the UK was facilitated by the complete absence of controls on Irish entry up to the present day, and on New Commonwealth citizens until the 1960s. Irish citizens make up about two-thirds of the estimated one million EC workers in the UK, according to the 1987 Labour Force Survey. By contrast in West Germany almost all non-EC workers entered subject to control and were specifically recruited. Shorn of these somewhat facilitated migrations, UK foreign labour begins to look more in proportion with modest UK economic performance since the war. The UK has stood in the middle of the EC labour sending–receiving spectrum, neither a major receiver (like West Germany) nor a major sender (like Italy). For example, the stock of French immigrants in Britain, recorded by the LFS, is low, just 34,000 in 1987. Except for the Huguenots, French presence in Britain has been modest since 1066. The biggest European contingent is the 77,000 Italians, settled especially in London. Numbering about 20,000 after World War II they had expanded to 97,000 by the 1966 census, but already then the Italian emigration stream had been diverted first to France then to West Germany (Salt 1976). The Italian population in Britain shows evidence of its post-war surge, followed by stagnation—very few children, with the working population (about 50,000) concentrated in the over-45s.

The German-born settlement in Britain is heterogeneous and has produced an odd age structure. Among the older population are refugee German Jews who arrived in the 1930s. The extraordinary number of children—36.2 per cent are below age 20—are for the most part the offspring of the large British army contingent in Germany. The number of 'real' Germans in Britain is therefore smaller than the 1981 census suggests, according to the Labour Force Survey about 52,000 in 1987.

In terms of numbers, the US population in Britain is the most impressive after the Irish and Indian—110,000 (excluding military personnel) according to the LFS. Despite the length of the US contact and the high degree of inter-marriage it is a constantly renewing young population, highly transient (many students) and non-settling.

With the exception of Italians, there is no tradition of 'Mediterranean' immigration into Britain. Communities from this region are therefore a novelty. The number of work permits issued to Iberians and Greeks has been low, but there is a tradition of entry for casual work in the leisure industry, which helps explain the stocks of these nationalities (table 11.2).

Immigration to Britain from the New Commonwealth and Pakistan

Post-war immigration

Most immigrants from the New Commonwealth and Pakistan (NCWP) are non-white (Mediterraneans are the major exception); almost all non-white immigrants in the UK are from the NCWP (Arabs are the only major exception). Colour identifies NCWP population and unifies them in the popular mind. Non-white immigrants to Britain are none the less a diverse group and their migration streams have been separate. These separate migration streams will be considered in two stages: their rapid increase before the 1962 Commonwealth Immigrants Act and the slow and erratic decline after it.

The 1951 census records 156,827 NCWP-born residents; most of these were white. Only the 16,188 born in the West Indies, or most of them, were non-white, together with long-standing colonies in Liverpool, Cardiff and other cities, some descended from West African seamen and white women and their children. The non-white population at that time cannot have been greater than 20,000, almost all born overseas. It has grown more than a hundredfold since, to reach 2.5 million in 1987, only about half of whom were born overseas.

The arrival of 492 intending immigrants from Jamaica on the converted troopship *Empire Windrush* in 1948 is usually taken to mark the beginning of West Indian settlement in the 'home country', though during the Second World War several thousand volunteers from the Caribbean colonies had served in the armed forces or worked in war industries (Patterson 1963). To some extent this migration followed new restrictions on entry to the USA, especially after the McCarran Walter Act in 1952. Numbers grew fast, from an estimated 2,000 per year in 1952/3 to 30,000 in 1956 and 66,000 in 1961, averaging over 50,000 a year during the 1950s.

Statistics are vague, but using various sources Peach (1968) has constructed the best set of estimates we are likely to get (table 11.3).

The 1961 census could not give a direct estimate of the coloured NCWP population because it includes NCWP-born whites, especially from India. The Home Office estimated a net inflow of 161,450 from the West Indies from 1955 to 1960, and 33,070 from India and 17,120 from Pakistan. By 1961 the census recorded 550,933 NCWP-born residents, including 172,379 from the West Indies, although Peach (1966) suggests there was a 20 per cent under-enumeration.

Migration from the Indian subcontinent had a much longer history among the good and great, a shorter one among the poor and lowly.

Table 11.3. Figures for arrivals from the West Indies

Year	Total arrivals, MSD	Total arrivals, Home Office	Net inward movement, Home Office
1951	898		
1952	1,281	2,200	
1953	2,285	2,300	
1954	10,261	9,200	
1955	24,473	30,370	27,500
1956	26,441	33,400	29,800
1957	22,473	27,620	23,020
1958	16,511	20,710	15,020
1959	20,397	32,390	16,390
1960	45,706	57,170	49,670
1961	61,749	74,590	66,290

Source: Peach (1968).

The English ruling class found Rajahs and Maharajas congenial; they were guests at court and at country houses, and were much applauded in first-class cricket. Indian mass migration began in wartime contacts, cheap travel, and again the open door of the 1948 Act. However, only 15 per cent of Pakistanis and 25 per cent of Indians present in 1971 had entered the country before 1961, compared with 43 per cent of West Indians (table 11.4).

The debate on the 1962 Act and its attendant publicity stimulated a great movement of population to Britain to 'beat the ban', so from 1959 a new wave of NCWP immigration took numbers to an all-time high in 1961. The 1971 census, like its predecessors, considerably underestimated the newly arrived NCWP population (Peach and Winchester 1974) but it suggested that in the eighteen months from January 1961 to June 1962, 98,000 West Indians arrived, 42,000 Indians, and 50,000 Pakistanis. Even at this time West Indian immigration had a balanced sex ratio, reflecting a general preference for family settlement. Indian migrants, by contrast, were predominantly male.

The 1962 Act may have transformed the Indian labour migration into a more permanent settlement by casting a shadow on the chances of future movement and the ease with which dependants might be brought across. The legislation was a watershed: before it West Indians always outnumbered Asians, afterwards Asian numbers grew faster not only as dependants, but also as applicants to the various categories of work vouchers instituted by the Act.

Table 11.4. Persons born outside the UK, by year of entry and country of birth, 1984 ('000s)

Country of birth	Year of entry					Total entrants	Percentage white
	Pre-1955	1955–64	1965–74	1975–84	No reply		
Irish Republic	243	136	61	27	76	544	98
Old Commonwealth	32	15	27	46	5	125	98
New Commonwealth and Pakistan	147	379	509	288	77	1,400	21
East African CW	6	16	113	49	9	192	13
Rest of African CW	7	9	22	30	7	75	31
Caribbean CW	18	146	52	8	18	242	5
India	61	87	148	64	23	382	18
Bangladesh	0	5	10	20	2	38	0
Far East CW	10	23	44	38	3	118	36
Mediterranean CW	33	40	30	7	3	112	94
Remainder of New Commonwealth	8	12	19	9	4	51	36
Pakistan	5	41	72	63	9	189	2
Other European Community	92	70	62	78	23	326	98
Other Europe (excluding USSR)	105	37	47	25	14	229	96
Rest of the world (including USSR)	88	39	75	181	18	400	93
All outside UK[a]	769	746	863	718	213	3,310	57

[a] Includes 287,000 persons who gave a year of entry but did not state their country of birth.

Source: Labour Force Survey.

The 1961 peak has never been rivalled again. The influx of 24,000 refugee Ugandan Asians in 1973, the third wave of NCWP migration, was only a fifth of the size. Overall the trend has been downward but erratic, for example, a major increase in immigration after 1977. Some primary migration continued after 1962 through the voucher system; it was characteristic of the tentative British approach to immigration control that for Commonwealth citizens it should use a different method of regulating labour migration from the work permit system adopted for aliens since 1920, and that even the statistical procedures for counting should be different.

NCWP immigration after 1962

West Indian migration never recovered from the 1962 limitations; furthermore in 1965 US immigration was liberalized and a large West Indian migration stream moved there instead and remains substantial today. By 1969 West Indian emigration from Britain more or less equalled immigration. Although it has been positive most years since there has been no major influx. Asians displaced West Indians in the voucher queues. Subsequently most Asian migrants were dependants. Rules for dependants were tightened in 1965 amid growing evidence that large numbers of friends and relations were being admitted improperly under the dependant categories. Nevertheless, the great majority—about three-quarters of all the Asians, Africans, and Hong Kong Chinese now in Britain—arrived after the 1962 legislation. There were differences within the Asian migration pattern itself. Indian immigration remained between twenty and thirty thousand arrivals a year during the 1960s; Pakistan migrants declined after 1967 and Bangladeshis came later.

The successive arrival in the UK of the different immigrant groups is summarized in table 11.4. About half of those people born in the Irish Republic and a similar proportion of those from other European countries outside the EC (principally Poland) had entered the UK by the mid-1950s. In contrast, of those people born in the NCWP who stated their year of entry, only 10 per cent—mostly white people born in the Mediterranean Commonwealth or India—entered before 1955. The majority of those born in the West Indies came into the UK between the mid-1950s and the mid-1960s, and the corresponding peak for people born in India came in the late 1960s and early 1970s. Bangladeshis are the most recent group, over a third of them entering during the 1980s.

The 1971 Act completed the transformation of the migration stream from primary migrant workers to dependants, almost all Asians. The only major exceptions were Asian doctors for whom work permits were readily issued. Despite various projections as to the maximum number of dependants still in Asia (Eversley and Sukdeo, 1969), estimates remained stubbornly high and the rules defining dependants were progressively tightened. Official reports claim that a high proportion of applications, especially from Bangladesh, include an element of fraud. The immigrant effect of the original colonizers was thereby multipled two- or threefold and is the main reason why immigration continued at a high level throughout the 1970s, 1980s, and into the 1990s.

The 1971 census counted 1,121,000 NCWP-born people in England and Wales, including 302,000 from the West Indies and 618,000 from the Asian and Oceanic Commonwealth (table 12.1). Once again the data were inflated by Indian-born whites and deflated by underenumeration (Peach and Winchester 1974). For the first and the last time the census asked a question on parental birthplace to try and extract

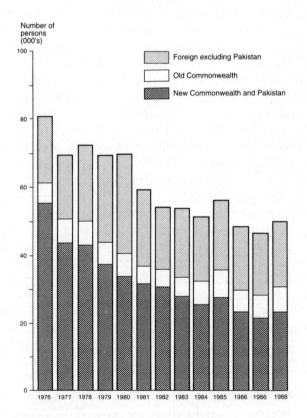

Source: Home Office.

Fɪɢ. 11.2. All acceptances for settlement, summary 1978–1988

ethnicity out of nativity, with the additional aid of surnames. The NCWP 'ethnic group' population (including the births in the UK and minus the white Asians) was estimated to be 1.3 million. The 1981 census recorded 1,474,000 born in the NCWP, and the high fertility of this group—quite variable between its component parts but all higher than the native born—has further multiplied the original representation. In the late 1980s the NCWP group, irrespective of birthplace, stood at about 2.5 million, or 4.5 per cent of the population.

In recent years there has been a steady decline in acceptance for settlement (figure 11.2). Foreign national and Old Commonwealth numbers have remained fairly stable while those of NCWP origin have declined most; the result is that the percentage of the total coming from the NCWP has fallen from around 60 per cent in the 1970s to around 50 per cent. In 1987 the number of persons accepted for settlement was 46,000, the lowest calendar year figure since 1962, but in 1988 it increased again to 49,100. The fall in 1986 and 1987 was attributable to a large extent to the new immigration rules introduced in 1985 which temporarily reduced acceptances of wives and children. A breakdown by category of immigrant for 1988 shows that wives and children accounted for half of acceptances, husbands were one in seven (figure 11.3). Other categories were relatively minor: only 10 per cent were primary migrants on the basis of work permit issue and only 12 per cent were refugees. The small number of special voucher holders, about 2,000 a year, are almost all East African Asians who hold UK passports.

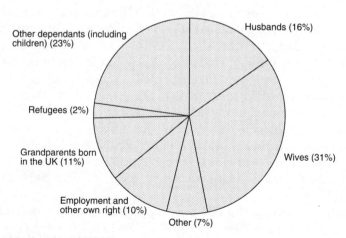

Note: Total number of people 49,280.

Source: Home Office

FIG. 11.3. Acceptances for settlement by category, 1988

Increasingly large numbers of young men and women of Asian origin born in the UK are reaching marriageable age. Some of them and/or their parents wish to follow traditional practice in arranging marriage with a suitable spouse from the home area (Jones and Shah 1980). In the 1987 age-structure, cohort size among young Asians doubles from 75,000 in the 15–19 age-group to 151,000 0–4-year-olds. This age-structure has the potential for substantial increases in migration for purposes of marriage. During 1969–74 there were few restrictions on Asian men wanting to bring in fiancées, although the privilege was not extended to women. In 1974 and again in 1980 the rules were changed to reduce the number of people entering through marriage. Women continued to be disadvantaged in that only those who were UK-born could bring in a fiancé. P. R. Jones (1982*a*) showed that in 1979 the UK-born comprised 28 per cent of the 15–19-year-olds, but 91 per cent of the 0–4-year-olds. The need to concur with EC policy on sex equality led to the two sexes being put on equal footing in 1985, extending the right of settlement to husbands of non-British citizens settled in the UK. However the intended migrant must show that the primary purpose of entry is marriage and not migration. So far, however, the trend in numbers entering for marriage has not been commensurate with the potential which is implicit in the age-structure.

11.5 Labour Migration and the British Economy

Inter-war recruitment of foreign workers

Restrictions on foreigners seeking work in Britain were brought in for security reasons during the First World War. A system of work permits was introduced in 1919 (the Aliens Restriction (Amendment) Act) and 1920 (the Aliens Order) which laid down conditions to regulate the employment of foreigners that essentially remain today. To obtain permits employers had to show that the proposed employment of a foreigner was reasonable and necessary, that adequate efforts had been made to find indigenous labour, and that wages and conditions were not less favourable than those accorded to British employees for similar work. However, no restrictions were imposed on immigration from the Empire and Commonwealth, including the Irish Free State after its independence in 1923.

Despite restrictions the UK borders proved quite porous to labour immigrants. Between 1921 and 1930 an average of 6,650 aliens with work permits, together with their dependants, landed in Britain each year; despite the recession the number rose to 16,500 per annum during

1931–40. Meanwhile the Southern Irish continued to arrive, the net inflow during 1924–39 being 239,203 (DE 1977).

Wartime brought new needs. The main pool tapped was Southern Ireland, and by July 1944 99,000 Irish workers were employed in Britain. Some workers from the Commonwealth, particularly the West Indies and India, were brought to the UK for training and employment in essential industries. A much larger number of people from these countries, including 7,000 West Indians who enlisted in the Royal Air Force, came as members of the Armed Forces. Their experiences of conditions in the mother country helped to stimulate subsequent New Commonwealth immigration. The war also brought new streams of migrants. Some of them became permanent. For example, most of the Poles of General Anders's army did not want to return to a newly Communist homeland.

Labour recruitment 1945–1972

The need to rebuild Europe's shattered economy after 1945 led to labour shortages in a number of countries, including the UK. Between 1946 and 1950 about 100,000 Poles and a further 77,000 displaced persons from Eastern Europe (European Volunteer Workers) were placed in employment. In addition, during the same period nearly 136,000 aliens with work permits and their dependants landed in Britain, an average of about 23,000 a year compared with 16,500 a year during the 1930s. Italians, Germans, and Swiss were the main nationalities, though substantial numbers of Austrians, Dutch, and French also came in. After 1947 numbers of work permits issued each year gradually rose, from 27,000 to over 50,000 in 1960, at which date the main recipients were Italians 10,688, Germans 9,911, Spaniards 6,694, and Swiss 4,684.

Despite early post-war labour immigration the UK was not to become the magnet for foreign workers that characterized other countries in North-Western Europe. From the late 1940s both Sweden and Switzerland, their economies not war-damaged, began to import workers in large numbers to satisfy the burgeoning demand created by reconstruction in Europe. Subsequently France and the Benelux countries followed suit in a trend massively reinforced after 1958 as the West German 'economic miracle' proved to have an almost insatiable appetite for immigrant labour. By 1973 France and West Germany both had about two and a half million foreign workers, Switzerland 600,000, and the Benelux countries a third of a million (Salt 1976). Most of the jobs on offer required low skill levels, many were dirty, dangerous, and boring, and shunned by the indigenous population (Castles and Kosack 1973). Migrants were expected to be temporary residents only, regulated by a series of work contracts. Apart from Finns going to Sweden, the countries around the Mediterranean basin provided the supply, first Italy, then Iberia, Greece, Yugoslavia, and Turkey (Salt 1976).

There is no doubt that these immigrations conferred enormous economic benefits on the countries of immigration (Böhning and Maillat 1974). They prevented bottlenecks in labour supply that might have slowed economic growth, and they kept down production costs by inhibiting cost-push inflation. But the immigration also brought built-in social problems related to family settlement and long-term assimilation. Even after a general halt was called throughout Western Europe to new recruitment of low-skilled labour after the 'oil crisis' of 1973, immigration did not stop. Workers already in the destination countries, fearful that if they left they would not be allowed back, responded by bringing in their families to join them in greater numbers than had been the case before (OECD annual). During the remainder of the 1970s numbers of immigrants in many countries continued to rise, with stocks of foreign population following suit (table 11.5).

The UK has largely escaped both the benefits and problems of large-scale labour immigration experienced on the other side of the Channel and North Sea. Much earlier than its European neighbours it took steps to curb its recruitment of overseas workers. The 1962 Act established a system of employment vouchers for all those wishing to come to the UK to work, including for the first time Commonwealth citizens. Initially there were three categories of vouchers: Category A for those with specific jobs to come to, Category B for those with a skill or qualification needed in Britain, and Category C for others. After the 1965 White Paper the last category was discontinued and the other two became increasingly restricted, so that overall issues fell from 41,001 in 1963 to 4,283 in 1972. An increasing proportion of vouchers went to people with skills, especially those with professional qualifications; by 1972 two-thirds of category B vouchers were given to doctors.

New Commonwealth migration and the post-war British economy

Immigration from the NCWP was not the organized guestworker phenomenon characteristic of other West European countries. In so far as employment was the main incentive for NCWP primary immigration, discussion of its relationship with the British economy has focused on two issues: the association of migration with economic trends and the

Table 11.5. Available information on stocks of foreign population in selected OECD countries, 1978–1987 ('000s)

	1975	1976	1977	1978	1979	1980	1981	1982	1983	1984	1985	1986	1987
Austria				—	—	282.7	299.2	302.9	275.0	268.8	271.7	275.7	283.0
Belgium	835.6	851.6	869.7	876.6	890.0	903.7	878.6	885.7	891.2	890.9	897.6	846.5	853.2
France	3442.4	—	—	—	—	—	—	3714.2	—	—	3752.2	—	—
Germany	4089.6	3948.3	3948.3	3981.1	4143.8	4453.3	4629.8	4666.9	4534.9	4363.7	4378.9	4512.7	4630.2
Netherlands	350.5	376.3	399.8	431.8	473.4	520.9	537.6	546.5	552.4	558.7	552.5	568.0	591.8
Sweden	409.9	418.0	424.0	424.2	424.1	421.7	414.0	405.5	397.1	390.6	388.6	390.8	401.0
Switzerland	1012.7	958.6	932.7	898.1	883.8	892.8	909.9	925.8	925.6	932.4	939.7	956.0	978.7

Source: OECD (1988).

demand for labour, and the consequences for structural characteristics of the economy such as unemployment, inflation, and productivity.

The overall relation of immigration, particularly from NCWP countries, to the growth and decline of the UK economy is still rather unclear. Peach (1978/9) shows a very close correlation between the inverse of UK unemployment and West Indian net immigration, estimated from Home Office net balances. The relationship, greatly disrupted in 1961, weakens with more recent data—as it should given the decline of work vouchers after 1962. This general finding is not too surprising since a sample survey of West Indians in the 1950s revealed that 90 per cent came to the UK to find work. A later survey (Smith 1977) estimated only 60 per cent of male Commonwealth migrants came to the UK specifically for job reasons and only 12 per cent had a specific job to go to. Despite the attractive power of employment, however, it is notable that even when British unemployment was at its highest, both in the 1960s and in the 1980s, West Indian immigration never went substantially into reverse as might have been expected.

The other side of the equation is the constant push of poverty and the pull of a developed welfare economy on a rapidly growing Third World population. West Indian emigration, for example, was unmistakedly related to national income in each island (Davison 1962). This factor seems particularly important in Asian migration, whose pattern of migration to Britain correlates much less well with British economic trends and whose more opportunistic character has been referred to earlier. The West Indian migration, too, becomes much less well correlated with British economic trends in the 1970s (Peach 1978/9; Jones 1980). The push factor behind the migration is illustrated by the diversion of these migration streams elsewhere as the British door has closed. West Indians have gone to the US while Asian migration streams have shifted to the Gulf states and to North America.

It has been suggested that the economic consequences of Commonwealth immigration have been neglected compared to the social ones (Jones and Smith 1970). The labour force contribution of NCWP migrants was never as great in the UK as that of the foreign workers in Continental Europe because the numbers were smaller. It was, however, considerable since initially most were male; furthermore, in 1961 93 per cent of West Indians, 92 per cent of Asians, and 86 per cent of the total NCWP population were of working age compared with 76 per cent of the indigenous British. Activity rates among women were high too: 55 per cent of West Indians, 34 per cent of Asians, and 32 per cent of women in Britain as a whole went out to work. Unemployment rates among NCWP immigrants have always been higher than those of the rest of the population, however.

The impact of NCWP immigration on the economy is strongly affected by the kind of jobs they have occupied. In only a few industries, like foundries and textiles and clothing, did their proportions of the work-force exceed 4 per cent of the total. The most salient labour concentrations have, in fact, been regional. In 1969 10 per cent of hospital domestic staff were non-white, but in London teaching hospitals the figure rose to 37 per cent. British Rail in London and also London Transport were favoured employers for the non-white population.

The most comprehensive review of the role of immigrant workers in the UK labour market was carried out in the mid-1970s (DE 1977). It showed that immigrants tended to be concentrated in jobs to which it was difficult to attract other workers and that firms and industries employing appreciable numbers of immigrants had often been faced with manpower shortages in those semi- and unskilled occupations in which immigrants were mainly employed. Even then though, the employment situation was changing as the attitudes of ethnic minorities changed. It was becoming more difficult to rely upon immigrants and their descendants to perform those job roles that the native population found unattractive. As the aspirations of young members of the minority population changed, it was also apparent that structural changes in the economy were leading to job losses in just those older sectors and less skilled occupations in which immigrants had found a niche. This combination has underlain many of the contemporary unemployment problems of the coloured population discussed in Chapter 12.

Labour immigration in the 1980s

The 1987 Labour Force Survey recorded 814,000 foreign nationals working in the UK, of whom 401,000 were from EC countries, including 258,000 Irish nationals (table 11.6). These stocks are continually being replenished. During 1987 91,000 labour migrants came into the UK. Of these, 40,000 (45 per cent) were foreign nationals, the rest UK citizens. Amongst the former, 19,000 (47 per cent) were from EC countries, split fairly evenly between those from Eire and those from other Community countries. Other developed market economies (Australasia, North America, Japan, non-EC Europe) supplied 13,000 (33 per cent of foreign workers). These figures are broadly consistent with work permit issues to non-EC nationals, of which there were 20,348 in 1987 (table 11.7). The UK economy therefore proves still to be surprisingly receptive to overseas workers, despite a quarter century of stringent labour immigration controls.

Table 11.6. Foreign nationals working in the UK, 1987 (thousands)

All nationalities	24,629
UK (incl. Ch. Isles & IOM)	23,584
Foreign nationals	814
EC countries	401
EC countries (excl. Eire)	144
of which:	
Irish Republic	258
Belgium & Denmark & Netherlands	14
France	18
Italy	50
Germany (Fed. Rep.)	14
Germany (part not stated)	13
Portugal and Greece	19
Spain	17
USSR and Eastern Europe[a]	21
Northern and Central Europe[b]	18
Other Mediterranean Europe[c]	16
Eastern Africa[d]	15
Western Africa[e]	16
Other Africa	12
Israel and Turkey	11
Middle East[f]	14
Bangladesh	11
India	73
Pakistan	14
Sri Lanka	13
Malaysia, Philippines, Singapore, and Japan	17
Other Asia	12
Canada	14
USA	41
Jamaica	45
Other W. Indies/Caribbean and Guyana[g]	27
Australia and New Zealand	21
Rest of World/not stated/not known	234

[a] Albania, Bulgaria, Czechoslovakia, East Germany, Hungary, Poland, Romania, Yugoslavia.
[b] Finland, Iceland, Norway, Sweden, Austria, Switzerland.
[c] Malta, Gozo, Cyprus.
[d] Kenya, Malawi, Seychelles, Tanzania, Uganda, Zambia, Mauritius.
[e] Gambia, Ghana, Niger, Nigeria, Sierra Leone.
[f] Bahrain, Iran, Iraq, Jordan, Kuwait, Lebanon, Oman, Qatar, Saudi Arabia, Syria, United Arab Emirates, North Yemen, South Yemen.
[g] Antigua and Barbuda, Bahamas, Cuba, Dominica, Dominican Republic, Grenada, Guadeloupe, Haiti, Martinique, Netherlands Antilles, Puerto Rico, St. Kitts-Nevis, St. Lucia, St. Vincent and The Grenadines, Barbados, Trinidad and Tobago.

Note: Figures exclude armed forces.

Source: Labour Force Survey (unpublished).

Table 11.7. Work permits and first permission issued, 1969–1988

Date	Long term	Annual % change	Short term	Annual % change	Trainee	Annual % change	Total	Annual % change
1969	67,093[a]				8,312		75,405	
1970	66,470[a]				7,549		74,019	−1.8
1971	56,031[a]				6,399		62,430	−15.7
1972	46,987[a]				5,712		52,669	−15.6
1973	20,716		12,123		3,697		36,536	−30.7
1974	20,695	−0.1	12,350	1.9	2,903	−21.5	35,948	−1.6
1975	18,664	−98	11,414	−7.6	3,136	8.0	33,214	−7.6
1976	11,925	n/a	8,545	n/a	2,651	n/a	25,271[b]	−23.9
1977	10,613	n/a	7,801	n/a	3,164	n/a	21,578	−14.6
1978	9,686	−8.7	9,463	21.3	3,662	15.7	22,811	5.7
1979	8,344	−13.9	9,649	2.0	4,010	9.5	22,003	−3.5
1980	6,423	−33.7	8,238	−14.6	4,152	3.5	18,813	−14.5
1981	5,906	−8.0	6,866	−16.6	3,088	−25.6	15,860	−15.7
1982	5,672	−4.0	7,225	5.2	2,557	−17.2	15,454	−2.6
1983	6,438	13.5	7,108	−1.6	2,361	−7.7	15,907	2.9
1984	6,801	6.0	6,244	−12.2	2,646	12.0	15,691	−1.4
1985	7,067	4.0	6,571	15.1	2,937	11.0	16,575	6.6
1986	7,915	12.0	7,947	20.9	2,826	−3.8	18,688	12.7
1987	8,063	1.9	9,385	18.1	2,900	−2.5	20,348	8.9
1988	10,391	28.9	11,793	25.7	3,790	30.7	25,974	27.6

[a] Figures include long and short term permits.
[b] Includes 2,150 issues unanalysed owing to industrial action.

Source: Salt (1990a).

It is likely that data from the LFS considerably underestimate total in-flows of foreign workers; for one thing they do not include many of those who stay for less than a year (Salt 1990*a*). Department of Social Security data suggest the total figure is around 100,000 per year, about half from the EC. Even this may be on the low side since the self-employed are excluded.

The 1971 Immigration Act ended the voucher system, introducing instead a system whereby similar employment controls operated for non-patrial Commonwealth citizens as for foreign workers (except, as usual, from the Irish Republic). Accession to the European Community in 1973, however, meant that EC nationals ceased to be subject to the full requirements of the Immigration Rules and became, for work permit purposes, part of the resident labour force. They were free to come and go as they pleased, seeking and taking employment. Hence, two distinct types of movement have developed, one controlled the other not. This has meant that flows of EC workers and those from the rest of the world differ in composition. The latter, requiring work permits, are much more highly skilled.

Labour entry under the work permit scheme

The United Kingdom uses work permits selectively, and for full employment they are now available only for overseas workers holding recognized professional qualifications or having a high degree of skill or experience. Allied to the main scheme is the Trainee and Work Experience Scheme. Its primary purpose is to help developing countries by providing training or work experience which is not readily available in the applicant's own country. Employment under TWES does not qualify the worker for permanent settlement, though case studies show that a number of TWES 'students' are granted permission to remain and work in the UK on completion of training or work experience.

Since 1969, when records of admissions for work became available, there has been a general reduction in numbers entering (table 11.7), although the three main components have not always behaved in the same way. During the early 1980s, for example, issues of long-term work permits (for over twelve months) were falling while short-term ones (for under twelve months) were going up. This reflects the nature of the occupations for which permits are granted; most short-term ones are to entertainers and sportspeople, and at times of recession the circuses continue. Never the less, over the period 1969–87 there was a clear negative relationship between total work permit issues and the state of the national economy, as measured by unemployment rate

($r = -0.92$): indeed, this relationship has held for all classes of permits (Salt and Kitching 1989).

The characteristics of those granted long-term work permits indicate a select group. In recent years 85 per cent have been in managerial or professional occupations, and two-thirds have come in on company transfers. Over half are American or Japanese, reflecting the UK's main trading links. Most come to London, and most of the rest to elsewhere in South-East England. They are well-paid too: a sample in 1988 averaged a salary of £28,400 per year (Salt and Kitching 1989).

Workers from the European Community

Nationals of the European Community working in the UK do not display such selectivity. Data for them are less good, coming as they do from the Labour Force Survey. They show for 1987 a more disparate group than those coming in with work permits. Youth is to the fore: 48 per cent of EC foreign nationals coming in were aged 16–24. Many of these are known to undertake casual and part-time work in the hotel and catering industry. This form of employment is reflected in their socio-economic structure, only 18 per cent being in professional and managerial occupations (SEGs 1–4), half in manual work (table 11.8).

Social and economic differences occur between the sexes and

Table 11.8. European Community workers in the UK, 1987: social group (%)

	Professional and managerial	Other non-manual	Manual
All			
EC	18.0	25.5	56.5
Irish	15.2	25.0	59.8
Rest of EC	23.0	26.3	50.7
Males			
EC	30.0	11.6	62.4
Irish	20.4	12.4	67.2
Rest of EC	37.5	10.0	52.5
Females			
EC	9.4	40.4	50.2
Irish	9.0	40.2	50.8
Rest of EC	10.1	40.8	49.1

Source: Labour Force Survey (unpublished).

between the Irish and other member nationals. European Community men are more than three times as likely to be in high status groups as EC women, the latter being found especially in a range of junior and intermediate non-manual jobs. The Irish are more likely to fill manual roles, 67 per cent of the men compared with 53 per cent of those from other EC countries. The Irish, too, distribute themselves more widely, only a third working in London compared with 44 per cent of other EC nationals.

11.6 Refugees in the UK

The principal refugee movements

Refugees constitute a special problem and may be regarded as a separate category from ordinary settlement or labour migration, although the distinction may be less clear than is often thought. They may flee from persecution while still keeping their eyes on their main chance. We cannot be sure how many refugees there are in the UK. The United Nations High Commission for Refugees suggests a total of 140,000, though it is unclear who is included in the figure. It is presumed to encompass many of those who arrived before and after the Second World War, though it is unknown how many refugees have become British citizens or gone back home or abroad (British Refugee Council 1987). It is also unclear how many family members of admitted refugees have subsequently arrived.

Refugee movements are usually characterized by their unpredictability, though not always so. Jewish migration (over 100,000) from Eastern Europe at the end of the nineteenth century occurred over thirty years during a long period of dispossession. In contrast Jewish refugees in the 1930s had more immediate fears; about 30,000 came to Britain. The Poles after the Second World War may be regarded in that light as well, though there is no doubt that many of them could have gone home safely had they wished. The smaller numbers of Hungarians and Czechs in 1956 and 1968 may rightly be regarded as fleeing persecution; in general it is true to say they were relatively easily assimilated into the UK.

The biggest acute refugee movement since then was the Ugandan air lift of 1972–3 when more than 20,000 Asians were expelled by the Amin government in Uganda in order to 'Africanize' the economy and confiscate the property of those expelled. A number of the British passport holders went to India in the first instance and only came to Britain as secondary migrants. Under the circumstances, the quota arrangement which in 1968 had been designed to prevent this kind of major influx was overruled and 27,000 were accepted. More recently, and after initial reluctance, 17,000 'boat people' have also been accepted, people of Chinese origin escaping from Vietnam. While it is clear that their position in Vietnam had worsened and many had indeed undergone very severe danger and privation at sea, later research (P. R. Jones 1982b) suggests that there was also a powerful economic motive behind their departure. This has not stopped those resettled in the UK finding the going difficult, their average unemployment rate still being 18 per cent in 1988, double that of the rest of the population. Their counterparts in the USA—always the preferred destination—have done better. Currently the special programme for Vietnamese resettlement is less than 250 per year, despite around fifty thousand in the 'closed camps' in Hong Kong. By 1989 British policy towards Vietnamese refugees in Hong Kong was in a state of flux. Officially it was one of repatriation, using force if necessary, since most of the 'refugees' were regarded as economic migrants.

Predicting further waves is difficult. Since the UK is located in a stable part of the world's political map it is unlikely that it will become a place of first asylum for those seeking escape from persecution. Of greater concern is the possibility of large numbers of British citizens overseas wanting to return as a result of political change where they are living. For example, in Hong Kong there are about 20,000, half of Chinese descent, who have a right of abode in the UK which they may wish to take up as 1997 approaches. Countries which wish to expand their populations, including Australia, Canada, and Singapore, are already recruiting highly skilled workers and rich entrepreneurs from Hong Kong. Some of these are among the five million or so other inhabitants of Hong Kong who include about three and a half million British Dependent Territories and British Overseas citizens who have no automatic right of entry to the UK. An estimated 250,000 of these will be allowed to settle in the UK as a result of the British Nationality (Hong Kong) Act. South Africa, too, is a potential source of people vacating insecurity. The Home Office estimates about 800,000 there are British or can claim full British citizenship under the patrial provisions of the 1971 Act.

Refugees in the 1980s

One of the important trends in international migration during the 1980s has been the growing numbers of those seeking asylum. Almost all countries in Western Europe and North America have experienced

Table 11.9. Applications for asylum, 1980–1987

	1980	1981	1982	1983	1984	1985	1986	1987	Total
Austria	9,300	34,500	6,300	5,900	7,200	6,700	8,700	11,400	90,000
Belgium	2,700	2,400	2,900	2,900	3,400	5,300	7,700	6,000	33,300
Denmark	—	—	—	800	4,300	8,700	9,300	2,100	25,200
France	13,700	9,200	12,600	14,300	15,900	25,800	23,400	24,800	139,700
Germany	107,800	49,400	37,200	19,700	35,300	73,900	99,700	57,400	480,400
Greece	1,800	2,300	1,200	500	800	1,400	4,300	7,000	19,300
Italy	2,500	3,600	3,200	3,100	4,600	5,400	6,500	10,900	39,800
Netherlands	3,200	1,600	1,800	2,000	2,600	5,700	5,900	14,000	36,800
Norway	—	—	—	200	300	900	2,700	8,600	12,700
Portugal	—	—	—	1,500	400	100	300	200	2,500
Spain	—	—	2,500	1,400	1,100	2,400	2,300	2,500	12,200
Sweden	—	—	—	3,000	12,000	14,500	14,600	18,500	62,600
Switzerland	6,100	5,200	7,200	7,900	7,500	9,700	8,600	10,900	63,100
United Kingdom	10,000	2,900	3,600	5,500	3,300	5,500	3,900	4,200	38,900
TOTAL	157,100	111,100	78,500	68,700	98,700	166,000	197,900	178,500	1,056,500

Source: United Nations High Commission for Refugees (unpublished).

increased applications (OECD annual). Often the refugee status of many asylum seekers has been dubious. Many are would-be economic migrants seeking to exploit loopholes in immigration control systems. Destination countries which allow in applicants while their cases are being reviewed are especially attractive. West Germany is perceived to be a particularly soft touch; its political past has made it unusually generous to refugee applicants. Its system of reviewing applications— now itself under review—can take anything up to two years, so it has undoubted attractions to those whose cases are dubious, and helps explain why in 1986 West Germany dealt with 100,000 applications. In consequence, there has been a general tightening up in control procedures for granting asylum and the UK is no exception.

No one can be sure how many genuine refugees (i.e. those with a real fear of persecution) there are in the world, but the figure is probably around 15–20 million. Most of these originate in Third World countries and that is where most find a place of first (and usually last) asylum. In fact, the UK has escaped relatively lightly in the number of asylum applications it has received. Across Western Europe as a whole data from the UN High Commission for Refugees show there have been over a million applications for asylum in the 1980s (table 11.9). Compared with neighbouring countries, the level of applications to the UK has been low, and during most of the 1980s has not shown the tendency to rise experienced by Sweden, Belgium, and France, for example. In 1989, however, applications for asylum in the UK trebled to 15,500. A better index of 'demand' for asylum than simple numbers

Table 11.10. Asylum-seekers in selected countries as percentage of population

	Population (millions)	Asylum applications 1983–7	Asylum-seekers 1983–7 as % of population
Sweden	8.3	62,600	0.75
Switzerland	6.5	44,600	0.69
Austria	7.5	39,000	0.52
Denmark	5.1	25,000	0.49
Germany	61.0	286,000	0.47
Norway	4.1	13,000	0.32
Belgium	9.9	25,600	0.26
Netherlands	14.5	30,200	0.21
France	55.2	104,200	0.19
United Kingdom	56.6	22,400	0.04

Table 11.11. Applications received for refugee status or asylum, by nationality, 1979 to 1988

Nationality	1979	1980	1981	1982	1983	1984	1985	1986	1987	1988[a]	Total
Afghanistan	30	86	82	43	16	39	49	64	67	35	510
Czechoslovakia	30	53	55	55	26	19	18	4	10	25	295
Ethiopia	189	97	90	90	126	135	209	212	266	230	1,640
Ghana	122	29	13	407	689	337	175	220	153	155	2,300
Hungary	44	62	21	44	26	21	17	8	21	35	300
India	—	2	1	8	8	60	32	86	126	310	630
Iran	797	1,421	1,547	2,280	1,862	1,310	1,126	1,119	942	555	12,955
Iraq	65	146	14	271	298	348	350	269	326	315	2,405
Lebanon	9	9	—	3	24	28	34	37	102	165	410
Libya	—	41	41	48	26	78	60	125	72	60	550
Pakistan	83	38	79	63	36	133	114	265	459	220	1,490
Poland	42	55	92	494	127	109	71	59	57	85	1,190
Seychelles	—	15	19	20	25	31	66	90	201	65	530
Somalia	—	14	11	14	50	83	244	214	356	390	1,375
South Africa	1	27	62	54	61	54	53	73	73	35	495
Sri Lanka	1	18	12	16	380	548	2,306	1,332	774	340	5,730
Sudan	1	3	14	11	19	57	27	27	42	35	235

Turkey	6	21	1	38	43	61	34	111	210	855	1,385
Uganda	38	28	99	66	199	165	203	189	440	565	1,990
Zaïre	—	2	—	2	4	11	8	18	63	100	210
Other countries by geographical region											
Africa	17	32	43	49	80	130	120	102	85	110	770
Americas	12	74	68	51	58	23	28	35	51	80	480
Middle East	23	13	6	23	22	27	19	53	56	40	280
Remainder of Asia	18	22	7	22	25	11	3	27	13	25	170
Europe	35	43	42	50	49	26	34	27	42	45	395
Other nationalities including stateless	—	1	6	1	17	25	44	45	153	235[b]	525
TOTAL	1,563	2,352	2,425	4,223	4,296	3,869	5,444	4,811	5,160	5,105	39,245

[a] Provisional estimates.
[b] Includes an estimated remaining 120 applications at ports.

Source: Home Office 1989.

is their size relative to the national population. For the UK there are only four applications for every hundred residents, compared with 75 for Sweden, 47 for West Germany, and 21 for the Netherlands (table 11.10).

Between 1979 and 1988 there were 39,245 applications for asylum or exceptional leave to remain (the latter subject to periodic review), according to Home Office figures. Of these, 9,600 were granted refugee status, 12,000 exceptional leave to remain. In addition, 20,500 South-East Asian refugees were accepted for settlement. This high proportion admitted has led some to suggest that the phenomenon of 'economic refugee' is of small importance as far as the UK is concerned (British Refugee Council 1987). A large majority of those admitted as refugees have come from just seven countries: Iran, Iraq, Sri Lanka, Poland, Ghana, Ethiopia, and Uganda (table 11.11). Among Tamils from Sri Lanka particularly, numbers have fluctuated depending upon conditions. The origins of refugees coming to the UK have changed considerably during the 1980s in response to political circumstances abroad. The most notable increase has been of Sri Lankans who accounted for 6 per cent of applications in 1983, 12 per cent in 1984, and 42 per cent in 1985. Iranians were the biggest single group from 1979 to 1984 following the fall of the Shah in 1979 but have since declined. Ghanaian applications have also gone down following greater political stability. The British Refugee Council argues that in recent years increase or decline in refugee numbers appears to correlate directly with circumstances such as war and conflict rather than with the economic situation, and that if asylum seekers followed the path of economic migration applications would be more evenly distributed from a wide range of poorer countries.

UK policy towards refugees

Until 1987 refugee policy in the UK was based on an interpretation of the UN Convention of 1951 in which each application was treated on its merits by interview at the port of entry. Fear of rising pressure from fraudulent asylees prompted the UK government to pass the Immigration (Carrier's Liability) Act in 1987. Under the provisions of this law transport companies may be fined £1,000 for each passenger who is allowed to travel to the UK without the necessary documents, even if that person subsequently applies for and is granted refugee status. In the first two months of operation carriers—mainly the airlines—were fined on 600 occasions for bringing to the UK persons without proper visas. The legislation is thus designed to keep would-be refugees away from the UK until a right of entry has been established at a consulate overseas.

As the world-wide refugee crisis has increased and as the 'economic refugee' loophole has been exploited all Western European governments have looked hard at their admission policies for asylees. Discussions are currently going on within the EC to co-ordinate national policies, especially on the concept of first asylum. From 1992 when the Single European Act comes into force refugees accepted by one member country will be able to move freely within the Community. It is clearly important to have a commonly agreed policy and set of rules before then.

12   Ethnic Minority Populations

12.1 Introduction

Immigrants and ethnic minorities

Immigration, which was discussed in the last chapter, has a direct and obvious effect upon population size and structure. It also tends to make populations more diverse. If immigrants succeed in preserving their distinctive cultural attributes and transmitting them to children born in their new adopted country, they may then establish a new ethnic minority which may be demographically distinct from the majority population. This chapter focuses on the demography and distribution of ethnic minorities in the UK, and on their changing characteristics.

A distinction should be made between 'immigrants' and 'ethnic minorities'. An 'immigrant' is readily defined demographically, conventionally as a person who, having been absent for at least a year, enters a country with the intention of staying at least a year. An ethnic minority is usually defined as a group of people self-consciously aware of membership of a culturally defined group at least nominally claiming descent from common ancestors and distinguished from the majority of the national population by characteristics such as language, religion or other value systems, social and family structure. These may be (but are not necessarily) associated with a characteristic demographic regime of fertility, mortality, marriage, and kinship derived from the original country of origin. Ethnic minorities may or may not be distinguished by distinctive racial (biological, genetically inherited) characteristics such as colour, physique, or socially invisible population differences in genetic markers such as blood groups and other biochemical differences (Cavalli-Sforza and Bodmer 1971). In this chapter the term 'racial' refers to biological, genetically inherited characteristics which may be found more frequently in one population than another, the term 'ethnic' to cultural characteristics. Ethnicity is not easy to define in ways which command universal agreement, but the reader is referred elsewhere (Bulmer 1980, A. Wilson 1981, 1984, A. D. Smith 1986) for further discussion.

Not all ethnic minorities arise from migrant populations (see Kirkwood, Herbertson, and Parkes 1983). International boundary changes or successful invasions by larger populations may turn 'nations' or parts of them into ethnic minorities. Immigrants from a particular place may comprise a coherent and distinctive group and thereby create an 'instant' ethnic minority, even without a second generation, if they are present in sufficient numbers to sustain a coherent social life. An immigrant population will turn itself into an ethnic minority if it succeeds in transmitting distinctive ethnic characteristics to the generations born in the host country, or some modification of them. Then they may permanently change the demography of the total population, making it more diverse.

Ethnic homogeneity in pre-twentieth-century Britain

In general, before this century immigrants to Britain did not establish substantial ethnic minority populations which preserved in the long term distinctive new forms of language, religion, or way of life. Since the Anglo-Saxon invaders of the sixth and seventh centuries drove the original Celtic speaking Britons into Wales and Cornwall and confined others to the Scottish highlands England has been ethnically homogeneous compared to most other European countries. As the previous chapter on immigration noted, there have frequently been immigration streams of varying size into Britain, although never on the scale of post-war Commonwealth immigration. The larger immigrant streams sometimes caused much public concern, but with the exception of the Jewish immigration from the 1880s, little thought seems to have been given to the idea that the new populations would radically alter the structure of the British population (but see Dickinson 1967). Almost all previous migrants (apart from the Jews) came from other West European countries, from similar economies and demographic regimes, and were not racially distinguishable from the mass of the population. There were few barriers to the assimilation of the immigrants themselves, and particularly of their children.

There have always been immigrant populations in Britain, mostly in larger towns. Many were well organized. Some received corporate royal protection of their privileges, because of the valuable specialist services they rendered, especially in finance (Lombards, Jews) or textiles (Flemings). The latter had been encouraged to move to England, poached from the Low Countries by Henry I and Edward III to found and revive the medieval textile industry (Nicolson 1976). A tax survey of 1440 counted 16,000 foreigners. This suggests a population of up to 30,000, about 1 per cent of the total population. The leading groups were Flemings, Brabanters, and Germans (24 per cent), French (22 per cent), Irish (16 per cent), and Scots (19 per cent) (Thrupp 1957). From the sixteenth century, migration was dominated by Protestant refugee groups from the Low Countries and France, such as the 10,000 'Poor Palatines' of 1709. Their entry had been facilitated by the Whigs' 'General Naturalization Act', which was rapidly repealed by the Tories who succeeded them (Dickinson 1967). More important were the French Protestants, the 'Huguenots' of the sixteenth and seventeenth century, who received an unusually warm welcome. They represented much of the military, academic, commercial, and industrial talent of France. Initially they may have numbered 80,000–100,000, although many moved on to Ireland, Holland, or the American colonies (see Scouloudi 1938).

All these and many other groups have ceased to exist as social groupings. They survive now only in the form of distinctive surnames (Fleming, Courtauld, Paul, Dolland, Brunel) and in the case of the Huguenots, the Huguenot Society, a learned society devoted to archives rather than to revanchist politics or to the pursuit of ethnic minority grants from the Urban Programme. Indeed the dates at which the distinctive Huguenot and other Protestant congregations became extinct or amalgamated with neighbouring English congregations in the eighteenth century can be precisely determined. For the most part, the Italians and Germans and others who came in the nineteenth century to work as stonemasons, clerks, and engineers have likewise left no organized communities. Instead they have vanished into the general population through assimilation, migration and intermarriage. The substantial number of black people of the eighteenth century, most slaves imported to become servants in London, and ex-sailors, seem to have died out without trace. This impoverished population, almost entirely male, may have numbered 10,000 at its peak (Shyllon 1977). Some were repatriated to Freetown in Africa (Sierra Leone) or as free labourers to the West Indies. Today's indigenous mixed-race black populations of Liverpool and Cardiff have nineteenth-century origins, the former from West African sailors and white (mostly Irish) women.

From the nineteenth century the Irish formed the greatest migration stream. An Irish presence is still an important dimension of life in many British towns, but for the most part it is sustained by continued immigration, not by the transmission to generations born in the UK of any strong sense of being distinctively Irish. People of Irish descent in the UK greatly outnumber the Irish-born. But most are distinguished, if at all, only by surname and, often, adherence to Roman Catholicism. Jews have assimilated culturally to a more variable degree but apart from small 'defensively structured' (Siegel 1970) groups such as the Hassidim, people with Jewish ancestry in Britain substantially exceed recorded synagogue membership. A book on the demography of Britain in the 1930s might have dealt with immigrants, and with groups defined by religion or in the case of Welsh and Gaelic speakers, by language; it would have been odd to have included a chapter on 'ethnic minorities'.

The rise of ethnicity in the twentieth century

The arrival after the 1940s of large numbers of immigrants from Third World countries with populations which differed sharply by colour and race and (with the exception of the West Indians) by language and religion as well, was a break with the past. These multiple cultural differences, relative poverty, and hostility to the newcomers on the part of the natives have kept them distinctive and partly segregated within the UK.

Their arrival coincided with radical changes in attitudes to race and Empire (Rich 1986), at least among people in public life. The Empire was abandoned in just twenty years. Its place was taken by a multi-racial Commonwealth of independent states whose citizens still retained rights of entry to the UK through the provisions of the British Nationality Act 1948. Britain's relative economic and military strength was in retreat and with it confidence in old attitudes and in-stitutions. Religion and nationalism declined. In intellectual circles at least cultural relativism took their place: a refusal to acknowledge the superiority or preferability of one culture over others. This has gone hand in hand with a rise of ethnic consciousness which is one of the major political novelties of the twentieth-century world, both among European minorities within the West and outside it (Barth 1969, A. D. Smith 1986). The more assertive and confident traditional Third World cultures which have come with immigration, with their near-universal religious faith and more rigid social relations, have thereby moved into a more accommodating social environment than would previously have been the case. These new attitudes have also helped to slow the apparently inexorable decline of our own indigenous minority lan-guages. The use of the Welsh language declined only slightly between the censuses of 1971 and 1981 (to 503,000 over age 3), as new measures of law and new practices promoted Welsh speaking.

The spread of anti-discrimination measures into all areas of life following the first Race Relations Act of 1965 and its successors, including the more militant wing of 'anti-racism', has given practical force to new attitudes. They are reinforced by substantial public spending on ethnic minority culture, language, and religion—about £140 million per year from the government's 'Urban Programme' and 'Section 11' grant, from the Department of Education and Science, and from local government. This support is helping to preserve some well-assimilated groups which were previously disappearing from view. Poles and Italians for example, are just two of the populations benefiting from public spending on language conservation, as well as more recent immigrant populations speaking Gujarati, Urdu, Turkish, and other languages.

12.2 Definition and Measurement of British Ethnic Minority Populations

We now have a multi-racial and a multi-ethnic society, even though the native population of British origin still accounts for over 90 per cent of the total. What the new categories of people should be called, and how their numbers and characteristics should be measured (or even if they ought to be measured) have presented major problems in demography, often with strong political overtones.

Ethnic categories in Britain (including language)

Devising sensible categories for ethnic groups in Britain has been a constant source of difficulty. Those which seem to work in practice are shown in figure 12.1. They are hybrid classifications in that they include colour categories ('white', 'black'), national categories ('Indian'), and ethnic categories coincident with language as well as broad geographical origin ('Arab', 'Chinese'). Here a single question is trying to do the same job as three related questions in the US census (on 'race', 'ethnic origin', and 'Hispanic origin', Lowry 1980). The hybrid list has been objected to on principle. In practice, Third World migration to Britain is so recent that a population defined on a national basis includes more or less the same people as ethnic or racial or linguistic categories would do, and has the advantage of being in common use. Such terms disguise the ethnic heterogeneity of the populations, especially those from the Indian subcontinent. But some hierarchical grouping is essential, and the Asian groups are more different from the native British population than they are from each other. Categories must represent a group with which individuals are prepared to identify. Indeed any ethnic group only exists if individuals will identify themselves with it (or are so identified).

Some people are reluctant to identify with specific, or any, ethnic

11 Racial or ethnic group

Please tick the appropriate box to show the racial or ethnic group to which the person belongs.

If the person was born in the United Kingdom of West Indian, African, Asian, Arab, Chinese or 'Other European' descent, please tick one of the boxes numbered 2 to 10 to show the group from which the person is descended.

1 ☐ English, Welsh, Scottish or Irish
2 ☐ Other European
3 ☐ West Indian or Guyanese
4 ☐ African
5 ☐ Indian
6 ☐ Pakistani
7 ☐ Bangladeshi
8 ☐ Arab
9 ☐ Chinese
10 ☐ Any **other** racial or ethnic group, or if of **mixed** racial or ethnic descent (please describe below)

(a) 1979 Test census

4. **SHOW CARD A**

To which of the groups listed on this card do you consider you belong?

White 0
West Indian or Guyanese 1
Indian 2
Pakistani 3
Bangladeshi 4
Chinese .... 5 → Q5
African 6
Arab.. 7
Mixed Origin (SPECIFY) 8

Other (SPECIFY) 9

(b) 1981 Labour Force Survey (and subsequent)

Ethnic group

Please tick the appropriate box.

White ☐ 0
Black-Caribbean ☐ 1
Black-African ☐ 2
Black-Other ☐
please describe

Indian ☐ 3
Pakistani ☐ 4
Bangladeshi ☐ 5
Chinese ☐ 6
Any other ethnic group ☐
please describe

If you are descended from more than one ethnic or racial group, please tick the group to which you consider you belong, or tick the 'Any other ethnic group' box and describe your ancestry in the space provided.

(c) 1991 census

Source: 1991 Census.

FIG. 12.1. Some official classifications of ethnicity

group categories. Others object to any classification of people on the basis of race or colour, for any reason. Many of the people who objected to the proposed question in the 1979 Test Census were West Indians and older Eastern European Jews (Sillitoe 1978b). West Indians are the only major NCWP immigrant group whose native language is English and who may have been inclined to identify themselves as 'British'. In fact there have been repeated suggestions that a category 'black British' be introduced for the census and surveys, and as a result of later fieldwork the term 'black' has been adopted for the 1991 census (figure 12.1, Sillitoe 1987, White 1990). The census question differs in unhelpful ways from the LFS question; for example it excludes the category 'mixed'. Whether Asians wish to identify themselves as 'black' is a controversial matter. Some radical groups wishing to brigade immigrant and ethnic minority opinion use the term to include all non-white ethnic minority groups. But it seems that the majority of Asians do not regard themselves as 'black'. Africans (not East African Asians) who have racial affinities to West Indians are content to be called black. But Africans have very different social and demographic characteristics from West Indians, and it makes no cultural or demographic sense to group them together as the OPCS and other agencies are inclined to do. Turks (mostly from Cyprus) find it difficult to locate themselves in any of the categories (Sillitoe 1978b).

The broad divisions of religion and of language tend to coincide with national boundaries, even though there are further divisions within them. Most Bangladeshis (116,000 in Britain in 1987) and Pakistanis (392,000) are Muslim: Indians (762,000) are Sikh, Hindu, or Muslim (12 per cent in India) with a few Christians. Of the 116,000 Africans in Britain perhaps a quarter are Muslim, almost all the 79,000 Arabs may be assumed to be. Altogether this gives about 700,000 Muslims in Britain. The often repeated claim that there are two million has no foundation (see Peach 1990). South Asian respondents are often keen to specify their membership of language or religious categories in detail (Sillitoe 1978b). This reflects the fragmented nature of South Asian society, subdivided even at the local level vertically and horizontally by caste, language, and religion, which define social position and social relations. Religious affiliation was considered for the census question for 1981 and 1991. Most immigrants to Britain come from a small selection of the large number of ethnic groups in the very heterogenous Indian subcontinent; in part a consequence of chain migration from a relatively small number of villages. For example, most Indians are Gujarati Hindus or Sikhs, most from quite circumscribed areas of Gujarat and Punjab. Many Pakistanis come from

Mirpur; most Bangladeshis are from the districts of Sylhet and Campbellpur. Most Chinese in Britain are from a few villages in Kowloon.

More closely defined ethnic or religious groups are usually studied by specially designed surveys, which may rely on the 'snowballing' of contacts with that community, or information from religious institutions, rather then conventional survey methods: for example Sikhs (Simons 1982*a*), various South Asian groups (Robinson 1986), Roman Catholics (Spencer 1982), and Jews (Kosmin 1987). Elementary statistics are collected by some local authorities which see it as their responsibility to identify ethnic groups and promote their interests with grants and other special provision. For example the ILEA recorded 143 different languages in use in its schools.

Most of the British population would probably deny that they belonged to an ethnic group. Ethnicity is regarded, if it is considered at all, as something to do with minority groups of immigrants, especially coloured immigrants. Furthermore there is little interest in England in the social or economic differences (if any) between people of English, Scots, Welsh, Italian, or Polish origins. In Scotland and Wales themselves, of course, there are important nationalist political parties which emphasize language and other cultural differences in their bid to mobilize support for more independence. In the same areas, demographic differences on those lines are either non-existent or trivial compared to the substantial differences between all of them and the Third World populations. Such national categories for whites were used in the 1979 LFS and some local authorities still use them. But their token nature was obvious, and the term 'white' is a much simpler catchall. In this discussion the original white Celtic populations in the UK tend to get overlooked. As groups their demography has been ignored (as opposed, for example, to their local political significance). But there is no evidence that the Welsh and Gaelic speaking people in the UK are demographically distinct, over and above the characteristics expected from their occupations and residence (for the most part) in remote rural areas.

Minorities defined by religion

No official routine data on religious adherence are collected in Great Britain. Data on religious adherence come from unofficial surveys or from religious organizations themselves (Brierley 1988, Currie *et al.* 1977). Some religious organizations set up statistical bureaux to monitor trends in numbers. In England the Newman Demographic Survey performed this function from 1953 to 1964 (Spencer 1964). Jews have kept such records for even longer (see Lindfield 1931): in Britain the Board of Deputies set up its Statistical and Demographic Research unit in 1965. Concern about numbers becomes particularly acute when a minority fears it is declining. Quite apart from the problem of marriage partners, in each settlement there is a minimum population needed to sustain the infrastructure of social life—religious communities, shops, organizations, and so on—and ultimately to preserve organized religious observance itself.

Generally in Britain religious observance is only followed by a minority. In a survey in 1981 24 per cent denied any faith, compared with 35 per cent in the Netherlands and 42 per cent in Denmark (Simons 1986*a*). Some religious differences were originally linked to broader ethnic differences, being imported with immigrants. Most of the five million Roman Catholics in Britain are descended from Irish immigrants of the nineteenth and twentieth centuries. Most Jews are descendants of the East European immigrants from the 1880s. Many people change their religious affiliation, acquire one or lose one, entirely on personal grounds by conversion or schism as well as by intermarriage. Roman Catholicism gained numbers fast through conversion up to the 1960s (Brierley 1988); Methodism and other Low Church sects owe their existence entirely to such processes, although there is a tendency for such new movements to be more successful in regions already socially or ethnically distinct (Wales and Scotland). The religious affiliations of more recent immigrants from the Third World, however, are more demographically significant. Data on specifically religious affiliation are scanty but can be inferred with reasonable accuracy, at least with respect to South Asians, from ethnic estimates. Partly because of Islam's prescriptions limiting the position of women in society, Muslim populations tend to have higher fertility than other cultures in the same society and Muslim nations tend to have higher fertility than other, economically comparable nations (Breton 1988, Weeks 1988).

Data on country of birth from the census

Chapter 10 described the development of statistics on immigration in the twentieth century, and noted the absence of any continuing collection of statistics on the population of immigrants once they had been given the right to settle in the UK. Elsewhere, e.g. Germany and Holland, especially where there are continuous population registers, such populations are recorded as 'foreign', unless they acquire local nationality, and are readily distinguished in statistics. In the UK data on birthplace can serve as a substitute to some extent. Place of birth has been asked in the census since 1841 and routinely in other enquiries and on the registration of birth and death since 1969. Birthplace data from the census and Labour Force Survey provides a measure of the net contribution to the British population from overseas migration and the characteristics of the foreign born. It is the only substantial source of information on past and present UK residents born in the Republic of Ireland (table 12.1) and on nineteenth-century immigration.

In some of the earlier censuses answers on nationality were used in combination with answers on birthplace to estimate the size of foreign populations ('aliens'): for example, the Jewish immigrants from Eastern Europe from the 1880s to the First World War. The General Register Office responded in an imaginative way to enumerate the new population, many of whom were illiterate in English. From the census of 1881 to 1921 census schedules were prepared in Yiddish for use in areas of Jewish concentration, mostly in the East End of London (e.g. Registrar-General 1904). Rabbinical support was mobilized to persuade the Jewish population to support the census. Volunteers helped to publicize it and gave assistance in filling in census forms.

No question on religion or on race was asked either then or subsequently in any census of Great Britain (OPCS/CRO 1977). (Religion is asked on a voluntary basis in Northern Ireland; the 'religious census' of 1851 was a separate, voluntary enquiry.) An attempt was made to correct underenumeration by analysing the surnames on the census schedule. This technique depends on persons of particular national, ethnic, religious or language minority origin having characteristic surnames (for a technical discussion see Goldman et al. 1988). It has been widely used for purposes of ethnic identification and progressively refined, most recently by local authorities such as the London Borough of Redbridge (Chard 1988) and by the Research Unit of the Board of Deputies of British Jews (Waterman and Kosmin 1986) in response to the lack of any census data on ethnicity. It is claimed that this technique allows 95 per cent of the surnames on the electoral register to be allocated to the appropriate group, and for a classification to be adopted which most usefully reflects the local distribution of minorities in more detail than the general LFS categories permit, to estimate the size of Muslim, Hindu, and Jewish communities, Tamils, Gujaratis, Chinese, and others (Chard 1988). Confidence in such use of surnames is reinforced by the astonishing constancy of the frequency distribution of the most common surnames in England over more than a century (Ammon 1976).

Undercounting is a classic problem in the enumeration of poor

Table 12.1. Birthplace of the population, England and Wales, 1841–1981 ('000s)

	1841	1851	1861	1871	1881	1891	1901	1911	1921	1931	1951	1961	1971	1981
All countries	15,907	17,928	20,066	22,712	25,975	29,003	32,528	36,070	37,887	39,952	43,758	47,105	48,750	48,522
UK	15,836	17,816	19,891	22,497	25,672	28,654	32,048	35,529	35,161	38,929	41,836	43,642	45,585	45,303
S. Ireland	}291	520	601	567	562	458	427	375	365	451	492	683	676	580
N. Ireland										70	135	188	216	209
Old Commonwealth								49	64	70	88	89	129	137
New Commonwealth (All Comm/Empire before 1921)	17	34	51	71	94	112	136	162	204	226	202	571	1,121	1,292
West Indies								11	11	10	16	172	302	294
India								}63	}74	87	111	157	313	383
Pakistan, Bangladesh											11	31	136	230
Foreign born	39	62	102	139	174	233	339	374	306	308	914	760	929	1,209
of which not British subjects														
British subjects		50	84	101	118	198	248	285	228	180	378	417	228	—
France			13	18	15	21	31	39	33	29	30	30	35	37
Germany			21	33	37	51	65	65	22	28	99	121	148	169
Italy			4	5	7	10	20	22	21	20	33	81	103	93
Poland (Russian Poland until 1921)			4	7	11	21	21	37	42	44	152	120	104	88
Russia/USSR (includes Poland before 1921)			5	10	14	45	93	108	62	36	76	53	46	34

Notes: Table excludes some categories of birthplace, including 'not stated', so columns will not sum to 'All countries' total. Categories used and totals differ somewhat between censuses. S. Ireland included with UK until 1931. Ireland 'part not stated' included with S. Ireland.

Sources: 1841 Census Enumeration Abstract Preface pp. 143–23; 1851 Census Population Tables II Vol. I Summary Tables p.cclxxxvii 7. XXXVIII; 1861 Census Volume II Population Tables. Summary Tables p.lxxiv T.XXV, p.lxxv, T.XXVII; 1871 Census Volume III Summary Tables p.xlix T.XX, p.li T.XXIII; also General Report and Appendix A p. 70–83 for earlier censuses; 1881 Census Volume III, Summary Tables p.xxiv T.9; 1891 Census Summary Tables p.xxvii T.7, p.xxxii T.9; 1901 Census Summary Tables p. 246 Table XLIV, p. 260 T.XLVI; 1911 Census General Report p. 204 T.XCIV, Appendix D p. 352. T.7; 1911 Census Vol. IX Birth places; 1921 Census General Tables p. 181 T.46, p. 178 T.45; 1931 Census General Tables p. 179 T.30; 1951 Census General Tables p. 114 T.32, p. 118 and 119 T.33; 1961 Census Birthplace and Nationality Tables T1, 2, 7, 1971 Census Country of Birth Tables p. 6 T.1; 1981 Census Country of Birth Tables pp. 4, 5 T.1 (usually resident population)

immigrants or minority populations from the Third World, because of their patterns of residence concentrated in multiply occupied housing, a tendency to be illiterate in the language of the host country, and deliberate evasion arising from hostility to official authority or fear of discrimination. Peach estimated at least a 20 per cent undercount of persons born in the West Indies in the 1961 census, about 18 per cent in 1966, and between 11 and 14 per cent in 1971, and an undercount in 1971 of about 4 per cent of the Indian-born and 29 per cent of the Pakistani-born (Peach 1966, Peach and Winchester 1973). The 1981 census figures on birthplace give figures close to those reported in 1971, updated by births, deaths, and migration (Population Statistics Division, OPCS 1986a) except for children, probably from under-counting by the International Passenger Survey.

Approaches to 'ethnicity' in the census and surveys

Until the 1971 census, questions related to immigrant populations con-centrated solely on first generation immigrants, through the questions on birthplace and on previous residence. Subsequent generations had been assumed to assimilate into British society and to be of no further concern to the census in respect of their origins. But in the 1960s it became apparent that the New Commonwealth immigrants and their children seemed likely to retain distinct cultural, social, and demo-graphic characteristics for some time into the future. They were forming substantial 'ethnic minority' populations. Birthplace data were becoming rapidly obsolete as a measure of their size or characteristics. Accordingly, the need was felt to enumerate these ethnic group popu-lations on other criteria.

In response the 1971 census added questions on parental birthplace and date of entry into the UK to the question on birthplace. A direct ethnic or origin question was considered to be too sensitive. Instead, the additional questions provided a complicated and roundabout way of identifying people of New Commonwealth ethnic origin who were themselves born in Britain. The immigration was then too recent for any further generations to be numerically important. People of British origin, born in the New Commonwealth but whose parents were born in the UK, could similarly be removed from the estimates, especially the considerable number of people of British origin born in India. The 1971 estimates of the New Commonwealth and Pakistani ethnic group population (table 12.2) were refined by reference to an analysis of surnames (Immigrant Statistics Unit 1977), which are distinctive in New Commonwealth immigrant groups except West Indians.

Table 12.2. NCWP population estimates, 1951–1986 ('000s)

Mid-year to mid-year	Population at beginning of period	Components of change				Change in year	Population at end of period	Percentage of GB population at end of period
		Birth[a]	Deaths[b]	Natural increase	Net migration			
1951	—	—	—	—	—	—	200	0.4
1961	—	—	—	—	—	—	500	1.0
1971–2	1,371	+49	−4	+45	+37	+82	1,453	2.7
1972–3	1,453	+47	−5	+42	+52	+94	1,547	2.8
1973–4	1,547	+44	−5	+39	+29	+68	1,615	3.0
1974–5	1,615	+44	−5	+39	+37	+76	1,691	3.1
1975–6	1,691	+45	−5	+40	+40	+80	1,771	3.3
1976–7	1,771	+47	−5	+42	+33	+75	1,846	3.4
1977–8	1,846	+50	−6	+44	+30	+74	1,920	3.5
1978–9	1,920	+56	−6	+50	+43	+93	2,013	3.7
1979–80	2,013	+60	−6	+54	+37	+91	2,104	3.9
1980–1	2,104	+60	−6	+54	+25	+80	2,183	4.0
1984–6	—						2,432	4.5
average		+64	−6	+58	+24	+82		

[a] 1971–81 only cover births where at least one parent was overseas-born; precise information is not available about the number of births to parents of NCWP ethnic origin both of whom were UK-born.

[b] Includes an estimate of deaths of children of NCWP ethnic origin born in Great Britain.

Note: The 'NCWP Ethnic group population estimates' derived from population accounting were only made from 1971 to 1981 (see PP 1 83/2). The 1951 and 1961 estimates are internal OPCS estimates (Shaw 1988b); those for 1984–6 are the average of LFS results. They include births to UK-born mothers of NCWP origin and (unlike the OPCS figures) include births to Mediterranean CW mothers but not to non-CW ethnic minorities.

Sources: OPCS Monitor PP1 81/6 (1971–80 data). OPCS Monitor PP1 83/2 (1980–1 data). Shaw 1988a, table 2 (Population Trends 51) (1951, 1961, 1984–6). Shaw 1988b, Box 1 (Population Trends 52) (1984–6 components).

The categories generated were far from watertight, especially those of mixed birthplaces. They could not be expected to be useful for more than one or two censuses because of the increasing numbers of births expected to occur in the UK to parents of ethnic minority descent who were themselves born in the UK. A direct ethnic question seemed to be needed for the 1981 census. Despite reasonably successful field trials (Sillitoe 1978*b*) and initial support from both main political parties, the question was eventually abandoned in 1980 after difficulties in later trials (Sillitoe 1980) and after the relative failure of the 1979 Test Census in Haringey (OPCS 1980*c*). The area was known from previous surveys to have low response rates; and a political campaign was waged against the test in the run-up to the 1979 General Election. In the US adventurous publicity and language helped to secure the success of the much more detailed racial and ethnic questions in the 1980 census (Lowry 1980).

The arguments in favour of a question on ethnicity—mostly concerned with welfare and housing demands on local authorities—have not gone away. The Home Affairs Committee (1982) proposed one for the 1986 sample census (which was cancelled) and again for the 1991 census. This has been accepted (figure 12.1). A direct ethnic question similar to that proposed for the 1981 census has been used successfully in the 1977–8 National Dwelling and Housing Survey (OPCS 1980*a*), in the 1979 Labour Force Survey, and in an improved form in the Labour Force Surveys from 1981 onwards (OPCS 1986*d*). The LFS is now the chief source of data on ethnic minority populations (Shaw 1988). The General Household Survey only records interviewers' impressions of colour (white/coloured only) and asks questions on birthplace and date of entry into the UK. Some NCWP populations (e.g. Mediterranean) are not normally regarded as coloured; some coloured persons in the UK are not of NCWP origin. The OPCS estimates now exclude Cypriot and other Mediterranean populations and births. Greeks and Turks are not regarded as coloured but do form self-conscious ethnic minorities with characteristic language, religion, and family structure. By excluding them the OPCS is treating 'NCWP ethnic minority' as synonymous with 'non-white'.

Meanwhile the 1981 Census can only provide ethnic data by inference: on persons in households headed by persons born in the New Commonwealth and Pakistan (OPCS 1983*b*). OPCS surveys suggest that 90 per cent of all persons of NCWP ethnic origin will be enumerated in such households (OPCS 1982*c*); indeed most of the UK-born ethnic minority population are still dependent children. But the 1981 LFS indicated that 15 per cent of people in such households may not be of NCWP ethnic origin, being overseas-born British or partners in mixed marriages (OPCS 1983c).

Data from vital registration, and NCWP population estimates

The 1971 census estimates of the 'New Commonwealth and Pakistani (NCWP) ethnic group population' were updated annually until 1981 by deaths, migration, and births (OPCS 1981b, 1983d) from the vital registration system and the International Passenger Survey (IPS). During that decade the NCWP population grew from 1,371,000 (2.7 per cent of the population of Great Britain) to 2,104,000 (4.0 per cent). Registration of vital events records only the birthplace of the mother or of the deceased (since 1969, OPCS 1983c), not ethnicity. Migrants are recorded in the IPS by nationality and country of last residence. Ethnicity of births has been noted by a few local authorities (e.g. City of Birmingham 1983) and in special surveys. Adjustments have had to be made to the vital registration data to make them more appropriate as 'ethnic' estimates, by inspection of surnames (Immigrant Statistics Unit 1977). The NCWP population still has a young age structure with correspondingly few deaths. A proportion of these deaths are of elderly NCWP-born persons of British origin, now an ageing population. A correction was made on the basis of a sample of surnames, yielding an estimate of annual deaths from 4,000 per year in 1971 to 6,000 in 1981. It was assumed that most migrants between the UK and the New Commonwealth and Pakistan are of New Commonwealth and Pakistani ethnic origin. This appears to be substantially true, but the IPS does not record ethnicity or colour.

Throughout the 1970s annual births to mothers born in the NCWP rose to 50,000, 8 per cent of the total in England and Wales. In 1985 they reached 51,700. But classifying births according to the NCWP birthplace of the mother is increasingly underestimating births of NCWP ethnicity. There are errors in both directions. In 1985 7,900 out of the 52,700 births to women born in the NCWP were estimated to be to 'white' mothers. This total includes 2,900 born to women born in the Mediterranean Commonwealth (see Shaw 1988, OPCS 1989c), most of them Cypriots. Surnames help to correct such errors. Conversely births to mothers of New Commonwealth and Pakistani origin who were themselves born in Britain will not be included. Between 10,000 and 25,000 children had been born in the UK up to 1981 with parents born in the UK but of NCWP ancestry (OPCS 1981b), the majority West Indian. In the mid-1980s, there were probably between 5,000 and 10,000 such births a year, to add to a total of about over 50,000 a year

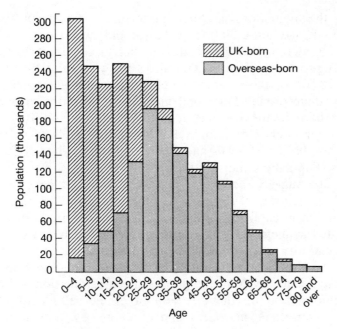

Source: Shaw 1988a: 7, fig. 9.

Fig. 12.2. Age structure of ethnic minority population, 1984–1986 average

to mothers born in the NCWP. In 1984–6 there were about 600,000 ethnic minority women in Great Britain of childbearing age (15–44). Overall, 60 per cent were born in the NCWP, 30 per cent in the UK. Most of the latter are young; 70 per cent of ethnic minority women aged 15–19 were born in the UK; only 5 per cent of those aged 30–44. These proportions differ greatly according to ethnic group; about half of West Indian women over age 15 were born in the UK, only 15 per cent of South Asians. These proportions will change rapidly with time (figure 12.2).

The Labour Force Survey can provide estimates of the numbers of ethnic minority children with UK born mothers. In 1984, 15 per cent (96,000 out 655,000) of non-white children aged 0–14 born in the UK had mothers also born in the UK. Where the mother's birthplace was known, about 21 per cent of West Indian children had mothers born in the UK, 3 per cent of Indian, Pakistani, and Bangladeshi children, and 60 per cent of children of mixed origin (OPCS 1985a). In all about a half of these children of UK-born mothers are of mixed or West Indian origin, but the numbers of Asian origin will increase rapidly as successively larger cohorts of UK-born Asian girls become older. In general, the number of such children is increasing rapidly: in 1984 there were 47,000 aged 0–4, 30,000 aged 5–9, and 19,000 aged 10–14. All things considered, the non-white population of Great Britain was probably producing about 62,000 births per year from 1982 to 1985. About 58,000 of these births were to the non-white population of NCWP ethnic origin. That total includes 5,000 births to non-white mothers born in the UK and a further 5,000 to non-white fathers (mostly to mothers born in the UK). It excludes the 3,000 or so births to mothers born in Cyprus and Malta and other white NCWP-born mothers (Population Statistics Division 1986*b*).

LFS data suggest there were 263,000 persons of mixed origin in 1987, three-quarters of them born in the UK. The 1986-based OPCS figures on births explicitly assume that all births of mixed origin should be counted as members of the appropriate ethnic minority group. In fact the majority are described as being of mixed origin by their parents, and most of the rest as 'white' (see section 12.6). The omission of this 'mixed' category from the proposed census question will deprive us of information on the direction of ethnic self-identification in Britain. Inter-ethnic marriages and other unions, and the children resulting from them, are a major indicator of ethnic assimilation.

The absence of ethnic or parental birthplace questions in the 1981 census ended the series of NCWP ethnic group population estimates in 1981 (OPCS 1983*d*). Since then the LFS has taken over this function (OPCS 1986*d*). For 1987 it estimated the non-white population of Great Britain at 2.48 million, about 4.6 per cent of the population. The LFS is vulnerable to the same problems of under-enumeration as a census, as well as sampling error. Internal analysis (e.g. on the age and sex distribution) reveals a low response by young West Indian males, also apparent in other surveys (Brown 1984, Hollis 1982, D. Coleman 1985) and paralleled by the regular undercount of young black males in the US census. It must also be assumed that most illegal immigrants evade such surveys. It is not known whether their numbers are in tens or hundreds of thousands. A glimpse of the possible scale was given in 1990 when official investigations suggested that 13,000 people had gained entry in one year from West Africa through bogus marriages.

12.3 Geographical Distribution of Immigrants and Ethnic Minority Populations

Immigrant populations are strongly concentrated geographically. This concentration is a function of the jobs they have found, the availability of suitable accommodation, and of the location of initial settlements close to ports of entry. Accordingly different immigrant populations tend to have different geographical distributions. Irish immigrants are concentrated in the North-West (13 per cent), particularly Manchester, in the West Midlands (13 per cent), and especially in London (33 per cent) and the South-East (50 per cent). NCWP immigrants are concentrated in major cities and conurbations, especially London, and therefore in the regions where the conurbations are situated (table 12.3) particularly the South-East (56 per cent). Very few have settled in Wales (1 per cent), Scotland (3 per cent), or Northern Ireland or in the Newcastle (Tyne and Wear) conurbation (0.6 per cent). Most members of NCWP ethnic minority groups still live in households headed by persons who are themselves immigrants from the New Commonwealth. So the distribution of the ethnic population, including people born in the UK, closely resembles that of immigrants. As a consequence mothers born in the NCWP are now producing between a fifth and a half of all births in some major urban areas: in 1987 21 per cent in Greater London; 46 per cent in Tower Hamlets, 42 per cent in Brent (table 12.4).

The conurbations dominate the spatial structure of the immigrant population. Very few migrants settled in the countryside or have subsequently moved there. Most of them came from villages as peasant cultivators, small traders, or craftsmen, so the migration both from Ireland and even more from the New Commonwealth and Pakistan has been a rural–urban migration as well as an international migration. Three-quarters of the West Indian-born population, two-thirds of the Pakistanis, and half the Indian-born live in the seven conurbations, compared to only a third of the British born. Not all the conurbations, though, have a high proportion of NCWP immigrants. They were not attracted to areas where unemployment was already high: Glasgow, Tyneside and, initially, Liverpool. The regional concentrations of different New Commonwealth immigrants and their descendants are quite different. Sixty-four per cent of British residents of African origin lived in London in 1983–5, 57 per cent of the West Indians, 54 per cent of Bangladeshis, 14 per cent of Pakistanis.

Very few immigrants live in the new towns or in those new peripheral estates in suburban areas which have grown fastest since the Second World War. West Indians are highly concentrated in areas where population has been declining and are much less often found in areas of population growth—much the same is true of the Asian population (Peach 1982, Peach, Robinson, Maxted, and Chance 1988), although high Asian birth-rates have started to reverse population decline in, for example, Bradford and some London boroughs.

Table 12.3. Country of birth: resident population of Great Britain, 1981 ('000s)

	Irish Republic	All NCWP	West Indies	India	Pakistan	Bangla-desh	East Africa	West Africa	Mediterranean
Great Britain	607.4	1513.4	295.2	391.9	188.1	48.5	197.2	52.7	129.6
England & Wales	580.4	1473.7	293.6	382.8	181.7	47.9	192.8	50.8	126.5
North	8.1	20.7	0.8	5.2	3.6	0.8	1.8	0.7	1.9
Tyne and Wear	2.7	8.8	0.3	2.4	1.4	0.6	0.6	0.4	0.6
Yorkshire and Humberside	29.4	98.8	13.1	22.2	37.8	3.2	6.5	1.7	4.3
S. Yorkshire	5.7	15.9	3.5	2.3	5.6	0.5	0.7	0.3	0.9
W. Yorkshire	18.0	71.6	10.0	17.5	31.5	2.3	4.5	0.9	1.5
East Midlands	30.4	98.8	14.6	34.1	7.1	1.5	26.0	1.0	4.9
East Anglia	9.9	24.3	3.3	5.0	2.5	0.6	3.3	0.5	3.5
South-East	305.3	850.8	195.9	198.7	59.7	28.1	118.2	39.3	90.6
Greater London	199.4	630.9	167.4	139.1	35.6	22.1	91.6	34.0	69.0
South-West	27.5	56.2	8.9	12.9	2.9	0.7	5.9	1.5	8.7
West Midlands	76.9	193.9	41.8	72.4	38.3	6.6	17.1	1.7	5.1
WM Metropolitan	60.5	164.1	37.7	63.1	33.8	5.9	13.5	1.2	2.8
North-West	79.3	110.1	13.2	28.3	28.3	5.3	11.8	3.5	5.2
Greater Manchester	45.3	64.0	10.1	15.1	17.0	3.9	6.8	1.9	2.4
Merseyside	15.0	10.8	1.3	2.1	0.4	0.3	0.8	1.0	1.0
Wales	13.4	20.1	2.0	4.0	2.0	1.0	2.1	0.9	2.3
Scotland	28.0	39.7	1.5	9.1	6.5	0.6	4.4	1.8	3.1
Central Clydeside	14.4	14.9	0.4	4.0	4.4	0.3	1.0	0.7	0.6

Notes: NCWP = New Commonwealth and Pakistan. 'Irish Republic' includes 'Ireland, part not stated'. The conurbation data are included in the appropriate regional totals.

Sources: OPCS 1983b. Census 1981 Country of Birth Tables, table 1.

Table 12.4. Proportion of births to mothers born in the NCWP (%)

Area of mother's usual residence	1971	1976	1981	1985	1987
Metropolitan counties					
Greater London	17	21	22	21	21
Inner London	24	27	27	25	25
Tower Hamlets	18	31	41	45	46
Outer London	12	17	19	19	18
Brent	34	42	46	45	42
Greater Manchester	5	7	9	9	8
Bolton	8	13	16	16	·
Merseyside	1	1	1	1	1
South Yorkshire	3	3	4	4	4
Tyne and Wear	1	2	2	2	3
West Midlands	15	19	21	18	16
Birmingham	20	24	28	25	23
West Yorkshire	9	12	15	14	12
Bradford	17	21	27	27	24
Other urban districts with over 20% in 1985					
Luton	13	17	25	24	22
Slough	27	31	38	37	31
Blackburn	15	27	31	28	23
Leicester	20	30	32	32	31
England and Wales	6	7	8	8	8

Note: Selected areas only.

Sources: OPCS Monitor FM1 86/4, FM1 83/3, FM1 77/2. FM1 Births volume 1974 and unpublished data. OPCS Birth Statistics 1987 series FM1 no 16 t. 9.2.

Within the conurbations immigrants tend to concentrate in inner city areas, the only sources of cheap housing reasonably readily available. Discrimination against immigrants has been claimed as a major concentrating factor (Rex and Moore 1967). But many immigrants need cheap housing and strongly prefer to live together in order to recreate home conditions as far as possible (Robinson 1986): to re-establish familiar surroundings, to be near to relatives and to their own shops and places of worship, to establish a settlement which is, in effect, an internal colony. Immigrants were not immediately eligible for council housing because their short-term residence in the country did not enable them to qualify under the local authorities' allocation rules. Initially they were concentrated in private rented accommodation, most of which is in older property in inner city areas. Asians rapidly become owner-occupiers—partly to meet the needs of their large households and for proximity to the extended family. Immigrant concentrations have been aided by the tendency for whites to move out of areas which are becoming dominated by immigrant communities, although unlike the experience of US cities, there seems to be no critical point of concentration at which 'white flight' turns into a rout (Woods 1979b).

Consequently, immigrant colonies have grown up so that their distribution by local authority areas is highly skewed, more so than with the Irish, Jews, and other immigrants of the past (Walter 1980). South Asians have been relatively more economically successful than other minorities. Many East African Asians in particular brought professional, business, and entrepreneurial skills with them. A higher proportion of South Asians now own their own homes than do whites. This has helped their diffusion to suburban districts. Bangladeshis, the most recent migrants and the poorest, unlike other South Asian groups are mostly in local authority housing; in Tower Hamlets over 80 per cent of households accepted as statutorily homeless were Bangladeshi. West Indians have been less economically successful or upwardly mobile than Asians. They are concentrated in local authority tenure; both of these factors have tended to keep them concentrated in inner urban areas (Lee 1977).

From 1961 to 1981 there was relatively little change in the degree of segregation in the London boroughs (Peach et al. 1981). Individual minority groups, however, displayed different patterns. Bangladeshis have very high levels of segregation in Britain (20 per cent of the total enumerated Bangladeshi-born population in Britain live in the borough of Tower Hamlets), being more segregated from Pakistanis and Indians than from the population as a whole. Cypriots also show very high levels of segregation. West Indians are generally less segregated than others from the NCWP.

The Irish-born in Britain remain concentrated in certain urban centres, although they are more widely dispersed than immigrants from the New Commonwealth (Walter 1980). But their case is different. Because of long-term settlement and high levels of intermarriage, there is a larger population of part-Irish ancestry, mostly Roman Catholic, widely distributed in the social structure and throughout the country (see Hornsby-Smith 1987). Nineteenth-century Irish immigrants settled mainly in the heavy manufacturing areas of Scotland and the North-West, some parts of the industrial North-East, and London. Since the Second World War it has been the South-East and the Midlands that have been attractive to immigrants from Ireland, Scotland hardly at all. The Irish-born only show residential segregation in the biggest areas of settlement such as Camden Town in London; socially they remain concentrated in social class V (21 per cent in 1971 compared with only 10 per cent in classes I and II), particularly in building and general labouring.

12.4 Demography of Jews, Irish, and Catholics in Britain

Immigrants can import new and unfamiliar demographic regimes. The Jewish immigrants of the late nineteenth century for example, did not share the West European marriage pattern of the host population, had a more complex family structure and larger household and family size. Fertility in Ireland has not fallen in line with the decline general elsewhere, so it is not surprising that the fertility of Irish-born women remains somewhat higher than average. New Commonwealth immigrants brought to Britain for the first time the fertility, mortality, and family patterns typical of Third World demographic regimes. There is not one New Commonwealth immigrant demography; there are several. In fact some overseas Chinese populations, notably in Hong Kong and Singapore, are now ahead of European demographic trends, with lower fertility and mortality than Britain's (table 12.5). Particular

Table 12.5. Contrast between demographic regimes of countries sending immigrants to Britain and British national averages, c.1988

Country of origin	TFR	e_o	IMR	Household size
England and Wales	1.8	75	9	2.4
Irish Republic	2.5	72	9	3.1
Jamaica	2.8	74	20	3.0
India	4.3	58	104	5.2
Pakistan	6.5	54	121	6.3
Bangladesh	5.8	52	135	6.0
Hong Kong	1.3	76	8	3.5

Note: TFR = Total Fertility Rate; e_o = expectation of life at birth (both sexes); IMR = Infant mortality rate.

Sources: Mean household size for Pakistan, Bangladesh from 1976, 1975 World Fertility Survey. Population Reference Bureau (1989), *World Population Data Sheet*, Washington DC, Population Reference Bureau Inc. Kabir, M. (1980). *Demographic Characteristic of Household Populations*, World Fertility Survey Comparative Studies no. 6, London, International Statistical Institute. United Nations (1973), *The Determinants and Consequences of Population Trends*, New York, United Nations.

components are discussed below. The characteristics of populations descended from the older immigrations of Irish and Jews are quite different from those of the post-war migrants from the Third World. They will be considered first.

The Jews

The Jews of medieval Britain were expelled in 1290, after despoilation and massacre. Small numbers of Sephardi Jews, fleeing persecution in Portugal, were admitted by the Lord Protector in 1665 and their position was confirmed by Charles II. Many became Anglicized, a number became prominent in politics, banking, and science (see Roth 1978, Nicolson 1976). There were about 60,000 in Britain by 1881 (figure 12.3). Most Jews in Britain today are descended from the mass migration from Eastern Europe during the 1880s. Only about 3 per cent of British Jews today belong to Sephardi synagogues. Starting from decidedly non-Western European marriage and household patterns, the nineteenth-century Jewish population assimilated fast to British demographic norms. Average age at marriage increased rapidly in the late nineteenth and early twentieth century to reach the national average. In some respects the Jews had overtaken the indigenous population in the demographic transition to low birth- and death-rates (Kosmin 1982).

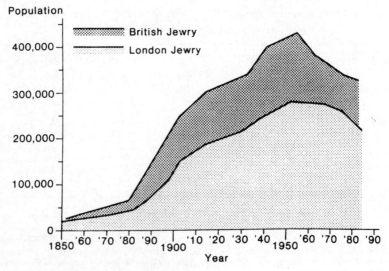

Source: Waterman and Kosmin 1986, fig. 1.

FIG. 12.3. The changing population of British Jewry, 1850–1985

Over 150,000 Jews came to Britain in that period. The immigration stream was slowed by the Aliens Act of 1905 and stopped by the First World War. Post-war immigration legislation and political changes in Eastern Europe prevented its resumption, except for about 30,000 refugees from Germany in the 1930s. By 1918 the Jewish population of the United Kingdom is estimated to have been 300,000 (Waterman and Kosmin 1986). The population grew to a peak of 430,000 in the 1950s (figure 12.3), about 70 per cent living in London. This may be an exaggerated figure. The earlier population estimates are more reliable, as the population was then more homogeneous and geographically concentrated. It is more difficult to give a population figure today. Most estimates are based on synagogue records of membership and burials and marriages from the Board of Deputies.

The population is blurred at the edges. In 1976, it was estimated that there was a 'core' population of about a quarter of a million. This 'religious' population known to synagogues, mostly of entirely Jewish origin, is a lot smaller than the wider population with at least some Jewish origins. Because of intermarriage, many who consider themselves Jewish will not have uniquely Jewish origins. Many who do have such origins may not consider themselves Jewish, especially if descent is through the father and not the mother, in which case other Jews will not consider them Jewish. Whether practising or not, it is believed that most Jews who regard themselves as Jews wish to be buried by religious rites (see Haberman, Kosmin, and Levy 1983). The 1985 population estimate based on 4,844 deaths gives a population of 330,000—a decline of 25 per cent since the 1950s (Waterman and Kosmin 1986).

Today the Jewish population as recorded through religious observance is in decline. The population is ageing: 18.1 per cent of the population in 1975–9 was aged 65 or over compared with 14.5 per cent of the population of England and Wales. The national birth-rate is estimated (1980–3) at 10.4 per thousand (England and Wales 13.0); local studies suggest fertility rates certainly no higher than the national average and possibly lower. As the death-rate (14.4 per thousand) is higher than the birth-rate, the population is in a state of natural decline of 0.4 per cent per year. Synagogue marriages, except the ultra-Orthodox, have declined faster than marriages in general and since the late 1970s faster than other kinds of religious marriage. Only about half the birth cohorts of British Jews born in the 1950s and 1960s who could have married in a synagogue did so in the early 1980s. In 1983 there were 18,000 Israeli Jews born in Britain or of British descent—about 5 per cent of the British Jewish population. In all, British Jews now living abroad amount to about 12 per cent of the home population of Jews.

The Jewish population remains highly urbanized and metropolitan. 201,000 British Jews live in London (61 per cent of the UK total), the next biggest centre being Manchester (30,000, 9 per cent). Within this urban pattern of settlement there has been a general dispersal to the suburbs away from the earlier inner-city areas of settlement. This may well have been accompanied by a drift away from observance. The population in such centres as Sheffield has declined to about a third of its 1918 total and is correspondingly elderly (Kosmin, Bauer, and Grizzard 1976). In London the population is now concentrated in a few major suburban centres, especially the London Borough of Barnet, where Jews comprise about 17 per cent of the population on the basis of an 'ethnic names' analysis, also Hackney (11 per cent) and Redbridge (5 per cent). The original Jewish population of the East End has declined to about 10,000. Education has transformed the Jewish immigrants who were concentrated in manual work, especially in the clothing trade, into a population of professionals, small businessmen, and self-employed workers. Jews are greatly over-represented in medicine, accountancy, the universities; also law, dentistry, clothing, estate agency, and property. Regional surveys show that few British Jews today are unskilled or semi-skilled manual workers; up to 55 per cent are self-employed. In Redbridge, employers and managers and junior non-manual workers comprised by far the biggest groups. About a third of London taxi drivers are Jews (see Waterman and Kosmin 1986).

Irish and Roman Catholics

In Britain, most people born in Ireland (900,000 in 1981) are Catholics (82 per cent according to Cartwright 1978). Most of the approximately five million Catholics in Britain (11 per cent of the English population, 25 per cent of the Scots) have some Irish ancestry (Spencer 1972), even though only 16 per cent were born in Ireland. Another 14 per cent of the British-born Catholics had at least one Irish-born parent in 1978. This being the case, these related populations show in a striking way the degree to which characteristics and attitudes can change as immigrant groups diffuse into the wider population.

The resurrection of Roman Catholicism in Britain followed the mass migration from Ireland to Britain after the 1840s. Catholics of Irish descent greatly outnumber the descendants of the indigenous Roman Catholics who held out in rural Lancashire and the North-West of Scotland and among the recusant gentry and aristocracy. Their numbers had probably shrunk to about 40,000 by the mid-eighteenth century (Spencer 1975). Indigenous numbers began to grow with the progressive lifting of restrictive legislation (a remnant of which survives from the Bill of Rights of 1689). Conversions to Catholicism ran at a high level after the debate begun by the Oxford Movement in the 1860s until their precipitate decline in the 1960s, together with conversions on marriage. About 10 per cent of the present Catholic population are converts. Recusants and recruits from conversion have typically come from different social origins from the Irish Catholics, who initially provided almost all the clergy.

Roman Catholics still comprised 21 per cent of the population of the North-West region in 1978, compared to 12 per cent in the South-East and 7 per cent in the South-West and Wales (Hornsby-Smith and Lee 1979, see also Gay 1971). But the occupational distribution of Roman Catholics is now only slightly different from the general population. In 1978 11 per cent of the Catholic population was in the AB socio-economic status compared to 13 per cent nationally, and 35 per cent in the DE category compared to 31 per cent nationally (Hornsby-Smith and Lee 1979). (These categories roughly correspond to social classes I and II, and IV and V respectively.) This is less true of the Irish-born; 80 per cent were manual workers in 1971 compared with 65 per cent of the general population, with about a third employed in the building industry and about double the national average of unemployment. Social mobility, as well as social status, is also substantially lower among the Irish-born compared with the Roman Catholic population. (Hornsby-Smith 1987).

From at least the early nineteenth century Ireland has been characterized by late marriage and high proportions of bachelors and spinsters, combined with high marital fertility. This produced lower overall fertility than elsewhere in Europe in the nineteenth century, but has changed much less, so fertility in Ireland was the highest in Europe outside Albania (TFR 2.5 in 1985, 3.2 in 1980, 3.9 in 1970). During the 1980s fertility has fallen rapidly, to 2.1 in 1989 (Coleman forthcoming *a*). The dominance of the Roman Catholic Church in Irish national life is one of many reasons for the slow spread of small family norms and family planning practices in Ireland. It is not surprising therefore that the fertility of Irish-born mothers has typically been higher than the British average: at the 1971 census 2.8 live births at 15–19 years' marriage duration compared with a national average of 2.3. Live births to Irish-born mothers have none the less fallen sharply—23,500 (3.0 per cent of all births) in 1970 compared with 9,200 (1.4 per cent) in 1980 and 6,000 (0.9 per cent) in 1987, partly because of lower migration rates. By 1975 overall patterns of contraceptive usage among Irish-born

Table 12.6. Age structure of selected overseas-born populations resident in England and Wales, 1981

Age-group	Birthplace						
	UK	Irish Republic	Northern Ireland	Caribbean	Pakistan	USSR	USA
0–4	6.3	0.3	1.0	0.3	3.1	0.2	5.4
5–15	16.8	1.4	6.8	2.0	13.7	0.7	17.4
16–19	6.7	1.1	3.6	2.7	6.6	0.2	7.1
20–4	7.2	3.4	6.3	10.6	14.7	0.3	12.9
25–9	6.5	6.0	8.9	11.0	15.8	0.5	11.5
30–4	7.4	8.7	10.0	8.2	9.7	0.9	12.1
35–9	6.2	10.2	10.1	10.6	6.9	1.7	8.5
40–4	5.5	10.8	8.2	14.9	8.8	2.3	4.9
45–pension	19.3	36.8	28.3	34.4	18.0	53.1	12.7
pensionable	18.2	21.3	16.9	5.4	2.6	40.0	7.3
All ages	100	100	100	100	100	100	100
Number	580,384	209,042	293,632	181,739	34,470	105,852	

Source: OPCS (1983*b*). 1981 Census Country of Birth Tables.

women in Britain were not substantially different from the general population (Cartwright 1978), but the use of the pill, rhythm method, and female sterilization were more common among the Irish women, and the sheath and IUD less so. Roman Catholicism does not of itself keep fertility high; Italian fertility is the lowest in Europe. Any 'Catholic effect' tends to be evident where Catholics are in a minority (Day 1968). The disappearance of specific 'Roman Catholic' fertility differentials since the 1970s has also been noted in the United States and elsewhere. It does not make sense to talk of the English Catholic population having a distinctive subculture (Hornsby-Smith 1987), as to an increasing extent their religion is all that distinguishes them from their fellow citizens.

Most marriages involving Irish-born people and Roman Catholics in Britain are now mixed marriages (Spencer 1975, Caulfield and Bhat 1978, Coleman 1983). In the GB 1971 census only 30 per cent of people born in Ireland had an Irish-born spouse. Of all legitimate births in Britain with at least one Irish-born parent, the parents were both Irish-born in 34 per cent of such births in 1970, 26 per cent in 1988. The proportion of marriages solemnized in Roman Catholic churches with a non-Catholic partner was already as high as 46 per cent in 1958 and had risen to 64 per cent by 1972 (Spencer 1975). This does not include religiously mixed marriages solemnized in other churches or register offices (see Hornsby-Smith 1987).

The Irish is Britain have become a relatively elderly group (table 12.6) thanks to slackening emigration from the Republic and some return migration during the 1970s. Most of them were over 45 (58 per cent compared to 38 per cent of the UK-born) in 1981. There were few Irish-born children—the under-20s comprised 3 per cent of the total of the Irish-born compared with 30 per cent of the UK-born. The proportion of children born in England and Wales to mothers born in the Irish Republic fell from 3 per cent in 1971 to 1 per cent in 1988. The Ulster-born population is different. More are in working age-groups, although the population is still concentrated over the age of 45 (45 per cent). The heavy immigration is much more recent. Protestants now predominate among migrants from Northern Ireland; it appears that a relatively high proportion of the small number of mixed marriages (6 per cent: Compton and Coward 1989) which occur in the province end up living in Britain.

Fertility differences in Northern Ireland

This picture of assimilation and convergence between Protestants and Catholics is not repeated in Northern Ireland, which shows perhaps the sharpest demographic contrast between any two neighbouring communities in Europe outside Kosovo. Two different demographic regimes are preserved by a religious and political divide. The historical background to the community divide is well known. Roman Catholics are a substantial minority—about 40 per cent in 1981, 34 per cent in 1926. Almost all are of Irish origin and birth; there is very little migration (except return migration) into Northern Ireland. The Protestants—of different denominations—are almost all of Irish birth but ultimately many are of Scottish ancestry. There is a voluntary religious question in the Northern Ireland census although in 1971 10 per cent did not reply to it (mostly Catholics according to Compton 1982*a*) and a higher proportion did not reply in 1981. Residential segregation is so strong (Boal 1981, Boal and Douglas 1982) that estimates of relative fertility of the religious groups can be made from the local geography of births. There are also religious sources (Spencer 1977) using baptisms (there are hardly any conversions). The first fertility survey was held in 1983 (Compton and Coward 1989).

Overall, fertility in Northern Ireland is high by British standards. The TFR was 4.6 in 1961, 4.1 in 1971, 2.5 in 1981, 2.4 in 1988. The religious differential first became apparent at the 1911 census (O'Grada 1984), had become substantial by the 1930s, and has widened considerably since the 1960s. Since then, Protestant fertility has fallen closer to the British average, while until recently Catholic fertility only declined slowly. In 1961 the total marital fertility rate for Catholics in Northern Ireland was 5.2 compared to the Protestants' 3.3; in 1971 the difference was 4.2 to 2.9; in 1981 3.9 to 2.6. In the 1983 Northern Ireland Fertility Survey average family size (all marriage durations) was 3.3 among Catholics, 2.3 among Protestants (Compton and Coward 1989). However measured, Catholic fertility is between 40 and 50 per cent higher than Protestant (Compton 1981) and if the figures are standardized for marriage the difference is expanded. In fact Catholic fertility in Northern Ireland in 1971 was slightly higher than in the Republic (4.2 compared with 4.0), part of which may be explained as a 'minority' effect (Coward 1980*a*).

Higher Catholic fertility within Northern Ireland is not mainly due to the socio-economic characteristics of the Catholics compared with Protestants. Instead most of the difference is due to cultural and religious factors in a province where religious observance is much higher than anywhere else in the UK. Catholic ideal family size is 3.9, Protestant 2.9 and the more religious the respondent, the higher the ideal. Again unlike the rest of the UK, there are big denominational differences in ever-usage of family planning and methods used (Compton and Coward 1989). Because Roman Catholic natural increase was three times that of Protestant in 1971 (1.8 per cent to 0.6 per cent) there has been speculation that the Catholics will 'out-breed' the Protestants and eventually form the majority (Kennedy 1973). If most Catholics remained republican in sympathy, a democratic vote could then go in favour of union with the Republic, against the present wishes of most of the Protestants. Until the present wave of terrorism began after 1969, the Catholic 'advantage' in natural increase was more or less eliminated by their higher emigration rate. But the Protestant emigration has gone up since then. The proportion of Catholics has risen from 34 per cent in 1926 to 38 per cent in 1985. At 1981 rates a majority of the population might be Catholic by 2011–31, and a majority of voters by 2026–46 (Compton 1981). Demographic differentials seemed to be closing during the 1980s, and fertility in the Republic also fell fast over the same period. Convergence of fertility of the two denominations has been forecast for the marriage cohorts of the turn of the century.

12.5 Demographic Characteristics of New Commonwealth Ethnic Minority Populations

Because of high fertility and continued immigration, New Commonwealth minority populations have increased rapidly from negligible numbers in 1945 to about 2.5 million in 1987 (table 12.7). This represents an annual growth rate of about 5.2 per cent from 1971 to 1987. Over this period the population has doubled through natural increase and immigration (table 12.2). Initially West Indians were the largest single group; thanks to their later migration Indians now hold that position. Bangladeshis doubled from 1981 to 1985. Unlike the indigenous population, men still outnumber women in these populations; sex ratios are especially high among Pakistanis and Bangladeshis, Africans and Arabs (table 12.8). This reflects different immigration patterns and the extent to which family reunion has still to take place. The Bangladeshis were the last to arrive and family reunion is still proceeding rapidly. Many African immigrants are students who come without their families. The very low West Indian sex ratio is an artefact of low response rates by young West Indian males.

Overall, 42 per cent (one million) of the non-white population were born in the UK. Over half of the West Indian and Guyanese populations were born in the UK, and three-quarters of the population of mixed origins. One half of those born outside the UK described themselves as white. Most of the 289,000 white persons born in the NCWP were from Mediterranean countries, although there was still a

Table 12.7. Components of the NCWP ethnic group population, Great Britain 1971–1986

Ethnic origin	1971		1981		1985 –7			
	No.	%	No.	%	No.	%	% born UK	% born NCWP
White	—	—	50,914	—	51,333	—	96	4
All NCWP	1,371	100	2,166[a]	100	2,473	100	43	54
West Indian	553	40	519	24	521	21	53	45
African	69	5	65	3	105	4	35	62
Asian African	68	5	192[b]	—				
Indian	307	22	719	33	745	30	36	61
Pakistani	} 171 } 12		283	13	404	16	42	56
Bangladeshi			52	2	111	4	31	61
Mediterranean	140	10	171[b]	—	—	—	—	—
Chinese	} 63 } 5		81	4	120	5	24	76
Arab			36	2	71	3	11	87
Mixed			234	11	255	10	74	24
Other			177	8	141	6	28	68
Not stated	—	—	608	—	570	—	—	—

[a] Not including Mediterranean or Asian African.
[b] 1980 figures, not included in NCWP total.

Note: Sources differ from year to year and may be incompatible. Percentages of 'UK born' etc. may not cast to 100% because of non-response. They refer to 1984–6, not 1985–7.

Sources: 1971, Immigrant Statistics Unit 1977, t. 6 (NCWP estimates); 1981, OPCS Monitor LFS 83/1 (Labour Force Survey 1981); 1984–6, Shaw 1988 t. 3 (1984–6 Labour Force Survey); (1980 OPCS Monitor PP1 81/1; Sources of Statistics on Ethnic Minorities). 1985–7, OPCS (1989k) t. 5.29 (1987 Labour Force Survey).

significant number of mainly elderly white persons who were born in India. Virtually all people born in the Caribbean Commonwealth were of West Indian or Guyanese origin. Most people born in Pakistan and Bangladesh were of the corresponding ethnic origin. But only a minority of people born in the African Commonwealth were 'African'. The vast majority from East Africa were Asian; whereas most people born in Central and West Africa are indeed 'African'. Almost all 'Arabs' were born in the Middle East. About one in four of the Chinese population was born in China or Vietnam (not Hong Kong or Singapore)

Age structure

The NCWP minority population is a young one (table 12.8, figure 12.2). In 1985–7 34 per cent of the ethnic minority population as a

Table 12.8. Age structure and sex ratio of NCWP population Great Britain, 1985–1987 (%)

Ethnic group	Age					All persons	Males	Females	Males per 100 females
	Under 16	16–29	30–44	45–64 (men) 45–59 (women)	65 and over (men) 60 and over (women)				
Percentages									
White	20	22	20	19	19	100	49	51	96
All ethnic minority groups	34	28	20	14	4	100	51	49	104
West Indian or Guyanese	25	33	15	22	5	100	46	54	85
African	26	31	29	12	2	100	51	49	104
Indian	31	27	24	14	4	100	53	47	113
Pakistani	43	25	18	13	1	100	56	44	127
Bangladeshi	50	21	14	14	1	100	53	47	113
Chinese	29	25	30	11	5	100	57	43	133
Arab	21	36	27	13	3	100	73	27	270
Mixed	55	26	10	7	2	100	53	47	113
Other	27	27	30	12	4	100	46	54	85
Not stated	29	23	18	15	15	100	48	52	94
All groups	21	22	20	19	18	100	49	51	96

Note: Age-structure data refer to 1985. Sex ratio data refer to 1985–7.

Sources: OPCS (1986*d*) Monitor LFS 86/2, Labour Force Survey 1985: Ethnic Group and Country of Birth. (1985 data) OPCS (1989*k*) t. 5.30 (1985–7 data).

whole was under 16 compared with 20 per cent of the white population (see Haskey 1989*c*). Conversely, the 'greying' of the non-white population is less: only 3 per cent being over pensionable age compared with 19 per cent of the white population. Differences occur between the various minority groups; Pakistanis and Bangladeshis have very youthful populations. Over half (51 per cent) of the Bangladeshi population is under age 16, and 43 per cent of Pakistanis (the latter the same as in the country of origin) compared with 26 per cent of West Indians and Guyanese, and 27 percent of Chinese. The mixed population has the youngest age structure of all, over half aged under 16 and fully 80 per cent under 30.

This youthful population lives in above average size households. This follows both from higher fertility and from the greater complexity of Asian households, which frequently include relatives outside the nuclear family, or more than one family. In 1985–7 the average size of a household with a white head was 2.5 persons, about half the average for households with a Pakistani or Bangladeshi head. Some 60 per cent of all Pakistani or Bangladeshi households contained five or more persons compared with 36 per cent of Indian households, 18 per cent of West Indian or Guyanese, and only 8 per cent of white households (table 12.9). Conversely, one-person households accounted for almost one in four of those with a white head while the corresponding figure for households with an Indian, Pakistani, or Bangladeshi head was about one in twenty.

Mortality

High mortality in the Third World arises from a very unfavourable environment of poverty and malnutrition, poor public hygiene and health care, where infectious diseases remain a serious threat to life. Expectation of life at birth in India in 1988 was about 58 years, in Bangladesh about 52. But male Third World immigrants to Britain, except Africans, suffer about the same mortality level as the British general population, or even lower. All these comments refer to immigrants because birthplace, but not ethnicity, is recorded on death certificates. The gap has been bridged, almost at once, by high UK living standards, the absence of major public health risks, and free medical coverage. On top of this there is the expected 'migrant effect'; male migrants are self-selected for health and possibly for enterprise and activity as well. But migrants are only a selected group at the time of their migration. This initial advantage is progressively lost as time elapses after the initial arrival. These generalizations do not seem to apply to immigrants to England and Wales from Scotland and

Table 12.9. Household size of NCWP ethnic groups, Great Britain, 1985–1987 (%)

Ethnic group of head of household	Household size (percentages)						All households (thousands = 100%)	Average household size
	1	2	3	4	5	6 and over		
White	25	33	17	17	6	2	20,358	2.5
West Indian or Guyanese	20	25	22	18	9	6	191	2.9
Indian	6	13	18	26	17	19	192	4.0
Pakistani or Bangladeshi	6	9	11	16	19	39	110	4.9
Other	22	23	17	21	10	7	202	3.0
Not stated	27	33	14	17	6	3	180	2.6
All ethnic groups	24	33	17	17	6	3	21,231	2.6

Source: OPCS (1989*k*), t. 5.41.

Ireland, whose average mortality is worse than the British average. It has been suggested that the 'selection effect' does not apply there—and may apply in reverse—because the movement is short-range and without difficulty, and involves a high proportion dependent on welfare.

The pattern of mortality and disease among ethnic minorities is somewhat different (Marmot, Adelstein, and Bulusu 1983) both by cause and in respect of the social class pattern (Marmot 1986). West Indian males have a lower propensity to heart attack than the rest of the population of England and Wales, even though smoking is popular among West Indians. Asians of both sexes, and West Indian females, have a higher level of circulatory disease. Asians have a higher incidence of stroke than the average population and they are also more prone to suffer from tuberculosis. Much of the latter—like malaria—is a chronic infectious hangover from the home country or caught on return visits. Cancer risks are lower in almost all the NCWP groups. Whether these differences are genetic or dietary in origin is not yet known (Beevers 1983). Immigrants from the Mediterranean Commonwealth have consistently lower mortality for all causes in both sexes. Immigrants from Italy and Spain, who do not have particularly high social status, have lower mortality than the average in England and Wales, even lower than immigrants from France and Germany. This may be a further example of the 'Mediterranean effect' on mortality mentioned in Chapter 7.

There are also minor differences of a specifically racial nature. Blacks (i.e. people of African racial origin) have high frequencies of the sickle-cell haemoglobin gene. Mediterranean Commonwealth immigrants, and many from Asia, have high frequencies of the Thalassaemia gene (Bittles, in press). These genes are harmless or nearly so in single dose; but the small minority who inherit two genes (at an incidence which is the square of the gene frequency) suffer severe or lethal chronic anaemia. The conditions are vanishingly rare in North-West Europeans. The genes are common in many tropical populations as an evolutionary response to the heavy mortality burden of malaria (Livingstone 1981). The gene in single dose causes no harmful side effects but protects the blood from attack by the malaria parasite.

The dietary habits of Asians, including Chinese, should help protect them against cancer and heart disease. Traditionally the diet is sparse, with little meat and fat, and the wholemeal flour used is high in fibre. The vitamin D deficiency in Glasgow Asians was mentioned in Chapter 8. Smoking trends, too, may be increasing in New Commonwealth populations in Britain and may cause mortality problems in the future; although smoking (and alcohol) is forbidden to Muslims.

Table 12.10. Infant mortality rates for babies born
to immigrant women, 1975–1977 and 1985

Birthplace of mother	Infant mortality rate	
	1975–7	1985
All birthplaces	14.4	9.2
UK	14.1	9.0
Irish Republic	13.6	12.0
Australia, Canada, NZ	11.3	8.9
NCWP		11.1
India	16.8	10.0
Bangladesh		7.1
Pakistan	23.5	14.8
East Africa	17.8	9.1
West Africa		11.7
West Indies	18.7	15.0
Mediterranean	—	5.4

Source: OPCS Monitor DH3 87/1 'Infant and perinatal
mortality 1985' t. 6(*b*). Davies 1980, t. 2.

High infant mortality is the outstanding health problem among some
New Commonwealth immigrant groups, particularly among Pakistanis
(see Gillies 1984, Kirji and Edouard 1984, Bittles in press) (table
12.10). Data are only available about the risks to babies (the majority)
born to women who were themselves born in the New Commonwealth.
High fertility, poor accommodation, infrequent use of NHS facilities,
especially ante-natal visits, and adherence to traditional habits by
secluded and often illiterate women all contribute to high infant mortality rates. Perinatal mortality rates in the early 1980s were higher for the
babies of NCWP-born mothers compared with mothers born in the
UK—83 per cent higher for Bangladeshi-born mothers, for example.
However post-neonatal mortality, of which 'cot death' is the single
most important cause (42 per cent), shows a different pattern. Here the
average for mothers born in the UK and the Republic of Ireland was
4.1 deaths per 1,000 live births. Births to mothers born in Pakistan had
a much higher post-neonatal death rate (6.4 per 1,000) but babies born
to mothers from India, East Africa, and Bangladesh have significantly
lower than average risks: 3.9, 3.0, and 2.8 respectively. In the case
of babies of Bangladeshi mothers, this advantage reduces their IMR

below the national average. This advantage stands despite an unfavourable birthweight distribution and it survives standardization for age, parity, and social class. It is unexpected and not yet understood. Babies born to mothers from the Indian subcontinent (but not from the Caribbean) suffer very low levels of cot death; and also of respiratory disease with which cot death is sometimes confused. In these populations, congenital malformations are much more important: 26 per cent of the post-neonatal deaths from Indian mothers, 31 per cent from Pakistani mothers, 36 per cent from Bangladeshi mothers (Balarajan, Raleigh, and Botting 1989). The high frequency of cousin marriage among Pakistanis may contribute to their high infant mortality (Bundey *et al.* 1990). Consanguineous marriages tend to raise infant deaths and malformations by increasing the chance of children inheriting two identical copies of harmful recessive genes. For example the offspring of single first cousin marriages have a one in sixteen chance of inheriting identical pairs of each of their genes through the effect of inbreeding alone. Double first cousin marriage and uncle/niece marriage, also practised, raise this figure to one in eight (see Bundey and Roberts 1988).

Fertility

Sparse data make the fertility of ethnic minorities difficult to analyse. Moreover, the tempo and quantum of their family building is changing fast and that makes it difficult to trust conventional summary measures. Total Fertility Rates can be calculated from birth statistics derived from vital registration together with estimates of women in various age-groups at risk derived from the Labour Force Survey. In 1987 these TFRs varied from 5.2 for women born in Bangladesh and Pakistan to 1.9 for women born in the West Indies. The latter is only just above the national average (table 12.11). But further analysis by birth order on 1979 data showed that the TFRs implied that each Indian mother would have 1.6 first births and 1.2 second births, which is clearly impossible (Thompson 1982). This paradox arises because families are still being united by continued immigration of wives and dependants from the Indian subcontinent into the UK. This makes Asian family building patterns unstable. Women settled here are having first births young and at the usual high rate, while women who have been separated from their husbands or fiancés by the process of immigration control are having their first babies later in life than would otherwise be the case. Despite these problems of analysis all measures show that family size in most New Commonwealth groups is substantially greater than the British average, especially among South Asians.

Table 12.11. Total fertility rate of women born in the NCWP, for England and Wales, 1971–1987

Birthplace	1971[a]	1981	1983	1985	1987
Total	2.4	1.8	1.8	1.8	1.8
UK	2.3	1.7	1.7	1.7	1.8
Total outside UK	—	2.5	2.4	2.5	2.4
New Commonwealth and Pakistan	4.0	2.9	2.8	2.9	2.8
India	4.3	3.1	2.8	2.9	2.7
Pakistan and Bangladesh	9.3	6.5	6.1	5.6	5.2
East Africa	2.7	2.1	2.0	2.1	2.0
Rest of Africa	4.2	3.4	3.1	3.0	3.2
West Indies	3.4	2.0	1.8	1.8	1.9
Malta, Gibraltar, Cyprus	} 2.7	2.1	2.1	2.2	2.0
Hong Kong, Malaysia, Singapore, Brunei		1.7	1.9	2.0	1.8
Rest of New Commonwealth		2.3	2.4	2.3	2.5
Rest of world	n.a.	2.0	1.9	2.0	1.9

[a] OPCS Monitor, Series FM1 84/9.

Sources: OPCS Birth Statistics 1985, Series FM1 no. 12 table 9.5. OPCS Birth Statistics 1987 Series FM1 no. 16 table 9.5.

The distribution of births by birth order confirms that marital family size is declining in West Indians (table 12.12). However, looking at births within marriage only, 14 per cent of all births to West Indian born mothers are fourth or higher order, compared with 8 per cent in the general population. A high proportion (55 per cent) of West Indian women are in the work-force (more than the Asian and the British average) and this tends to inhibit family size. These figures relate only to the 51 per cent of births which are legitimate. It is not known if these trends are also shared in West Indian single-parent families. Many West Indian women are the heads of one-parent households, primarily through illegitimacy rather than divorce, as in the West Indies. In 1985–7 42 per cent of families headed by West Indians in Britain were lone-parent families.

Asian fertility is still high: originally equivalent to about 5 children per woman, the most recent data show an overall decline to an average just below 3. But among the predominantly Muslim Pakistanis and Bangladeshis the TFR is still over 5. The distribution of births by birth order suggests that Indian family size is declining: the percentage of fourth and higher births within marriage is the same as among West

Table 12.12. Births to women born in the NCWP, by birth order, England and Wales, 1987 (% of total births)

Country of birth of mother	Year	Total births (= 100%)	All legitimate births	Birth order within marriage				Illegitimate births
				1	2	3	4+	
All countries	1971	783,155	91.6	36.2	30.7	14.3	10.4	8.4
	1976	584,270	90.8	37.2	34.8	12.1	6.6	9.2
	1981	634,492	87.2	35.3	32.4	13.0	6.5	12.8
	1984	636,818	82.7	33.0	30.3	12.7	6.6	17.3
	1985	656,417	80.8	32.3	29.4	12.6	6.5	19.2
	1987	681,511	76.8	30.8	27.8	11.9	6.2	23.2
Caribbean CW	1971	12,544	63.7	13.1	13.1	11.6	25.8	36.3
	1976	7,171	51.6	15.2	16.6	8.2	11.6	48.4
	1981	6,247	50.0	15.4	15.0	10.4	9.3	50.0
	1984	5,255	50.4	14.5	18.0	10.5	7.4	49.6
	1985	4,851	51.4	16.1	17.2	10.9	7.3	48.6
	1987	4,565	51.3	14.3	18.4	10.6	4.8	48.7

India	1971	13,389	98.3	29.9	26.8	16.1	25.6	1.7
	1976	12,044	98.9	33.6	29.2	17.8	18.2	1.1
	1981	12,402	98.8	32.8	36.0	15.7	14.3	1.2
	1984	11,102	98.5	31.2	34.0	20.1	13.1	1.5
	1985	11,110	98.2	30.8	33.4	19.7	14.3	1.8
	1987	9,991	98.2	31.6	32.4	20.9	13.2	1.8
Pakistan	1971	8,200	99.2	17.3	20.9	17.0	43.0	0.8
	1976	8,173	99.3	27.2	20.3	16.4	35.4	0.7
	1981	13,349	99.5	21.8	22.9	19.6	35.0	0.5
	1984	13,399	99.3	19.6	19.7	20.0	40.0	0.7
	1985	13,643	99.3	20.2	19.2	18.9	40.9	0.7
	1987	12,919	99.1	18.8	20.8	18.8	40.7	0.9
Bangladesh	1971	—	—	—	—	—	—	—
	1976	1,415	99.4	20.4	17.9	14.7	46.4	0.6
	1981	3,079	99.6	17.2	19.5	21.1	42.2	0.4
	1984	4,067	99.6	15.3	16.7	17.7	49.9	0.4
	1985	4,238	99.7	18.6	15.7	16.6	48.7	0.3
	1987	4,845	99.6	15.9	16.8	16.1	50.9	0.4

Sources: OPCS Monitor FM1 86/5 Births by birthplace of parent, 1985, t. 4. OPCS Birth Statistics 1987 series FM1 no. 16 t. 9.6.

Indians. But there is no decline at all in the proportion of fourth and higher births to mothers born in Pakistan or Bangladesh. These remain at about 40 per cent and 49 per cent of their respective totals. Youthful marriage helps to keep fertility high. Marriage is young and almost universal. In 1984–6, 45 per cent of Pakistani and Bangladeshi males aged 16–29 were already married, and 76 per cent of females, compared with the British average of 29 per cent and 45 per cent respectively. But there may also be an increase in average age of marriage. Techniques developed for rectifying inadequate Third World demographic data (Brass 1982) suggested that Asian fertility had declined to about three births per woman and is falling to such an extent that it will approach the English level by the turn of the century. This seems likely to be premature.

Future trends in fertility

The circumstances of life in Britain may have removed whatever economic rationality there may have been in high fertility in India (low UK mortality, existence of a welfare state and pensions, compulsory education and the prohibition of child labour, opportunities for married women to work in the non-agricultural work-force). None the less, Asian extended family arrangements and the prevalence of family enterprises may make high fertility seem less disadvantageous than among West Indians. Marked sex preferences for boys, evident in most Third World countries, are still apparent at least in London Sikhs (Simons 1982*a*). This tends to keep up family formation until the requisite number of male children have appeared. Asian women tend to be illiterate even in their own language; only about a third are competent in spoken English. Muslim women tend to be reticent about sexual matters and ignorant of contraception, especially those recently arrived from Pakistan and Bangladesh, where contraceptive use is low—about 7 and 25 per cent of couples respectively (Mauldin and Segal 1988). Only a small proportion of married Asian women go out to work. The concentration of the New Commonwealth populations in the manual social classes may also help keep fertility higher until they are more evenly distributed throughout the country's social and educational structure.

There is unresolved debate about the causes, and likely future of ethnic minority fertility differences. One school of thought suggests that such differences are primarily due to coincident socio-economic differences—usually because the minorities are poorer and less well educated. In the USA, for example, despite two centuries of co-residence,

US blacks still have considerably higher fertility than US whites, rising and falling in the same way with economic trends but at a higher level (Coleman 1983). These occupational differences certainly exist in Britain. West Indians and Bangladeshis are particularly concentrated in manual occupations. But overall the distribution is becoming closer to the national average, and East African Asians are over-represented in professional and other higher status occupations (DE 1988).

Where minorities feel threatened by absorption or assimilation, a 'minority effect' may make acceptance of family planning difficult and retard convergence in fertility. This may operate among Northern Irish Roman Catholics, and among Hassidic Jews (Siegel 1970). Other minorities, especially those with more positive attitudes towards education, may consciously limit their fertility in order to overcome the economic disadvantages which they experience: The rapid convergence of most Jewish fertility in British and the USA, sometimes to below average levels, may be one example. In the USA, highly educated blacks, and Chinese and Japanese in general, have fertility below the national average. Alternatively, autonomous cultural differences, fundamentally linked with all aspects of the community's life, may have effects upon fertility. The limited role outside the home prescribed for women by Islam may sustain higher than average fertility under most economic circumstances. Preferred family and household structures and a strong role for kin in social life, in so far as they can be sustained in a Western setting, may have a similar effect. No New Commonwealth ethnic minority group in Britain has yet achieved below average fertility.

12.6 Intermarriage and the Population of Mixed Origins

In the end, the persistence of distinctive ethnic groups in Britain will depend upon the transmission of culture across generations to children sufficiently numerous to replace their parents. The effects of low fertility and of intermarriage, for example, mean that Jews (known to synagogues) are only replacing themselves to the extent of about 80 per cent per generation (Kosmin 1976). Low fertility is unlikely to undermine the new multiracial society developing in Britain, because none of the new immigrant groups is yet following the Jewish road to low fertility (Kosmin 1982). Neither at the moment is intermarriage sufficiently common to bring about rapid assimilation.

Overall, about 1 per cent of all current marriages are ethnically mixed. About 10 per cent of current marriages with at least one ethnic minority partner are ethnically mixed. Almost all of these are with whites (figure 12.4). Non-white men are more likely to be married to

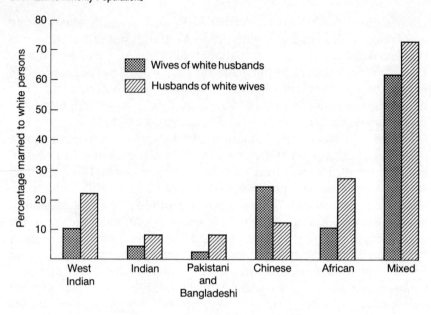

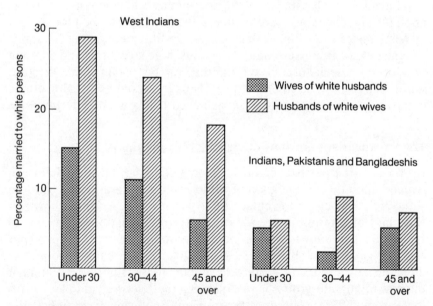

Note: (a) fertility and mortality continuing at 1933 levels (TFR = 1.73, NRR = 0.73, e_o males = 58.9, e_o females = 62.8) (b) fertility continuing to decline at rates current in Sweden from 1921–31, then remaining constant after 1985 (for details see source).

Sources: Coleman 1985, figs. 1, 2.

FIG. 12.4. Ethnic intermarriage in Great Britain, 1981

white women than vice versa, reflecting past imbalances in the sex ratio and the more secluded lives of Asian immigrant women. Of all the ethnic minority groups, West Indians and Africans are most likely to be married to whites—about 25 per cent in each case, although the undoubted under-enumeration of West Indian men in the LFS from which these data come casts some doubt on the figure (Coleman 1985). Other research, for example, obtained by 'snowball' interviews in ethnic minority communities only, suggests a lower figure (Brown 1984).

South Asians are much less likely to marry whites (or anyone else outside their own group). This is not surprising in view of the much bigger differences in religion, language, and way of life. Most white people disapprove of inter-ethnic marriage; even more Asians do so (Brown 1984). Arranged marriage with strict regard to religion and caste is insisted on by parents, even though the young have more ambivalent feelings (Ballard 1978). Partly for this reason, arranged marriages are still generating a considerable primary migration stream. Almost all such marriages are endogamous (Jones and Shah 1980). However, despite the increase in the population of young UK-born Asians, migration for purposes of marriage is not increasing.

Inter-ethnic marriage or liaisons seem to have been quite common among Asians and West Indians in the early 'boarding house' stage of migration in the 1950s, when the immigrant population was still quite small and still mostly male. Since then South Asian intermarriage became less common, as immigrant populations became larger, more self-contained, and more balanced in sex ratio. West Indian inter-marriage seems to be increasing. There is some evidence that UK-born Asians and West Indians have a higher tendency to marry whites than had their immigrant parents (Coleman in press).

A substantial mixed-race population has arisen from these unions. Problems of definition have made estimates of its size difficult and in general the question of self-identity and of recognition as a group, or groups, by others may be substantial (see A. Wilson 1981, 1984). In the 1970s the mixed-race population was estimated to be about 250,000, in 1981 about 170,000, and 263,000 in 1987 (Population Statistics Division OPCS 1986a). Most are the offspring of white native/Commonwealth immigrant unions (particularly West Indian men and white women), not two different minority groups. Most people of mixed origin (77 per cent) were born in the UK. Their age-distribution is the most youthful of all the ethnic minority 'groups'; in 1984–6 62 per cent were aged under 16. The major exception are the Anglo-Indians, a long-standing, now rather homogeneous group of originally mixed origins dating from

British rule in India in the eighteenth and nineteenth centuries. The marital choice of people of mixed origin themselves is of some consequence for forecasting the effects of inter-ethnic marriage. Almost all marry whites, and each group of mixed origin does not intermarry with the others (D. Coleman 1985).

This may not speed up assimilation if those who marry whites become socially and geographically marginalized. They tend, for example, to live at the geographical edges of immigrant settlement (Brown 1984) isolated from social contact with either, so the centres of such settlement will be little influenced by their example. The loss of the 'deviants' can easily be 'spared' when population growth rates are so high. It is not clear with which groups the offspring of mixed unions tend to identify, although about 40 per cent of parents in mixed unions classify their children as white (Shaw 1988), especially where one parent is white and one mixed. Most of the rest classify their children as 'mixed'. What happens here will be of considerable importance for the future of ethnic minority populations and race relations generally. The exclusion of a 'mixed origin' category from the 1991 census question will not help resolve this important issue.

12.7 Population Projections

Future fertility and immigration are the key to projecting the future size and composition of the new ethnic minorities. The present pattern of fertility is unstable and there is no certain basis for estimating the number of births to UK-born mothers of NCWP origin. An earlier section suggested reasons why births to some South Asian ethnic minorities might not decline fast. Continued immigration has contributed almost half of the population increase in ethnic minority populations since 1964, despite the controls in the legislation of 1962, 1968, 1971, and 1988 (see Chapter 10). The projection of future migration patterns (see OPCS 1979b) is particularly difficult. It is subject to unpredictable political changes. For example, the present government's policy to restrict immigration was weakened by a ruling of the European Court of Human Rights in 1985 to apply its regulations on the entry of fiancés equally to each sex, as discussed in Chapter 10, and by its decision in 1990 to admit up to 50,000 additional households from Hong Kong.

No adequate estimate of the total of intending migrants exists, and there is no general model of the migration streams. Previous estimates of the likely number of dependants of the NCWP population settled in the UK who may wish to come to the UK have usually turned out to be substantial underestimates (e.g. Eversley and Sukdeo 1969). Quotas, or registers of dependants, were recommended by one parliamentary committee (Parliamentary Group 1977), promised but not delivered by the government in 1979, and rejected by another parliamentary committee (Home Affairs Committee 1982). Such quotas or registers might have provided some data, but they would probably also have had an effect on the migration system itself.

The Home Affairs Committee suggested that the data on applications and queues for entry clearances in the Indian subcontinent (published in the Control of Immigration Statistics), which are all in decline, provide a more sure and responsive measure of potential migration than trends in migration itself. The other substantial source of future migration from the Indian subcontinent—fiancés of men and women settled here—depends on future changes in the Immigration Rules and on whether arranged marriages with partners from the home country continue among Asians settled in Britain (P. R. Jones 1982b). The lack of upward trend in such arrivals suggests that arranged marriages may be becoming less popular.

Official projections, obsolete but not replaced (Immigrant Statistics Unit 1979), projected total NCWP population from a 1976 base. The lower variant totals of wholly NCWP descent were 2.22 million by 1986 and 2.47 million by 1991. The latter has already been equalled by the 1985 estimate of 2.43 (which includes 0.25 million persons of mixed origin). The higher variant is more on target; it projected 2.47 million by 1986 and 2.94 million by 1991. Other projections based on a low and fast falling estimate of NCWP fertility (Brass 1982) have forecast 3 million by 2001. This total will be within reach by 1991. Since 1971 NCWP population has grown on average at 5.2 per cent per year—by up to 94,000 people per year—and has roughly doubled every fourteen years. Further substantial increase is inevitable because the youthful age structure guarantees more young people of childbearing age for the next quarter century. This effect alone, even with replacement fertility and an immediate stop to immigration, will ensure an increase of 50–60 per cent—to about 3.5 million. Simple projections based on a decline of fertility to replacement levels and an end to immigration in fifteen years' time would generate a final NCWP population size of about 4.5 million.

13 The Political Economy of Demographic Change

13.1 Introduction

In the last decade, politicans and the public have again discovered that population matters. This has happened before. The 1930s fear of population decline and the Royal Commission on Population, the early 1960s concern about overpopulation and the South-East Study, and the later 1970s school closure programme, all reflected movements in the nation's demographic foundations. Since the late 1980s the coming shortage of teenagers has been alarming institutions which depend upon recruiting the young; from the Royal College of Nursing to the Norwich Union Insurance Society and the armed forces. Specific demographic aspects of problems are now frequently cited by politicians and journalists in a way unimaginable a decade ago: divorce as a cause of homelessness, the baby boom as a contributor to unemployment, the future growth of the elderly population as a challenge to welfare and pensions policy.

Some demographic trends can indicate that a response is needed. Sometimes the direction is clear: everyone is in favour of lower death-rates, even though there may be no consensus about means (Chapter 7). Where the concerns relate to fertility and marriage, or to immigration, there is much less agreement over what signal the data are giving and what kind of policy response, if any, is appropriate. Discussing demographic differences by class, race, or region in public can seriously damage political health. Sir Keith Joseph got into trouble in 1975 after speaking on the proportion of illegitimate and unwanted births produced by teenage girls from unskilled manual backgrounds. Enoch Powell discovered in 1968 that quotations from Virgil were little appreciated in modern Britain; his forecast that large immigrant populations were likely to cause trouble in urban areas led to his permanent banishment from the Shadow Cabinet. Mrs Edwina Currie, unabashed by her suggestions that Northerners should blame their higher mortality on their dietary habits, in the end provoked the food industry once too often. This chapter will look at the impact of demographic trends on our society and economy, the principal policy problems raised by the new demography, and whether policies should or can influence demographic behaviour.

13.2 Malthus at Bay: Facing Demographic Stagnation

No population policy please, we're British

This century, concern about the direction of overall population growth, and its implications for national welfare, has been as volatile as the course of fertility itself. By the mid-nineteenth century Malthusian pessimism about the ill consequences of population growth had evaporated in a new confidence about the ability of science, industry, and empire to raise living standards, and to demand more labour, not to create more poor. Steam power and free trade were to consign Malthusian economic pessimism on the limits to rates of growth to a footnote in economic history. But the 'Great Depression' of the 1870s, and Britain's chronically worsening relative economic position put a question mark against indefinite population growth. Concern about the numbers of the poor had never gone away, and millions of families were already starting to limit their own family size.

By the beginning of this century it was becoming clear that the decline of the birth-rate from the 1870s was no fluke or hiccup but a serious and probably permanent trend. Concern switched to the problem of low fertility partly for old-fashioned mercantilist reasons, partly because some social classes had begun to limit fertility before others. The consequent shift in the social origins of the next generation was felt to have worrying social, political, and economic implications. These concerns were shared by the left as well as by the right and, reinforced by fears of national physical unhealthiness revealed by the recruitment for the Boer War, helped to prepare the way for legislation to improve child health and family welfare in 1906 and 1911 (see Teitelbaum and Winter 1985).

The 1920s and 30s were the golden age of the fear of depopulation. As the birth-rate fell more and more pamphlets and books appeared on race-suicide, the twilight of parenthood, and national decline (Charles 1936, Hogben 1938) suitably illustrated with horrendous population projections (figure 13.1). Concern was given added point by contrast with the growing economic and military strength of the new Bolshevik state and of the increasing power and ambitions of Japan in the Far East, both with healthy, positive net reproduction rates (table 13.1) and a strong interest in heavy industry (although fears of overpopulation were current in Japan at the same time).

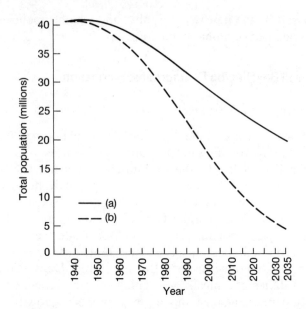

Note: (a) fertility and mortality continuing at 1933 levels (TFR = 1.73, NRR = 0.73, e_o males = 58.9, e_o females = 62.8) (b) fertility continuing to decline at rates current in Sweden from 1921–31, then remaining constant after 1985 (for details see source).

Source: Charles 1938, Fig. 1.

FIG. 13.1. 1930s forecasts of population decline

Table 13.1. Reproduction rates in the 1930s

Nation	Year	GRR	NRR	CBR 1935	NRR 1986
England and Wales	1935	0.866	0.764	14.7 ⎫	0.86
Scotland	1935	1.057	0.909	17.8 ⎭	
Sweden	1934	0.815	0.727	13.8	0.86
Germany	1933	0.801	0.698	18.9	0.63
France	1935	1.003	0.866	15.2	0.88
Italy	1930/2	1.607	1.243	23.3	0.72
Australia	1932/4	1.047	0.955	16.6	0.89
New Zealand	1933	1.053	0.978	16.1	0.94
Canada	1931	1.555	1.319	20.2	0.80
South Africa	1933	1.427	1.212	24.8	—
USA	1933	1.044	0.940	16.9	0.87
Ukraine	1926/7	2.485	1.676	—	0.91
Japan	1929/31	2.324	1.540	31.6	0.81

Note: GRR = Gross reproduction rate; NRR = Net reproduction rate; CBR = Crude birth-rate

Sources: Glass and Blacker 1938, t. 5, Council of Europe 1989 t. 6b. Annual Statistical Yearbooks of Australia, New Zealand, Canada, USA, USSR, and Japan.

Elsewhere worries were expressed in sharper policy terms. In Germany, fertility wilted under an epidemic of illegal abortions, which exceeded live births in the 1920s as unemployment and hyperinflation hit family budgets. Policies to encourage larger families through propaganda, welfare, and tax advantages became almost universal in Continental Europe. In France, for example, draconian legislation in 1920 forbade the advertisement or dissemination of contraceptive devices or information (Ogden and Huss 1982). In Nazi Germany substantial marriage loans were payable if the wife left the work-force and were progressively cancelled on the birth of successive children (Glass 1940). In response to earlier failed attempts, the French *Code de la Famille* of 1939, still the basis of French family support, introduced generous welfare benefits linked to family size, not exceeded until the pronatalist policies of post-war East European Communist regimes (David 1982). Britain, whose economy had been less seriously damaged by the war or the peace showed little official interest in following any of these examples. Then as now, the lack of any clear official view on which demographic trends are desirable is a further example of the British exceptionalism mentioned at the beginning of the book.

The 1911 census confirmed what had previously been suspected. Not only was fertility declining but the better educated classes, in the vanguard of family limitation, were progressively less represented in each generation than the less educated (see Chapter 4). On top of that, the flower of the nation was believed to have fallen on the battlefields of the First World War, a view which statistics to some extent support (Winter 1985). Today's relatively flat curve of fertility in relation to occupational status has taken much of the heat out of the problem (Chapter 4). But early childbearing and high fertility of a small minority of mothers is still linked with a concentration of social problems, some of them evidently inherited from their own backgrounds (Rutter and Madge 1976, Madge 1988).

13.3 The Debate on Population

The Royal Commission welcomed population stabilization but feared population decline. With its Family Census and its pioneering family planning enquiry, it was a landmark in demographic and economic analysis. Its analysis of the pros and cons of population growth has much in common with that of the Population Panel's report thirty years later (Central Policy Review Staff 1973).

According to these analyses, population problems tend to resolve themselves into concern about economic consequences; lack of demand versus diversion of investment, fear of overcrowding and loss of amenity, and the international consequences of a shrinking economy and armed forces. Land was considered the most serious problem. As Mark Twain remarked, they ain't making it any more. Population growth diminishes the area of land per head of population. Increasing numbers demand capital investment, for example in housing, which diverts productive resources from increasing living standards. On the other hand an increase in numbers encourages economies of scale and stimulates technical improvement, generates a younger population (Boserup 1981, Simon 1981), and increases the nation's international influence and its capacity to defend itself.

Some of these effects are consequences of size (land, economies of scale); others are consequences of growth (the stimulus to investment, the age structure). The advantages to investment and business confidence of a growth rate which in Britain has seldom been more than 0.5 per cent per year this century must always have been rather marginal, although this argument is still prominent in the US with its higher population growth rate. Keynes wondered in the 1930s if in 'chaining up the Malthusian devil P of population that we might not be unleashing the devil U of unemployment' (Keynes 1936), through a failure of demand. But lower population growth may encourage more per capita spending beyond subsistence needs, also more saving and capital accumulation. Growth in real incomes and short-term changes in consumer spending have generally swamped the effects of population growth at the national level. Most emphasis nowadays is on the relative growth of different sectors of the population with different patterns of consumption (the growth of the elderly market, the twilight of the adolescent).

The Commission concluded '[we have] good reason to be thankful that no further large increases in our population are probable' (p. 224). Responses to more recent opinion polls have shown that the British public of the 1970s and 1980s shared the same view. The British nineteenth-century economic boom had been a temporary fluke sustained by cheap food imports (Langer 1975) paid for by an eroding monopoly of British manufactured goods and overseas investments (e.g. Argentine Railways)—a view echoed more recently (Royal Commission 1950, Wiener 1989, Barnett 1986). Overseas investments had been liquidated to pay for the Second World War, after which Britain faced, in Keynes's words, a 'financial Dunkirk' (Kennedy 1988). It was felt that the population growth supported in the nineteenth century could not be supported in the twentieth with any increase in per caput living standards. Dominant British shares of the market in manufactured goods, protected by the *Pax Britannica*, had kept the terms of trade exceptionally favourable. But competition from newer industrial powers reduced this pre-eminent position. In fact, the economy was to grow more rapidly than the Commission's pessimism thought possible. In the 1950s and 1960s Gross Domestic Product increased by up to 3.5 per cent per year, and after the recession of the early 1980s, to even higher levels from 1983–8. Even though this progress has been modest compared to that of many competitors, its corresponding effects on real incomes (figure 4.2) and wealth have enabled a majority of households to enjoy a standard of living and financial security previously restricted to a minority.

In the Commission's view the Malthusian problems of the 1830s had been translated, on a wider scale, into the balance of payments crises of the 1930s and beyond. The pressure of population against resources could be deferred for a century or so, but not for ever. Food resources were in the long run vulnerable to increased consumption by the food exporting countries themselves and their richer and growing populations. Consequently the report put a premium on self-sufficiency in food, a conclusion spurred by wartime experience. Britain has been digging for victory ever since, and is now largely self-sufficient in temperate foodstuffs, thanks to £2.4 billion per year subsidies to farming. Despite the Royal Commission's pessimism there is still a considerable world market in food, at 10 per cent lower prices than those current in the EC. But much of it comes from just a few sources; notably Canada and the United States (see Gilland 1983, Hendry 1988).

The Commission correctly predicted an adverse trend in the age structure following the new low fertility, which would double the relative number of pensioners to taxpayers. Early retirement and higher real pensions have compounded the matter since. Declining numbers of children were expected to increase standards of living, but the decline in the number of young men would be serious for national defence. This concern returned in the 1980s, although the abolition of conscription after 1957 reduced the size of the armed forces much more dramatically than any demographic effect.

Neither the Royal Commission nor anyone else predicted the post-war baby boom of 1950–64 (Holmans 1963). They saw no reason to expect a return to fertility substantially above replacement because of its adverse consequences on family income and living standards. This remains true today (Chapter 4). The great difference between the perceptions of population in the 1930s and those of today is in the international arena. Then the Empire and Commonwealth were regarded as the basis of Britain's prosperity and power. It was feared that lower population growth would lead to lower emigration to the Commonwealth and thereby diminish the proportion of their population of British origin (Chapter 11). This would weaken their propensity to buy British goods or support Britain internationally. This prediction has certainly been borne out. But political changes in the Commonwealth have been more important (McIntyre 1976). The Dominions have matured. More of their population is native-born. They have strengthened their ties with the economically and militarily dominant United States. Today, their migrants are selected on the basis of family connections or on economic grounds and come from many countries and ethnic backgrounds to join what are becoming self-consciously multi-cultural nations, no longer British ones (although not without considerable domestic dissent).

As the Union Jack has been hauled down a third of the world's flagpoles since 1947, attention has switched to immigration. The Royal Commission felt that low population growth might create a demand for immigration to strengthen the labour force, but there were few obvious sources in Europe. Non-European people, of alien race and religion, were regarded as unassimilable in large numbers. The Royal Commission never dreamt that 2.5 million coloured immigrants and their descendants would be living in Britain just thirty years after their report.

13.4 Malthus Revived: Growth, Land, and the Environment

The post-war baby boom, together with heightened interest in global population trends (Ehrlich and Ehrlich 1970, Meadows *et al.* 1972) displaced fear of population decline with concern about population growth. A shower of books (e.g. Taylor 1970, Brooks 1974, Parry 1974) and pamphlets (Goldsmith *et al.* 1972) of the late 1960s and 1970s linked UK population concern firmly with wider fears about the adequacy of material resources and with environmental protection. Malthus suddenly found himself dressed in green. These views were not without their critics (Cole 1973); notably from French mercantilists (Sauvy 1975) and from the left (Hawthorn 1970), keen to debunk what they regarded as Malthusian evasions of the central problem of the ownership and distribution of resources. Opinion polls showed a majority of the nation believed the country was over-populated. New housing threatened to cover the countryside with bricks and concrete, especially in the South—a problem still concerning people today, fortified by a healthy regard for property prices. The South-East Study (1964) was carried out specifically to decide where to put the growing population, in a political environment then much given to national and regional plans of every kind. The 1960s fashion for tower blocks was in part a response to these worries about the undue pressure of population on land. Pollution and traffic congestion were also linked to population growth. There was and is indeed a connection, but about two-thirds of the extra post-war land used for housing came from population redistribution and more living space per person—an improvement in living standards primarily responsible for the growth of traffic too. The standing Royal Commission on Environmental Pollution was set up around this time. It is clear, however, that economic growth at 3–5 per cent per year and technical change arising from the demands of higher productivity or new legislation are the crucial factors in the increase and the decline of environmental pollution, rather than the slow (< 1 per cent) population growth of industrial countries in the late twentieth century.

The Select Committee on Science and Technology chose population growth as the subject of its first report (1971). Its papers are an interesting combination of academic analysis, pressure group agitation, and official complacency. It concluded excitedly that 'The Government must take action to ensure that the consequences of growth do not become intolerable.' Government response was one of comprehensive indifference, for which it was severely taken to task by the Select Committee (Fifth Report, 1973). In a sense the government was right, as fertility had already begun its downturn to the low levels which have lasted to the present. But it was right for the wrong reasons; not through any prescience but because the subject was beyond its ken.

However to keep the agitators quiet it did set up a government committee (The Population Panel) under the aegis of the Central Policy Review Staff to report on the effects of contemporary population growth on the nation's society and economy. Developing many of the arguments of the Royal Commission, the Panel's thoughtful report concluded that a stationary population was preferable to one which was growing, and would make the long-term solution of problems easier, although it declined to specify an optimum despite pressure from the environmentalists. Population growth and trends in distribution made their most serious impact on land and the countryside. But the country could, if necessary, accommodate any likely increase over the next few decades. Population policies were not a panacea for social ills; there was no need for policies actively to reduce growth further. Rapid decline was to be avoided. There is much sense in all this, although

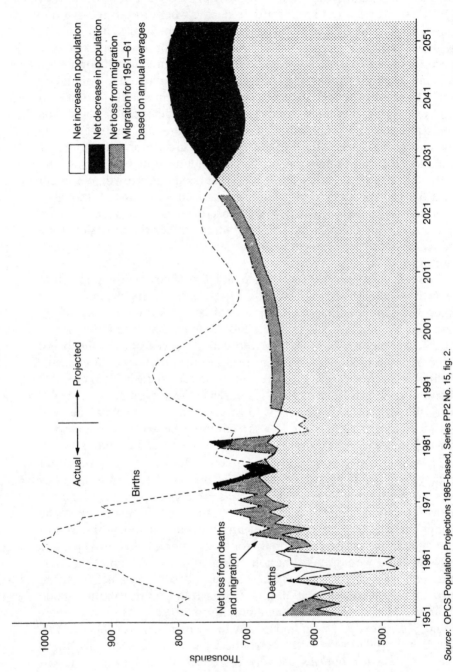

Source: OPCS Population Projections 1985-based, Series PP2 No. 15, fig. 2.

Fig. 13.2. Projections of births, deaths, and migration, UK, 1951–2055

Table 13.2. Age structure of the projected population, England and Wales, 1987–2027 (%)

Age-group	1987	1991	1996	2001	2011	2021	2027
0–14	18.7	19.1	20.0	20.3	18.7	18.4	18.8
15–29	23.6	22.4	19.9	18.3	19.7	19.5	18.4
30–44	20.6	21.2	21.6	22.4	19.1	18.1	19.2
45–59	16.2	16.6	18.0	18.7	20.2	20.1	17.7
60–74	14.2	13.8	13.3	12.8	14.8	16.0	17.0
75+	6.7	7.1	7.2	7.5	7.5	7.9	8.9
60+/65+[a]	18.4	18.4	18.2	18.0	19.3	21.0	22.6
Total (per cent)	100.0	100.0	100.0	100.0	100.0	100.0	100.0
Total (millions, E & W)	50.2	50.9	51.8	52.6	53.5	54.4	55.1
Total (millions, GB)	55.4	56.0	56.9	57.6	58.4	59.2	59.6
Total (millions, UK)	56.9	57.6	59.3	60.1	60.9	61.2	61.3

[a] % over pensionable age, 65 for men, 60 for women.

Source: OPCS (1989*a*) Appendix 1, microfiche 87021 (1987-based).

since then the demographic ground has shifted and with it the emphasis on problems. The 1970s was marked by the cancellation of several large new town projects designed to accommodate the population growth envisaged in the plans of the 1960s (Chapter 10). In concentrating on total population, the report failed to address those areas of population change which were developing rapidly and many of which did need urgent policy responses.

13.5 Contemporary Demographic Problems: The Threat of Population Decline?

Fertility has been below replacement rate ever since the publication of the Panel's report in 1973. The TFR has been around 1.8 since the late 1970s. Briefly in 1977 deaths exceeded births for the first time in peacetime for over two centuries. None the less the population has continued to increase slowly (from 1988 to 1989 by about 170,000 people, or about 0.3 per cent per year) thanks to the inertia of age structure, improvements in survival, and, from 1983, net positive immigration. Eventual population decline is implicit in such low fertility levels. Official projections still forecast a gradual increase in the population of Great Britain from 55.4 million people in 1987 to 59.6 million by the year 2027 (OPCS 1989*a*). Around that time the population growth will cease. These projections (table 13.2, figure 13.2) assume a total fertility rate stabilizing at 2.0 (a 10 per cent increase) and zero net migration replacing the positive contribution of about 50,000 people per year which immigration made to British population totals in the middle 1980s. Expectation of life is assumed to increase to 75.7 years for men and 80.5 years for women by 2026–7, compared with 72.1 and 77.8 years respectively in 1985–6. If those fertility assumptions are right, then unlike many other industrial countries we will not face population decline until about 2030 (figure 13.2). By then, the thirty or forty years of sub-replacement fertility which will have passed will make it difficult to reverse the decline quickly.

In Britain there is no apparent political concern for the general implications of overall population trends (Eversley 1980), in marked distinction to the 1940s (Hansard 1943a,b) and the Continent today (McIntosh 1983, Davis *et al.* 1986). There is no overall population policy, despite frequent official references to such problems as the ageing of the population and the forthcoming shortage of young re-cruits to the labour force. No quantitative goals have ever been set for population size or growth-rate. Brief official statements accept that the solution of many problems may be assisted by the absence of popula-tion growth, but conclude that the present position requires no action (Whitehead 1991). Public interest and political controversy is focused on components of the population, immigration and minorities, house-hold growth, migration, and the overcrowding of the South-East.

France, with a similar fertility to our own, maintains its traditional high anxiety on the subject, even on behalf of others (Chesnais 1991). Successive presidents irrespective of political hue assure the French people that population (its failure to grow) is one of the four great problems facing the nation. M. Chirac insisted during his 1988 pres-idential campaign that 'Our population can become the biggest in Europe in a few decades as long as we have a policy that encourages families.' The Germans had more reason to be concerned, with almost the lowest fertility in Europe and a population declining by 0.1 per cent per year until re-unification in 1990. But the history of the Nazi era (Bleuel 1976) inhibits the discussion and the implementation of pronatalist policies even half a century later (McIntosh 1983). Al-though the Federal Government set up a commission into the matter, opinion was divided over whether falling population was a problem or a welcome relief to an overcrowded national territory whose boundaries had been constricted since 1945 (Höhn 1987). Denmark is losing popu-lation, but Danish opinion seems as relaxed about that as about every-thing else despite four government commissions on population ageing and family policy since 1978. East European Communist regimes showed no such reticence and attempted to prop up fertility with massive income and other support for larger families (David 1982). Hungary and East Germany nevertheless continued to lose population. Modern contraception is little developed; legal (and therefore controllable) abortion is a primary mean of family planning.

The West German Government has always encouraged the return of ethnic Germans still living in the Soviet Union and elsewhere in Eastern Europe. After the general collapse of East European Communist regimes in 1989, the trickle of population from East Germany (population 17 million) to West Germany became a flood. In 1989, West Germany received 344,000 migrants from East Germany as well as 377,000 from the rest of Eastern Europe and the USSR. In the first six months of 1990, a further 464,000 entered from East Germany. This unstoppable migration was one of the factors that made the union of Germany inevitable. Re-unified Germany has 79 million inhabitants, about the same as the Reich in 1939 within its larger pre-war frontiers. This makes Germany once again demographically pre-eminent in Europe; with a population equal to over 70 per cent of the combined total of France and the UK (112 million). German economic performance will make the total GNP of a united Germany greater than that of France and the UK put together. A return to the demographic and economic balance of the early twentieth century may revive some of its old political alignments as well.

In the United States population is still growing at almost 1 per cent per year thanks to a youthful age structure and heavy immigration (up to one million per year) despite sub-replacement fertility (TFR in 1987 = 1.8). There, the people that brought us the 'baby boom' (Russell 1987) have now turned their publicity talents to the 'birth dearth' (Wattenberg 1987) which in the US promises to be all the more impressive because of its contrast with the protracted period of higher fertility which preceded it. Such trends are taken more seriously because US business is already the best demographically educated in the world. Concern is also expressed in the US that much of the population growth in the future, and the origins of a growing proportion of the population, will come from Hispanic migrants (Glazer 1985). In the USSR comparable worries about its rapidly growing Asian population have prompted the development of a two-sided population policy since 1979, in the teeth of ideological opposition and accusations of racism.

The more mercantilist concerns about population growth have not survived the apparent irrelevance of population growth to the success of European economies. Economic progress in Western European countries is independent of their rate of population growth and of their population size although there is a school of thought which believes that population growth is a necessary stimulant to economy and technical innovation (Simon 1981). West Germany and Sweden—the former with eight times the population of the latter—have had two of the most successful economies and two of the slowest growing populations, although reinforced by labour migrants.

Markets for some products greatly exceed the size of national populations. The whole of Western Europe (population over 340 million) can only accommodate three or four unsubsidized volume car manufacturers. The whole of the Western industrial world (population 630 million, with Japan 740 million, and reaching a total market over 1,000 million) may only be able to support two substantial civil airliner manufacturers. For over a century the economic unit for a growing number of products and services has not been the population size of the nation state, but rather super-power economic states or groupings such as the USA (246 million population in 1988), the Soviet Union (286 million population in 1988), or the EC (325 million population in 1988). The implementation of the Single European Act in 1992 is intended to make the EC much more of a single market than it is at present. In a system which encourages free trade and competition and the removal of regulations, the way to expand the size of markets will be to join such groupings rather than strive for an impossible and much slower increase in domestic population.

Within groups of states of roughly equivalent economic level, international influence and security are still likely to depend upon the size of the national population. As the prospect of decisive superiority in military technology by one side or another seemed increasingly elusive, the size of armed forces and the demographic as well as the economic resources which sustain them were subjects of lively interest in security circles (Clarke 1989). The diminution of the successive cohorts of young men throughout the Western world means that the size of forces in conscript or volunteer armies can only be maintained by increasing the length of service or by reducing the standards of recruiting. The former option has encountered strong opposition in West Germany, for example. The Ministry of Defence has discovered demography and its severe effect on the size of infantry battalions and responded with MARILYN (Manpower and Recruiting in the Lean Years of the Nineties; MoD 1989). In 1990 the Royal Navy announced it was sending women to sea for the first time. While not facing the same overall demographic problem of size and with a healthy growth rate of 1 per cent per year, the Soviet Union faces other difficulties arising from the concentration of this growth among Muslim Asians, of uncertain Soviet loyalty, who will form a third of its conscript cohorts early next century. The spectacular collapse of the Warsaw Pact as an effective military alliance in 1989 and 1990 must abate demographic defence worries for the West, although not necessarily for the Soviets.

13.6 Population and Household Distribution and the South-East Problem

Government policies affecting migration and population distribution

British governments, although reluctant to try to influence national population trends, have certainly attempted to control trends in migration and settlement pattern. Labour migration policy was discussed in Chapter 10. The Royal Commission on the Distribution of the Industrial Population (The 'Barlow Report', 1940) proposed the decentralization of industrial activities and the industrial population, and the dispersal of some of London's central functions, on grounds of health and amenity, security from air attack, and the promotion of regional economic development. The Abercrombie Report (1944) created novel public sector new towns for some of London's population. Milton Keynes, the last of these, continues to advertise to Londoners. Until the mid-1970s the government's Location of Offices Bureau tempted enterprises and their workers out of London, although by the time of its abolition in 1980 it was already trying to tempt them back. The government itself had exiled many of its functions to the provinces in the 1930s. The policy was pursued with renewed vigour in the 1960s and again in the 1980s to help revive less favoured areas, and to save on London's high rents and costs.

The Town and Country Planning legislation developed from the 1930s may have had the most powerful demographic effect. The planning structure it created has limited migration directly by limiting the areas where houses can be built and employment created, indirectly by inflating house prices, particularly in the South-East. Green Belts, first set in place around London in the 1930s, now occupy in all an area greater than Wales. Planning restrictions in the South-East region cover 80 per cent of the land surface. Land for house building has correspondingly become even more expensive—£21,000 per plot in the South-East in 1986—and makes the North–South gradient in house prices even steeper (Evans 1988). Planning policies, contrary to their original intention, are already beginning to force up urban—or more usually suburban—population densities. About a quarter of the land used for housing in the South-East in 1987—1,300 acres—came from suburban back gardens. In suburban parts of the capital, such as Harrow, in-fill developments have become a major political issue.

National population trends may not catch public attention in Britain, such regional population pressures certainly do: the North/South contrast in population growth and economic activity, the depopulation of urban centres, the pressure of growing small towns and suburbs on their surrounding countryside.

Some of the fiercest controversies arise because the geographical

Table 13.3. Household/dwelling balance in England and major regions, 1981 (1000s)

	England	Greater London	Rest of South	Midlands and North
Housing stock				
(1) Total	18,003	2,720	6,312	8,971
(2) less: secondary residences	−191	−22	−108	−61
(3) less: vacant dwellings being repaired	−170	−37	−50	−83
(4) less: turnover vacancies (2%)[a]	−387	−82	−126	−179
(5) 'Available' main residences	17,255	2,579	6,028	8,648
Households				
(6) Total	17,285	2,650	6,037	8,598
(7) less: sharing households not wanting separate accommodation	−68	−32	−20	−16
(8) plus: concealed families wanting separate accommodation	+137	+26	+44	+67
(9) Households and concealed families wanting separate accommodation	17,354	2,644	6,061	8,469
Balance (line 5 minus line 9) (rounded)	−100	−65	−35	0

[a] 3% in London.
Source: 1981 Census, Dept. of the Environment.

distribution of employment, economic growth, and population matches quite badly the geographical distribution of housing inherited from previous decades. The migration and development needed to bring them into line, mostly in southern, rural areas, encounters strong local objections. In the 1980s, for the first time, an overall gross surplus of dwellings over households has been achieved. None the less there is still a housing shortage in some areas of the country, notably in the South-East (table 13.3). And apparent surpluses may disguise an emergent mismatch between available housing and the accommodation and tenure needs of households, which are fast changing in their size and composition (Dicks 1988, Murphy 1989).

The projected increase in household formation over the next fifteen years will make the relative position in the South-East even worse at present building rates. London is particularly attractive to young people. And because there is still a much greater supply of rented accommodation in London (about a sixth of the capital's population live in privately rented accommodation—Whitehead and Kleinman 1986), young people can leave home and set up household there in a way which is more difficult elsewhere.

The South-East population problem

Planning policies and conservation interests are colliding with pressure for development to meet growing domestic household formation, and labour migration to the nation's main economic engine-room in the South. The need to preserve countryside and encourage urban revival, while at the same time to free the economy and work-force to invest and to move where returns are highest presents the most serious conflict of policy for the present government (see Champion 1989). Public concern seems to be dominated by fears that without the strictest controls on development, the population of the North is poised to pour down the map into the South, so requiring most of it to be built over, Areas of Outstanding Natural Beauty and all, in the interests of employment and economic growth. In fact, North–South migration is not the major source of pressure (Chapter 10). The net annual movement across the North–South divide has been about 62,000 from 1983 to 1986, an increase from about 49,000 in 1979–83, when national migration rates were at their lowest for many decades (Rees 1989). This is only slightly higher than net international migration into the South-East. In particular, most migrants settling in the South-East come from elsewhere in the South-East or from adjacent regions. Labour shortages are specialist, not for large numbers of unskilled

Percentage change 1985–2001

- Increase of 10 per cent or more
- Increase of 5 per cent but less than 10 per cent
- Increase of less than 5 per cent
- Decrease of less than 5 per cent
- Decrease of 5 per cent but less than 10 per cent

Note: The Highland Region, Orkney, Shetland, and Western Isles Island Areas of Scotland are grouped together.

Source: *Population Trends*, 52: 43.

Fig. 13.3. Projected population change between 1985 and 2001 in counties of England and Wales, regions of Scotland, and Northern Ireland

workers. Overall, the South-East suffers a small net loss from internal migration, and gross immigration into the South-East from overseas is almost as great as that from all the rest of England put together.

For some years the most rapidly growing region has been East Anglia, not the South-East. Most future population growth is projected to occur in a diagonal belt taking in East Anglia, the East Midlands, the north-west corner of the South-East and most of the South-West avoiding most major cities (figure 13.3), much of it in commuting range of London. In part this is a consequence of artificial constraints upon development and house building and its effects on costs. There appears to be no estimate of the extra volume of migration expected under specified additional provisions of housing. In fact a high proportion of interregional labour migration is not speculative. Instead it is arranged by large employing organizations (Chapter 10). If estimates of potential movement into the South could be made at various levels of increase in supply of housing—and there are obvious difficulties in preparing them (Coopers and Lybrand 1987)—then they might reveal a more manageable potential influx than is generally feared. As Chapter 6 pointed out, the pressure could not in any case be permanent.

A direct estimate of this kind does not appear to have been made. However, the planning system may raise house prices in the South by between 50 per cent for the largest to 10 per cent for the smallest houses compared to the North. Three-quarters of a million households are thereby unable to afford owner-occupation, and the average plot size for houses in the South is reduced by 60 per cent compared to what families would prefer (Cheshire and Sheppard 1989).

The 1985-based projections of South-Eastern household growth (see Chapter 6) show that the major pressure is internal, from faster than expected household formation underpinned by faster than expected population growth from improved survival and positive immigration from overseas (DoE 1988a, OPCS 1987c). These projections show a 14 per cent increase (923,000) from 6,649,000 households in 1986 in the number of households expected in the South-East by 2001 even under today's restrictive planning regime. Almost all this projected increase (699,000, an 18 per cent increase) is outside London (figure 13.4). This was 230,000 more than those projected just two years earlier. The consortium of South-East region planning authorities (SERPLAN) has accordingly raised its estimates for 1991–2001 for an additional 560,000–580,000 dwellings, up 100,000 from the previous guidance (SERPLAN 1989), with a corresponding effect on the temperature of debate on South-East planning and conservation.

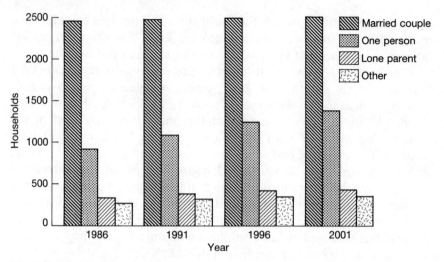

Source: Department of the Environment 1988a, t. 5.

FIG. 13.4. Household projections, Rest of South-East, 1985-based

Their upward revision strengthens the hand of those who argue that many existing Structure Plans cannot accommodate even local increase in household numbers (Evans 1988) and will encourage an unhelpful increase in house prices and private rents. Even though house prices are falling at the time of writing (1990) their average level had reached a multiple of income (almost 5) at a record high from the conventional expectation of about 3.5. Furthermore regional differences in house prices are the highest of any regional cost. Some analysts have suggested that high houseprices, especially in the South-East, have driven up wage claims, have driven out population from the South-East, and may even reverse net inward overseas migration in the near future (Muelbauer and Murphy 1988). If such high costs drove population and investment away from the South-East that might meet one government aim; but the population would not necessarily move to the North, some investment might move to France, and life would be made difficult for the much larger number of intending first-time home buyers in the South-East, a third of whom are apparently incapable of buying at current prices. Once again new towns are being proposed for the South-East countryside to meet these needs, although this time they are private sector and relatively small scale (about 13,000 population). They are violently opposed by pressure groups for countryside protection. So far, none has been approved. It is likely that the next set of population and household projections (1991) will forecast further increases, and other estimates are even higher (section 6.5).

One argument for taking action is that the processes behind the projected increases in household numbers will have shot their bolt by the end of the century. They can therefore be responded to without a commitment to limitless new building. Most of the increase (60 per cent) occurs in the early 1990s. Numbers in the younger age-groups most likely to form new households are eventually projected to fall. Much of the housing demand arises from non-married couple households whose needs do not necessarily run to traditional family houses. None of the increase is projected to come from married couple households, which decline slightly, especially in the younger age-groups. Instead the projected increase is in one-person (40 per cent) and lone-parent (30 per cent) households (see Chapter 6).

13.7 Rural Decline—and Renaissance?

Rural population has declined from the middle nineteenth century. In the 1930s the agricultural depression drove even more off the land. Paradoxically, this occupational and geographical shift was accentuated by the higher productivity encouraged by the government after the war to make good agricultural deficits. Today even in rural districts only 14 per cent of the population works in agriculture.

Such declines can threaten the survival of small communities. Below a critical population, services, shops, transport, and schools cannot be supported on an economic basis. Population composition changes as manual workers with little future in agriculture leave the villages to be replaced by commuters, weekenders with second homes, or retired couples. Planning restrictions prevent a general increase in housing supply in most rural areas. This artificial shortage contributes further upward pressure to house prices which rise generally in the area, above the level affordable on local wages. In Britain, because rent control has marginalized private renting, council tenure has become the only, and limited, alternative although now housing associations are developing in rural areas.

Some unviable rural communities have been shut down. There is nothing new about abandoned villages: at least 2,000 ancient sites are known which have long reverted to fields (Beresford and Hurst 1971). In Durham and Northumberland in the 1930s mining villages dependent upon the local pit for employment lost their reason for existence when the pit closed. Families were resettled with compensation and the villages abandoned. One or two of the Outer Hebrides have been evacuated at the request of their inhabitants. But generally policy has been to support marginal settlements directly or indirectly. In Britain the virtues of rural life are deeply embedded in language and literature (Newby 1985, Williams 1985). Town living has long been second best for those that can afford to choose (Girouard 1985). Rural areas are widely seen as the heartland of decent attitudes, sturdy independence, and national tradition (Waldegrave 1978), on the Continent as well as in Britain. The preservation of farming communities with their supposedly conservative views, however inefficient their farming, was and remains one of the main political aims of the Common Agricultural Policy. Small farmers are a much more important component of the demography—and the electorate—in West Germany and in France. In Britain less than 3 per cent of the work-force are now engaged in agriculture.

Most support for rural populations comes from price and other subsidies to farmers (£2.4 billion in 1988), which raise EC food prices at least 10 per cent above the world market price. Many holdings would be uneconomic without them. It is hardly possible to put spade to ground without turning up an agricultural subsidy. Farmers in remote upland areas, belonging to the most vulnerable communities, have benefited most. Ten thousand crofters (whose numbers are regulated) receive special attention in Scotland. Special premiums apply to upland sheep. Until 1988 substantial tax benefits were given to the plantation of economically useless forests in environmentally sensitive areas, in the mistaken belief that it would encourage local employment, a testimony to the remarkable durability of the 'plant for victory' campaign of 1915. A government agency, English Estates, promotes the limited development of rural light industry and services, to help preserve communities which the ebb tide of agriculture has left stranded. Now that the problems of overproduction are recognized further subsidies have been given to farmers since 1987 to conserve the countryside and to set aside some fields from cultivation altogether. The rural population turn-around since 1970, discussed in Chapter 3, is particularly marked in the growth of small country towns, now a favourite location for new small and high technology industries. It owes nothing to agriculture.

13.8 The Inner Cities

Policy questions are also raised by the other side of the population turnaround, i.e. the decline of inner cities, discussed in Chapter 3. Until quite recently, inner cities had problems of poverty (associated more with low wages than with unemployment) and overcrowded and insanitary housing. Rebuilding at lower density and population decentralization was the obvious solution. The growth of suburbia was a natural response to the overcrowding of the central city. The national policy of encouraging local authority public housing, particularly after 1945, led to the biggest public housing sector in the Western world (Holmans 1987) and made it possible for local authorities to plan population location on the largest scale. Peripheral council housing estates, starting in the 1920s and 1930s, and the new towns following the Abercrombie Plan of 1944 realized in concrete this policy of dispersal. Local authority powers of compulsory purchase and capital expenditure for new building replaced private renting with council housing as the ordinary urban tenure. This determined the location of millions of households and influenced demographic behaviour in ways which have recurred throughout this book (Chapters 4, 5, 7, 9, and 10).

Three new factors have turned this retreat from the city into a rout since the 1960s (see Chapters 9 and 10). Heavy industries and textiles, whose nineteenth-century growth created the cities and conurbations that now lie around them, progressively collapsed. Traditional British industry had become overmanned, underproductive, poorly trained and managed, and underinvested compared to its more modern and competitive European counterparts (Wiener 1981, Barnett 1986, Kennedy 1988). By the 1950s this low productivity had turned Britain into the most heavily industrialized nation ever in terms of the pro-portion of the work-force (about 50 per cent) engaged in manufacturing (Martin and Rowthorn 1986). Textiles from the 1950s, steel, shipyards, and coal in successive decades, progressively failed to meet challenges from overseas competition, the slump in demand after the oil shocks of 1973 and 1979, and the removal of subsidies in the new economic policy from 1979. Unlike the 1930s, there was no chance for their revival in place and no substantial new employment elsewhere. Heavy un-employment therefore became an extra urban problem, particularly pronounced in Northern cities with a heavy manufacturing base and no local tradition of mobility, thanks in part to a heavy concentration in council tenure. Out-migration has been selective. It is the younger, better-off, and more skilled members of the middle ranks of society who leave. The relict population left in the inner cities is top heavy with old age pensioners, deficient in people aged from their 30s to retire-ment age, and has a disproportionate number with low skills or who are unemployed. In a few areas of 'gentrification' the proportions of people in social class I (professionals) and II (business and administrative) have gone up. But it has not made much of a statistically measurable impact on the overall urban scene, only on particular areas such as London Docklands.

The third factor has been the arrival into this deteriorating urban scene of 1.3 million immigrants from the New Commonwealth and Pakistan, reinforced by their 1.2 million British-born offspring. As almost all this population is urban, and most of it inner urban, their demographic impact has been substantially to counteract the net movement out of the inner city described above. They have, to some extent, replaced the departing native population, although in many areas (especially in London) they have competed for housing with the indigenous inhabitants, and probably hastened their departure. There has never been a housing surplus in inner London. The geographical concentration of immigrant populations (Chapter 12) has transformed the social and cultural environment of many inner city boroughs and wards. The low-wage labour supply has been kept buoyant, but partly because many initially went to obsolescent labour-intensive indus-tries—foundries and textiles—immigrant unemployment has subse-quently been higher than average. Corner shop and other small scale services have expanded. But the arrival of a poor 'replacement' popu-lation with large household size has hampered the solution of urban overcrowding by deconcentration. The growth in the Bangladeshi population, still arriving at about 7,000 a year, has created exceptional housing problems in Tower Hamlets, where most settle. Eighty per cent of all registered homeless there are Bangladeshi; no rehousing is possible of families who are not statutorily homeless (Home Affairs Committee 1986). The Immigration Act 1988 was in part a response to this problem. In a few areas of ethnic minority, especially Muslim concentration—notably in Bradford and some London boroughs—the high birth-rate has reversed the previous decline in urban births.

Since the 1970s government policy has concentrated on the need to reverse the decline in urban numbers and economic activity. The 1977 White Paper 'Policy for the Inner Cities' marked the turning point. It aimed to preserve urban communities and reduce unemployment. Layers of policy initiatives have been laid upon each other since the 1960s to subsidize urban investment, improve urban housing and environment, and ease the problems of Commonwealth immigrants. Initially most of this aid was channelled via the Urban Programme (1968) through local authorities. Since 1979 priorities have been to revive urban private business activity to reduce unemployment and to encourage urban housebuilding, especially private housebuilding, to diversify the social mix of cities, and to channel population location away from the countryside (DoE 1988d). By 1989 total annual expenditure on the urban block of programmes was about £750 million, or £3 billion if all the Urban Development Corporation expenditure is counted. Strict countryside protection seeks to force as much development as possible back to cities. In some areas, notably London Docklands, subsidies and relaxed planning regimes have had some success, in business if not in demographic terms. Local populations are often ill equipped to participate in these revivals and their views command little attention.

These problems are shared with many US but with few Continental inner cities. The latter conform more to the expectations of some theorists that inner urban areas naturally attract the better-off rather than the poor, a feature common in pre-industrial cities. Segregation of activities by planning can be less strict on the Continent, and the acceptance of private renting as a normal tenure enables many people to live a truly urban life, only available to the very rich in London, by living in apartments over shops and businesses. If the present government's housing policies work and increase housing choice and mobility by increasing the supply of private tenancies, it may help create such conditions and paradoxically reduce urban densities as more people choose to move out. It does not seem realistic to try to preserve forever the distribution of population and economic activity bequeathed by last century's industrial revolution. But well advised or not, successful or not, and intended or not, policies to arrest urban decay, rehouse the urban poor, and protect the countryside are the most powerful policies affecting population distribution and regional composition which this country has experienced.

13.9 The Challenge of the Age Structure

The changing age distribution provides the greatest demographic challenge to public policy. As we saw in Chapters 2 and 4, long-term and short-term processes both contribute to present and future age structures. The dominant long-term process follows from the substantial decline in fertility since the nineteenth century, and the progressive improvement in survival. Declining fertility was primarily responsible for the ageing of the population: the relative shrinkage of the child age-groups and the tripling in relative size of the old age-groups. And as survival past reproductive age is now 96 per cent, further reductions in mortality now contribute more to population ageing. Superimposed on that are the short-term processes which can speed up or retard the underlying ageing process. One of these is the highly uneven age structure, a novelty of the last fifty years. Almost immediate control over the timing of births in response to changing circumstances has enabled the numbers of births to vary by over 30 per cent within five

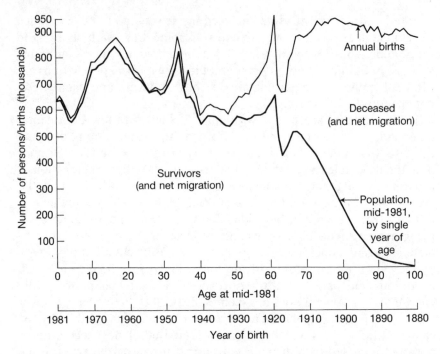

Source: Craig 1983, fig. 1, p. 29.

Fig. 13.5 Age distribution compared with past births, England and Wales, mid-1981

years (figure 13.5). These bulges and troughs, as they move upwards through successive age-groups, cause serious problems of alternating scarcity and surplus in the services and structures appropriate to each age-group and in the balance between age-groups which typically produce and those which typically consume. The British people can make babies much easier than the British economy can create jobs or reorganize its maternity or school services.

Supporting the elderly: pensions and pensioners

The burden of dependency in a population, and therefore on the average household, as defined by demography is the ratio of the numbers of dependent children and retired persons to the numbers in 'productive' age-groups, usually taken to be from school leaving age to retirement. Conventional age-limits of 15 and 65 are usually adopted. More strictly economic analysis concentrates on the smaller numbers in the actual work-force (i.e. taxpayers). At the moment the baby boom and its surrounding birth deficits occupy a favourable position in the

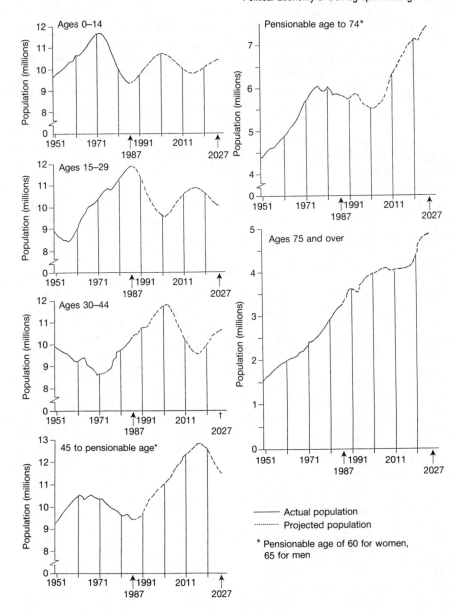

Source: OPCS 1989b, fig. 1.

FIG. 13.6. Actual and projected home population by age-group (in millions), England and Wales, 1951–2027

age structure. Dependent schoolchildren are declining in number. The
work-force has absorbed the baby boom and unemployment is consequently tending to decline, other things being equal. The large birth
cohorts of the pre-First World War period have already been absorbed
into the pensioner age-group, although they are swelling the numbers
of the over 75s, who are more likely to need intensive—and expen-

Table 13.4. Broad age-groups as a percentage of population, England and Wales, and
Scotland, 1901–1991

Year	The young 0–14	Persons of working age 15–64	The elderly 65 and over	All ages	Dependency[b] ratio
England and Wales					
1901	32.4	62.9	4.7	100	59.6
1911	30.6	64.2	5.2	100	55.8
1921	27.7	66.2	6.0	100	50.9
1931	23.8	68.8	7.4	100	45.3
1939	20.6	70.2	9.2	100	42.5
1951	22.1	66.8	11.0	100	49.6
1961	23.0	65.1	11.9	100	53.6
1971	23.7	62.9	13.3	100	58.8
1981[a]	20.5	64.5	15.0	100	55.0
1991	19.1	65.0	15.9	100	53.9
Scotland					
1901	33.4	61.7	4.8	100	61.9
1911	32.3	62.3	5.4	100	60.5
1921	29.5	64.5	6.0	100	55.0
1931	26.9	65.8	7.3	100	52.0
1939	24.1	67.2	8.7	100	48.8
1951	24.6	65.4	10.0	100	52.9
1961	25.9	63.5	10.6	100	57.5
1971	25.9	61.8	12.3	100	61.8
1981[a]	21.4	64.5	14.1	100	55.0
1991	18.9	66.2	15.0	100	51.2

[a] 'Usually resident' population
[b] (0–14) + (65 and over)/(15–64)

Note: The 1939 estimate includes an allowance for non-enumerated servicemen. The 1991 figures
are derived from 1987-based population projections

Source: *Statistical Abstract of the United Kingdom* relevant years up to 1931. *Annual Abstract of
Statistics* relevant years from 1951. *National Register 1939*. OPCS (1989a) Appendix 1. (for 1991
only).

sive—support. The new recruits to pensionable age come from the small cohorts of the 1920s and 1930s and the population of pensionable age in Britain will remain at just over ten million for the rest of the century. So in the short run, the population is not ageing very fast (figure 13.6). Much of the cost of population ageing has already been paid. The ratio of people of working age to pensioners in the 1920s was about 8 to 1. It has already declined to about 3.3 to 1. There it will stay until early next century.

The future size of the elderly population is a cause for concern because of its implications for pensions and the dependency ratio and other welfare costs especially medicine and residential care. If fertility were at replacement rate, sufficient to create a stationary population in the long run, then at present survival about 18 per cent of the population will be expected to be aged 65 and over. We have almost reached that position already (table 13.4). If fertility remains slightly below replacement (2.0) then the expected constant proportion of over-65s is about 20 per cent. At the turn of the century pensioners numbered about 5 per cent of the population. This ageing really became apparent in the 1930s, half a century after the fertility decline began. The dependency ratio has changed less, because the increase in the elderly has to some extent been balanced by the decline in the number of dependent children and of births (table 13.4). On average an elderly dependant costs at least three times as much as a dependent child (International Labour Office 1989). Nevertheless at (unrealistic) constant real expenditure per head, total medical costs may not increase more than 12 per cent up to 2027 for solely demographic reasons, mostly after 2006 (Ermisch 1990).

In the short and medium term, fluctuations in the age structure are much more important in determining the numbers of pensioners than long-term ageing. Thanks to birth-rate fluctuations, the next fifteen years will remain unexpectedly favourable from the viewpoint of age structure. In the 1990s, men who will enter retirement at age 65 were born in the 1920s and 1930s after the baby boom at the end of the First World War. That boom was sharp but short; the number of babies born in 1919 was 30 per cent greater than the number born in 1920. From these years on, the number of births, and therefore the number of people entering pensionable age, gradually declines over about a decade. Ratios of the work-force to pensioners stay favourable (table 13.5), as the work-force is expanded by the recruitment of the baby boom generation (Chapter 9).

Therefore there is no contemporary crisis arising from a substantial increase in the total numbers of the elderly. That happens early next

Table 13.5. Trends in elderly dependency ratios, 1911–2026
(a) *Ratios of elderly population to population of working age, 1911–1988, England and Wales* (000s)

Year	15–64 (A)	65+ (B)	Working agea (C)	Pensionable ageb (D)	A:B	C:D
1911	23,200.6	1,883.0	23,200.6	1,883.0	12.3	12.3
1921	24,897.8	2,185.1	23,268.2	2,814.7	11.4	8.6
1931	27,594.2	2,856.3	26,699.9	3,750.6	9.7	7.1
1939	28,788.2	3,731.9	27,724.5	4,795.6	7.7	5.8
1951	29,249.0	4,813.0	28,042.0	6,020.0	6.1	4.7
1961	30,076.8	5,513.0	28,720.8	6,869.0	5.5	4.2
1971	30,903.7	6,591.8	29,387.4	8,108.1	4.7	3.6
1981	31,995.5	7,548.3	29,795.9	8,928.2	4.2	3.3
1985	32,791.0	7,633.7	30,571.5	9,098.7	4.3	3.4
1988	33,048.8	7,936.0	31,019.6	9,287.3	4.2	3.3

a 15–64 in 1911. 15–64/59 from 1921 to 1971. 16–64/59 for 1981 and 1985.
b 65 and over in 1911. 65/60 and over for remaining years.

(b) *Ratio of elderly population to population of working age, and of National Insurance contributors to pensioners, 1984–5 to 2025–6.*

Year	Ratio of persons of working age to persons of pensionable age	Number of National Insurance Contributors per pensioner
1984–5	3.3	2.3
1995–6	3.3	2.2
2005–6	3.4	2.2
2015–6	3.1	2.0
2025–6	2.7	1.8

Sources: OPCS Monitor, PP2 83/1; OPCS Monitor PP1 89/1 (Revised) Mid-1988 population estimates for England and Wales, t. 13, t. 9. DHSS (1984) Population, Pension Costs and Pensioners' Income, Table 1, table 2.37, and unpublished OPCS data.

century. Instead the elderly population is itself ageing fast, with rapid growth in numbers of age 75 and older. This population was born in the years of increasing births before the First World War and their numbers are further increased by the substantial gains in survival achieved over the last few years, which are expected to continue. As a consequence, the number of people aged 75 and over in England and Wales is forecast to increase by 0.7 million or 20 per cent from 1987 to 2001, to

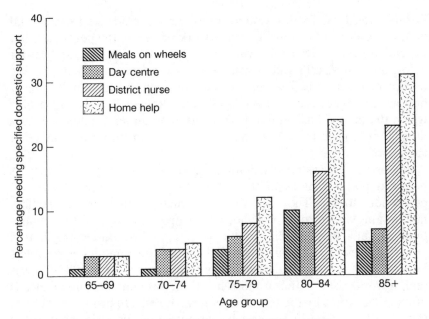

Note: 19 per cent of persons aged 85 and over were resident in institutions in 1981.

Source: Social Trends, 17 (1987), t. 7.30.

FIG. 13.7. Use of domestic support by the elderly, Great Britain, 1984

4.3 million; the number of persons of 85 and over by 369,000 or 54 per cent, and the number of persons aged 90 or over by 151,000 or 80 per cent (OPCS 1989*a*). As this is occurring at a time when the over-65 population as a whole, and especially that aged 65–74, has almost ceased to grow, the average age of the elderly population will increase particularly fast in the next few years.

The costs of supporting the elderly rise exponentially with age (figure 13.7), like the sickness rate and death-rate itself. Average NHS costs per person aged 75 and over in 1984 were £1,087 per year compared with £473 for persons aged 65–74 and £130 for persons aged 5–15 (the lowest; *Social Trends* 17). The ability of modern medicine to relieve suffering and to prolong life among the elderly is one of the fastest growing areas in medicine. Its costs are increasing faster than inflation. Especially in the last decade, death-rates have been declining quite fast in the old age-groups—between 1 and 2 per cent per year. So even without changes in demography or in social policy, costs of dependency will rise.

These changes in numbers and age structure are particularly important because most State pension schemes, including the British system, operate on a pay-as-you-go basis. So do most other welfare income transfers. In this system, pensions are paid not from a fund based on contributions made during working life by the pensioner, but instead on direct transfers from taxpayers. It is an instant transfer across generations. Private pension schemes, on the other hand, having no power to tax, need to set up funds into which individuals' contributions are paid. The accumulated total, together with any profits which the money has earned, is then (usually) either handed over as a lump sum or used to buy an annuity for the recipient on the day he or she retires.

Pay-as-you-go systems depend upon a large number of taxpayers being in place decades in the future to pay for promises made to pensioners today. They are therefore highly vulnerable to fertility fluctuations and fertility decline, which upset the optimistic assumptions, usually made earlier in this century, of continued population growth preserving a favourable ratio between the numbers of taxpayers in work and the number of pension recipients (Keyfitz 1985). Taxes then have to rise, or the promise has to be broken. This imbalance is often made worse by the tendency of governments to bribe older voters today with pension increases which future taxpayers, irrespective of their numbers, will have to pay for if they are to be honoured. This has been a constant feature of British political life since the 1950s, and it has destroyed any connection between the size of contributions to the state pension and the size of the pension received. A funding requirement would certainly have ruled out the State Earnings Related Pension Scheme (SERPS) discussed below.

On top of the underlying demographic change, the boundaries of the dependent age-groups themselves have shifted, squeezing the producer population between an expanding minimum leaving age population of young people on the one hand, and early retirement on the other. Fourteen per cent of 18-year-olds now go on to further education. Compared with fifty years ago, very few men now work on beyond retirement age. Work-force participation has declined fast from 55 onwards as early retirement has become more popular, funded by employers, especially in the public sector, wishing to reduce their work-force. The rise of work-force participation by married women, although substantial, has compensated for these reductions. Unemployment, increasing from 6 per cent in 1979 to a peak of 13 per cent—before falling again to 6 per cent in 1990—has also reduced the effective size of the taxpaying population. These are further reasons why the ratio of taxpayers' contributions to beneficiaries has worsened faster than the ratios of the respective age-groups (table 13.5).

Nevertheless we have reached a temporary lull in the rate of change of the numbers of pensioners and workers. Serious pension problems start when the boom generation reaches age 65. This is one of the biggest foreseeable problems facing all the Western industrial nations (International Labour Office 1898, Johnson, Conrad, and Thomson 1989). The problem cannot be averted; all the elderly population and most of the future work-force for that period have already been born. By 2020 the ratio of taxpayers to beneficiaries worsens from 3.0 to a low of 2.5. Even with only 6 per cent unemployment, national insurance contributions would have to rise from their current 9 per cent of employee's earnings to 20 per cent or more (and *pro rata* on employers' payrolls) quite apart from income tax (DHSS 1984). This is why the government, reacting for once to a long-term threat beyond the horizon of the next election, attempted in 1986 to ditch its inherited commitment to the State Earnings Related Pension Scheme (SERPS) which was created in 1975, although without complete success (Kay 1988). By 2010 the unmodified SERPS would have cost an additional £9.6 billion per year, by 2035 about £23 billion extra (1985 prices). SERPS is still in place but its terms are less generous and the government has offered tax bonuses for those who opt out of SERPS into private, funded schemes. The US state pensions scheme, which is partly funded, has increased its contributions rate so that it is building up a huge nominal surplus (but invested only in government debt) for the baby boom to deplete when it retires next century.

Private pensions might be thought to solve the problem. In the UK workers are being given wider opportunities to opt out into private, portable pension schemes. But flexible private schemes tend to have higher administrative costs. Depending on the market they may return more, but may also return less than occupational pension schemes, which usually pay a fixed proportion of salary. The demands on dividends by pensioners receiving private pensions will go up just as the demands on taxes by state pensioners. Either way, pensioners depend upon the active part of the economy. To weather this inevitable problem without damage will require further improvements in European and US productivity.

The success of the pensioners and welfare lobbies in limiting SERPS reform brings attention to another effect of population bulges. Pensioners will be likely to have some of their way in any confrontation with taxpayers as they will number about a quarter of the electorate. The growth of pensioners in the population this century has been matched by the importance of their representation in the electorate. That is why politicians have been paying increasing attention to them. As late as 1942 the Beveridge Report, which set out the modern

Welfare State, paid rather little attention to pensioners; in the more youthful population of those days the unemployed, and the needs of families, were the most pressing problem. These problems are reflected by the crisis of the middle-aged family. Now, for the first time in history, in line with the age structure, couples aged around 40 have more living parents than children. This may force them to realign their time-budgets and spending in respect of dependants.

Conflict between generations

We are all now familiar with the notion that membership of large cohorts minimizes life chances, lifetime income, and so on through increased competition for niches and promotion (Easterlin 1980). There is some empirical evidence for this view, although more from the USA than the UK.

More recently attention has been drawn to a countervailing effect; that members of large cohorts can help themselves in modern states through the public sector by voting for larger welfare benefits targeted at their own age-group. In this respect pensioners have a strong advantage over child dependants, who have no vote. Their electoral influence is already enhanced by the greater propensity of older people, at least up to retirement age, to vote. Pensioner incomes from all sources have increased fastest of any age-groups, and in the USA at least, where this analysis has gone furthest, they have done particularly well compared to young families with children (Preston 1984) and are expected to continue to do so as long as they form a large and growing population compared to other dependant (child) groups and the population of taxpayers as a whole. In respect of state provision it may pay to belong to a large cohort; in private competition (e.g. work-force entrance and wage rates) to a small one.

These forces are leading to a transfer of resources across generations; not from the elderly to the younger generations, as was normal, although that continues at the family level through inheritance, but from younger people to the elderly (see Johnson, Conrad, and Thomson 1989). It is claimed that the welfare generation has captured the welfare state, turned it from a child-centred to an age-centred process. So far in Britain there is little evidence that the elderly have gained at the expense of families (Johnson and Falkingham 1988). But the average age of consumers in the UK is now 5 years older than the average age of producers assuming a stationary population and economy (Ermisch 1989). The interaction of changes in taxation, welfare benefits, and cohort size may create generations of winners and losers. Today's older middle-aged and elderly may be winners. They have made small contributions and can make relatively big claims on welfare systems. But the generations born after the 1950s face the prospect of handing over about a third of their lifetime earnings. This high risk and deferment requires high trust in state welfare systems which may not be forthcoming. This has made several commentators suggest that the implicit contract in the welfare state may no longer be workable because the returns to today's younger contributors will be too small. The contract may therefore be up for renegotiation in 2000, with more private choice in prospect, and weakening of the entitlement to early retirement or to automatic rises in state pensions and other aspects of the 'institutionalization of the lifespan'. For example, disability insurance is very important in financing early withdrawal from work-force in the UK and many other industrial countries (up to 50 per cent of those reaching retirement age). Since the 1970s in most European countries, special unemployment help for over-60s makes it easier for companies to dismiss workers. Orthodox retirement has been losing its central function of regulating labour-force withdrawal. In the future, these special provisions may be expected to be more limited. The notion of a fixed retirement age may go as well, or the age of entitlement to automatic state pensions may be pushed back. In 1987 the USA abolished all age-limits for holding jobs.

The increase in the elderly population is not all bad news. Until almost the middle of the next century the retired baby boom generation will be in the 'young elderly' age-group of 65–75. Most old people can still look after themselves, stay in good health, and even keep in part-time employment—in 1987 there were 400,000 employed over age 65. Many of the fit 'young' elderly provide services for people older than they are, and for people still active in the labour force: caring for grandchildren and, in some cases, their own divorced children, as well as doing welfare work (Thane 1989). They will be particularly needed because recruitment to voluntary services has been hit by the decline in the single population and the rise in the number of married women going out to work. As these cohorts mature into retirement age they will take with them an unprecedentedly high degree of self-sufficiency. Their owner-occupation rate is likely to approach 80 per cent, compared to 47 per cent of household heads over 65 who were owner-occupiers in 1985. And in 1983 75 per cent of men over 55 in full-time employment belonged to occupational pension schemes, compared with just 60 per cent a decade earlier. A high proportion should have ample capital resources, because of the growing number who will benefit in middle age from the inheritance of mostly

unmortgaged property from their parents, whose generation was the
first major home-owning cohort (Morgan Grenfell 1987). Such people
can only be regarded as dependants if they receive tax transfers in
retirement, rather than paying for them through working. Cohorts now
approaching middle age will, when they enter old age, be much
healthier than their peers today. They will have enjoyed better
nutrition, they will have smoked less, they will have had more effective
medical care. This should improve their expectation of life and keep
them healthier and independent for longer. Old age now begins in the
mid-70s.

13.10 The Middle Years: Consumers and Work-Force in the Future

The numbers of adults of employable age dominate the demographic
effects of population change. Because working adults account for much
consumption as well as almost all production, their numbers and
behaviour moderate the impact of the demands made by dependent
children and the elderly. The demographic limits of the future
work-force can be projected with some confidence (DE 1987). Its
overall numbers, though not its age structure, are settled until the end
of the century now that the baby boom has been absorbed into it.

The size of the work-force is expected to remain constant for the rest
of the century, at about 27 million. Relatively small numbers of
departures, at their lowest from 1992–4 (the births of the 1920–30s)
will be balanced by relatively small numbers of entrants (the births
of 1970–90). The internal age distribution will shift upwards: the
growth of the 45–65 age-group (the boom) balanced by a decline of
20–4-year-olds. This will make the future early retirement pattern
particularly important. In common with the rest of the industrial world,
participation rates of men 55–64 have fallen in the last fifteen years
(60–70 per cent down to 50–60 per cent). The increase of married
women in the work-force accounts for 71 per cent of projected
work-force increase, but it will put a premium on growth in child
care/tax reliefs; otherwise their participation may be at the expense of
the size of future birth cohorts and the future labour force. Economic
activity rates of woman below age 25 are likely to rise because of
delayed childbearing; with a later corresponding decline in the activity
rates of 25–34 age-groups. More modest declines in male activity rates
aged 60–4 and 65+ are projected for the 1990s than in the 1980s as
early retirement is no longer encouraged by the Job Release Scheme
and is unlikely to be encouraged by employers increasingly anxious
about recruitment.

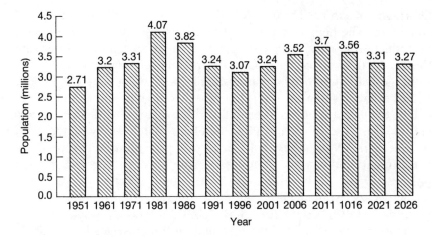

Note: Change of scale after 1981.

Source: OPCS 1989b t.4, 1971 Census Age, Marital Conditions, and General Tables, t. 9

FIG. 13.8. Population aged 15–19, England and Wales, 1951–2026

The current demographic sensation is the trough of small cohorts born since the early 1970s, which will create a novel shortage of young workers. Although long predicted, it only started to be discussed publicly in Britain during 1988. Then the Royal College of Nursing and the Norwich Union Insurance Company began the teenager scare by forecasting substantial shortfalls in future recruits for nurses and clerks. Such a sharp fall in potential teenage recruits is without precedent (figure 13.8). Typically, births for the last decade have been 20–5 per cent lower than at their peak in the mid-1960s. Therefore the available young work-force entrants (assumed to be 18 years old) of the early 1990s and beyond will be 20–5 per cent fewer than employers have become used to. Some of this effect is already apparent; cohorts of 18-year-olds were already 10 per cent down from their 1970s peak by 1987. Some years will show particularly severe reductions; births dropped to a twentieth-century low in Britain and many European countries around 1977; the work-force entry cohort of 1995 will be 35 per cent smaller than that of 1982. However, the decline in the numbers of entrants will bottom out in around 1993 and will then fluctuate slightly. By 2001, births to children of the baby boom are expected to relieve the shortage temporarily and teenage numbers will rise again to almost the present level. In general, smaller recruitment cohorts are here to stay, but the decline must be kept in perspective. The current reduction only takes the numbers back to those of the 1960s and 1970s.

Shortages of young workers will not be equal at different levels of education. The higher education projections discussed below envisage no reduction in entry because it is proposed to expand to 30 per cent the proportion of each age-group attending tertiary education. The shortage may therefore be concentrated upon young people who have left school with some 'A' levels but who do not go on to take a degree.

For the last two decades employers have been able to pick and choose from the unusually large numbers of teenagers of the baby boom years. Now, they will have to open up other sources of recruitment and supply. Employers will have to reconsider their policies towards early retirement, make employment conditions more attractive for women with children, and retrain those with few or redundant skills (NEDO 1988, CBI 1989). Pressure on wage rates will be strongly upwards. Trade unions may find themselves in a stronger bargaining position than for some time. Incentives for older workers in large cohorts may compare unfavourably with those offered to secure the services of the scarce young, although their numbers will block promotion. Malthus insisted that workers would improve their position most effectively by reducing the supply of labour in this way. Rarely before has it happened so dramatically. Renewed capital investment may be one way out for employers who may attempt to minimize their conventional work-force, or expand output. This impending shortage of workers could be turned to advantage. One of Britain's chronic economic problems has been low labour productivity and high unit costs of production. Renewed capital investment, given appropriate interest rates, is one way out for employers to minimize their work-force or expand output with a higher capital ratio. That might help create a new high-wage, high-output economy.

Alternatively, as in the past, attempts may be made to evade the problem by importing labour. There will be calls for a reconsideration of immigration policies by government, to remedy deficits in the labour force and the age structure (see Espenshade 1987). Electorates are unlikely to agree. In this context the application of Turkey to join the EC (and for its citizens to enjoy freedom of movement within it) becomes highly significant. Turkey had a population of 53 million in 1987, growing at 2 per cent per year. Its natural increase of 1.2 million per year is bigger than that of all the EC countries put together. Even without further immigration a higher proportion of the future work-force will be of immigrant ethnic minority origin. Although their fertility has showed some decline, immigrant mothers and most ethnic minorities (e.g. Asians in Britain, Hispanics, Turks elsewhere), maintain higher fertility than the native population. About 13 per cent of births in the UK, West Germany, USA and some other industrial countries are to immigrant mothers. The teenage shortage may help solve some problems of ethnic minority unemployment, and of some inner city areas in general. It may also help solve some of Northern Ireland's employment problems, both in the province itself and by migration to areas of high demand. In that province, as in the Republic of Ireland, high fertility has created a youthful age structure. The Roman Catholic population has been growing about 50 per cent faster than its Protestant counterpart and much faster than job creation has been possible (Compton and Coward 1989, J. Smith 1987). Now, the age structure it has created may supply some labour shortages in Britain and, for the first time this century, bring fertility within the capacity of the domestic Northern Ireland economy.

The middle-aged person has a paramount importance as consumer as well as producer. The ageing baby boom will keep the demand high especially for private sector goods and services (as opposed to schools and old people's homes). High demand for owner-occupied housing from this age-group has been blamed for part of the unusual inflationary spiral of houseprices in the 1980s. But as the bulge moves upwards in the age-groups it will expand demand in goods and services which are characteristic of older age-groups and leave business closures behind it. Consumer patterns change fast during adolescence. The very characteristic teenage market has seen its consumers decline by a quarter in the last decade, with little opportunity to remarket its goods elsewhere: grown-ups do not want pop records or fluorescent T shirts. The volume of demand tends to increase as a person ages and income grows. Older working adults buy better quality and more expensive goods of all kinds. The balance of consumption also alters with the family life cycle. Small fast cars and small convenient flats suitable for single or early married life give way to the purchase of estate cars and larger suburban dwellings in early middle life. Consumption patterns change again when children leave home in the 'empty nest' phase. Marketing departments now pay great attention to likely shifts in the demand for their products arising from age-structure changes. 'Business demographics' is becoming big business in the USA, and the ideas are now catching on in Britain (BSPS 1988). The centre of gravity of the baby boom in 1990 is still in the 15–29 age-group (figure 13.6). It is 2.7 million people bigger than the 15-year age-group which follows it. By the 1990s it will have moved into the 30–44 age-group; around the end of the century it will have made the later middle-aged group of over 45s the most potent force in the marketplace.

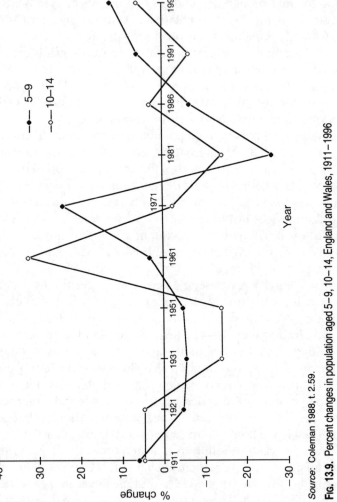

Source: Coleman 1988, t. 2.59.

Fig. 13.9. Percent changes in population aged 5–9, 10–14, England and Wales, 1911–1996

13.11 Educating the Young

Rational planning of education and other local authority based services is already made difficult by the overwhelming importance of migration—inadequately measured and less predictable—on local demography (Rhodes and Naccache 1977, Campbell 1976, Armitage 1986). Recent changes in age structure have compounded these difficulties by changing the underlying national demographic patterns as well.

School attendance is compulsory from age 5 to 16, so demand for schools up to that age is directly determined by the age structure of the population (figure 13.9). First primary, then secondary schools were obliged to expand by 30 per cent or more from the 1960s; since the late 1970s they have had to respond to the unprecedented problems of falling rolls, contraction, and amalgamation. As the number of teachers has not declined to the extent of the school population itself, the average pupil/teacher ratio has increased to its most favourable level ever. Likewise the provision of buildings expenditure has not fallen commensurate with the numbers enrolled, so although the amount spent per child is also at an all-time high, most of it goes on teachers' salaries and building costs (see CIPFA 1986).

The pressure on schools has been made worse by two other factors. The first is the continued depopulation of inner city areas and some rural areas in the 1960s and 1970s and the consequent increased demand for schools in suburbs and small towns. The second is the sluggishness with which government responded to the warnings inherent in the age structure through adjustment of school provision and teacher training. It is only since the late 1970s (DES 1977, Central Policy Review Staff 1977) that much thought has been given to the effect of demographic changes on education and social services.

Local authorities' new powers to respond to declining rolls by amalgamating schools (together with the government's other policies, for example on enhanced parental choice of school) has caused fierce local disputes about which under-patronized schools to close. Some Local Educational Authorities have responded to these uncertainties by holding a stock of 'Portakabin' class rooms to be used wherever necessary. Attempts are now being made (Diamond 1989) to make the best possible use of other relevant demographic data for forecasting pupil numbers at local level.

The baby boom has now moved on to stir up political controversy in higher education. From the 1970s to the 1980s the bulge was accommodated without a decline in the participation rate, but also without much increase in the higher education establishment. The debate in the 1980s has concentrated on how to manage the following slump in student numbers, and on whether the participation rate should not be expanded instead. This has become connected with parallel debate about the adequacy of the participation rate itself. Critics insist that the present participation rate in higher education (14 per cent) is less than that of our major industrial competitors and cannot produce an adequately trained higher level work-force. However, participation rates compare better if higher drop-out rates which are now planned to double abroad are taken into account.

The initial official forecast for higher education (DES 1982) was based on simple extrapolation of the age structure. But three other factors complicate the picture: more girls now take up higher education as the number taking and passing A levels has risen to that of boys; more mature students go back to it; most important, the substantial shift in the social class structure of the population (Chapter 4) powerfully affects demand. The sex ratio of girls to boys with two or more A level passes has risen from 75 : 100 in 1970 to 95 : 100 in 1982; the corresponding sex ratio for university entrance has risen from 40 to 70 (Diamond 1989). On the social class factor, the initial government projections may have underestimated likely future demand by 20–30 per cent (Royal Society 1983). Children of middle-class parents comprise three-quarters of university entrants. Children with parents in professional occupations are four times as likely to apply for higher education as children with parents in clerical occupations, eight times as likely as those with parents in manual occupations. Upwardly mobile parents are almost four times as likely to apply for higher education for their children than are downwardly mobile parents (Diamond 1989). All three factors have now been taken into account (DES 1986) and the final estimate of numbers is almost 60 per cent greater than that in the 1982 report. The 1987 White Paper on Higher Education (DES 1987) did not allude to demographic decline at all in the context of the constraints on student numbers.

13.12 One or Two Parents?

Many British population trends are shared with the rest of the industrial world: long-term ageing, low and volatile fertility, uncertainty about the attractions of marriage, the risks of divorce, the high proportion of people living by themselves. All these are becoming incorporated into the emerging demographic regimes of late industrial and post-industrial society. They are maintained by high incomes, universal education, the permanent absorption of women into the work-force; the minimizing of risk though welfare systems.

In divorce and illegitimacy, Britain has become rather exceptional compared to European averages. Our divorce rate is the highest in Europe (although almost all are now high) and second only to that of the United States. The proportion of births which are illegitimate is two to four times the proportions in countries such as Germany, Belgium, the Netherlands, and Italy, although they are matched by those of France, Austria, and Norway, and greatly exceeded by Sweden and Denmark (Council of Europe 1989, see Chapters 5 and 6).

This situation appears in part to be an artefact of British tax, welfare, and housing systems. There are few advantages in tax or welfare arrangements for couples who choose to marry rather than to cohabit (although the married persons' allowance to be introduced in 1991 will change that), and few fiscal benefits in marrying compared to remaining single, especially for people on low incomes. For example, according to 1988–9 Income Support rates, an unemployed couple with a baby receive £68.35 in all, while as lone mother and baby (£54), and father living separately (£33.40) they would be £19.05 per week better off, not counting the threefold increase in earnings limit and priority access to council housing for the mother. Comparing families on low pay (£100 in 1988–9), a single mother's net spending power of £91.15 is £4.90 more than that of a conventional family because she receives the same family credit as a married couple and extra One-Parent Benefit (National Family Trust 1989). Despite this circumstantial evidence, it is not known from direct evidence how people respond to these economic differentials. An analysis of the 1980 Women and Employment Survey did not show that welfare payments tended to prolong the duration of lone parenthood (single and divorced women together), but that being in work did so (Ermisch and Wright 1989).

In housing, too, tax relief and systems of allocation have not favoured marriage or conventional childbearing. Until August 1988 cohabiting couples could obtain tax relief on a total of £60,000 of a new mortgage—a subsidy of up to about £2,600 per year—compared with a £30,000 limit for a married couple. Cohabiting couples with such mortgages who wish to marry will immediately lose half their subsidy. In most countries private renting is the normal tenure for new households. Britain's private rented sector is the smallest in Europe; accordingly more new households are forced into the financial burdens of owner-occupation at an earlier stage than in any other country (see Boléat 1989). Those with no ambitions or hope of ownership look instead to the system of publicly subsidized but rationed rented housing, access to which is speeded up by dependency, including single-parent status. Cohabitation also makes sense for other reasons (see Chapter 5): for example the general lack of pre-marital contracts in Britain to safeguard rights to property brought into the marriage by each partner.

In 1989 birth registration data suggested that about 28 per cent of all illegitimate births were of the 'traditional' illegitimate type; the remainder being to cohabiting unions. This means that about 7 per cent of all births are 'traditionally' illegitimate, 19 per cent are in cohabiting unions, 74 per cent in marriage.

There are two reasons why this fairly new demographic development may be unwelcome. The first is economic. It represents a further transfer through the welfare system from earners to dependants. It is also a transfer from earners to fathers who have abandoned, or refused to support, their children.

With 28 per cent of births now illegitimate, and about 20 per cent of children likely to experience the break-up of their parents' marriage before age 16, altogether 45 per cent of children are likely to spend some part of their childhood in an unorthodox family setting which in many cases will be dependent on welfare transfers. Children may not stay in this position; a study of the illegitimate children in the 1958 birth cohort showed that the majority were living in a two-parent family of some sort within seven years of birth; through adoption or the subsequent marriage or cohabitation of their mother (Crellin 1971). In a 1980 sample, 50 per cent of lone mothers who were previously married remarried within five years; 50 per cent of single mothers had partners within three years (Ermisch and Wright 1989).

None the less, Relate, formerly the Marriage Guidance Council, estimated in 1989 that marital breakdown costs a minimum £1.25 billion per year (Relate 1989), of which £950 million is in Income Support and One-Parent Benefit. This excludes private sector costs. In separate calculations, the government has estimated that welfare support for one-parent families of all kinds will amount to £1.85 billion in 1990, and that support for unmarried mothers alone cost £700 million in 1988 (Hansard 1990). Most absent fathers make little or no contribution: their payments amount to about 8 per cent of the welfare support costs of single-parent families. They can marry or cohabit again. The welfare system appears to subsidize over-consumption by men of marriage, and perhaps a less reflective attitude to producing or abandoning children, by reducing their costs.

The second concern is that children brought up in single-parent households may suffer more than their fair share of difficulties when growing up. The higher infant and perinatal mortality rates of illegitimate children—about 50 per cent—are long established (OPCS 1987*d*, 1988*d*). They are not accounted for entirely by social class factors; for example, the below average height and weight of the mothers. In part they are a consequence of other demographic characteristics of illegitimate birth, such as youth of the mother and the fact that a high proportion are first births. Concealed pregnancy and generally low levels of ante-natal care also contribute (see Gill 1977). Perhaps surprisingly, children born to cohabiting unions also have a higher post-neonatal mortality rate (5.2 deaths per 1,000 births in 1982–5), intermediate between legitimate (3.4) and 'conventional' illegitimate births (7.2). Accordingly it was suggested that illegitimacy, even when the birth is registered by both parents, should substitute for social class V origin as an indicator of social deprivation of infants (Gordon 1990). Subsequent physical development of illegitimate children, however, shows no disadvantage.

Most studies which have followed up the lives of illegitimate children show that they have a higher than average risk of experiencing learning difficulties and doing less well at school. Illegitimate children are more likely to be in local authority care. Prolonged institutional care is believed to risk damage to a child's intellectual and emotional development and leave it vulnerable to later stress (Mapstone 1969). In the 1960s up to 50 per cent of the children in long-term care were illegitimate. Illegitimate children are more likely to suffer from a higher frequency of depression and other disorders, although up to age 7 at least, social adjustment can be superior to children from other backgrounds (Crellin *et al.* 1971). Many studies show that illegitimate children are more likely to become delinquent and involved in crime (Wilson and Herrnstein 1985). Problems of delinquency and maladjustment are also reported from cohort studies of children in homes broken by divorce (Wadsworth 1979). Some (small-scale) studies, however, have not found these effects (Riley and Shaw 1985) and emphasize that quality of parenting is paramount irrespective of the form of family.

Some of these problems also affect children who have experienced the break-up of their parental home, although the consequences of divorce for children are not well understood (Walczak and Burns 1984). Loss of a father through death seems more damaging than through divorce (Gill 1977), which may in some cases improve the emotional life of mother and children. Two-parent upbringing may be restored by remarriage. However, step-relationships are evidently not always easy to negotiate (Maddox 1975, Brown 1982). Child abuse is relatively more frequent in stepfamilies (Daley and Wilson 1981,

Russell 1984). Their financial circumstances tend to be more fragile (Maclean and Ekelaar 1983), with higher than average risks of divorce (see Chapter 5).

A number of factors may contribute to these difficulties. On average, lone mothers are likely to experience downward social mobility and a lower income if they keep their child. Divorcees are likely to move from owner-occupation to council tenancy, from higher to lower status areas, to a lower income level based on a lower status job than that provided by the former husband or which they occupied when they could work full time. Lone mothers are about twice as likely to go out to work than married mothers (although the proportion is declining), and single working mothers are the most likely to leave their children with child-minders, who are known to offer the least stimulating care. These effects are more substantial on women and children from non-manual backgrounds.

Many of the studies which support these generalizations are over a decade old. Interest in illegitimacy has waned since then; the decline of the stigma associated with it has gone with a reluctance to envisage deleterious consequences arising from alternative lifestyles. It is not known if the handicaps associated with 'traditional' illegitimacy also apply to any degree to the now more common illegitimacy where both parents register the birth of the child. If parents do stay together there seem no obvious reasons arising from the family situation itself why the child should suffer disadvantage, although the risk of subsequent parental break-up seems to be high. A high proportion of the nation's children will be brought up in new circumstances the consequences of which we know little.

So far the welfare system has been demand-led in these respects. Little attention has been given to the prospects of changing it to moderate demand, or even if this is possible. Reform of divorce law, most recently in 1984, responded to the needs of partners, not to needs of children or welfare costs. Alternative policies have been urged to rearrange tax and welfare incentives to help ensure that as many children as possible, irrespective of legitimacy, are brought up with the financial and emotional support of two parents (National Family Trust 1989). The notion of obliging absent fathers to pay a higher proportion of the costs of their children has been much discussed in 1990. It has been suggested that genetic fingerprinting techniques now make determination of parenthood easy; although it is less certain that computerized record linkage will make it easier to trace the location of individuals.

Support for families and children cannot be considered apart from the growing demand, by women and by many employers, for women to go out to work or to return to it after having children. Women's participation in the labour force is its only component likely to grow in future. Concern about the 'teenager shortage' has thrown this debate into sharp relief. The 1990 budget introduced a modest novelty to encourage mothers with children to continue working or to return to work, in removing tax from the value to mothers of nurseries provided at work. This only affects a few thousand women in 1990. Evidence abroad suggests that other measures, such as the right to return to a relinquished job, is at least as important as financial compensations in encouraging women back into the work-force after childbearing. Other things being equal, such measures might also be expected to have a mild pronatalist effect. The continued movement of women into the work-force seems to be assured. The future production of children is not.

13.13 The Shape of the Future

Three kinds of challenge emerge from the demographic groundswell. The first is the problems of single-parent families and the growth of one-person households arising from new trends in household and family formation and dissolution, some of which were discussed above. The other two are on a different scale. One is the legacy of the perturbations in fertility which characterized the half century from the 1930s to the present day: the baby bulge and the trough which followed, the challenges it presents in education, the labour force, pensions, and the demographic underpinning of the welfare system. The other is the long-term spectre of low fertility and of declining population. For over a decade, fertility in the developed world has been settled at rates well below replacement level. Since the 1980s Western Europe has been joined by Southern Europe and the newly industrialized countries of the Far East in what looks like a world-wide trend. Some societies, notably Germany and its neighbours, have maintained levels of between 1.3 to 1.6 for years; in Germany and Denmark consequent population decline has already begun. Others, including France, Britain, the USA, the Dominions and Japan have kept fertility around 1.8. Britain is not accustomed to thinking about population policy. It may not need one (see Chapter 4). But it is quite reasonable to suppose that the average woman will produce less than 2 children in the forseeable future. If fertility does not increase beyond 2.0 then our population will acquire an age distribution looking like figure 13.10. That may be the picture of the British demographic future.

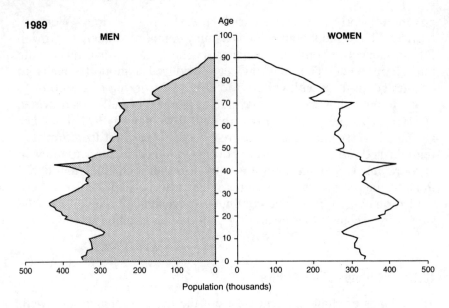

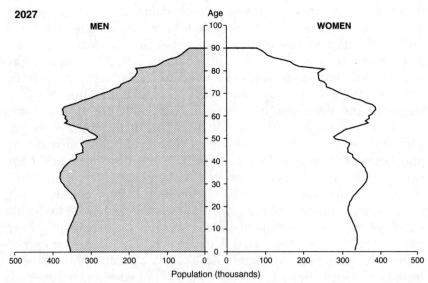

Sources: Data from OPCS (1989a), OPCS (1990f).

FIG. 13.10. Age structure of the population of England and Wales, 1989, 2075 up to age 90.

APPENDIX

Major Sources of Demographic Data in Britain

(1) OPCS annual publications

Series	Subject
AB	Legal Abortions
CEN	Census
DH1	Mortality Statistics general
DH2	Mortality Statistics cause
DH3	Mortality Statistics childhood and maternal
	Mortality Statistics perinatal and infant—social and biological factors.
DH4	Mortality Statistics accidents and violence
DH5	Mortality Statistics area
DH6	Mortality Statistics childhood
DS	Decennial Supplements (following each census)
EL	Electoral Statistics
FM1	Birth Statistics
FM2	Marriage and Divorce Statistics
MB1	Cancer Statistics registration
MB2	Communicable Diseases Statistics
MB3	Congenital Malformation Statistics
MB5	Morbidity Statistics from General Practice
MN	International Migration
	Internal Migration
PP1	Population Estimates
PP2	Population Projections (usually 2-yearly)
PP3	Population Projections area
VS	Key Population and Vital Statistics for local authority areas

OPCS Monitors (same series, published quarterly or occasionally)

AB	Legal Abortions (quarterly and annual)
DH2	Deaths by Cause (quarterly)
DH3	Infant and Perinatal Mortality (DHAs) (quarterly)
	Sudden Infant Deaths (biennially)
DH4	Deaths from Accidents and Violence;
	Fatal Accidents during Sporting and Leisure activities.
EL	Electoral Registration: local government (quarterly)
MB2	Infectious Diseases: quarterly notifications
PP1	Population estimates: national, local government, and health areas (annual)

SS   General Household Survey: preliminary results (annual)

Others may be published in addition. (See OPCS Monitors Subscription Factsheet 1990)

(2) Other OPCS publications

Census (decennial since 1801 except for 1941) HMSO
Longitudinal Study Series LS (occasional) HMSO
Population Trends (quarterly) HMSO
Studies in Medical and Population Subjects Series SMPS (occasional) HMSO
OPCS Occasional Papers OPCS

(3) Other annual official statistical reviews relevant to population, all with commentary as well as tables (all HMSO)

Annual Report of the Registrar-General for Scotland
Annual Report of the Registrar-General for Northern Ireland
Economic Trends
Health Trends
Regional Trends
Social Trends

(4) Annual Government surveys (HMSO)

General Household Survey
Labour Force Survey
International Passenger Survey (continuous, data in OPCS Series MN)

Home Office Control of Immigration Statistics (annual), HMSO
Home Office Immigration and Nationality Department Annual Report, Home Office

(5) International

Council of Europe (annual) Recent Demographic Developments in the Member Countries of the Council of Europe, Strasburg, Council of Europe

Eurostat (annual) Demographic Statistics (Theme 3, Population and Social Conditions; Series C, Accounts Surveys and Statistics), Luxemburg, EC.

SOPEMI (Système d'Observation Permanente sur les Migrations), Annual Report, Paris, OECD (continuous reporting system on migration).

United Nations (annual) Demographic Yearbook, New York, United Nations.

Population Reference Bureau, Inc. (annual), World Population Data Sheet, Washington DC, Population Reference Burean, Inc.

References

ABERCROMBIE, P. (1945), *Greater London Plan, 1944*, London, HMSO.

ACHESON, E. D. (1989), 'Breast cancer screening'. *Journal of the Royal Society of Medicine*, 82 (Aug.–July), 455–7.

ACHESON, R. M. (1988), 'Prevention versus cure: use of resources in the National Health Service', in Keynes, Coleman, and Dimsdale (1988).

—— and SANDERSON, C. (1978), 'Strokes: social class and geography', *Population Trends*, 12: 13–17.

ADAMS, J. G. U. (1985), *Risk and Freedom: The Record of Road Safety Regulation*, Transport Publishing Projects.

ADDY, D. P., and MATHEW, P. M., (1981), 'Malaria in children in Birmingham in the 1970s', *Postgraduate Medical Journal*, 57: 781–3.

ADELSTEIN, A. (1977), 'Tuberculosis deaths: a generation effect', *Population Trends*, 8: 20–3.

—— DAVIES, I. M. M., and WEATHERALL, J. A. C. (1980), *Perinatal and Infant Mortality: Social and Biological Factors 1975–77*, Studies on Medical and Population Subjects No.41, London, HMSO.

—— and LOY P. (1979), 'Fatal adverse effects of medicine and surgery', *Population Trends*, 17: 17–22.

—— and MARDON, C. (1975), 'Suicides 1961–74', *Population Trends*, 2: 13–18.

—— and WHITE, G. (1976*a*), 'Leukaemia 1911–1973: cohort analysis', *Population Trends*, 3: 9–13.

—— —— (1976*b*), 'Alcoholism and mortality', *Population Trends*, 6: 7–13.

ALDERSON, M. R. (1976), *An Introduction to Epidemiology*, London, Macmillan.

—— (1982), 'The span of life: a comment', *Journal of the Institute of Actuaries*, 109: 355.

—— and ASHWOOD, F. (1985), 'Projection of mortality rates for the elderly', *Population Trends*, 42: 22–9.

—— LEE, P. N., and WALSH, R. (1985), 'Risks of lung cancer, chronic bronchitis, ischaemic heart disease and stroke in relation to type of cigarette smoked', *Journal of Epidemiology and Community Health*, 39: 286–93.

ALFORD, B. W. E. (1973), *WD &HO Wills and the Development of the UK Tobacco Industry 1786–1965*, London, Methuen.

AMMERMAN, A. J., and CAVALLI-SFORZA, L. (1973), 'A population model for the diffusion of early farming in Europe', in C. Renfrew *et al.* (eds.), *The Explanation of Cultural Change: Models in Prehistory*, Research Seminar in Archaeology and Related Subjects, London, Duckworth.

—— —— (1984), *The Neolithic Transition and the Genetics of Population in Europe*, Princeton, NJ, Princeton University Press.

AMMON, L. (1976), 'Smith and Jones: 1853 and 1975', *Population Trends*, 4: 9–11.

ANDERSON, B. A., and SILVER, B. D. (1986), 'Infant mortality in the Soviet Union: regional differences and measurement issues', *Population and Development Review*, 12: 705–38.

—— (1989), 'The changing shape of Soviet mortality 1958–1985: An evaluation of old and new evidence', *Population Studies*, 43: 243–65.

ANDERSON, M. (1980), 'Quantitative indicators of family change', in M. Anderson (ed.), *Sociology of the Family*, Harmondsworth, Penguin.

—— (1983), 'What is new about the modern family: an historical perspective', in *The Family*, OPCS/BSPS Occasional Paper No. 31, London, OPCS.

ANDERSON, P. (1988), 'Excess mortality associated with alcohol consumption', *British Medical Journal*, 297: 824–6.

ANDERSON, R. M., and MAY, R. M. (1988), 'Epidemiological parameters of HIV transmission', *Nature*, 333: 514–19.

—— —— and McLEAN, A. R. (1988), 'Possible demographic consequences of AIDS in developing countries', *Nature*, 332: 228–34.

ANDORKA, R. (1978), *Determinants of Fertility in Advanced Societies*, London, Methuen.

APPLEBY, A. B. (1979), Grain prices and subsistence crises in England and France 1590–1740', *Journal of Economic History* 39: 865–87.

—— (1980a), 'The Disappearance of plague: a continuing puzzle', *Economic History Review*, 33: 161–73.

—— (1980b), 'Epidemics and famine in the little Ice Age', *Journal of Interdisciplinary History*, 10: 643–63.

ARGYLE, M., and HENDERSON, M. (1985), *The Anatomy of Relationships and the Rules and Skills to Manage them Successfully*, London, Heinemann.

ARIES, P. (1962), *Centuries of Childhood*, London, Jonathan Cape.

—— (1983), 'Two successive motivations for the declining birth rate in the West', in C. Hohn and R. Mackensen (eds.), *Determinants of Fertility Trends: Theories Re-examined*, Liège, Éditions Ordina, 123–30.

ARMITAGE, R. I. (1986), 'Population projections for English local authority areas', *Population Trends*, 43: 31–40.

—— (1987), 'English regional fertility and mortality patterns, 1975–1985', *Population Trends*, 47: 16–23.

ASHFORD, J. R., READ, K. L. Q., and RILEY V. C. (1973), 'An analysis of variations in perinatal mortality amongst local authorities in England and Wales', *International Journal of Epidemiology*, 2: 31–46.

ASKHAM, J. (1975), *Fertility and Deprivation: A Study of Differential Fertility Amongst Working-Class Families in Aberdeen*, Cambridge, Cambridge University Press.

Association of Scientific, Technical and Managerial Staffs (1980), *The Prevention of Industrial Cancer: An ASTMS Policy Document*, London, ASTMS (now Manufacturing, Scientific and Finance (MSF)).

ATKINSON, J. (1987), 'Relocating managers and professional staff', IMS Report No. 139, Institute of Manpower Studies, University of Sussex.

ATSATT, M. (n.d.), 'Population estimates for England and Wales from the Eleventh to the Nineteenth Centuries' (mimeo), Berkeley, University of California.

AUSTIN, C. R., and SHORT R. V. (eds.) (1980), *Human Sexuality*. Cambridge, Cambridge University Press.

AYKROYD, W. R. (1973), 'The consumption of sugar', *British Nutrition Foundation Bulletin*, 8: 21–9.

BAINES, D. (1985), *Migration in a Mature Economy: Emigration and Internal Migration in England and Wales 1861–1900*, Cambridge, Cambridge University Press.

BALL, K. P., and PURCELL, H. (eds.) (1984), 'Recent trends in coronary mortality and their implication for the UK', Coronary Prevention Group Conference, *Postgraduate Medical Journal*: 1–46.

BALARAJAN, R., RALEIGH, V. S, and BOTTING, B. (1989), 'Sudden Infant Death syndrome and postneonatal mortality among immigrants in England and Wales', *British Medical Journal*, 298: 716–20.

BALLARD, C. (1978), 'Arranged marriages in the British context', *New Community*, 6: 3.

BANKS, J. A. (1954), *Prosperity and Parenthood: A Study of Family Planning Among the Victorian Middle Classes*, London, Routledge & Kegan Paul.

——(1981), *Victorian Values: Secularism and the Size of Families*, London, Routledge & Kegan Paul.

——and BANKS, O. (1954), 'The Bradlaugh–Besant trial and the English newspapers', *Population Studies*, 8: 33.

————(1964), *Feminism and Family Planning in Victorian England*, Liverpool, Liverpool University Press.

BARKER, D. J. P. (1989), 'The Rise and Fall of Western diseases', *Nature*, 338, 30 Mar.: 371–2.

——OSMOND, C., GOLDING, J., KUH, D., and WADSWORTH, M. E. J. (1989), 'Growth in utero, Blood pressure in childhood and adult life, and mortality from cardiovascular disease', *British Medical Journal*, 298: 564–7.

BARKER, T., and DRAKE, M. (eds.) (1982), *Population and Society in Britain 1880–1980*, Batsford Academic.

BARNETT, C. (1970), *Britain and her Army*, Harmondsworth, Penguin.

——(1972), *The Collapse of British Power*, London, Eyre Methuen.

——(1986), *The Audit of War*, London, Macmillan.

BARRETT, J. C., and Brass, W. (1974), 'Systematic and chance components in fertility measurement', *Population Studies*, 20: 473–93.

BARTH, F. (ed.) (1969), *Ethnic Groups and Boundaries*, Oslo, Oslo University Press.

BAUM, F., and COPE, D. R. (1980), 'Some characteristics of intentionally childless wives in Britain', *Journal of Biosocial Science*, 12/3: 287–99.

BEAGLEHOLE, R. (1986), 'Medical management and the decline in mortality from coronary heart disease', *British Medical Journal*, 292: 33–8.

BEAN, J. M. W. (1963), 'Plague, population and economic decline in England in the later middle ages', *Economic History Review*, 2nd series, 15: 423–37.

BEARD, R. W. (1981), 'Technology in the care of mother and baby: an essential safeguard', in R. Chester, P. Diggory, and M. B. Sutherland (eds.), *Changing Pattern of Child-Bearing and Child-Rearing*, London, Academic Press: 1–12.

BEAUMONT, P. B. (1976), 'Assisted labour mobility policy in Scotland 1973–74, *Urban Studies*, 13: 75–9.

BEAVER, M. W. (1973), 'Population, infant mortality and milk', *Population Studies*, 27: 243–54.

BECKER, G. S. (1973), 'A theory of marriage, Part I, Part II', *Journal of Political Economy*, 81/4: 812–46.

—— (1981), *A Treatise on the Family*, Cambridge, Mass., Harvard University Press.

—— LANDES, E. M., and MICHAEL R. T. (1977), 'An economic analysis of marital instability', *Journal of Political Economy*, 85: 1141–87.

BEDDOES, J. (1885), *The Races of Britain*, Bristol, Arrowsmith.

BEEVERS, D. G. (ed.) (1983), 'Ethnic differences in common diseases', *Postgraduate Medical Journal*, 59: 615–71.

BELLOC, N. B. (1973), 'Relationship of health practices and mortality', *Preventive Medicine*, 2: 67–81.

—— and L. BRESLOW, (1972), 'Relationship of physical health status and health patterns', *Preventive Medicine*, 1: 409–21.

BENEDICTOW, O. J. (1987), 'Mortality in historical plague epidemics', *Population Studies*, 41/3: 401–31.

BENJAMIN, B. (1964), 'The urban background to public health changes in England and Wales 1900–1950', *Population Studies*, 17/3; also *Public Health and Urban Growth*, London, Centre for Urban Studies.

—— (1982), 'Smoking and mortality', In S. Preston (ed.), *Biological and Social Aspects of Mortality and the Length of Life*, Liège, Éditions Ordina: 443–48.

—— (1989), *Population Statistics: A Review of UK Sources*, London, Gower.

—— and OVERTON, E. (1981), 'Prospects for mortality decline in England and Wales', *Population Trends*, 23: 22–8.

BENJAMIN, B., and WALLIS, C. (1963), 'The mortality of widowers', *Lancet*, 2: 454.

BENSON, S. (1981), *Ambiguous Ethnicity: Inter-racial Marriages in London*, London, Cambridge University Press.

BERAL, V., and KAY, C. R. (1977), 'Mortality among oral-contraceptive users', *Lancet*, 2: 727–33.

BERESFORD, S. A. A. (1985), 'Is nitrate in the drinking water associated with the risk of cancer in the urban UK?', *International Journal of Epidemiology*, 14: 57–63.

BERESFORD, M. W., and HURST, J. G. (1971), *Deserted Medieval Villages*, London, Butterworth.

BERKMAN, L. F., and BRESLOW, L. (1983), *Health and Ways of Living: The Alameda County Study*, New York, Oxford University Press.

BERRY, B. J. L. (1976), 'The counter-urbanization process: urban America since 1970', *Urbanizaton and Counter-Urbanization*, Urban Affairs, Annual Review, II, London, Sage, 17–30.

BINGHAM, S., WILLIAMS, D. R. R., COLE, T. J. and JAMES, W. P. T. (1979), 'Dietary fibre and regional large bowel cancer mortality in Britain', *British Journal of Cancer*, 40: 456–63.

BIRABEN, J.-N. (1977), 'Current medical and epidemiological views on plague', in *The Plague Reconsidered*, *Local Population Studies* Supplement. 25–36.

BILD, I. (1984), *The Jews in Britain*, London, Batsford.

Bird's Eye Report (1987), *Britain's Eating Habits: The Pace of Change*, Walton-on-Thames, Bird's Eye Walls Ltd.

BIRKIN, M. (1981), *Mortality in England and Wales 1916–1976: Causes of Trends and Trends in Causes*, School of Geography Working Paper No.315, University of Leeds, School of Geography.

Birth Control Trust (1984), *Teenage Pregnancy in Britain*, London, Birth Control Trust.

Bissenden, J. G., Scott, P. H., and Wharton, B. A. (1981), 'Effects of Nutrition in Asian and European pregnancies', *Postgraduate Medical Journal*, 57: 787–9.

Bittles, A. H. (in press), *The Genetics, Demography, and Health of Minority Populations*, London, Macmillan.

——and Collins, K. J. (1986), *The Biology of Human Ageing*, Cambridge, Cambridge University Press.

——and Sambuy, Y. (1986), 'Human cell culture systems in the study of ageing', in Bittles and Collins (1986).

Black, D., Morris, J. N., Smith, C., and Townsend, P. (1982), *Inequalities in Health: The Black Report*, ed. P. Townsend and N. Davidson, Harmondsworth, Penguin.

Blake, J. (1968), 'Are Children Consumer Durables? A critique of the economic theory of fertility motivation', *Population Studies*, 22: 1–26.

Blaxter, M. (1986), 'Longitudinal Studies in Britain relevant to inequalities in health', in R. G. Wilkinson (ed.), *Class and Health*, London, Tavistock: 125–216.

Bleuel, H. P. (1976), *Strength Through Joy: Sex and Society in Nazi Germany*, London, Secker and Warburg (1973); Pan (1976).

Blum, A. (1989), *Démographies de l'URSS et des pays de l'Est. Continuité ou rupture?* Notes et Études Documentaires No. 4891–2, INED, Paris.

——and Pressat, R. (1987), 'Une nouvelle table de mortalité pour l'URSS (1984–1985)', *Population*, 42: 6, 843–62.

Blunden, J. (1985), *The Changing Countryside*, London, Croom Helm.

Boal, F. W. (1981), 'Ethnic residential segregation, ethnic mixing and racial conflict: a study in Belfast, Northern Ireland', in Peach, Robinson, and Smith (1981).

——and Douglas, J. N. H. (eds.) (1982), *Integration and Division: Geographical Perspectives on the Northern Ireland Problem*, London, Academic Press.

Bohning, W. R. (1972), *The Migration of Workers in the United Kingdom and the European Community*, London, Oxford University Press.

——and Maillat, D. (1974), *The Effects of the Employment of Foreign Workers*, Paris, OECD.

Boléat, M. (1989), *Housing in Britain* (2nd edn.), London, The Building Societies' Association.

Bone, M. (1978a), *The Family Planning Services: Changes and Effects*, London, HMSO.

——(1978b), 'Recent trends in sterilisation', *Population Trends*, 13: 12–16.

——(1982), 'The pill scare and fertility in England and Wales', *IPPF Medical Bulletin*, 16/4: 2–4.

——(1986), 'Trends in single women's sexual behaviour in Scotland', *Population Trends*, 43: 7–14.

Bongaarts, J., Burch, T., and Wachter, K. (eds.) (1987), *Family Demography: Methods and their Application*, Oxford, Oxford University Press.

——and Potter, R. G. (1983), *Fertility, Biology and Behaviour: An Analysis of the Proximate Determinants*, New York, Academic Press.

——and Way, P. (1989), *Geographic Variation in the HIV Epidemic and the*

Mortality Impact of AIDS in Africa, Research Division Working Papers No. 1, New York, The Population Council.

BORGERHOFF-MULDER, M. (1987), 'Resources and reproductive success in women with an example from the Kipsigis of Kenya', *Journal of Zoology*, 213: 489-505.

BOSERUP, E. (1981), *Population and Technological Change: A Study of Long-term Trends*, Chicago, Chicago University Press.

BOSTON, G. F. P. (1984), *Occupation, Industry, Social Class and Socio-Economic Groups 1911–1981*. Unpublished working paper available from OPCS Titchfield, Hants.

BOURGEOIS-PICHAT, J. (1951), 'La Mesure de la mortalité infantile', *Population*, 6: 233–48, 459–80.

BRADLEY, L. (1977), 'Some medical aspects of plague', in *The Plague Reconsidered, Local Population Studies* supplement.

BRADSHAW, J., EDWARDS, H., LAWTON, D., STADEN, F., WEALE, J., and WEEKES, A. (1982), 'Area variations in infant mortality 1975–7', *Journal of Epidemiology and Community Health*, 36: 11–16.

——WEALE, J., and WEATHERALL, J. (1980), 'Congenital Malformations of the Central Nervous System', *Population Trends*, 19: 13–18.

BRAH, A. (1978), 'South Asian teenagers in Southall: new perspectives of marriage, family and ethnic identity', *New Community*, 613: 197–206.

BRASS, W. (1974), 'Perspectives on population prediction, illustrated by the statistics of England and Wales', *Journal of the Royal Statistical Society*, 137: 532–8.

——(1982), 'The future population of New Commonwealth immigrant descent: numbers and demographic implications', in D. A. Coleman (ed.) *The Demography of Immigrants and Minority Groups in the United Kingdom*, London, Academic Press.

——(1983), 'The formal demography of the family: an overview of the proximate determinants', in *The Family*, OPCS Occasional Paper No.31, London, OPCS.

——(1989), 'Is Britain facing the twilight of parenthood?', in H. Joshi (ed.), *The Changing Population of Britain*, Oxford, Basil Blackwell.

——and KABIR, M. (1978), 'Regional variation in fertility and child mortality during the demographic transition in England and Wales', in J. Hobcraft, and P. Rees (eds.), *Regional Demographic Development*, London, Croom Helm: 71–88.

BRAY, J. (1972), *Politics of the Environment*, London, Fabian Society.

BRENNER, M. E., and LANCASHIRE, R. (1976), 'Association of childhood mortality with housing status and unemployment', *Journal of Epidemiology and Community Health*, 32: 28–33.

BRENNER, M. H. (1979), 'Mortality and the national economy: a review and the experiences of England and Wales 1936–1976', *Lancet*, Sept.: 568.

Brewers' Society (1989), *Brewers' Society Statistical Handbook*, London, Brewery Publication Ltd.

BRIDBURY, A. R. (1981), 'English provincial towns in the later middle ages', *Economic History Review*, 34: 1–24.

——(1986), 'Dr. Rigby's comment: a reply', *Economic History Review*, 39: 417–22.

BRIERLEY, P. (1988), 'Religion', in A. H. Halsey (ed.) *British Social Trends since*

1900, London, Macmillan: 519–60.

British Medical Journal Editorial (1980*a*), 'Alcoholism: an inherited disease?', *British Medical Journal*, 281: 1301–2.

——(1980*b*), 'Heart disease in different ethnic groups', *British Medical Journal*, 281: 469–70.

British Refugee Council (1987), *Asylum-Seekers in the United Kingdom: Essential Statistics*, London.

British Society for Population Studies (1988), Local Area Demography in Business and Government, Conference Papers, Nottingham 1988, London, BSPS.

BRITTEN, N., and HEATH, A. (1984), 'Women's jobs do make a difference', *Sociology*, 18: 475–90.

BRITTON, M. (1976), 'Women at work', *Population Trends*, 2: 22–5.

——(1980), 'Recent trends in births', *Population Trends*, 20: 4–8.

——(1986), 'Recent population changes in perspective', *Population Trends*, 44: 33–41.

——(1990), 'Mortality and Geography: A review in the mid-1980s England and Wales', Series DS No. 9, London, HMSO.

BROOKS, E. (1974), *This Crowded Kingdom*, London, Charles Knight.

BROTHWELL, D. (1972), 'Paleodemography and earlier British populations', *World Archaeology*, 4/1: 75–87.

BROWN, A. (1986), 'Family circumstances of young children', *Population Trends*, 43: 18–23.

——and KIERNAN, K. (1981), 'Cohabitation in Great Britain: evidence from the General Household Survey', *Population Trends*, 25: 4–10.

BROWN, C. (1984), *Black and White Britain*, London, Policy Studies Institute/ Heinemann Educational Books.

BROWN, D. (1982), *The Step-Family: A Growing Challenge for Social Work*, Social Work Monographs No. 4, Norwich, University of East Anglia/Social Work Today.

BROWN, M., and MADGE, N. (1982), *Despite the Welfare State*, London, Heinemann/SSRC.

BROWNLEE, J. (1916), 'The history of the birth and death rates in England and Wales taken as a whole, from 1570 to the present time', *Public Health*, June: 211–22.

——(1925), 'The health of London in the 18th century', *Proc. Royal Society of Medicine*, 18, Epidemiology section: 76.

BRYCE, R., STANLEY, F., and BLAIR, E. (1989), 'The effects of intrapartum care on the risk of impairment in childhood', in I. Chalmers, M. Enkin, and M. J. N. C. Keirse (eds.) *Effective Care in Pregnancy and Childbirth*, Oxford, Oxford University Press.

BUCKATZSCH, E. J. (1951), 'The autonomy of local populations and migration in England and Wales before 1800', *Population Studies*, 5: 62–9.

BULLOUGH, V. L. (1981), 'Age at menarche: a misunderstanding', *Science* 213: 365–6.

BULMER, M. (ed.) (1979*a*), *Censuses, Surveys and Privacy*, London, Macmillan.

——(1979*b*), 'Introduction' and 'Parliament and the British census since 1920', in M. Bulmer (1979*a*): 124–31,158–83.

——(1980), 'On the feasibility of identifying "race" and "ethnicity" in Censuses and Surveys', *New Community*, 8: 3–16.

—— (1986), 'The ecological fallacy: its implications for social policy analysis', in M. Bulmer (ed.), *Social Science and Social Policy*, London, Allen and Unwin, 223–46.

BULUSU, L. (1989), 'Migration in 1988', *Population Trends*, 58: 33–9.

—— and ALDERSON, M. (1984), 'Suicides 1950-82', *Population Trends*, 35: 11–17.

BUNDEY, S. (1978) 'Possible revision of the law relating to incest', *Eugenics Society Bulletin*, 10/3: 80–4.

—— and ROBERTS, D. F. (1988), 'Health and consanguinity in immigrant populations in Britain', *Biology and Society*, 5: 12–37.

—— ALAM, H., KAUR, A., MIR, S., and LANCASHIRE, R. J. (1990), 'Race, consanguinity and social features in Birmingham babies: a basis for a prospective study', *Journal of Epidemiology and Community Health*, 44: 130–5.

BURCH, T. K., and MATTHEWS, B. J. (1987), 'Household formation in developed societies', *Population and Development Review*, 13: 495–511.

BURGOYNE, J., and CLARK, D. (1988), 'Parenting in step-families', in R. Chester, P. Diggory, and M. B. Sutherland (eds.) *Changing Patterns of Child-Bearing and Child-Rearing*, London, Academic Press: 133–47.

BURKITT, B., and ROSE, H. (1981), 'Why be a wife?', *Sociological Review*, 29/1: 67–76.

BURKITT, D. P. (1971), 'Epidemiology of cancer of the colon and rectum', *Cancer*, 28/1: 3–11.

BURNETT, J. (1968), *Plenty and Want: A Social History of Diet in England from 1815 to the Present Day*, Harmondsworth, Penguin.

—— (1986), *A Social History of Housing 1815-1985*, (2nd edn.), London, Methuen.

BURNEY, P. (1988), 'Asthma deaths in England and Wales 1931-85: evidence for a true increase in asthma mortality', *Journal of Epidemiology and Community Health*, 42: 316–20.

BURY, J. (1984), *Teenage Pregnancy in Britain*, London, Birth Control Trust.

BUSFIELD, J. (1972), 'Age at marriage and family size: social causation and social selection hypotheses', *Journal of Biosocial Science*, 4/1: 117–34.

—— and PADDON, M. (1977), *Thinking about Children: Sociology and Fertility in Post-War England*, Cambridge, Cambridge University Press.

BUTLER, N. P., GOLDING, J., and HOWLETT, B. (1986), *From Birth to Five: A study of the Health and Behaviour of Britain's Five Year Olds*, Oxford, Pergamon.

BUTZ, W. P., and WARD, M. P. (1979), 'Will US fertility remain low? A new economic interpretation', *Population and Development Review*, 5/4: 663–89.

BYTHEWAY, W. R. (1981), 'Variation with age of age differences in marriage', *Journal of Marriage and the Family*, 43: 923–7.

CAIN, M. (1981), 'Risk and insurance: perspectives on fertility and agrarian change in India and Bangladesh', *Population and Development Review*, 7: 435–74.

CALDWELL, J. C. (1982), *Theory of Fertility Decline*, London, Academic Press.

CALHOUN, C. A., and ESPENSHADE, T. J. (1988), 'Childbearing and wives' foregone earnings'. *Population Studies*, 42: 5–38.

CALOT, G., and THOMPSON, J. (1981), 'The recent up-turn in fertility in England and Wales, France and West Germany', *Population Trends*, 23: 8–9.

CAMERON, G. C. (ed.) (1980), *The Future of the British Conurbations: Policies and*

Prescription for Change, London, Longman.

CAMPBELL, B. (1984), *Wigan Pier Revisited*. London, Virago Press.

CAMPBELL, E. (1985), *The Childless Marriage*, London, Tavistock Publications.

CAMPBELL, R. (1976), 'Local population projections', *Population Trends*, 5: 9–12,

CARRIER, N. H., and JEFFERY, J. R. (1953), *External Migration: A Study of the Available Statistics 1815–1950*, GRO Studies in Medical and Population Subjects No. 6, London, HMSO.

CARR-HILL, R. A., HARDMAN, G. F., and RUSSELL, I. T. (1987), 'Variations in avoidable mortality and variations in health care resources', *Lancet* 1. 787–92.

CARR-SAUNDERS, A. (1922), *The Population Problem: A Study in Human Evolution*, Oxford, Clarendon Press.

CARTER, C. O. (ed.) (1983), *Developments in Human Reproduction and Their Eugenic Ethical Implications*, Proceedings of the 19th Annual Symposium of the Eugenics Society, London 1982, London, Academic Press.

CARTER, H. (1956), 'Population changes in Wales 1931–51, *Geography*, 41: 120–3.

CARTWRIGHT, A. (1976), *How Many Children?*, London, Routledge & Kegan Paul.

——(1978), *Recent Trends in Family Building and Contraception*, Studies in Medical and Population Subjects No. 34, London, HMSO.

CARTWRIGHT, R. A. (1980), 'Social class and disease', in Clegg and Garlick (1980): 145–56.

CASELLI, G., and EGIDI, V. (1979), 'La Géographie de la mortalité italienne: differences térritoriales et milieu', *Genus*, 35: 1–2, 101–53.

——————(1981), *New Trends in European Mortality*, Strasburg, Council of Europe.

CASTLES, S., and KOSACK, G. (1973), *Immigrant Workers and Class Structure in Western Europe*, Oxford, Oxford University Press.

CATFORD, I. C., and FORD, S. (1984), 'On the state of the public ill health: premature mortality in the United Kingdom and Europe', *British Medical Journal*, 289: 1668–70.

CAULFIELD, B., and BHAT, A. (1978), 'The Irish in Britain: intermarriage and fertility levels 1971–75', *New Community*, 9/1: 73–85.

CAVALLI-SFORZA, L. L. and BODMER, W. (1971), *The Genetics of Human Populations*, San Francisco, Freeman.

CBI (1989), *Managing the Skills Gap*, London, Confederation of British Industry.

Census Commissioners (1831), *Comparative Account of the Population of Britain 1831*, pp. xviii, 15, London, HMSO.

Central Policy Review Staff (1973), *Report of the Population Panel*, Cmnd. 5258, London, HMSO.

——(1977), *Population and the Social Services*, London, HMSO.

——(1978), *Social and Economic Implications of Microelectronics*, London, HMSO.

——/CSO (1980), *People and Their Families*, London, HMSO.

Central Statistical Office (1951), *Statistical Digest of the War: History of the Second World War*, United Kingdom Civil series, ed. W. K. Hancock, London, HMSO.

CHADWICK, E. (1842), *Report of the Sanitary Conditions of the Labouring Population of Great Britain* (see Flinn 1965).

CHALMERS, I. (1981), 'The limitation of audit by death', in R. Chester, P. Diggory, and M. B. Sutherland (eds.), *Changing Patterns of Child-Bearing and Child-*

Rearing, London, Academic Press: 39–56.

—— (1989*a*), 'Evaluating the effects of care during pregnancy and childbearing', in I. Chalmers, M. Enkin, and M. J. N. C. Keirse (eds.), *Effective Care in Pregnancy and Childbirth*, Oxford, Oxford University Press.

—— ENKIN, M., and KEIRSE, M. J. N. C. (1989), 'Effective care in pregnancy and childbirth: a synopsis for guiding practice and research', in Chalmers, Enkin, and Keirse (eds.).

CHAMBERLAIN, G., and GARCIA, J. (1983), 'Pregnant women at work', *Lancet*, 29 Jan.: 228–30.

CHAMBERS, J. D. (1953), 'Enclosure and labour supply in the industrial revolution', *Economic History Review*, 2nd ser., V, 319–43. Also in Glass and Eversley (1965): 308.

—— (1957), 'The Vale of Trent 1670–1800: a regional study of economic change', *Economic History Review*, Suppl. 3.

—— (1972), *Population, Economy and Society in Pre-industrial England*, Oxford, Oxford University Press.

CHAMPION, A. G. (1976), 'Evolving patterns of population distribution in England and Wales 1951–71, *Transactions, Institute of British Geographers*, NS 1/4: 401–20.

—— (1981), 'Population trends in rural Britain', *Population Trends*, 26: 20–3.

—— (1983), 'Population trends in the 1970s', in Goddard and Champion (1983).

—— (1987), *Population Deconcentration in Britain 1971–1984*, Seminar Paper No.49. Department of Geography, University of Newcastle-upon-Tyne.

—— (1989), 'Internal migration and the spatial distribution of population', in H. Joshi (ed.), *The Changing Population of Britain*, Oxford, Basil Blackwell.

—— CLEGG, K., and DAVIES, R. L. (1977), *Facts about the New Towns: A Socio-Economic Digest*, Cambridge, Retailing and Planning Associates.

—— and GREEN, A. (1987), 'The booming towns of Britain: the geography of economic performance in the 1980s', *Geography*, 315/72/2: 97–108.

—— —— (1988), *Local Prosperity and the North–South Divide: Winners and Losers in 1980s Britain*, Warwick, Institute for Employment Research, University of Warwick.

—— —— Owen, D. W., Ellin, D. J., and Coombes, M. G. (1987), *Changing Places*, London, Edward Arnold.

CHANDLER, T. J. (1976), 'Human settlements and the atmospheric environment', in Harrison and Gibson (1976): 49–73.

CHARD, R. I. (1988), 'Estimating numbers of persons in cultural minorities', paper presented to the British Society for Population Studies meeting, Nottingham University, Sept. Copies available from BSPS, c/o London School of Economics.

CHARLES, E. (1936), *The Menace of Under-Population*, London, Watts & Co.

—— (1938), 'The effects of present trends in fertility and mortality upon the future population of Great Britain and upon its age composition', in Hogben (1938): 73–105.

CHARLTON, J. R. H., HARTLEY, R. M. SILVER, R., and HOLLAND, W. W. (1983), 'Geographical variation in mortality from conditions amenable to medical intervention in England and Wales', *Lancet*, 1: 691–6.

CHEESEMAN, E. A., MARTIN, W. J., and RUSSELL, W. T. (1938), 'Disease and Environment', *Biometrika*, 30: 341.

CHERLIN, A. J. (1978), 'Remarriage as an incomplete institution', *American Journal of Sociology*, 84: 634–50.

CHERRY, S. (1972), 'The role of a provincial hospital: the Norfolk and Norwich hospital 1771–1880', *Population Studies*, 26/2: 291–306.

—— (1980), 'The hospitals and population growth: the voluntary general hospitals, mortality and local populations in the English provinces in the 18th and 19th centuries', *Population Studies*, 34/1: 59–76; 34/2: 251–66.

CHESHIRE, P., and SHEPPARD, S. (1989), 'Planning policy and access to housing: some empirical estimates', *Urban Studies*, 26: 469–85.

CHESNAIS, J. C. (1991), *Les Théories et pratiques du développement économique et leur influence possible sur la baisse séculaire de la fécondité*, Proceedings of UN/IUSSP Expert Group Meeting on the International Transmission of Population Policy Experience, UN, New York.

CHESTER, R. (1971), 'The duration of marriage to divorce', *British Journal of Sociology*, 22: 172–82.

CHILVERS, C. (1978), 'Regional mortality 1969–73', *Population Trends*, 11: 16–20.

—— and ADELSTEIN, A. (1978), 'Cancer mortality: the regional pattern', *Population Trends*, 12: 4–9.

CHINN, S., ELEREY, C. D., BALDWIN, I. G., and GOUZIL, M. (1981), 'The relation of mortality in England and Wales 1969–73 to measurements of air pollution', *Journal of Epidemiology and Community Health*, 35: 174–9.

CHIN RE-CHI and BROWN, S. (1968), 'A comparison of the size of families of Roman Catholics and Non-Catholics in Great Britain', *Population Studies*, 22: 51–60.

CICRED (1984), *Socio-Economic Differential Mortality in Industrial Countries*, New York, World Health Organization, United Nations.

CIPFA (Chartered Institute of Public Finance and Accountancy) (1986), *Education Statistics: 1986–87 Estimate*, London, CIPFA.

City of Birmingham (1983), *Ethnic Origins of Birmingham Children born in 1981*, The last in a series of annual reports, Central Statistical Office, City of Birmingham.

—— Central Intelligence Unit (1975), *Immigrant and 'All Non-European' Pupils on the Registers of Schools Maintained by the Birmingham Education Authority*, Survey 1975.

CLAPHAM, Sir J. (1932), *An Economic History of Modern Britain*, ii: *Free Trade and Steel 1850–1886*, Cambridge, Cambridge University Press.

CLARK, P. (1972), 'The migrant in Kentish Towns 1580–1630', in P. Clark, and J. Slack (eds.), *Crisis and Order in English Towns*, London, Routledge and Kegan Paul.

CLARKE, S. (1989), 'Demographics and the military balance: NATO in the nineties', *Orbis*, Spring.

CLEARIE, A. F., HOLLINGSWORTH L. A., JAMES, M. Q., and VINCENT, M. L. (1985), 'International Trends in Teenage Pregnancy: an overview of 16 countries', *Biology and Society*, 2/1: 23–30.

CLEGG, E. J., and GARLICK, J. P. (eds.) (1980), *Disease and Urbanisation*, London, Taylor and Francis.

CLELAND, J. (1985), 'Marital fertility decline in developing countries: theories and the evidence', in Cleland and Hobcraft (1985).

——and HOBCRAFT, J. (eds.) (1985), *Reproductive Change in Developing Countries: Insights from the World Fertility Survey*, Oxford, Oxford University Press.

——and WILSON, C. (1987), 'Economic theories of the fertility transition: an iconoclastic view', *Population Studies*, 41: 5–30.

COALE, A. J. (1973), *The Demographic Transition Reconsidered*, IUSSP International Population Conference, Liège, i. 53–71.

——and WATKINS, S. C. (1986), *The Decline of Fertility in Europe*, Princeton, NJ, Princeton University Press.

COHEN, S. B., and SWEET, J. A. (1974), 'The impact of marital disruption and remarriage on fertility', *Journal of Marriage and the Family*, 36: 87–96.

COLE, H. S. D. (1973), *Thinking About the Future: A Critique of the Limits to Growth*, London, Chatto and Windus.

COLEMAN, A. (1985), *Utopia on Trial*, London, Hilary Shipman.

COLEMAN, D. A. (1977*a*), 'Assortative Mating in Britain', in R. Chester and J. Peel (eds.), *Equalities and Inequalities in Family Life*, London, Academic Press.

——(1977*b*), 'The geography of marriage in Britain 1920–1960', *Annals of Human Biology*, 4/2: 101–32.

——(1979), 'A study of the spatial aspects of partner choice from a human biological viewpoint', *Man*, NS 14: 414–35.

——(1980*a*), 'A note on the frequency of consanguineous marriages in Reading, England in 1972–3', *Human Heredity*, 30: 278–85.

——(1980*b*), 'Recent trends in marriage and divorce in Britain and Europe', in Hiorns (1980): 83–125.

——(1981), 'The effect of socio-economic class, regional origin and other variables on marital mobility in Britain, 1920–1960', *Annals of Human Biology*, 7/1: 55–76.

——(1982), 'The population structure of an urban area in Britain', in H. H. Crawford and J. H. Mielke (eds.), *Current Developments in Anthropological Genetics*, New York, Plenum Press.

——(1983), 'The demography of ethnic minorities', in Kirkwood, Herbertson, and Parkes (1983):

——(1984), 'Marital choice and geographical mobility', in A. J. Boyce, *Migration and Mobility*, London, Taylor and Francis: 19–56.

——(1985), 'Ethnic intermarriage in Great Britain', *Population Trends*, 40: 4–10.

——(1986), 'Population regulation: a long range view', in D. A. Coleman and R. S. Schofield (eds.), *The State of Population Theory*, Oxford, Basil Blackwell: 14–41.

——(1987/8), 'United Kingdom Statistics on immigration: development and limitations', *International Migration Review*, 21: 1138–69.

——(1988), 'Population', in A. H. Halsey (ed.), *British Social Trends since 1900*, London, Macmillan, 36–134.

——(1989*a*), 'The new Housing Policy: a critique', *Housing Studies* 4/1: 44–57.

——(1989*b*), 'The contemporary pattern of remarriage', in E. Grebenik, C. Hohn, and R. Mackensen (eds.), *Later Phases of the Family Cycle: Demographic Aspects*, Oxford, Oxford University Press.

——(1990*a*), 'The demography of social class', in Mascie Taylor (1990).

——(in press *a*), 'The Demographic Transition in Ireland in International Context', in J. Goldthorpe, and C. Whelan (eds), *The Development of Industrial*

Society in Ireland, Oxford, Oxford University Press for the British Academy.

—— (in press *b*), 'Inter-ethnic marriage', in A. H. Bittles (ed.), *The Genetics, Demography, and Health of Minority Populations*, London, Macmillan.

—— and HASKEY, J. (1986), 'Marital distance and its geographical orientation in England and Wales 1979', *Transactions' Institute of British Geographers*, NS 2: 337–55.

COLLINGWOOD, R. G., and MYRE, J. N. L. (1936), *Roman Britain and the English Settlements*, Oxford, Oxford University Press.

COLLINS, K. J. (1987), 'Effects of cold on old people', *British Journal of Hospital Medicine*, Dec.: 506–14.

COLLEY, J. R. T. and REID, D. D. (1970), 'Urban and social origins of childhood bronchitis in England and Wales', *British Medical Journal*, 2: 213–17.

Commission on Population Growth and the American Future (1972), *Population and the American Future: Report and 6 other volumes*, Washington, DC, US GPO.

Commission for Racial Equality (1980), *1981 Census: Why the Ethnic Question is Vital*, London, Commission for Racial Equality.

Committee on Child Health Services (1976), *Fit for the Future: The Report of the Committee on Child Health Services* (Court Report), Cmnd. 6684, London, HMSO.

Committee on Medical Aspects of Food Policy (COMA) (1986), *Diet and Coronary Heart Disease*, DHSS Report on Health and Social Subjects, London, HMSO.

Communicable Disease Surveillance Centre (1986), 'Sexually transmitted disease surveillance in Britain: 1984'. *British Medical Journal*, 293: 942–53.

COMPTON, P. A. (1976), 'Religious affiliation and demographic variability in Northern Ireland', *Transactions' Institute of British Geographers*, NS 1/4: 433–52.

—— (1978), *Northern Ireland: A Census Atlas*, Dublin, Gill and Macmillan.

—— (ed.) (1981), *The Contemporary Population of Northern Ireland and Population Related Issues*, Belfast, Institute of Irish Studies, Queen's University.

—— (1982), 'The changing population', in R. J. Johnston, and J. C. Doornkamp, *The Changing Geography of the United Kingdom*, London, Methuen: 37–74.

—— (1982*a*), 'Fertility, nationality and religion in Northern Ireland', in D. A. Coleman, *The Demography of Immigrants and Minority Groups in the UK*, London, Academic Press.

—— (1982*b*), 'The changing population', In R. J. Johnston and J. C. Doornkamp (eds.), *The Changing Geography of the UK*, London, Methuen: 37–74.

—— (1985), Rising mortality in Hungary', *Population Trends*, 39: 71–86.

—— and COWARD, J. (1989), *Fertility and Family Planning in Northern Ireland*, Aldershot, Avebury.

CONGDON, P. (1980), 'Forecasting births in Greater London: an application of the Easterlin Hypothesis', *Population Studies*, 34/2: 267–78.

—— and CHAMPION, A. (1989), 'Trends and structure in London's migration and their relation to employment and housing markets', In P. Congdon and P. Batey (eds.), *Advances in Regional Demography*, London, Pinter: 180–204.

CONNELL, K. H. (1950*a*), *The Population of Ireland 1750–1845*, Oxford, Oxford University Press.

—— (1950*b*, 1965), 'Land and population in Ireland', *Economic History Review*, 2;

in Glass and Eversley (1965): 423–33.

CONQUEST, R. (1970), *The Nation Killers*, London, Macmillan.

—— (1990), *The Great Terror* (rev. edn.), London, Hutchinson.

COOK-MOZAFFARI P. J., ASHWOOD, F. L., VINCENT, T., FORMAN, D., and ALDERSON, M. (1987), *Cancer Incidence and Mortality in the Vicinity of Nuclear Installations: England and Wales 1959–1980*, Studies in Medical and Population Subjects 51, London, HMSO.

DE COOMAN, E., ERMISCH, J., and JOSHI, H. (1987), 'The next birth and the labour market: a dynamic model of births in England and Wales', *Population Studies*, 41/2: 237–68.

————————(1988), *Econometric Modelling of the Birth Rate*, Centre for Economic Policy Research Discussion Paper series 213, London, CEPR.

COOPER, C. L. (1980), 'Work stress in white and blue collar jobs', *Bulletin of the British Psychological Society*, 33: 49–51.

COOPER, R. (1981), 'Rising death rates in the Soviet Union', *New England Journal of Medicine*, 304: 1259–65.

—— (1982), 'Smoking in the Soviet Union', *British Medical Journal*, 285: 549–51.

Coopers and Lybrand Associates (1987), *Land Use Planning and Indicators of Housing Demand*, A Report by Coopers and Lybrand Associates, London, Department of the Environment.

CORNWALL, J. (1967), 'Evidence of Population Mobility in the Seventeenth Century', *Bulletin of the Institute of Historical Research*, 40: 143–52.

—— (1970), 'English population in the early 16th century', *Economic History Review*, 23: 32–44.

Council of Europe (1978), '*Population Decline in Europe*', London, Edward Arnold.

—— (1979), *Recent Demographic Developments in the Member States of the Council of Europe*, Strasburg, Council of Europe.

—— (1979), *Recent Trends in Attitudes and Behaviour Affecting the Family in Council of Europe Member States*, Strasburg, Council of Europe.

—— (1981), *European Migration in the 1980s: Trends and Policies*, Conference of European Ministers responsible for migration affairs, Strasburg, Council of Europe.

—— (1989), *Recent Demographic Developments in the Member States of the Council for Europe*, Strasburg, Council of Europe.

COWARD, J. (1980*a*), 'Recent characteristics of Roman Catholic fertility in Northern and Southern Ireland', *Population Studies*, 34/1: 31–44.

—— (1980*b*), 'Regional variation in family size in the Republic of Ireland', *Journal of Biosocial Science*, 12: 1–14.

—— (1981), 'Ideal family size in Northern Ireland', *Journal of Biosocial Science*, 13: 443–54.

COX, B. D., BLAXTER, M., BUCKLE, A. C. J., *et al.* (1987), *The Health and Lifestyle Survey*, Health Promotion Research Trust, London/School of Clinical Medicine, University of Cambridge.

COX, D. R. (1988), *Short Term Predictions of HIV Infection and AIDS in England and Wales*, London, HMSO.

—— ANDERSON, R. M., and HILLIER, H. C. (eds.) (1989), 'Epidemiological and statistical aspects of the AIDS epidemic', *Philosophical Transactions of the Royal*

Society B, 325;37–187.

Cox, P. R. (1976), *Demography* (5th edn.), Cambridge, Cambridge University Press.

Crafts, N. F. R. (1982), 'Illegitimacy in England and Wales in 1911', *Population Studies*, 36: 327–31.

—— (1978), 'Average age at first marriage for women in mid-19th century England and Wales: a cross-section study', *Population Studies*, 32/1: 21–6.

Craig, J. (1983), 'The growth of the elderly population', *Population Trends*, 32.

—— (1986), 'The most densely populated areas of England and Wales', *Population Trends*, 45: 34–41.

—— (1987), 'Changes in the population composition of England and Wales since 1841', *Population Trends*, 48: 27–36.

Crawford, M. D., Gardner, M. J., and Morris, J. N. (1971), 'Cardiovascular disease and the mineral content of drinking water', *British Medical Bulletin*, 27: 21–9.

—— Doyle, W., Craft, I. L., and Lawrence, B. M. (1986), 'A comparison of food intake during pregnancy and birth weight in high and low social economic groups', *Progress in Lipid Research*, 25: 249–54.

Craxford, S. R., and Weatherley, M-L. P. M. (1971), 'Air pollution in towns in the United Kingdom', *Phil. Trans. Royal Society A*, 269: 503–13.

Creighton, C. (1891–4), *History of Epidemics in Britain*, vol. ii, Cambridge, Cambridge University Press.

Creighton, S. (1988), *Child Abuse Deaths*, NSPCC Information Brief No. 5, London, NSPCC.

Crellin, E., Kellmer Pringle, M. L., and West, P. (1971), *Born Illegitimate: Social and Educational Implications*, Windsor, National Foundation for Educational Research.

Cressy, D. (1970), 'Occupation, migration and literacy in East London 1580–1640', *Local Population Studies*, 5: 53–9.

Crimmins, F. (1981), 'The changing pattern of America's mortality decline 1940–1977', *Population and Development Review*, 7: 229–54.

Crosland, A. (1970), 'No need for population policy', in *New Scientist*, 28 May: 11.

Cruickshank, D., and Burton, N. (1990), *Life in the Georgian City*, London, Viking.

Cullingworth, J. B. (1965), *English Housing Trends*, Occasional Papers on Social Administration, No. 13, London.

—— (1969), *Housing and Labour Mobility: A Preliminary Report*, Paris, OECD.

Cummins, R. O., Shaper, A. G., et al. (1981), 'Smoking and drinking by middle-aged British men: effects of social class and town of residence', *British Medical Journal*, 283, 5 Dec.: 1497–502.

Cunningham, A. (1980), 'Breast feeding and mortality in industrialised communities: an update', *Advances in International Maternal–Child Health*, 1: 128–68.

Cunningham, W. (1969), *Alien Immigrants to Britain*, 2nd edn., London, Frank Cass & Co. Ltd.

Currie, R., Gilbert, A., and Horstey, L. (1977), *Churches and Churchgoers: Patterns of Church Growth in the British Isles since 1700*, Oxford, Clarendon Press.

CURDS (1984), *Population Distribution 1971–81*, Factsheet 9, University of Newcastle-upon-Tyne.

CURWEN, M., DUNNELL, K., and ASHLEY, J. (1990), 'Hidden influenza deaths: 1989–90', *Population Trends*, 61: 31–3.

DAHYA, B. (1974), 'The nature of Pakistani ethnicity in industrial cities in Britain', In A. Cohen, (ed.), *Urban Ethnicity*, London, Tavistock.

DALEY, A., and BENJAMIN, B. (1964), 'London as a case study', *Population Studies*, 17: 3.

DALEY, M., and WILSON, M. I. (1981), 'Child maltreatment from a sociobiological perspective', *New Directions for Child Development*, 11.

DARBY, H. C. (1973*a*), 'The Anglo-Scandinavian foundations', in H. C. Darby (ed.), *A New Historical Geography of England*, Cambridge, Cambridge University Press.

——(1973*b*), 'The age of the improver 1600–1800', in H. C. Darby (ed.), *A New Historical Geography of England*, Cambridge, Cambridge University Press: 302.

D'ARCY, F. (1977), 'The Malthusian League and the resistance to birth control propaganda in late Victorian Britain', *Population Studies*, 31/3: 429–48.

DAUNTON, M. J. (1987), *A Property-Owning Democracy? Housing in Britain*, Historical Handbook, London, Faber and Faber.

DAVID, H. P. (1982), 'Eastern Europe: pronatalist politics and private behaviour', *Population Bulletin*, 36/6, Washington, DC, Population Reference Bureau.

DAVIES, I. M. (1980), 'Perinatal and infant deaths: social and biological factors', *Population Trends*, 19: 19–21.

DAVIS, C., and FESHBACH, M. (1980), *Rising Infant Mortality in the USSR in the 1970s*, US Department of Commerce, Bureau of the Census International Population Reports P. 95, No. 74.

——HAUB, C., and WILLETTE, J. (1983), 'US Hispanics: changing the face of America', *Population Bulletin*, 38/3.

DAVIS, G., and MURCH, M. (1988), *Grounds for Divorce*, Oxford, Oxford University Press.

DAVIS, K. (1945), 'The world demographic transition', *Annals of the American Academy of Political and Social Science* 273: 1–11.

——(1963), 'The theory of change and response in modern demographic history', *Population Index*, 21: 345–66.

——BERNSTAM, M. S., and RICARDO-CAMPBELL, R. (1986), 'Population decline in developed societies', *Population and Development Review*, Supplement to vol. xii, New York, Population Council.

DAVISON, R. B. (1962), *West Indian Migrants*, Oxford, Oxford University Press.

DAY, L. H., 'Nationality and ethnocentrism: some relationships suggested by an analysis of Catholic–Protestant differentials', *Population Studies*, 22: 27–50.

DAYKIN, C. D. (1981), 'The recent trend of mortality in Great Britain', *Journal of the Institute of Actuaries*, 108, Part 3 (440): 413–22.

DEAKIN, N., and UNGERSON, C. (1977) *Leaving London—Planned Mobility and the Inner City*, London, Heinemann.

DEANE, P. (1979), *The First Industrial Revolution*, 2nd edn., Cambridge, Cambridge University Press.

——and COLE, W. A. (1969), *British Economic Growth 1888–1959*, Cambridge, Cambridge University Press.

DELAMOTHE, T. (1989), 'Statistics today: urgent need to depoliticize official figures', *British Medical Journal*, 299: 1543–4.

DENNIS, R. J. (1977), 'Distance and social interaction in a Victorian city', *Journal of Historical Geography*, 3: 237–50.

DENNISON, S. R. (1939), *The Location of Industry and the Depressed Areas*, Oxford, Oxford University Press.

Department of Education and Science (1977), *Falling Numbers and School Closures*, Circular 5/77, London, HMSO.

——(1982), *Pupil Numbers and School Leavers: Future Numbers*, London, HMSO.

——(1986), *Projections of Future Student Numbers*, London, HMSO.

——(1987), *Higher Education: Meeting the Challenge*, White Paper on Higher Education, Cm. 114, London, HMSO.

Department of Employment (1977), *The Role of Immigrants in the Labour Market*, London, Unit for Manpower Studies.

——(1984), 'Labour force outlook for Great Britain', *Employment Gazette*, 92: 56–64.

——(1987), 'Labour force outlook for Great Britain', *Employment Gazette*, May: 253–63.

——(1988), 'Ethnic Groups and economic status', *Employment Gazette*, Mar.: 164–77.

——(1989), '1987 Census of Employment', *Employment Gazette*, 97: 624–32.

——(1990a), 'Labour force outlook to 2001', *Employment Gazette*, 98: 186–98.

——(1990b), 'Regional labour force outlook to the year 2000', *Employment Gazette*, 98: 9–19.

Department of the Environment (1976), *British Cities: Urban Population and Employment Trends 1951–71*, Research Report 10, London, HMSO.

——(1983), *Lead in the Environment: The Government's Response to the Ninth Paper of the Royal Commission on Environmental Pollution*, Pollution Paper No. 19, London, HMSO.

——(1986), *Nitrate in Water*, Pollution Paper No. 26, London, HMSO.

——(1988), *English House Condition Survey 1986*, London, HMSO.

——(1988a), *1985-Based Estimates of Numbers of Households in England, the Regions, Countries, Metropolitan Districts and London Boroughs 1985–2001*, London, HMSO.

——(1988b), *Household Projection Service: Explanatory Notes*, London, DoE.

——(1988c), *UK Terrestrial Effect Review Group: First Report*, London, HMSO.

——(1988d), *Action for Cities*, London, HMSO.

——(1989), *Digest of Environmental Protection and Water Statistics*, xi, London, HMSO.

——(1990a), 'Local authorities' actions under the homelessness provisions of the 1985 Housing Act: England, Statistics for the fourth quarter of 1989', London, DoE.

——(1990b), *This Common Inheritance: Britain's Environmental Strategy* (The Environment White Paper), Cm. 1200, London, HMSO.

Department of Health and Social Security (1974a), *Report on Health and Social Subjects 7: Diet and Coronary Heart Disease*, London, HMSO.

——(1974b), *Report of the Committee on One Parent Families*, vol. i, Cmnd. 5629,

London, HMSO.

—— (1976), *Prevention and Health: Everybody's Business*, London, HMSO.

—— (1981), *Prevention and Health: Drinking Sensibly*, London, HMSO.

—— (1984), *Population, Pension Costs and Pensioners' Income*, London, HMSO.

—— (1988), *On the State of the Public Health 1987: The Annual Report of the Chief Medical officer of the Department of Health and Social Security*, London, HMSO.

Department of Transport (1989), *Road Accidents, Great Britain 1988*, London, HMSO.

DESPLANQUES, G. (1976), *La Mortalité des adultes suivant le milieu social 1955–1971*, Paris, Collections d'INSEE No. 195.

DEVIS, T. (1984), 'Population movements measured by the NHS Central Register', *Population Trends*, 36: 18–24.

—— and Mills, I. (1986), *A Comparison of Migration Data from the National Health Service Central Register and the 1981 Census*, OPCS Occasional Paper 35, London, HMSO.

DE VRIES, J. (1986), 'The population and economy of the preindustrial Netherlands', in R. I. Rothberg and T. K. Rabb (eds.) *Population and Economy*, Cambridge, Cambridge University Press: 101–22.

DIAMOND, I. (1989), '*Education and the changing numbers of young people*', in H. Joshi (ed.), *The Changing Population of Britain*, Oxford, Basil Blackwell: 72–89.

DINKEL, R. H. (1985), 'The seeming paradox of increasing mortality in a highly industrialised nation: the example of the Soviet Union', *Population Studies*, 39: 87–98.

DICKINSON, H. T. (1967), 'The Tory Party's Attitude to Foreigners: a note on Party Principles in the Age of Anne', *Economic History Review*.

DIEHL, A. K. and GAU, D. W. (1982), 'Death certification by British Doctors: a demographic analysis', *Journal of Epidemiology and Community Health*, 36: 146–9.

DICKS, M. J. (1988), 'The demographics of housing demand: household formations and the growth of owner-occupation', Discussion Paper No. 22, London, Bank of England.

DIGBY, A. (1983), 'Malthus and Reform of the Poor Law', in J. Dupaquier, A. Fauve-Chamouk, and E. Grebenik (eds.) *Malthus Past and Present*, London, Academic Press, 97–110.

DIGGORY, P. (1981), 'The long-term effect upon the child of perinatal events', The Galton Lecture 1980, in R. Chester, P. Diggory, and M. B. Sutherland (eds.) *Changing Patterns of Child-bearing and Child-Rearing*, London, Academic Press, 23–37.

DIGHT, S. (1976), *Scottish Drinking Habits*, London, HMSO.

DIMSDALE, N.H. (1984), 'Employment and real wages in the inter-war period', *National Institute Economic Review*, 110: 96–102.

DOBBS, J., and MARSH, A. (1985), *Smoking Among Secondary School Children in 1984*, OPCS Social Survey Division, London, HMSO.

DOBSON, T. and ROBERTS, D. F. (1970), 'Historical population movement and gene flow in Northumberland parishes', *Journal of Biosocial Science*, 3: 193–208.

DOBSON, M. (1980), '"Marsh Fever": the geography of malaria in England', *Journal of Historical Geography*, 6/4: 357–89.

DODGSHON, R. A., and BUTLIN, R. A. (eds.) (1978), *An Historical Geography of England and Wales*, 2nd edn., 1990, London, Academic Press.

DOLL, R. (1982), *Prospects for Prevention*, The Harveian Oration of the Royal College of Physicians, London, Royal College of Physicians.

——(1987), 'Major epidemics of the 20th Century, : from coronary thrombosis to Aids', *Journal of the Royal Statistical Society A*, 150: 373–90.

——and PETO, R. (1976), 'Mortality in relation to smoking: 20 years' observations in male British doctors', *British Medical Journal*, 2: 1525–36.

————(1981), *The Causes of Cancer*, Oxford, Oxford Medical Publications.

DONKIN, R. A. (1973), 'Changes in the early middle ages', in H. C. Darby (ed.), *A New Historical Geography of England*, Cambridge, Cambridge University Press.

DONNAN, S. P. B., and HASKEY, J. (1977), 'Alcoholism and cirrhosis of the liver', *Population Trends*, 7: 18–24.

——and LAMBERT, P. M. (1976), 'Appendicitis: incidence and mortality', *Population Trends*, 5: 26–8.

DONNISON, D. V. (1961), 'The movement of households in England', *Journal of the Royal Statistical Society*, A, 124: 60–80.

——COCKBURN, C., CULLINGWORTH, J. B., and NEVITT, A. A. (1964), *Essays on Housing*, Occasional Papers on Social Administration No. 9, London.

DOUGLAS, M. M. (1972), 'Deciphering a meal', *Daedalus* (Winter), 61–81.

DOYAL, L. *et al.* (1983), *Cancer in Britain: The Politics of Prevention*, London, Pluto Press.

DRAKE, M. (1972), 'The census 1801–1891', in E. Wrigley (ed.), *Nineteenth Century Society*, Cambridge, Cambridge University Press.

DRAPER, G. J., BIRCH, J. M., BITHELL, J. F., KINNIER WILSON, C. M., LEETE, I., MARSDEN, H. B., MORRIS JONES, P. H., STICKER, C. A., and SWINDELL, R. (1982), *Childhood Cancer in Britain: Incidence, Survival and Mortality*, Studies in Medical and Population Subjects No. 37, London, HMSO.

DRUMMOND, J. C., and WILBRAHAM, A. (1938), *The Englishmen's Food*, London, Jonathan Cape.

DUDGEON, J. A. (1983), 'Immunization against rubella', *IPPF Medical Bulletin*, 17/2, Apr.: 2–4.

DUGMORE, K. (1975), 'The migration and distribution of socio-economic groups in Greater London: evidence from the 1961, 1966 and 1971 censuses', Intelligence Unit Research Memorandum 443, Greater London Council.

DUNNELL, K. (1979), *Family Formation 1976*, London, HMSO.

DUPAQUIER, J., HELIN, E., LASLETT, P., LIVI-BACCI, M., and SOGNER, S. (1981), *Marriage and Remarriage in Populations of the Past*, London, Academic Press.

DUTTON, J. (1979), 'Changes in Soviet mortality patterns 1959–1977', *Population and Development Review*, 5: 267–92.

DYHOUSE, C. (1981), 'Working-class mothers and infant mortality in England 1895–1914', in W. Webster (ed.), *Biology, Medicine and Society 1840–1940*, Cambridge, Cambridge University Press: 73–98; also *Journal of Social History*, 12(1978): 248–67.

EASTERLIN, R. A. (1961), 'The American baby boom in historical perspective', *American Economic Review*, 51: 869–911.

——(1968), *Population, Labour Force and Long Swings in Economic Growth*, New York, National Bureau of Economic Research.

——(1978), 'What will 1984 be like? Socio-economic implications of recent trends in Age-Structure', *Demography*, 15: 397–421.

——(1980), *Birth and Fortune*, London, Grant MacIntyre.

——and CONRON, G. A. (1976), 'A note on the recent fertility swing in Australia, Canada, England and Wales, and the United States', in H. Richards (ed.), *Population: Factor Movements and Economic Development: Studies Presented to Brinley Thomas*, Cardiff, University of Wales Press.

EDWARDS, G., GRASS, M., KELLER, M., MOSER, J., and ROOM, R. (1977), *Alcohol Related Disabilities*, Geneva, WHO.

EDWARDS, R. G. (1983), 'The Current Clinical and Ethical situation of Human Conception *in vitro*', in C.O. Carter (ed.), *Developments in Human Reproduction and their Eugenic, Ethical Implications*, London, Academic Press: 53–116.

EEKELAR, J., and MACLEAN, M. L. (1986), *Maintenance after Divorce*, Oxford, Oxford University Press.

EHRLICH, P. R., and EHRLICH, A. H. (1970), *Population, Resources, Environment*, San Francisco, W. H. Freeman & Co.

ELDRIDGE, S., and KIERNAN, K. (1985), 'Declining first marriage rates in England and Wales: a change in timing or a rejection of marriage?', *European Journal of Population*, 1: 327–45.

EMERY, F. V. (1973), 'England circa 1600', in H. C. Darby (ed.), *A New Historical Geography of England*, Cambridge, Cambridge University Press.

Employment and Immigration Canada (1987), *Annual Report to Parliament on Future Immigration Levels*, Ottawa.

EPSTEIN, F. H. (1984), 'Lessons from falling coronary heart disease mortality in the United States', *Postgraduate Medical Journal*, 60: 15–19.

——and SWARTZ, J. B. (1981), 'Fallacies of lifestyle cancer theories', *Nature*, 289: 127–30.

ERICKSON, C. (1981), 'Emigration from the British Isles to the USA in 1831', *Population Studies*, 35/2: 175–98.

ERMISCH, J. F. (1979), 'The relevance of the Easterlin hypothesis and the "New Home Economics" to fertility movement in Great Britain', *Population Studies*, 33: 39–58.

——(1980), 'Women's economic position and demographic changes', in OPCS Occasional Paper 19, *Implications of Current Demographic Trends for the UK of Social and Economic Policy*, London, HMSO: 19–34.

——(1981), 'Economic opportunities, marriage squeezes and the propensity to marry: an economic analysis of period marriage rates in England and Wales', *Population Studies*, 35: 347–56.

——(1983), *The Political Economy of Demographic Change*, London, Heinemann.

——(1988), *Purchased Child Care, Optional Family Size and Mothers' Employment: Theory and Econometric Analysis*, CEPR discussion paper series No. 238, London, CEPR.

——(1989), 'Demographic change and intergenerational transfers in industrialised countries' in P. Johnson, C. Conrad, and D. Thomson (eds.) (1989), 18–32.

——(1990), *Fewer Babies, Longer Lives*, York, Joseph Rowntree Foundation.

——and OVERTON, E. (1984), 'Minimal household units', *Population Trends*, 35: 18–22.

—and Wright, R. E. (1989), 'The duration of lone parenthood in Britain', Centre of Economic Policy Research Discussion Papers No. 302, London, CEPR.

Espenshade, T. (1980), 'Raising a child can now cost $85,000', *Intercom*, 8: 9,1,10–12.

—(1987), 'Population replacement and immigrant adaptation: new issues facing the West', *Family Planning Perspectives*, 19/3: 1215–18.

Eugenics Society (1978), *The Provision of Services for the Prenatal Diagnosis of Fetal Abnormality in the United Kingdom*, Supplement to the *Eugenics Society Bulletin* (1978), No. 3.

Evans, A., and Eversley, D. (1980), *The Inner City: Employment and Industry*, London, Heinemann.

—and Richardson, R. (1980), 'Urban unemployment: interpretation and additional evidence', *Scottish Journal of Political Economy*, 28: 107–24.

Evans, E. (1988), *No Room: No Room! The Costs of the British Town and Country Planning Systems*, London, Institute of Economic Affairs.

Eversley, D. E. C. (1971), 'Population changes and regional policies since the war', *Regional Studies*, 5: 211–27.

—(1980), 'Social policy and the birth rate', *New Society*, 3 Apr.: 9–11.

—(1980), 'Does Britain need a population policy?', *Policy Studies*, 1: 1.

—(1989), *Religion and Employment in Northern Ireland*, London, Sage Publications.

—and Köhlmann, W. (eds.) (1982). *Population Change and Social Planning*, London, Edward Amold.

—and Sukdeo F. (1969), *The Dependants of the Coloured Commonwealth Population of England and Wales*, London, Institute of Race Relations.

Eversley, Lord (1907), 'The decline of the numbers of agricultural labourers in Great Britain', *Journal of the Royal Statistical Society*, 70: 267–319.

Farr, W. (1840), *Third Annual Report of the Registrar-General 1839–40*.

—(1863), *1861 Census of England and Wales*, vol. iii, General Report BPP 1863, vol. iv.

—(1864), 'Letter to the Registrar-General', *Supplement to the 25th Annual Report of the Registrar-General*, London, HMSO: pp. xxxi–xxxvi, 440.

—(1875), *Supplement to the 35th Annual Report of the Registrar-General*, London, HMSO: 448.

Feinstein, C. H. (1976), *National Income Expenditure and Output in the UK 1855–1965*, Cambridge, Cambridge University Press.

Ferguson, T. (1964), 'Public health in Britain in the climate of the nineteenth century', in *Public Health and Urban Growth*, Centre for Urban Studies Report No. 4; also in *Population Studies*, 17/3.

Feshbach, M. (1982), 'The Soviet Union: population trends and dilemmas', *Population Bulletin*, 37/3: 44, Washington DC, Population Reference Bureau Inc.

Festy, P., and Prioux, F. (1975), 'Le Divorce en Europe depuis 1950', *Population*, 30/6: 975–1003.

Feyerabend, C., Higginbottam, M., and Russell, A. H. (1982), 'Nicotine concentrations in urine and saliva of smokers and non-smokers', *British Medical Journal*, 284: 1002–4.

FIELDING, A. J. (1982), 'Counterurbanisation in Western Europe', *Progress in Planning*, 17/1: 1–52.

FILDES, V. (1980), 'Neonatal feeding practices and infant mortality during the 18th century', *Journal of Biosocial Science*, 12: 313–24.

——(1988), *Wetnursing: A History from Antiquity to the Present*, Oxford, Basil Blackwell.

FINDLAY, A., and STEWART, A. (1985), 'The new nomads: a survey of British expatriates returning from the Middle East', Paper presented to the Population Geography Study Group Conference, Sept. 1985, University of Liverpool.

FINLAY, R. A. P. (1981), *Population and Metropolis*, Cambridge, Cambridge University Press.

FLEISHMAN, A. B. (1985), *The Significance of Small Doses of Radiation to Members of the Public*, Series R175, Chilton, NRPB.

FLETCHER, B. C. (1983), 'Marital relationships as a cause of death: an analysis of occupational mortality and the hidden consequences of marriage: some UK data', *Human Relations*, (New York) 36/2: 123–33.

FLEURE, H. J. (1951), *A Natural History of Man in Britain*, London, Collins.

FLEURY, M., and HENRY, L. (1956), *Des registres parroissiaux et l'histoire de la population: nouveau manuel de dépouillement et d'exploitation sommaire de l'état civil ancien*, Paris.

FLINN, M. W. (ed.) (1965), *Report on the Sanitary Conditions of the Labouring Population of Great Britain, by Edwin Chadwick 1842*, Edinburgh, Edinburgh University Press.

——(1981), *The European Demographic System 1500–1820*, Baltimore, Johns Hopkins University Press.

——(1982), 'The population history of England 1541–1871' (review), *Economic History Review*, 35: 443–57.

——*et al.* (1977), *Scottish Population History from the 17th Century to the 1930s*, Cambridge, Cambridge University Press.

FLOUD, R., WACHTER, K., and GREGORY, A. (1990), *Height, Health and History: Nutritional Status in the UK 1750–1980*, Cambridge, Cambridge University Press.

FLOWERDEW, R., and SALT, J. (1979), 'Migration between labour market areas in Great Britain, 1970–71', *Regional Studies*, 13: 211–31.

FOGEL, R. W., ENGEMAN, S. L. and R. F. (1983), 'Secular changes in American and British stature and nutrition', *Journal of Interdisciplinary History*, 14: 445–81.

FOGELMAN, K. (ed.) (1983), *Growing Up in Great Britain*, Papers from the National Child Development Study, London, Macmillan.

FORBES, J. F., BODDY, F. A., PICKERING, R., and WYLLIE, M. M. (1982), 'Perinatal mortality in Scotland 1970–9', *Journal of Epidemiology and Community Health*, 36: 282–8.

FORD, J. A., COLHOUN, E. M., McINTOSH, W. B. and DUNNIGAN, M. G. (1972), 'Rickets and osteomalacia in the Glasgow Pakistani community 1961–71', *British Medical Journal*, 2: 677–80.

FORMAN, D., AL-DABBAGH, S., and DOLL, R. (1985), 'Nitrates, nitrites and gastric cancer in Great Britain', *Nature*, 313: 620–5.

FOTHERGILL, S., and GUDGIN, G. (1982), *Unequal Growth*, London, Heinemann.

FOX, A. J. (1977), 'Occupational mortality 1970–72', *Population Trends*, 9: 8–15.

—— (1978), 'Household mortality from the OPCS Longitudinal Study', *Population Trends*, 14: 20–7.

—— (1989) (ed.), *Health Inequalities in European Countries*, Aldershot, Gower.

——BULUSU, L., and KINLEN, L. (1979), 'Mortality and age differences in marriage', *Journal of Biosocial Science*, 11: 117–31.

—— and GOLDBLATT, P. O. (1982*a*), *Longitudinal Study, 1971–75: Socio-demographic Mortality Differentials*, OPCS Series LS No. 1, London, HMSO. For a summary see Fox and Goldblatt 1982*b*.

———— (1982*b*), 'Socio-demographic differences in mortality', *Population Trends*, 27: 8–13.

———— (1986), 'Have inequalities in health widened?' Working Paper No. 47, Social Statistics Research Unit, The City University.

———— and JONES, D. R. (1986), 'Social Class Mortality differentials: artefact, selection or life circumstances?', in R. G. Wilkinson. (ed.), *Class and Health*, London, Tavistock: 34–49.

—— and LEON, D. A. (1988), 'Disadvantage and mortality: new evidence from the OPCS Longitudinal Study', in Keynes, Coleman, and Dimsdale (1988).

FREEMAN, H. (1984), *Mental Health and the Environment*, Singapore, Longman.

FREMLIN, J. (1987), *Power Production: What are the Risks?*, Oxford, Oxford University Press.

FRERE, S. (1974), *Britannia*, London, Sphere Books.

FRIEDLANDER, D. (1983), 'Demographic responses and socioeconomic structure: population processes in England and Wales in the 19th century', *Demography*, 20: 249–72.

—— and ROSHIER, R. J. (1966*a*), 'Internal migration in England and Wales 1851–1951', *Population Studies*, 19: 239–80.

———— (1966*b*), 'A study of internal migration in England and Wales, Part 2', *Population Studies*, 20/1: 45–59.

FRIES, J. F. (1980), 'Ageing, natural death and the compression of mortality', *New England Journal of Medicine*, 303: 130–5.

FROBEL, F., HEINRICHS, J., and Kreye, O. (1980), *The New International Division of Labour*, Cambridge, Cambridge University Press.

FRYER, P. (1965), *The Birth Controllers*, London, Secker and Warburg.

FUCHS, R. G. (1987), 'Legislation, poverty and child abandonment in 19th century Paris', *Journal of Interdisciplinary History*, 18: 55–80.

FURTH, D., and HARDING, P. (1989), 'Sugar and health', *New Scientist*, 10 March: 25–9.

GALBRAITH, N. S., FORBES, P., and MAYON-WHITE, R. T. (1980), 'The changing pattern of communicable disease in England and Wales', *British Medical Journal*, 281.

GALBRAITH, V. G., and THOMAS P. S., (1941), 'Birth rates and the inter-war business cycle', *Journal of American Statistical Association*, 36: 465–76.

GALE, A.H. (1959), *Epidemic Diseases*, Harmondsworth, Penguin.

GALLOWAY, P. R. (1985), 'Annual variations in deaths by age, deaths by cause, prices and weather in London 1670 to 1830', *Population Studies*, 39: 487–505.

Gallup Poll (1986), *Gallup Political Index*, Report 307, Mar., table 24, London, Gallup Poll.

GALPIN, O. P., WHITAKER, C. J., WHITAKER, R., and KASSAB, J. Y. (1990), 'Gastric cancer in Gwynedd: possible links with bracken', *British Journal of Cancer*, 61: 737–40.

GALTON, Sir F. (1872), 'Statistical enquiries into the efficacy of prayer', *Fortnightly Review*, 23: 353–7.

GARDNER, M. J., and DONNAN, S. (1977), 'Life expectancy: variations among regional health authorities', *Population Trends*, 10: 10–12.

——WINTER, P. D., and ACHESON, E. D. (1982), 'Variation in cancer mortality among local authority areas in England and Wales: relationship with environmental factors and search for causes', *British Medical Journal*, 284: 784–7.

————TAYLOR, C. P., and ACHESON, E. D. (1983), *Atlas of Cancer Mortality in England and Wales 1968–1978*, Chichester, John Wiley.

——SNEE, M. P., HALL. A. J., POWELL, C. A., DOWNES, S., and TERRELL, J. D. (1990), 'Results of case-control study of leukaemia and lymphoma among young people near Sellafield nuclear plant in West Cumbria', *British Medical Journal*, 300: 423–9.

GARLAND, J. A. (1971), *The English and Immigration 1880–1910*, Cambridge, Cambridge University Press/Institute of Race Relations.

GARTNER, L. P. (1973), *The Jewish Immigrant in England, 1870–1914* (2nd edn.), London, Simon Publications.

GARVEY, D. (1985), 'The history of migration flows in the Republic of Ireland', *Population Trends*, 39: 22–30.

GAUTIER, E., and HENRY, L. (1958), *La Population de Crulai, paroisse normande*, Paris.

GAY, J. D. (1971), *The Geography of Religion in England*, London, Duckworth.

GB Census (1911), *Census of England and Wales 1911*, xiii: *Fertility and Marriage*, London, HMSO.

GEE, F. A. (1972), *Homes and Jobs for Londoners in New and Expanding Towns*, London, HMSO.

General Household Survey (annual reports) (1977–89), London, HMSO.

General Register Office (1969), *Registration and Vital Statistics in England and Wales*, London, HMSO.

GIBSON, C. (1974), 'The association between divorce and social class in England and Wales', *British Journal of Sociology*, 25: 79–83.

GILBOY, E. W. (1936), 'The cost of living and real wages in 18th century England', *Review of Economic Statistics*, 18; also in Taylor (1975): 1–20.

GILJE, E. K. (1975), 'Migration patterns in and around London', *Research Memorandum Rm 470*, London, Greater London Council.

GILL, D. (1977), *Illegitimacy, sexuality and the status of women*, Oxford, Basil Blackwell

GILLAND, B. (1983), 'Population and food supply', *Population and Development Review*, 9: 203–12.

GILLESPIE, A. E., and OWEN, D. W. (1981), 'Unemployment trends in the current recession', *Area*, 13(B): 189–96.

GILLIES, D. R. N. (1984), 'Analysis of ethnic influences on stillbirths', *Journal of Epidemiology and Community Health*, 38/3: 214–17.

GILLIS, C. R., HOLE, D. J., and BOYLE, P. (1988), 'Cigarette smoking and male lung cancer in an area of very high incidence', *Journal of Epidemiology and Community Health*, 42: 38–43, 44–8.

GIROUARD, M. (1985), *Cities and People: A Social and Architectural History*, London, Yale University Press.

GLASS, D. V. (1936), *The Struggle for Population*, Oxford, Oxford University Press.

—— (1938), 'Marriage frequency and economic fluctuation in England and Wales 1851–1934', in Hogben (1938).

—— (1940, 1967), *Population Policies and Movements in Europe*, Oxford, Oxford University Press.

—— (1963), 'John Graunt and his "Natural and Political Observations"', *Proceedings of the Royal Society B*, 159/974, 10 Dec.

—— (1964), 'Some indicators of differences between urban and rural mortality in England and Wales and Scotland', in *Public Health and Urban Growth*, London, Centre for Urban Studies.

——— (1965*a*): 'Two papers on Gregory King', in Glass and Eversley (1965): 159–220.

—— (1965*b*), 'Population and population movement in England and Wales 1700–1850', in Glass and Eversley (1965).

—— (1971), *Components of Natural Increase in England and Wales*, First Report of the Select Committee on Science and Technology, also in 'Towards a Population Policy for Britain', supplement to *Population Studies*, May.

—— (1973), *Numbering the People*, Farnborough, Saxon House.

—— (1976), 'Recent and prospective trends in fertility in developed countries', *Philosophical Transactions of the Royal Society B*, 274: 1–52.

—— and BLACKER, C. P. (1938), *Population and Fertility*, London, Population Investigation Committee

—— and GREBENIK, E. (1954), *The Trend and Pattern of Fertility in Great Britain: A Report on the Family Census of 1946*, Papers of the Royal Commission on Population, vol. vi: Part I Report; Part II Tables, London, HMSO.

—— and EVERSLEY, D. E. C. (eds.) (1965), *Population in History*, London, Arnold.

GLAZER, N. (ed.) (1985), *Clamor at the Gates: The New American Immigration*, San Francisco, Institute of Contemporary Studies Press.

GLEAVE, D. and CORDEY-HAYES, M. (1977), 'Migration dynamics and labour market turnover', *Progress in Planning*, 8.

GLEIBERMANN, L. (1973), 'Blood pressure and dietary salt in human populations', *Ecology of Food and Nutrition*, 2: 143–56.

GLICK, P. D. (1977), 'Updating the life cycle of the family', *Journal of Marriage and the Family* 39, 5–13.

GLYN-Jones, A. (1975), *Growing Older in a South Devon Town*, Exeter, University of Exeter.

GODDARD, J. B. and CHAMPION, A. G. (eds.) (1983), *The Urban and Regional Transformation of Britain*, London, Methuen.

GOLDACRE, M., and GRIFFIN, K., (1983) *Performance Indicators: A Commentary on the Literature*, Oxford, Unit of Clinical Epidemiology, University of Oxford.

GOLDBLATT, P. (1988), 'Changes in social class between 1971 and 1981: could these affect mortality differences among men of working ages?', *Population Trends*, 51: 9–17.

—— (1989), 'Mortality by Social Class 1971–85, *Population Trends*, 56: 6–15.

——(1990), 'Mortality and alternative social classifications', in P. Goldblatt (ed.), *Longitudinal Study: Mortality and Social Organization*, OPCS Series LS No. 6, London, HMSO.

——and Fox, J., (1978), 'Household mortality from the OPCS Longitudinal Study', *Population Trends*, 14: 20–27.

GOLDMAN, A. J., BRAUN, T., and GALLAGHER, R. P. (1988), 'The classification of ethnic status using surnames', *Journal of Epidemiology and Community Health*, 42: 390–5.

GOLDMAN, L., and COOK, E. F. (1984), 'The decline in Ischaemic Heart Disease mortality rates: an analysis of the comparative effects of medical intervention and changes in lifestyle', *Annals of Internal Medicine*, 101: 825–36.

GOLDSMITH, E., ALLEN, R., ALLABY, M., DAVOLL, J., and LAWRENCE, S. (1972); 'A blueprint for survival', *Ecologist*, 2/1.

GOLDTHORPE, J., and HOPE, K. (1974), *The Social Grading of Occupations: A New Approach and Scale*, Oxford, Oxford University Press.

GOODHART, C. B. (1973), 'On the incidence of illegal abortion, with a reply to Dr. W. H. James'. *Population Studies*, 27: 207–33.

GOODY, J. (1983), *The Development of the Family and Marriage in Europe*, Cambridge, Cambridge University Press.

GORDIS, E., TABAKOFF, B., GOLDMAN, D., and BERG, K. (1990), 'Finding the gene(s) for alcoholism', editorial, *Journal of the American Medical Association*, 263, 2094–6.

GORDON, I. (1979), 'The analysis of motivation specific migration streams', *Environment and Planning A*, 14. 5–20.

GORDON, R. R. (1990), 'Postneonatal mortality among illegitimate children registered by one or both parents', *British Medical Journal*, 300: 236–7.

GOUDIE, A. S. (1983), *Environment Change*, 2nd edn., Oxford, Oxford University Press.

GRAHAM, H. (1988), 'Women's smoking and family health', *Social Science and Medicine*, 25: 47–56.

GREBENIK, E., and ROWNTREE G. (1963), 'Factors associated with age at marriage in Britain', *Proceedings of the Royal Society B*, 159: 178–97.

——HÖHN, C., and MACKENSEN, R., (eds.) (1989). *Later Phases of the Family Cycle: Demographic Aspects*, Oxford, Oxford University Press.

GREEN, A. E. (1984), 'Considering long-term unemployment as a criterion for regional policy aid', *Area*, 16/3: 209–18.

——OWEN, D. W., CHAMPION, A. G., GODDARD, J. B., and COOMBES, M. G. (1985), 'What contribution can labour migration make to reducing unemployment?' Discussion Paper 73, University of Newcastle-upon-Tyne, Centre for Urban and Regional Development Studies.

——(1986), 'The likelihood of becoming and remaining unemployed in Great Britain, 1984', *Transactions, Institute of British Geographers*, NS, 11: 37–56.

GREENWOOD, M. (1935), *Epidemics and Crowd Diseases*, London, Williams and Norgate.

GRENFELL, B. T. and ANDERSON, R. M. (1988), 'Pertussis in England and Wales: an investigation of transmission dynamics and control by mass vaccination', *Proceedings of the Royal Society B*, 236: 213–52.

GRIFFITH, G. TALBOT (1926, 1967), *Population Problems of the Age of Malthus*, 1st and 2nd edns., London, Frank Cass.

GRIGG, D. B. (1980), *Population Growth and Agricultural Change: An Historical Perspective*, Cambridge, Cambridge University Press.

GRISCLAUDE, A., LUX, B., VAN HOVIE-MINET, M., and WUNSCH G. (1979), 'Mortalité régionale et compartements différentiels: les déterminants de la mortalité masculine', *Population et famille*, 3: 1–44.

GROSSKURTH, A. (1985), 'Rent Acts now widely ignored', *Roof*, Mar–Apr,: 10.

GRUNDY, E. M. D. (1986), *Demographic Change, Household Evaluation and Housing Need*, paper presented to conference on Comparative Population Geography of the UK and the Netherlands, Oxford 1986.

——and Fox, A. J. (1985), 'Migration during early married life', *European Journal of Population*, 1: 237–63.

HABAKKUK, H. J. (1953, 1965), 'English population in the 18th century', *Economic History Review*, 6: 117–33, reported in Glass and Eversley, (1965): 269–84.

——(1971), *Population Growth and Economic Development since 1750*, Leicester, Leicester University Press.

HABERMAN, S. and BLOOMFIELD, D. S. F. (1987), 'Social class differences in mortality in Great Britain around 1981, Longitudinal Study Working Paper No. 55, London, City University.

——KOSMIN, B. A. and LEVY, C. (1983), 'Mortality patterns of British Jews, 1975–79: insights and applications for the size and structure of British Jewry, *Journal of the Royal Statistical Society*, Part 3, 146: 294–310.

HAINES, M. R. (1979), *Fertility and Occupation: Population Pattern in Industrialisation*, New York, Academic Press.

HAJNAL, J. (1950), 'Births, marriages and reproduction in England and Wales, 1938–1947', *Papers of the Royal Commission on Population*, ii: *Reports and Selected Papers of the Statistics Committee*, London, HMSO.

——(1953), 'Age at marriage and proportions marrying', *Population Studies*, 7: 1.

——(1964), 'Concepts of random mating and the frequency of consanguineous marriages', *Proceedings of the Royal Society B*, 150: 125–77.

——(1965), European marriage patterns in perspective', in Glass and Eversley (1965).

——(1982) 'Two kinds of pre-industrial houshold formation systems', *Population and Development Review*, 8: 449–94.

HAKIM, C. (1978), 'Sexual divisions within the labour force: occupational segregation', *Employment Gazette*, 92: 1264–78.

HALL, P. (ed.) (1981), *The Inner City in Context*, London, Heinemann.

——and HAY, D. (1980), *Growth Centres in the European Urban System*, London, Heinemann.

——and MARKUSEN, A. (1985), *Silicon Landscapes*, Boston, Allen & Unwin.

——THOMAS, R., GRACEY, H., and DREWETT, R. (1973), *The Containment of Urban England*, 2 vols. London, Allen & Unwin.

HALLAM, H. E. (1961), 'Population density in medieval Fenland', *Economic History Review*, 2nd series, 14: 71–81.

——(1972), 'The Postan thesis', *Historical Studies* (Melbourne) 15: 221.

HALSEY, A. H. (1987), 'Social trends since World War II', *Social Trends*, 17 (1987 edn.), London, HMSO: 11–19

——(ed.) (1988), *British Social Trends Since 1900*, London, Macmillan.

HAMMOND, W. H. (1955), 'Measurement and interpretation of subcutaneous fat with norms for children and young adult males', *British Journal of Preventive and Social Medicine*, 9: 201–11.

HAMNETT, C. (1984), 'Housing the two nations: socio-tenurial polarisation in England and Wales', *Urban Studies*, 43: 389–405.

HANNAN, M. T. (1982), 'Families, markets and social structures: an essay on Becker's "A treatise on the family"', *Journal of Economic Literature* (Nashville, Tenn.), 20/1: 65–72.

Hansard (1943*a*), 16 July (391/90), cols. 544–653 (trend of population).

Hansard (1943*b*), House of Lords, 8 June (127/68), cols. 891–930 (population problems).

Hansard (1980*a*) (House of Commons Official Report, Parliamentary Debates), 30 Apr. (983/165) col. 1301–37 (Census Order 1980).

Hansard (1980*b*); 27 Oct. (991/231).

Hansard (1981), 31 July (9/153).

Hansard (1982), 6 Dec. (33/24).

Hansard (1990), 8 Jan. (1506), col. 691.

HARRIS, A. I., and CLAUSEN, R. (1967), *Labour Mobility in Great Britain*, 1953–1963 Social Survey, London, HMSO.

HARRISON, G. A. (1980), 'Urbanisation and Stress', in Clegg and Garlick (1980): 55–72.

——and GIBSON, J. G. (1976), *Man in Urban Environments*, Oxford, Oxford University Press.

——HIORNS, R. W., and KÜCHEMANN, C. F. (1971), 'Social class and marriage patterns in some Oxfordshire parishes', *Journal of Biosocial Science*, 3/1: 1–12.

HART, R. A. (1970), 'A model of inter-regional migration in England and Wales', *Regional Studies*, 4: 279–96.

HART, TUDOR J. (1984), 'Hypertension and the prevention of coronary heart death in general practice', *Postgraduate Medical Journal* 60: 34–7.

HARVEY, B. F. (1966), 'The population trend in England between 1300 and 1348', *Transactions of the Royal Historical Society*, 16: 23–42.

HASKEY, J. (1982*a*), 'The proportion of marriage ending in divorce', *Population Trends* 27: 4–8.

——(1982*b*), 'Widowhood, widowerhood and remarriage', *Population Trends*, 30: 15–20

——(1983*a*), 'Children of divorcing couples', *Population Trends*, 31: 20–6.

——(1983*b*), 'Marital status before marriage and age at marriage: their influence on the chance of divorce', *Population Trends*, 32: 4–14.

——(1983*c*), 'Remarriage of the divorced in England and Wales: a contemporary phenomenon', *Journal of Biosocial Science*, 15: 253–71.

——(1983*d*), 'Social class patterns of marriage', *Population Trends*, 34: 12–19.

——(1984), 'Social class and socio-economic differentials in divorce in England and Wales', *Population Studies* 38: 419–38.

——(1986*a*), 'One parent families in Great Britain', *Population Trends*, 45: 5–13.

——(1986*b*), 'Recent trends in divorce in England and Wales: the effects of legislative changes' *Population Trends* 44: 9–16.

——(1987*a*), 'Social class differences in remarriage after divorce: results from a forward linkage study', *Population Trends*, 47: 36–42.

—— (1987*b*), 'One person households in Great Britain; living alone in the middle years of life', *Population Trends*, 50: 23–31.

—— (1988), 'Mid-1985 based population projections by marital status', *Population Trends*, 52: 30–2.

—— (1989*a*), 'Current prospects for the proportion of marriages ending in divorce', *Population Trends*, 55: 34–7.

—— (1989*b*), 'One-parent families and their children in Great Britain: numbers and characteristics', *Population Trends*. 55, 27–33.

—— (1989*c*), 'Families and households of the ethnic minority and white populations of Great Britain', *Population Trends*, 57: 8–19.

—— BALARAJAN, B., and DONNAN, S. P. (1983), 'Regional variations in alcohol-related problems in the United Kingdom', *Community Medicine*, 5: 208–19.

—— and COLEMAN, D. A. (1986), 'Cohabitation before marriage: a comparison of information from marriage registration and the General Household Survey', *Population Trends*, 43: 15–17.

—— and KIERNAN, K. (1989), 'Cohabitation in Britain—characteristics and estimated numbers of cohabiting partners', *Population Trends*, 58: 23–32.

HASLUCK, C. (1987), *Urban Unemployment, Local Labour Markets and Employment Initiatives*, London, Longman.

HATCHER, J. (1977), *Plague, Population and the English Economy 1348–1530*, London, Macmillan.

—— (1986), 'Mortality in the fifteenth century: some new evidence', *Economic History Review*, 39: 19–38.

HATTON, T. J. (1984), *Trends in the Labour Force 1850–1980*, London, Centre for Economic Policy Research.

—— (1986), *Female Labour Force Participation: The Enigma of the Interwar Period'* CEPR Discussion Paper No. 113, London, CEPR.

Health and Safety Executive (1987), *Health and Safety Statistics 1984–85*, London, HMSO.

HEASMAN, M.A., and LIPWORTH, L. (1966), *Accuracy of Certification of Cause of Death: A Report of a Survey Conducted in 1959 in 75 Hospitals of the National Health Service to obtain Information as to the Extent of Agreement between Clinical and Post-mortem Diagnoses*, Studies in Medical and Population Subjects, No. 20, London, HMSO.

HELLEINER, K. F. (1957, 1965), 'The Vital Revolution reconsidered', In *Canadian Journal of Economic and Political Science*, 23/1; reprinted in Glass and Eversley (1965).

—— (1967), 'The population of Europe from the Black Death to the eve of the vital revolution', in *Cambridge Economic History of Europe*, vol. iv.

HELLIER, J. (1977), 'Perinatal mortality 1950 and 1973,' *Population Trends*, 10: 13–15.

HENRY, L. (1956), *Anciennes familles genevoises, étude démographique des XVI–XXe siècles*, Paris, Presses Universitaires de France.

—— (1961), 'La Fertilité naturelle: Observations, théories, résultats', *Population*, 16/4: 625–36, Oct.–Dec.

HENDERSHOT, G. E., and PLACEK, P. J. (eds.) (1981), *Predicting Fertility: Studies of Birth Expectation*, Lexington, Mass., D. C. Heath.

HENDRY, P. (1988), 'Food and population: beyond five billion', *Population*

Bulletin, 43, no. 2: 40.

HILL, A. B. (1937), *Principles of Medical Statistics*, London, Lancet (see also recent editions).

HIMES N. E. (1936), *The Medical History of Contraception*, Baltimore, Williams and Wilkins.

——(ed.) (1967), *Illustrations and Proofs of the Principle of Population by Francis Place*, London, Allen and Unwin.

HINDE, P. R. A., and WOODS, R. I. (1983), 'Variations in historical natural fertility and the measurement of fertility controls', *Journal of Biosocial Science*, 16: 304–21.

HIORNS, R. W. (ed.) (1980), *Demographic Patterns in Developed Societies*, London, Taylor and Francis.

HIRAYAMA, T. (1981), 'Non-smoking wives of heavy smokers have a high risk of lung cancer: a study from Japan', *British Medical Journal*, 282: 183–5.

HIRO, D. (1971), *Black British, White British*, London, Eyre and Spottiswoode.

HIRST, L. F. (1953), *The Conquest of Plague: A Study in the Evolution of Epidemiology*. Oxford, Oxford University Press.

HJERMANN, I., BYRE, V., HOLME, I., LEREN, P, (1981), 'Effect of diet and smoking intervention on the incidence of coronary heart disease', *Lancet*, 12 Dec., 1303–10.

HM Government (1903); *Report of Royal Commission on Alien Immigration*, London, HMSO.

——(1973), *Security of the Census of Population*, Cmnd. 5365, London, HMSO.

——(1978), *The 1981 Census of Population*, Cmnd. 7146, London, HMSO.

——(1982), *The Government Reply to the Fifth Report from the Home Affairs Committee Session 1980–1981*, HC424: Racial Disadvantage, Cmnd. 8476, London, HMSO.

——(1984), *The Government Reply to the Second Report from the Home Affairs Committee Session 1982–83*, HC33–1: Ethnic and Racial Questions in the Census, Cmnd. 9238, London, HMSO.

HOBCRAFT. J. (1989), 'People and services: central assessment of local needs', in H. Joshi (ed.), *The Changing Population of Britain*, Oxford, Basil Blackwell.

——MENKEN, J., PRESTON, S. (1982), 'Age, period of cohort effects in demography: a review, *Population Index* 48: 4–43.

HOBHOUSE, H. (1985), *Seeds of Change: Five Plants that Transformed Mankind*, London, Sidgwick and Jackson.

HODGSON, J. T. and JONES, R. D. (1986), 'Mortality of asbestos workers in England and Wales 1971–81', *British Journal of Industrial Medicine*, 43: 158–64.

HOGARTH, T., and DANIEL, W. W. (1988), *Britain's New Industrial Gypsies*, London, Policy Studies Institute.

HOGBEN, L. (ed.) (1938), *Political Arithmetic*, London, Allen & Unwin.

HÖHN, C. (1987), 'Population policies in advanced societies: pronatalist and migration strategies', *European Journal of Population*, 3: 459–81.

HOLE, W. V., and POUNTNEY, M. T. (1971), 'Trends in population, housing and occupancy rates 1861–1961', *Department of the Environment/Building Research Station*, London, HMSO

HOLLAND, W. W., and REID, D. D. (1965), 'The urban factor in chronic bronchitis', *Lancet*, 1: 445–8.

HOLLINGSWORTH, M. F., and HOLLINGSWORTH, T. H. (1971), 'Plague mortality rates by age and sex in the Parish of St. Botolphs without Bishopsgate, London, 1603', *Population Studies*, 25.

HOLLINGSWORTH, T. H. (1957, 1965), 'A demographic study of the British ducal families', *Population Studies*, 11/1: 4–26; reprinted in Glass and Eversley (1965): 354–78.

—— (1964), 'The demography of the British peerage', *Population Studies*, 18 Supplement.

—— (1976), *Historical Demography*, Cambridge, Cambridge University Press.

—— (1982), review of 'The population history of England 1541–1871: a reconstruction', by E. A. Wrigley and R. S. Schofield, *Population Studies*, 36: 495.

HOLLIS J. (1982), 'New Commonwealth ethnic group populations in Greater London', in D. A. Coleman (ed.), *The Demography of Immigrants and Minority Groups in the United Kingdom*, London, Academic Press.

HOLMANS, A. E. (1963), 'Current population trends in Britain', *Scottish Journal of Political Economy*, 11: 31–56.

—— (1987), *Housing Policy in Britain: A History*, London, Croom Helm.

—— NANDY, S., and BROWN, A. C. (1987), 'Household formation and dissolution and housing tenure: a longitudinal perspective', *Social Trends*, 17: 20–8.

HOLMES, T. H. and RAHE, R. H. (1967), 'The social readjustment rating scale', *Journal of Psychosomatic Research*, 11: 213–18.

Home Affairs Committee (1982), *Report on Ethnic and Racial Questions in the Census*, House of Commons Paper No. 33/1, vol. i, May 1983, London, HMSO.

—— (1986), *First Report Session 1986–87: Bangladeshis in Britain*, i: *Report and Proceedings*, London, HMSO.

Home Office (1989*a*), *Control of Immigration: Refugee Statistics*, London, HMSO.

—— (1989*b*), *Criminal Statistics 1988*, London, HMSO.

HORNSBY-SMITH, M. P. (1987), *Roman Catholics in England: Studies in Social Structure since the Second World War*, Cambridge, Cambridge University Press.

—— and LEE, R. M. (1979), *Roman Catholic Opinion: A Study of Roman Catholics in England and Wales in the 1970s—Final Report*, Guildford, Dept. of Sociology, University of Surrey.

HOSKINS, W. G. (1963), *Provincial England: Essays in Social and Economic History*, London, Macmillan.

HOUSE, J. S., LANDIS, K. R., and UMBESON, D. (1988), 'Social Relationships and Health', *Science*, 241: 540–5.

House of Commons Social Services Committee (1979–80), *Perinatal and Neonatal Mortality*, i: *Report* (Second Report), vols. ii, iii, iv: *Evidence*, vol. v: *Appendices*, London, HMSO (the Short Report).

HOWE, G. M. (1970), *National Atlas of Disease Mortality in the U.K.*, 2nd edn., London, Nelson.

—— (1972), *Man, Environment and Disease in Britain: A Medical Geography Through the Ages*, Harmondsworth, Penguin.

HOWELL, N. (1986), 'Feedbacks and buffers in relation to scarcity and abundance', in D. A. Coleman and R. S. Schofield (eds.), *The State of Population Theory*, Oxford, Basil Blackwell.

HOWIE, P. W., FORSYTH, J. S., OGSTON, S. A., CLARK, A., and FLOREY, C. du V. (1990), 'Protective effect of breast feeding against infection', *British Medical*

Journal, 300: 11–16.

HUBER, J., and SPITZE, G. (1980), 'Considering divorce: an explanation of Becker's theory of marital instability', *American Journal of Sociology*, 86/1: 75–86.

HUGHES, G., and McCORMICK, B. (1981), 'Do council housing policies reduce migration between regions?' *Economic Journal*, 919–37.

————(1984), 'Migration intentions in the UK: which households want to migrate and which succeed?', *Economic Journal (Supplement)*, 95: 113–23.

HUGHES, J. S. *et al.* (1989), *The Radiation Exposure of the UK Population: 1988 Review*, Series R227, Chilton, NRPB.

HUNT, S. P., O'RIORDAN, J. L. H., WINDO, J., TRUSWELL, A. S. (1976), 'Vitamin D status in different subgroups of British Asians, *British Medical Journal*, 2: 1351–4.

HUNTER, D. (1969), *The Diseases of Occupations*, London, English UP.

HURST, R. (1989), 'A million home truths', *Search*, 2, 20–1.

HUZEL, J. P. (1980), 'The demographic impact of the old Poor Law: more reflections on Malthus', *Economic History Review*, 33/3: 367–87.

ILLSLEY, R, (1986), 'Occupational class, selection and the production of inequalities in health', *Quarterly Journal of Social Affairs*, 2: 151–65.

——and LE GRAND, J. (1987), 'The measurement of inequality in health', in A. Williams (ed.), *Health and Economics*, London, Macmillan.

Immigrant Statistics Unit, OPCS (1977), 'New Commonwealth and Pakistani population estimates', *Population Trends*, 9: 4–7.

——(1978), 'Marriage and birth patterns among the New Commonwealth and Pakistani populations', *Population Trends*, 11: 5–9.

——(1979), 'Population of New Commonwealth and Pakistani ethnic origin: new projections', *Population Trends*, 16: 22–7.

Industrial Society (1989), *Catering prices, costs and subsidies and other information*, London, The Industrial Society.

INEICHEN, B. (1972), 'Home ownership and manual working life-styles', *Sociological Review*, 20: 391–412.

——(1979*a*), 'Housing factors in the timing of weddings and first pregnancies', in *Sociology and the Family: New Directions for Britain*, University of Keele Sociological Review Monograph 28.

——(1979*b*), 'The social geography of marriage', in M. COOKE. and G. Wilson (eds.), *Love and Attraction*, Oxford, Pergamon Press: 145–9.

INMAN, W. H. W., ADELSTEIN, A.H. (1969), 'Rise and fall of asthma mortality in England and Wales in relation to the use of pressure aerosols', *Lancet* 2: 279–85.

INNES, J. A. (1981), 'Tuberculosis in Asians', *Postgraduate Medical Journal*, 57: 779–80.

INNES, J. W. (1938), *Class Fertility Trends in England and Wales 1876–1934*, Princeton, NJ, Princeton University Press.

International Labour Office (1989), *From Pyramid to Pillar: Population Change and Social Security in Europe*, Geneva, ILO.

International Planned Parenthood Federation (1983), The Pill and cancer-IPPF response (editorial), *IPPF Medical Bulletin*, 17: 1–2.

ISIS-2 Collaborative Group (1988), 'Randomized trial of intravenous streptokinase, and aspirin, both or neither among 17,187 cases of suspected acute myocardial infarction', *Lancet* 2: 349–60.

JACKSON, J. A. (ed.) (1969), *Migration*, Cambridge, Cambridge University Press.

JAMES, W. H. (1971), 'The incidence of illegal abortion', *Population Studies*, 25: 327–39.

—— (1980), 'Secular trend in reported sperm counts', *Andrologia*, 12: 381–8.

—— (1982), 'Second survey of secular trends in twinning rates', *Journal of Biosocial Science*, 14: 481–97.

JENKINS, C., and SHERMAN, B. (1979), *The Collapse of Work*, London, Eyre Methuen.

JOHANSSON, S. R. (1987), 'Status anxiety and demographic contraction of privileged populations', *Population and Development Reviews*, 13: 439–69.

JOHNSON, A. M., and GILL, O. N. (1989), 'Evidence for recent changes in sexual behaviour in homosexual men in England and Wales', *Philosophical Transactions of the Royal Society B*, 325: 153–61.

JOHNSON J. H. (1974), *Suburban Growth: Geographical Processes at the Edge of the Western City*, London, Wiley.

—— and SALT, J. (1980a), 'Labour migration within organizations: an introductory study', *Tijdschrift voor economische en sociale geographie*, 71: 277–84.

—— —— (1980b), 'Employment transfer policies in Great Britain', *Three Banks Review* 126: 18–39.

—— —— (1981), 'Population redistribution policies in Great Britain', in J. W. Webb, A. Naukkarinen, and L. A. Kosinski (eds.), *Policies of Population Redistribution*, Oulu, Geographical Society of Northern Finland, 77–92.

—— —— and WOOD, P. A. (1974), *Housing and the Migration of Labour in England and Wales*, Farnborough, Saxon House.

JOHNSON, P. and FALKINGHAM, J. (1988), 'Intergenerational Transfers and public expenditure on the elderly in modern Britain', CEPR Discussion Paper No. 254, London, CEPR.

—— CONRAD, C., and Thomson, D. (eds.) (1989), *Workers versus Pensioners: Intergenerational Justice in a Changing World*, Manchester, Manchester University Press.

JONES, B. (1982), *Sleepers, Wake! Technology and the Future of Work*, Brighton, Wheatsheaf.

JONES, D. R., and GOLDBLATT, P. (1987), 'Causes of death in widow(ers) and spouses', *Journal of Biosocial Science* 19: 107–21.

JONES. E., and GRUPP, F. W. (1983), 'Infant mortality trends in the Soviet Union', *Population and Development Review* 2: 213–46.

JONES, E. F. (1981), 'The impact of women's unemployment on marital fertility in the U.S. 1970–1975', *Population Studies*, 35/2: 161–74.

JONES, E. L. (1987), *The European Miracle: Environments, Economies and Geopolitics in the History of Europe and Asia* (2nd edn.), Cambridge, Cambridge University Press.

JONES, H. R., CAIRD, J., BERRY, W., and DEWHURST, J. (1986), 'Peripheral counter-urbanisation: findings from an integration of census and survey data in Northern Scotland,' *Regional Studies*, 20/1: 15–26.

JONES, K., and SMITH, A. D. (1970), *The Economic Impact of Commonwealth Immigration*, Cambridge, NIESR.

JONES, K. L., and SMITH, D. W. (1973), 'Recognition of the foetal alcohol syndrome in early pregnancy', *Lancet* 2: 999–1001.

JONES, P. N. (1978), 'The distribution and diffusion of the coloured population in

England and Wales 1961–71', *Transactions' Institute of British Geographers*, NS 3: 515–32.

JONES, P. R. (1982a), 'Ethnic intermarriage in Britain', *Ethnic and Racial Studies*, 5.

——(1982b), *Vietnamese Refugees*, Research and Planning Unit Paper 13, London, Home Office.

——(1982c), 'Some sources of current immigration', in D. A. Coleman (ed.), *The Demography of Immigrants and Minority Groups in the United Kingdom*, London, Academic Press.

——(1984), 'Ethnic intermarriage in Britain: a further assessment', *Ethnic and Racial Studies*, 7: 398–405.

——and SHAH, S. (1980), 'Arranged marriages: a sample survey of the Asian case', *New Community*, 8/3: 339–43.

JONES, R. E. (1980), 'Further evidence on the decline in infant mortality in pre-industrial England: North Shropshire 1561–1810', *Population Studies* 34/2: 239–50.

JOSEPH, G. (1983), *Women at Work*, Oxford, Philip Allen.

JOSHI, H. (1985), *Participation in Paid Work: Multiple Regression Analysis of the Incomes and Employment Survey*, CEPR Discussion Paper No. 40, London, CEPR.

——(1987a), *The Cash Opportunity Cost of Child-Bearing: An Approach to Estimation using British Data*, Paper No. 208, London, CEPR.

——(1987b), 'The cost of caring', in C. Glendenning and J. Millar (eds.), *Women and Poverty in Britain*, Brighton, Wheatsheaf Books.

——(1989), *The Changing Population of Britain*, Oxford, Blackwell.

——and OWEN, S. (1985), *Does Elastic Retract? The Effect of Recession on Women's Labour Force Participation*, CEPR Discussion Paper No. 64, London, CEPR.

JOWELL, R., and AIREY, C. (1986), *British Social Attitudes 1986*, Aldershot, SCPR/Gower.

——WITHERSPOON, S., and BROOK, L. (1987), *British Social Attitudes: The 1987 Report*, Aldershot, SCPR/Gower.

JOZAN, P. (1986), *Recent Mortality Trends in Eastern Europe'*, paper presented to BSPS meeting 23 June 1986, London.

KARASEK, R. A., THEORELL T. G., SCHWARTZ, J., PEIPER, C., and ALFREDSSON, L. (1982), 'Job psychological factors and coronary heart disease: Swedish prospective findings and US prevalence findings using a new occupational inference method', *Advances in Cardiology*, 29: 62–7.

KARN, V. A. (1977), *Retiring to the Seaside*, London, Routledge & Kegan Paul.

KAY, J. (1988), 'The welfare crisis in an ageing population', in Keynes, Coleman, and Dimsdale (1988).

KAY, J. and HOLMES, J. (1989), 'Changes in seasonal mortalities with improvement in home heating in England and Wales from 1964 to 1984; *International Journal of Biometeorology*, 33: 71–6.

KEATINGE, W. R., COLESHAW, S. R. K., COTTER, F., MATTOCK, M., MURPHY, M., and CHELLIAH, R. (1984), 'Increases in platelet and red cell counts, blood viscosity and arterial pressure during mild surface cooling: factors in mortality from coronary and cerebral thrombosis in winter', *British Medical Journal*, 289: 1405–8.

Keeble, D. E. (1980), 'Industrial decline, regional policy and the urban–rural manufacturing shift in the UK', *Environment and Planning A*, 12: 945–62.

Keegan, J. (1976), *The Face of Battle*, London, Jonathan Cape.

——(1985), *Soldiers*, London, Hamish Hamilton.

Kelsall, R. K. (1970), *Population* (rev. edn.), London, Longman

——(1989), *Population in Britain in the 1990s and beyond*, Stoke-on-Trent, Trentham.

Kelsey, J. L. (1979), 'A review of the epidemiology of human breast cancer', *Epidemiological Reviews*, 1: 74–109.

Kennedy, P, (1988), *The Rise and Fall of Great Powers*, London, Unwin Hyman.

Kennett, S. (1977), 'Migration and "Million City" labour markets 1966–71', Working Report 52, Urban Change in Britain Project, Dept. of Geography, London School of Economics.

——and Randolph, W. (1978), 'The differential migration of socio-economic groups 1966–71', Discussion Paper 66, Graduate School of Geography, London School of Economics.

Keyfitz, N. (1985), 'The demographics of unfunded pensions', *European Journal of Population*, 1: 5–30.

Keynes, J. M. (1936), 'The economic consequences of a declining population' *Eugenics Review* 29: 13–17.

Keynes, M., Coleman, D. A., and Dimsdale, N. H. (eds.) (1988), *The Political Economy of Health and Welfare*, London, Macmillan.

Keys, A (1980), 'Overweight, obesity, coronary heart disease and mortality', *Nutrition Review*, 38: 297–307.

Kiernan, K. (1980a), *Patterns of Family Formation and Dissolution*, OPCS Occasional Paper 19/2, London, HMSO: 21–35.

——(1980b), 'Teenage motherhood: associated factors and consequences: the experiences of a British birth cohort', *Journal of Biosocial Science*, 12: 393–405.

——(1983), 'The structure of families today: continuity or change?', *The Family*, OPCS Occasional Paper No. 31, London, HMSO.

——(1986), 'Leaving home: living arrangements of young people in six West European countries', *European Journal of Population*, 2: 177–84.

——(1987), 'Demographic experiences in early adulthood: a longitudinal study', Ph.D. Thesis, University of London.

——(1989a), 'Who remains childless?', *Journal of Biosocial Science*, 21: 387–498.

——(1989b), 'The departure of children', in E. Grebenik, C. Höhn, and R, Mackensen (eds.), *The Later Stages of the Family Cycle*, Oxford, Oxford University Press.

——(1989c), 'The family: formation and fission', in H. Joshi, (ed.), *The Changing Population of Britain*, Oxford, Basil Blackwell.

——and Diamond, I. (1982), *Family Origin and Educational Influences on Age at First Birth: The Experiences of a British Birth Cohort*, CPS Research Paper No. 82–1, London, London School of Hygiene and Tropical Medicine.

King, D. (1986), *1983-Based Department of Environment Household Projections: A Critical Review*, Population and Housing Research Group Information Note 7, Essex Institute of Higher Education.

King Edward's Hospital Fund for London (1989), *The Nation's Health: A strategy for the 1990s*, London, King Edward's Hospital Fund.

Kinlen, L. (1982), 'Diet and cancer', in R. Schoenatal and T. A. Conners (eds.),

Dietary Influences on Cancer: Influences Traditional and Modern, Boca Raton, Fla., CRC Press: 91–107.

——(1982), 'Meat and fat consumption and cancer mortality: a study of strict religious orders in Britain', *Lancet*, 946–9.

KIRJI, K. H., and EDOUARD, L. (1984), 'Ethnic difference in pregnancy outcome', *Public Health*, 98: 205–8.

KIRK, D. (1942), 'The relation of employment levels to births in Germany', *Millbank Memorial Fund Quarterly*, Apr.

KIRKMAN, K., (1985), 'Mid-nineteenth century rural change: the case of Pinner', *Local Historian*, 17: 199–204.

KIRKWOOD, K., HERBERTSON, M., and PARKES, A. (eds.) (1983), 'Biosocial aspects of ethnic minorities', Supplement to *Journal of Biosocial Science*, Cambridge, Galton Foundation.

KIRKWOOD, T. B. L., and HOLLIDAY, R. (1986), 'Ageing as a consequence of natural selection', in Bittles and Collins (1986).

KIRWAN, F. X. (1981), 'Recent Irish migration: a note on a neglected data source', *European Demographic Information Bulletin* (The Hague) 12/2: 56–62.

—— and NAIRN, A. G. (1983), 'Migrant employment and the recession: the case of the Irish in Britain', *International Migration Review*, 17: 672–81.

KITCHING, R. T. (1990), 'Migration behaviour among the unemployed and low skilled', in J. H. Johnson and J. Salt (eds.), *Labour Migration*, London, David Fulton, 172–90.

KLEIN, M. (1965), *Samples from English Culture*, vol. i, London, Routledge & Kegan Paul.

KLEIN, R. (1983), *The Politics of the NHS*, London, Longman.

——(1984), 'Auditing health care policies', *British Medical Journal*, 288: 1021–2.

KNIGHT, I. (1984), *The Heights and Weights of Adults in Great Britain: Report of a Survey Carried out on behalf of the DHSS*, OPCS Social Survey Division, London, HMSO.

KNODEL, J., and VAN DE WALLE, E. (1967), 'Breast feeding, fertility and infant mortality: an analysis of some early German data', *Population Studies*, 31: 109–32.

KNOX, E. G., MARSHALL, T., KANE, S., GREEN, A., and MALLETT, R (1980), 'Social and health care determinants of area variations in perinatal mortality', *Community Medicine*, 2: 282–90.

KOGEVINAS, M., MARMOT, M. G., and FOX, A. J. (1988), 'Socio-economic status and cancer: results from the OPCS Longitudinal Study', LS Working Paper No. 50, London, City University.

—— GOLDBATT, P. O., and PUGH, H. (1989), 'Socio-economic status and breast cancer in England and Wales', LS Working Paper No. 63, London, City University.

KOMAROV, B. (1978), *The Destruction of Nature in the Soviet Union*, Armonk, M.E. Sharpe.

KOSMIN, B. A. (1976), *The Structure and Demography of British Jewry in 1976*, London, World Zionist Organisation.

——(1982), 'Nuptiality and fertility pattern of British Jewry 1850–1980: an immigrant transition', in D. A. Coleman (ed.), *The Demography of Immigrant and Minority Groups in the UK*, London, Academic Press.

——BAUER, M., and GRIZZARD, N. (1976), *Steel City Jews*, London, Board of Deputies of British Jews.

——and DE LANGE, D. (1978), *Synagogue Affiliation in the United Kingdom 1977*, London, Research Unit, Board of Deputies of British Jews.

KRAUSE, J. (1957), 'The medieval household: large or small?', *Economic History Review*, 2nd series, 4: 420–32.

——(1965), 'The changing adequacy of English Registration 1690–1837', in Glass and Eversley (1965): 379–93.

KREAGER, P. (1988), 'New light on Graunt', *Population Studies*, 42: 129–40.

DE KRUIF, P, (1926), *The Microbe Hunters*, New York, Harcourt Brace.

KUDAT, A., and SABUNCUOGLU, M. (1980), 'The changing composition of Europe's guest worker population', *Monthly Labor Review*, Oct.: 10–17.

KUNZEL, R. (1974), 'The connection between the family cycle and divorce rates: an analysis based on European data', *Journal of Marriage and the Family*, 36: 379–88.

KUNST, A. E., CASPAR, W. N., MACKENBACH, L. and J. P. (1988), 'Medical care and regional mortality differences within the countries of the European Community', *European Journal of Population*, 4, 223–45.

KUSSMAUL, A. (1981), *Servants in Husbandry in Early Modern England*, Cambridge, Cambridge University Press.

KVALE. G., Heuch, I., ELDE, E. (1987), 'A prospective study of reproductive factors and breast cancer, I: Parity', *American Journal of Epidemiology*, 126: 831–41.

LAMB, H. H. (1982), *Climate, History and the Modern World*. London, Methuen.

LAMBERT, P. (1976), 'Perinatal mortality: social and environmental factors', *Population Trends*, 4: 4–8.

LANDERS, J. (1987), 'Mortality and Metropolis: the case of London 1675–1825', *Population Studies*, 41: 59–76.

LANGER, W. L. (1964), 'The Black Death', *Scientific American*, 210, Feb.

——(1972), 'Checks on population growth 1750–1850', *Scientific American*, 226/2: 92–9, Feb.

——(1975), 'American foods and European population growth 1750–1850', *Journal of Social History*, 9: 51.

LANGFORD, C. M. (1976), *Birth Control Practice and Marital Fertility in Great Britain*, London, Population Investigation Committee, London School of Economics.

——(1978), 'A consideration of some retrospective data on breast feeding in Britain', *Journal of Biosocial Science*, 10: 389–400.

——(1982), 'Family size from the child's point of view', *Journal of Biosocial Science*, 14/3: 319–27.

LASKER, G.W. (1985), *Surnames and Genetic Structure*, Cambridge, Cambridge University Press.

LASLETT, P. (1969), 'Size and structure of the household in England over three centuries', *Population Studies*, 23/2: 199–223.

——(ed.) (1972), *Household and Family in Past Time: Comparative Studies in the Size and Structure of the Domestic Group over the Last Three Centuries*, Cambridge, Cambridge University Press.

——(1977), 'Long-term trends in bastardy in England', in *Family Life and Illicit*

Love in Earlier Generations, Cambridge, Cambridge University Press: 102–55.

——(1983), *The World We Have Lost*, 3rd edn., Cambridge, Cambridge University Press.

——and HARRISON, J. (1963), 'Clayworth and Cogenhoe', in H. E. Bell and R. L. Allard (eds.), *Historical Essays 1600–1750 presented to David Ogg*, London, A. & C. Black, 157–84.

——OOSTERVEEN, K., and SMITH, R. M. (eds.) (1980). *Bastardy and its Comparative History: Studies in the History of Illegitimacy and Marital Nonconformism in Britain, France, Sweden, North America, Jamaica, and Japan*, London, Arundel.

LAURITSEN, J. G. (1982), 'The cytogenetics of spontaneous abortion', *Research in Reproduction* 14/3: 3–4, London, International Planned Parenthood Federation.

LAW, C. M. (1967), 'The growth of urban population in England and Wales 1801–1911', *Transactions of the Institute of British Geographers*, 41: 125–43.

——and WARNES, A. M. (1976), 'The changing geography of the elderly in England and Wales', *Transactions Institute of British Geographers*, NS 1/4: 453–71.

————(1980), 'The characteristics of retired migrants', in D. T. Herbert and R. J. Johnston (eds.), *Geography and the Urban Environment*, Chichester, Wiley: 177–222.

————(1982), 'The destination decision in retirement migration', in A. M. Warnes, (ed.), *Geographical Perspectives on the Elderly*, London.

LAWTON, R. (1968), 'The journey to work in Britain: some trends and problems', *Regional Studies*, 2: 27–40.

LAWTON, R. (1967), 'Rural depopulation in nineteenth-century England', in R. W. Steele and R. Lawton (eds.), *Liverpool Essays in Geography*, London, Longmans: 227–55.

——(1977), 'People and work', in J. W. House (ed.), *The UK Space: Resources, Environment and the Future*, 2nd edn., London, Weidenfeld, Nicholson: 109–213.

——(1978), 'Regional population trends in England and Wales 1750–1971', in J. Hobcraft and P. Rees (eds.), *Regional Demographic Development*, London, Croom Helm: 29–70.

LEATHARD, A. (1980), *The Fight for Family Planning*, London, Macmillan.

LEE, P. N. (ed.) (1976), *Statistics of Smoking in the United Kingdom*, Research Paper No. 1, 7th edn., London, Tobacco Research Council.

LEE, R, (1973), 'Population in pre-industrial England: an econometric analysis', *Quarterly Journal of Economics*, 87.

——(1974), 'Estimating series of vital rates and age structure from baptisms and burials: a new technique with applications to pre-industrial England', *Population Studies*, 28: 495–512.

——(1976), 'Demographic forecasting and the Easterlin hypothesis', *Population and Development Review*, 2: 459–68.

——(1986), 'Population homoeostasis and English demographic history', in R. I. Rothberg and T. K. Rabb (eds.), *Population and Economy*, Cambridge, Cambridge University Press: 75–100.

LEE, T. R. (1977), *Race and Residence: The Concentration and Dispersal of*

Immigrants in London, Oxford, Oxford University Press.

LEE, W. R. (ed.) (1979), *European Demography and Economic Growth*, London, Croom Helm.

LEETE, R. (1976), 'Some comments on the demographic and social effects of the 1967 abortion act', *Journal of Biosocial Science*, 8: 229–51.

——(1978), 'One parent families: numbers and characteristics', *Population Trends*, 13: 4–9.

——(1979), *Changing Patterns of Family Formation and Dissolution in England and Wales 1964–1976*, Studies in Medical and Population Subjects No. 39, London, HMSO.

——and ANTHONY, S. (1979), 'Divorce and remarriage: a record linkage study', *Population Trends*, 16: 5–11.

——and FOX, J. (1977), 'Registrar-General's social classes: origin and uses', *Population Trends*, 8: 1–7.

LEFCOURT, H. M. (ed.) (1983), *Research with the Locus of Control Construct*, ii, *Development and Social Problems*, New York, Academic Press.

LE GRAND, J. (1984), *Inequalities in Health and Health Care*, Nuffield/York Portfolios, London, Nuffield Provincial Hospitals Trust.

——(1987), *An International Comparison of Inequalities in Health*, Welfare State Programme Paper No. 16, STICERD, London, London School of Economics.

LEON, A. S., *et al.* (1979), 'Effects of a vigorous walking programme on body composition and carbohydrate and lipid metabolism of obese young men', *American Journal of Clinical Nutrition*, 32: 1776–87.

LEON, D. A. (1988), 'Cancer mortality by social class and occupation 1851–1971', Studies in Medical and Population Subjects 44, London, HMSO.

——and WILKINSON, R. G. (1985), 'Inequalities in prognosis: socioeconomic differences in cancer and heart disease survival'. paper for European Science Foundation Workshop, London, City University.

LERIDON, H. and MENCKEN, J. (1982), *Natural Fertility: Patterns and Determinants*, Liège, Éditions Ordina.

LE ROY LADURIE, E. (1971), *Times of Feast, Times of Famine: A History of Climate since the Year 1000*, London, Croom Helm.

——(1972), 'History and climate', in P. Burke (ed.), *Economy and Society in Early Modern Europe*, London, Routledge & Kegan Paul: 134–69.

LESTHAEGHE, R. (1980): 'On the social control of human reproduction'. *Population and Development Review*, 6: 527–48.

——(1983), 'A century of demographic and cultural change in Western Europe: an explanation of underlying dimensions', *Population and Development Review*, 9/3: 411–35.

——and MEEKERS, D. (1986), 'Value changes and the dimensions of familism in the European Community', *European Journal of Population*, 2: 225–68.

——and SURKYN, J. (1988), 'Cultural Dynamics and Economic Theories of Fertility Change', *Population and Development Review*, 14: 1–45.

LEWES, F. (1983), 'William Farr and cholera', *Population Trends*, 31: 8–12.

LEVI, L. (ed.) (1971). *Society, Stress and Disease*, Oxford, Oxford University Press.

LEWIS, B., HAMMETT, F., KATAN, M., KAY, R. M., MERKX, I., NOBELS, A., MILLER, N. E., SWAN, A, V. (1981), 'Towards an improved lipid-lowering diet: additive effects of changes in nutrient intake', *Lancet*, 2: 1310–13.

LEWIS-FANING, E. (1949), *Report of an Enquiry into Family Limitation and its Influence on Human Fertility During the Past Fifty Years*, Papers of the Royal Commission on Population, vol. i. London, HMSO.

LINDFIELD, H. S. (1931), *Statistics of Jews 1931*, New York, The American Jewish Committee. Reprinted from the *American Jewish Year Book*, vol. 32.

LIVI-BACCI, M. (1983), 'The nutrition mortality link in past times: a comment', *Journal of Interdisciplinary History*, 14/2: 293–8.

LIVINGSTONE, F. B. (1981), 'National selection and the origin and maintenance of genetic marker systems', *Yearbook of Physical Anthropology*, 23: 25–42.

Local Population Studies (Supplement) (1977), *The Plague Reconsidered*, Local Population Studies/SSRC Cambridge Group.

LOGAN, W. P. D. (1982), *Cancer Mortality by Occupation and Social Class 1851–1971*, Studies on Medical and Population Subjects No. 44, London, HMSO.

LORING, J., and Holland, M. (1978), *The Prevention of Cerebral Palsy: The Basic Facts*, London, Spastics Society.

LOSCH, A. (1937), 'Population cycles as a cause of business cycles', *Quarterly Journal of Economics*, Aug.

LOWRY, I. S. (1980), *The Science and Politics of Ethnic Enumeration*, Santa Monica, Rand Corporation.

LUNN, K. (ed.) (1980), *History, Immigrants and Minorities: Historical Responses to Newcomers in British Society 1810–1914*, Folkestone, Dawson.

MCAULEY, W. J., and NUTTY, C. L., (1985), 'Residential satisfaction, community integration and the risk across the family life cycle', *Journal of Marriage and the Family*, 47: 125–9.

MCCARTHY, J. F. (1978), 'A comparison of the probability of the dissolution of first and second marriages', *Demography*, 15: 345–59.

MACLEAN, M., and EKELAAR, J. (1983), *Children and Divorce: Economic Factors*, Oxford, Oxford University Press.

MCCORMICK, A. (1989), 'Estimating the size of the HIV epidemic by using mortality data', *Philosophical Transactions of the Royal Society B*, 325: 125–36.

MCDOWALL, M. (1981), 'Long term trends in seasonal mortality', *Population Trends*, 26: 16–19.

——(1983), 'William Farr 1807–1883: his work in the field of occupational mortality', *Population Trends*, 31: 12–14.

——GOLDBLATT, P. O., and FOX, A. J. (1981), 'Employment during pregnancy and infant mortality', *Population Trends*, 26: 12–15.

MCEVEDY, C., and JONES, R. (1978), *Atlas of World Population History*, Harmondsworth, Penguin.

MCFALLS, J. A., and MCFALLS, M. H. (1984), *Disease and Fertility*, London, Academic Press.

MACFARLANE, ALAN (1978), *The Origins of English Individualism*, Oxford, Basil Blackwell.

——(1986), *Marriage and Love in England 1300–1840*, Oxford, Basil Blackwell.

MACFARLANE, ALISON (1976), 'Daily deaths in Greater London', *Population Trends*, 5: 20–5.

——(1979), 'Child deaths from accidents: place of accident', *Population Trends*, 15: 10–15.

——(1982), 'Infant Deaths After Four Weeks', *Lancet*, 23 Oct. 1982, pp. 929–30.

—— and WHITE, G. (1977), 'Heart attack deaths: the weekly cycle', *Population Trends*, 7: 7–8.

—— and MUGFORD, B. (1980), *Birth Counts*, London, HMSO.

—— and CHALMERS, I (1982), 'Birth, death and the way we live', *The Health Service*, 14 May 1982, pp.12–13.

—— and Fox, J. (1978), 'Child deaths from accidents and violence', *Population Trends*, 12: 22–7.

MACFARLANE BURNET, Sir F. (1980), *Endurance of Life: The Importance of Genetics for Human Life*, Cambridge, Cambridge University Press.

MACGREGOR, G. A., MARKANDU, N. D., SAGNELLA, G. A., SINGER, D. R. J., and CAPPUCCIO, F. P. (1989), 'Double-blind study of three sodium intakes and long-term effects of sodium restriction in essential hypertension', *Lancet*, 2: 1244–7.

McINTOSH, C. A. (1983), *Population Policy in Western Europe: Responses to Low Fertility in France, Sweden and West Germany*, New York, M. E. Shape Inc.

McINTYRE, W. D. (1976), *Colonies into Commonwealth* (rev. edn.), London, Blandford.

MACKAY, D. I., BODDY, D., BRACK, J., DIACK, J. A., and JONES, N., (1971), *Labour Markets under Different Employment Conditions*, London, George Allen & Unwin.

McKEOWN, T. (1976a), *The Role of Medicine: Dream, Mirage or Nemesis*, London, The Rock Carling Fellowship Nuffield Provincial Hospitals Trust.

—— (1976b), *The Modern Rise of Population*, London, Arnold.

—— (1978), 'Fertility, mortality and causes of death', *Population Studies*, 32/3: 535–42.

—— (1988), *The Origins of Human Disease*, Oxford, Basil Blackwell.

—— and BROWN, R. G. (1955), 'Medical evidence related to English population changes in the eighteenth century', *Population Studies*, 9: 119–41.

—— and RECORD, R. G (1963), 'Reasons for the decline in mortality in England and Wales during the 19th century', *Population Studies*, 16: 113–22.

—— (1972), 'An interpretation of the modern rise of population in Europe', *Population Studies*, 26: 345–82.

—— and TURNER, R. D. (1975), 'An interpretation of the decline in mortality in England and Wales during the 20th century', *Population Studies*, 29/3: 391–422.

MACKINNON, A. V. (1987), 'The origin of the modern epidemic of coronary artery disease in England', *Journal of the Royal College of General Practitioners*, 37: 174–6.

McLAREN, A. (1978), *Birth Control in 19th Century England*, London, Croom Helm.

—— (1990), *A History of Contraception from Antiquity to the Present Day*, Oxford, Basil Blackwell.

McNEILL, W. H. (1977), *Plagues and Peoples*, Oxford, Basil Blackwell.

MADDOX, B. (1975), *The Half-Parent*, London, André Deutsch.

MADGE, N. (1988), 'Inheritance, chance and choice in the transmission of poverty', in Keynes, Coleman, and Dimsdale (1988): 26–35.

MAKOWER, H., MARSCHAK, J., and ROBINSON, E. A. G. (1939), *Studies in the Mobility of Labour*, Parts I & II *Oxford Economic Papers* I and II, 83–123, 70–97.

MALTHUS, T. R. (1826), *Essay on the Principle of Population*, 6th edn., ii. 95,

London, repr. Ward Lock 1980.

——(1830), *A summary View of the Principle of Population*, London, John Murray, and in A. Flew (ed.) (1970), *The Principle of Population*, Harmondsworth, Penguin.

——(1836), *Principles of Political Economy considered with a View to their Practical Application* (2nd edn.), London, William Pickering.

MANN, M. (1973), *Workers on the Move*, Cambridge, Cambridge University Press.

MANT, D., VESSEY, M., and LONDON. N. (1988), 'Social class differences in sexual behaviour and cervical cancer', *Community Medicine*, 10/1: 52–6.

MAPLE, P. A. C., HAMILTON-MILLER, J. M. T., and BRUMFITT, W. (1989), 'World antibiotic resistance to methicillin-resistant staphylococcus aureus', *Lancet*, 1: 537–40.

MAPSTONE, E. (1969), 'Children in care', *Concern* 3: 23–8.

MARKUSEN, A. (1985), 'High-tech jobs, markets and economic development: evidence from California', in P. Hall and A. Markusen (eds.) *Silicon Landscapes*, Boston, Allen & Unwin: 35–48.

MARMOT, M. G. (1980), 'Affluence, urbanisation and coronary heart disease', in Clegg and Garlick (1980): 127–44.

——(1984), 'Lifestyle and national and international trends in coronary heart disease mortality', *Postgraduate Medical Journal*, 60: 3–8.

——(1986), 'Social inequalities in mortality: the social environment', in R. G. Wilkinson (ed.), *Health and Class*, London, Tavistock.

——*et al.* (1981*a*), 'Changes in heart disease mortality in England and Wales and other countries', *Health Trends*, 13: 33–8.

——— ROBINSON, N., and ROSE, G. (1978), 'Changing social class distribution of heart disease', *British Medical Journal*, 2: 1109–12.

——and McDOWALL, M. E. (1986), 'Mortality decline and widening social inequalities', *Lancet*, 2: 274–6.

——ROSE, G., SHIPLEY, M., and HAMILTON, P. J. S. (1978), 'Employment grade and coronary heart disease in British Civil Servants', *Journal of Epidemiology and Community Health*, 32: 244–9.

——ADELSTEIN, A., and BULUSU, L. (1983), 'Immigrant mortality in England and Wales 1970–1978', *Population Trends*, 33: 14–17.

——*et al.* (1981*b*), 'Alcohol and mortality: a U-shaped curve', *Lancet*, 14 Mar.: 580–3.

——and SMITH, G. D. (1989), 'Why are the Japanese living longer?', *British Medical Journal*, 299: 1547–51.

——and THEORELL, T. (1989), 'Social class and cardiovascular disease: the contribution of work', *International Journal of Health Services*, 18: 659–74.

MARSHALL, J. and COOPER, C. (1976), *The Mobile Manager and his Wife*, Bradford, MCB Monographs.

MARSHALL, J. D. (1968), *The Old Poor Law 1795–1834*, London, Macmillan.

MARSHALL, J. N. (1988), *Services and Uneven Development*, Oxford, Oxford University Press.

MARSHALL, L. M., 'The rural population of Bedfordshire 1671–1921', *Bedfordshire Historical Records Society*, 16.

MARTIN, J. (1978), *Infant Feeding 1975: Attitudes and Practice in England and Wales*, London, HMSO.

——and Monk, J. (1982), *Infant Feeding 1980*, OPCS Social Survey Division, London, HMSO.

——and Roberts, C. (1984), *Women and Employment: A Lifetime Perspective*, London, HMSO.

Martin. P. L., and Richards, A. (1980), 'International migration of labor: boon or bane?', *Monthly Labor Review*, Oct.: 4–10.

Martin, R. L. (1984), 'Redundancies, labour turnover and employment contraction in the recession: a regional analysis', *Regional Studies*, 18/6: 445–58.

——and Rowthorn, B. (eds.) (1986), *The Geography of De-industralisation*, London, Macmillan.

Mascie-Taylor, C. G. N. (ed.) (1990), *The Biology of Social Class*, Cambridge, Cambridge University Press.

Massey, D. (1984), *Spatial Divisions of Labour*, London, Macmillan.

——and Meegan, R. (1982), *The Anatomy of Job Loss*, London.

Mathias, P. (1972*a*), *Science and Society 1600–1900*, Cambridge, Cambridge University Press.

——(1972*b*), 'Who unbound Prometheus? Science and technical change 1600–1800', in Mathias (1972*a*).

Matras, J. (1965), 'Social strategies of family formation: data from British female cohorts from 1831–1906', *Population Studies*, 19: 167–82.

Mauldin, W. P., and Segal, S. J. (1988), *World Trends in Contraceptive Use, by Method, and their Relationship to Fertility*, Center for Policy Studies Working Papers No. 139, New York, The Population Council.

May, R. and Anderson, R. M. (1987), 'Transmission dynamics of HIV infection', *Nature*, 326: 137–42.

Meade, J. E. (1968), *The Growing Economy: Population Growth and the Standard of Living*, London, Allen & Unwin: 147–87.

Meadow, R. (1989), 'Suffocation', *British Medical Journal*, 298: 1572–3.

Meadows, D. H., Meadows, D. L., Randers, J., and Behrens, W. W (1972), *The Limits to Growth*, London, Earth Island Press.

Medical Council on Alcoholism (1987), *Hazadous Drinking: A Handbook for Medical Practitioners*, London, Medical Council on Alcoholism.

Medical Statistics Division, OPCS (1978), *Social and Biological Factors in Infant Mortality 1975–76*, OPCS Occasional Paper 12, London, HMSO.

Meek, R. L. (ed.) (1953), *Marx and Engels on Malthus*, London, Lawrence and Wishart.

Melia, R. J. W., Florey, C. du V., Altman, D. G., and Swan, A. V. (1977), 'Association between gas cooking and respiratory disease in children', *British Medical Journal*, 2: 149–52.

Menefee, S. P. (1981), *Wives for Sale: An Ethnographic Study of British Popular Divorce*, Oxford, Basil Blackwell.

Menken, J. (1985), 'Age at fertility: how late can you wait?', *Demography*, 22: 4.

Mercer, A. J. (1985), 'Smallpox and the epidemiological–demographic change in Europe: the role of vaccination', *Population Studies*, 39: 287–307.

Metcalf, D. (1975), 'Urban unemployment in England', *Economic Journal*, 85: 578–89.

——and Richardson, R. (1980), 'Unemployment in London', A. Evans and D. Eversley (1980), 193–203.

MICKLEWRIGHT, F. H. (1961), 'Rise and decline of English Malthusianism', *Population Studies*, 15: 32.

MILHAM, S. (1983), *Occupational Mortality in Washington State 1950–1979*, Cincinnati, US Dept. of Health and Human Services.

MILLS, I. (1987), 'Developments in census-taking since 1841', *Population Trends*, 48: 37–44.

MILNER, A. D. (1987), 'Recent theories on the causes of cot death', *British Medical Journal*, 295: 1366–8.

MINFORD, P. (1983), *Unemployment: Cause and Cure*, Oxford, Robertson.

——PEEL, M., and ASHTON, P. (1987), *The Housing Morass: Regulations, Immobility and Unemployment*, Hobart Paperbacks 25, London, Institute of Economic Affairs.

Ministry of Health (1954), *Mortality and Morbidity During the London Fog of December 1952*, Reports on Public Health and Medical Subjects No. 95, London, HMSO.

Ministry of Works and Planning (1942), *Report of the Committee on Land Utilisation in Rural Areas* (Scott Report), Cmd. 6378, London, HMSO.

MITCHELL, B. R. (1980), *European Historical Statistics 1750–1975*, 2nd (revised) edn., London, Macmillan.

MITCHISON, R. (1977), *British Population Change Since 1860*, London, Macmillan.

MOISLEY, H. A. (1962), 'Population changes and the Highland problem 1951–61', *Scottish Studies*, 6: 194–200.

MONTESQUIEU, C. L. DE S., Baron de la (1729, 1964), *Œuvres complètes*, Paris, Éditions du Seuil.

Morgan Grenfell Economics (1987), 'Housing Inheritance and Wealth', *Morgan Grenfell Economic Review*, 45: 22.

MORRILL, R. L., and PITTS, F. R. (1967), 'Marriage, migration and the mean information field: a study of uniqueness and generality', *Annals of the Association of American Geographers*, 57: 401–22.

MORRIS, C. (1971), 'The plague in Britain', *Historical Journal*, 14/1: 205–15.

MOSER, C. A. (1972), 'Statistics about immigrants: objectives, sources, methods and problems', *Social Trends*, 3: 20–30.

MOSER. K. A., GOLDBLATT, P. O., FOX, A. J., and JONES, D. R. (1987), 'Unemployment and mortality: comparison of the 1971 and 1981 Longitudinal Study census samples', *British Medical Journal*, 294: 86–90.

MOSS, P. (1980), *Patterns of Child Care and Child Rearing Practice: The Effects on them of Recent Social and Demographic Movements for Women*, BSPS Conference on the Implications of Current Demographic Trends in the UK for social and economic policy, OPCS Occasional Paper 19/2, London, HMSO.

MUELLBAUER, J., and MURPHY, A. (1988), *UK House Prices and Migration: Economic and Investment Implications*, London, Shearson, Lehman, Hutton Securities.

Multiple Risk Factor Intervention Trial Research Group (MRFIT) (1982), 'Multiple risk factor intervention trial', *Journal of the American Medical Association*, 248: 1465–8.

MURIE, A. (1974), *Household Movement and Housing Choice*, Centre for Urban and Regional Studies, Occasional Paper 28, University of Birmingham.

MURPHY, J. F., NEWCOMBE, R. G., and SIBERT, J. R. (1982), 'The epidemiology of sudden infant death syndrome, *Journal of Epidemiology and Community Health*, 36: 17–21.

MURPHY, M. (1983), 'The life course of individuals in the family: describing static and dynamic aspects of the contemporary family', in *The Family*, OPCS Occasional Paper No. 31, London, OPCS, 50–70.

—— (1985*a*), 'Marital breakdown and socio-economic status: a reappraisal of the evidence from recent British sources', *British Journal of Sociology*, 36: 81–93.

—— (1985*b*), 'Demographic and socio-economic influences on recent British marital breakdown patterns', *Population Studies*, 39: 441–60.

—— (1987), 'Differential family formation in Great Britain', *Journal of Biosocial Science*, 19: 463–81.

—— (1989), 'Housing the people: from shortage to surplus?', in H. Joshi (ed.), *The Changing Population of Britain*, Oxford, Basil Blackwell: 90–109.

—— and SULLIVAN, O. (1985), 'Housing tenure and family formation in contemporary Britain', *European Sociological Review*, 1: 230–43.

MUTHESIUS, S. (1982), *The English Terraced House*, New Haven, Conn., Yale University Press.

National Audit Office (1989), *Report for the Comptroller and Auditor General NHS: Coronary Heart Disease*, London, HMSO.

National Birth Rate Commission (1916), *The Declining Birth Rate: Being the First Report and Evidence of the National Birth Rate Commission 1916*, London, National Birth Rate Commission.

—— (1920), *Problems of Population and Parenthood: Being the Second Report of the Commission and Evidence 1920*, London, National Birth Rate Commission.

National Board for Health and Welfare (1980), *The Swedish Cancer Environment Registry 1961–1973*, Stockholm.

National Center for Health Statistics (1989), *Induced Termination of Pregnancy; Reporting States 1985 and 1986*, Monthly Vital Statistics Report 37, 12 (PHS) 89–1120, Public Health Service, Maryland.

National Consumer Council (1984), *Moving Home*, London, National Consumer Council.

National Dwelling and Housing Survey (1979, 1980). *Phase II and III*, Department of Environment, London, HMSO.

National Family Trust (1989), *Facing up to Family Income: Reversing the Economic Disvestment of the Family*, London, National Family Trust.

National Food Survey Committee, Ministry of Agriculture, Fisheries and Food (1952–89), *Household Food Consumption and Expenditure 1950–1988*, Annual Reports of the National Food Survey Committee, London, HMSO.

National Housing Forum (1989), *Housing Needs in the 1990s*, London, National Federation of Housing Associations.

National Mobility Office (1987), *Annual Report*, London, National Mobility Office.

National Radiological Protection Board (NRPB) (1986), *Living with Radiation*, Didcot, NRPB.

—— (1987), *Exposure to Radon Daughters in Dwellings*, Series GS6, Chilton, NRPB.

Nationwide Building Society (1982), *House Buyers Moving*, London.

—— (1983), *Home Owners on the Move*, London.

—— (1987), *House Prices: The North/South divide: Who gains: Who loses?*, London, Nationwide BS.

NEDO (1988), *Young People and the Labour Market: A Challenge for the 1990s*, London, National Economic Development Office.

NEWBY, H. (1985), *Green and Pleasant Land? Social Change in Rural England*, London, Wildwood House.

NEWCOMBE, R. (1978), *Perinatal Mortality and Low Birthweight 1965–73*, OPCS Occasional Paper 7, London, HMSO.

NEWELL, C. (1988), *Methods and Models in Demography*, London, Belhaven Press.

NEWMAN, D. (1978), *Practical Problems of Sampling in the Census of Population/ Techniques for Ensuring the Confidentiality of Census Information in Great Britain*, OPCS Occasional Paper 4, London, HMSO.

NEWMAN BROWN, W. (1986), 'The receipt of poor relief and family situation: Aldenham, Hertfordshire 1630–90' in R. M. Smith (ed.), *Land, Kinship and Life Cycle*, Cambridge, Cambridge University Press.

NEWSHOLME, A., and STEVENSON, T. H. C. (1906), 'The decline in human fertility in the United Kingdom and other countries, as shown by the corrected birth-rates', *Journal of the Royal Statistical Society*, 69: 34–87.

Ní BHROLCHÁIN, M. (1986*a*), 'The interpretation and role of work-associated accelerated childbearing in post-war Britain', *European Journal of Population*, 2: 135–54.

—— (1986*b*), 'Women's paid work and the timing of births: longitudinal evidence', *European Journal of Population*, 2: 43–70.

—— (1987), 'Period parity progression ratios and birth intervals in England and Wales 1941–1971: a synthetic life table analysis', *Population Studies*, 41: 103–26.

NICHOLLS, P. (1989), speech to Health Education Authority, London, June 19.

NICHOLSON, K. G., and WISELKA, M. J. (1989), 'Infectious diseases: a review', *Journal of the Royal College of Physicians of London*, 23: 147–51.

NICOLSON, C. (1976), *Strangers to England: Immigration to England 1100–1952*, London, Wayland.

NILSSON, T. (1985), 'Les Ménages en Suède 1960–1980', *Population*, 40/2: 223–48.

NIXON, P. G. F. (1982), 'Stress and the cardiovascular system', *Practitioner*, 226.

NIZARD,, A. and PRIOUX, F. (1975), 'La Mortalité départementale en France', *Population*, 4–5.

NORA, S., and MINC, A. (1978), *L'Informatisation de la société*, Paris, La Documentation française.

NOTESTEIN, F. W. (1945), 'Population: the long view', in T. W. Schultz (ed.), *Food for the World*, Chicago University Press.

NOVE, A. (1990), 'How many victims in the 1930s? II', *Soviet Studies*, 42: 811–18.

Nuffield Provincial Hospitals Trust (1987), *Report of a Confidential Inquiry into Perioperative Deaths*, London, Nuffield Provincial Hospitals Trust.

NUGENT, J. B. (1985), 'The old age security motive for fertility', *Population and Development Review*, 11: 75–98.

ODDY, D. J. (1982), 'The health of the people', in T. Bowker, and M. Drake (eds.), *Population and Society in Britain 1850–1980*, London, Batsford: 120–39.

OECD (annual), *Report of the SOPEMI Committee*, Paris, OECD.

Office of Health Economics (OHE) (1988), *HIV and AIDS in the United Kingdom*,

OHE Briefing No. 23, Jan., London, OHE.

OGBORN, M.E. (1962), *Equitable Assurances*, London, Allen & Unwin.

OGDEN, P. E. (1973), *Marriage Patterns and Population Mobility: A Study in Rural France*, Oxford, School of Geography Research Paper 7.

—— and HUSS, M. (1982), 'Demography and pronatalism in France in the 19th and 20th centuries', *Journal of Historical Geography*, 8/3: 283–98.

OGILVY, A. A. (1979), 'Migration: the influence of economic change', *Futures*, 11/5: 383–94.

—— (1980), *Inter-regional Migration since 1971: An Appraisal of Data from the NHS Central Register and Labour Force Surveys*, OPCS Occasional Paper 16, London, HMSO.

—— (1982), 'Population migration between the regions of Great Britain 1971–9, *Regional Studies*, 16/1: 65–73.

O'GRADA, C. (1984), *Did Catholics always have Larger Families? Religion, Wealth and Fertility in Rural Ulster before 1911*, CEPR Discussion Paper No. 6, London, CEPR.

—— (1985), *On Two Aspects of Postwar Irish Immigration*, CEPR Discussion Paper No. 52, London, CEPR.

OLIVER, F. R. (1964), 'Inter-regional migration and unemployment, 1951–61, *Journal of the Royal Statistical Society*, Series A. 127: 42–75.

OLIVER, M. F. (1982), 'Does control of risk factors prevent coronary heart disease?', *British Medical Journal*, 285: 1065–6.

OPCS (1978), *Demographic Review: A Report on Population in Great Britain*, Series DR No. 1, London, HMSO.

—— (1978a), *Trends in Mortality 1951–1975*, Series DH 7, No.3, London, HMSO.

—— (1978b) *Occupational Mortality 1979–1972*, Series DS, No. 1, London, HMSO.

—— (1979a), *Area Mortality Tables: The Registrar-General's Decennial Supplement for England and Wales 1969–1973*, Series DS, No. 3, London, HMSO.

—— (1979b), *Projections of the New Commonwealth and Pakistani Population*, OPCS Monitor PP2 79/1, London, HMSO.

—— (1980), *Population and Health Statistics in England and Wales*, London, OPCS.

—— (1980a), *The National Dwelling and Housing Survey 1977–78*, London, HMSO.

—— (1980b), *The Classification of Occupations 1980*, London, HMSO.

—— (1980c), *Tests of an Ethnic Question*, OPCS Monitor CEN 80/2, London, OPCS.

—— (1981a), *Trends in Respiratory Mortality 1951–1975*, Series DH1 No. 7, London, HMSO.

—— (1981b), *OPCS Monitor PP1 81/6: Mid-1980 Estimates of the Population of New Commonwealth and Pakistani Ethnic Origin*, London, OPCS.

—— (1981c), *Area Mortality Decennial Supplement 1969–73*, Series DS, No. 4, London, HMSO.

—— (1981d), *Adult Height and Weights Survey 1980*, Monitor SS 81/1, London, HMSO.

—— (1982a), *OPCS Monitor MB3 82/1: Congenital Malformations and Parents' Occupations*, London, OPCS.

—— (1982*b*), 'Family and household statistics from the 1981 Census', *Population Trends*, 27: 14.

—— (1982*c*), 'Sources of statistics on ethnic minorities', *Population Trends*, 28: 1–8 (editorial); also pub. as *OPCS Monitor PP1 82/1*, London, OPCS.

—— (1983), *Congenital Malformation Statistics: Notifications 1971–1980*, Series MB3, No. 1, London, HMSO.

—— (1983*a*), *Fertility Report from the 1971 Census: Decennial Supplement*, Series DS, No. 5, London, HMSO.

—— (1983*b*), *Census 1981: Country of Birth Great Britain*, CEN 81 CB, London, HMSO.

—— (1983*c*), *OPCS Monitor LFS 83/1: Labour Force Survey 1981: Country of Birth and Ethnic Origin*, London, OPCS.

—— (1983*d*), *OPCS Monitor PP1 83/2: Mid-1981 Estimates of the Population of New Commonwealth and Pakistani Ethnic Origin*, London, OPCS.

—— (1983*e*), *Mortality Statistics 1978 (Sample): Comparisons of 8th and 9th Revisions of the International Classification of Diseases*, Series DH1, No. 10, London, HMSO.

—— (1983*f*), *Cancer Registration 1979 and 1980 (Estimates)*, OPCS Monitor MB1 83/1, London, OPCS.

—— (1983*g*), *Drinking Behaviour and Attitudes in Great Britain*, Monitor SS 83/1, London, OPCS.

—— (1983*h*), *Recently Moving Households: A Follow-up to the 1978 National Dwelling and Housing Survey*, London, HMSO.

—— (1984), *Trends in Conceptions to Women Resident in England and Wales 1970–1980*, OPCS Monitor FMI, London, OPCS.

—— (1985*a*), *OPCS Monitor LFS 85/1: Labour Force Survey 1984: Country of Birth, Ethnic Group, Year of Entry and Nationality*, London, HMSO.

—— (1985*b*), *William Farr 1807–1883: Commemorative Symposium*, OPCS Occasional Paper 33, London, OPCS.

—— (1986*a*), *Births by Birthplace of Parent 1985*, OPCS Monitor FM1 86/5, London, OPCS.

—— (1986*b*), *Fertility Trends in England and Wales 1975–1985*, Monitor FM2 86/3, London, OPCS.

—— (1986*c*), *Occupational Mortality: The Registrar-General's Decennial Supplement for Great Britain 1979–80, 1982–83*, Series DS, No. 6, Part 1 Commentary, Part 2, Microfiche Tables, London, HMSO.

—— (1986*d*), *OPCS Monitor LFS 86/2: Labour Force Survey 1985: Ethnic Group and Country of Birth*, London, OPCS.

—— (1987*a*), *People Count: A History of the General Register Office*, London, HMSO.

—— (1987*b*), *Trends in Conceptions to Women Resident in England and Wales: 1975–85*, Monitor FM1 87/2, London, OPCS.

—— (1987*c*), *Population Projections: 1985 Based*, Series PP. 2, No. 15, London, HMSO.

—— (1987*d*), *English Life Tables No. 14, 1980–1982*, Series DS, No. 7, London, HMSO.

—— (1987*e*), *Morbidity Statistics from General Practice*, London, HMSO.

—— (1987*f*), *Mortality Statistics 1985: Accidents and Violence*, Series DH4, No.

11, London, HMSO.

—— (1987*g*), *Mortality Statistics 1985: Area*, Series DH5, No.12, London, HMSO.

—— (1987*h*), *Monitor DH3 87/4: Infant and Perinatal Mortality 1986: DHAs*, London, OPCS.

—— (1987*i*), *Communicable Disease Statistics 1985: Statistical Tables*, Series MB2, No. 12, London, HMSO.

—— (1987*j*). *Mortality Statistics 1985: Childhood*, Series DH3, No. 19, London, HMSO.

—— (1987*k*), *Mortality Statistics: Serial Tables: Review of the Registrar-General on Deaths in England and Wales 1841–1980*, Series DH1, No. 15, London, HMSO.

—— (1987*l*), *Mortality Statistics 1985*, Series DH1, No. 17, London, HMSO.

—— (1987*m*), *Birth Statistics: Historical Series of Statistics from Registrations of Births in England and Wales 1837–1983*, Series FM1, No.13, London, HMSO.

—— (1988*a*), *Congenital Malformation Statistics 1981–1985: Notification*, Series MB3, No. 2, London, HMSO.

—— (1988*b*), *Census 1971–1981: The Longitudinal Study*, London, HMSO.

—— (1988*c*), *Occupational Mortality Supplement 1979–80, 1982–83 (Childhood)*, Series DS, No. 8, London, HMSO.

—— (1988*d*), *Mortality Statistics 1986 Perinatal and Infant: Social and Biological Factors*, Series DH3, No. 20, London, HMSO.

—— (1989*a*), *Population Projections: Population Projections by Sex and Age for United Kingdom, Great Britain and Constituent Countries from Mid-1987*, Series PP2, No. 16, London, HMSO.

—— (1989*b*), *Population Projections: Mid-1987 Based*, Monitor PP2 89/1, London, OPCS.

—— (1989*c*), *Birth Statistics 1987*, Series FM1, No. 16, London, HMSO.

—— (1989*d*), *Marriage and Divorce Statistics 1987*, Series FM2, No. 14, London, HMSO.

—— (1989*e*), *Mortality Statistics 1987:Cause*, Series DH2, No. 14, London, HMSO.

—— (1989*f*), *Communicable Disease Statistics 1987*, Series MB2, No. 14, London, HMSO.

—— (1989*g*), *Mortality Statistics 1987:General*, Series DH1, No. 20, London, HMSO.

—— (1989*h*), *Monitor DH3 89/1: Infant and Perinatal Mortality 1988: DHAs*, London, OPCS.

—— (1989*i*), *Mortality Statistics 1988: Area*, Series DH5, No. 13, London, HMSO.

—— (1989*j*), *Mortality Statistics 1841–1985: Serial Tables*, Series DH1, No. 19, London, HMSO.

—— (1989*k*), *Labour Force Survey 1987*, Series LFS, No. 7, London, HMSO.

—— (1990*a*), *Congenital Malformation Statistics 1988: Notifications*, Series MB3, No.4, London, HMSO.

—— (1990*b*), *Monitor SS90/3: General Household Survey: Preliminary Results for 1989*, London, OPCS.

—— (1990*c*), *Mortality Statistics 1988 Cause*, Series DH2, No. 15, London, HMSO.

—— (1990*d*), *Communicable Disease Statistics 1988*, Series MB2, No. 15, London, HMSO.

—— (1990*e*), *Monitor SS90/2: Cigarette Smoking 1972 to 1988*, London, OPCS.

—— (1990*f*), *Monitor PP1 90/1: Mid-1989 Population Estimates for England and Wales*, Lonodn, OPCS.

—— /BSPS (1983), *The Family*, OPCS Occasional Paper No. 31, in conjunction with the British Society for Population Studies, London, OPCS.

—— /GRO (Scotland) (1977), *Guide to Census Reports: Great Britain 1801–1966*, London, HMSO.

—— Population Statistics Division/Home Office Statistical Department (1979), *Immigration Statistics: Sources and Definitions*, London, HMSO.

OPPENHEIMER, V. K. (1976), 'The Easterlin Hypothesis: another aspect of the echo to consider', *Population and Development Review*, 2: 433–58.

—— (1982), *Work and the Family: A Study in Social Demography*, New York, Academic Press.

O'RIORDAN, M. C. (1988), 'Notes on radon risks in houses', *Radiological Protection Bulletin*, 89: 13–14.

OSBORN, A. F., BUTLER, N. R., and MORRIS, A. C. (1984), *The Social Life of Britain's Five-Year-Olds: A Report of the Child Health and Education Study*, London, Routledge & Kegan Paul.

—— and MORRIS, T. C., 'The rationale for a composite index of social class and its evaluation', *British Journal of Sociology*, 30: 39–60.

OSMOND, C., GARDNER, M. J., and Acheson, E. D. (1982), 'Analysis of trends in cancer mortality in England and Wales during 1951–1980 separating changes associated with period of birth and period of death', *British Medical Journal*, 284: 1005–8.

OVERTON, E., and ERMISCH, J. (1984), 'Minimal Household Units', *Population Trends*, 35: 18–22.

OWEN, D. W., GILLESPIE, A. E., and COOMBES, M. G. (1984), 'Job shortfalls in British local labour market areas: a classification of labour supply and demand trends, 1971–81', *Regional Studies*, 18/6: 469–88.

PAHL, R. E. (1984), *Divisions of Labour*, Oxford, Basil Blackwell.

PAIN, A. J., and SMITH, M. (1984), 'Do marriage horizons accurately measure migration? A test case from Stanhope Parish, County Durham', *Local Population Studies*, 33: 44–8.

PAMUK, E. R. (1988), 'Social class inequality in infant mortality in England and Wales from 1921 to 1980', *European Journal of Population*, 4: 1–21.

PARKER, G. (1988), *The Military Revolution*, Cambridge, Cambridge University Press.

PARKER, S. (1975), 'Assisted Labour Migration', OPCS Social Survey Division (unpublished).

PARKES, A. S. (1976), *Patterns of Sexuality and Reproduction*, Oxford, Oxford University Press.

PARKES, C. M., BENJAMIN, B., and FITZGERALD, R. G. (1969), 'Broken heart: a statistical study of increased mortality among widowers', *British Medical Journal* 1: 740–3.

Parliamentary Group on the Feasibility and Usefulness of a Register of Dependants (1977), *Reports*, Cmnd. 6698, London, HMSO.

PARRY, H. B. (ed.) (1974), *Population: A Plain Man's Guide*, Oxford, Oxford University Press.

PASSMORE, R., and EASTWOOD, M. A. (1986), *Davidson's Human Nutrition and*

PATTEN, J. (1973), *Rural–Urban Migration in Pre-Industrial England*, Oxford, School of Geography Research Paper No. 6.

PATTERSON, S. (1963), *Dark Strangers*, London, Tavistock.

PEACH, G. C. K. (1966), 'Under-enumeration of West Indians in the 1961 census', *Sociological Review, 14: 73–80.*

——*(1968), West Indian Migration to Britain: A Social Geography*, London, Oxford University Press for Institute of Race Relations.

——(1978/9), 'British unemployment cycles and West Indian immigration 1955–74', *New Community*, 7: 40–4.

——(1981), 'Ins and outs of Home Office and IPS migration data', *New Community*, 9: 117–19.

——(1982), 'The growth and distribution of immigrant population in the United Kingdom', in D. A. Coleman (ed.), *The Demography of Immigrants and Minority Groups in the United Kingdom*, London, Academic Press.

——(1990), 'The Muslim population of Great Britain', *Ethnic and Racial Studies*, 13: 414–19.

ROBINSON, V., MAXTED, J., and CHANCE, J. (1988), 'Immigration and ethnicity', in A. H. Halsey (ed.), *British Social Trends since 1900*, London, Macmillan.

——and WINCHESTER, S. W. C. (1974); 'Birthplace, ethnicity and the under-enumeration of West Indians, Indians and Pakistanis in the Census of 1966 and 1971', *New Community*, 3: 386.

——and SMITH, S. (eds.) (1981), *Ethnic Segregation in Cities*, London, Croom Helm.

PEARCE, D. (1983), 'Population in communal establishments', *Population Trends*, 33: 14–17.

——and BRITTON, M. (1977), 'The decline in births: some socio-economic aspects', *Population Trends*, 7: 9–14.

——and FARID, S. (1977), 'Illegitimate births: changing patterns', *Population Trends*, 9: 20–3.

PEARCE, J. L. (1981), 'Care of the premature baby: needs and prospects', in R. Chester, P. Diggory, and M. B. Sutherland (eds.), *Changing Patterns of Child-Bearing and Child-Rearing*, London, Academic Press.

PEARLIN, L. I. and SCHOOLER, C. (1978), 'The structure of coping', *Journal of Health and Social Behaviour*, 19: 2–21.

PECK, F. W. (1984), 'An analysis of publicly-announced redundancies within named UK corporations', paper presented at Annual Conference, Institute of British Geographers, Durham.

PELLER, S. (1965), 'Births and deaths among Europe's ruling families since 1500', in Glass and Eversley (1965).

PENHALE, B. (1989), 'Association between unemployment and fertility among young women in the early 1980s', LS Working Paper No. 60, London, City University.

PERRY, R., DEAN, K., and BROWN, B. (1986), *Counterurbanisation: International Case Studies of Socio-economic Changes in Rural Areas*, Norwich, Geobooks.

PETERSEN, W. (1975), *Population* (3rd edn.), London, Macmillan.

PETO, R. (1980), 'Distorting the epidemiology of cancer: the need for a more balanced overview', *Nature* 284: 297–300.

PEYTON, S. A. (1915), 'The village population in Tudor lay subsidy rolls', *English*

Historical Review, 30: 234–50.

PHARAOH, P. O. D., and MACFARLANE, A. J. (1982), *Recent Trends in Postneonatal Mortality: Studies in Sudden Infant Death*, Studies in Medical and Population Subjects No. 45, London, HMSO.

—— COOKE, T., ROSENBLOOM, I., and COOKE, R. W. I. (1987), 'Trends in the birth prevalence of cerebral palsy', *Archives of Diseases in Childhood*, 62: 379–89.

PHELPS BROWN, E. H. and HOPKINS, S. V. (1955), 'Seven centuries of building wages', in E. M. Carus-Wilson (ed.) *Essays in Economics History*, ii: 167–78, London.

PHILLIPS, G. A., and MADDOCK, R. T. (1973), *The Growth of the British Economy 1918–68*, London, Allen & Unwin.

PHILLIPS, R. (1988), *Putting Asunder: A History of Divorce in Western Society*, Cambridge, Cambridge University Press.

PIKE, M. C., HENDERSON, B.E., KRAILO, M.D., DUKE, A., and ROY, S. (1983), 'Breast cancer in young women and the use of oral contraception: possible modifying effect of formulation and age at use', *Lancet*, 2: 926–9.

PISA, Z., and VEMUCA, K. (1982), 'Trends of mortality from IHD and other cardiovascular disease in 27 countries 1968–1977', *World Health Statistics Quarterly*, 35: 11.

PLUMB, J. H. (1950), *England in the Eighteenth Century*, Harmondsworth, Penguin.

—— (1976), 'The New World of children', *Listener*, 26 Feb.: 232–3.

POCOCK, S. J., and ASHBY, D. (1985), 'Environmental lead and children's intelligence: a review of recent epidemiological studies', *Statistician*, 34: 31–44.

—— SHAPER, A. G., COOK, D. G., PACKHAM, R. F., LACEY, R. F., POWELL, P., and RUSSELL, P. F. (1980), 'British regional heart study: geographic variations in cardiovascular mortality and the role of water quality', *British Medical Journal*, 280: 1243–9.

POIKOLAINEN, K. (1982), 'Alcohol use and mortality', in S. Preston (ed.), *Biological and Social Aspects of Mortality and the Length of Life*, Liège, Éditions Ordina: 417–32.

Political and Economic Planning (PEP) (1948), *Population Policy in Great Britain*, London, PEP.

POLLARD, A. H., YUSUF, F., and POLLARD, G. N. (1981), *Demographic Techniques* (2nd edn.), Oxford, Pergamon.

Population Reports (1983), 'Infertility and sexually transmitted disease: a public health challenge', *Population Reports*, Series L, No. 4 (July).

Population Statistics Division, OPCS (1982), 'Recent population growth and the effect of the decline in births', *Population Studies*, 27: 18–24.

—— (1986a), 'Estimating the size of the ethnic minority populations in the 1980s', *Population Trends*, 44: 23–7.

—— (1986b), 'Ethnic minority populations in Great Britain', *Population Trends*, 46: 18–21.

—— /Statistical Division, Home Office (1979), *Immigration Statistics: Sources and Definitions*, OPCS Occasional Paper 15, London, HMSO.

POSTAN, M. M. (1950), 'Some economic evidence of declining population in the later middle ages', *Economic History Review*, 2: 221–46.

—— (1966), 'Agrarian society in its prime: England: the land, population', in M.

M. Postan (ed.), *Cambridge Economic History of Europe, The Agrarian Life of the Middle Ages*, 2nd edn., Cambridge, Cambridge University Press: 549–76.

——(1972), *The Medieval Economy and Society*, London, Weidenfeld and Nicholson.

POTTS, M., DIGGORY, P., and PEEL, J. (1977), *Abortion*, Cambridge, Cambridge University Press.

POTTS, W. T. W. (1987), 'Blood group analysis and the history of settlement in Ireland', *Biology and Society*, 4/1: 12–28.

POUAK, R. A., and WALES, T. S. (1981), 'Demographic variables in demand analysis', *Econometrica*, 49/6: 1533–51.

POWER, A. (1988), *Council Housing: Conflict, Change and Decision Making*, Discussion paper WSP/27, STICERD, London, London School of Economics.

PRATT, O. (1981), 'Alcohol and the woman of child-bearing age: a public health problem', *British Journal of Addiction*, 76: 383.

PRESTON, B. (1978), 'Further statistics of inequality', *Sociological Review*, 27/2: 343–50.

PRESTON, P., HALL, P., and BEVAN, N. (1985), *Innovation in Information Technology Industries in Great Britain*, Geographical Papers 89, University of Reading, Dept. of Geography.

PRESTON, S. H. (1975), 'The changing relation between mortality and level of economic development', *Population Studies*, 29: 231–48.

——(1976), *Mortality Patterns in National Population with Special Reference to Recorded Causes of Death*, London, Academic Press.

——(1982) (ed.), *Biological and Social Aspects of Mortality and the Length of Life*, Liège, Éditions Ordina.

——(1984), 'Children and the elderly: divergent paths for America's dependents', *Demography*, 21: 435–57.

——and NEBAN, V. E. (1974), 'Structure and change in causes of death: an international summary', *Population Studies*, 28: 1.

PRICE, R., and BAIN, G. S. (1988), 'The labour force', in A. H. Halsey (ed.), *British Social Trends since 1900*, London, Macmillan.

Public Attitude Surveys Ltd. (1989), *PAS Drinks Market Survey*, High Wycombe, Public Attitude Surveys Ltd.

Public Health Laboratory Service (1988a), Report from the PHLS Communicable Diseases Surveillance Centre, *British Medical Journal*, 296: 778–90.

——(1988b), 'Human Immunodeficiency virus infection in the UK: Quarterly Report 2', *Journal of Infection*, 17: 71–82.

PUGH, H., POWER, C., and GOLDBLATT, P. (1989), 'Smoking, class and lung cancer mortality among women', LS Working Paper No. 62, London, City University.

PUSKA, P., et al. (1979), 'Changes in coronary risk factors during comprehensive five year community programme to control cardiovascular disease (North Karelia project), *British Medical Journal*, 2: 1173–8.

RACKHAM, O. (1985), *The English Countryside*, London, J. M. Dent.

RAPOPORT, R., and RAPOPORT, R. N. (eds.), (1981), *Families in Britain*, London, Routledge & Kegan Paul.

RAVENHOLT, R. T. (1990), 'Tobacco's global death march', *Population and Development Review*, 16: 213–40.

RAYNER, M. (1989), 'The truth about the British diet', *New Scientist*, 22 July: 44–7.

RAZI, Z. (1980), *Life, Marriage, and Death in a Medieval Parish: Economy, Society and Demography in Halesowen 1270–1400*, Cambridge, Cambridge University Press.

RAZZELL, P. E. (1965), 'Population change in 18th century England: a reappraisal', *Economic History Review*, 18: 315–6.

——(1974), 'An interpretation of the modern rise of population in Europe: a critique', *Population Studies*, 28: 5–18.

——(1977), *The Conquest of Smallpox*, Firle, Sussex, Caliban Books.

REDCLIFFE-MAUD, Lord (1969), *Royal Commission on Local Government in England*, Cmnd. 4039, London, HMSO.

REDDAWAY, W. B. (1939), *The Economics of a Declining Population*, London, Allen & Unwin.

REES, M. (1987), 'The sombre view of AIDS', *Nature*, 326: 343–5.

——(1990), 'Short-term prediction of HIV infection and AIDS: a critique of the Working Group's Report to the Department of Health', *International Journal of STD and AIDS*, 1: 10–17.

REES, P. H. (1979), *Migration and Settlement*: i: *United Kingdom*, Laxenburg, IIASA.

——(1986), 'A geographical forecast of the demand for student places', *Transactions' Institute of British Geographers*, 11/1: 5–26.

——(1989), 'Where is the population headed?', paper presented to BSPS meeting, London School of Economics, June.

Registrar-General (1848), *Ninth Annual Report of the Registrar-General* (for 1846) Parliamentary Papers 1847–8 XXV [996.], London, HMSO.

——(1849), *Appendix to Ninth Annual Report*, Parliamentary Papers XXI [1087.], London, HMSO.

——(1853), *Fourteenth Annual Report of the Registrar-General* (for 1851), Parliamentary Papers 1852–3 XL [1665.], London, HMSO, pp. xv–xxiii

——(1885), *Forty Sixth Annual Report of the Registrar-General (abstracts of 1883)*, Parliamentary Papers 1884–5 XVIII [C.4424], London, HMSO.

——(1893), *Census of England and Wales 1891 Volume IV: General Report*, Parliamentary Papers 1893–4 CVI [C.7222], London, HMSO: 5–7.

——(1904), *Census of England and Wales 1901: General Report*, Parliamentary Papers 1904 CVIII [Cd. 2174], London, HMSO.

——(1933), *Registrar-General's Statistical Review* 1931: Part 3—Commentary, London, HMSO: 102.

——(1954), *Registrar-General's Statistical Review of England and Wales, 1946–1950: Text, Civil*, London, HMSO.

——(1963), *Registrar-General's Statistical Review for 1961: Part III—Commentary*, London, HMSO.

——(1970a), *Registrar-General's Statistical Review 1966: Part 3—Commentary*, London, HMSO.

——(1970b), The International Passenger Survey, *Registrar-General's Statistical Review 1966, Part 3—Commentary*, London, HMSO: 10–5

——(1971), *Registrar-General's Statistical Review 1967: Part III—Commentary*, London, HMSO.

——(1971a), *Decennial Supplement England and Wales 1961, Occupational Mortality Tables*, London, HMSO.

Registrar-General for Northern Ireland (1990), *Seventy-seventh Annual Report of the Registrar-General 1988*, Belfast, HMSO.
Registrar-General for Scotland (1981), *Occupational Mortality 1969–1973*, Edinburgh, General Register Office.
——(1990), *Annual Report 1988*, Edinburgh, HMSO.
REID, D. D., HAMILTON, P. J. S., McCARTNEY, P. ROSE, G., JARRELT, R. J., and KEEN, H. (1976), 'Smoking and other risk factors for cardiovascular heart disease in British Civil Servants', *Lancet* 7993: 979–84, 6 Nov.
REISCHAUER, E. O. (1981), *The Japanese*, Cambridge, Mass., Harvard University Press.
Relate (1989), *Annual Report*, Rugby, Relate (formerly Marriage Guidance Council).
RENFREW, C. (1987), *Archaeology and Language*, London, Jonathan Cape.
Resource Allocation Working Party (RAWP) (1976), *Report: Sharing Resources for Health in England*, London, HMSO.
REX, J. A., and MOORE, R. (1967), *Race, Community and Conflict*, Oxford, Oxford University Press.
RHODES, T. and NACCACHE, J. A. (1977), 'Population forecasting in Oxfordshire', *Population Trends*, 7: 2–6.
RICH, E. E. (1950), 'The population of Elizabethan England', *Economic History Review*, 2nd Series 11/3: 247–65.
RICH, P. B. (1986), *Race and Empire in British Politics*, Cambridge, Cambridge University Press.
RICKMAN, J. (1802), *Observations on the Results of the Population Act 41 Geo III*, London, HMSO.
——(1843), *Enumeration Abstract*, 1841 Census (Preface): 34–7.
RILEY, D., and SHAW, M. (1985), *Parental Supervision and Juvenile Delinquency*, Home Office Research Study Report No. 83, London, Home Office.
ROBERTS, D. F., and CHESTER, R. (eds.) (1981), *Changing Patterns of Conception and Fertility.*, London, Academic Press.
——and SUNDERLAND, E. (eds.) (1973), *Genetical Variation in Britain*, London, Taylor and Francis.
——and THOMSON, A. M. (eds.), (1976), *The Biology of Human Fetal Growth*, London, Taylor and Francis.
ROBERTS, H., and BARKER, R. (1987), 'What are people doing when they grade women's work?', LS Working Paper No. 52, London, City University.
ROBERTS, J., LYNCH, M. A., and GOLDING, J. (1980), 'Post-neonatal mortality in children from abusing families', *British Medical Journal*, 281: 102–4.
ROBINSON, G. (1979), *Housing Tenure and Labour Mobility in Scotland*, Edinburgh, Scottish Economic Planning Dept.
ROBINSON, M. J., and PALMER, S. R., AVERY, A., JAMES, C. E., BEYNON, J. L., and TAYLOR, R. W. (1982), 'Ethnic differences in perinatal mortality: a challenge', *Journal of Epidemiology and Community Health* 36: 22–6.
ROBINSON, V. (1986), *Transients, Settlers and Refugees: Asians in Britain*, Oxford, Oxford University Press.
——(1980), 'Patterns of South Asian ethnic exogamy and endogamy in Britain', *Ethnic and Racial Studies*, 3: 427–43.
——(1982), 'Assimilation, interpretation or encapsulation: prospects for the

coloured population of the United Kingdom', in D. A. Coleman (ed.) *The Demography of Immigrants and Minority Groups in the United Kingdom*, London, Academic Press.

RODRIGUES, L., and BOTTING, B. (1989), 'Recent trends in postneonatal mortality in England', *Population Trends*, 55: 7–15.

ROGERS, S. C., and WEATHERALL, J. A. C. (1976), *Anencephalus, Spina Bifida and Congenital Hydrocephalus, England and Wales 1964–72*, Studies in Medical and Population Subjects No. 32, London, HMSO.

ROLL, J. (1986), *Babies and Money: Birth Trends and Costs*, London, Family Policy Studies Centre.

RONA, R. J., and CHINN, S. (1982), 'National study of health and growth: social and family factors and obesity in primary school children', *Annals of Human Biology*, 9/2: 131–45.

—— and MORRIS, R. W. (1982), 'National study of health and growth: social and family factors and overweight in English and Scottish parents', *Annals of Human Biology*, 9/2: 147–56.

ROSE, G. A. (1976), 'Epidemiological evidence for the effects of urban environment', in Harrison and Gibson (1976).

ROSENMAN, R. H., FRIEDMAN, M., STRAUS, R. JENKINS, C. D., ZYZANSKI, S. J., and WURM, M. (1970), 'Coronary disease in the Western Collaborative Group study: a follow up experience of 4½ years', *Journal of Chronic Diseases*, 23: 173–90.

ROSING, K. E. and WOOD, P. A. (1971), *Character of a Conurbation: A Computer Atlas of Birmingham and the Black Country*, London, University of London Press.

ROTH, C. (1978), *A History of the Jews in England*, Oxford, Oxford University Press.

ROTHBERG, R. I., and RABB, T. K. (eds.) (1985), Hunger and History: *The Impact of Changing Food Production and Consumption on Society*, Cambridge, Cambridge University Press.

ROUTH, G. (1980), *Occupation and Pay in Great Britain 1906–1979*, London, Macmillan.

—— (1987), *Occupations of the People of Great Britain, 1801–1981*, London, Macmillan.

ROWE, C. (1986), *People and Chips: The Human Implications of Information Technology*, London, Paradigm.

ROWNTREE, G. (1970), 'Some aspects of marriage breakdown in Britain in the last thirty years', *Population Studies*, 23: 147–63.

—— and CARRIER, N. (1958), 'The resort to divorce in England and Wales, 1857–1957', *Population Studies*, 11.

—— and PIERCE, R. M. (1961), 'Birth control in Britain', *Population Studies*, 15: 3–9.

ROXBY, P. M. (1912), 'Rural depopulation in England during the nineteenth century', *Nineteenth Century and After*, 71: 174–90.

Royal College of General Practitioners, OPCS, DHSS (1979), *Mortality Statistics from General Practice 1971–76: Second National Study*, Studies on Medical and Population Subjects No. 36, London, HMSO.

—— (1982), *Mortality Statistics from General Practice 1970–71: Socio-economic Analysis*, Studies in Medical and Population Subjects No. 46, London, HMSO.

Royal College of Obstetricians and Gynaecologists (1984), *Late Abortions in England and Wales: Report of a National Confidential Study*, London, Royal College of Obstetricians and Gynaecologists.

Royal College of Physicians (1962), *Smoking and Health*, London, Pitmans Medical Publishing.

—— (1971), *Smoking and Health Now: A New Report*, London, Pitmans Medical Publishing.

—— (1976), *Fat and Heart Disease*, London, Pitmans Medical Publishing.

—— (1978), *Smoking or Health: The 3rd Report*, London, Pitmans Medical Publishing.

—— (1983*a*), *Health or Smoking?*, Follow-up report.

—— (1983*b*), 'Obesity: a report of the Royal College of Physicians', *Journal of the Royal College of Physicians of London*, 17: 3–58.

—— (1987*a*), *A Great and Growing Evil: The Medical Consequences of Alcohol Abuse*, Report of a Working Party on Alcohol, London, Royal College of Physicians.

—— (1987*b*), *The Sun on your Skin: Adapted from a Report of the Royal College of Physicians on Links between Exposure to Ultraviolet Radiation and Skin Cancer*, London, Royal College of Physicians.

—— (1989), *Prenatal Diagnosis and Genetic Screening: Community and Service Implications*, London, Royal College of Physicians.

——/Royal College of Pathologists (1982), 'Medical aspects of death certification', *Journal of Royal College of Physicians of London*, 16: 4.

Royal College of Psychiatrists (1979), *Alcohol and Alcoholism: Report of a Special Committee on Alcohol and Alchoholism*, London, Tavistock.

Royal College of Surgeons (1989), *Report of the Working Party on the Management of Patients with Major Injuries*, London, Royal College of Surgeons.

Royal Commission on the Depression of Trade and Industries (1886), *Final Report*, Parliamentary Paper 1886, 23.

Royal Commission on the Distribution of the Industrial Population (1940), *Report* (Barlow Report), Cmnd. 6153, London, HMSO.

Royal Commission on Environment Pollution (1983), *Ninth Report: Lead in the Environment*, Cmnd. 8852, London, HMSO.

—— (1984), *Tenth Report: Tackling Pollution Experience and Proposals*, Cmnd. 9149, London, HMSO.

Royal Commission on Local Government in England, (1969), *Report*, vol. i (Maud Report), Cmnd. 4040, London, HMSO.

Royal Commission on Population (1949), *Report*, Cmnd. 7965, London, HMSO.

—— (1950), *Report of the Economics Committee*, Papers of the Royal Commission on Population, vol. iii, London, HMSO.

Royal Society (1983), *Demographic Trends and Future University Candidates: A Working Paper*, London, Royal Society.

RUDDY, S. (1969), *Industrial Selection Schemes: An Administrative Study*, Centre for Urban and Regional Studies Occasional Paper No. 5, University of Birmingham.

Runnymede Trust (1977), *Briefing Paper 5/77: The Role of Immigrants in the Labour Market: A Summary of a Report by the Unit for Manpower Studies at the Department of Employment*, London, Runnymede Trust.

—— (1979), *Census 1981: The Race Question*, Proceedings of a one-day seminar, London, Runnymede Trust.

RUSSELL, C. (1987), *100 Predictions for the Baby Boom: The Next 50 Years*, New York, Plenum Press.

RUSSELL. D. E. H. (1984), 'The prevalence and seriousness of incestuous abuse', *Child Abuse and Neglect*, 8/1: 15–22.

RUSSELL, J. C. (1948), *British Medieval Population*, Albuquerque, N. Mex., University of New Mexico Press.

—— (1958), 'Late ancient and medieval populations', *Transactions of the American Philosophical Society*, 48/3.

—— (1985), 'Late ancient and medieval population control', *Memoirs of the American Philosophical Society*, 160.

RUSSELL, J. K. (1981), 'Medical and social hazards of teenage pregnancy', in Roberts and Chester (1981).

RUTTER, M., and MADGE, N. (1976), *Cycles of Disadvantages*, London, Heinemann Educational.

RYDER, N. B. (1979), 'The future of American fertility', *Social Problems*, 26/3: 359–70.

—— (1980), 'Components of temporal variations in American fertility', in Hiorns, (1980).

SALAMAN, R. N. (ed.) (1989), *The History and Social Influence of the Potato*, Cambridge, Cambridge University Press.

SALT, J. (1973), 'Workers to the work?', *Area*, 5/4: 262–6.

—— (1976), 'International labour migration: the geographical pattern of demand', in Salt and Clout (1976): 80–125.

—— (1983), 'High level manpower movements in Northern Europe and the role of careers: an explanatory framework', *International Migration Review*, 17: 633–52.

—— (1984), 'Labour migration within multi-locational organisations in Britain', *Final Report*, ESRC Grant F/00/23/0027.

—— (1985), 'The geography of unemployment in the UK in the 1980s', *Espaces, populations, sociétés*, 7: 349–56.

—— (1990a), *Foreign Labour Immigration and the UK Labour Market*, Report to the Dept. of Employment, London.

—— (1990b), 'Organisational labour migration: theory and practice in the United Kingdom', J. H. Johnson and J. Salt (eds.), *Labour Migration*, London, Fulton: 53–70.

—— and CLOUT, H. (eds.) (1976), *Migration in Post-War Europe*, London, Oxford University Press.

—— and FLOWERDEW, R. (1980), 'Labour migration from London', *London Journal*, 6/1: 36–50.

—— and KITCHING, R. T. (1989), *United Kingdom Labour Immigration and the Work Permit System in the 1980s*, Working Paper No. 1, Migration Research Unit, University College, London.

—— (1990), 'Foreign workers and the UK labour market', *Employment Gazette*, (Nov.) 538–46.

SALTMARSH, J. (1941), 'Plague and economic decline in England in the late middle ages', *Cambridge Historical Journal*, 7: 23–41.

SALWAY, P. (1981), *Roman Britain*, Oxford, Oxford University Press.

SAUER, R. (1978), 'Infanticide and abortion in 19th-century Britain', *Population Studies*, 32: 81–94.

SAUNDERS, M. N. K. (1985), 'The influence of job vacancy advertising upon migration: some empirical evidence', *Environment and Planning A*, 17: 1581–9.

SAUVY, A. (1975), *Zero Growth?*, Oxford, Basil Blackwell.

SAVELAND, W., and GLICK, P. C. (1969), 'First marriage decrement tables, by color and sex for the United States in 1958–60', *Demography*, 6: 243–60.

SAVILLE, J. (1957), *Rural Depopulation in England and Wales 1851–1951*, London, Routledge & Kegan Paul.

SCHOEN, R. and NELSON, V. E. (1974), 'Marriage, divorce and mortality: a life table analysis', *Demography*, 11/2: 267–90.

SCHOFIELD, M. (1965), *The Sexual Life of Young People*, Harmondsworth, Penguin.

SCHOFIELD, R. S. (1970), 'Age specific mobility in an eighteenth-century rural English parish', *Annales de démographie historique*, 261–4.

—— (1972), 'Crisis mortality', *Local Population Studies*, 9: 10–21.

—— (1973), 'Dimensions of illiteracy 1750–1850', *Explanations in Economic History*, 10: 437–54.

—— and COLEMAN, D. A. (1986), 'Introduction: the state of population theory', in D. A. COLEMAN and R. S. SCHOFIELD (eds.), *The State of Population Theory*, Oxford, Basil Blackwell.

SCHULTZ, T. P. (1981), *Economics of Population*, Reading, Mass., Addison-Wesley.

SCOBIE, J. (1972), *Black Britannia: A History of Blacks in Britain*, Chicago, Ill., Johnson.

SCOTT, J. (1987), 'Oncogenes in atherosclerosis', *Nature*, 325: 574–5.

SCOTT, P. P., and WILLIS, P. A. (1985), *Road Casualties in Great Britain during the First Year with Seat Belt Legislation*, Transport and Road Research Laboratory Research Report 9, Crowthorne, TRRL.

SCOULOUDI, I. (1938), 'Alien immigration into and alien communities in London 1558–1640', *Proceedings of the Huguenot Society* 16: 27–49.

SCRIMSHAW, N. S., TAYLER, C. E., and GORDON, J. E. (1968), *International Nutrition and Infection*, Geneva, World Health Organization.

SEEMAN, M., and SEEMAN, T. E. R. (1983), 'Health behaviour and personal autonomy', *Journal of Health and Social Behaviour*, 24: 144–59.

Select Committee on Science and Technology (1971), *First Report Population of the United Kingdom*, London, HMSO.

—— (1973), *Fifth Report*, London, HMSO.

SELMAN, P. F. (1989), *Reviews of UK Statistical Sources*, xxv: *Family Planning*, London, Chapman and Hall.

SERPLAN (London and South East Regional Planning Conference) (1989), *Housing Provision in the South East: Report to SERPLAN on a Revised Distribution for the 1990s* (W. S. Grigson, Consultant), London, SERPLAN.

SEVER, P. S. (1981), 'Racial differences in blood pressure: genetic and environmental factors', *Postgraduate Medical Journal*, 57: 755–9.

—— GORDON, D., PEART, W. S., and BEIGHTON, P. (1980), 'Blood pressure and its correlates in urban and tribal Africa', *Lancet* 2: 60–4.

SHANNON, G., and NYSTUEN, J. (1972), 'Marriage, migration and the measurement of social interaction', in W. P. Adams and F. M. Helleiner (eds.), *International Geography 1972: 22nd International Geographical Congress*.

SHAPER. A. G., POCOCK, S. J., *et al.* (1981), 'British regional heart study: cardiovascular risk factors in middle-aged men in 24 towns', *British Medical Journal*, 283: 179–86.

—— WANNAMETHEE, G., and WALKER, M. (1988), 'Alcohol and mortality in British men: explaining the U-shaped curve', *Lancet*, 2: 1267–73.

SHAW, C. (1988*a*), 'Latest estimates of ethnic minority populations', *Population Trends*, 51: 5–8.

—— (1988*b*), 'Components of growth in the ethnic minority population', *Population Trends*, 52: 26–30.

—— (1989), 'The sex ratio at birth in England and Wales', *Population Trends*, 57: 26–9.

SHEPHARD, R. J. (1981), *Ischaemic Heart Disease and Exercise*, London, Croom Helm.

—— (1982), *The Risks of Passive Smoking*, London, Croom Helm.

SHEPHARD, J. WESTAWAY, J., and LEE, T. (1974), *A Social Atlas of London*, Oxford, Oxford University Press.

SHERLOCK, S. (1983), 'Current problems in alcoholic liver disease', *Alcohol and Alcoholism*, 18/2: 99–118.

SHORTER, E., KNODEL, J., and VAN DE WALLE, E. (1971), 'The decline of non-marital fertility in Europe 1880–1940', *Population Studies*, 25: 375–93.

SHREWSBURY, J. F. D. (1970), *A History of Bubonic Plague in the British Isles*, Cambridge, Cambridge University Press.

SHRYOCK, H. S., and SIEGEL, J. S. (1976), in E. G. Stockwell (ed.), *The Methods and Materials of Demography*, New York, Academic Press.

SIEGEL, B. J. (1970), 'Defensive structuring and environmental stress', *American Journal of Sociology*, 76: 11.

SIGSWORTH, E. M. (1972), 'Gateways to death? Medicine, hospitals and mortality, 1700–1850', in Mathias (1972).

SILLITOE, K. (1978*a*), 'Ethnic origins: the search for a question', *Population Trends*, 13: 25–9.

—— (1978*b*), *Ethnic Origins 1, 2, 3*, OPCS Occasional Paper 8, 9, 10, London, OPCS.

—— (1981), *Ethnic Origins 4: An Experiment in the Use of a Direct Question about Ethnicity for the Census*, London, OPCS.

—— (1987), 'Questions on race/ethnicity and related topics for the census', *Population Trends* 49: 5–11.

SILMAN, A. J. (1981), 'Routinely collected data and ischaemic heart disease in the United Kingdom', *Health Trends*, 13: 39–42.

SILVERSTONE, J. T. (1968), 'Psycho-social aspects of obesity', *Proceedings of the Royal Society of Medicine* 61: 371–5.

SIMMIE, J. M. (1972), 'The sociology of internal migration', University Working Paper 15, London, Centre for Environmental Studies.

SIMMS, D. L. (1986), 'Towards a scientific basis for regulating lead contamination', *Science of the Total Environment*, 58: 209–24.

SIMMS, M. (1982), 'Teenage mothers by chance, not choice', *Family Planning Today*.

SIMONS, J. (1974), 'Population policy in developed countries: Great Britain', in B. Berelson (ed.), *Population Policies in Developed Countries*, New York, McGraw-Hill: 592–646.

——(1982a), 'Attitudes to fertility among the Sikhs in London' in D. A. Coleman (ed.), *The Demography of Immigrants and Minority Groups in the United Kingdom*, London, Academic Press.

——(1982b), *Reproductive Behaviour as Religious Practice*, CPS Research Paper No. 82–3, London, London School of Hygiene and Tropical Medicine, also in C. Hohn and R, Mackensen (eds.), *Determinants of Fertility Trends: Theories Re-examined*, Liège, IUSSP, Éditions Ordina: 131–46.

——(1986a), 'Culture, economy and reproduction in contemporary Europe', in D. A. Coleman and R. S. Schofield (eds.), *The State of Population Theory*, Oxford, Basil Blackwell.

——(1986b), 'How conservative are British Attitudes to Reproduction?', *Quarterly Journal of Social Affairs*, 2/1: 41–54.

SIMON, J. (1981), *The Ultimate Resource*, Princeton, Princeton University Press.

SIMPSON, D. (1984), 'Trends in major risk factors 1: cigarette smoking', *Postgraduate Medical Journal*, 60: 20–5.

SLACK, P, (1982), *Death and Disease in Early Modern Europe*, Harvester.

——(1985), *The Impact of Plague in Tudor and Stuart England*, London, Routledge & Kegan Paul.

SLATER, P. E., and EVER-HADANI, P. (1983), 'Mortality in Jerusalem during the 1983 doctors' strike', *Lancet*, 2: 1306.

SMIL, V. (1989), 'Coronary heart disease, diet, and western mortality', *Population and Development Review*, 15: 399–424.

SMITH, A. D. (1986), *The Ethnic Origins of Nations*, Oxford, Basil Blackwell.

SMITH. D. J. (1977), *Racial Disadvantage in Britain*, Harmondsworth, Penguin.

SMITH, D. P. (1981), 'A reconsideration of Easterlin cycles', *Population Studies*, 35/2: 247–64.

SMITH, F. (1931), *A History of English Elementary Education 1760–1902*, London, University of London Press.

SMITH, J. (1987), *Equality and Inequality in Northern Ireland: Employment and Unemployment*, London, Policy Studies Institute.

SMITH, R. (1987), *Unemployment and Health: A Disaster and a Challenge*, Oxford, Oxford University Press.

SMITH, R. M. (1978), 'Population and its geography in England 1500–1730', in Dodgshon and Butlin (1978): 199–237.

——(1981), 'Fertility, economy and household formation in England over three centuries', *Population and Development Review*, 7: 595–622.

——(1986), 'Transfer incomes, risk and security: the roles of the family and the collectivity in recent theories of fertility change', in D. A. Coleman and R. S. Schofield (eds.), *The State of Population Theory*, London, Academic Press.

——(1988), 'Welfare and the management of demographic uncertainty', in Keynes, Coleman, and Dimsdale (1988).

——(1990), 'Demographic developments in rural England, 1300–48: a survey', in B. M. S. Campbell (ed.), *Before the Black Death*, Manchester, Manchester University Press.

——(1990a), 'Monogamy, landed property and demographic regimes in pre-industrial Europe: regional contrasts and temporal stabilities', in J. Landers, and V. Reynolds (eds.), *Fertility and Resources*, Cambridge, Cambridge University Press.

—— (1990*b*), 'Geographical aspects of population change in England, 1500–1730', in R. A. Dodgshan and R. A. Butlin (eds.), 1990.

SMITH, T. E. (ed.) (1981), *Commonwealth Migration: Flows and Policies*, London, Macmillan.

Social Services Committee (1980), *Report on Perinatal and Neonatal Mortality*, London, HMSO.

Social Trends (annual), An annual publication of the Central Statistical Office, London, HMSO.

SOLOWAY, R. A. (1982), *Birth Control and the Population Question in England 1877–1930*, London, University of Carolina Press, Chapel Hill.

SOMERVILLE, S. M., RONA, R. J., and CHINN, S. (1988), 'Passive smoking and respiratory conditions in primary school children', *Journal of Epidemiology and Community Health*, 42: 105–10.

SOUTHGATE, B., BINGHAM, S., WILLIAMS, D. R. M., COLE, T. J., and JAMES, W. P. T. (1979), 'Dietary fibre and regional large-bowel cancer mortality in Britain', *British Journal of Cancer*, 40: 456–63.

Spastics Society (1970), *Towards Healthy Babies: The Prevention of Cerebral Palsy*, London, Spastics Society.

—— (1981), *Who's Holding the Baby Now?*, London, Spastics Society.

—— (1982), *Smoking in Pregnancy: A Review*, London, Spastics Society.

SPENCE, N. A., GILLESPIE, A. E., GODDARD, J. B., KENNET, S. R., PINCH, S. P. and WILLIAMS A. M. (1982), *British Cities: An Analysis of Urban Change*, Oxford, Pergamon.

SPENCER, A. E. C. W. (1964), 'The Newman demographic survey 1953–1964: reflections on the birth life and death of a Catholic institute for social-religious research', *Social Compass*, 11/3–4: 31–7.

—— (1972), 'The Catholic community as a British melting pot', *New Community*, 2: 125–31.

—— (1975), 'Demography of Catholicism', *Month*, 236/1291: 100–5.

—— (1977), *The Relative Fertility of the Two Religious–Ethnic Communities in Northern Ireland 1947–1977*, Transactions of the Sociological Association of Ireland 1977–8: Joint meeting with the Royal Statistical Society.

—— (1982), 'Catholics in Britain and Ireland: regional contrasts', in D. A. Coleman, (ed.), *The Demography of Immigrant and Minority Groups in the UK*, London, Academic Press.

SPENGLER, J. J. (1972), 'Demographic factors and early modern demographic development', in D. V. Glass and R. Revelle (eds.), *Population and Social Change*, London, Arnold.

STALLONES, R. A. (1980), 'The rise and fall of ischaemic heart disease', *Scientific American*, 243/5: 43–9.

STATHER, J. W., DIONIAN, J., BROWN, J., FELL, T. P., and MUIRHEAD, P. (1986), *The Risks of Leukaemia and Other Cancers in Seascale from Radiation Exposure*, Addendum to NRPB-R171, Chilton, National Radiological Protection Board.

—————————————— (1988), *The Risk of Childhood Leukaemia near Nuclear Establishments*, Series R-215, Chilton, National Radiological Protection Board.

STERN, J. (1983), 'The relationship between unemployment, morbidity and mortality in Britain', *Population Studies*, 37: 61–74.

STEVENSON, J., and COOK, C. (1979), *The Slump*, London, Quartet Books.

STEVENSON, T. H. C. (1923), 'The social distribution of mortality from four different causes in England and Wales, 1910–1912', *Biometrika*, 15: 382–400.

—— (1928), 'The vital statistics of wealth and poverty', *Journal of the Royal Statistical Society*, 91: 207–20.

STILLWELL, J. C. H. (1983), 'Migration between metropolitan and non-metropolitan regions in the UK', paper presented at the Anglo-Dutch migration symposium, Soesterberg, Netherlands, Sept.

—— and BODEN, P. (1989), 'Internal migration: the United Kingdom', in J. C. H. Stillwell and H. J. Scholten (eds.), *Contemporary Research in Population Geography*, Dordrecht, Kluwer: 64–75.

STOCKS, P. (1934), 'The association between mortality and density of housing', *Proceedings of the Royal Society of Medicine*, 27/2: 1127–46.

STOECKEL, J., and CHOWDHURY, A. K. M. A. (1980), 'Fertility and socio-economic status in rural Bangladesh: differentials and linkages', *Population Studies*, 34: 519–24.

STONE, L. (1966), 'Social mobility in England 1500–1700', *Past and Present*, 3: 29–33.

—— (1977), *The Family, Sex and Marriage in England, 1500–1800*, London, Weidenfeld and Nicholson.

—— (1981), 'Family history in the 1980s: past achievements and future trends', *Journal of Interdisciplinary History*, 12: 51–87.

STONIER, T. (1982), *The Wealth of Information: A Profile of the Post Industrial Society*, London, Methuen.

STUART-HARRIS, C. H. (1980), 'The ecology of chronic lung disease', in Clegg and Garlick (1980): 73–92.

STUDLAR, D. T. (1980), 'Élite responsiveness or élite autonomy: British immigration policy reconsidered', *Ethnic and Racial Studies*, 3: 207–23.

Study Commission on the Family (1982), *Values and the Changing Family: A Final Report from the Working Party on Values*, London, Study Commission on the Family.

SUNDERLAND, E., and CARTWRIGHT, R. A. (1974), 'Some genetic inter-relationships in England and Wales: a methodological investigation', *Human Heredity*, 24: 540–53.

—— and MURRAY, V. (1978), 'ABH secretion in the population of Pembrokeshire, Wales', *Annals of Human Biology*, 5/5: 483–5.

SURAULT, P. (1979), *L'Inégalité devant la mort*, Paris, Economica.

SUSSER, M. W., and STEIN, Z. A. (1962), 'Civilisation and peptic ulcer', *Lancet*, 1: 115–9.

SUTHERLAND, I. (1972), 'When was the Great Plague', in D. V. Glass and R. Revelle (eds.), *Population and Social Change*, London, Arnold.

SWERDLOW, A. J. (1987), '150 years of Registrar-General's medical statistics', *Population Trends*, 48: 20–6.

SZRETER, S. R. S. (1984), 'The genesis of the Registrar-General's social classification of occupations', *British Journal of Sociology*, 35: 522–46.

—— (1986), *The Importance of Social Intervention in Britain's Mortality Decline c1850–1914: A Re-interpretation*, CEPR Discussion Paper No. 121, London, CEPR.

TANNER, J. M. (1962), *Growth at Adolescence*, Oxford, Basil Blackwell.

——(1978), *Fetus into Man: Physical Growth from Conception to Maturity*, London, Open Books.

TAYLOR, A. J. (ed.) (1975), *The Standard of Living in Britain in the Industrial Revolution*, London. Methuen.

TAYLOR, C. E. (1983), 'Synergy among mass infections, famines and poverty', *Journal of Interdisciplinary History*, 14: 483–501.

TAYLOR, L. R. (ed.) (1970), *The Optimum Population for Britain*, London, Academic Press.

TAYLOR, R. C. (1969), 'Migration and motivation: a study in determinants and types', in Jackson (1969): 99–133.

TEITELBAUM, M. S. (1984), *The British Fertility Decline*, Princeton, NJ, Princeton University Press.

——and WINTER, J. (1985), *The Fear of Population Decline*, London, Academic Press.

TEPER, S. (1975), 'Recent trends in teenage pregnancy in England and Wales', *Journal of Biosocial Science*, 7: 141–52.

——and SYMONDS, E. M. (1985), 'Artificial insemination by donor: problems and perspectives', in C. O. Carter (ed.), *Developments in Human Reproduction and their Eugenic, Ethical Implications*, London, Academic Press: 19–52.

TERRY, P. B., and CONDIE, R. G. (1981), 'Ethnic differences in perinatal mortality', *Postgraduate Medical Journal*, 57: 790–1.

THACKRAH, C. T. (1831), *The Effects of the Principal Acts, Trades and Professions, and of Civic States and Habits of Living, on Health and Longevity, with Suggestions for their Removal*, reprinted 1957, Edinburgh, Livingstone.

THANE, P. (1989), 'Old age: Burden or Benefit?', in H. Joshi (ed.), *The Changing Population of Britain*, Oxford, Basil Blackwell: 56–71.

THATCHER, R. (1981), 'Centenarians in England and Wales', *Population Trends*, 25: 11–14.

THELLE, D.S., SHAPER, A. G., WHITEHEAD, T. P., BULLOCH, D. G., ASHBY, D., and PATEL, I. L. A. (1983), 'Blood lipids in middle-aged British men', *British Heart Journal*, 49: 205–13.

THIRSK, J. (1959), 'Sources of information of population 1500–1760', *Amateur Historian*, 4/4 and 5: 129–33, 182–5.

THOMAS, B. (1986), 'Escaping from constraints: the industrial revolution in a malthusian context', in R. I. Rothberg and T. K. Rabb (eds.), *Population and Economy*, Cambridge, Cambridge University Press: 169–93.

THOMAS, D. S. (1927), *Social Aspects of the Business Cycle*, New York, Gordon and Breach.

THOMPSON, F. M. L. (1968–9), 'The second agricultural revolution 1815–1880', *Economic History Review*, 21: 62–77.

THOMPSON, Sir G. H. (1946), *The Trend of National Intelligence: The Galton Lecture 1946*, Occasional Papers in Eugenics No. 3, London, The Eugenics Society (now The Galton Institute).

THOMPSON, J. (1980), 'The age at which child-bearing starts', *Population Trends*, 21: 10–13.

——(1982), 'Differential fertility in ethnic minority populations in Great Britain', in D. A. Coleman (ed.), *Demography of Immigrant and Minority Groups in the United Kingdom*, London, Academic Press.

THOMPSON, W. S. (1929), 'Recent trends in World population', *American Journal of Sociology*, 34: 959–79.

THORNES, B., and COLLARD, J. (1979), *Who Divorces?*, London, Routledge & Kegan Paul.

THRUPP, S. (1957), 'A survey of the alien populations of England in 1440', *Spectrum*, 32: 262–73.

TICKELL, C. (1978), *Climate Change and World Affairs*, Oxford, Pergamon.

TIETZE, C. (1979), 'Anti-pill scare', *International Family Planning Perspectives*, 5: 8.

TITMUSS, R. M. (1943), *Birth, Poverty and Wealth: A Study of Infant Mortality*, London, Hamish Hamilton.

TITOW, J. Z. (1961), 'Some evidence of the thirteenth century population increase', *Economic History Review*, 14: 218–24.

——(1969), *English Rural Society 1200–1350*, London, Allen & Unwin.

Tobacco Research Council (1976), *Statistics of Smoking in the United Kingdom*, Research Paper 1, 7th edn., ed. P. N. Lee, London, Tobacco Advisory Council.

TOWNSEND, A. R. (1982), 'Recession and the regions in Great Britain 1976–80: analysis of redundancy data', *Environment and Planning A*, 14: 1389–404.

——(1986), 'The location of employment growth after 1978: the surprising significance of dispersed centres', *Environment and Planning A*, 18: 529–45.

TOWNSEND, P., and DAVIDSON, N. (1982), *Inequalities in Health: The Black Report*, Harmondsworth, Penguin.

——PHILLIMORE, P., and BEATTIE, A. (1988), *Health and Deprivation: Inequality and the North*, London, Croom Helm.

TRANTER, N. (1979), *Population since the Industrial Revolution: The Case of England and Wales*, London, Croom Helm.

TROST, J. (1979), 'Dissolution of cohabitation and marriage in Sweden', *Journal of Divorce*, 2/4: 415–21.

TROWELL, H. C., and BURKITT, D. P. (1981), *Western Diseases: Their Emergence and Prevention*, London, Edward Arnold.

TRUETT, J., CORNFIELD, J., and KANNEL, W. B. (1967), 'A multivariate analysis of the risk of coronary heart disease in Framingham', *Journal of Chronic Diseases*, 20: 511–24.

TRUSSELL, J., and WESTOFF, C. F. (1980), 'Contraception practice and trends in coital frequency', *Family Planning Perspectives*, 12/5: 246–9.

——and WILSON, C. (1985), 'Sterility in a population with natural fertility', *Population Studies*, 39: 2.

TRUSWELL, A. S. (1982), 'Epidemiology of over-nutrition', in S. Preston (ed.), *Biological Aspects of Mortality and the Length of Life*, Liège, Éditions Ordina: 393–416.

TUCHMAN, B. W. (1979), *A Distant Mirror: The Calamitous 14th Century*, Harmondsworth, Penguin.

TUNSTALL-PEDRE, H., SMITH, W. C. S., and TAVENDALE, R. (1989), 'How-often-that-high graphs of serum cholesterol', *Lancet*, 1: 540–2.

TURNER, R. J., and NOH, S. (1983), 'Class and psychological vulnerability among women', *Journal of Health and Social Behaviour*, 24: 2–15.

TURNOCK, D. (1968), 'Depopulation in N. E. Scotland, with reference to the countryside', *Scottish Geographical Magazine*, 84: 256–68.

UK Health Departments (1977), *Reducing the Risk: Safer Pregnancy and Child Birth*, London, HMSO.

United Nations (1979), *Trends and Characteristics of International Migration Since 1950*, UN Department of Economic and Social Affairs Demographic Study No. 64, New York, United Nations.

—— (1983), *International Migration: Policies and Programmes: A World Survey*, Population Studies No. 80, New York, United Nations.

US Dept. of Commerce (1983), *Ancestry of the Population by State: 1980*, Bureau of the Census Supplementary Report, PC80-S1-10, Washington, DC, USGPO.

US Dept. of Health and Human Services (1987), *Fecundity, Infertility and Reproductive Health in the United States 1982*, Hyattsville, Md., Public Health Service.

US National Academy of Sciences (1989), *Diet and Health*, Washington, DC, National Academy of Sciences.

US Surgeon-General (1982), *The Health Consequences of Smoking: Cancer*, Report of the Surgeon-General.

—— (1983), *The Health Consequences of Smoking: CVD*, Report of the Surgeon-General.

—— (1988), *Report on Nutrition and Health*, US Public Health Service, Rockville, Md.

VAN DE KAA, D. J. (1987), 'Europe's second demographic transition', *Population Bulletin*, 42/1.

VAN DE WALLE, F. (1986), 'Infant mortality and demographic transition', in A. J. Coale and S. C. Watkins (eds.), *The Decline of Fertility in Europe*, Princeton, NJ, Princeton Univeristy Press.

VESSEY, M. P. (1988), 'Oral contraception and cancer', in M. Filshie and J. Guillbaud (eds.), *Contraception Science and Practice*, London, Butterworth.

—— and GRAY, M. (1987) *Cancer Risks and Prevention*, Oxford, Oxford University Press.

—— LAWLESS, M., McPHERSON, K., and YEATES, D. (1983), 'Neoplasms of the cervix uteri and contraception: a possible adverse effect of the pill', *Lancet*, 2: 930–34.

—— McPHERSON, K., and JOHNSON, B. (1977), 'Mortality among women participating in the Oxford FPA contraceptive study', *Lancet*, 2: 731–3.

—— VILLARD-MACKINTOSH, L., McPHERSON, K., and YEATES, D. (1989), 'Mortality among oral contraceptive users: 20 year follow-up of women in a cohort study', *British Medical Journal*, 299: 1487–91.

VINCE, S. W. E., (1955) 'The rural population of England and Wales 1801–1951', Ph.D. thesis, University of London.

VINING, D. R., and KONTULY, T. (1978), 'Population dispersal from major metropolitan regions: an international comparison', *International Regional Science Review*, 3/1: 49–73.

VLASSOFF, M. (1980), 'Economic utility of children and fertility in rural India', *Population Studies*, 36: 45–59.

WACHTER, K. W., HAMMEL, E. A., and LASLETT, P. (1978), *Statistical Studies of Historical Social Structure*, New York, Academic Press.

WADSWORTH, M. E. (1979), *Roots of Delinquency*, London, Martin Robertson.

——(1987), 'Follow-up of the first national birth cohort: findings from the Medical Research Council National Survey of Health and Development', *Paediatric and Perinatal Epidemiology*, 1: 95–117.

WALCZAK, Y., and BURNS, S. (1984), *Divorce: The Child's Point of View*, Milton Keynes, Open University Press.

WALD, N. (1983), 'Possible prevention of neural tube defects by vitamin supplementation', in J. Dobbing (ed.), *Prevention of Spina Bifida and Other Neural Tube Defects*, London, Academic Press.

——(1984), 'Neonatal-tube defects and vitamins: the need for a randomised clinical trial', *British Journal of Obstetrics and Gynaecology*, 91: 516–23.

——NANCHAHAL, K., THOMPSON, S. G., and CUCKLE, H. S. (1986), 'Does breathing other people's tobacco smoke cause lung cancer?', *British Medical Journal*, 293: 1217–22.

WALDEGRAVE, W. (1978), *The Binding of Leviathan*, London, Hamish Hamilton.

WALES, T. (1984), 'Poverty, poor relief and the life cycle: some evidence from seventeenth century Norfolk', in R. M. Smith (ed.) *Land, Kinship and Life Cycle*, Cambridge, Cambridge University Press.

WALKER, C. L. (1984), 'Trends in major risk factors 2: the national diet', *Postgraduate Medical Journal*, 60: 26–33.

——and CANNON, G. (1984), *The Food Scandal*, London, Century.

WALL, R. (1979), 'Regional and temporal variation in English household structure from 1650', in J. Hobcraft and P. Rees (eds.), *Regional Demographic Development*, London, Croom Helm.

——(1983), 'The household: demographic and economic change in England 1650–1970', in R. Wall, J. Robin, and P. Laslett (eds.), *Family Forms in Historic Europe*, Cambridge, Cambridge University Press.

——(1989), 'The Residence Patterns of the Elderly in Europe in the 1980s', in E. Grebenik, C. Höhn, and R. Mackensen (eds.), *Later Phases of the Family Cycle: Demographic Aspects*, Oxford, Oxford University Press.

——(1988), *Leaving Home and Living Alone: An Historical Perspective*, CEPR Discussion Paper No. 211, London, CEPR.

——and PENHALE, B. (1989), 'Relationships within households in 1981', *Population Trends*, 55: 22–6.

WALSH, B. (1968), *Some Irish Population Problems Reconsidered*, Paper 41, Economic and Social Research Institute, Dublin.

WALTER, B. (1980), 'Time-space patterns of second-wave Irish immigration into British towns', *Transactions' Institute of British Geographers*, NS 5/3: 297–317.

WALTER, J. and SCHOFIELD, R. (1989), *Famine, Disease and the Social Order in Early Modern Society*, Cambridge, Cambridge University Press.

WARD, R. H., and WEISS, K. M. (eds.) (1976), *The Demographic Evolution of Human Population*, London, Academic Press.

WARNES, A. M. (1983), 'Migration in late working age and early retirement', *Socio-economic Planning Science*, 17: 291–302.

——and LAW, C. M. (1984), 'The elderly population of Great Britain: locational trends and policy implications', *Transactions' Institute of British Geographers*, NS, 9: 37–59.

WATERMAN, S., and KOSMIN B. (1986), *British Jewry in the Eighties: A Statistical and Geographical Study*, London, Board of Deputies of British Jews.

WATKIN, E. I., (1957), *Roman Catholicism in England from the Reformation to 1950*, London, Oxford University Press.

WATTENBERG, B. J. (1987), *The Birth Dearth: What Happens When People in Free Countries Don't Have Enough Babies?*, New York, Phoses Books.

WEATHERALL, J. A. C. (1975), 'Infant mortality: international differences', *Population Trends*, 1: 9–12.

——and HASKEY, J. (1976), 'Surveillance of malformations', *British Medical Bulletin*, 32: 1.

WEBB, S. (1907), *The Decline in the Birth Rate*, Fabian Tract No. 131, London, Fabian Society.

——and WEBB, B. (1927), *English Poor Law History*, Part I: *The Old Poor Law*; Part II(vols. i and ii): *The Last Hundred Years*, London, Frank Cass (repr. 1963).

WEED, J. (1980), *National Estimates of Marriage Dissolution and Survivorship, United States*, Hyattsville, Md., US Department of Health and Human Services, National Center for Health Stations Analytic Studies Series 3, No. 19.

WEEKS, J. R. (1988), 'The demography of Islamic nations', *Population Bulletin*, 43/4.

WERNER, B. (1982), 'Recent trends in illegitimate births and extra-marital conceptions', *Population Trends*, 30: 9–15.

——(1984), 'Fertility and family background: some illustrations from the OPCS Longitudinal Study', *Population Trends*, 35: 5–10.

——(1985), 'Fertility trends in different social classes 1970–83', *Population Trends*, 41: 5–12.

——(1986), 'Family building intentions of different generations of women: results from the General Household Survey', *Population Trends*, 44: 17–23.

——(1987), 'Fertility statistics from birth registrations in England and Wales 1837–1987', *Population Trends*, 48: 4–10.

——(1988), 'Birth intervals: results from the OPCS Longitudinal Study 1972–84', *Population Trends*, 51: 25–9.

WESTOFF, C. F., HAMMERSCLOUGH, C. R., and PAUL, C. (1987), 'The potential impact of improvements in contraception and fertility in Western countries', *European Journal of Population*, 3: 7–32.

WHITE, J. R., and FROEB, H. F. (1980), 'Small-airways dysfunction in nonsmokers chronically exposed to tobacco smoke', *New England Journal of Medicine*, 27 Mar.: 720–3.

WHITE, P. (1990), 'A question on ethnic group for the Census: findings from the 1989 census test', *Population Trends*, 59: 11–19.

——and WOODS, P. (1982), 'Migration and the formation of ethnic minorities', in A. S. Parkes (ed.), *Biosocial Aspects of Ethnic Minorities*, Cambridge, Galton Foundation.

WHITEHEAD, C. M. E., and KLEINMAN, M. (1986), 'Private renting in London: is it so different', *Journal of Social Policy*, 16: 319–48.

WHITEHEAD, F. (1991), *Population Policy in the United Kingdom*, Proceedings of UN/IUSSP Expert Group Meeting on the International Transmission of Population Policy Experience, UN, New York.

WHITEHEAD, M. (1987), *The Health Divide: Inequalities in Health in the 1980s*, London, Health Education Council.

WHITELAW, A. G. L. (1971), 'The association of social class and sibling numbers with skinfold thickness in London schoolboys', *Human Biology*, 43: 414–20.

WIENER, M. J. (1981), *English Culture and the Decline of the Industrial Spirit*, Cambridge, Cambridge University Press.

WILKINSON, R. G. (1986), 'Income and mortality', in R. G. Wilkinson (ed.), *Class and Health: Research and Longitudinal Data*, London, Tavistock: 88–114.

—— (1988), 'Health, inequality and social structure', in Keynes, Coleman, and Dimsdale (1988): 207–20.

WILLATS, E. C., and NEWSON, M. G. C. (1953), 'The geographical pattern of population change in England and Wales, 1921–51, *Geographical Journal*, 99: 442–50.

WILLEKENS, F. J., SHAH, J., SHAH, J. M., and RAMACHANDRAN, P. (1982), 'Multi-state analysis of marital status life tables: theory and application', *Population Studies*, 36: 129–44.

WILLIAMS, R. (1985), *The Country and the City*, London, Hogarth Press.

WILLIAMS, R. M. (1978), *British Population*, 2nd edn., London, Heinemann Educational.

WILLIAMS, S. (1985), *A Job to Live*, Harmondsworth, Penguin.

WILLIS, K. G. (1970), 'Differential migration in selected areas of north-east England', Ph. D. Thesis, University of Newcastle-upon-Tyne.

WILLIS, P. E. (1977), *Learning to Labour*, Farnborough, Saxon House.

WILLIS, R. J. (1973), 'A new approach to the economic theory of fertility behaviour', *Journal of Political Economy*, 81/2: 514–64.

WILLMOTT, P. (1976), 'The role of the family', in M. Buxton and E. Craven (eds.), *The Uncertain Future*, London, Centre for Studies in Social Policy: 51–8.

—— (1986), *Social Networks, Informal Care and Public Policy*, London, Policy Studies Institute.

WILSON. A. (1981), 'Mixed-race children: an exploratory study of racial categorisation and indentity', *New Community*, 9: 36–43.

—— (1984), ' "Mixed race" children in British society: some theoretical considerations', *British Journal of Sociology*, 35: 42–61.

WILSON, C. (1984), 'Natural fertility in pre-industrialised England 1600–1799', *Population Studies*, 38/2: 225–40.

WILSON, E. O. (1975), *Sociobiology*, Cambridge, Mass., Harvard University Press.

WILSON, J. Q., and HERRNSTEIN, R. J. (1985), *Crime and Human Nature*, New York, Simon and Schuster.

WILSON, P. (1980), 'Drinking habits in the United Kingdom', *Population Trends*, 22: 14–18.

WINCH, D. (1987), *Malthus*, Oxford, Oxford University Press.

WINIKOFF, B. (1983), 'Weaning, nutrition, morbidity and mortality consequences', in S. Preston (ed.), *Biological and Social Aspects of Mortality and the Length of Life*, Liège, Éditions Ordina: 113–50.

WINTER, J. M. (1976), 'Some aspects of the demographic consequences of the First World War in Britain', *Population Studies*, 30/3: 539–51.

—— (1977*a*), 'Britain's "lost generation" of the First World War', *Population Studies*, 31: 449–66.

—— (1977*b*), 'The impact of World War I on civilian health in Britain', *European Historical Review*, 30/3: 487–507.

—— (1980), 'Military fitness and civilian health in Britain during the First World War', *Journal of Contemporary History*, 15: 211–44.

—— (1984), 'Unemployment, nutrition and infant mortality in Britain 1920–1950', in J. M. WINTER (ed.), *The Working Class in Modern British History*, Cambridge, Cambridge University Press.

—— (1985), *The Great War and the British People*, London, Macmillan.

—— (1988), 'Public health and the extension of life expectancy in England and Wales 1901–60', in Keynes, Coleman, and Dimsdale (1988): 184–206.

WOOD, J. C. (1981), 'The psyche and the heart', *New Scientist*, 12 Mar.

—— (1984), *Living in Overdrive*, London, Fontana.

WOOD, P. A. (1974), 'Urban manufacturing: a view from the fringe', in Johnson (1974): 129–54.

—— (1976), 'Inter-regional migration in Western Europe: a reappraisal', in Salt and Clout (1976): 52–79.

WOODS, R. I. (1979*a*), *Population Analysis in Geography*, London, Longman.

—— (1979*b*), 'Ethnic segregation in Birmingham in the 1960s and 1970s', *Ethnic and Racial Studies*, 2: 455–76.

—— (1982), 'The structure of mortality in mid-nineteenth century England and Wales', *Journal of Historical Geography*, 8/4: 373–94.

—— (1987), 'Approaches to the fertility transition in Victorian England', *Population Studies*, 41: 283–311.

—— and HINDE, P. R. A. (1987), 'Mortality in Victorian England: models and patterns', *Journal of Interdisciplinary History*, 18: 27–54.

—— and SMITH, C. W. (1983), 'The decline of marital fertility in the late 19th century: the case of England and Wales', *Population Studies*, 37: 207–26.

—— WATTERSON, P. A., and WOODWARD, J. H. (1988–9), 'The causes of rapid infant mortality decline in England and Wales, 1861–1921, Parts I, II', *Population Studies*, 42: 343–66; 43: 113–32.

WOODWARD, J. H. (1974), *To do the Sick no Harm: A Study of the British Voluntary Hospital System to 1875*, London, International Library of Social Policy, Routledge.

WOOLF, M. (1967), *The Housing Survey in England and Wales, 1964*, London, HMSO.

—— (1971), *Family Intentions*, London, HMSO.

—— and PEGDEN, S. (1976), *Families Five Years On*, Social Survey Report SS. 449. London, HMSO.

Woolwich Building Society (1988), *Cost of Moving Survey*, London.

Working Group on Inequalities in Health (1980), *Report of the Working Group on Inequalities in Health* (The Black Report), London, DHSS.

World Health Organization (1977, 1978), *International Classification of Diseases*, Ninth Revision (ICD-9), vols. I and II, Geneva, World Health Organization.

—— (1982), *Prevention of Coronary Heart Disease*, WHO Technical Report Series 678, Geneva, World Health Organization.

—— (1986), *Atlas of Cancer in Scotland 1975–80*, Oxford, Oxford University Press.

—— (1987), *AIDS Surveillance in Europe*, Quarterly Report No. 15, Sept., WHO Collaborating Centre on AIDS, Paris, Hôpital Claude Bernard.

WRIGHT, F. J., and BAIRD, J. P. (1971), *Tropical Diseases*, 4th edn. (Supplement to

S. Davidson and J. Macleod, *The Principles and Practice of Medicine*, 10th edn.), London, Churchill Livingstone.

WRIGLEY, E. A. (1966*b*), 'Family limitation in pre-industrial England', *Economic History Review*, 2nd series, 18: 82–109.

——(1966*a*) (ed.), *An Introduction to English Historical Demography*, London, Weidenfeld and Nicholson.

——(1967), 'A simple model of London's importance in changing English society and economy 1650–1750', *Past and Present*, 37: 44–70.

——(1968), 'Mortality in pre-industrial England: the example of Colyton, Devon, over three centuries', *Daedalus*, 97: 546–80.

——(1969), *Population and History*, London, Weidenfeld and Nicholson.

——(1972), 'The process of modernisation and the industrial revolution in England', *Journal of Interdisciplinary History*, 3: 225–59, reprinted in E. A. Wrigley, *People, Cities and Wealth*, Oxford, Basil Blackwell, 1987.

——(1977), 'Births and baptisms: the use of Anglican baptism registers as a source of information about the numbers of births in England before the beginning of Civil Registration', *Population Studies*, 31: 281–312.

——(1983), 'The growth of population in eighteenth-century England: a conundrum resolved', *Past and Present, 98: 121–50.*

——*(1985a)*, 'Urban growth and agricultural change: England and the continent in the early modern period', *Journal of Interdisciplinary History*, 15: 683–728.

——(1985*b*), 'The fall of marital fertility in nineteenth-century France: exemplar or exception?', *European Journal of Population*, 1: 31–66.

——(1986), 'Elegance and experience: Malthus at the bar of history', in D. A. Coleman and R. S. Schofield (eds.), *The State of Population Theory: Forward from Malthus*, Oxford, Basil Blackwell: 46–64.

——and SCHOFIELD, R. S. (1983), 'English population history from family reconstitution: summary results 1600–1799', *Population Studies*, 37/2: 157–84.

——and SOUDEN, D. (eds.) (1986), *The Works of Thomas Robert Malthus*, 8 vols., London, William Rickering.

WROBLEWSKI, B. M., SINEY, G. P., and WHITE, R. (1990), 'Seasonal variation in fatal pulmonary embolism after hip arthroplasty', *Lancet*, 335: 56.

WUNSCH, G., and LAMBERT. A. (1981), 'Life styles and death styles: differentials and consequences of mortality trends', *BSPS Essex Conference*, 16–18 Sept.

WYNNE. M. (1970), *Family Policy*, London, Michael Joseph.

YOUNG, M., and WILLMOTT, P. (1954), *Family Life and Kinship in East London*, London, Routledge & Kegan Paul.

YUDKIN, J. (1972), *Sweet and Dangerous*, London, Bantam.

YULE, G. U. (1906), 'On the changes in the marriage and birth rates in England and Wales during the past half century: with an inquiry as to their probable causes', *Journal of the Royal Statistical Society*, 69: 88–132.

ZIEGLER, P. (1968), *The Black Death*, London, Collins.

ZINNSER, H. (1935), *Rats, Lice and History*, New York, Little Brown.

Author Index

General Index

Immigrants Acts (1962, 1968) 437,
439–40, 448, 451, 456; General
Naturalization Act 474;
Immigrant Appeals Act
(1969) 440; Immigration Acts
(1971, 1985, 1988) 440–1, 451,
462, 465, 540; Immigration
(Carrier's Liability) Act
(1987) 470–1; Imperial Act
(1914) 439
local government, Local
Government Act 60
marriage and divorce 562; Divorce
Act (1857) 193; Divorce Reform
Act (1969) 196, 206; Family Law
Reform Act (1969) 186;
Matrimonial Causes Act
(1937) 194; Matrimonial and
Family Proceedings Act (1984)
197–8, 200
private acts of Parliament 49, 129
property 4, 34
religion, Bill of Rights (1689) 497
town and country planning 531
trade, Corn Laws (1846) 82
welfare: Old Age Pensions Act 58;
poor laws 16, 25, 32, 44, 66, 232;
New Poor Law (1834) 58;
overseers 44, 47; Speenhamland
(1795) 58
Europe: Bills of Mortality 9; Court
of Human Rights 441, 516;
industrial hazards 302; sex
equality 454; Single European
Act (1992) 471, 530
France, *Code de la Famille* (1939)
521
USA, McCarran Walter Act (1952)
448
Leicester, Leics. 42, 99
Leightonstone Hundred, Essex 26
Letchworth, Herts. 94
life expectation 61, 238–9, 243, 315–
16, 339
future projections 303–4, 528, 552
HIV virus and AIDS 250
pre-twentieth century 9, 19–20, 39–
42, 53

USSR and Eastern Europe 283
women 39, 53, 243, 303–4, 528
Lincolnshire 94
Liverpool, Merseyside 41–2, 57–8, 79,
103, 391, 412
ethnic population 474, 489
mortality differentials 331, 334
local authorities 60, 83, 88, 396
children in care 561
ethnic birth surveys 486
ethnicity statistics collection 479
family planning 75
housing allocation 491
mortality trends 298
planning 234, 535, 557
Regional Health Authorities
(RHAs) 321, 337, 363, 396
see also council housing
Location of Offices Bureau 98, 531
lodgers 217–18, 221–2
London 397, 410–15, 425, 531–5,
540–1
Docklands 539, 541
East End 410, 481
employment/unemployment 372–4,
382–6
immigrant and ethnic
population 459, 474, 489, 492–3,
495–6
mortality 288–9, 331–2
population distribution changes
83–6, 89, 93, 96, 103–10
pre-twentieth century 9, 27, 57, 60,
79, 82
London, Greater 372, 383–6, 411–14,
429, 489, 532
Abercrombie's Greater London Plan
(1944) 412
internal migration 406–7, 409
respiratory disease 333
smoking 333, 346
London Transport 459
longitudinal studies and surveys:
Child Health and Education 310
fertility 167–8
internal migration 400
mortality 309–11, 315–17, 338,
361

mortality (*cont.*)
 suicide 52, 263, 268, 272, 300, 334
 trends in age-specific 40
 women 241, 309, 312, 323–30, 345,
  361; childbirth 46, 52, 55, 276,
  328; pre-twentieth century 39, 52;
  social class and regional variation
  315–17, 321–3, 328–34, 345
 see also accidents: infancy, mortality:
  violence

National Birth Control Association 75
National Birth Rate Commission 115
National Health Service 75, 238, 318,
 358, 507
 allocation of resources 363
 contraception 122
 cost of the elderly 547
 funding and staffing 297–9, 444, 459
 inadequate blood screening 250
National Mobility Office 431, 611
National Secular Society 147
Netherlands 34, 143, 474, 480, 559
New Commonwealth and Pakistan
 (NCWP) 157, 437–59, 478–93,
 501–17, 540
 *see also under names of countries and
 regions*
New York City, USA 272
New Zealand 50, 442–3, 446, 459,
 507, 521
Newcastle, Tyne and Wear 27, 102,
 103, 363, 391, 420, 489
Newcastle, University of 102
Newtownards, Down 102
Nigeria 441
Nightingale, Florence 45
North America 31, 61, 82, 458
 see also Canada: USA
North Clay, Notts. 26
Northampton, Northants. 399, 412–
 13, 422
Northamptonshire, England 26
Northern Ireland 93, 96, 102, 534
 age structure 86–7, 89, 555
 employment/unemployment 372,
  384, 388–9, 555
 fertility 499–501

immigrant and ethnic population 489
migration loss 411, 415
mortality 272, 283, 321, 333–4, 350,
 363–4
Northumberland 215, 363, 410, 537
Norway 47, 269, 339, 466, 559
Norwich, Norfolk 86
Norwich Union Insurance Society 518,
 553
Nottingham, Notts. 58, 102, 103,
 334–5
nutrition, *see* diet and nutrition: food

Oakland, USA 338
occupation 31, 67
 agricultural labour 67, 537
 business and administrative 327–8,
  382, 387, 539
 classification and composition 305,
  309, 316, 375–6
 clerical 375–6, 387, 463, 558
 employers and managerial 159, 315,
  326–8, 344, 347, 356, 402, 405
 of husband 312–13, 317, 330, 333
 immigrant and ethnic
  population 474, 496, 512–13
 intermediate 159, 344, 347, 356, 402,
  405
 see also manual workers; military
  personnel: professional people:
  servants
occupational hazards 261, 302, 305–11,
 332–4
 asbestos 261, 302, 308, 310–11, 332
 fatal injuries 302, 310
 industrial conflict 311
 radiation 292–3
Ohta 73
Okehampton, Devon 41
Oldham, Lancs. 331, 333
OPCS (Office of Population Censuses
 and Surveys) viii–ix, 553, 565–6,
 613–16
 abortion statistics 127
 contraception 125
 employment 371
 ethnic minorities 477, 481–91, 488,
  498, 502–11

differentials 311–19, 334–40,
350–3, 355–63; smoking and
drinking 344–5
see also middle classes, professional
people: socio-economic groups:
working classes: manual workers
social services 89
Society for Constructive Birth Control
and Racial Progress 72
socio-economic groups 68, 375–6,
401–6, 420, 463, 558
immigrant and ethnic population 512
migration 404–6
mortality differentials 313–15, 339,
344, 347, 350, 356
see also manual workers: middle
classes: occupation: professional
people: social class: working
classes
Solent region 86
South Africa 443, 446, 465, 521
South America 446
South East Region Planning
Authorities (SERPLAN) 535
South Korea 365
South Shields, Tyne and Wear 332
Southampton, Hants 99, 332
Southwark, Greater London 333
Southwark and Vauxhall Water
Company 59
Soviet Union, *see* USSR
Spain 19, 65, 365, 445–7, 456, 463
mortality 506
Spanish immigrants 455–6
Speenhamland, Berks. 58
Sri Lanka 441, 446, 468, 470
Standard Metropolitan Labour Areas
(SMLAs) 98, 100–2, 416–17, 420
standardized mortality ratios
(SMRs) 53, 239, 306–9, 326–9,
332–4, 362
general social class and geographical
variations 312, 314–15, 317,
320–1
statistics, demographic 59
Stepney, Greater London 75
Stevenage, Herts. 99, 331–2
Stevenson, T. H. C. viii

Stoke-on-Trent, Staffs. 319
Stopes, Marie 72–3
Strathclyde, Scotland 107
students 405–6, 408–9, 409
Study Commission on the Family
(1982) 186
Suffolk, England 94
Sunderland, Tyne and Wear 59, 334,
420
surnames 26–7, 214, 452–3, 481, 486
Protestant refugees 474
Surrey, England 420
surveys and studies:
British Regional Heart Study 343
Family Formation (1976) 187
Health Education Council
(1981) 301
Health and Lifestyle 358, 360
Health and Safety Executive
(1987) 310
Housing and Labour Mobility Study
(1972) 399, 402, 421
International Passenger (IPS) 84,
437–8, 483, 486
London Statistical Society (1841) 57
Manchester (1840) 41
National Consumer Council
(1984) 424
National Dwelling and Housing 485
National Food (1985, 1988,
1989) 284, 286, 352, 354
National Movers (1977–8) 423
Newman Demographic (1953–64)
479
Organizational Labour Migration
Study (early 1980s) 400, 428
Population Investigation Committee
(1967–8) 124
South East Study (1964) 518, 525
tax survey (1440) 473
Women and Employment (1980) 559
Europe, Princeton study 66
USA: Alameda County, California
(1965–74) 338, 362; Multiple Risk
Factor Intervention Trial (MR
FIT) (1982) 274–5
World Fertility Survey 493
see also General Household surveys: